LEADING CHANGE

IN GIFTED EDUCATION

LEADING CHANGE

IN GIFTED EDUCATION

THE FESTSCHRIFT OF DR. JOYCE VANTASSEL-BASKA

EDITED BY
BRONWYN MACFARLANE, PH.D., AND TAMRA STAMBAUGH, PH.D.

PRUFROCK PRESS INC.
WACO, TEXAS

Library of Congress Cataloging-in-Publication Data

Leading change in gifted education : the festschrift of Dr. Joyce Vantassel-Baska / edited by Bronwyn MacFarlane and Tamra Stambaugh.
    p. cm.
 Includes bibliographical references.
 ISBN-13: 978-1-59363-376-9 (pbk.)
 ISBN-10: 1-59363-376-9 (pbk.)
 1. Gifted children--Education. I. VanTassel-Baska, Joyce. II. MacFarlane, Bronwyn, 1974- III. Stambaugh, Tamra.
 LC3993.L393 2009
 371.95'3--dc22
                 2008054401

On the Cover
Pictures left to right clockwise:
- Top left: Mihyeon Kim, Joyce VanTassel-Baska, and Bronwyn MacFarlane collaborating in the doctoral program at The College of William and Mary (circa 2006).
- Top right: Joyce VanTassel-Baska with gifted children enrolled in the Summer Enrichment Program at The College of William and Mary.
- Bottom right: Joyce VanTassel-Baska, Toledo Public Schools English Teacher (circa 1968).
- Center: Joyce VanTassel-Baska, Director of The William and Mary Center for Gifted Education, visiting Petsworth Elementary School in Gloucester, VA (circa 2004).
- Bottom left: Joyce VanTassel-Baska reading with gifted children enrolled in the Saturday Enrichment Program at The College of William and Mary.

Copyright © 2009 Prufrock Press Inc.
Edited by Jennifer Robins
Cover and Layout Design by Marjorie Parker

ISBN-13: 978-1-59363-376-9
ISBN-10: 1-59363-376-9

Printed in the United States of America.

At the time of this book's publication, all facts and figures cited are the most current available. All telephone numbers, addresses, and Web site URLs are accurate and active. All publications, organizations, Web sites, and other resources exist as described in the book, and all have been verified. The authors and Prufrock Press Inc. make no warranty or guarantee concerning the information and materials given out by organizations or content found at Web sites, and we are not responsible for any changes that occur after this book's publication. If you find an error, please contact Prufrock Press Inc.

Prufrock Press Inc.
P.O. Box 8813
Waco, TX 76714-8813
Phone: (800) 998-2208
Fax: (800) 240-0333
http://www.prufrock.com

DEDICATION

This festschrift is dedicated to the work and contributions of Dr. Joyce VanTassel-Baska, a pioneer in leading change in gifted education.

CONTENTS

STRAND I: FOUNDATIONAL THEORIES AND CONSTRUCTS IN GIFTED EDUCATION

Section I: Basic Constructs

Section II: Threats to Optimizing Abilities

STRAND II: APPLICATIONS TO SCHOOL-BASED PRACTICE IN GIFTED EDUCATION

Section III: Applications to School Practice

STRAND III: THE INFRASTRUCTURE OF GIFTED EDUCATION: THE TIES THAT BIND

Section IV: The Infrastructure

ACKNOWLEDGEMENTS

We would like to acknowledge the support of Steve Coxon and Jennifer Axsom for their work on the preparation of this volume.

Thank you to Joel McIntosh, Jennifer Robins, Marjorie Parker, Lacy Compton, and Richard Restaino of Prufrock Press for their generosity, tenacity, and willingness to publish this book in honor of Dr. VanTassel-Baska.

—Bronwyn MacFarlane and Tamra Stambaugh

FOREWORD

by

VIRGINIA
L. MCLAUGHLIN

I am honored to contribute to this text for the festschrift of Joyce VanTassel-Baska. What a wonderful tribute to Joyce to have so many major scholars in the field—who are her friends as well as her colleagues and former students—share their expertise in this single volume, *Leading Change in Gifted Education*. I will leave it to these experts to address Joyce's legacy to the field of gifted education. Having known Joyce since 1987, I will focus more specifically on her contributions to The College of William and Mary and our School of Education.

Joyce's accomplishments have been phenomenal by any measure. Her success as founder and executive director of the Center for Gifted Education has reflected her ability not only to align with our collective vision and values but to actively shape and enliven them through innovative practices. Those of us in NCATE-accredited institutions use conceptual frameworks to communicate our particular visions and values. William and Mary's conceptual framework includes four key components: content expertise, reflective practice, collaboration, and leadership. We claim these as hallmarks of our education programs. When I think of Joyce's legacy to William and Mary, I recognize and celebrate the myriad ways that she has actualized, enriched, and expanded our vision over the past two decades. Briefly, I will highlight some of these.

The first strand of William and Mary's conceptual framework involves content expertise. Foundational to Joyce's success as a teacher, scholar, and leader has been a knowledge base of remarkable breadth and depth. Her understanding of teaching and learning always has been firmly grounded in the liberal arts. With deep respect for the structure of disciplines, Joyce has brought important perspective to curriculum issues in gifted education. Her concern for *what* should be taught has been coupled with equal concern for *how* content can be taught most effectively to learners with diverse needs. Joyce's expertise in curriculum development is unique and internationally acclaimed.

The commitment to content expertise also has been pervasive throughout the Center for Gifted Education. Faculty, students, and staff have come from diverse backgrounds with a range of concentrations and work experiences. Their common ground has been the pursuit of intellectual rigor in their own work and in their work on behalf of gifted learners. Perhaps the strongest evidence of the focus on content expertise is apparent in the research agenda of the Center. Its continual efforts to test, validate, and improve assessment, program, curriculum, and instructional practices have significantly advanced the knowledge base of our profession.

The second strand of our conceptual framework, reflective practice, represents the ongoing application of theory, research, and practice in authentic settings. With its emphasis on intentional, systematic planning, and problem solving, reflective practice might simply be defined as "Joyce in action." Her entire approach to life has been characterized by an indefatigable quest for excellence. Seldom accepting ideas at face value, Joyce questions and probes until ideas worth pursuing become more coherent and compelling. Some might find this annoying, but those of us who have been privileged to work with Joyce have seen how she holds her own work to even greater scrutiny, and we know that her nudging us through such interactions stretches our own capacity for reflective practice. Talent development at work!

Agenda setting for the Center for Gifted Education has always been a reflective process as well. In-depth planning, careful implementation, and thorough evaluation are habitual activities throughout the Center. Its models for curriculum development and for student problem-based learning are, in essence, well-refined examples of reflective practice.

The collaboration strand of the conceptual framework is fully embodied in the work of the Center for Gifted Education. Even a quick glance at the list of its publications and products reveals that nearly all of the work has been a group effort. I can assure you that in the Center for Gifted Education, coauthoring has not been an automatic practice or nominal gesture. Having observed closely and on occasion been part of a project team for the Center, I know the level of engagement that has been expected of all partners. Faculty, staff, and students have quickly realized, first, that no one can possibly keep up with Joyce, and, then, in even trying to keep up with her, everyone works harder and contributes more than ever thought possible. Work in the Center for Gifted Education has not been for the faint-hearted.

Yet, along with the high expectations has been an amazing level of support. Joyce has created in the Center for Gifted Education a powerful community of practice where persons with great capacity and commitment have worked together to tackle significant issues and accomplish complex tasks well beyond what any might have achieved independently.

The faculty, students, and staff who work at the Center have been core members of this community of practice and regularly included others in their collaborative projects. From the beginning, the Center for Gifted Education has been an interdisciplinary effort. School of Education faculty in curriculum and instruction, foundations and research, educational leadership, and other areas have contributed to Center initiatives. Deep collaborative relationships with faculty in arts and science departments have been critical to the curriculum work of the Center. These collaborative relationships have extended well beyond the William and Mary community. Key leaders in gifted education have served on the Center's National Advisory Committee and contributed greatly to strategic planning and evaluation efforts. Members of the National Advisory Committee and other experts frequently have presented for Center conferences and contributed to collaborative publications. Central to all of these accomplishments over the past two decades have been partnerships with public schools. Through well-established local, national, and international networks, states, districts, schools, teachers, and administrators have participated actively in curriculum development and research.

The fourth strand of William and Mary's conceptual framework focuses on leadership, another great strength of the Center for Gifted Education evident throughout its academic programs, research and development, and advocacy efforts. The program in gifted education at the doctoral level is offered as a concentration within the Ph.D. in educational policy, planning, and leadership. As such, students are prepared explicitly for leadership roles in school districts, state agencies, higher education, and other settings. Those at the master's level who prepare primarily for teaching specialist roles also build leadership capacity as they develop curriculum, consult with teachers, serve on school-based teams, and advocate for children's needs. Whatever leadership preparation these students have received in their formal coursework and clinical and research experiences has been magnified through their work in the Center for Gifted Education. Students at all levels have gotten directly involved in research and development, program and conference coordination, journal editing, professional association activities, and other leadership responsibilities.

With Joyce at the helm, the Center for Gifted Education has assumed a strong leadership role within the profession and policy arena. By tackling some of the most pressing issues of the field, the Center has charted new directions in assessment and curriculum development. Projects Athena and Clarion, for example, have demonstrated that rigorous, problem-based curriculum typically reserved for high-ability learners can benefit all students in heterogeneous classes in Title I elementary schools. A comprehensive, performance-based assessment system designed for the state of South Carolina serves as a model for identifying high-ability students, particularly those from traditionally underrepresented groups.

Any discussion of leadership must focus ultimately on Joyce herself. Major leadership awards from the National Association for Gifted Children and Mensa International have acknowledged her extraordinary career-long contributions, yet even these prestigious awards cannot do justice to her achievements. The publication of this festschrift may come closest to capturing what Joyce has meant to the profession.

Joyce leaves a rich and enduring legacy at The College of William and Mary. Since her arrival in 1987, she has set the pace for the School of Education and helped us as a faculty to expand our research and service horizons. Our current conceptual framework reflects many of the values and aspirations that Joyce has articulated and modeled over the years. Her work at the Center for Gifted Education has made our vision come alive and, once again, set a very high standard to which we must aspire.

Virginia L. McLaughlin
Dean and Chancellor Professor
School of Education
The College of William and Mary

FOREWORD

by

Patricia O'Connell Johnson

Recently, I received a final report for one of Joyce's Javits-funded projects, and I reviewed it with particular interest because I knew Joyce was retiring and that it would be the last report I would receive from her after many years—needless to say, it was on time, interesting, and complete, as always. I also knew that I had the honor of writing this foreword for Joyce's festschrift book and had fitfully, even anxiously, been considering what I could say that would sum up my feelings about her and her work. There, in the middle of a 6-inch binder stuffed with materials produced out of this project, was a brief summary of her work over the past 20 years. Even though I knew this history, having been involved in helping to fund a good deal of it, I was amazed. The work is impressive and important, and all the more astonishing because I know how hard it is to sustain high-quality work over a long period of time, especially with erratic funding sources.

So, allow me to stroll down memory lane. I was hired to be the first director of the Javits program when it was created in 1989. It was a hectic beginning. We were simultaneously running a grant competition and a competition for the first national research center. About 4 months into the fiscal year, Congress passed a supplemental budget and the Javits program received an additional $1 million. Green as I was in the ways of Washington, I had no idea how unusual this was, but in the almost 20 years since then I have never seen another program receive, unasked for, additional funds in the middle of the fiscal year. Given the timing, the only way we could get the funds awarded to the field was through a contract for some specialized work. I had this idea that the field needed more attention to the disciplinary content of gifted programs. This was a time when many programs focused on process skills and extracurricular activities. I struggled with describing the needed work in the solicitation—I knew in general terms what was needed but because it didn't really exist yet, it was hard to describe in bureaucratic language, and I wasn't sure what was required to create them. Thankfully, when we read Joyce's proposal, I could exhale. I could tell that she understood what we were trying to create and had the wherewithal to manage it. She brought fresh ideas to the project that we hadn't considered but which greatly improved on our original notions. This was the beginning of the problem-based learning curricula that is a hallmark of the Center for Gifted Education at The College of William and Mary. Under impossibly tight time limitations, she created an outstanding team and plowed ahead developing high-level, challenging curricula in science and language arts. She has built on this beginning by expanding into other disciplines, has tested the impact of the materials on students' learning, and won national awards and honors for the work from a many quarters. Thousands of children around the country have benefited from the William and Mary curriculum. What more can a bureaucrat ask for from a government investment?

Over the life of the Javits program, Joyce has been successful in winning discretionary grants that continued her work in curriculum and allowed her to contribute to another of her passions—improving the educational opportunities of low-income students who are gifted and talented. She has done the tough empirical work to determine what professional development, curricula, materials and support, and assessments work in improving the chances of disadvantaged students with great potential. Her work embodies high standards and great opportunities for these students. She never underestimated what these students could do.

I've learned a lot from Joyce. Here are but a few of these lessons:

▶ Intellectual enthusiasm coupled with hard work and tenacity is a powerful combination. Joyce always has a new idea that she's been thinking about or something wonderful she's read. Where she is different from most, however, is that she also thinks about how to use these ideas and integrate them into work that helps teachers and students. Although this complexifies what she started out with and makes her project more difficult to do, ultimately the work is stronger and richer for it.

▶ Surround yourself with strong people with diverse talents and the work will be better. Over the 20 years I've worked with the Center, the staff has always been hard working, committed, strong-minded, and smart. The quality and quantity of the work of the Center depended on her exceptional staff.

▸ One can have strong, even controversial beliefs, but if you state them in gracious ways you are more likely to be heard. Joyce holds strong opinions but the door is always open for discussion and reflection.

The field of gifted and talented education will miss Joyce's daily presence, but I expect we will continue to benefit from her wisdom and advice for years to come. I know that the Javits program has been greatly enhanced by the quality of her work.

Patricia O'Connell Johnson
United States Department of Education

CHAPTER 1

TRANSFORMING GIFTEDNESS TO EMINENCE:

Patterns of Influence on a Developmental Path From Publication to Policy Center

by

RENA
F. SUBOTNIK,

MELANIE
FRANK,

LUCAS
COOK,

ROCHELLE
RICKOFF,

AND

ASHLEY
EDMISTON

As individuals become older, more educated and established in a career, ability appears to become less of a factor in distinguishing the gifted from their colleagues.
—Joyce VanTassel-Baska (1989)

INTRODUCTION

Scholars relish their simple pleasures. One of the most delightful is finding an article or book chapter that coalesces thoughts and gives direction to one's work. This chapter honors the impact of "Characteristics of the Developmental Path of Eminent and Gifted Adults," authored by Joyce VanTassel-Baska. It appeared in a book she coedited with Paula Olszewski-Kubilius, entitled, *Patterns of Influence on Gifted Learners* (1989). The chapter sheds light on a central conundrum of our field: Children we identify as gifted in childhood often do not demonstrate truly exceptional performance in adulthood, *and* exceptional adults often report that others did not view them as gifted children or educate them as such. VanTassel-Baska discusses many potential explanations for this puzzle including: (1) the trajectory of some domains starts later than childhood, (2) professionals may not be using the appropriate identification schema, and (3) practitioners may not be offering the appropriate educational stimuli to promote talent development of gifted children.

We organize this chapter as follows. First, we provide a summary of the VanTassel-Baska chapter (while encouraging those of you who have not read it in a while to go back to the original). Next, we offer a logic chain for the research conducted by Subotnik and colleagues that led to the establishment of the American Psychological Association's (APA) Center for Gifted Education Policy. Third, we describe the work of the Center in light of this logic chain, including the description of three major projects that explore educational and social paths to eminence.

DEVELOPMENTAL PATH OF GIFTED AND EMINENT ADULTS

A wealth of research has been conducted to inform what schools should do with gifted students. A much smaller proportion of the gifted literature is devoted to eminence later in life, including links between giftedness in youth and eminence in adulthood. Joyce VanTassel-Baska (1989) provided an outstanding synthesis of the eminence literature nearly 20 years ago. In the article, she defined childhood giftedness as " . . . advanced development in intellectual areas, or as exemplary performance in a specific area . . . " (p. 146). Concurrently, VanTassel-Baska identified adult giftedness as measured by national and international recognition through high-quality and important work in one's field. She argued that eminence cannot be predicted on childhood giftedness alone, and that eminence is culture-bound so that factors that lead to eminence in one time and place may not be relevant in another context. She also stated that eminence may be obtained after death (as in the case of Emily Dickinson) and that in some cases achieving eminence may have a negative effect on production of subsequent works (as with Ernest Hemingway).

VanTassel-Baska further developed a model for the transformation of giftedness into eminence over a person's lifetime in the course of four stages:

- early childhood (developing talent),
- middle childhood (nurturing talent),
- adolescence/adulthood (displaying extraordinary achievement), and
- adulthood/old age (producing "prodigious acts and life's work"). (p. 157)

She presented the first two stages as a "constellation of variables" (VanTassel-Baska, 1989, p. 157), where the development and nurturance of talent can depend on factors such as schooling, community, family support, and position within the family. As a child moves from early to middle childhood, skills, knowledge, attitudes, behaviors, personal characteristics, and higher order thinking skills emerge as tangible results of the interplay between the aforementioned factors (VanTassel-Baska, 1989, p. 158).

As gifted children enter into adolescence, then adulthood and old age, they build a framework around them that shifts and supports this constellation of variables. A "recreated family" (VanTassel-Baska, 1989, p. 158) replaces their home family structure as gifted individuals seek out other bright peers and mentors associated with their talents. The workplace replaces schooling as the arena for demonstrating abilities. Factors such as timing, perceptions of events and experiences, and the role of significant others influence the framework.

Innate intelligence is important only as a starting point in the model: Other psycho-social factors such as family, home life, parental involvement, personal traits, and perceptions become just as important, if not more important, over time. VanTassel-Baska (1989) stated that coming from a middle-class background and having parents who are highly educated professionals, as well as gaining early access to role models and large home libraries, are good indicators for eminence. She also presented evidence that both a stable home life and an unstable home life can be predictors of eminence, but for different reasons. For example, VanTassel-Baska cited a Goertzel and Goertzel (1962) study showing that out of 400 childhood homes that produced eminent adults only 58 could be considered untroubled. The researchers argued that troubles early in childhood, if dealt with in a healthy way, give children the skills to deal with life's hardships.

Notably, researchers have shown that traditional schooling in the primary and secondary grades can have little impact on gifted children's abilities to become eminent adults. In fact, VanTassel-Baska (1989) noted that 60% of those in Goertzel and Goertzel's 1962 study had serious schooling issues. This might be explained by the tendency of some gifted children to develop a particular passion that becomes so prominent that it can overshadow and inhibit other areas of learning (VanTassel-Baska, 1989).

The central factors of adult eminence reported by VanTassel-Baska (1989) are personal traits and perceptions. Gifted children may have talents but never properly develop them without the passion, determination, and confidence to pursue their goals. These personal traits become increasingly important as gifted children reach adulthood and rise in their respective fields. In elite fields, there are fewer differences between levels of talent among peers, so personal traits and perceptions about chances of success play a larger role in achieving more public success. VanTassel-Baska noted that perceptions about chances of success and perceptions about previous successes are greater predictors of future accomplishments than actual evidence of past achievement.

The development of eminence is a topic of particular interest for the APA Center for Gifted Education Policy (CGEP). Our work is committed to promoting the educational and social skills necessary for adolescents with demonstrated talent to become successful in their chosen fields. The more we know about what factors are important in fostering eminence, the more we can promote these factors through education and policy to help the next generation of gifted youth stay on track to reach their full potential.

LINKAGES OF CGEP AND
VANTASSEL-BASKA (1989)

In 1986, the first author and some colleagues (Subotnik, Kassan, Summers, & Wasser, 1993) began a study of the high-IQ graduates (1948–1960) of Hunter College Elementary School, a publicly funded, highly selective school in New York City. The researchers compared 210 participants, with a mean IQ of 157 (Stanford-Binet L-M) at age 4, to the Terman group by using the Terman-Oden midlife questionnaire (Terman & Oden, 1959). These grown-up gifted children experienced many advantages associated with the fulfillment of talent: educated parents, enriched schooling, and challenging peers. We expected our study participants to be major contributors to the arts, sciences, and professions. However, the paths they chose to midlife did not deviate from what might have been expected from bright, upper middle class students. They were upstanding and productive citizens, content with their professional lives, and enjoyed good mental and physical health. However, the Hunter graduates were not exceptionally eminent in their fields. Subotnik and her colleagues attributed this outcome to ambition neutralized by general life satisfaction. In order to explain the outcomes better, we looked to the literature on lifespan development, including VanTassel-Baska's 1989 chapter. We concluded that high IQ and an enriched home and school environment were not sufficient to generate eminence.

Concurrently, Subotnik pursued her longitudinal study of Westinghouse (now Intel) Science Talent Search (STS) winners. STS is the most prestigious U.S. high school science award, and only can be attained by demonstrating hard work, commitment, and creativity, and finding a mentor/sponsor. In order to better understand the variables that predicted continuing participation in the elite science pipeline, Subotnik and her colleagues (Subotnik, Duschl, & Selmon, 1993; Subotnik, Maurer, & Steiner, 2001) conducted a 13-year longitudinal study of the 1983 STS cohort. This group came from less economically enriched backgrounds than the Hunter group, and at age 17 aspired to be successful research or applied scientists (including doctors and engineers). Most achieved their goals of attending top U.S. universities to study science disciplines. Once there, however, they encountered a number of hurdles that quenched the ambition of a significant proportion of this group, particularly the women. The first setbacks came in the form of large and impersonal science and mathematics courses. At the most elite institutions, these exceptionally talented young scientists perceived that professors and peers viewed them as no more unique than any other freshman. They felt dismayed that the institutions made no effort to capitalize on their experience in top labs at the frontiers of science while in high school. Even by the second year of college, many could not gain entry to a laboratory or access to a sponsor/mentor.

After their university studies, those Westinghouse study participants who had successfully majored in the sciences continued into graduate engineering, medicine, and science research. By age 35, however, none of the female scientists were engaged full-time as researchers, having chosen to devote more energy to developing a family. Only a small minority of the men were able to find academic positions in the mid 1990s, as they faced a shortage of openings for research scientists both in academe and in industry.

In 1995, just as the last round of Westinghouse longitudinal data came in, Subotnik (2004) began a 3-year study of elite classical musicians' training and preparation. How were young people of the same level of ability as the Westinghouse cohort educated when they entered a conservatory at age 18? Indeed, she found stark differences between the university and conservatory programs. Each conservatory student had a teacher (often an active professional performer) assigned to him or her, and that teacher usually had fewer than 10 students at any time in his or her studio. In addition to individual lessons, conservatory students had the equivalent of doctoral seminars in the form of master classes. Students tested their own motivation and drive every week during lessons, and each year with a juried performance in front of the entire faculty associated with their instrument. Explicit presentation of tacit knowledge emerged as the second important difference between conservatory preparation and university education. Each student took courses, also reinforced in individual lessons, about how to select a repertoire for performance, how to dress, where to get headshots or agents, and the like. Students also lived in dormitories with artists from other departments, including dance and drama. These arrangements helped stave off the loneliness that dogged earlier generations of musicians who became increasingly isolated in their practice rooms. Finally, students reported that the prevailing ethos of the institution was that playing and creating music were the most important and valuable life pursuits. As a corollary, conservatory students shared the notion that it was natural to experience setbacks and sacrifices in order to achieve the life to which they aspired.

A second study at three conservatories explored the psychosocial variables associated with success in music careers (Subotnik & Jarvin, 2005; Subotnik, Jarvin, Moga, & Sternberg, 2003). The researchers interviewed 74 members of the conservatory community, including students, teachers, and administrators, with regard to a set of 17 variables. Six gatekeepers (newspaper critics, artistic directors, and agents) also responded to the interview protocol. As a result of this data collection, the researchers developed a model of talent development that demonstrated the importance of social skills and other psychosocial variables in successful performance careers, beyond the demonstration of talent and technique. Although the first publication of this work appeared in 2003, researchers collected and analyzed the data before the American Psychological Association (APA) established the Center for Gifted Education Policy in 2001. The theoretical and empirical framework of the Center derived from Subotnik's work, as well as that of Bloom (1985), Feldman (1986), Gagné (2005), Sternberg (1998), Tannenbaum (1986), and Zuckerman (1979), with a special focus on variables outside the home. A key spark for the work was the 1989 VanTassel-Baska publication.

CGEP's MODELS FOR DOMAIN SPECIFIC GIFTED YOUTH

The mission of the American Psychological Association's Center for Gifted Education Policy is to generate public awareness, advocacy, clinical applications, and cutting-edge research ideas that will enhance the achievement and performance of children and adolescents with special gifts and talents in all domains, including the academic disciplines, the performing arts, sport, and the professions. In the area of talent development and gifted education, CGEP has initiated several programs that support the goal of transforming adolescent talent into the next generation of eminent scholars or artists. The American Psychological Foundation (APF) first created and funded the Center in order to bring more attention to the topic of giftedness, particularly to psychological scientists and practitioners. Since 2004, the APF and grants from the Jack Kent Cooke Foundation, the Camille and Henry Dreyfus Foundation, and the National Science Foundation have supported CGEP's work.

CGEP first developed the Pinnacle Model and later the Catalyst Project, whose goals align with our mission to foster talent development while drawing upon several of the factors VanTassel-Baska (1989) mentioned as important components in promoting talent.

The Pinnacle Model

Martin Seligman conceived of the Pinnacle Model as emblematic of Positive Psychology (Seligman & Csikszentmihalyi, 2000). Seligman, in partnership with CGEP director Rena Subotnik, developed the Pinnacle Project. This year-long program teamed an eminent master in the fields of art, science, or other professions with a gifted high school student who had demonstrated high-level interest and talent in that field. The Pinnacle Project brought together developed and developing talent in order to:

- ▸ provide an opportunity for highly gifted adolescents to learn from and be guided by mentors in their fields of interest, including planning investigations that would serve as a basis of these mentoring relationships;
- ▸ establish a venue of fertilization for creativity and exploration in the design and execution of a year long project; and
- ▸ discuss in a safe forum the joys, psychological stresses, and expectations associated with talent development at the very highest levels and gain access to tacit knowledge as could only be provided by a true master.

The participants of the model included (1) *Masters*, eminent scholars across a series of domains; (2) *Associates*, rising stars in their domain; and (3) *Scholars*, high-school-aged individuals who have exhibited outstanding achievement in one of those fields as a result of their commitment of time and talent.

As part of the Pinnacle Project, the Masters design their own application targeting the factors they consider most important in selecting their scholars. For example, our chemical engineering Master sought candidates who had conducted projects where an idea conceived in their head was translated through their hands. Applicants also show their interest by providing evidence of enrollment in academic classes and participation in competitions and projects that show they went beyond normal academic expectations. Masters normally prefer students who possess a high level of ambition and intellectual curiosity over high marks, as these personality traits set apart future achievers from their more average counterparts (Terman & Oden, 1959, as cited by VanTassel-Baska, 1989).

During a summer week known as the *Summit*, Masters, Associates, and Scholars participate in domain-specific activities and interdisciplinary discussions and project planning on a college campus in the Berkshire Mountains. Each day includes team meetings (where Masters, Associates, and Scholars generate the beginnings of a yearlong project), Masters' lectures or demonstrations, round table discussions, and cultural and recreational activities.

VanTassel-Baska found the inclusion of a mentor to be an important indicator of eminence and cited several scholars (Bloom, 1985; Simonton, 1978; Zuckerman, 1979) whose work supports the significance of a role model in the course of emerging talent. The Pinnacle Project encourages mentoring relationships to flourish during team meetings where Scholars select their project designs. Mentoring continues to be an important part of the model throughout the year as Masters provide guidance on the projects, helping to negotiate academics and life as well. This process transitions Scholars from a learning into a mastery stage, as described in Bloom's (1985) model of talent development. The Pinnacle Project also grants Scholars an opportunity for risk-taking and failure, both important factors in achieving eminence in any of the disciplines (Ochse, 1990). The Pinnacle Model strives to show the creative parallels among professional fields as a source of inspiration and risk-taking for students as they undertake their own projects, no matter what the domain.

A third key element to the model is the tacit knowledge shared by both Masters and Associates. In addition to the yearlong mentoring relationship based on a project, team meetings at the Summit offer career guidance and other forms of insider knowledge. These meetings and meal-time round table discussions provide opportunities for discussions relating to giftedness, as well as the expectations that come along with it. Round table discussions offer the opportunity to flesh out ideas in a more casual format. Topics have ranged from the current state of mathematics and science education in the schools to when it is best to take a professional risk. Over the years, the Pinnacle Model has evolved into several new mentoring programs. The most recent is the Catalyst Program.

The Catalyst Program

Supported by the Camille and Henry Dreyfus Foundation, the Catalyst Program is an out-of-school plan and course for adolescents with deep interests in and commitment to the arts or sciences. Over a 3-year span that began during the summer of 2007, Catalyst has immersed more than 100 participants into experiences that develop young artists and scientists, combining intensive exploration in a specific discipline with intergenerational professional advice and consultation, as well as interdisciplinary creative stimulation.

Catalyst uniquely focuses on the disciplines of art and chemistry, drawing on the multidisciplinary approach of the Pinnacle Project. Although it seems like an unusual coupling, there are meaningful connections between success as a scientist and evidence of success as an artist of various mediums (Root-Bernstein et al., 2008).

The purpose of Catalyst is to provide team-based support for transforming adolescent talent into the next generation of important innovators. Like the Pinnacle Project, the participants of the program are composed of Masters (four chemists and three artists), Associates, and Scholars. Each Master works with three Scholars (rather than one in the Pinnacle Model) in order to increase the number of Scholars impacted by the program and to provide additional peer support for participating Scholars. VanTassel-Baska (1989) noted the difficulty that many gifted adolescents can face in forming meaningful relationships with other students their own age. Although not targeted as a social program, Catalyst does provide a platform for Scholars to interact with peers who share motivation, interests, and abilities. Scholars are free to express their ideas and fortify their self-perceptions as scholars or artists, something VanTassel-Baska noted as an important factor in predicting eminence later in life. Other planned activities, such as attending high-caliber artistic presentations (performing, visual, and music) and subsequent discussions led by a Catalyst Master in the same or similar field are important for eliciting creative connections among disciplines and showing the parallels in the creative process between art and science.

The mentoring aspect remains the core of the program and Masters and their Associates sustain a relationship with "their" Scholars through regular lab visits and correspondence, in order to complete projects discussed and/or developed during the Summit. The following year, Scholars, Masters, and Associates return to the Summit to where the Scholars present their projects and everyone interacts with members of a new Catalyst cohort. The return of the previous cohort creates a growing community of individuals who help one another by providing connections, information, recommendations, and creative collaborations.

CGEP's Research Project on Specialized STEM High Schools

The difficulty in recognizing and supporting talented American students in the disciplines of science, technology, engineering, and mathematics (STEM) has surfaced as a recent challenge for many researchers and policymakers (Andreescu, Gallian, Kane, & Mertz, 2008; National Academy of Sciences, National Academy of Engineering, & Institute of Medicine of the National Academies, 2007; Tai, Liu, Maltese, & Fan, 2006). In addition, both researchers and practitioners lament the startling observation that young and talented STEM students often choose not to pursue STEM fields as a career (Lee, 1998; Subotnik et al., 1993). Several states have responded with widespread funding for specialized STEM high schools to support their high-achieving math and science students. However, thus far, no studies have shown that students who attend specialized STEM schools instead of their traditional high schools are more likely to choose STEM majors during college, enter into STEM careers, or ultimately achieve eminence in such fields.

CGEP has embarked on a 3-year investigation to examine the contributions of specialized STEM high schools to the development of scientific researchers in the life, physical, and behavioral sciences. In partnership with Robert H. Tai of the University of Virginia, and with funding through the National Science Foundation (NSF), CGEP will oversee a comprehensive survey of 5,000 STEM high school graduates 4–6 years out versus similarly talented students (participants in the Midwest Academic Talent Search) who attend conventional high schools. The study will track graduates and ask them to remark on their high school experiences and outcomes. Are specialized STEM high school graduates more likely to remain in the science, math, engineering, or technology fields than students with similar academic ability and interests who attended traditional public high schools? Which instructional practices used by specialized STEM high schools are associated with keeping students in the science, mathematics, and technology tracks in college and higher rates of entrance into science-, mathematics-, or technology-related professions? Do specialized STEM high school graduates possess perspectives on professional success and ethical scientific behavior that differ from their non-STEM counterparts?

VanTassel-Baska (1989) identified some specific characteristics that seem to increase the likelihood of eminence. She noted, for example, that eminent individuals have reported the importance of early access to role models throughout their development (p. 149). She acknowledged Zuckerman's (1979) study of Nobel Laureates, which found that access to "an elite network of scientists through apprenticeships was a key pattern in their lives" (VanTassel-Baska, 1989, p. 149). As such, CGEP hypothesizes that whether or not a student talented in science attends a specialized school environment or a traditional school, those who locate such mentors are more likely to stay in the science pipeline. Given that specialized schools have integrated these apprenticeships into their curriculum, the opportunity for apprenticeships or mentorships may be more accessible in STEM schools.

VanTassel-Baska (1989) noted that highly gifted children and adolescents commonly refuse to conform to "normal societal pressure" of their age-mates (p. 153). CGEP estimates that STEM schools provide a greater pool of students with similar and advanced interests, allowing gifted students the chance for more or deeper friendships and schoolwork that will satisfy their need for challenge (VanTassel-Baska, 1989, p. 154).

It may be that STEM schools provide positive prototypes of science-related careers that support student self-perceptions within their school environment—not just within their academic course selections—increasing the likelihood that gifted students will pursue science and mathematics college majors. In the third stage of VanTassel-Baska's (1989) conceptual model for the development of eminence, she indicated a transition between adolescence and adulthood. In the course of this transition, individuals seek out new support systems to help them develop their interests. Throughout the upcoming NSF study, CGEP intends to test several of these factors to see how or whether they make a specialized school experience for gifted STEM students a more likely path to eminence.

CGEP expects that the results of our research project will contribute to a greater understanding of what leads to eminence in STEM fields. If particular aspects of STEM schools prove important to the development of future scientists, mathematicians, and researchers, it may be possible to emulate some of these characteristics in traditional public high schools. VanTassel-Baska has taken a close look at the difficulties of connecting gifted children to eminent adults. CGEP's work continues this tradition of identifying particular educational practices or environments that appear to be most strongly associated with eminence in STEM disciplines.

CONCLUSION

We are grateful for Joyce VanTassel-Baska's insights in guiding the direction of our Center. In the course of our work, we have developed more confidence in responding to her three disconnects between the generation of eminence on the part of gifted children and the childhood biographies of eminent individuals:

1. *The trajectory of some domains starts later than childhood.* For this reason, CGEP has focused attention on identifying students no younger than 14, and basing our predictions of potential only starting from that age.
2. *We may not be using the appropriate identification schema.* We focus on authentic, content-valid, domain-specific evidence of interest, motivation, and creativity.
3. *We may not be offering the appropriate educational stimuli to promote talent development of gifted children.* We are testing the Pinnacle/Catalyst Models and the specialized high school models of talent development for their effectiveness.

VanTassel-Baska's (1989) chapter directed attention to the importance of bridging the gap between childhood giftedness and the kind of creative invention and productivity that defines eminence. CGEP continues to expand on VanTassel-Baska's seminal synthesis in this arena by researching the psychological and educational factors associated with eminence and using that research to inform its programs for adolescents.

References

Andreescu, T., Gallian, J. A., Kane, J. M., & Mertz, J. E. (2008). Cross-cultural analysis of students with exceptional talent in mathematical problem-solving. *Notices of the American Mathematical Society, 55,* 1248–1260.

Bloom, B. S. (1985). *Developing talent young people.* New York: Ballantine Books.

Feldman, D. H. (1986). *Nature's gambit: Child prodigies and the development of human potential.* New York: Basic Books.

Gagné, F. (2005). From gifts to talents: The DMGT as a developmental model. In R. J. Sternberg & J. E. Davidson (Eds.), *Conceptions of giftedness* (2nd ed., pp. 98–119). New York: Cambridge University Press.

Goertzel, V., & Goertzel, M. G. (1962). *Cradles of eminence.* Boston: Little, Brown.

Lee, J. D. (1998). Which kids can "become" scientists? Effects of gender, self-concepts, and perceptions of scientists. *Social Psychology Quarterly, 61,* 199–219.

National Academy of Sciences, National Academy of Engineering, & Institute of Medicine of the National Academies. (2007). *Rising above the gathering storm: Energizing and employing America for a brighter economic future.* Washington, DC: National Academies Press.

Ochse, R. (1990). *Before the gates of excellence: Determinants of creative genius.* New York: Cambridge University Press.

Root-Bernstein, R., Allen, L., Beach, L., Bhadula, R., Fast, J., Hosey, C., et al. (2008). Arts foster scientific success: Avocations of Nobel, National Academy, Royal Society and Sigma Xi members. *Journal of Psychology of Science and Technology, 1*(2), 51–63.

Seligman, M. E. P., & Csikszentmihalyi, M. (2000). Positive psychology: An introduction. *American Psychologist, 55,* 5–14.

Simonton, D. K. (1978). Multiple discovery and invention: Zeitgeist, genius, or chance? *Journal of Personality and Social Psychology, 37,* 1603–1616.

Sternberg, R. J. (1998). Abilities are forms of developing expertise. *Educational Researcher, 27,* 11–20.

Subotnik, R. F. (2004). Transforming elite musicians into professional artists: A view of the talent development process at the Juilliard School. In L. V. Shavinina & M. Ferrari (Eds.), *Beyond knowledge: Extracognitive aspects of developing high ability* (pp. 137–166). Mahwah, NJ: Erlbaum.

Subotnik, R. F., Duschl, R., & Selmon, E. (1993). Retention and attrition of science talent: A longitudinal study of Westinghouse Science Talent Search winners. *International Journal of Science Education, 15,* 61–72.

Subotnik, R. F., & Jarvin, L. (2005). Beyond expertise: Conceptions of giftedness as great performance. In R. J. Sternberg & J. E. Davidson (Eds.), *Conceptions of giftedness* (2nd ed., pp. 343–357). New York: Cambridge University Press.

Subotnik, R. F., Jarvin, L., Moga, E., & Sternberg, R. (2003). Wisdom from gatekeepers: Secrets of success in music performance. *Bulletin of Psychology and the Arts, 4,* 5–9.

Subotnik, R. F., Kassan, L., Summers, E., & Wasser, A. (1993). *Genius revisited: High IQ children grown up.* Norwood, NJ: Ablex.

Subotnik, R. F., Maurer, K., & Steiner, C. L. (2001). Tracking the next generation of the scientific elite. *Journal of Secondary Gifted Education, 13,* 33–43.

Tai, R. H., Liu, C. Q., Maltese, A. V., & Fan, X. (2006). Planning early for careers in science. *Science, 312,* 1143–1144.

Tannenbaum, A. J. (1986). Giftedness: A psychosocial approach. In R. J. Sternberg & J. E. Davidson (Eds.), *Conceptions of giftedness* (pp. 21–52). New York: Cambridge University Press.

Terman, L. M., & Oden, M. H. (1959). *The gifted group at mid-life: 35 years' follow-up of the superior child.* Stanford, CA: Stanford University Press.

VanTassel-Baska, J. (1989). Characteristics of the developmental path of eminent and gifted adults. In J. VanTassel-Baska & P. Olszewski-Kubilius (Eds.), *Patterns of influence on gifted learners: The home, the self, and the school* (pp. 146–162). New York: Teachers College Press.

Zuckerman, H. (1979). *Scientific elite: Nobel Laureates in the United States.* New York: The Free Press.

CHAPTER 2

EMINENCE AND CREATIVITY IN SELECTED VISUAL ARTISTS

by

JANE
PIIRTO

I dream of painting and then I paint my dream.
—Vincent Van Gogh

Who is eminent? How does one qualify to be eminent? In what does eminence consist? Eminence (n.d.) is defined as "distinguished superiority, elevated rank as compared with others; in reputation, intellectual or moral attainment, or the possession of any quality, good, or (sometimes) bad; acknowledgement of superiority; an excellence." Simonton (1999b) defined eminence as having "made a name" for oneself (p. 647). Some speak of true eminence being defined as the person having made an original contribution to the talent domain, as opposed to high achievement, which consists of continuing old thought in the domain; thus, eminence is viewed as the highest level of the development of one's talent.

People know who is eminent in the talent domains with which they are familiar, or in which they work, but eminence also exists in domains with which most people are not familiar. Eminent people have biographies written about their lives; they are cited in journals, magazines, newspapers, and other media. Simonton (1999b) noted that predicting eminence from mere prominence depends on certain criteria. In terms of individual differences, the productivity, intelligence level, personality attributes, and degree of psychopathology are somewhat distinctive in eminent people. In terms of development, the family pedigree, childhood precocity, birth order, presence of early trauma, the presence of role models and mentors, and formal education and training are important. In terms of the sociocultural context, the political, economic, cultural, and ideological contexts are vital. Most of the research on eminence has focused on men (Albert, 1992; Cattell, 1903; Goertzel, Goertzel, Goertzel, & Hansen, 2004; Simonton, 1999a; Smith, 1938; Terman & Oden, 1959); Simonton (1999b) stated that fewer than 3% of eminent people throughout history were women, Marie Curie notwithstanding. The U.S. Inventors Hall of Fame includes few women, as do most other Halls of Fame. This has led researchers and feminists to propose their own lists (Kronberg, 2008; Piirto, in press-a).

And what about creativity? To put it simplistically, there are several ways to approach creativity. Creativity research focuses on the *person*—who is creative?; the *process*—what happens when one is being creative?; the *product*—what does the creative person make?; and the *press*—what is the environmental pressure on person, process, product (Rhodes, 1961)? One judges a product "creative" and then looks at the person who has produced that product to see what forces operated in the creation of that product and what that person is like. Another approach tests a child through paper and pencil or through observation, pronouncing him or her potentially or really more creative than others, on a presumed normal curve of creativity, as a construct which supposedly exists within everyone to some degree or another.

Domain-based studies of creators have been a focus of research since the 1950s, with the landmark studies of the Institute of Personality Assessment and Research (IPAR) at Berkeley (Barron, 1968, 1972; MacKinnon, 1975). Ghiselin (1952) presented an anthology of creators in various domains discussing their creative process. Feldman and Goldsmith (1986) studied six child prodigies in various domains. VanTassel-Baska (1989) noted that there are certain "necessary but not sufficient" characteristics necessary for creators in domains (p. 146). She also commented on domain-based creativity in 2005, summarizing the research on creativity in domains. Gardner (1993) did case studies of exemplars for seven of his eight intelligences. Creativity in domains also was prominently featured in the *Encyclopedia of Creativity* (Runco & Pritzker, 1999).

My approach has been to look at the creative person and the creative press. Elsewhere I studied creative writers (Piirto, 1998, 2002, in press-b). VanTassel-Baska (1996) also has studied creative writers, exploring themes in the lives of Charlotte Brontë and Virginia Woolf. (Note: This correspondence between Joyce VanTassel-Baska's interests and mine is striking, as my own master's thesis (Piirto, 1966), studied Charlotte Brontë's novel *Villette*.) With much yet to be said about creativity in creative writers, the present chapter looks at persons who have produced creative products in the visual arts. What are their backgrounds, their personalities, their experiences, and their ways of looking at the world?

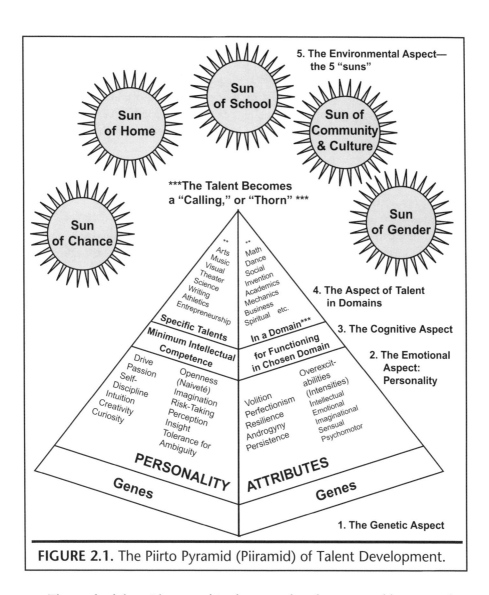

FIGURE 2.1. The Piirto Pyramid (Piiramid) of Talent Development.

The methodology I have used in the research to be presented here is qualitative and archival. Scholarly biographies, autobiographies, memoirs, and published interviews have formed the basis for this research. The findings in qualitative research are inductive. In doing the massive reading necessary for writing a synoptic textbook, I formulated my first version of the Piirto Pyramid in 1994. This model has since guided my work on talent in domains (Piirto, 1992, 1994, 2000, 2004). It is a contextual framework for a biographical method that considers person, process, and product, as well as press, or environmental factors (see Figure 2.1).

THE PIIRTO PYRAMID (PIIRAMID) OF TALENT DEVELOPMENT

The eight basic assumptions of the Piirto Pyramid include (1) creativity is domain based; (2) environmental factors are extremely important; (3) talent is an inborn propensity; (4) creativity and talent can be developed; (5) creativity is not a general aptitude, but is an attribute of personality, dependent on the demands of the domain; (6) each domain of talent has its own rules and ways in which talent is developed; (7) these rules are well-established and known to experts in the domain; and (8) talent is recognized through certain early *predictive behaviors*, that is, certain patterns that are common to those who enter the same field. Along with these predictive behaviors are certain crystallizing experiences (Feldman, 1982). Crystallizing experiences are unique to the individual, while predictive behaviors are common to the field. The crystallizing experience lets the person know that this particular domain is the one for him and sets him on the path.

1. The Genetic Aspect and the Emotional Aspect: Personality Attributes

Many studies have emphasized that successful creators in all domains have certain *personality attributes* in common (e.g., Baird, 1985; Feist, 1999). These make up the base of the model, the affective aspects of what a person needs to succeed. These rest on the foundation of *genes*. Among these are androgyny; creativity; imagination; insight; introversion; intuition; naiveté, or openness to experience; overexcitabilities; passion for work in a domain; perceptiveness; persistence; preference for complexity; resilience; risk-taking; self-discipline; self-efficacy; tolerance for ambiguity; and volition, or will (see Piirto, 1992, 1994, 2000, 2004). This list is by no means discrete or complete, but shows that creative adults have achieved effectiveness partially by force of personality, and talented adults who achieve success possess many of these attributes. One could call these the foundation, along with the genetic aspect, and one could go further and say that these may be innate but to a certain extent they also can be developed and directly taught.

2. The Cognitive Aspect

The *cognitive* dimension in the form of an IQ score has been overemphasized. The IQ test often is an abstract, "out there" screen that served to obfuscate our efforts, and IQ is a *minimum* criterion, mortar and paste, with a certain level of intellectual ability necessary for functioning in the world. Having a really high IQ is not necessary for the realization of most talents. Rather, college graduation seems to be necessary (except for professional basketball players, actors, and entertainers), and as Simonton (1999a) said, most college graduates have above-average IQs but not stratospheric IQs. Theoretical physicists and philosophers may need the highest IQs.

3. Talent in Domains

The *talent* itself—inborn, innate, mysterious—also should be developed. Each school has experts in most of the talent domains that students will enter. The talent domain is the tip of the Pyramid. The talents are quite well-defined academically, and people can go to school to study in any of them. Most talents are recognized through certain predictive behaviors, for example, voracious reading for linguistically talented students or a preference to be class treasurer for mathematically talented students. These talents are demonstrated within domains that are socially recognized and valued within the society, and thus may differ from society to society.

4. Environmental "Suns"

These four levels described could theoretically be called the individual person. In addition, each individual is influenced by five "suns." These suns may be likened to certain factors in the environment. The three major suns refer to a child's being (1) in a positive and nurturing *home* environment, and (2) in a *community and culture* that conveys values compatible with the educational institution, and that provides support for the home and the school. The (3) *school* is a key factor, especially for those children whose other suns may have clouds in front of them. Other, smaller suns are (4) the influence of *gender*, for there have been found few gender differences in personality attributes in adult creative producers; and (5) what *chance* can provide. Chance can be improved by manipulating oneself so that one can indeed be in the right place at the right time. The presence or absence of all or several of these make the difference between whether a talent is developed or whether it atrophies. Many people's "suns" have clouds before them, and their progress in the development of their talents is obfuscated by circumstance.

5. Talent Multipotentiality: Feeling the Call, or the "Thorn"

However, although absolutely necessary, the presence of talent is not sufficient. Many people have more than one talent, and wonder what to do with them. What is the impetus, what is the reason, for one talent taking over and capturing the passion and commitment of the person who has the talent? A useful explanation comes from Socrates, who described the inspiration of the Muse (Plato, *Ion*). Carl Jung (1965) described the passion that engrosses; Csikszentmihalyi (1990) described the process of flow; and depth psychologist James Hillman (1996) described the presence of the *daimon* in creative lives. All of these provide clues as to what talent a person will choose to develop. This is similar to the notion of vocation or call. I would call it inspiration or passion for the domain. Philosophers would call it soul, and depth psychologists would agree (Reynolds & Piirto, 2005, 2007). Thus, I have put an asterisk, or "thorn" on the pyramid to exemplify that talent is not enough for the realization of a life of commitment. Suffice it to say that the entire picture of talent development ensues when a person is pierced or bothered by a thorn, which is similar to the *daimon* (Jung, 1965), the acorn (Hillman, 1996) or the call (vocational psychology)—that leads to commitment.

6. Crystallizing Experiences and Catalysts

Much evidence exists that the creative person decides to pursue the development of his or her talent after some catalyst reveals that this is what must happen. It may be winning a contest or receiving praise or may come after a long period of thought and meditation. The creative person recognizes that the thorn is pricking and the call must be answered. In this chapter, I will elucidate only one of the talent domains, visual arts, using the Piirto Pyramid as a framework.

DOMAIN: VISUAL ARTS

Vasari (1561) began the consideration of eminence in visual arts with his classic books, *Lives of the Most* Eminent *Artists* (emphasis added). Throughout this medieval text, themes that are still current in the lives of artists show up, especially in the presence of the predictive behavior of compulsive drawing during childhood.

1. The Genetic Aspect

The evidence shows that talent in visual arts runs in families (Goertzel et al., 2004) with the families of Calder, Duchamp, Renoir, Picasso, O'Keeffe, Kahlo, Raphael, Bernini, and Utrillo as examples. Nochlin (1988) pointed out that in the 17th and 18th centuries,

> the transmission of the artistic profession from father to son was considered a matter of course; . . . a large proportion of artists, great and not so great, in the days when it was not normal for sons to follow in their fathers' footsteps, had artist fathers. (p. 156)

Greer (1979) pointed out that female visual artists frequently came from dynasties of artists, but their works often went unsigned.

2. The Emotional Aspect: Personalities of Visual Artists

Studies (Barron, 1972; Sloane & Sosniak, 1985) have shown that visual artists care little about social conformity, have a high need to achieve success independently, and are flexible. Personality attributes recognized through biographical studies (as cited in Piirto, 2004) were androgyny, risk-taking, depression, tolerance for ambiguity, preference for complexity, naiveté, nonconformity, intuition, ambition or drive, and interests and values that resemble those of other people in the arts.

3. The Cognitive Aspect in Visual Artists

The intelligence of visual artists is spatial intelligence (Gardner, 1993), or figural intelligence (Guilford, 1967). As Vincent Van Gogh, in his letters to his brother, said, "It is at bottom fairly true that a painter as man is too much absorbed by what his eyes see, and is not sufficiently master of the rest of his life" (Stone & Stone, 1937, p. 45). The Getzels and Csikszentmihalyi (1976) study of visual artists revealed that their cognition is most aptly described as problem finding, rather than problem solving. Problem finding precedes problem solving.

4. The Domain "Thorn" in Artists

Art is a vocation, a sacred calling, and those who heed the call have a certain character besides interest and talent. The decision to commit their careers to making art—to being artists—came "as a progressive or sequential revelation," according to Sloane and Sosniak (1985, p. 130). For example, N. C. Wyeth as a child was driven by a "constant need to draw," and he put a drawing table in his bedroom (Michaelis, 1998, p. 32). His schoolbooks and notebooks were filled with sketches in the margins. He begged his merchant father to pay $10 for art lessons from a local woman who had graduated from the state art school. As another example, de Kooning also displayed his early talent, and at age 12, when he finished his academic education in Rotterdam, he began working for a design firm. They were so impressed with his talent that they paid for him to attend the local art school (Stevens & Swan, 2006).

Biographical evidence (Piirto, 2004) indicates that there are certain predictive behaviors for the visual artists, including precocity, or creating art like older children do, being known as the class artist, using drawing as a means to communicate and to self-comfort, keeping sketchbooks, winning art contests, continuing to draw when other children stop because they can't achieve verisimilitude, and demonstrating interest in the work of other artists. For example, Salvador Dali described his battle at the age of 8 with his parents for a playroom in which he could paint (Dali, 1942, p. 174). Nochlin (1988) cited several mythic stories that accompany stories of artists' childhoods, such as doodling in the margins of their schoolbooks, the "mysterious inner call in early youth, the lack of any teacher but Nature herself . . . the fairy tale of the discovery by an older artist or discerning patron of the Boy Wonder," usually in the guise of a shepherd (p. 154).

5. Environmental "Suns" for Visual Artists

Sun of Home. No outstanding demographic patterns have surfaced as to the professions of the parents. As many fathers were professionals as were blue-collar workers. Coincidentally, both Dali's and Marcel Duchamp's fathers were notaries in their hometowns (Etherington-Smith, 1995; Tomkins, 1998). Families were both encouraging and discouraging (Getzels & Csikszentmihalyi, 1976; Goertzel et al., 2004). The elder Duchamp gave each of his three artist sons 150 francs per month while they established themselves. The elder Dali did the same for his son. The genetic aspect seems to apply, especially historically, where whole families were engaged in the business of making art. Childhoods were both idyllic and traumatic. de Kooning, who grew up in Rotterdam, experienced the divorce of his parents, moving 14 times in 7 years, extreme poverty, and the necessity to be a child laborer (Stevens & Swan, 2004), while Duchamp grew up in pleasantness and security (Tomkins, 1998).

Sun of Community and Culture. Cross-fertilization and cross-cultural influences among artists is common (e.g., Matisse and Picasso). Artists do not create in a vacuum. It is a myth that artists do not respond to community and culture. For example, Picasso's repeating theme of the Minotaur had a profound influence on Jackson Pollock (Naifeh & Smith, 1989). Getzels and Csikszentmihalyi (1976) used the term *loft culture* to describe the interactions among artists in art centers in urban areas. They stated that the artist often must move from the setting that inspired the art to a place where one can make one's name among the artists and the galleries.

It is difficult to make a living making visual art, and the art collector is an important part of the community and culture, or the press (Rhodes, 1961) of the milieu of the visual artist. Saarinen (1958) described the collecting passion and patronage of individuals and families such as Mrs. Potter Palmer of Chicago; Isabella Stewart Gardner of Boston; J. Pierpont Morgan of New York City, who "purchased by the carload" (p. 75); as well as Gertrude Stein and her siblings, who kept a famous salon in Paris that was memorialized in Hemingway's (1964) *A Moveable Feast* and other memoirs of the time.

Art critics and art galleries also are important in making the public aware of the work being done. An entry-level gallery and a group show are the first steps, and the visual artists move progressively to higher level galleries, one-person shows, and higher prices for their works. The artists who are not darlings of the critics or who do not win the prizes often band together to do shows that are outside the mainstream, but which eventually become recognized and accepted into the mainstream such as the Surrealists in Paris (Etherington-Smith, 1995).

Sun of School. In both academic school and art school, visual artists showed intense drawing and the emphasis on products, on making the drawings realistic and recognizable representations. Regular academic school often is a challenge, with apocryphal stories abounding: Dali being so dreamy that he never learned to read until his teenage years; Picasso's father taking him out of academic school so he could paint and draw at home; Jackson Pollock almost flunking out of high school. The childhood of Mark Rothko is anomalous amidst the stories of how poorly many visual artists did in academic school; in fact, his childhood resembles that of creative writers, who are often good academic students in verbal areas (Breslin, 1993).

Sun of Chance. In order to enhance their chances of eminence, visual artists must rent or buy a loft, move to an art center such as New York City, Los Angeles, Paris, or London, and be in juried art shows. They must try for a one-man/woman show and begin with group shows. An alternate strategy is to continue studying to get a master of fine arts, and to try to become art professors or teachers, although the danger of teaching is that it may suck the creative juices needed for doing art. Good luck follows proximity to the world of art. Proximity may be enhanced by attractiveness, as it was for Georgia O'Keeffe, who attracted Alfred Stieglitz with her beauty as well as her talent.

Sun of Gender. Women are and have been less likely to become well-known artists. Greer (1979) commented that historically, women were not permitted to sign their paintings (thus the plethora of paintings by Anon.), and were relegated by their brothers and fathers in artistic families to paint miniatures of the easel portraits painted by their male relatives. The very lack of existence of scholarly biographies on women artists other than Mary Cassatt (Hale, 1975), Georgia O'Keeffe (Robinson, 1989), and Frida Kahlo (Herrera, 1991) speaks to this marginalization. Women also are more likely to go into art education than into fine arts, perhaps for practical reasons, including the reason that many creative women use—the mommy imperative—how can I be in the creative arts and still be a mother (Piirto, 1992)?

Feminist critic Linda Nochlin (1988) pointed out that women were not permitted to study in the academies as late as the early 20th century, but in the 20th century, the barriers began to be broken down. In the 1950s in New York City, in the abstract expressionist school, the few women artists who hung around with the men at the cafes and bars were, as Stevens and Swan (2004) stated, quite strong:

> The strongest female figures of the period refusing to be pitied, became remarkably tough survivors. They often did so not by rejecting the macho of the period, but by embracing it, showing the world that they could out-boy the boys. (p. 345)

EXAMPLE OF WILLEM DE KOONING (1904–1997)

As an example of how one eminent visual artist's life is illuminated when utilizing the Piirto Pyramid of Talent Development (see Figure 2.1) as a biographical method, let us focus on the creativity of Willem de Kooning (Stevens & Swan, 2004).

Regarding de Kooning's genetic aspect, he was good-looking, sturdy, and from a working class Dutch family. The personality attributes/emotional aspect attributed to de Kooning included (1) intense ambition—always thinking of his career and his art; (2) skill at defusing tension from experiences in his childhood home atmosphere; (3) a strong work ethic, clean and neat, and pride in being Dutch; (4) willingness to endure poverty for long periods of his adult life; (5) melancholy—he often battled with alcohol and depression; (6) his introversion: he preferred to work alone and he did not like to go to parties; (7) intensity: he was always described as intense; (8) tolerance for ambiguity: "poetic elusiveness and joy in paradox" (Stevens & Swan, 2004, p. 108); (9) persistence: he continued to paint even when he was not validated as an artist and painted until 1988; (10) shrewdness: he kept the end result in mind when dealing with people; (11) stubbornness: he would not change his style at the whim of the art world; (12) perceptiveness; (13) intuition; (14) risk-taking; and (15) generosity: he gave away drawings, paintings, and financially helped many. In regards to the cognitive aspect, de Kooning (1) was academically talented and always in the top three of his grammar school class; (2) was always well read in philosophy and art criticism, having read Wittgenstein for entertainment; (3) sought to relate his work to art of the European past; and (4) first admired what Picasso was doing and later acknowledged the influence of Rubens and Matisse.

de Kooning's talent in the artistic domain was exhibited through (1) drawing on walls as a child and drawing as a constant throughout his life; (2) a scholarship to Rotterdam design arts academy; and (3) the creation of a few drawings after immigration that resulted in being hired over many others by Eastman Brothers as stage designer. The "thorn" for the artistic domain was demonstrated through (1) his need to draw from an early age; (2) seeking out the company of artists rather than house painters when he illegally immigrated to U.S., even though he made less money as a commercial artist; (3) his decision that he had to paint (clutched stomach when talking about need) in early 1930s; (4) an experience of an epiphany in 1932 at Gorky's studio—he was overwhelmed and became dizzy at true metaphysics of art; (5) model of meeting a serious artist who made art the center of his life; and (6) his passion for painting even when economic disaster ensued.

Influences upon de Kooning from the environmental suns included the following. The Sun of Home included (1) a poor family in Rotterdam with constant financial problems; (2) his father left to live with and start another family; (3) his mother remarried and took in wash, and his stepfather kept a tavern; (4) violence in the home: his mother had screaming fits and beat her children with wooden shoes; (5) he suffered borderline malnourishment and rotted teeth; (6) he moved 14 times between age 4 and 13; (7) he rented his first "loft" in 1932 and always had one because of a hatred of small, chintzy apartments; (8) he lived with multiple women, some simultaneously, several of whom had multiple abortions; (9) he had one child, Lisa; (10) he had many bouts with severe alcoholism that were life threatening; and (11) he painted in isolation in his studio on Long Island except for assistants.

The Sun of School included (1) teachers noticed his gift for drawing; (2) formal academic education ended at age 12, as was typical for most working-class people; (3) began to work as apprentice in decorating firm at age 12; (4) given drawing scholarship to technical arts academy in Rotterdam by owners of decorating firm at age 13 and was the best student in the class; (5) returned on scholarship to academy and went to 5th form, then quit; and (6) never returned to formal education, although he taught art at Yale and Black Mountain.

The Sun of Community and Culture included (1) his first mentor (Bernard Romein, store display designer) at age 16, who showed him Mondrian, Frank Lloyd Wright, and Dostoevsky and introduced him to commercial art; (2) he hung around in extreme poverty with the "bohemian" crowd on docks in Rotterdam, went with two friends into Belgium, and worked as sign painter; (3) moved to Greenwich Village after illegal immigration, in search of "artists" and was friends with Pollock, Kline, Rothko, Rosenberg, and Noguchi; (4) emigré artists at Eastman Brothers formed a group of highly intelligent, talented outsiders; (5) spent summers at artist colonies at Woodstock, Provincetown, Southampton, and Black Mountain; (6) was profoundly influenced by Arshile Gorky, Stuart Davis, John Graham, Picasso, Matisse, and Rubens; (7) regularly visited galleries and museums; (8) was part of the "downtown scene" for many years until moving to Long Island, where he socialized with high society, while always treasuring his working class origins; and (9) changed gallery representation and vastly improved financial status on advice of friend Eastman.

The Sun of Chance included (1) stowing away on a British ship bound for America in 1926 (he didn't become a U.S. citizen until 1962); (2) his design background and talent would always help him get a job—house painting, signs, design, and carpentry; (3) WPA's artist program made him finally stop "side jobs" and declare he was a full-time painter in 1935 and poverty ensued; (4) his first one-man show in New York City in 1948 did not sell any art but was a turning point that made the art world conscious of him—the critics, galleries, and museums take notice, and this became the turning point for his career; and (5) eventually winning the Presidential Medal of Freedom and many other national and international awards.

The Sun of Gender included (1) his paintings of men indicate insecurity and vapidness; (2) his paintings of women indicate deep misogyny and mistrust, anger, rage, and fascination; (3) like other artistic men of his generation, he viewed his art as primary, often neglecting his daughter and didn't think it important she attend school; and (4) he had many women as muses.

de Kooning's creative process was characterized with the following: (1) being a slow worker, scraping and rescraping his work many times; (2) the use of exercise such as walking and bicycling to meditate on his work; (3) drawing multiples while watching television, similar to automatic writing: "In this way the drawing comes from something deeper" (Stevens & Swan, 2004, p. 245); (4) talking about technical aspects of his work—palette knives, paint chemistry—with other artists; and (5) his inspiration from travel, nature, and women.

CONCLUSION

This very brief introduction to the biographical method I have employed to elucidate themes in the lives of creators in domains is, perhaps, too simplistic. After all, individual lives are complex, and each human is unique. However, certain patterns do exist among creators in domains. My students' studies have confirmed these themes. Hundreds of my graduate students, teachers studying to be teachers of the gifted and talented, and my undergraduate students in general studies have completed biographical case studies that have mostly confirmed the themes I have discussed here.

COMMENTARY

I have known of Joyce VanTassel-Baska since she was Joyce VanTassel. I was finishing my dissertation at Bowling Green State University in 1977, and had taken a job as a gifted coordinator in Hardin County. One of my professors, in hearing that I had entered the field of the education of the gifted and talented, told me he had a graduate student at the University of Toledo in the joint doctoral program that the two universities had at that time named Joyce VanTassel, who was the gifted coordinator for the city of Toledo. Both of us graduated from that program with our doctorates in educational administration and supervision. Joyce went to Illinois, and I went to Michigan and then to New York City, and then back to Ohio. I followed her career from then on, and we connected at various conferences. Over the years, we have become friends, having lunch and dinner together at conferences here and abroad, and we have shared our similar backgrounds and our passions for literature and the arts. Joyce asked me to speak at several of the curriculum conferences at William and Mary, and I have required my graduate students in the curriculum class in our endorsement program to buy and to prepare to teach one of the William and Mary units. We stay in touch. I am very honored to be asked to contribute a chapter to this volume, and to celebrate the transition of my friend from the present to the future, where she will break new ground, I am sure.

REFERENCES

Albert, R. S. (Ed.). (1992). *Genius and eminence* (2nd ed.). Oxford, UK: Pergamon Press.

Baird, L. L. (1985). Do grades and tests predict adult accomplishment? *Research in Higher Education, 23*(1), 3–85.

Barron, F. (1968). *Creativity and personal freedom.* New York: Van Nostrand.

Barron, F. (1972). *Artists in the making.* New York: Seminar Press.

Breslin, J. E. B. (1993). *Mark Rothko: A biography.* Chicago: University of Chicago Press.

Cattell, J. M. (1903). A statistical study of eminent men. *Popular Science Monthly, 62,* 359–377.

Csikszentmihalyi, M. (1990). *Flow: The psychology of optimal experience.* New York: Cambridge University Press.

Dali, S. (1942). *The secret life of Salvador Dali.* New York: Dial Press.

Eminence. (n.d.). In *Oxford English dictionary.* Retrieved on November 13, 2008, from http://dictionary.oed.com

Etherington-Smith, M. (1995). *The persistence of memory: A biography of Dali.* New York: Da Capo Press.

Feist, G. H. (1999). Influence of personality on artistic and scientific creativity. In R. Sternberg (Ed.), *Handbook of creativity* (pp. 273–296). New York: Cambridge University Press.

Feldman, D. H. (1982). A developmental framework for research with gifted children. In D. Feldman (Ed.), *New directions for child development: Developmental approaches to giftedness and creativity* (pp. 31–46). San Francisco: Jossey-Bass.

Feldman, D. H., & Goldsmith, L. (1986). *Nature's gambit.* New York: Basic Books.

Gardner, H. (1993). *Creating minds: An anatomy of creativity seen through the lives of Freud, Einstein, Picasso, Stravinsky, Eliot, Graham, and Gandhi.* New York: Basic Books.

Getzels, J., & Csikszentmihalyi, M. (1976). *The creative vision: A longitudinal study of problem finding in art.* New York: Wiley.

Ghiselin, B. (1952). *The creative process.* New York: Bantam.

Goertzel, V., Goertzel, M. G., Goertzel, T. G., & Hansen, A. M. W. (2004). *Cradles of eminence* (2nd ed.). Scottsdale, AZ: Great Potential Press.

Greer, G. (1979). *The obstacle race: The fortunes of women painters and their work.* New York: Farrar Straus Giroux.

Guilford, J. P. (1967). *The nature of human intelligence.* New York: McGraw Hill.

Hale, N. (1975). *Mary Cassatt.* New York: Addison-Wesley.

Hemingway, E. (1964). *A moveable feast.* New York: Bantam.

Herrera, H. (1991). *Frida: A biography of Frida Kahlo.* New York: Perennial.

Hillman, J. (1996). *The soul's code: In search of character and calling.* New York: Random House.

Jung, C. G. (1965). *Memories, dreams, reflections.* New York: Vintage.

Kronberg, L. (2008). *Talent development of eminent Australian women.* Unpublished doctoral dissertation, Monash University, Victoria, Australia.

MacKinnon, D. (1975). IPAR's contribution to the conceptualization and study of creativity. In I. A. Taylor & J. W. Getzels (Eds.), *Perspectives in creativity* (pp. 60–89). Chicago: Aldine.

Michaelis, D. (1998). *N.C. Wyeth: A biography.* New York: Alfred A. Knopf.

Naifeh, S., & Smith, G. W. (1989). *Jackson Pollock: An American saga.* New York: Clarkson Potter.

Nochlin, L. (1988). *Women, art, and power, and other essays.* New York: Harper & Row.

Piirto, J. (1966). *Charlotte Brontë's* Villette. Unpublished master's thesis, Kent State University, Kent, OH.

Piirto, J. (1992). *Understanding those who create.* Tempe, AZ: Gifted Psychology Press.

Piirto, J. (1994). *Talented children and adults: Their development and education.* New York: Macmillan.

Piirto, J. (1998). Themes in the lives of contemporary U.S. women creative writers at midlife. *Roeper Review, 21,* 60–70.

Piirto, J. (2000). The pyramid of talent development. *Gifted Child Today, 23*(6), 22–29.

Piirto, J. (2002). *My teeming brain: A psychology of creative writers.* Cresskill, NJ: Hampton Press.

Piirto, J. (2004). *Understanding creativity.* Scottsdale, AZ: Great Potential Press.

Piirto, J. (in press-a). Eminent women. In B. Kerr (Ed.), *Encyclopedia of giftedness, creativity, and talent.* Thousand Oaks, CA: Sage.

Piirto, J. (in press-b). Themes in the lives of creative writers using the Piirto Pyramid as a framework. In E. Grigorenko, E. Mambrino, & D. Preiss (Eds.). *Handbook of writing: A mosaic of perspectives and views. New York: Psychology Press.*

Reynolds, F. C., & Piirto, J. (2005). Depth psychology and giftedness: Finding the soul in gifted education. *Roeper Review, 27,* 164–171.

Reynolds, F. C., & Piirto, J. (2007). Honoring and suffering the thorn: Marking, naming, initiating, and eldering: Depth psychology, II. *Roeper Review, 29,* 45–53.

Rhodes, M. (1961). An analysis of creativity. *Phi Delta Kappan, 42,* 305–310.

Robinson, R. (1989). *Georgia O'Keeffe: A life.* New York: Harper & Row.

Runco, M., & Pritzker, S. (Eds.). (1999). *Encyclopedia of creativity* (2 vols). San Diego, CA: Academic Press.

Saarinen, A. B. (1958). *The proud possessors*. New York: Conde Nast Publications.

Simonton, D. K. (1999a). *Origins of genius: Darwinian perspectives on creativity*. New York: Oxford University Press.

Simonton, D. K. (1999b). Eminence. In M. Runco & S. Pritzer (Eds.), *Encyclopedia of creativity* (Vol. 1, pp. 646–649). San Diego, CA: Academic Press.

Sloane, K. D., & Sosniak, L. A. (1985). The development of accomplished sculptors. In B. Bloom (Ed.), *Developing talent in young people* (pp. 90–138). New York: Ballantine Books.

Smith, M. (1938). The general formal education of eminent men. *Scientific Monthly, 46,* 551–560.

Stevens, M., & Swan, A. (2004). *De Kooning: An American master*. New York: Alfred A. Knopf.

Stone, I., & Stone, J. (Eds.). (1937). *Dear Theo*. New York: Doubleday.

Terman, L. M., & Oden, M. H. (1959). *The gifted group at mid-life: 35 years' follow-up of the superior child*. Stanford, CA: Stanford University Press.

Tomkins, C. (1998). *Duchamp: A biography*. New York: Henry Holt.

VanTassel-Baska, J. (1989). Characteristics of the developmental path of eminent and gifted adults. In J. VanTassel-Baska & P. Olszewski-Kubilius, P. (Eds.), *Patterns of influence on gifted learners: The home, the self, and the school* (pp. 146–162). New York: Teachers College Press.

VanTassel-Baska, J. (1996). The talent development process in women writers: A study of Charlotte Brontë and Virginia Woolf. In K. D. Arnold, K. D. Noble, & R. F. Subotnik (Eds.), *Remarkable women: Perspectives on female talent development* (pp. 295–316). Cresskill, NJ: Hampton Press.

VanTassel-Baska, J. (2005). Domain-specific giftedness: Applications in school and life. In R. J. Sternberg & J. E. Davidson (Eds.), *Conceptions of giftedness* (2nd ed., pp. 358–376). New York: Cambridge University Press.

Vasari, G. (1561). *Lives of the most eminent painters, sculptors, and architects*. (Gaston C. De Vere, Trans.) London: Philip Lee Warner. Retrieved from http://www.efn.org/~acd/vite/VasariLives.html

CHAPTER 3

ANNE FRANK:

The Development of an Eminent Writer

by

SUZANNA
E. HENSHON

Writing can be an antidote to the oppressiveness of everyday life.
—Joyce Van Tassel-Baska

INTRODUCTION

Anne Frank's *The Diary of a Young Girl* has received a great deal of attention since its publication in 1947. The diary has been translated into 55 languages, and it has sold 25 million copies worldwide. Each year 600,000 people flock to The Anne Frank House in Amsterdam, where Anne and seven other people hid during World War II. Anne Frank is a recognizable brand name, but is she truly eminent?

When defining an eminent person, researchers do not prescribe this quality lightly. Britney Spears, Madonna, and Michael Jackson are famous. Thomas Jefferson, Abraham Lincoln, and Eleanor Roosevelt are eminent. Becoming an eminent person takes years of talent development and training. Eminent people are the subject of biographies, films, and ongoing attention.

Eminence is a "high level of achievement and societal recognition, usually marked by a contribution that has historical significance in a given field or across several fields" (Van Tassel-Baska, 1989, p. 146). Persistence and motivation are key factors in the development of writing talent. In the case of Anne Frank, there was little time for intense training; she wrote all of her work during a 2-year period (between the ages of 13–15) before perishing in the Holocaust.

Walking through the Anne Frank House 10 years ago, I imagined a young woman crafting a life for herself as an artist in this setting. She did not have a room of her own, and it would be difficult for any writer to be inspired by the air raids in the near vicinity while sharing personal space with a middle-aged man. Considering the conditions under which she worked, Anne Frank's diary is a remarkable achievement. But, it is important to note that there is a clear link between adverse conditions in childhood and later eminence (Goertzel & Goertzel, 1962). Like many eminent writers, Anne Frank channeled her personal adversity into a creative product that has lasting value.

BIOGRAPHY OF ANNE FRANK

Annelies Marie "Anne" Frank (June 12, 1929–March 1945), a Jewish girl, was born in Frankfurt, Germany. In 1933, the Frank family moved to Amsterdam after the Nazis came into power.

On Anne's 13th birthday, she received a writing book from her parents. This book became Anne's diary, and she used it to record her experiences in hiding during World War II. The Frank family went into hiding in July 1942 as persecution increased against Jewish populations across Europe. In August 1944, the group was betrayed and sent to concentration camps.

Anne Frank became famous after her diary was published posthumously. The diary depicts her life from June 12, 1942 to August 1, 1944. Anne's diary has been published around the world, and it has been adapted into plays and films. Because of the quality of her writing, Anne Frank has become one of the most famous Holocaust victims.

In March 1945, Anne and her sister, Margot, died from typhus at the Bergen-Belsen concentration camp. Otto Frank, the only surviving member of the family, returned to Amsterdam at the end of the war and discovered that Anne's diary and the family photo album had been saved. He published his daughter's diary in 1947, and it soon became an international bestseller.

THE PUBLICATION OF THE DIARY

When Anne and the other occupants of the Secret Annex (as Anne called the place where the Frank family hid) were arrested on August 4, 1944, Miep Gies returned later that day and saved Anne's diary. She carefully stored this diary with the hope of returning it to Anne when the war ended.

In July 1945, the Red Cross confirmed that Anne and Margot Frank had died in Bergen-Belsen. After learning that news, Miep Gies presented Anne's diary to her father. Otto Frank was surprised at the depth and complexity of his daughter's writing and decided to publish the diary.

During her time in hiding, Anne prepared the diary for publication. She created a second diary, a revised version of the first one. Anne's original diary begins with the lines, "I hope I will be able to confide everything to you, as I have never been able to confide in anyone, and I hope you will be a great source of comfort and support" (Frank & Pressler, 1996, p. 1). Later Anne returned to the diary and added the following comment, which is published on the first page of *Anne Frank: The Diary of a Young Girl: The Definitive Edition*:

> So far you truly have been a great source of comfort to me, and so has Kitty, whom I now write to regularly. This way of keeping a diary is much nicer, and now I can hardly wait for those moments when I'm able to write in you. Oh, I'm so glad I brought you along! (Frank & Pressler, 1996, p. 1)

Initially, Otto Frank was unable to find a publisher, so he gave a copy of the diary to Professor Jan Romein, who wrote an article titled "Kinderstem" ("A Child's Voice"), which appeared in the newspaper *Het Parool* on April 3, 1946. Professor Romein stated,

> By coincidence I came across a diary that was written during the war. The Netherlands State Institute for War Documentation already has about 200 of such diaries, but it would surprise me if there was one other which was as pure, as intelligent, and yet as human as this one. (van der Rol & Verhoeven, 1993, p. 105)

When the diary was published in 1947, Otto Frank served as the general editor. Although Anne had planned on publishing the diary, she did not finish revising it during her lifetime. As a result, Otto Frank had two diaries to work with; he combined the original diary with the revisions in an attempt to follow Anne's intentions. According to Lee (2008), "Despite the various constraints, and with no background in writing or publishing, Otto's editing of his daughter's diary was ingenious" (p. 216). In 1952, *Anne Frank: The Diary of a Young Girl* was published in the United States, and the 5,000 copies printed sold out in just a few hours. Anne quickly became a literary superstar and a hot commodity for television and movie producers.

After Otto Frank's death in 1980, he willed his daughter's manuscripts to the Netherlands State Institute for War Documentation. The diary was carefully examined and authenticated before *The Critical Edition* was published (1986); it contains versions of the original diary, Anne's edited diary, and the third and shortened version that readers know as *The Diary of a Young Girl*. The Anne Frank-Fonds (Anne Frank Foundation) in Switzerland decided to publish this new, expanded diary (*The Diary of Anne Frank: The Critical Edition*) for readers; the 1986 edition contains 30% more material than the original version.

In 2003, *The Diary of Anne Frank: The Critical Edition* was updated to include five pages that had never before been published (Lee, 2008). These pages included Anne's introduction and a controversial statement about her parent's marriage, dated February 8, 1944. Many readers are familiar with Otto Frank's edition, which was translated and in wide circulation for 40 years. But, the new version of the diary includes more material, painting a different picture of Anne than was available to previous generations of readers.

TALENT DEVELOPMENT AND THE WRITING PROCESS

Talent development in any field is a complicated and lengthy process. Bloom (1985) delineated three major phases of talent development: the early years, the middle years, and the later years. The early years occur when children are first exposed to their talent field. In the middle years, students refine their talent while training with a more specialized teacher. During the later years, adults attain high levels of training and are able to innovate and contribute to the greater field. Young teenagers like Anne Frank generally would be in the second stage of talent development.

Although Bloom (1985) studied general talent development trends, VanTassel-Baska (1996) specifically analyzed writing talent development in her seminal study of Charlotte Brontë and Virginia Woolf. VanTassel-Baska described a four-stage developmental process for eminent writers. These stages are (1) being born into a family that values literary and intellectual life; (2) informal early development of the craft of writing; (3) active experimentation with various forms/genres of writing; and (4) progressive development of mature form and ideas in successive works. VanTassel-Baska's guidelines can be applied to Anne Frank, who was born into a literary family, wrote at an early age, and composed work in different genres during her time in the Secret Annex. During her time in hiding, Anne Frank wrote short stories, diary entries, and the beginning of a novel.

Teenagers rarely attain mastery in the field of writing because it is a lengthy process, but Anne Frank's isolation from peers served her talent development well because it allowed her to focus specifically on the craft of writing in a way that many young people cannot. Gagné (1995) theorized that talents emerge from the transformation of aptitudes "into well-trained and systematically developed skills characteristic of a particular field of human activity or performance" (p. 107). Gagné emphasized the importance of intrapersonal and environmental influences on a person's life, and their role as catalysts in the development of talent. Follow-ing Gagné's conceptual model, Anne Frank wrote every day and read rigorous materials during her time in hiding. She attained adult levels of competency, and her writing progressed remarkably; she was inquisitive and demonstrated curiosity about her immediate surroundings. She not only developed technical skills, she also transformed her life experiences into creative work. Her diary is a canvas for complex thoughts, observations, and narrative techniques. In contrast to the Nazis (who tattooed numbers upon their victims), Anne Frank defines herself through letters and words.

THE DIARY AS A DOCUMENT OF TALENT DEVELOPMENT

Anne Frank's work offers a unique glimpse into talent development and the creative writing process. *Anne Frank's Tales From the Secret Annex* (Mok, 1983) is a collection of prose fiction and nonfiction that she wrote during her time in hiding. It was first published in 1949, and it is now included in *The Diary of Anne Frank: The Revised Critical Edition* (Netherlands Institute for War Documentation, 2003). *Anne Frank: The Diary of a Young Girl* is more than 300 pages long and includes Anne's observations from 1942–1944, the time she spent in hiding in Amsterdam. Modern scholars have 500 pages of Anne Frank's writing to study; these materials can be used to analyze her talent development and to estimate the writer she might have become.

Anne Frank's Tales from the Secret Annex (Mok, 1983) includes fables, short stories, and part of a novel. The short story "Kitty" is interesting to read because Anne also called her diary Kitty. Anne begins:

> Kitty is the girl next door. In fair weather, I can watch her playing in the yard through our window. Kitty has a wine-red velvet frock for Sundays and a cotton one for every day; she has pale-blond hair with tiny braids, and clear blue eyes.
>
> Kitty has a sweet mother, but her father is dead. The mother is a laundress; sometimes she is gone during the day, cleaning other people's houses, and at night she does the wash for her customers. (p. 11)

Like Anne Frank, Kitty is a dreamer and is constantly cultivating her imagination. There also is a section of essays which includes, "Do You Remember? Reminiscences About My School Days," which Anne composed on July 7, 1943. At the time she wrote this essay, Anne had been in hiding for nearly a year, never having the chance to say goodbye to classmates she had known since kindergarten. She writes poignantly:

> Do you remember? I spent happy hours talking about school, the instructors, our adventures, and—boys. When we still were part of ordinary, everyday life, everything was just marvelous. That one year in Lyceum was sheer bliss for me; the teachers, all that they taught me, the jokes, the prestige, the romances, and the adoring boys. (p. 99)

In the early days, Anne describes school, girlfriends, boys, and everyday life. Early entries are fairly typical, and reflect what many young women might write:

> I'll begin from the moment I got you, the moment I saw you lying on the table among my other birthday presents. (I went along when you were bought, but that doesn't count.) On Friday, June 12, I was awake at six o'clock, which isn't surprising, since it was my birthday. (June 12, 1942)

In the early pages of the diary, Anne is every 13-year-old girl, carefree and unconcerned about the future. But, just a month later, Anne writes in a serious tone, "I put in the craziest things with the idea that we were going into hiding, but I'm not sorry, memories mean more to me than dresses" (July 8, 1942).

Anne lives in constant fear of being discovered and arrested; she hears bombs and gunfire on a daily basis. Her life experiences are the catalyst for her psychological development, which is expressed in her writing. Anne describes this fear perfectly, "I can't tell you how oppressive it is never to be able to go outdoors, also I am very afraid we will be discovered and shot" (September 28, 1942). Anne also is troubled to hear that, "Countless friends and acquaintances have gone to a terrible end . . . Nobody is spared, old people, children, babies, expectant mothers, the sick each and all join in the march of death" (November 19, 1942). Just 6 months after beginning the diary, Anne returns to her original entries and comments:

> When I look over the diary today, 1 ½ years on, I cannot believe that I was ever such an innocent young thing . . . I still understand those moods, those remarks about Margot, Mummy, and Daddy so well that I might have written them yesterday, but I no longer understand how I could write so freely about other things. (January 22, 1944)

During her time in hiding, Anne observes the world from an outsider's perspective. She develops observational skills that are essential to writing high-quality pieces, and the following is one example:

> It's lovely weather again and I've quite perked up since yesterday. This morning, when I went up to the attic again, Peter was busy cleaning it up. He was finishing very quickly and when I sat down on my favorite spot on the floor, he joined me. Both of us looked at the glorious blue of the sky, the bare chestnut trees on whose branches little raindrops shone, at the seagulls and other birds that looked like silver in the sun. . . He stood and I sat, we breathed the fresh air, and both felt like the spell should not be broken. (February 23, 1944)

Anne develops a close friendship with Peter, and one night they talk for a long time in the attic of the Secret Annex:

I was standing on the left side of the open window; I went and stood on the right side, and we talked. It was much easier to talk beside the open window in semidarkness than in bright light and I believe Peter felt the same. We told each other so much, so very very much, that I can't repeat it all, but it was lovely, the most wonderful evening I have ever had in the "Secret Annex." (March 19, 1944)

Anne creates tension within a few lines of exposition. One night there is a frightening burglary at the Secret Annex, and we can feel the fear experienced by occupants of the Secret Annex when we read Anne's words:

Then, at quarter past 11, a bustle and noise downstairs. Everyone's breath was audible, in other respects no one moved. Footsteps in the house, in the private office, kitchen, then . . . on our staircase, no one breathed audibly now, 8 hearts thumped, footsteps on our staircase, then a rattling of the swinging cupboard. This moment is indescribable: "Now we are lost!" I said and could see all fifteen of us being carried off by the Gestapo that very night. (April 11, 1944)

In her final entry, Anne reconciles the carefree girl of her childhood with the serious writer she has become:

I have already told you before that I have, as it were, a dual personality. One half embodies my exuberant cheerfulness, making fun of everything, vivacity, and above all the way I take everything lightly . . . This side is usually lying in wait and pushes away the other; which is much better, deeper, and purer. No one knows Anne's better side. (August 1, 1944)

During the years in which she writes her diary, Anne Frank emerges as a young woman with thoughts, feelings, and distinct visions, a sharp contrast to the talkative and vivacious girl she was in early 1942. By writing in her diary every day, Anne progressively develops the wisdom and vision that is essential for a successful career in writing.

THE DIARY AND ITS OFFSPRING

Because Anne Frank never became an adult, it is difficult to compare her achievements to Maya Angelou, John Steinbeck, or Ernest Hemingway. Anne Frank's writing is limited to the time she spent in hiding between the ages of 13 and 15. Can Anne Frank, eternally 15, be an eminent person in the world's eyes? To gauge her influence, it is essential to look at the myriad of products connected with the diary.

Like many eminent people, Anne Frank has been marketed to a broad spectrum of readers from early childhood to adulthood. Anne Frank has become a consumer product for young readers of David Adler's (1996) *A Picture Book of Anne Frank* and Ruth Ashby's (2005) *Anne Frank: Young Diarist* in the Childhood of World Figures series. Among adults, she is featured in the Greenhaven Press Literary Companion of World Literature alongside Herman Melville, F. Scott Fitzgerald, and Emily Dickinson. She is the subject of dozens of biographies for readers of all ages.

Readers also can purchase books about people and sites connected with the diary. Miep Gies (the young woman who worked to bring food and supplies to the Secret Annex and later saved Anne's diary) has published her story, *Anne Frank Remembered: The Story of the Woman Who Helped to Hide the Frank Family* (Gies, 1986). In 1993, the Anne Frank House produced *Anne Frank: Beyond the Diary* (van der Rol & Verhoeven); the book includes photographs of Anne, images of the Secret Annex, and reproduced pages of the diary. During the past 60 years, Anne also has been the subject of stage plays, movies, and documentaries.

If Anne Frank had survived World War II and moved to New York City, she might have published the diary at a later time. It might have attracted a following, and become the foundation of her writing career. But, part of what makes the diary so precious is that it represents what Anne Frank could have been, the writer she might have become.

Since the publication of the diary in 1947, Anne Frank has attained worldwide fame; the diary is a compelling account of a young girl living in Amsterdam during World War II. Anne effectively records the outside events, the conflicts, and the context of the times. She describes a "slice of life" that resonates with many Holocaust survivors. There were more than 25,000 people hiding in Amsterdam, and two thirds survived the war; many people had comparable experiences during that era.

As an autobiography of adolescence, Anne's diary is a vivid account of what it means to be a teenager; waiting for menstruation, feeling sexual attraction, and wishing to grow up are hallmarks of female adolescence. But, this alone would not account for Anne's fame and widespread following.

When I reread the diary this year, I was struck by Anne's ability to create drama. For an interesting comparison, we can look at Elie Wiesel's *Night*. Many people experienced the Holocaust and had close encounters with death, but Wiesel's account is outstanding because he dramatizes suspense perfectly; he takes the reader into the horror of the moment. Many chapters in this memoir include a conflict, a climax, and a resolution; Wiesel's details enhance the plot without weighing it down. In the same way, Anne Frank's dynamic writing takes readers to the heart of the action so that the emotional development of a young woman attains universal qualities.

ANNE FRANK AS AN EMINENT PERSON

Like many eminent people, Anne Frank's public persona has shifted over the years. There are two different representations of Anne to critique: the way she was defined in 1947, and the manner in which she has been redefined during the past 20 years. It is not uncommon for eminent people to be "repackaged" for different audiences; new biographies often highlight previously untold stories of a famous person's background, emphasizing some threads of their lives over others.

Had she survived, Anne Frank would be almost 80 years old today. Perhaps she could have used her diary as a launching point for a career in journalism or as a novelist. Unfortunately, the trajectory of all biographies ends in March 1945; whether we view her as a young victim, a girl in the middle of a sexual awakening, or as a future journalist, we can only study Anne Frank as a child and young teenager. Our analysis is limited to 500 pages of writing and eyewitness accounts of people who knew the Frank family.

We cannot study Anne's juvenile writing in reference to later pieces as we can with the Brontë sisters. We are even robbed of the full biography of Anne's life—the middle and ending of her story. We only can read the existing body of her work and contemplate the person Anne Frank would be today.

Eminence is an elusive label, and cannot easily be quantified. Although Anne Frank was not granted the gift of time, she did have the gift of words and a deep understanding of human nature. After the war, she might have written a memoir like *Night* that would have taken the world by storm, an account that would represent the culmination of talent development intensified by tragic life experiences.

We will never know what the exact outcome of Anne Frank's life would have been, but we can see the beginning of eminence when we visit the Secret Annex and we can read her promising future in the pages of her diary.

After studying with Joyce VanTassel-Baska, my understanding of eminence is redefined. My vision of eminence includes not only fame and impressive feats but talent development and persistence across the lifespan. As an eminent scholar, Joyce VanTassel-Baska has inspired a generation of gifted scholars and scholars of gifted education; I am privileged to be one of her lifetime students.

REFERENCES

Adler, D. (1996). *A picture book of Anne Frank*. New York: Holiday House.

Ashby, R. (2005). *Anne Frank: Young diarist*. New York: Aladdin.

Bloom, B. (1985). *Developing talent in young people*. New York: Ballantine Books.

Frank, A. (1952). *Anne Frank: The diary of a young girl*. New York: Doubleday.

Frank, A. (1986). *The diary of Anne Frank: The critical edition*. New York: Doubleday.

Frank, O., & Pressler, M. (Eds.). (1996). *The diary of a young girl: Anne Frank: The definitive edition*. New York: Anchor Books.

Gagné, F. (1995). From giftedness to talent: A developmental model and its impact on the language of the field. *Roeper Review, 18,* 103–111.

Gies, M. (with Gold, A. L.). (1986). *Anne Frank remembered: The story of the woman who helped to hide the Frank family.* New York: Simon and Schuster.

Goertzel, V., & Goertzel, M. G. (1962). *Cradles of eminence.* Boston: Little, Brown.

Lee, C. A. (2008). *The hidden life of Otto Frank.* New York: Paw Prints.

Mok, M. (Trans.). (1983). *Anne Frank's tales from the secret annex.* New York: Washington Square Press.

Netherlands Institute for War Documentation. (2003). *The diary of Anne Frank: The revised critical edition.* New York: Doubleday.

van der Rol, R., & Verhoeven, R. (1993). *Anne Frank: Beyond the diary.* New York: Puffin Books.

VanTassel-Baska, J. (1989). The development of eminent and gifted adults. In J. VanTassel-Baska & P. Olszewski-Kubilius (Eds.), *Patterns of influence: The home, the self, and the school* (pp. 146–162). New York: Teachers College Press.

VanTassel-Baska, J. (1996). The talent development process in women writers: A study of Charlotte Brontë and Virginia Woolf. In K. Arnold, K. D. Noble, & R. F. Subotnik (Eds.), *Remarkable women: Perspectives on female talent development* (pp. 295–316). Cresskill, NJ: Hampton.

Wiesel, E. (2006). *Night.* New York: Farrar, Straus and Giroux.

CHAPTER 4

DEVELOPING CREATIVITY IN GIFTED AND TALENTED STUDENTS

by

KYUNG HEE KIM

If an individual does not produce creative work when his or her intellectual and/or artistic powers are at their height, he or she may never be able to do so at an older age.
—Joyce VanTassel-Baska (1989)

INTRODUCTION

Traditionally, giftedness has been viewed as being highly intelligent, which leads to the view that IQ tests can be used to identify the gifted. However, IQ tests have many deficiencies; among them is the suspicion that they favor the socially dominant classes and may discriminate ethnically. Further, IQ tests correlate positively to academic success, but academic success may not highly correlate to success later in life. Historically, many eminent people have possessed something more than high ability or high IQ; they also have exhibited creativity. New definitions of giftedness have incorporated the concept that giftedness is more than mere intelligence.

THE DEFINITION OF CREATIVITY

An idea or product must be original to be considered creative, and originality must be defined within a particular sociocultural group to provide a meaningful criterion (Simonton, 1999). What may be original in one society or culture may be more commonplace in other societies or cultures. An original idea or product cannot be creative unless it has social value, aesthetic appeal, and appropriateness (Runco, 1993). Without these sociocultural attributes, originality may be characterized as a bizarre or inappropriate work or behavior (Runco & Charles, 1993). Thus, creativity is the ability to produce work that is both original and appropriate or useful (Barron, 1995). Further, the recipients, not the originator, judge the usefulness of an original idea or product (Simonton, 1999).

THE CONDITIONS FOR CREATIVE PRODUCTIVITY: THE FOUR P'S OF CREATIVITY

According to Rhodes (1961), the four P's explain the multifaceted construct of creativity: person, process, product, and press. *Person* includes cognitive abilities and biological, biographical, and personalogical traits; *process* describes the mental processes operative in creating ideas, which include preparation, incubation, illumination, and verification; *product* includes ideas expressed in the form of language or craft; and *press* includes the relationship between a person and his or her environment (Rhodes, 1961). Creative products are the outcome of creative processes engaged in by creative persons, which is supported by creative press.

The First P for Creative Productivity: Person

Many characteristics underlie and contribute to the creativeness of a person: cognitive abilities and biographical and personalogical traits. Thus, the person as a whole must be considered to understand creativity.

Cognitive abilities. Creativity and intelligence are separate constructs; that is, a highly intelligent person is not necessarily highly creative. Some studies illustrate that creative potential is independent of IQ (Getzels & Jackson, 1958; Torrance, 1977a). Many researchers adhere to the "threshold theory," which assumes that above an IQ score of 120 there is no correlation between measured creativity and intelligence (Getzels & Jackson, 1962; MacKinnon, 1967; Walberg & Herbig, 1991). However, Kim's (2005) meta-analysis found that the relationship between creativity test scores and IQ ($r = .17$) is negligible at any IQ level. This finding undermines the threshold theory, but supports the belief that creativity and intelligence are separate constructs.

Biological traits. The human brain behaves differently when a person is being creative as evidenced by brain patterns measured with electroencephalography (EEG; Fink & Neubauer, 2006; Jaušovec, 2008; Mölle, Marshall, Wolf, Fehm, & Born, 1999). Creative tasks cause higher EEG complexity than less creative tasks (Mölle et al., 1999). Creative tasks are accompanied by an increase of alpha activity and lower levels of analytic mental activity, and less creative tasks are accompanied by decreased alpha activity and higher analytic mental activity (Fink & Neubauer,

2006). Creative persons are more anxious and show higher levels of basal arousal than the less creative on physiological measures but show lower levels of cortical arousal than the less creative while performing creative tasks (Martindale & Hines, 1975). When resting, creative persons show more decoupling of brain areas, but the less creative show more intense cooperation (Jaušovec & Jaušovec, 2000).

Personalogical traits. Creative persons tend to have a sense of humor, have a childlike approach to problems (Getzels & Jackson, 1962), and have artistic interests (Davis & Subkoviak, 1978). They tend to be perceptive (Tardif & Sternberg, 1988); be independent (Eiduson, 1962; Rushton, Murray, & Paunonen, 1987); take risks (Farley, 1986); be energetic (Taylor, 1988); be curious (Eiduson, 1962); be attracted to complexity and novelty; be open-minded (Eysenck, 1995; Walberg & Herbig, 1991); and have needs for privacy or alone time (Storr, 1988). Creative persons tend to be less interested in the details or facts than most ordinary people are (MacKinnon, 1975); have a wider range of interests than the less creative (Barron & Harrington, 1981; Prentky, 1980); and tend to categorize ideas in different ways than the less creative (Dykes & McGhie, 1976). Motivationally, creative persons tend to be self-confident, ambitious, and persistent (Martindale, 1989). They find it difficult to begin a task; however, once started, they find it difficult to stop doing a task. Further, high motivation leads to arousal seeking and adventurousness, which are essential for creative productivity (Farley, 1986).

The Second P for Creative Productivity: Process

The creative process involves identifying a problem, gathering necessary data or developing a background in the fields needed to address the problem, allowing ideas to gel into a workable idea and then, testing the idea. Wallas (1926) identified this creative process, stating that it includes preparation, incubation, illumination, and verification. Preparation includes defining the problem and gathering experience and ideas. Incubation is a maturation phase, which results in the insight that occurs when a subconscious connection between ideas fits so well that it is forced into awareness (Csikszentmihalyi, 1996). Often these connections come when the person is relaxing or taking a break and not when the person is tired or actually working (Ochse, 1990; Wallas, 1926). Illumination is a creation of insights and the inspiration phase that is closely associated with the incubation phase. During illumination, the promising idea breaks through to conscious awareness—the "aha" moment. Verification is the execution and evaluation phase, which includes evaluating, refining, and testing the idea (Lubart, 2001).

The Third P for Creative Productivity: Product

The product of creative activity determines its success (Feldhusen & Goh, 1995). MacKinnon (1978) insisted that creativity research should first evaluate the products of creative activity to learn the differences between creative and mundane products. However, evaluating the products of creative activity is dependent on the environment (e.g., press). In the Western environment, the view of creativity focuses on tangible forms of creative products (Hughes & Drew, 1984). Creativity is the ability to produce work that is novel, or original, appropriate, useful, or adaptive concerning task constraints (Barron, 1995; Lubart, 1994). In the Eastern environment, the view of creativity is not oriented toward tangible products. Eastern people define creativity as a state of personal fulfillment and the expression or understanding of an inner sense of ultimate reality (Kuo, 1996). In the Eastern environment, creativity is the reinterpretation of traditional ideas, whereas in the Western environment, creativity is a break with tradition (Kristeller, 1983). Regardless of the difference in view between Eastern and Western environments, creativity results in a product that is new, unique, and not mundane to that culture.

The Last P for Creative Productivity: Press

Although a person follows the creative process and completes a creative product, if environmental conditions do not value or reproach the creativity, the person's creative productivity is not recognized. Thus, press is not only the starting point in encouraging creativity but also is the ending point in evaluating the creative product and determining whether it will be recognized as creative. Csikszentmihalyi (1988) described creativity as an interaction among a person, a field, and a culture. Culture is a critical environmental condition that encourages or discourages creative persons and assigns value to creative products. Cross-cultural studies can illustrate the ways culture and creativity interacts. Such studies (e.g., Lim & Plucker, 2001; Seo, Lee, & Kim, 2005; Yue & Rudowicz, 2002) have shown cultural diversity in both the expression of creativity and the degree that a culture values its expression. Creative behaviors may conflict with cultural norms, so cultures create barriers to creativity such as social influence, expectations, and conformity pressures (Davis, 1992; Torrance, 1963, 2002). Alternatively, if a culture considers creative behaviors valuable, such behaviors will be encouraged.

A NEW SYNTHESIS OF DEFINITIONS OF GIFTEDNESS IN RELATION TO CREATIVITY

Some students may be highly intelligent but not necessarily creative, while others may be creative but not necessarily highly intelligent. Academically successful students are those who have domain-specific knowledge or skills, task commitment, and high intelligence, whereas highly creative students are those who have domain-specific knowledge or skills, task commitment, and high creativity. Both academically successful and creative students require task commitment and domain-specific knowledge or skills. A person must first learn the elements relevant to a domain to have creative ideas. Eminent creators possess a certain level of knowledge in a field; however, a curvilinear relationship exists between knowledge and creativity, indicating that too much knowledge leads to entrenchment and an inability to conceptualize the field in a radically different light (Batey & Furnham, 2006).

As Figure 4.1 shows, the students who are both highly academic and highly creative are the person. When the person is in an environment (e.g., press) that

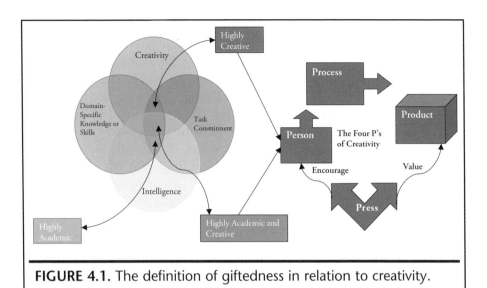

FIGURE 4.1. The definition of giftedness in relation to creativity.

encourages the person's creativity, the person follows the creative process, originates a creative product, and depending on whether the press values the product,
the creative productivity becomes successful. The new synthesis of definitions of
giftedness should be expansive rather than limiting. Both highly academically successful students and highly creative students are gifted. Each individual student's
strengths should be recognized and used to identify him or her as gifted. These
strengths can be high intelligence, talent in a specific area, or high creativity. Gifted
programs should emphasize the development of creativity based on each student'
strengths and weaknesses.

HIGHLY CREATIVE STUDENTS AND/OR HIGHLY ACADEMICALLY SUCCESSFUL STUDENTS

Creativity is important to the development of gifted students because it has
the power to transform giftedness into eminence (Khatena, 1983). Bright students who also are creative outperform students who have high IQs (Cropley &
Urban, 2000). Highly creative students have distinctive characteristics conducive
to originating creative ideas or products. Unfortunately, some of these characteristics are conducive to having difficulties in traditional school settings. Many highly
creative students have trouble in traditional school environments (Amabile, 1989),
and 60% of 400 eminent creative people had serious school problems (Goertzel
& Goertzel, 1960). Eminent creators often exhibited behaviors that resulted in
school problems due to their qualities that enabled the transformation of giftedness into eminence (Cramond, 1995). The energy of Thomas Edison and Nikola
Tesla got them into trouble in childhood but undoubtedly aided them in working
long hours (Cheney, 1981). Virginia Woolf and Samuel Taylor Coleridge were

constant talkers, an often-problematic trait in school, yet this verbal ability was clearly an asset to their writing. Robert Frost's daydreaming was not seen as creative; instead, he was expelled from school. Frank Lloyd Wright was prone to trancelike daydreams and had to be shouted at or slapped to get his attention. Inattention caused problems for these highly creative individuals in school, but it may have enabled their imaginations (Cramond & Kim, 2007).

Highly creative students exhibit characteristics that many teachers find undesirable in traditional school environments (Davis & Rimm, 1994; Torrance, 1962). Highly creative students forced into traditional school environments routinely become troublesome to teachers; disruptive in the classroom; and resent the constraining structure of the classroom, excessive rules, and the press for conformity. Torrance (Gowan, Khatena, & Torrance, 1979) referred to highly creative students as "creatively handicapped" because their creativity, although an asset in their lives, creates a situation that makes achievement in most classrooms extremely difficult.

Teachers are apt to prefer students who are achievers and teacher pleasers rather than disruptive or unconventional creative students (Davis & Rimm, 1994; Rudowicz, 2003; Rudowicz & Yue, 2000; Scott, 1999). Teachers often see creative children as a source of interference and disruption (Scott, 1999), and thus teachers' judgment of their favorite students is negatively correlated with creativity (Westby & Dawson, 1995). Teachers prefer students who exhibit traits that make them easy to manage in the classroom such as unquestioning acceptance of authority, conformity, logical thinking, and responsibility. Teachers' images of the ideal student emphasize conformist and socially acceptable traits (Torrance, 1963). Teachers rate students with high IQs as more desirable, better known, or understood, and more studious than students with high creativity (Torrance, 1962). In both Eastern and Western societies, teachers' perceptions of an ideal student do not fit a creative child model. In Eastern societies, the top ranked traits for an ideal student were honest, self-disciplined, responsible, and respects parents; followed by diligent, unselfish, humble, and obedient (e.g., Rudowicz, 2003; Rudowicz & Yue, 2000). The mismatch between teachers' preferences and the characteristics of highly creative students can lead to a wide gap between classroom expectations and the educational needs of creative students. Ultimately, this gap can stifle creativity and lead to significant underachievement of highly creative students. Moreover, due to their desire for conformity, teachers may misidentify energetic and unconventional students, a description fitting many highly creative students, as having attention deficit hyperactivity disorder (Cramond, 1994).

DEVELOPING CREATIVITY IN CLASSROOM

Researchers disagree whether creativity is fixed or developmental and is general or domain-specific. Currently, most researchers see creativity as dynamic (Cramond & Kim, 2007), which Runco (2004) describes as a syndrome or complex to

Table 4.1 MEAN EFFECT SIZES BY TYPES OF CREATIVITY PROGRAM		
Type	% of the 51 Studies	Effect Size
Creative Problem Solving Program	8.1%	1.13
Named Creative Training Programs	17.7%	0.82
Other Creative Training Programs	19.4%	0.67
School Programs	19.4%	0.61
Other Techniques Related to Creative Thinking	24.2%	0.78
Other Techniques Related to Humor, Cognition, etc.	11.3%	0.76

emphasize its intricate and changeable nature. Most researchers agree that creative thinking can be taught, but important questions remain about what is being taught by creativity programs and how these programs might best enhance creativity. Some research indicates that a part of creativity, innate creative abilities, cannot be taught, whereas another part of creativity, creative skills, can be taught (e.g., Huang, 2005; Rose & Lin, 1984). Other research indicates that creativity programs enhance creativity in general (e.g., Scott, Leritz, & Mumford, 2004). Most likely, some components of creativity cannot be significantly affected by creativity programs and can be thought of as innate abilities; however, creativity programs can enhance other aspects of creativity such as skills and dispositions. Several reviews of research have incorporated measures of creative potential and showed that creativity-training programs can enhance creativity. The mean effect sizes by types of creativity programs based on meta-analytic studies are reported in Table 4.1. As Table 4.1 shows, creativity programs can improve participants' scores on measures of creative thinking.

Successful creativity programs have cognitive and emotional functioning components and provide motivation and opportunities for involvement. Additionally, motivating and facilitating conditions make a difference in scores on creative potential, but differences are greatest and most predictable when deliberate teaching is involved (Huang, 2005; Rose & Lin, 1984; Scott et al., 2004). Further, creativity programs are found to have a strong positive effect on measures of creative potential at all ages (children to adults), in all situations (academic or occupational), and across all intelligence levels (low achievers to gifted students).

VanTassel-Baska's Contributions to Developing Creativity in Gifted and Talented Students

VanTassel-Baska has contributed to nurturing creativity in gifted and talented students by developing curriculum that infuses creativity into content. She suggests teaching creativity-relevant skills and embedding those skills in selected content; encouraging creative behaviors (risk-taking, openness, multiple answers); teaching higher order concepts that embrace creative thinking; developing content-based creative projects; and using performance-based and portfolio assessment approaches to document authentic learning (VanTassel-Baska, 2003, 2008).

VanTassel-Baska (1996a) examined the lives of Charlotte Brontë and Virginia Woolf to study talent development in writers. She explained that Brontë and Woolf used their pursuit of writing as a way to create meaning and make sense of their lives, which ultimately stimulated their talent to its optimal development. She identified eight common themes that influenced the process of talent development in Brontë and Woolf as writers: adversity, auto-didacticism, practice of the craft, needs for emotional support, a defined philosophy of being, influence of place, loneliness, and search for a mother figure. From this research, VanTassel-Baska (1996b) developed practical suggestions for parents and educators to facilitate writing talent: encourage early writing behaviors; provide a supportive network of young writers to test ideas; encourage reflection and writing on the students' life experiences; encourage bookmaking; develop artistic interest as an analogue to literary talent; and provide emotional support for the writing process.

NEW DIRECTIONS OF DEVELOPMENT OF CREATIVITY IN GIFTED AND TALENTED STUDENTS

Creativity should be the most important developing topic in the education of gifted and talented children. The purposes of gifted education should be to help gifted students become more self-actualized creative individuals and to better enable them to make creative contributions to society (Davis & Rimm, 2004). However, creative students are more likely to be seen in a negative light by teachers, and their behaviors often are seen as symptomatic of problems. Thus, highly creative students may face personal and societal losses due to the pain of being different, alienated, and alone. If this field can recognize students' creativity and encourage them to express it in positive ways, gifted education can help alleviate this pain, which may result in encouraging positive methods of dealing with stress, developing the highly creative, and ultimately helping society. Economists warn that our educational system must change for us to remain competitive in the global economy. The Internet has antiquated our old fact-based, content-divided teaching methods. To find solutions for the problems facing us, we must rely upon creative responses. Educational planners must use theories that include creative positives as a part of their facts and generalizations. Additionally, they must realize that many of our most creative students are missed when tested in traditional ways, thereby failing to nurture their most valuable resources (Cramond & Kim, 2007). Our culturally diverse society makes it imperative that giftedness not be restricted to high achievement or IQ. In creativity assessment, individuals respond from their own knowledge base rather than from a predetermined knowledge base; therefore, especially when verbal components are minimized, they are fairer to individuals from diverse cultures (Torrance, 1977b). Using a creativity test as an option to identify giftedness has proven effective in identifying students from underrepresented populations (Williams, 2000). The future direction of creativity research in gifted and talented education should focus on developing creativity in underrepresented populations. To promote the optimal development of underrepresented populations, educators must be aware of possible sources of ethnic or cultural bias to provide academic and psychological support to all students.

REFERENCES

Amabile, T. M. (1989). *Growing up creative: Nurturing a lifetime of creativity.* Williston, VT: Crown House Publishing Limited.

Barron, F. (1995). The disposition toward originality. *Journal of Abnormal and Social Psychology, 51,* 478–485.

Barron, F., & Harrington, D. M. (1981). Creativity, intelligence, and personality. *Annual Review of Psychology, 32,* 439–476.

Batey, M., & Furnham, A. (2006). Creativity, intelligence, and personality: A critical review of the scattered literature. *Genetic, Social, and General Psychology Monographs, 132,* 355–429.

Cheney, M. (1981). *Tesla: Man out of time.* New York: Prentice Hall.

Cramond, B. (1994). Attention-deficit hyperactivity disorder and creativity: What is the connection? *Journal of Creative Behavior, 28,* 193–210.

Cramond, B. (1995). *The coincidence of attention deficit hyperactivity disorder and creativity* (RBDM 9508). Storrs: University of Connecticut, The National Research Center on the Gifted and Talented.

Cramond, B., & Kim, K. H. (2007). The role of creativity tools and measures in assessing potential and growth. In J. VanTassel-Baska (Ed.), *Alternative assessments with gifted and talented students* (pp. 203–225). Waco, TX: Prufrock Press.

Cropley, A. J., & Urban, K. K. (2000). Programs and strategies for nurturing creativity. In K. A. Heller, F. J. Mönks, R. J. Sternberg, & R. F. Subotnik (Eds.), *International handbook of giftedness and talent* (2nd ed., pp. 485–498). New York: Pergamon Press.

Csikszentmihalyi, M. (1988). Society, culture, and person: A systems view of creativity. In R. J. Sternberg (Ed.), *The nature of creativity: Contemporary psychological perspectives* (pp. 325–339). New York: Cambridge University Press.

Csikszentmihalyi, M. (1996). *Creativity: Flow and the psychology of discovery and invention.* New York: HarperCollins.

Davis, G. A. (1992). *Creativity is forever* (3rd ed.). Dubuque, IA: Kendall/Hunt.

Davis, G. A., & Rimm, S. B. (1994). *Education of the gifted and talented* (3rd ed.). Needham Heights, MA: Allyn & Bacon.

Davis, G. A., & Rimm, S. B. (2004). *Education of the gifted and talented* (5th ed.). Boston: Pearson Education.

Davis, G. A., & Subkoviak, M. J. (1978). Multidimensional analysis of a personality-based test of creative potential. *Journal of Educational Measurement, 12,* 37–43.

Dykes, M., & McGhie, A. (1976). A comparative study of attentional strategies of schizophrenic and highly creative normal subjects. *British Journal of Psychiatry, 128,* 50–56.

Eiduson, B. T. (1962). *Scientists: Their psychological world.* New York: Basic.

Eysenck, H. J. (1995). Creativity as a product of intelligence and personality. In D. Saklofske & M. Zeidner (Eds.), *International handbook of personality and intelligence: Perspectives on individual differences* (pp. 231–247). New York: Plenum Press.

Farley, F. H. (1986). The big T in personality. *Psychology Today, 20,* 45–52.

Feldhusen, J., & Goh, B. E. (1995). Assessing and accessing creativity: An integrative review of theory, research, and development. *Creativity Research Journal, 8,* 231–247.

Fink, A., & Neubauer, A. C. (2006). EEG alpha oscillations during the performance of verbal creativity tasks: Differential effects of sex and verbal intelligence. *International Journal of Psychophysiology, 62,* 46–53.

Getzels, J. W., & Jackson, P. W. (1958). The meaning of "giftedness": An examination of an expanding concept. *Phi Delta Kappan, 40,* 75–77.

Getzels, J. W., & Jackson, P. W. (1962). *Creativity and intelligence.* New York: John Wiley & Sons.

Goertzel, M. G., & Goertzel, V. H. (1960). Intellectual and emotional climate in families producing eminence. *Gifted Child Quarterly, 4,* 59–60.

Gowan, J. C., Khatena, J., & Torrance, E. P. (1979). *Educating the ablest: A book of readings on the education of gifted children.* Itasca, IL: Peacock.

Huang, T.-Y. (2005). Fostering creativity: A meta-analytic inquiry into the variability of effects. *Dissertation Abstracts International, 66*(04A), 2348A.

Hughes, A. O., & Drew, J. S. (1984). A state creative? *Papers in the Social Sciences, 4,* 1–15.

Jaušovec, N. (2008). Differences in cognitive processes between gifted, intelligent, creative, and average individuals while solving complex problems: An EEG study. *Intelligence, 28,* 213–237.

Jaušovec, N., & Jaušovec, K. (2000). Differences in resting EEG related to ability. *Brain Topography, 12,* 229–240.

Khatena, J. (1983). What schooling for the gifted. *Gifted Child Quarterly, 27,* 51–56.

Kim, K. H. (2005). Can only intelligent people be creative? A meta-analysis. *Journal of Secondary Gifted Education, 16,* 57–66.

Kristeller, P. O. (1983). "Creativity" and "tradition." *Journal of the History of Ideas, 44,* 105–114.

Kuo, Y.-Y. (1996). Taoistic psychology of creativity. *Journal of Creative Behavior, 30,* 197–212.

Lim, W., & Plucker, J. A. (2001). Creativity through a lens of social responsibility: Implicit theories of creativity with Korean samples. *Journal of Creativity Behavior, 35,* 115–130.

Lubart, T. I. (1994). Creativity. In R. J. Sternberg (Ed.), *Thinking and problem solving* (pp. 290–332). San Diego, CA: Academic Press.

Lubart, T. I. (2001). Models of the creative process: Past, present, and future. *Creative Research Journal, 13,* 295–308.

MacKinnon, D. W. (1967). Educating for creativity: A modern myth? In P. Heist (Ed.), *Education for creativity* (pp. 1–20). Berkeley, CA: Center for Research and Development in Higher Education.

MacKinnon, D. W. (1975). IPAR's contribution to the conceptualization and study of creativity. In I. A. Taylor & J. W. Getzels (Eds.), *Perspectives in creativity* (pp. 60–89). New York: Aldine.

MacKinnon, D. W. (1978). *In search of human effectiveness: Identifying and developing creativity.* Buffalo, NY: Creative Education Association.

Martindale, C. (1989). Personality, situation, and creativity. In J. A. Glover, R. R. Ronning, & C. R. Reynolds (Eds.), *Handbook of creativity: Perspectives on individual differences* (pp. 211–232). New York: Plenum Press.

Martindale, C., & Hines, D. (1975). Creativity and cortical activation during creative, intellectual, and EEG feedback tasks. *Biological Psychology, 3,* 71–80.

Mölle, M., Marshall, L., Wolf, B., Fehm, H. L., & Born, J. (1999). EEG complexity and performance measures of creative thinking. *Psychophysiology, 36,* 95–104.

Ochse, R. (1990). *Before the gates of excellence: The determinants of creative genius.* New York: Cambridge University Press.

Prentky, R. A. (1980). *Creativity and psychopathology: A neurocognitive perspective.* New York: Praeger.

Rhodes, M. (1961). An analysis of creativity. *Phi Delta Kappan, 42,* 305–310.

Rose, L. H., & Lin, H. T. (1984). A meta-analysis of long-term creativity training programs. *Journal of Creative Behavior, 18,* 11–22.

Rudowicz, E. (2003). Creativity and culture: A two way interaction. *Scandinavian Journal of Educational Research, 47,* 273–290.

Rudowicz, E., & Yue, X.-D. (2000). Compatibility of Chinese and creative personalities. *Creativity Research Journal, 14,* 387–394.

Runco, M. A. (1993). Operant theories of insight, originality, and creativity. *American Behavioral Scientists, 37,* 54–67.

Runco, M. A. (2004). Creativity. *Annual Review of Psychology, 55,* 657–687.

Runco, M. A., & Charles, R. E. (1993). Judgments of originality and appropriateness as predictors of creativity. *Personality and Individual Differences, 15,* 537–546.

Rushton, J. P., Murray, H. G., & Paunonen, S. V. (1987). Personality characteristics associated with high research productivity. In D. Jackson & J. P. Rushton (Eds.), *Scientific excellence* (pp. 129–148). Beverly Hills, CA: Sage.

Scott, C. L. (1999). Teachers' biases toward creative children. *Creativity Research Journal, 12,* 321–328.

Scott, G., Leritz, L., & Mumford, M. (2004). The effectiveness of creativity training: A quantitative review. *Creativity Research Journal, 16,* 361–388.

Seo, H.-A., Lee, E. A., & Kim, K. H. (2005). Korean science teachers' understandings of creativity in gifted education. *Journal of Secondary Gifted Education, 16,* 98–105.

Simonton, D. K. (1999). *Origins of genius: Darwinian perspective on creativity.* New York: Oxford University Press.

Storr, A. (1988). *Solitude: A return to the self.* New York: Free Press.

Tardif, T. Z., & Sternberg, R. J. (1988). What do we know about creativity? In R. J. Sternberg (Ed.), *The nature of creativity: Contemporary psychological perspectives* (pp. 429–440). New York: Cambridge University Press.

Taylor, D. W. (1988). Various approaches to and definitions of creativity. In R. J. Sternberg (Ed.), *The nature of creativity* (pp. 99–121). New York: Cambridge University Press.

Torrance, E. P. (1962). *Guiding creative talent.* Englewood Cliffs, NJ: Prentice-Hall.

Torrance, E. P. (1963). The creative personality and the ideal pupil. *Teachers College Record, 65,* 220–226.

Torrance, E. P. (1977a). *Creativity in the classroom.* Washington, DC: National Education Association.

Torrance, E. P. (1977b). *Discovery and nurturance of giftedness in the culturally different.* Reston, VA: Council for Exceptional Children.

Torrance, E. P. (2002). *The manifesto: A guide to developing a creative career.* West Westport, CT: Ablex.

VanTassel-Baska, J. (1996a). Talent development in women writers: A study of Charlotte Brontë and Virginia Woolf. In K. Arnold, R. Subotnik, & K. Noble (Eds.), *Remarkable women: Perspectives on female talent development* (pp. 295–316). Cresskill, NJ: Hampton Press.

VanTassel-Baska, J. (1996b). The process of talent development. In J. VanTassel-Baska, D. T. Johnson, & L. N. Boyce (Eds.), *Developing verbal talent: Ideas and strategies for teachers of elementary and middle school students* (pp. 3–22). Boston: Allyn & Bacon.

VanTassel-Baska, J. (2003). *Curriculum planning and instructional design for gifted learners.* Denver, CO: Love.

VanTassel-Baska, J. (2008, January). *How can we infuse creative strategies into content?* Paper presented at the 2008 International Costa Rican Educational Adventure in Creativity Theory and Empiricism Conference, Costa Rica

Walberg, H. A., & Herbig, M. P. (1991). Developing talent, creativity, and eminence. In N. Colangelo & G. A. Davis (Eds.), *Handbook of gifted education* (pp. 245–255). Needham Heights, MA: Allyn & Bacon.

Wallas, G. (1926). *The art of thought.* New York: Harcourt Brace.

Westby, E., & Dawson, V. L. (1995). Creativity: Asset or burden in the classroom? *Creativity Research Journal, 8,* 1–10.

Williams, E. (2000). The history of the evolution of gifted identification procedures in Georgia. (Doctoral dissertation, University of Georgia, 2000). *Dissertation Abstracts International, 160,* 153.

Yue, X.-D., & Rudowicz, E. (2002). Perception of the most creative Chinese by undergraduates in Beijing, Guangzhou, Hong Kong, and Taipei. *Journal of Creative Behavior, 36,* 88–104.

CHAPTER 5

SOCIAL AND EMOTIONAL DEVELOPMENT OF STUDENTS WITH GIFTS AND TALENTS

by

TRACY L. CROSS,

JENNIFER RIEDL CROSS,

AND

ANDREW S. DAVIS

Every gift contains a danger. Whatever gift we have we are compelled to express. And if the expression of that gift is blocked, distorted, or merely allowed to languish, then the gift turns against us, and we suffer.

—L. Johnson

INTRODUCTION

The research base on the social and emotional development of students with gifts and talents has increased quite significantly over the past 25 years. In addition to the increase in the number of studies conducted, articles published, and literature reviews produced, the nature of the questions asked reflect a healthy broadening of the concepts used, making the current research increasingly more sophisticated in both its theoretical foundations and statistical analyses. This chapter provides a review of the research on this psychological construct.

Contemporary research in gifted studies includes two relatively distinct conceptions of the social and emotional development of students with gifts and talents: (1) a characteristics-based perspective, and (2) the interaction of characteristics and context perspective. The perspectives represent two larger conceptions of giftedness that have helped guide the field of gifted studies over the past 20 years or so: giftedness as *being* and giftedness as *doing*. Other similar descriptions include giftedness as an entity, something that exists (being), and giftedness as an incrementally developed outcome (doing). From the giftedness as being conception arises the assumption that students with gifts and talents exist and therefore we should study their endogenous characteristics (characteristics of the person). From the giftedness as doing conception arises the assumption that we should study the development of talent within specific contexts. This is more of an exogenous notion of giftedness.

Two exemplary theories of intelligence have guided our thinking about giftedness in general and social and emotional development more specifically. In his classic book *Frames of Mind*, Gardner (1983) described seven types of intelligences (interpersonal, intrapersonal, spatial, bodily kinesthetic, logical-mathematical, linguistic, musical) as unique domains. He has since added to the list of intelligences. He proposed that abilities can exist in these domains and are developed over time. Sternberg (1985) offered a triarchic conception of intelligence in which people possess three (practical, analytic, synthetic) largely distinct abilities that can be developed into heightened intelligences. These two theories encourage researchers to frame their questions in ways that are different from the past. Moreover, many professionals have treated social and emotional issues and development as one construct. Gardner's work, along with a host of others, has influenced us to study each type of intelligence on its own. Goleman (1995) built on Gardner's work, creating great interest in the construct of emotional intelligence. As a consequence, several new "intelligences" are now being pursued. Inherent to these major theories and the associated ones that have followed is that giftedness needs to be considered within a developmental framework and within varying contexts.

Approximately 25 years ago, the most common phrase used to discuss this topic was the *social/emotional needs* of gifted students. The term was created after the suicide of a gifted student in 1981 that garnered considerable attention (Neihart, 1999). The phrasing situates the thinking of the day, revealing that we conflated the two topics and thought of them in very practical terms. Moreover, we assumed students with gifts and talents actually have unique needs. Much of the research done at the time on this topic explored the self-concept of gifted students. Twenty-five years later, we speak more regularly in terms of development and with social and emotional domains representing related but distinct constructs.

To offer the broadest, most encompassing lens on students with gifts and talents, we prefer the term *gifted studies* rather than gifted education. Much of the important research that has been and remains to be conducted does not necessarily have application to curriculum or even pedagogy. The social/emotional needs construct circa 1983 typically had assumptions related to instruction. For example, a need/issue of adolescent students with gifts and talents may lie in college guidance matters. Although the actual issue at hand emerges out of the desire to transition into a college placement from high school, the true need may derive from an issue that may or may not have legitimate psychological ramifications. From this perspective, essential aspects of this need are contextual, school-related, and somewhat culturally limited. How to advise these students is based in part on educational needs rather than psychological characteristics—psychological characteristics situated within a context. Recent research has largely broken free from such assumptions.

Contemporary Research

To characterize contemporary research on the topic of the social and emotional development of students with gifts and talents, we will use an overarching category of the "psychology" of students with gifts and talents. To that end, we will characterize three bodies of research that answer important questions about the psychology of these students. They are: (1a) What are common psychological characteristics of students with gifts and talents? (1b) Are they the same as or different from the general population? (2a) What are the personalities of students with gifts and talents like? (2b) Are the personalities of students with gifts and talents the same as or different from the general population? (3) Are students with gifts and talents psychologically more or less healthy than the general population? The second part of this chapter will provide a detailed overview of new directions in research on the topic of the psychology of students with gifts and talents.

What are common psychological characteristics of students with gifts and talents? Are they the same as or different from the general population?

A considerable body of research exists on self-concept among students with gifts and talents, much of it conducted in the early 1980s through the late 1990s. Virtually all of this research was conducted with intellectually or academically gifted students. Many of the studies used convenience samples from which to gather data. By today's standard of sensitivity to diversity, much of the research would be criticized for loading heavily with middle- and upper class Caucasian students. The results of these studies are mixed, with some studies indicating no substantial differences of the self-concepts of students with gifts and talents and the general population (e.g., Bracken, 1980; Tong & Yewchuk, 1996) and other studies that did find some differences. Among those studies reporting differences, it was generally revealed that the self-concept of students with gifts and talents are more positive than in the general population (e.g., Ablard, 1997; Janos, Fung, & Robinson, 1985). Other studies found that the self-concept scores of students with gifts and talents are lower than that of the general population (e.g., Lea-Wood & Clunies-Ross, 1995). More recent research has investigated the relationship of contexts on self-concept of students with gifts and talents. These studies generally have found that schools that bring highly able students together may influence self-concept scores, causing them to decline slightly (e.g., Cross, Adams, Dixon, & Holland, 2004; Marsh & Hau, 2003). The results of these types of studies are too limited to draw conclusions at this time.

Perfectionism is another topic in which considerable interest has been shown. It can be defined as a tendency to set unreasonable expectations for oneself. More recent conceptions have delineated that perfectionism actually is multidimensional with three or more types, including self-oriented, socially oriented, and other (Hewitt & Flett, 1991). This line of research has led many to conclude that students with gifts and talents manifest a greater propensity for perfectionism than the general population (Cross, 1997). The most recent research (e.g., Dixon, Lapsley, & Hanchon, 2004; Speirs Neumeister, Williams, & Cross, 2007) is attempting to assess this construct using multidimensional instruments such as the Multidimensional Perfectionism Scale (Hewitt & Flett, 1991).

Another important psychological characteristic that is more common among students with gifts and talents than in the general population has been labeled *asynchronous development* (AD; Silverman, 1997). AD describes the difference between an extraordinary area of ability and other developmental areas. For example, the 7-year-old child who has a measured IQ of 150 and social skills on par with an average student exhibits AD. Such dramatic differences can create many difficulties for the child, especially as she navigates school situations that tend to be rigidly age-specific environments. Some believe that asynchronous development is actually a definition for giftedness because it is so common (Morelock, 1992).

What are the personalities of students with gifts and talents like? Are the personalities of students with gifts and talents the same as or different from the general population?

Some important research about students with gifts and talents of an endogenous nature has investigated questions about personality. To that end, a popular instrument—the Myers–Briggs Type Indicator (MBTI; Myers, 1980)—has been used many times. The MBTI identifies four dichotomous dimensions of personality: Extraversion/Introversion, Sensing/Intuitive (perception of one's surroundings is either taken in through the senses or intuited from a more holistic perspective), Thinking/Feeling (a preference for one over the other in making judgments), and Judging/Perceiving (organized, systematic or spontaneous, receptive; Sak, 2004). Some consistencies have been found that show signs of difference between students with gifts and talents and the general population of same-age children and adolescents. For example, although the general population has demonstrated approximately 73% to be extraverted and 27% introverted, research has shown that students with gifts and talents consistently demonstrate a 50/50 split on extraversion and introversion (Cross, Speirs Neumeister, & Cassady, 2007; Sak, 2004). This means that about twice the percentage of students with gifts and talents are more introverted than the general population. Some gender differences also have been found. More gifted girls tend to be Extraverts (rather than Introverts), Intuitive rather than Sensing (slightly); more are Thinking rather than Feeling, and more often gifted girls are Perceiving rather than Judging when compared to the general population.

Are students with gifts and talents more or less psychologically healthy than the general population?

Our attempts to address this question have credible data going back to the Terman (1925) studies, wherein he found that gifted students of the day were at least as healthy and strong on psychological and physical indicators as the general population. Current research has explored specific areas within the domain of mental health with findings consistent with Terman's claims (Coleman & Cross, 2005; Cross et al., 2004; Neihart, 1999). Although there have been a small number of exceptions, research has consistently demonstrated that students with gifts and talents are not less mentally healthy than their nongifted peers.

Depression is a very common condition of Western societies, regularly demonstrating numerous worrisome associations with other maladies. For example, depression is considered the most important correlate of suicidal behavior of people in general. Research to date has not established a meaningful correlation between IQ and depression in children and adolescents (Mash & Barkley, 1996). Moreover, research about levels of depression between students with gifts and talents and the general population have found that gifted students' levels tend to be the same as or lower than their comparison group (Baker, 1995; Bartell & Reynolds, 1986; Cross et al., 2004). Although there is reasonable evidence that risk of suicidal behavior and depression is no greater among students with gifts and talents than in the general population, other lenses offer different perspectives. In the area of suicidal behavior, research over the past 12 years has consistently revealed that there is little to no actual research suggesting that students with gifts and talents are engaging in suicidal behavior at a different rate than the general population (Cassady & Cross, 2006; Cross, Cassady, Dixon, & Adams, 2008; Dixon & Schekel, 1996; Gust & Cross, 1999). Moreover, this research on students with gifts and talents has revealed that the level of suicide ideation of students with gifts and talents is within a normal range, with no significant difference from the general population.

Researchers also have explored the hypothesis that rates of depression and anxiety are higher among students with gifts and talents. In studies comparing rates of depression between students with gifts and talents and their peers in the general population, the gifted have not been found to have a higher incidence (Baker, 1995; Berndt, Kaiser, & van Aalst, 1982; Neihart, 1991). Although most studies of young students with gifts and talents report lower measures of anxiety compared to the general population (Neihart, 1991; Reynolds & Bradley, 1983; Scholwinski & Reynolds, 1985), Tong and Yewchuk's (1996) high school sample found the opposite, suggesting a possible developmental relationship between giftedness and anxiety.

LIVED EXPERIENCE AND SOCIAL COPING

When characterizing the lived experience of students with gifts and talents, researchers have found that they often feel different from other students (Coleman

& Cross, 1988; Cross, Coleman & Terhaar-Yonkers, 1991). Extending the perceived differences based on the lived experiences of the students with gifts and talents is a body of research on their social coping behavior. Several studies have identified these behaviors (e.g., Coleman, 1985; Coleman & Cross, 1988; Cross, Coleman, & Stewart, 1993; Cross & Swiatek, in press; Swiatek, 1995). Swiatek (2001; Swiatek & Dorr, 1998) developed the Social Coping Questionnaire that has become widely used over the last decade to investigate the social coping of students with gifts and talents. These students may have more positive social coping skills than their counterparts in the general population (Barnett & Fiscella, 1985; Dauber & Benbow, 1990), but giftedness is not necessarily predictive of positive adjustment. Some evidence exists that students who are verbally gifted experience greater difficulty in adjustment and social acceptance than do students who are mathematically gifted (Cross et al., 1993; Swiatek, 1995).

NEW RESEARCH DIRECTIONS

As research continues utilizing traditional methods, the advent of brain imaging technologies has opened the door to new and potentially groundbreaking research on the biological bases of giftedness. On the horizon are studies that focus on the anatomy and neurological functioning of the brains of students with gifts and talents. Although a small number of such studies have been conducted, the scientific winds of change are shifting in this direction. Techniques used to examine or estimate neurological functioning tend to fall into two categories, direct and indirect measurement.

Perhaps the most common methodology for indirect measurement of neurological functioning involves neuropsychological and neurobehavioral testing. These approaches provide for an indirect measurement of neural activity by observing elicited or involuntary behavior. The clinician then extrapolates an estimate of neurological status, either in regard to specific areas of the central nervous system or functional output. Typically conducted by neurologists and neuropsychologists, this approach offers the advantage of being relatively inexpensive and noninvasive, with a rich empirical history. The second approach utilizes medical technology and allows for direct measurement of in-vivo real-time neural processing. These techniques include functional Magnetic Resonance Imaging (fMRI), Positron Emission Tomography (PET), and electroencephalography (EEG). These three techniques offer an advantage to older medical technology such as Computed Tomography (CT) and Magnetic Resonance Imaging (MRI), which limited examination to the *structure* of the brain. In essence, these older techniques provide static pictures of neural areas that allows for the investigation of lesions, tumors, and other anomalies. The newer techniques of fMRI, PET, and EEG actually show *functional* activity of the brain, as opposed to simple structure, allowing clinicians to directly observe neural processing.

There is a debate in the literature regarding the relative contribution of morphological brain differences and environmental factors to giftedness. Traditional psychological and neuropsychological nondirect measurement techniques are inherently flawed in addressing this issue because they measure behavioral/functional performance without regard for the etiology of the child's performance. This has led to recent research that combines the techniques of direct measurement techniques, such as EEG, with behavioral assessment measures. The combination of neuropsychological assessment and EEG increasingly is being used to provide evidence of construct validity for the neuropsychological tests and to examine if assessment approaches are yielding the same functional clinical data for different populations (Banaschewski & Brandeis, 2007). Such exploration could provide valuable comparisons between students with gifts and talents and their peers in the general population.

EEG also is being used to investigate the relationship between neurocognitive processing and neural activity. For example, van der Hiele et al. (2007) demonstrated that measures of EEG were related to neuropsychological test performance and may be useful in the measurement of cognitive decline and dementia. Most neuroscience research focuses on the measurement and interpretation of deficits, as this has direct clinical application to neurologists and neuropsychologists. The literature is less extensive in regard to examining neurological functioning in superior performing adults and children, such as those children identified with gifts or talents.

Some research has emerged linking EEG measures and neurocognitive functioning in gifted children, which is not surprising given that several studies have linked intelligence and faster nerve conduction (Henderson & Ebner, 1997). Jin, Kwon, Jeong, Kwon, and Shin (2007) compared the EEG results of 25 students with gifts and talents to 25 age-matched controls. They used a scientific hypothesis generation task, which could be considered a measure of mental flexibility, an important component of executive functions. They determined that, consistent with improved performance on the task, the students with gifts and talents were more able to effectively utilize cognitive resources. Although this is an important finding, it also demonstrates some of the methodological problems with previous studies exploring the results of EEG and neurocognitive processing in students with gifts and talents. Two of the problems pervasive in the literature are small sample size and inadequate cognitive processing tasks in regard to psychometric properties. In another study, Staudt and Neubauer (2006) split 31 adolescent students into four groups based on high and low intelligence and achievement. They determined that the level of intelligence and achievement resulted in different levels and locations of cortical achievement. Again, although this is an important finding, the small sample size in each group limits generalization. Additionally, the authors used psychometrically troubled instruments, starting with the fact that they were from the 1960s and 1970s, a significant problem given the well-documented rise in cognitive abilities over time.

In sum, the idea that neurocognitive processing can be assessed by EEG is well documented. What is less clear is the connection between measures of behavioral neurocognitive processing and EEG in special populations. This is more than an academic question. There are significant implications for practitioners and researchers as far as this relationship is concerned, including implications for early intervention, improving the identification of gifted children, and determining treatment and intervention efficacy. The different approaches required for treatment and interventions benefiting students with gifts and talents can be explored as physiological differences (or the lack thereof) between students with gifts and talents and their peers in the general population are identified through these advanced technologies.

CONCLUSION

Since Terman's classic study revealing important characteristics of students with gifts and talents almost 85 years ago, the field of gifted studies has gained momentum in its research. Terms have evolved with increasingly sophisticated conceptions guiding contemporary research. Those interested in the various aspects of the psychology of students with gifts and talents have evolved from describing basic qualities of the person, to intense study of the students within a myriad of contexts. More recently, although considerable overlap of these types coexist with the newer brain-based research, clearly, the baton is being handed to those who conduct neurophysiological research. The field of neuroscience has witnessed a movement from measuring matters indirectly with paper-and-pencil inventories, to much more direct measures using EEG and *f*MRI technologies. The next 25 years of research on the psychology of students with gifts and talents will contribute significant insight about the neurological functioning of these students that will help us serve them in ways not yet fully understood.

The history of research on the social and emotional development of students with gifts and talents traces a pattern of increasing refinement and sophistication of constructs and methodologies. From education to psychology, the social and emotional needs of this special population are being identified and addressed. A leader in the field of gifted education, a truly gifted individual herself, Dr. Joyce Van Tassel-Baska (2007) has noted the importance of understanding the social and emotional needs of students with gifts and talents in developing the learning communities they will inhabit. Her substantial work in affective curriculum has put into practice the findings of research on the social and emotional development of students, a testament to her dedication and the model she provides for generations of future researchers and educators.

References

Ablard, K. E. (1997). Self-perceptions and needs as a function of type of academic ability and gender. *Roeper Review, 20,* 110–115.

Baker, J. A. (1995). Depression and suicidal ideation among academically talented adolescents. *Gifted Child Quarterly, 39,* 218–223.

Banaschewski, T., & Brandeis, D. (2007). Annotation: What electrical brain activity tells us about brain function that other techniques cannot tell us: A child psychiatric perspective. *Journal of Child Psychology and Psychiatry and Allied Disciplines, 48,* 415–435.

Barnett, L., & Fiscella, J. (1985). A child by any other name . . . A comparison of the playfulness of gifted and nongifted children. *Gifted Child Quarterly, 29,* 61–66.

Bartell, N. P., & Reynolds, W. M. (1986). Depression and self-esteem in academically gifted and nongifted children: A comparison study. *Journal of School Psychology, 24,* 55–61.

Berndt, D. J., Kaiser, C. F., & van Aalst, F. (1982). Depression and self-actualization in gifted adolescents. *Journal of Clinical Psychology, 38,* 142–150.

Bracken, B. A. (1980). Comparison of self-attitudes of gifted children and children in a nongifted normative group. *Psychological Reports, 47,* 142–150.

Cassady, J. C., & Cross, T. L. (2006). A factorial representation of suicidal ideation among academically gifted adolescents. *Journal for the Education of the Gifted, 29,* 290–304.

Coleman, L. J. (1985). *Schooling the gifted.* New York: Merrill.

Coleman, L. J., & Cross, T. L. (1988). Is being gifted a social handicap? *Journal for the Education of the Gifted, 11,* 41–56.

Coleman, L. J., & Cross, T. L. (2005). *Being gifted in school: An introduction to development, guidance and teaching* (2nd ed.). Waco, TX: Prufrock Press.

Cross, T. L. (1997). Psychological and social aspects of educating gifted students. *Peabody Journal of Education, 72,* 180–200.

Cross, T. L., Adams, C. A., Dixon, F., & Holland, J. (2004). Psychological characteristics of academically gifted adolescents attending a residential academy: A longitudinal study. *Journal for the Education of the Gifted, 28,* 159–181.

Cross, T. L., Cassady, J. C., Dixon, F., & Adams, C. (2008). The psychology of gifted adolescents as measured by the MMPI-A. *Gifted Child Quarterly, 52,* 326–339.

Cross, T. L., Coleman, L. J., & Terhaar-Yonkers, M. (1991). The social cognition of gifted adolescents in schools: Managing the stigma of giftedness. *Journal for the Education of the Gifted, 15,* 44–55.

Cross, T. L., Coleman, L. J., & Stewart, R. A. (1993). The school-based social cognition of gifted adolescents: An exploration of the stigma of giftedness paradigm. *Roeper Review, 16,* 37–40.

Cross, T. L., Speirs Neumeister, K. L., & Cassady, J. C. (2007). Psychological types of academically gifted adolescents. *Gifted Child Quarterly, 51,* 285–294.

Cross, T. L., & Swiatek, M. A. (in press). Social coping among academically gifted adolescents in a residential setting: A longitudinal study. *Gifted Child Quarterly.*

Dauber, S. L., & Benbow, C. P. (1990). Aspects of personality and peer relations of extremely talented adolescents. *Gifted Child Quarterly, 34,* 10–14.

Dixon, D. N., & Schekel, J. R. (1996). Gifted adolescent suicide: The empirical base. *Journal of Secondary Gifted Education, 7,* 386–392.

Dixon, F., Lapsley, D., & Hanchon, T. (2004). A typology of gifted adolescent perfectionism. *Gifted Child Quarterly, 48,* 95–106.

Gardner, H. (1983). *Frames of mind: The theory of multiple intelligences*. New York: Basic Books.

Goleman, D. (1995). *Emotional intelligence*. New York: Bantam Books.

Gust, K. A., & Cross, T. L. (1999). An examination of the literature base on the suicidal behaviors of gifted students. *Roeper Review, 22,* 28–35.

Henderson, L. M., & Ebner, F. F. (1997). The biological basis for early intervention with gifted children. *Peabody Journal of Education, 72,* 59–80.

Hewitt, P. L., & Flett, G. L. (1991). Perfectionism in the self and social contexts: Conceptualization, assessment, and association with psychopathology. *Journal of Personality and Social Psychology, 60,* 456–470.

Janos, P. M., Fung, H. C., & Robinson, N. (1985). Self-concept, self-esteem, and peer relations among gifted children who "feel different." *Gifted Child Quarterly, 29,* 79–81.

Jin, S. H., Kwon, Y. J., Jeong, J. S., Kwon, S. W., & Shin, D. H. (2007). Differences in brain information transmission between gifted and normal children during scientific hypothesis generation. *Brain and Cognition, 62,* 191–197.

Lea-Wood, S. S., & Clunies-Ross, G. (1995). Self-esteem of gifted adolescent girls in Australian schools. *Roeper Review, 17,* 195–197.

Marsh, H., & Hau, K. T. (2003). Big-fish-little-pond effect on academic self-concept. *American Psychologist, 58,* 364–376.

Mash, E. J., & Barkley, R. A. (Eds.). (1996). *Child psychopathology*. New York: Guilford Press.

Morelock, M. J. (1992). Giftedness: The view from within. *Understanding Our Gifted, 4*(3), 1, 11–15.

Myers, I. B. (with Myers, P. B.). (1980). *Gifts differing*. Palo Alto, CA: Consulting Psychologists Press.

Neihart, M. (1991). Anxiety and depression and high ability and average ability adolescents. Unpublished doctoral dissertation, University of Northern Colorado.

Neihart, M. (1999). The impact of giftedness on psychological well-being: What does the empirical literature say? *Roeper Review, 22,* 10–30.

Reynolds, C. R., & Bradley, M. (1983). Emotional stability of intellectually superior children versus nongifted peers as estimated by chronic anxiety levels. *School Psychology Review, 12,* 190–194.

Sak, U. (2004). A synthesis of research on psychological types and gifted adolescents. *Journal of Secondary Gifted Education, 15,* 70–79.

Scholwinski, E., & Reynolds, C. R. (1985). Dimensions of anxiety among high IQ children. *Gifted Child Quarterly, 29,* 125–130.

Silverman, L. K. (1997). The construct of asynchronous development. *Peabody Journal of Education, 72,* 36–58.

Speirs Neumeister, K. L., Williams, K. K., & Cross, T. L. (2007). Perfectionism in gifted high-school students: Responses to academic challenge. *Roeper Review, 29*(5), 11–18.

Staudt, B., & Neubauer, A. C. (2006). Achievement, underachievement and cortical activation: A comparative EEG study of adolescents of average and above average intelligence. *High Ability Studies, 17,* 3–16.

Sternberg, R. J. (1985). *Beyond IQ: A triarchic theory of human intelligence*. New York: Cambridge University Press.

Swiatek, M. A. (1995). An empirical investigation of the social coping strategies used by gifted adolescents. *Gifted Child Quarterly, 39,* 154–161.

Swiatek, M. A. (2001). Social coping among gifted high school students and its relationship to self-concept. *Journal of Youth and Adolescence, 30,* 19–39.

Swiatek, M. A., & Dorr, R. M. (1998). Revision of the Social Coping Questionnaire: Replication and extension of previous findings. *Journal of Secondary Gifted Education, 10,* 252–259.

Terman, L. (1925). *Mental and physical traits of a thousand gifted children. Genetic studies of genius, Vols. 1 and 2.* Stanford, CA: Stanford University Press.

Tong, J., & Yewchuk, C. (1996). Self-concept and sex-role orientation in gifted high school students. *Gifted Child Quarterly, 40,* 15–23.

van der Hiele, K., Vein, A. A., Reijntjes, R. H. A. M., Westendorp, R. G. J., Bollen, E. L. E. M., van Buchem, M. A., et al. (2007). EEG correlates in the spectrum of cognitive decline. *Clinical Neurophysiology, 118,* 1931–1939.

VanTassel-Baska, J. (2007). Leadership for the future in gifted education. *Gifted Child Quarterly, 51,* 5–10.

CHAPTER 6

BUILDING GIFTS INTO TALENTS:

Detailed Overview of the DMGT 2.0

by

FRANÇOYS GAGNÉ

I have no special gift. I am only passionately curious.
—Albert Einstein

The Differentiated Model of Giftedness and Talent (DMGT) first appeared in French 25 years ago, 2 years before being formally described—and named—in an American publication (Gagné, 1985). Over the next two decades, I regularly introduced minor improvements to the model, mainly by enriching either of its components. During that period, but mainly after my official retirement in 2001, I began accumulating questions, suggestions, and addenda aimed at improving further the DMGT. As the 25th anniversary of the DMGT's birth approached, I decided to bring all of these bits and pieces together into a major update of the former model, progressively transformed into a talent development theory. The term *major* might be judged an overstatement because the core of the DMGT remained untouched, namely the basic distinction between gifts and talents, as well as the five major components linked dynamically to express the talent development process. Still, the large number of minor changes to each component, as well as new additions (e.g., the DMGT's underpinnings, the three subcomponents of the talent development component), could justify in an aggregate way its designation as a major update. A bit tongue-in-cheek, I followed the customs of the computer world, and named the updated theory DMGT 2.0.

No chapter-length text can encompass all of the details of the DMGT's contents and dynamics. Consequently, I propose the present text as a detailed overview—a potential oxymoron!—of the updated DMGT. This overview will cover five themes: (a) the DMGT's rationale; (b) the five components; (c) the "how many?" question; (d) the DMGT's biological underpinnings; and (e) some basic dynamic rules of talent development.

I. THE DMGT'S RATIONALE

The field of gifted education uses two key concepts, *gifted* and *talented*, to label its special population. Those who browse through the field's scientific and professional literature soon discover that the existence of these two terms does not mean the existence of two distinct concepts.

A Current Chaotic Situation

Most authors consider these two terms synonyms, just like in the common expression: "the gifted and talented are . . ." A few scholars (e.g., Joseph S. Renzulli, Robert Sternberg) even hesitate to use the term talent, focusing their whole conception of outstanding abilities on the concept of giftedness. When the two terms are differentiated, the distinction may take many forms. Some apply the term gifted to high cognitive abilities and the term talented to all other forms of excellence (e.g., arts, sports, technology). Others consider giftedness to represent a higher order of excellence than talent. Still others associate giftedness with some mature expression as opposed to a vision of talent as an undeveloped ability (U.S. Department of Education, 1993). In other words, if we were to extract from major publications in the field all of the proposed definitions for these two terms, we would end up with more than a dozen. It would not be too much of an exaggeration to associate the current status of our conceptual foundations with the biblical Tower of Babel.

As strange as it may seem, most of the field's scholars and professionals appear quite comfortable with this lack of consensus over the definition of our basic constructs. The most significant piece of evidence to that effect is a quasi-unanimous silence on that question. When specifically prodded, scholars will express either a doubt about the possibility of ever reaching some consensus or a strong opposition to any concerted effort in that direction. For instance, as part of a target article describing my positions on the nature of gifts and talents, I expressed my hope that my initiative would "launch an interactive process of discussion and debate" whose ultimate goal would be "to create a consensus among a large majority of professionals over scientifically clear and defensible positions concerning the meaning we give to the concepts of giftedness and talent" (Gagné, 1999b, p. 132). None of the five commentators reacted positively to this proposal. Two of them judged the priority of such an enterprise to be very low, while another associated my goal with a "quixotic quest whose futility is, I believe, guaranteed" (Borland, 1999, p. 141). He concluded: "I do not think his way of doing the impossible and, in my opinion, the undesirable, will work" (Borland, 1999, p. 145). (See also Gagné, 1999a, 2004.)

Exploiting a Fundamental Dichotomy

Whereas conceptions abound and often contradict one another, scholars keep mentioning one particular idea in almost every discussion of the giftedness construct. They acknowledge, implicitly or explicitly, a distinction between early emerging forms of giftedness with strong biological roots and fully developed adult forms of giftedness. That distinction is expressed through pairs of terms like potential/realization, aptitude/achievement, and promise/fulfillment. The DMGT was created to take advantage of that distinction; it became the basis for new differentiated definitions of these two terms. *Giftedness* designates the possession and use of outstanding natural abilities, called aptitudes, in at least one ability domain to a degree that places an individual at least among the top 10% of age peers. *Talent* designates the outstanding mastery of systematically developed abilities, called competencies (knowledge and skills), in at least one field of human activity to a degree that places an individual at least among the top 10% of age peers who are or have been active in that field.

These definitions reveal that the two concepts share three characteristics: (a) both refer to human abilities; (b) both are normative, in the sense that they target individuals who differ from the norm or average; and (c) both target individuals whose "nonnormal" status comes from outstanding behaviors. These commonalities help understand why so many professionals and laypersons confound them. Indeed, most dictionaries, even those specialized in the social sciences, commonly define giftedness as talent and vice-versa. Note that both definitions concretize the meaning of *outstanding* with precise estimates of prevalence: the "how many?" question. Assuming that most human abilities manifest themselves as normal—or bell curve—distributions, the DMGT states that gifted and talented individuals occupy the top 10% of any such ability distribution. From these two definitions, we can extract a simple definition for the talent development process: Talent development corresponds to the progressive transformation of gifts into talents.

These three components, giftedness (G), talent (T), and the talent development process (D), constitute the basic trio of components within the DMGT. Two additional components (see Figure 6.1) complete the structure of this talent development theory: intrapersonal catalysts (I) and environmental (E) catalysts.

II. The Five Components

Gifts (G)

Domains. The G component of the DMGT clusters natural abilities into six groups, called *domains*. Four of these domains belong to a mental subcomponent:

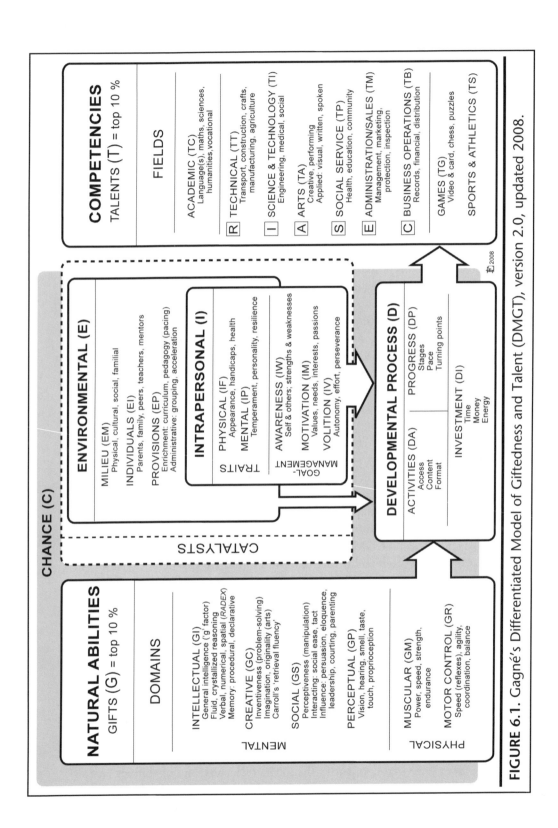

FIGURE 6.1. Gagné's Differentiated Model of Giftedness and Talent (DMGT), version 2.0, updated 2008.

intellectual (GI), creative (GC), social (GS), and perceptual (GP). Before the 2.0 update, the perceptual domain was embedded into a larger sensorimotor domain. Yet, although our knowledge of the outside world begins with sensory impressions, most of the treatment of that information happens within the brain, in areas devoted to each of the six senses, as well as the cortex. It is definitely much more mental than physical. On the other hand, even though they also begin as brain processes guiding neuronal impulses to the muscles, motor activities are directly observable in human movement. It justifies their recognized status as physical abilities. Examination of various category systems for physical abilities (e.g., Bouchard & Shepard, 1994; Burton & Miller, 1998) led to their subdivision into two major groups: muscular (GM) abilities devoted to large physical movements and abilities representing fine motor control and reflexes (GR). Both usually contribute to complex physical activities (e.g., tennis, baseball, gymnastics).

We can observe natural abilities in most tasks children confront in their daily activities and their schooling. Think, for instance, of the intellectual abilities needed to learn to read, speak a foreign language, or understand new mathematical concepts. Think of the creative abilities involved in writing a short story, composing a song, drawing an attractive poster, or playing with LEGO blocks. Notice also the social abilities children use in their daily interactions with classmates, teachers, and parents. Finally, perceptual and physical natural abilities guide activities in the schoolyard, in neighborhood sports, or arts (dance, sculpture, crafts).

Natural abilities are not innate; they do develop over the whole course of a person's life, but probably much more during the early part of that life (see Section IV). Gifts manifest themselves more easily and directly in young children because only limited systematic learning activities have begun transforming them into specific talents. Still, we can observe them in older children and adults through the facility and speed with which individuals acquire new knowledge and skills. We can assume that the easier or faster the learning process, the higher the underlying natural abilities. Many scholars have stressed the link between natural abilities and learning pace. For instance, Gottfredson (1997) stated: "Although researchers disagree on how they define intelligence, there is virtual unanimity that it reflects the ability to reason, solve problems, think abstractly, and acquire knowledge" (p. 93). Carroll (1997) similarly affirmed: "Experts have largely neglected what seems to be an obvious conclusion to be drawn from the evidence from IQ tests: that IQ represents the degree to which, and the rate at which, people are able to learn" (p. 44).

Measures. Three domains, the intellectual and both domains of the physical subcomponent, have developed psychometrically valid measures of natural abilities. IQ tests, administered either in groups or individually, are generally recognized as the most reliable and valid assessments of general cognitive functioning. In the two motor domains, one finds complex batteries of tests to assess the physical fitness of children in elementary or junior high schools (President's Council on Physical Fitness and Sports, 2001). The creative domain also has tests, but their psychometric qualities remain well below those of IQ tests, especially in terms of convergent validity (Plucker & Renzulli, 1999). Because of its more recent exploration, the social domain lags behind in terms of psychometrically sound measures; available instruments predominantly revolve around self-assessments or peer judgments. Finally, some measures can be associated with the perceptual domain—for example, tests of auditory discrimination used to assess musical aptitudes.

Talents (T)

Fields. Before the 2.0 update, the DMGT figure illustrated the diversity of talent fields with examples applicable to high school students. No effort had been made to use an exhaustive taxonomy of occupations. I chose the ACT's World-of-Work map taxonomy (ACT, 2008). It has its source in John Holland's well-known RIASEC work-related classification of personality types: Realistic, Investigative, Artistic, Social, Enterprising, and Conventional (RIASEC). These six basic types lead to the six major occupational groups in the center of the Talent component in Figure 6.1. Occupations are further subdivided into 26 smaller groups summarily identified within each of the RIASEC categories. The World-of-Work map omits three major talent fields: (a) K–12 academic subject matters, (b) games, and (c) athletics and sports. Their addition in Figure 6.1 should make the DMGT's talent taxonomy fairly complete. Note the lack of elitism in the DMGT's concept of talent. Contrary to most scholars, who tend to borrow their examples from eminent achievements in elite professions (e.g., inventors, internationally renowned artists, prize winners), I have defined the concept of talent in such a way that it ensures the presence of many individuals—the top 10%—in almost every human occupation.

Measures. An appropriate survey of assessment measures of developed skills would require covering hundreds of distinct occupations. Only general guidelines here are possible. Basically, the measurement of talent is a straightforward enterprise: Talent simply corresponds to outstanding performance in the use of the specific skills of any occupational field. During the developmental phase of any talent, whether academic, artistic, technological, or athletic, many occasions for normative assessments present themselves: teachers' exams, achievement tests, competitions, scholarships, and so forth. After individuals have completed their training, performance rankings usually disappear. How will you know if the plumber you have called is below or above average compared to peers? How about the mechanic working on your car, the dentist repairing a filling, the accountant preparing your income tax return, or the coach managing your child's hockey team? Most of the time, the only guideline will be word of mouth. Even when assessments are available, their validity often is partly questionable because they rely mostly on peer or superiors' ratings (Anastasi & Urbina, 1997). Athletics and sports stand out as the only major field in which talent assessment remains possible over the whole career of its members. As anyone could observe during the recently completed 2008 Olympics, individual differences between athletes is evidenced clearly on scoreboards. Only professional athletes have to deal with constant normative comparisons of their performances!

The Talent Development Process (D)

Until the present update, the talent development component had received much less attention than the others since the creation of the DMGT. I had said little about it beyond mentioning that it comprised four distinct processes: maturation, spontaneous learning, systematic but unstructured (autodidactic) skill development, and systematic and structured (e.g., school, team, conservatory) talent development. A review of the literature on talent development, not just in academics, but also in arts and sports, led to a more formal definition of the talent development process than the brief one proposed earlier in this chapter. *Talent development* is the systematic pursuit by talentees, over a significant period of time, of a structured program of activities aimed at a specific excellence goal. The neologism *talentee*—analogous to mentoree—labels anyone actively involved in a talent development program in any field. Based on my classification of the information I had gathered on the talent development process, I subdivided the D component into three main subcomponents (see Figure 6.1): Activities (DA), Investment (DI), and Progress (DP). Then, I further subdivided each of these three subcomponents into more specific elements. Here is a brief overview of the result of that differentiation.

Activities (DA). The talent development process begins when a child, an adolescent, or an adult accesses (DAA), through identification or selection, a systematic, talent-oriented and long-term program of activities. The talent development activities include a specific content (DAC), the curriculum, offered within a specific learning environment (DAF or format). That learning environment may be either unstructured (autodidactic learning) or structured (e.g., school, conservatory, sport organization).

Investment (DI). This subcomponent serves to illustrate *quantitatively* the intensity of the talent development process in terms of time (DIT), money (DIM), or psychological energy (DIE). These three indices usually lead to longitudinal curves showing increases or decreases over weeks, months, and years; they also can be used to compare talentees. The energy construct is not as easy to operationalize as the other two. It could be assessed as passion, concentration during practice, or determination to achieve; it parallels to a large extent the "deliberate" in Ericsson's concept of deliberate practice (Ericsson, Krampe, & Tesch-Römer, 1993).

Progress (DP). The progress of talentees from initial access to peak performance can be broken down into a series of stages (DPS). Researchers interested in the development of expertise often use a simple system of stages: novice, advanced, proficient, and expert. Sports and arts have adopted a geographically based system of stages: local excellence is the lowest rung, followed by regional, provincial/state, national, and international excellence (Oldenziel, Gagné, & Gulbin, 2003). Special access criteria and developmental activities characterize these different levels or stages. One of the best-known systems of stages found in education follows students from kindergarten through elementary school, high school, college, graduate, and postgraduate studies. Just completing either of its two highest levels could be considered a talented achievement.

The measurement of pace (DPP) constitutes the main quantitative representation of talentees' progress within and between developmental stages. We can assess pace with both ipsative and normative measures. Ipsatively, talentees can measure their progress over time, trying to improve on previous achievements or personal bests. But, within the context of talent development, normative assessments are the rule: how fast talentees are progressing with regard to peers who are pursuing a similar talent development program, at the same level of course.

Finally, the long-term developmental course of talentees will be marked by a series of more or less crucial turning points (DPT): being spotted by a teacher or coach, receiving an important scholarship, or accidents, as well as positive (falling in love) or negative (death of a close one) personal events impacting the developmental process. This element replaces a former environmental subcomponent called Events.

Intrapersonal (I) and Environmental (E) Catalysts

The 2.0 update of the DMGT has brought a few significant changes to the catalysts: (a) the repositioning of Chance outside the catalyst area, (b) the repositioning of the environmental catalysts on the same side, and partially behind, the intrapersonal catalysts, and (c) the already mentioned transfer of the Events subcomponent to the Progress subcomponent within the D component. I will discuss these changes later in this subsection.

Generalities. In chemistry, catalysts facilitate and accelerate a chemical process; they also remain unmodified after their contribution. Their DMGT metaphorical counterparts differ in two ways: (a) they may exert—by their presence or absence—both positive and negative influences, and (b) they may be permanently transformed through their involvement in the developmental process. With regard to the first difference, think of the various ways parents can impact, both positively and/or negatively, the talent development of their child. As for the second difference, there are so many examples of a talentee's motivation toward a field being permanently transformed, either positively or negatively, through his or her involvement in a talent development process.

Intrapersonal (I) catalysts. The set of intrapersonal catalysts went through an important update a few years before the recent 2.0 update (Gagné, 2003a). I partly borrowed the revised structure from a conception of self-management proposed by De Waele, Morval, & Sheitoyan (1993). This redefinition produced a new dichotomy among intrapersonal catalysts: (a) relatively stable physical and mental traits, and (b) goal-oriented processes.

Physical traits (IF) include general appearance, racial or ethnic traits, handicaps (think of the Paralympic Games), chronic illnesses, and so forth. These catalytic physical traits differ qualitatively (through their role) from physical characteristics that directly impact the level of natural physical and mental abilities (e.g., tallness in basketball, hand span in music, flexibility in dance). These templates help pinpoint young individuals who might succeed because of their specific "build." These ability-related physical characteristics belong to the DMGT's biological underpinnings (see Section IV).

Mental characteristics (IP) cluster around two major constructs: temperament and personality, which represent the nature and nurture poles respectively, or basic tendencies as opposed to behavioral styles (McCrae et al., 2000). Most personality researchers recognize the existence of five basic bipolar personality dimensions, called "The Big Five" (Digman, 1990) or the Five-Factor Model (FFM). There is growing evidence for a close relationship between temperament dimensions and adult personality traits; that relationship probably explains why all FFM dimensions have significant genetic underpinnings (Rowe, 1997).

The goal-management dimension includes three subcomponents: awareness (IW), motivation (IM), and volition (IV). Being aware of one's strengths and weaknesses, both within the G and I components, plays a crucial role in the planning of talentees' developmental activities; these strengths and weaknesses also concern environmental influences. Goal-oriented processes may be differentiated according to goal-identification activities (IM), as opposed to goal-attainment activities (IV): *what* we want to achieve and *how* we will go about reaching that goal. I borrowed this interesting dichotomy from Kuhl and Heckhausen's *Action Control* theory (see Corno, 1993). Note that the term *motivation* is given here a more restrictive definition than in lay language and most psychology textbooks, where it commonly covers both goal-identification and goal-reaching activities. The IM subcomponent includes the identification—and occasional reassessment—of an appropriate talent-development goal. Talentees will examine their values and their needs, as well as determine their interests or be swept by a potential—but rare—passion. The loftier the goal, the more difficulties talentees will encounter in their efforts (IV) to reach it. Long-term goals placed at a very high level will require an intense dedication, as well as daily acts of willpower to maintain practice through obstacles, boredom, and occasional failure.

Environmental (E) catalysts. In older versions of the DMGT, environmental catalysts appeared *below* a central arrow that graphically illustrates the developmental process as a progressive transformation of gifts into talents. In this 2.0 update, the E catalysts have been moved up and partially behind the intrapersonal catalysts. The partial overlap of the two catalysts signals the crucial *filtering* role that the I component plays with regard to environmental influences. The narrow arrow at left indicates some limited direct E influence on the developmental process. But, the bulk of environmental stimuli have to pass through the sieve of an individual's needs, interests, or personality traits. Talentees continually pick and choose which stimuli will receive their attention.

The E component comprises three distinct subcomponents. The first one, called *milieu* (EM), can be examined both at a macroscopic level (e.g., geographic, demographic, sociological) and a microscopic level (e.g., size of family, socioeconomic status, neighborhood services). For example, young gifted persons who live far from large urban centers do not have easy access to appropriate learning resources (e.g., sports training centers, music conservatories, magnet schools). Within the child's home environment, the parents' financial comfort, the absence of one of the caregivers, the number and age distribution of siblings within the family, as well as many other elements of the immediate environment can have some degree of impact on the child's talent development. The second subcomponent, *individuals* (EI), focuses on the influence of significant persons in the talentee's social environment. It includes, of course, parents and siblings, but also the larger family, teachers and trainers, peers, mentors, and even public figures adopted as role models by talentees. The significant impact of interpersonal influences is probably easier to imagine than that of any other source of influence within the environment. Moreover, the traditional environmentalist beliefs of most professionals in the social sciences, for whom nurture is a much more powerful agent than nature, increases the importance of humans as significant agents in the lives of their fellow humans. Thus, it is not surprising that a good percentage of the professional literature on talent development examines the potential influence of significant individuals in the immediate environment of gifted or talented youngsters.

The third subcomponent, *provisions* (EP), covers all forms of talent development services and programs. The two traditional subcategories of enrichment and administrative provisions directly parallel the *Content* (DAC) and *Format* (DAF) subcategories of the DA subcomponent earlier described. Here we adopt a broader outlook rather than examine provisions from the strict perspective of a given talentee's talent development course. *Enrichment* (EPE) refers to specific talent development curricula or pedagogical strategies; its best-known example is called enrichment in density or curriculum compacting. *Administrative* (EPA) provisions are traditionally subdivided into two main practices: (a) part-time (e.g., clusters, pull-out classes) or full-time ability grouping, and (b) accelerative enrichment (e.g., early entrance to school, grade skipping, Advanced Placement programs).

About the Chance Factor

I borrowed the chance factor from Tannenbaum (1983), the first scholar in the field to discuss its role in talent development. Chance's placement within the DMGT has evolved considerably over the years. It was first introduced as one of five environmental subcomponents. In the early 1990s, it became a qualifier of environmental factors, and was placed in the margin of that component. But, that solution did not satisfy me; chance did influence other components. After disappearing for a few years, chance came back as the third member of a trio of catalysts. Although its reappearance as a full-fledged component pleased a majority of DMGT aficionados, I remained dissatisfied with that solution. I finally realized that its true role was that of a *qualifier* of *any* causal influence, along with direction (positive/negative) and intensity (see Generalities above); chance represented the degree of control that talentees had over the various causal factors affecting their talent development.

A famous psychologist in motivation, John William Atkinson, once stated that all human accomplishments could be ascribed to two crucial "rolls of the dice" over which no individual exerts any personal control: the accidents of birth and background. Indeed, we do not control the genetic endowment received at conception; yet, that genetic endowment affects both our natural abilities (the G component) and our temperament, as well as other elements of the I component.

Moreover, we do not control in which family and social environment we are raised. These two impacts alone give a powerful role to chance in sowing the bases of a person's talent development possibilities.

Because of this redefined role, the chance factor should no longer appear in a visual representation of the DMGT. But, because of its popularity among DMGT fans—as well as my personal attachment to it—I created some room for it (see Figure 6.1) in the background of the components it influences.

III. Prevalence and Levels

How many people are gifted and/or talented? The prevalence question represents a crucial definitional element in the case of normative constructs, which, like giftedness and talent, target a small proportion of the whole population. Practically speaking, adopting a threshold of 10% instead of 1%—a tenfold difference in estimated prevalence—has a huge impact on selection practices and educational provisions!

Current Situation

The "how many?" question has no absolute answer; nowhere will we find a magical number that automatically separates those labeled gifted or talented from the rest of the population. The choice of an appropriate threshold requires that professionals come to a consensus. Nutritionists achieved such a consensus when they created the Body Mass Index, with its thresholds of 25 and 30 respectively to separate normal weight from overweight, and overweight from obesity (National Institute of Health, 1998). But, such a consensus does not exist in our professional field. It leaves room to a diversity of practical thresholds. Scholars' proposals can easily range from the 1% adopted by Terman (1925) with his threshold of a 135 IQ, or the 3% to 5% in the famous Marland (1972) definition, to the 20% advanced by Renzulli (1986) to create the talent pools in his Revolving Door model. What about the ratios used in school districts? In a survey of state policies, Mitchell (1988) pointed out that "states using intelligence and achievement test scores for identification generally use cut-off points which range between the 95th and 98th percentile levels" (p. 240).

The MB System

In the DMGT, the threshold for both the giftedness and talent concepts is placed at the 90th percentile (Gagné, 1998b). In other words, those who belong to the top 10% of the relevant reference group in terms of natural ability (for giftedness) or achievement (for talent) deserve the relevant label. This generous choice of threshold is counterbalanced by the recognition of levels or degrees of giftedness or talent. There are five hierarchically structured levels inspired by the metric system; each new level includes the top 10% (one decimal place) of the preceding level. This metric-based (MB) system of levels constitutes an intrinsic constituent of the DMGT. Within the top 10% of *mildly* gifted or talented persons, the four progressively more selective subgroups are labeled *moderately* (top 1%), *highly* (top 1:1,000), *exceptionally* (top 1:10,000), and *extremely* or *profoundly* (top 1:100,000). Note that the MB system of levels applies to every domain of giftedness and every field of talent. Because giftedness domains are not closely correlated, individuals gifted in one domain are not necessarily the same as those gifted in another. Consequently, the total number of gifted and talented individuals largely exceeds the 10% value. Some studies indicate that it might well be two or three times larger (Bélanger & Gagné, 2006; Gagné, 1998a).

Comment

An unfortunate habit of many keynote speakers in the field of gifted education consists in using examples of gifted or talented behaviors taken from children who show extraordinary precocity either in verbal, mathematical, scientific, moral, or social development. As attractive as such examples may be to impress an audience, they illustrate behaviors that the vast majority of gifted students identified in school districts—the *mildly* gifted or talented between the 90th and 99th percentiles—will rarely show. According to the DMGT's MB system of levels, the prevalence of *exceptionally* gifted individuals (intellectually), those with IQs of 155 or more, is approximately 1:10,000 within the general population. Because the DMGT defines the total gifted population as the top 10% (IQs ≥ 120) of the same-age general population, the prevalence of exceptionally gifted individuals *within the gifted population* does not exceed 1:1,000. It corresponds to one such student in 30 to 40 homogeneous groups of intellectually gifted students. Even full-time teachers of the gifted would, in the course of their 35-year professional career, encounter at best just a few of them. In short, exceptional giftedness or talent—and all the more *extreme* giftedness or talent—is a very rare phenomenon. Consequently, when we present extreme examples of behavior to groups of parents or teachers, we risk conveying a distorted image of who the "garden variety" of gifted and talented individuals really is. And, if we present giftedness and talent as very exceptional phenomena, we might tempt school administrators to judge that such a rare population does not require large investments of time and money to cater to their special needs.

IV. UNDERNEATH THE DMGT

The subject of the biological underpinnings of talent development originates from users' questions and personal observations. The questions addressed the absence in the DMGT of specific references to anatomical structure (e.g., tallness for basketball players, joint flexibility for gymnasts, or brain size for intelligence), physiological processes (e.g., speed of nerve impulses, VO_2max), or specific genetic effects as causal influences in the emergence of outstanding gifts or talents. The observations relevant to this question concerned a frequent misinterpretation by DMGT users of the giftedness vs. talent differentiation. They oversimplified that differentiation by opposing the terms *innate* and *systematically developed*. Judging natural abilities to be innate went far beyond recognizing a genetic origin for natural abilities.

About Innateness

When we say that little Mary is a "born" pianist, we are certainly not implying that she began playing the piano in the hospital nursery, nor that she was able to play a concerto within weeks of beginning her piano lessons. Describing her talent as innate only makes sense metaphorically. It will convey the idea that Mary progressed rapidly and seemingly effortlessly through her talent development program, at a much more rapid pace than that of her learning peers. The same applies to any natural ability. Intellectually precocious children develop their cognitive abilities by going through the same developmental stages as any other child. The difference resides in the ease and speed with which they will advance through these successive stages. The term *precocious* says it all: They reach a given level of knowledge and reasoning *before* the vast majority of learning peers. And, the higher their intellectual giftedness will be, the earlier these successive stages will be reached.

So, what does the term innate really mean? Researchers in behavioral genetics have given that term a very specific definition. At the behavioral level, it implies

> hard-wired, fixed action patterns of a species that are impervious to experience. Genetic influence on abilities and other complex traits does not denote the hard-wired deterministic effect of a single gene but rather probabilistic propensities of many genes in multiple-gene systems. (Plomin, 1998, p. 421)

Because of its restricted meaning, very few scientists use the term innate to describe any type of natural ability or temperamental characteristic. If natural abilities by themselves cannot be considered innate as defined above, what exactly is innate? Where does the "given" in giftedness reside? To answer that question, we need to look at the biological underpinnings of human behavior.

The DMGT's Basements

The biological underpinnings of human behavior—and by extension talent development—range in depth from gene activity at the deepest level to directly observable anatomical characteristics like tallness or body build. There are extremely complex causal paths linking these various levels of biological structures and processes. Now that the human genome has been decoded, researchers have reoriented their efforts toward pinpointing specific genes responsible for various human abilities and other personal characteristics. But, their scientific activities go well beyond the identification process itself. They try to reconstruct the complete biological chain of impacts from the proteins encoded by the identified genes to the specific intervening physiological structures and processes, all the way up to their impact on mental or physical abilities, as well as intrapersonal catalysts.

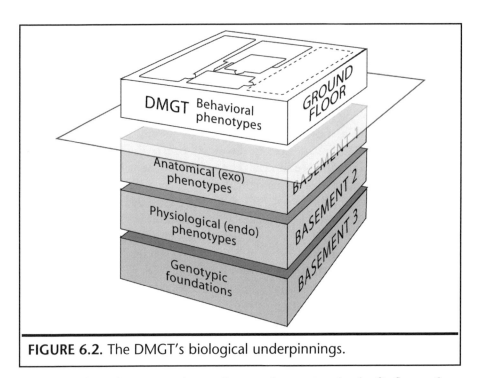

FIGURE 6.2. The DMGT's biological underpinnings.

Let us adopt a house metaphor to illustrate these various levels of influence from gene activity to behavioral expression. The house in question has a ground floor and a series of underground basements. As shown in Figure 6.2, the DMGT occupies the ground floor where directly observable and measurable behaviors manifest themselves. We often call them *phenotypes* to contrast them with gene-level, or *genotypic* activity. Every component and subcomponent we have described in Section II belongs to that ground level. Note that the talent component (T) appears as a broken line; it underlines the fact that the T component, because of its status as outcome of the talent development process, has no *direct* biological underpinnings.

A series of basements appear underneath that ground floor; they represent progressively deeper biological substrates. The number of these basements would probably provoke heated discussions among specialists. As an outsider, I gave myself the privilege of subdividing the whole gene-to-behavior substructure into three basements. At the deepest level (B-3), we find genotypic structures and processes (e.g., DNA, RNA, protein production). The second basement (B-2) contains a large diversity of physiological and neurological processes (called *endophenotypes*) that not only control a person's biological development from conception to death, but also ensure the proper functioning of body and brain. A certain number of such structures or processes already have been identified as influencing individual differences in cognitive processing, for instance, cerebral glucose metabolism or brain nerve conduction velocity (Hoppe & Stojanovic, 2008; Jensen, 1998). The highest basement (B-1) includes anatomical structures (e.g., brain size, tallness, joint flexibility) that have been associated with abilities and other personal characteristics. They are called *exophenotypes*. Most of the structures and processes associated with either basement have little bearing on the talent development process; only relevant ones would be included in an inventory of the DMGT's basements.

Where among these three subterranean levels do we find "innate" elements? Certainly not at the first (B-1) level. Most of these anatomical structures result from extensive development; they do not achieve their maturity until adolescence or adulthood; they are clearly not innate in the way we defined that term. If we go one basement down to the level of physiological processes, we might be in a gray zone where it becomes difficult to separate innate processes from those that result from development. What seems clear is that the lowest basement, devoted to gene activity, is almost completely under inborn control.

In conclusion, the present section should have made it clear that natural abilities are neither innate nor do they appear suddenly at some point during a person's early—or later—development. Just like any other type of ability, natural abilities need to develop progressively, in large part during a person's younger years; but they will do so spontaneously, without the structured learning and training activities typical of the talent development process.

V. The Dynamics of Talent Development

The DMGT is a talent-development model. It is *not* a model representing a person's total personal development; it was not designed to address questions of moral or ethical development, or consider the growth of personal maturity. Consequently, only elements that have a significant influence on the talentee's developmental process should be introduced.

Basic Dynamic Rules

Within the DMGT, natural abilities or aptitudes act as the "raw materials" or the constituent elements of talent. It follows from this relationship that talent necessarily implies the presence of well-above-average natural abilities; in most situations, one cannot become talented without first being gifted, or close to that threshold. The reverse is not true: High natural abilities may simply remain gifts, and not be translated into talents, as witnessed by the phenomenon of academic underachievement among intellectually gifted children. There also is a dynamic association between specific gifts and talents. Because of their status as raw materials, gifts represent generic abilities that can be molded into somewhat divergent skills, depending on the field of activity adopted by a talentee. For example, manual dexterity, one of many natural physical abilities, can be molded into the particular skills of a pianist, a dentist, a typist, or a video-game player. Similarly, analytical reasoning, one of many cognitive natural abilities, can be molded into the scientific reasoning of a chemist, the game analysis of a chess player, or the strategic planning of an athlete.

In most talent development situations, each of the four causal components (G, I, E, D) contributes positively to the emergence of talents. It is assumed that this positive contribution will become more intense as talentees attempt to reach higher talent goals. These contributions can vary a lot in intensity and continuity from one talentee's story to another. No two developmental paths look alike. This is why talent development is a very complex process, a process where the four causal components modify their interactions over the course of a talentee's developmental path. Think, for instance, of the close supervision many parents give to their children's homework in elementary school, and its virtual disappearance by the time the kids reach high school.

Illustrative Scenarios

Within the K–12 educational system, it is not rare to observe academically talented students who have invested little more in their schooling than their high natural intellectual gifts. Most of these students never show much intrinsic motivation for learning, need almost no environmental support, and invest little time in their schooling beyond presence in the classroom and occasional preexam cramming. Here are students who literally surf on their intellectual gifts. Conversely, a few students with barely above-average natural intellectual abilities may reach the bottom rung of the MB system of levels—mild academic talent—thanks to intense dedication and effort (IV), long hours of deliberate study (DI), and continuous support from both parents and teachers (EI). These two examples illustrate diverse dynamic interactions between the four causal components.

What Makes a Difference?

Do some components generally—on average—exercise more powerful influences on talent emergence? My own review of the existing literature has brought me to propose the following downward hierarchy among the four components: G, I, D, E. I have discussed this hierarchy in detail elsewhere (e.g., Gagné, 2003b). But, creating a causal hierarchy should not make us forget that in most situations all components play a crucial role in the talent development process. In a nutshell, talent emergence results from a complex choreography between the four causal components, a choreography that is unique to each individual.

VI. CONCLUSION

Four specific characteristics of the DMGT jointly make the model a distinct and unique conception of giftedness and talent.

1. The DMGT stands alone in its clearly differentiated definitions of the field's two key concepts. The separation of potentialities/aptitudes from realizations/achievements is well operationalized through a distinction between natural abilities and systematically developed skills, both concepts associated with the labels *giftedness* and *talent* respectively. This distinction leads to another clear definition, that of talent development, which becomes the transformation of specific natural abilities in one or more domains into the systematically developed skills typical of

an occupational field. Only in the DMGT does the concept of talent become as important as that of giftedness to understand the development of outstanding skills and knowledge. Finally, this differentiation between potentialities and realizations permits a much clearer definition of underachievement among gifted individuals. It becomes simply the *non*transformation of high natural abilities into systematically developed skills in a particular occupational field.

2. The introduction within the giftedness and talent definitions of prevalence estimates (top 10%) also constitutes a unique facet of the DMGT among existing conceptions of giftedness. Because it confronts the prevalence issue and proposes a metric-based system of five levels that applies to any giftedness domain or talent field, the DMGT helps maintain a constant awareness of differences *within* the subpopulations of gifted and talented individuals. The availability of clear thresholds and labels could facilitate not only the selection and description of study samples, but also the comparison of results from different studies. Moreover, the MB system of levels should remind educators in the field that the vast majority of gifted or talented individuals (90% of the top 10%) belong to the lowest or *mild* category, and that only a tiny fraction of those identified as talented in their youth will ever achieve eminence in their chosen field.

3. The DMGT's complex structure clearly identifies every significant causal factor of talent emergence, especially those located within the intrapersonal and environmental catalysts. But, that comprehensive outlook maintains the individuality of each component, clearly specifying its precise nature and role within this talent development theory. The giftedness construct remains well circumscribed, thus more easily operationalized. The catalysts are clearly situated outside the giftedness and talent concepts themselves. This sets the DMGT apart from many rival conceptions where disparate elements are lumped together in the giftedness definition itself. For instance, Feldhusen (1986) defined giftedness as follows: "Our composite conception of giftedness then includes (a) general intellectual ability, (b) positive self-concept, (c) achievement motivation, and (d) talent" (p. 112). Similarly, a group of professionals, calling themselves the Columbus Group, proposed the following definition: "Giftedness is asynchronous development in which advanced cognitive abilities and heightened intensity combine to create inner experiences and awareness that are qualitatively different from the norm" (Morelock, 1996, p. 8). Or, consider Renzulli's (1986) well-known definition: "Gifted behavior consists of behaviors that reflect an interaction among three basic clusters of human traits—these clusters being above average general and/or specific abilities, high levels of task commitment, and high levels of creativity" (p. 73).

4. Most published conceptions focus almost exclusively on intellectual giftedness (IG) and academic talent (AT), as well as academically based professions (e.g., scientists, lawyers, doctors, and so forth). That tendency led me to label IGAT the target population of most enrichment programs (Gagné, 1995). The DMGT follows an orientation adopted explicitly by only a few past scholars (e.g., DeHaan & Havighurst, 1961; Gardner, 1983; Marland, 1972), namely to broaden the concept of giftedness and acknowledge various qualitatively distinct manifestations. In that

respect, the DMGT stands almost alone in bringing physical giftedness within the fold of the giftedness construct, defining that domain much more broadly than Gardner's bodily-kinesthetic intelligence. This openness should foster closer ties between professionals focusing on academic talent development and those who devote their energies to the development of athletic talents.

Finally, there is one set of validating testimonies that this author is especially proud of. It comes from hundreds of professionals and teachers in the field of gifted education who, after discovering the DMGT, spontaneously say: "It makes so much sense."

AUTHOR'S NOTE

I consider as a great honor the invitation I received to participate in this memorial book celebrating the "official" completion of Joyce's immensely productive career as a professor, a researcher, an author, and a leader. From the first time we met 15 years ago in Iowa—guess where!—I have been one of her admirers and, hopefully, a good friend of hers. Our distinctly different professional interests have maintained our relationship more on a personal than a professional basis. As a psychologist by training, my interests lead me more spontaneously toward the DMGT's set of intrapersonal catalysts, whereas Joyce's career interests have given the lion's share to curriculum development, a clearly environmental provision (the DMGT's EPE subcomponent).

What has constantly fascinated me, year after year, is Joyce's unbounded energy and productivity, mixed with the subdued graciousness and gentility of a Southern Lady. Who would guess, at first glance, that her generous smile and ready friendliness are coupled with an iron hand and a will as strong as steel. That strong temperament regularly brought me to intense envy, thankfully of the positive, emulating type. But, just like my annual New Year vows, my regular self-promises of VanTassel-Baskaysian productivity never materialized. She is one of a kind, period! I wish her a happy well-deserved retirement, one as satisfying as the one I have enjoyed over the past 7 years. Yet, I still hope that she will regularly briefly put aside her new interests to offer us a few more of her pearls of wisdom.

REFERENCES

ACT. (2008). *World-of-work map.* Retrieved from http://www.act.org/wwm/index.html

Anastasi, A., & Urbina, S. (1997). *Psychological testing* (7th ed.). Upper Saddle River, NJ: Prentice Hall.

Bélanger, J., & Gagné, F. (2006). Estimating the size of the gifted/talented population from multiple identification criteria. *Journal for the Education of the Gifted, 30,* 131–163.

Borland, J. (1999). The limits of consilience. *Journal for the Education of the Gifted, 22,* 137–147.

Bouchard, C., & Shepard, R. J. (1994). Physical activity, fitness, and health: The model and key concepts. In C. Bouchard, R. J. Shepard, & T. Stephens (Eds.), *Physical activity, fitness, and health* (pp. 77–88). Champaign, IL: Human Kinetics.

Burton, A. W., & Miller, D. E. (1998). *Movement skill assessment.* Champaign, IL: Human Kinetics.

Carroll, J. B. (1997). Psychometrics, intelligence, and public perception. *Intelligence, 24,* 25–52.

Corno, L. (1993). The best-laid plans: Modern conceptions of volition and educational research. *Educational Researcher, 22,* 14–22.

DeHaan, R. F., & Havighurst, R. J. (1961). *Educating gifted children* (Rev. ed.). Chicago: University of Chicago Press.

De Waele, M., Morval, J., & Sheitoyan, R. (1993). *Self-management in organizations: The dynamics of interaction.* Seattle, WA: Hogrefe & Huber.

Digman, J. M. (1990). Personality structure: Emergence of the five-factor model. In M. R. Rosenzweig & L. W. Porter (Eds.), *Annual Review of Psychology* (Vol. 41, pp. 417–440). Palo Alto, CA: Annual Reviews.

Ericsson, K. A., Krampe, R. T., & Tesch-Römer, C. (1993). The role of deliberate practice in the acquisition of expert performance. *Psychological Review, 100,* 363–406.

Feldhusen, J. F. (1986). A conception of giftedness. In R. J. Sternberg & J. E. Davidson (Eds.), *Conceptions of giftedness* (pp. 112–127). New York: Cambridge University Press.

Gagné, F. (1985). Giftedness and talent: Reexamining a reexamination of the definitions. *Gifted Child Quarterly, 29,* 103–112.

Gagné, F. (1995). From giftedness to talent: A developmental model and its impact on the language of the field. *Roeper Review, 18,* 103–111.

Gagné, F. (1998a). The prevalence of gifted, talented, and multitalented individuals: Estimates from peer and teacher nominations. In R. C. Friedman & K. B. Rogers (Eds.), *Talent in context: Historical and social perspectives on giftedness* (pp. 101–126). Washington, DC: American Psychological Association.

Gagné, F. (1998b). A proposal for subcategories within the gifted or talented populations. *Gifted Child Quarterly, 42,* 87–95.

Gagné, F. (1999a). Is there any light at the end of the tunnel? *Journal for the Education of the Gifted, 22,* 191–234.

Gagné, F. (1999b). My convictions about the nature of human abilities, gifts and talents. *Journal for the Education of the Gifted, 22,* 109–136.

Gagné, F. (2003a, November). *Self-management: A crucial catalyst.* Paper presented at the 50th annual conference of the National Association for Gifted Children, Indianapolis, IN.

Gagné, F. (2003b). Transforming gifts into talents: The DMGT as a developmental theory. In N. Colangelo & G. A. Davis (Eds.), *Handbook of gifted education* (3rd ed., pp. 60–74). Boston: Allyn & Bacon.

Gagné, F. (2004). An imperative, but, alas, improbable consensus! *Roeper Review, 27,* 12–14.

Gardner, H. (1983). *Frames of mind: The theory of multiple intelligences.* New York: Basic Books.

Gottfredson, L. S. (1997). Why *g* matters: The complexity of everyday life. *Intelligence, 24,* 79–132.

Hoppe, C., & Stojanovic, J. (2008). High-aptitude minds. *Scientific American Mind, 19*(4), 60–67.

Jensen, A. R. (1998). *The 'g' factor: The science of mental ability.* Westport, CT: Preager.

Marland, S. P., Jr. (1972). *Education of the gifted and talented: Report to the Congress of the United States by the U.S. Commissioner of Education and background papers submitted to the U.S. Office of Education,* 2 vols. Washington, DC: U.S. Government Printing Office. (Government Documents, Y4.L 11/2: G36)

McCrae, R. R., Costa, P. T., Jr., Ostendorf, F., Angleitner, A., Hrebickova, M., Avia, M. D., et al. (2000). Nature over nurture: Temperament, personality, and life span development. *Journal of Personality and Social Psychology, 78,* 173–186.

Mitchell, B. M. (1988). The latest national assessment of gifted education. *Roeper Review, 10,* 239–240.

Morelock, M. (1996). On the nature of giftedness and talent: Imposing order on chaos. *Roeper Review, 19,* 4–12.

National Institute of Health. (1998). *Clinical guidelines on the identification, evaluation, and treatment of overweight and obesity in adults: The evidence report.* Bethesda, MD: National Institute of Health.

Oldenziel, K., Gagné, F., & Gulbin, J. (2003). *How do elite athletes develop? A look through the "rear-view mirror."* Canberra: Australian Institute of Sport, Australian Sports Commission.

Plomin, R. (1998). Genetic influence and cognitive abilities. *Behavioral and Brain Sciences, 21,* 420–421.

Plucker, J. A., & Renzulli, J. S. (1999). Psychometric approaches to the study of human creativity. In R. J. Sternberg (Ed.), *Handbook of creativity* (pp. 35–61). New York: Cambridge University Press.

President's Council on Physical Fitness and Sports. (2001). *President's challenge: Physical fitness program packet.* Retrieved from http://www.fitness.gov/challenge/challenge.html

Renzulli, J. S. (1986). The three-ring conception of giftedness: A developmental model for creative productivity. In R. J. Sternberg & J. E. Davidson (Eds.), *Conceptions of giftedness* (pp. 53–92). New York: Cambridge University Press.

Rowe, D. C. (1997). Genetics, temperament, and personality. In R. Hogan, J. Johnson, & S. Briggs (Eds.), *Handbook of personality psychology* (pp. 367–386). San Diego, CA: Academic Press.

Tannenbaum, A. J. (1983). *Gifted children: Psychological and educational perspectives.* New York: Macmillan.

Terman, L. M. (1925). *Mental and physical traits of a thousand gifted children. Genetic studies of genius, Vol. 1.* Stanford, CA: Stanford University Press.

U.S. Department of Education, Office of Educational Research and Improvement. (1993). *National excellence: A case for developing America's talent.* Washington, DC: U.S. Government Printing Office.

CHAPTER 7

THE IDEA OF "TALENT DEVELOPMENT":

How We Got There and Where We Are Going

by

PAULA OLSZEWSKI-KUBILIUS

It is time we woke up to the realities that talent development will not happen if it is left to chance, to the accident of birth, or the serendipity of a caring teacher at a critical point in life. It will only happen if we have the will to work together and the insight to work smarter so that our efforts truly benefit the society and the high-potential individuals within it that we all care about so deeply.

—Joyce VanTassel-Baska (2007)

INTRODUCTION

In 1983, when I entered the field of gifted education, there was a paradigm shift occurring. People were beginning to use the term *talent development* and, in fact, my center at Northwestern University was one of the first to incorporate the term into our title—The Center for Talent Development, or CTD. This was not just semantics, although it may have appeared so to outsiders, but indicative of an important conceptual shift in thinking among leaders in the field of gifted education and those who studied exceptional ability.

History of Talent Development

Renzulli (2005), with his focus on creative productivity and adult manifestations of giftedness, including noncognitive factors in his definition, set the stage for an openness to broader conceptions of gifted education. Another major impetus to the shift from gifted to talent development was the landmark study of Benjamin Bloom (1985). This study was crucial because Bloom investigated several different domains of talent, including artists, scientists, and tennis professionals, thereby immediately broadening the field. He also used the word *talent* in the title of his book rather than *gifted*. Via interviews, he and his colleagues looked comprehensively at the role of the family, school, and community in the development of elite levels of talent. Outcomes of this study included the perspective that talent develops differently in different fields; that the role of school varies depending on the field and may be relatively unimportant in some fields; that the role of the family is critical especially at the earliest stages of talent development and in fields where schooling is less important (e.g., families garner resources for child); and that for some fields, the role of the community and community resources (e.g., tennis clubs, coaches) are especially vital. Bloom's study revealed the developmental nature of talent development, particularly that as the child and talent matures and develops, different kinds of teachers are needed. This major study has had a profound and lasting impact on the field of gifted education.

The early 1980s were a very active period in the field in terms of major work on talent development and intelligence. Feldman (1986) studied child prodigies and developed his theory of co-incidence to account for how a young child can reach adult levels of performance and expertise in certain domains. He emphasized the complexity of the talent development process and the fact that many different factors in several different contexts had to line up in order for prodigious talent to be revealed and developed. Feldman's main contribution to our thinking about talent development was connecting it to other developmental phenomenon, particularly Piaget's stages of cognitive development. Thus, the abilities of prodigies do not develop in a qualitatively different manner than less gifted children, but they proceed through stages of cognitive development, only within the talent area, at a much faster rate before reaching higher levels.

Gardner (1983) expanded our notions about intelligence by including varying types. He asserted that rather than a general "g" intelligence factor that underlies all cognitive behavior, there are distinctly separate forms of intelligence. Gardner emphasized that each intelligence has its own symbol system or core set of operations, "end-state" performances, and evolutionary history, and that several intelligences are involved in creative production and high achievement within any particular field. A major outgrowth of Gardner's multiple intelligence theory was reaffirmation of the domain-specific nature of talent and ability. It is this idea that has had a profound impact on the field of gifted education and its focus on talent development.

Sternberg (2005) similarly expanded our thinking about the nature of intelligence. Like Gardner, he proposed different types of intelligence, but his were not domain specific. His triarchic theory of intelligence includes three types of intelligence: synthetic (akin to creative thinking), analytical, and practical. He defined the successful use of intelligence as the ability to use the three different types in order to adapt to, select, and shape one's environment. In his definition he recognized the relative nature of intelligence and that "intelligent behavior" is a function of one's culture and environmental circumstances. Gifted individuals are those who have high levels of those intelligences needed for success or achievement in their chosen fields. Sternberg later proposed that intelligence is the basis for creativity and both are needed for the development of wisdom.

The impact of new thinking about intelligence greatly expanded the ways in which we identify gifted and talented children including the spawning of alternative methods and tests. But, more importantly, these new conceptions changed our thinking about what ability and talent is—from a unidimensional, single focus on IQ and generalized intellectual ability, to a more multidimensional, domain-oriented view. We now talk more about mathematical talent and verbal talent as opposed to general ability.

TALENT DEVELOPMENT: WHAT DO WE KNOW?

A Theory to Guide Us

There are many factors that contribute to the development of talent. In Bronfenbrenner's (1979) ecological theory he contends that children exist within a series of settings or contexts: family, school, neighborhood, society, and the like. These contexts vary in their distance from the child but aspects of each influence the child's development. The degree to which each of these influences is synchronous, the more likely positive outcomes occur.

In terms of talent development, optimal conditions within the family, school, neighborhood, or society would certainly increase the likelihood that a child would achieve commensurate with or above his or her potential. But, many children do not have optimal environments, and research has shown that deficits in one area often can be compensated by "affordances" in others (Therival, 1999). It also is the case that individuals bring their own genetically determined personalities and temperaments that interact with and affect the impact of various factors within the environment. Similarly, environmental influences affect the further development of personality traits in children and these traits make them more or less able to fully take advantage of environmental supports or advantages or overcome negative environmental factors (see Olszewski-Kubilius, 2000, 2008).

The Context of the Family

The role of the family in talent development is absolutely critical and can be the determining factor as to whether a child's ability is developed to a high level or not. We all know very accomplished people who came from less than optimal family situations and very talented individuals who had optimal family situations but did not achieve. So, how does the family influence talent development?

Family history. Family history, including many generations back, can influence the degree to which a child is socialized and prepared for a particular role or profession. Some families (e.g., Kennedy family) have long histories of involvement in particular fields while others push multiple family members into the same field, particularly when an older sibling has been successful (e.g., Britney Spears and her sister Jamie Lynn). Family history also affects the educational, social, and financial resources available to provide a child with talent-developing opportunities. Family stability across at least three generations will likely result in knowledge of educational paths and careers, firsthand experience with education, knowledge of cultural institutions, social connections, and sufficient family income to support the needs of a talented child (Albert, 1994; Olszewski-Kubilius, 2000, 2008).

Family marginality. Family marginality, or the extent to which the family is different or vulnerable due to race, ethnicity, or socioeconomic level (e.g., poor and minority), affects the extent to which family members may endorse traditional paths to achievement versus recommending their children pursue nontraditional paths that they perceive to have higher payoffs (e.g., classical musical training versus becoming a rock star; Albert, 1994; Olszewski-Kubilius, 2000, 2008).

Birth order. Birth order is a seemingly superficial characteristic of a child, yet can have implications for talent development because it triggers psychological sets and expectations on the part of parents. Parents often socialize firstborn children for high academic achievement. Consequently, later-born children may be freer to determine their own paths and are more likely to choose creative endeavors and unusual careers (Albert, 1980, 1994; Olszewski-Kubilius, 2000, 2008).

Parental values and beliefs. Parental values and beliefs are communicated to children both verbally and through their actions. Values conducive to talent development include the importance of education, hard work, drive and persistence, excellence, striving to do one's best, active-recreational pursuits, and creative achievement as well as beliefs about self-efficacy, control over one's fate, and destiny. Values also are communicated and reinforced through parental actions. Providing students with a quiet place to study, limiting television viewing, advocating for children at school, and enriching children through visits to museums and other cultural institutions all have been found to be conducive to high achievement (Olszewski-Kubilius, 2008). Interestingly, a disconnect between the values parents espoused regarding achievement and their actions, such as promoting high achievement but only expressing frustration with their own work lives (Rimm & Lowe, 1988) or telling children that it is important to get a good education but not providing a quiet place to study, can result in under- or low achievement (Sampson, 2002).

Parental spin on, or interpretations of, events. Parental spin on, or interpretation of, events that affect children either directly or indirectly, influences the way children view the world and their subsequent decisions. Families serve as translators and filters for events inside and outside the family and they can, by their interpretations, cast a positive light on a negative situation or use it to motivate a child toward high achievement (Csikszentmihalyi & Beattie, 1979). Parents give messages and cues to their child about whether they can control their destiny or overcome obstacles. Parents also can model effective (or ineffective) coping strategies for difficult circumstances and events, thereby affecting their children's future actions.

The degree of conventional socialization. The degree of conventional socialization of children by parents can affect whether children choose traditional paths and ways of viewing the world, paths similar to their parents, or independently pursue less traditional directions. Parents can work hard to inculcate their values and beliefs in their children through deliberate teaching and expect and demand conformity to conventional values and the routines and traditions of society. These kinds of parents can expect to have children who achieve at high levels in academics, particularly in school. Or, they can promote independent thinking and expression of individual ideas, allow children to generate their own views of the world, and tolerate nontraditional interests and unconventional careers. Parents of the latter type tend to produce children who are creative and pursue creative and nontraditional careers (Albert, 1994; Simonton, 1992; Therival, 1999).

Family cohesion and closeness. Family cohesion and closeness affects the degree to which families can support children emotionally and psychologically as they pursue talent development activities including challenging courses and programs of study or demanding schedules of lessons and outside-of-school activities. Child-centeredness, particularly when children are young, is associated with talent development (Bloom, 1985). Close family relationships including positive affection and psychological connectedness, combined with a push for children to develop their individual talents and pursue their unique paths, is optimal for talented children (Csikszentmihalyi, Rathunde, & Whalen, 1993). Gifted children may have particularly close relationships with parents that they need and use to cope with the stress associated with high achievement. Some tension, competitiveness, or "wobble" between family members tends to promote psychological independence and creativity in children (Albert, 1978), although intense sibling rivalry and oppositional relationships between parents and children are associated with underachievement among gifted children (Rimm & Lowe, 1988).

Family processes. Many prominent researchers in the field of talent development agree that attributes of the individual, specifically personality and motivation, are the most important components of creative achievement and differentiate achievers and producers from others (Csikszentmihalyi, 1985; Ochse, 1993; Simonton, 1984, 1992). Csikszentmihalyi (1985) wrote, "The unifying similarity among geniuses and innovators is not cognitive or affective but motivational. What is common among them is the unwillingness or inability to strive for goals everyone else accepts—their refusal to live by a presented life theme" (p. 114). Winner (1996) wrote, "After a certain point, levels of ability play a less important role than personality and motivational factors" (p. 283). Ochse (1993) noted, "It is consistently recognized that the creator's most salient characteristic is persistent motivation" (p. 133).

Families, through their complex dynamics that include values, relationships, beliefs, and choices, affect the development of personality traits and motivations in their children that are critical for their talent development. The processes that occur within families determine whether children are motivated to achieve; are goal-directed, confident, and persistent; willing to spend the countless hours studying and practicing skills alone needed for success in their talent field; and able to cope with the stresses of pursuing excellence, the pressures associated with standing out from peers due to high achievement, and the tensions associated with being creative and having unusual thoughts and ideas.

School Contexts

School is, of course, another major context within which children spend considerable time, and it can have a tremendous impact on them. Interestingly, however, retrospective studies of eminent people reveal that many of them did not cite school as a major influential factor in their talent development and some found school to be a stifling, unchallenging, and demotivating experience (Simonton, 1992). Whether and in what ways schools influence talent development depends largely on the school and particularly its philosophy toward high-ability learners, including how knowledgeable its staff members are about gifted education and talent development, and the school's commitment of human and instructional resources to providing appropriate educational experiences for gifted students.

Previous research has documented the effectiveness of different types of accelerative programs and specifically that such programs enable bright children to learn at a sufficiently motivating and challenging pace; result in growth rates appropriate for their advanced abilities; do not result in burn-out, superficial learning, or poor preparation for subsequent classes; and are preferred by gifted children (Colangelo, Assouline & Gross, 2004; Kulik & Kulik, 1992; Lubinski & Benbow, 1995; Rogers, 2002). There also is evidence that homogenous grouping of gifted students is advantageous to their learning (Kulik & Kulik, 1992), as are enrichment programs (Kulik & Kulik, 1992; Rogers, 2002), problem-based learning approaches (Gallagher & Steppien, 1996), and specialized curricula (VanTassel-Baska, 2003). Lack of appropriate school services is especially detrimental to the talent development of low-income and minority gifted students whose families and communities may not be able to compensate for missing school programs. These students are less likely to be identified as gifted largely because they are significantly underreferred by teachers and less likely to be served appropriately in programs developed for primarily White and advantaged students with high levels of verbal ability, achievement, and accomplishment (Olszewski-Kubilius, 2006, 2007). Programs crafted specifically for underrepresented students that are designed to meet their needs and that prepare them for entrance into gifted programs are rare but successful (Olszewski-Kubilius, in press).

Community Contexts

The broader community in which a family lives also impacts the development of talent. First, gifted and talented teens' motivation and desire to experience challenge draws them to available community activities. Participation in cultural events is both a venue for recognition of their talent and predictive of later adult creative accomplishment and occupational choice (Hong, Milgram, & Whiston, 1993; Hong, Whiston, & Milgram, 1993). Second, retrospective studies of eminent individuals indicate that outside-of-school influences such as mentors, organized activities, or parental enrichment and teaching often play a more pivotal role in talent development than school-based programs (Bloom, 1985; Simonton, 1992). Third, research suggests that children's participation in extracurricular and outside-of-school activities fosters and augments parents' social networks and contacts that aids parents in obtaining appropriate educational resources and additional opportunities for their children (Horvat, Weininger, & Lareau, 2003). Fourth, positive effects of outside-of-school activities on overall educational attainment for heterogeneous groups (Olszewski-Kubilius & Lee, 2004a) as well as for academically talented students (Olszewski-Kubilius, 2003a, 2003b; Olszewski-Kubilius & Lee, 2008) are well documented.

Research has shown that talent search organizations in the United States have become the predominate provider of outside-of-school educational programs for academically gifted students (Lee, Matthews, & Olszewski-Kubilius, 2008) and that students who participate in these programs benefit in many ways including choosing more rigorous courses, having higher educational aspirations, choosing accelerative options more often during high school, earning more awards and honors, and pursuing advanced degrees in greater numbers (Olszewski-Kubilius & Lee, 2008). Academically talented children benefit from other programs as well that are available through organizations and institutions within communities, including distance-learning programs that enable gifted children to accelerate and take courses appropriately matched to their level of development and knowledge (Olszewski-Kubilius & Lee, 2004b); leadership programs that help adolescents to develop sensitivity to social problems and increase active involvement in their communities (Lee, Olszewski-Kubilius, Donahue, & Weimholt, 2007); weekend programs that challenge children, connect them with peers, and support parents in seeking appropriate educational programs for their children within their schools (Olszewski-Kubilius & Lee, 2004c); and supplementary programs for low-income minority gifted children that enable them to achieve on par with their more advantaged peers (Olszewski-Kubilius, Lee, Ngoi, & Ngoi, 2005). Thus, participation in outside-of-school activities has both direct and indirect effects on the talent development of gifted children.

Although many gifted children live in communities rich in opportunities for talent development, not all do. This particularly is a problem for rural children, due to geographic distances and possibly, also, due to family income. But, urban poor children also are at risk for taking advantage of what their communities can potentially provide in terms of talent development activities. It is not atypical that poor, urban gifted children live in blighted neighborhoods completely unaware of and unable to access the opportunities available only blocks away (Olszewski-Kubilius, in press).

The Context of the Broader Culture and Society

Finally, societal attitudes can affect the extent to which particular talents are valued and provided equitably to all members of society (Sternberg, 2005; Tannenbaum, 1986). Anti-intellectualism and beliefs about the capabilities of females, minorities, or those in poverty can severely diminish the probability that their talents will come to fruition as is evidenced by the underrepresentation of children of color and females in particular fields and levels of education (Miller, 2004). Similarly, attitudes, beliefs, and values within particular cultures also can limit who is afforded which opportunities, what talent fields are valued and promoted, how talent is demonstrated, and whether individual achievement versus teamwork and cooperation is rewarded (Castellano, 2003). Gifted children exist within these broader social contexts and their lives, and their talent development, are affected by them.

THE CONTRIBUTIONS OF JOYCE VANTASSEL-BASKA TO OUR THINKING ABOUT TALENT DEVELOPMENT

Joyce's work at The College of William and Mary has been so impressive that most people in the field do not know much about her work prior to that. But, I certainly do. The Center for Gifted Education was the second center that Joyce started; the Center for Talent Development (CTD) at Northwestern University was the first. As usual, Joyce was ahead of her time at CTD and her initiatives continue to be carried out some 20 years later. She started a focus on disadvantaged gifted, which remains today, and chose to name it the Center for Talent Development long before the conceptual shift was predominant. She has continued this emphasis at William and Mary and during her National Association for Gifted Children presidency.

At the College of William and Mary's Center for Gifted Education, Joyce contributed to the talent development of all children by creating, with graduate students and staff members, groups of specialized, high-powered curricula. But, even more critical is Joyce's prolific skill in researching the effectiveness of those curricula with different kinds of gifted learners using rigorous criteria such as student achievement on standardized tests and validated performance assessments (See *What Works: 20 Years of Curriculum Development and Research for Advanced Learners* [VanTassel-Baska & Stambaugh, 2008]) for a summary of this work and a listing of publications).

Overall, Joyce's work has demonstrated that schooling, and specifically, differentiated curricula combined with teacher training, can impact the achievement of gifted students, particularly for promising gifted students who are at risk for the development of their talent and typically underserved by their schools. This body of work significantly contributes to the talent development opportunities available to many children and augments our understanding of the process of talent development.

REFERENCES

Albert, R. S. (1978). Observation and suggestions regarding giftedness, familial influence and the achievement of eminence. *Gifted Child Quarterly, 28,* 201–211.

Albert, R. S. (1980). Family positions and the attainment of eminence: A study of special family positions and special family experiences. *Gifted Child Quarterly, 24,* 87–95.

Albert, R. S. (1994). The contribution of early family history to the achievement of eminence. In N. Colangelo, S. G. Assouline, & D. L. Ambroson (Eds.), *Proceedings from the 1993 Henry B. and Jocelyn Wallace National Research Symposium on Talent Development* (pp. 311–360). Dayton: Ohio Psychology Press.

Bloom, B. S. (1985). *Developing talent in young people.* New York: Ballantine Books.

Bronfenbrenner, U. (1979). *The ecology of human development: Experiments by nature and design.* Cambridge, MA: Harvard University Press.

Castellano, J. A. (2003). *Special populations in gifted education: Working with diverse gifted learners.* Boston: Pearson Education.

Colangelo, N., Assouline, S. G., & Gross, M. U. M. (Eds.). (2004). *A nation deceived: How schools hold back America's brightest students* (Vol. 2). Iowa City: The University of Iowa, The Connie Belin & Jacqueline N. Blank International Center for Gifted Education and Talent Development.

Csikszentmihalyi, M. (1985). Emergent motivation and the evolution of the self: Motivation in adulthood. In D. Kleiber & M. H. Maehr (Eds.), *Advances in motivation and achievement: Volume 4* (pp. 93–119). Greenwich, CT: JAI Press.

Csikszentmihalyi, M., & Beattie, O. (1979). Life themes: A theoretical and empirical exploration of their origins and effects. *Journal of Humanistic Psychology, 19*(1), 45–63.

Csikszentmihalyi, M., Rathunde, K., & Whalen, S. (1993). *Talented teenagers: The roots of success and failure.* New York: Cambridge University Press.

Feldman, D. H. (1986). Nature's gambit: Child prodigies and the development of human potential. In R. J. Sternberg & J. E. Davidson (Eds.), *Conceptions of giftedness* (2nd ed., pp. 98–119). New York: Cambridge University Press.

Gallagher, S. A., & Steppien, W. (1996). Content acquisition in problem-based learning: Depth versus breadth in American studies. *Journal for the Education of the Gifted, 19,* 257–275.

Gardner, H. (1983). *Frames of mind: The theory of multiple intelligences.* New York: Basic Books.

Hong, E., Milgram, R. M., & Whiston, S. C. (1993). Leisure activities in adolescents as predictor of occupational choice in young adults: A longitudinal study. *Journal of Career Development, 19,* 221–229.

Hong, E., Whiston, S. C., & Milgram, R. M. (1993). Leisure activities in career guidance for gifted and talented adolescents: A validation study of the Tel-Aviv Activities Inventory. *Gifted Child Quarterly, 37*(2), 65–68.

Horvat, E. M., Weininger, E. B., & Lareau, A. (2003). From social ties to social capital: Class differences in the relations between schools and parent networks. *American Educational Research Journal, 40,* 319–351.

Kulik, J. A., & Kulik, C. C. (1992). Meta-analytic findings on grouping programs. *Gifted Child Quarterly, 36,* 73–77.

Lee, S.-Y., Matthews, M. S., & Olszewski-Kubilius, P. (2008). A national picture of talent search and talent search educational programs. *Gifted Child Quarterly, 52,* 55–69.

Lee, S.-Y., Olszewski-Kubilius, P., Donahue, R., & Weimholt, K. (2007). The effects of a service-learning program on the development of civic attitudes and behaviors among academically talented adolescents. *Journal for the Education of the Gifted, 31,* 165–197.

Lubinski, D., & Benbow, C. P. (1995). The study of mathematically precocious youth: The first three decades of a planned 50-year study of intellectual talent. In R. F. Subotnik & K. D. Arnold (Eds.), *Beyond Terman: Contemporary longitudinal studies of giftedness and talent* (pp. 255–289). Norwood, NJ: Ablex.

Miller, L. S. (2004). *Promoting sustained growth in the representation of African Americans, Latinos, and Native Americans among top students in the United States at all levels of the education system* (Research Monograph No. 04190). Storrs: University of Connecticut, The National Research Center on the Gifted and Talented.

Ochse, R. (1993). *Before the gates of excellence: The determinants of creative genius.* Cambridge, UK: Cambridge University Press.

Olszewski-Kubilius, P. (2000). The transition from childhood giftedness to adult creative productiveness: Psychological characteristics and social supports. *Roeper Review, 23,* 65–71.

Olszewski-Kubilius, P. (2003a). Gifted educational programs and procedures. In W. Reynolds & G. E. Miller (Eds.), *Educational psychology* (Vol. 7, pp. 487–510). Hoboken, NJ: Wiley.

Olszewski-Kubilius, P. (2003b). Special summer and Saturday programs for gifted students. In N. Colangelo & G. A. Davis (Eds.), *Handbook of gifted education* (3rd ed., pp. 219–228). Boston: Allyn & Bacon.

Olszewski-Kubilius, P. (2006). Addressing the achievement gap between minority and nonminority children: Increasing access and achievement through Project EXCITE. *Gifted Child Today, 29*(2), 28–37.

Olszewski-Kubilius, P. (2007). Working with promising learners from poverty: Lessons learned. In J. VanTassel-Baska & T. Stambaugh (Eds.), *Overlooked gems: A national perspective on low-income promising learners* (pp. 43–46). Washington, DC: National Association for Gifted Children.

Olszewski-Kubilius, P. (2008). The role of the family in talent development. To appear in S. I. Pfeiffer (Ed.), *Handbook of giftedness in children. Psychoeducational theory, research, and best practice* (pp. 53–70). New York: Springer.

Olszewski-Kubilius, P. (in press). Working with academically gifted students in urban settings: Issues and lessons learned. In J. VanTassel-Baska (Ed.), *Patterns and profiles of promising learners from poverty.* Waco, TX: Prufrock Press.

Olszewski-Kubilius, P., & Lee, S.-Y. (2004a). The role of participation in in-school and outside-of-school activities in the talent development of gifted students. *Journal of Secondary Gifted Education, 15,* 107–123.

Olszewski-Kubilius, P., & Lee, S.-Y. (2004b). Gifted adolescents' talent development through distance learning. *Journal for the Education of the Gifted, 28,* 7–35.

Olszewski-Kubilius, P., & Lee, S.-Y. (2004c). Parent perceptions of the effects of the Saturday enrichment program on gifted students' talent development. *Roeper Review, 26,* 156–165.

Olszewski-Kubilius, P., & Lee, S.-Y. (2008). Specialized programs serving the gifted. In F. A. Karnes & K. S. Stephens (Eds.), *Achieving excellence: Educating the gifted and talented* (pp. 192–208). Columbus, OH: Pearson Education.

Olszewski-Kubilius, P., Lee, S.-Y., Ngoi, M., & Ngoi, D. (2005). Addressing the gap between minority and non-minority achievement by increasing access to gifted programs. *Journal for the Education of the Gifted, 28,* 127–158.

Renzulli, J. S. (2005). The three-ring conception of giftedness: A developmental model for promoting creative productivity. In R. J. Sternberg & J. E. Davidson (Eds.), *Conceptions of giftedness* (2nd ed., pp. 246–279). New York: Cambridge University Press.

Rimm, S., & Lowe, B. (1988). Family environments of underachieving gifted students. *Gifted Child Quarterly, 32,* 353–359.

Rogers, K. B. (2002). *Re-forming gifted education: Matching the program to the child.* Scottsdale, AZ: Great Potential Press.

Sampson, W. A. (2002). *Black student achievement: How much do family and school really matter?* Lanham, MD: Scarecrow Press.

Simonton, D. K. (1984). Artistic creativity and interpersonal relationships across and within generations. *Journal of Personality and Social Psychology, 46,* 1273–1286.

Simonton, D. K. (1992). The child parents the adult: On getting genius from giftedness. In N. Colangelo, S. G. Assouline, & D. L. Ambroson (Eds.), *Talent development: Proceedings from the 1991 Henry B. and Jocelyn Wallace National Research Symposium on Talent Development* (pp. 278–297). New York: Trillium.

Sternberg, R. J. (2005). The WICS model of giftedness. In R. J. Sternberg & J. E. Davidson (Eds.), *Conceptions of giftedness* (2nd ed., pp. 327–342). New York: Cambridge University Press.

Tannenbaum, A. J. (1986). Giftedness: A psychosocial approach. In R. J. Sternberg & J. E. Davidson (Eds.), *Conceptions of giftedness* (pp. 21–52). New York: Cambridge University Press.

Therival, W. A. (1999). Why are eccentrics not eminently creative? *Creativity Research Journal, 12*(1), 47–55.

VanTassel-Baska, J. (2003). *Curriculum planning and instructional design for gifted learners.* Denver, CO: Love.

VanTassel-Baska, J. (2007). Alternative programs and services: A creative response to the unmet needs of gifted students. In J. VanTassel-Baska (Ed.), *Serving gifted learners beyond the traditional classroom: A guide to alternative programs and services* (pp. 241–256). Waco, TX: Prufrock Press.

VanTassel-Baska, J., & Stambaugh, T. (Eds.). (2008). *What works: 20 years of curriculum development and research for advanced learners.* Waco, TX: Prufrock Press.

Winner, E. (1996). *Gifted children: Myths and realities.* New York: Basic Books.

CHAPTER 8

PERSONALIZED PROGRAMS FOR TALENT DEVELOPMENT:

The Johns Hopkins Model for Meeting Individual Needs

by

LINDA
E. BRODY

[High school and college provide the] last really systematic opportunity to explore the thoughts and creations of . . . some of the greatest thinkers and doers of all time. If they become too impatient to get on with technical matters, they will probably go through life as a craftsperson instead of a learned person. Because individuals must live with themselves 24 hours of every day, they need to cultivate themselves in many respects in order to be worth their own company over an entire lifetime.

—Julian Stanley (1989, p. 199)

For most of the last century, intelligence tests were the primary method of identifying students with the potential to excel academically, a process that was perhaps fueled by Terman's (1925) landmark *Genetic Studies of Genius*, which supported the use of IQ as a measure of ability that is stable over time and that predicted achievement among the subjects that were studied. Although this work had a positive influence on our thinking about giftedness, the implication that gifted students will inevitably become gifted adults may have negatively influenced the development of programs for the purpose of developing talent.

More recently, we have seen a shift in our field away from a focus on "gifted education" to one on "talent development," with the new terminology reflecting a growing realization that using a measure of general intellectual ability as a sole predictor of achievement is not adequate; rather, many factors contribute to an individual's potential for achievement (e.g., Simonton, 2008). The change also places greater emphasis on the importance of developing individual talents through programs and other experiences (e.g., Gagné, 2003).

Much of the initial shift away from screening for general intelligence can be attributed to the work in the 1970s of the late Julian Stanley. Believing IQ scores to be of little use "in planning academic experiences for brilliant children" (Stanley & Benbow, 1986, pp. 363–364) and noting that "a high IQ and 50 cents can buy you a 50-cent cup of coffee" (Hendricks, 1997, p. 36), Stanley focused on identifying exceptional reasoning abilities in specific academic areas rather than general ability. He also knew that many factors in addition to ability influence achievement, and believed that insight into these factors was necessary to effectively select the strategies most likely to help students develop their talents. Stanley founded the Study of Mathematically Precocious Youth (SMPY) at Johns Hopkins University to find and serve students with exceptional abilities in mathematics and the sciences, and he established university-based talent search centers throughout the United States to carry on this effort.

Variously referred to in the literature as the Johns Hopkins Model (Brody et al., 2001), the Talent Search Model, the Center for Talented Youth Model, and the MVT:D4 Model (Brody & Stanley, 2005; Stanley, 2005), the principles and practices of this approach are based on three principles from developmental psychology: (1) that learning is sequential and developmental; (2) that children learn at different rates; and (3) that effective teaching involves posing problems to students slightly exceeding the level already mastered (Brody & Stanley, 2005; Robinson, 1983; Stanley & Benbow, 1986). The implication of these principles is that, for students to develop their talents, "the pace of educational programs must be adapted to the knowledge of individual children" (Robinson, 1983, p. 140). MVT:D4 is an acronym that represents the four steps in implementing this model of talent development, and it is helpful to understand the role all four components play in meeting the needs of talented students.

MVT:D4

The first book that described SMPY's efforts to identify and serve mathematically talented students was entitled *Mathematical Talent: Discovery, Description, and Development* (Stanley, Keating & Fox, 1974). Abbreviated as MT:D3, the title was specifically intended to conceptualize the steps necessary for developing mathematical talent. As the work evolved, a 4th D, for *Dissemination*, was recognized as critical to the process (Stanley & George, 1980), and, when the talent search centers also began to serve verbally talented students, a V was added (Brody & Stanley, 2005). Thus, MVT:D4 refers to developing mathematical and verbal talents through discovery, description, development, and dissemination.

Discovery refers to identifying students with advanced academic abilities. In the talent search model, above-grade-level specific aptitude tests are administered to students who all score well on in-grade tests, and many years of testing have shown that the results are reflected in a full distribution of scores. They show which students, among the group of highly able students tested, are ready to master above-grade-level content, while others can be served with strong grade-level content. Talent search testing can lead to the *discovery* of students whose academic abilities are much more advanced than anyone would have recognized and provide the base for educational decision making.

In order to provide optimal experiences that match students' needs, however, it also is crucial to learn much more about them. Thus, the second step is *Description*, and this refers to gaining a broader understanding of the other characteristics and attributes that can affect students' achievement. Some of this information can be gleaned informally, such as interests and motivation, but some must be formally assessed. As Stanley (1977) noted, "Without intensive study of the aptitudes, achievement, interests, values, and attitudes of the youths who scored quite high on SAT-M, appropriate counseling would not be possible" (p. 96).

Development refers to helping the students who are identified as academically talented get the educational accommodations and programs needed to allow them to achieve their full potential. In this model, the goal is to achieve a match between a student's individual needs and the programs and strategies selected to meet those needs for developing talent. The pace and level of instruction should be adjusted so that it is appropriately challenging, and supplemental opportunities can augment school programs to facilitate academic, social, and emotional development. The emphasis on recognizing individual differences and utilizing a variety of in- and out-of-school options as intervention strategies to serve students is what sets this approach apart from so many school-based "gifted and talented" programs, where groups of students are identified for a single program and individual needs are not recognized.

The final D is *Dissemination*, which refers to sharing with educators, policy makers, researchers, and parents the principles, practices, and research results related to the strategies and options available to facilitate talent development so they will be open to this approach to talent development. A huge legacy of books and book chapters, articles, and presentations at conferences exist as testimony to the effectiveness of the talent search model and of the intervention strategies and programs the model supports. SMPY also believed strongly in communicating with the students who were being served directly and did so through personal communication and newsletters that were packed with information about challenging programs and opportunities. The Center for Talented Youth's (CTY) award-winning *Imagine* magazine, with its focus on resources and opportunities to serve academically talented students, evolved from the original SMPY newsletters.

Identifying Advanced Reasoning Abilities

In looking back at the growth of this model for talent development, Stanley called it a "saga of serendipity" (Stanley & Brody, 2001, p. 94) and a "quiet revolution" (Stanley, 2005, p. 5). It began quite by accident, almost 40 years ago, when Stanley, then a quantitative psychologist and professor at Johns Hopkins University, met Joe. Although it is fairly common today to see middle school students filling classrooms and dormitories on college campuses in the summer, it was very unusual in 1969. Somehow, though, 13-year-old Joe had found his way to a summer computer course at Johns Hopkins and was astounding his teachers with his knowledge.

Piqued with interest, Stanley set out to determine how advanced Joe really was and decided to try something that was quite radical at that time: administering the SAT to this eighth grader. The idea of giving a test developed for high school seniors to a 13-year-old was pretty unheard of, and it also was very unusual to assess a student's ability with something other than an IQ test. But, because the SAT offers separate mathematical and verbal scales, it seemed more appropriate than a general ability measure for identifying mathematical or verbal talent. Stanley also believed that the SAT would serve as a reasoning test for middle school students who had not been formally exposed to the subject matter on the test. With Joe, who was doing college-level work, Stanley wanted to assess whether his reasoning abilities were on a college level.

Joe excelled on the test, well beyond anyone's expectations, and the results suggested that he needed an advanced curriculum. But, Joe's high school was unwilling to adjust his schedule, and few other challenging options existed 40 years ago, so another radical idea was posed. Because his test scores on the aptitude measures (as well as on above-level achievement tests that Stanley also administered) were at or above the level of the typical Johns Hopkins freshman, perhaps Joe could enroll full time as an undergraduate at Hopkins. The 13-year-old freshman excelled from the start, and he earned bachelor's and master's degrees by age 17. Joe subsequently went on to earn a Ph.D. in computer science, and he has had a highly successful career since then. Soon after Joe enrolled at Johns Hopkins, a second exceptionally gifted student emerged on the scene, and then a third. These young men also scored extraordinarily well on the above-level assessments and enrolled at Johns Hopkins as early entrants (Stanley, 2005).

The accomplishments of these students suggested that the SAT, administered out-of-level, could be a good predictor of a student's readiness to master advanced content, especially in mathematics and math-related subjects. This sparked the idea of conducting a talent search to see how many other students might score similarly high. The first Johns Hopkins talent search, which was held in 1972 on the Johns Hopkins campus involving mostly Baltimore-area students, yielded many more students scoring at a higher level than the researchers expected, and SMPY replicated these results in subsequent searches, with students coming from an expanding geographic area, throughout the 1970s (Stanley, 2005; Stanley et al., 1974).

In 1979, the Center for Talented Youth was established at Johns Hopkins to conduct talent searches on an annual basis, with testing taking place at local testing centers so students could participate regardless of where they lived. Soon, centers that embraced the Hopkins model were established at Duke and Northwestern Universities and the University of Denver to serve students in their geographic regions (see Putallaz, Baldwin, & Selph, 2005; Olszewski-Kubilius, 2005; and Rigby, 2005, respectively). The talent search model using above-level tests for talent identification also has been adopted by educators in other countries, thus successfully demonstrating the robustness of this model to transcend geographic and cultural boundaries. Reportedly, more than 3 million students have participated in talent search testing since its inception (Lee, Matthews, & Olszewski-Kubilius, 2008).

It was Joyce VanTassel-Baska who took the model to the Midwest. She was attracted to Stanley's ideas when she was a young gifted program coordinator in Illinois. With great enthusiasm, she began with a statewide talent search in Illinois and expanded it to host a regional search in the Midwestern states. Wanting to establish a permanent university-based program, she sought Stanley's help and founded the Midwest Talent Search and Center for Talent Development (CTD) at Northwestern University. This Center continues to thrive today under the leadership of Paula Olszewski-Kubilius. The choice of CTD's name was quite meaningful as one of the first that reflected the emerging shift from gifted education to talent development (Olszewski-Kubilius, 2005). It should be noted that Stanley also avoided using the word *gifted* in most of his work, preferring terms like *precocious*, or *mathematically talented*, or referring to "students who reason exceptionally well mathematically."

DEVELOPING MATHEMATICAL AND/OR VERBAL TALENT

From the beginning, Stanley recognized that it was not enough to identify talent; it must be developed. Yet, when Stanley tested Joe, he found few opportunities to meet the needs of such an advanced student, and he turned to radical early entrance to college as the only option available. But, Stanley realized that rapid grade advancement might not be appropriate for all academically talented students. In fact, students who are identified based on their advanced reasoning abilities in a specific content area (e.g., mathematics) often need accelerative experiences in that content area, but not necessarily in other subjects. Recognizing that students varied much in their educational needs, many choices were needed.

Stanley established SMPY to "find youths who reason exceptionally well mathematically and to provide them the special, supplemental, accelerative 'smorgasbord' of educational opportunities they sorely need and . . . richly deserve for their optimal development" (Stanley 2005, p. 9). SMPY created numerous programs and opportunities to serve the students that were identified, experimenting with a variety of formats and settings to offer math and science in fast-paced and challenging ways. These efforts were research-based and provided much evidence in support of using the above-level SAT to identify students with advanced academic abilities and support of accelerative strategies for meeting the needs of these students (Benbow & Lubinski, 1996; Stanley et al., 1974). To help students choose the best programmatic options to meet their own unique needs, SMPY staff worked personally with many of the students they served. VanTassel-Baska (1996) observed that:

> Much of the best mentoring I have seen take place in the field of gifted education comes directly from Julian Stanley's approach with his SMPY students and their families. Through personal correspondence, a fine and comprehensive newsletter, and frequent personal contacts, SMPY has fostered the development of many individual students and placed them on the path to educational and career success. The focus for SMPY's mentoring is always on educational opportunities for which students are ready, coupled with sound advice for future possibilities that they should be considering. Mentoring becomes more than just the establishment of a one-to-one relationship with a well-chosen adult; it allows access to a network of options available through a carefully constructed talent search system (pp. 243–244).

Stanley's emphasis was not on creating school-based programs, but he advocated for curricular flexibility in schools, followed by articulation at the next level. This meant placing students at their appropriate instructional levels, not necessarily with age peers. SMPY "meant to be 'benignly insidious,' i.e. to burrow up under school systems to coerce receptivity to curricular flexibility and articulation of in-school with out-of-school educational experiences" (Stanley, 2005, p. 11).

With the establishment of CTY in 1979, as well as the other university-based talent search centers that followed, academic residential summer programs became their signature programs. Located on college campuses, they offer students the opportunity to accelerate their course taking or to take courses not offered in school, as well as a chance to interact with their intellectual peers (Olszewski-Kubilius, 2007). The talent search centers also offer online courses and other opportunities to serve students throughout the year.

THE JULIAN C. STANLEY STUDY OF EXCEPTIONAL TALENT

After establishing CTY in 1979, Stanley continued to focus his efforts on helping top students individually, specifically serving students who scored 700 or more on the mathematical portion of the SAT before age 13. This effort moved to CTY in 1991 as the Study of Exceptional Talent (SET), expanding its outreach to include high-verbal, as well as high-math, scorers. Later named in honor of Julian Stanley, SET carries on the tradition of personalized counseling that SMPY developed (Brody, 2005, 2007). The following principles underlie SET's counseling efforts and guide the nature of its recommendations.

- *Gifted students need an appropriately challenging educational program if they are to achieve their full potential.* Many people believe that gifted students will be fine without intervention, and even parents can be complacent as long as their children are earning good grades. However, students who are not challenged often fail to develop the goals, motivation, and study skills they will need to be successful in college and beyond, and exceptional talents may not be developed at all. SET's services are offered free of charge so that the cost doesn't limit access for any students who need these services.

- *The more talented the child, the greater the need for a differentiated program.* Because there are few students at the upper end of the ability continuum in any one school, a typical school program is unlikely to meet their needs, including gifted and talented programs developed for groups of moderately gifted learners. Consequently, exceptionally talented students often need a differentiated and accelerated program, and this is why SET focuses primarily on top scorers.

- *Above-grade-level assessments are crucial for evaluating a gifted student's level of ability and content knowledge.* Many years of talent search results have shown that huge differences can be found among students who all hit the ceiling on in-grade tests. Students who score very high on above-level tests, as SET students do, have very different educational needs than those who score lower.

- *Gifted students vary greatly in their specific abilities, content knowledge, interests, motivation, goals, personalities, and learning styles.* Although SET students all qualify with high SAT scores, they are quite heterogeneous in these other characteristics, resulting in very different educational needs. Formal or informal assessment of these variables is necessary to inform educational decisions.

- *Students need access to coursework that is at a level and pace appropriate for their abilities.* For students who exhibit advanced abilities and achievement, some acceleration in content and/or grade placement may be crucial for meeting their academic needs and keeping them engaged in learning.

- *School programs can be enhanced with curricular flexibility and articulation at the next level.* Schools often can meet the needs of advanced students if they are willing to let students test out of content they already know and be placed with older students in more advanced classes, allow students to work independently on more advanced work, and/or provide students with opportunities to work on in-depth projects in lieu of basic skills that they have already mastered.

- *Students can increase their learning opportunities through supplemental educational programs and extracurricular activities.* Summer programs, online courses, part-time college courses, internships, opportunities to work with mentors, and extracurricular activities offer exposure to content not available in school, and opportunities to interact with peers who share their interests and abilities.

▶ *Students should gain a broad background in the liberal arts.* Although it is crucial that students are challenged and encouraged to excel in their area of strength, a broad academic background also is needed for ultimate success in life. In addition to developing specific talents, SET students are encouraged to develop strong written and oral communication skills, have solid backgrounds in science, mathematics, global affairs, and the arts, and be fluent in several languages. Stanley (1989), known for facilitating the development of mathematical talent, strongly advocated for the importance of a general education (see introductory quote).

▶ *Students need to be able to interact with intellectual peers.* Social skills development also is critical to success in life, but students may fail to develop adequate social skills if they do not have access to peers who share their interests and abilities.

▶ *Students need access to role models and mentors.* Role models can inspire gifted students to pursue higher level goals, and mentors can be crucial teachers who share their passions for their subject areas.

SET's counselors work with students and their families to identify the strategies and programs that will meet the students' unique academic, social, and emotional needs. As much as possible, students are encouraged to define their own needs, make their own choices, and take responsibility for their own learning. SET's publications (*Imagine* magazine and *SET Precollege Newsletter*) and Internet resources (SET Web site at http://cty.jhu.edu/set/index.html and http://www.cogito.org) inform students about programs and encourage participation and link students to role models and to their intellectual peers. Although SET targets a particular group of top talent search students, others can use this approach in guiding the students they serve. Among those who have adopted this model is the Jack Kent Cooke Foundation's Young Scholars Program, which helps gifted students from low-income backgrounds find the opportunities they need to achieve their full potential (Brody, 2007).

EDUCATIONAL OPTIONS: THE SMORGASBORD

When Stanley was advocating for Joe, he found that there were few options for Joe to access an appropriately challenging educational program except to enroll in college at a radically young age. Since then, a smorgasbord of numerous programs has been established to serve students with advanced academic abilities.

For example, at least 18 early college entrance programs have emerged as an option for students who want to enter college early but do not quite have the academic background or emotional maturity to fully fend for themselves. These programs admit young students as a cohort and provide considerable academic and social support (Brody, Muratori, & Stanley, 2004).

More common than grade acceleration is the need for subject acceleration, especially among talent search participants who have been identified as having talent in a particular academic area. Subject acceleration may take many forms, but basically students are either placed with older students so they can access a more advanced curriculum or they are provided with a more advanced curriculum in their current grade placement. The advent of online courses has added to the viability of providing advanced coursework to students at home or in classrooms. The Advanced Placement (AP) program is a successful example of subject acceleration, and now offers 37 courses and exams in 22 content areas. Highly gifted students can increase their challenge in high school by not waiting until senior year to enroll in AP courses. As a result, they may leave high school with a large number of AP credits, credits that often transfer to colleges, and leave open the door to pursue other opportunities during their last year of high school such as doing an internship or in-depth project, taking some college courses, or possibly entering college early. Similarly, the International Baccalaureate (IB) program aims to offer college-level work to high school students, and dual enrollment legislation in many states financially supports programs where advanced high school students are simultaneously enrolled in high school and at a local college.

Academic summer programs also expand course-taking opportunities for students seeking challenging content. Students can either choose a course that allows them to accelerate their school program (e.g., take chemistry in the summer and enroll in AP chemistry in the fall) or one that is typically not offered in school such as cryptology, neuroscience, or philosophy. Summer programs that provide the opportunity for students to reside with other students can enhance building relationships with intellectual peers, relationships that often have lasting effects beyond the end of the summer.

Participation in extracurricular activities also can enhance talent development, help students connect with peers, and provide opportunities for leadership roles. For example, students can become involved at high levels in academic competitions, especially those at the national or international level, in the performing arts, community service, or writing and publishing original work (Brody, 2007). VanTassel-Baska (1989) observed that "opportunities to experience real-life extensions of academic subjects make the academic process more meaningful for gifted learners" (p. 303). A variety of out-of-school opportunities are profiled in VanTassel-Baska's recent (2007) book, *Serving Gifted Learners Beyond the Traditional Classroom.*

As we work to help gifted students modify, accelerate, or supplement their learning plans to meet their educational needs, a wide variety of strategies, options, and programs are available. However, to select those best suited for developing the talents of an individual student, his or her specific abilities, content knowledge, motivation and goals, passions and interests, and social and emotional concerns must be considered, along with the available resources in the school and community.

ADDRESSING SOCIAL AND EMOTIONAL NEEDS

An understanding of the social and emotional needs of the students served must be incorporated into any attempts to meet their educational needs. As a group, gifted students have been shown to have good social and emotional adjustment compared to age peers (Neihart, Reis, Robinson, & Moon, 2002), however, individual students may exhibit social and emotional problems that should not be overlooked. Extremely gifted students have been found to experience more difficulties than moderately gifted students, and verbally gifted students may have more social and/or emotional problems than those who are mathematically talented (Dauber & Benbow, 1990). Difficulties that arise when highly gifted students are ill-suited for their academic placement and lack access to intellectual peers often can be improved upon by placing them in more appropriate educational environments (Gross, 1993; Neihart et al., 2002). For example, a student who said he lacked friends at home said the following after attending a CTY summer program: "There I wasn't different. Everyone was 'that guy' from their school. I made more friends in 3 weeks than I had in 8 years of school."

THE ROLE OF ASSESSMENT IN DECISION-MAKING

Assessment is a crucial component in the SET talent development model, and the importance of above-level testing is demonstrated in the stories of Sam and Matthew. Both boys were recognized by their teachers as strong in math and science, but when they took the SAT as seventh graders in a talent search, Sam earned a 460 on the mathematical portion of the SAT, while Matthew earned a 780. Sam clearly demonstrated the ability to be a top student in challenging courses, but Matthew was functioning on a much more advanced level and was ready to master much more complex mathematical concepts. Although Sam continued to progress in math with age peers, Matthew was placed on a more accelerated track and was given opportunities to exchange ideas with other very advanced students. Matthew's results typify what Stanley referred to as discovering talent, because changes would not have been made without the test results.

Christopher and Rachel both demonstrated their exceptional mathematical abilities when they scored 720 and 730, respectively, in the talent search. But, placement tests showed that Christopher had mastered all of the precalculus topics and was ready to be placed in a calculus course, while Rachel had many gaps in her precalculus knowledge. Clearly, with her abilities, she could be expected to fill those gaps quickly, but it would have been a mistake for her to move immediately into calculus with Christopher. Content knowledge must be considered, along with ability, when making placement decisions.

We also might consider Sarah and James. Sarah earned a 760 on the math SAT and 720 in critical reading; James earned the same 760 in math but only 420 in reading. The difference in the reading scores suggested differing strategies for these two students. Unhappy with the pace of her middle school courses and lacking a compatible peer group, and given her exceptional performance on the SAT, Sarah embarked on an accelerated path to skip eighth grade and enter college after 2 years of high school AP courses. James stayed at his grade level, continuing to take humanities courses with his age peers throughout high school. But, he enrolled in online accelerated math courses, supplemented his coursework with heavy involvement in math and science competitions, and worked with a mentor on a physics project.

A student's choices or preferences also must be factored into any decision-making, which is why Stanley chose to work directly with students. Samantha's scores were similar to Sarah's, very high across the board, but she declined any acceleration. She attended a school with a great deal of flexibility and opportunities for leadership, and she had a peer group with whom she was close. She attended summer programs, took advanced courses and some independent study, assumed leadership roles in several activities, and planned to pursue a medical career, but she was in no hurry to leave high school. She could have moved faster, but her wishes, social needs, and the flexibility of the school she attended were factors that contributed to acceleration not being the answer for Samantha.

CONCLUSION

As a result of the work of such visionaries as Julian Stanley, Joyce VanTassel-Baska, and others, as well as the proven success of the talent search model for identifying students with exceptional academic abilities, a variety of strategies, programs, and other opportunities now exist to help talented students achieve their full potential. This talent development model requires a personalized approach to finding a match between a student's needs and the program options that will help him or her excel. It also requires flexibility on the part of schools to place students wherever they need to be for optimal learning and to recognize the value of out-of-school learning experiences. With the world facing so many problems, it is critical that we find ways to develop the talents of students who are likely to become our future leaders, innovators, and problem solvers, not only for their own fulfillment, but for the betterment of society.

REFERENCES

Benbow, C. P., & Lubinski, D. (Eds.). (1996). *Intellectual talent: Psychometric and social issues.* Baltimore: Johns Hopkins University Press.

Brody, L. E. (2005). The Study of Exceptional Talent. *High Ability Studies, 16*(1), 87–96.

Brody, L. E. (2007). Counseling highly gifted students to utilize supplemental educational opportunities: Using the SET program as a model. In J. VanTassel-Baska (Ed.), *Serv-*

ing gifted learners beyond the traditional classroom: A guide to alternative programs and services (pp. 123–143). Waco, TX: Prufrock Press.

Brody, L. E., Muratori, M. C., & Stanley, J. C. (2004). In N. Colangelo, S. G. Assouline, & M. U. M. Gross (Eds.), *A nation deceived: How schools hold back America's brightest students* (Vol. 2, pp. 97–107). Iowa City: The University of Iowa, The Connie Belin & Jacqueline N. Blank International Center for Gifted Education and Talent Development.

Brody, L. E., & Stanley, J. C. (2005). Youths who reason exceptionally well mathematically and/or verbally: Using the MVT:D4 model to develop their talents. In R. J. Sternberg & J. E. Davidson (Eds.), *Conceptions of giftedness* (2nd edition, pp. 20–37). New York: Cambridge University Press.

Brody, L. E., Stanley, J. C., Barnett, L. B., Juhasz, S. E., Gilheany, S., & Touron, J. (2001). Expanding the Johns Hopkins talent search internationally. *Gifted and Talented International, 16*(2), 94–107.

Dauber, S. L., & Benbow, C. P. (1990). Aspects of personality and peer relations of extremely talented adolescents. *Gifted Child Quarterly, 34,* 10–15.

Gagné, F. (2003). Transforming gifts into talents: The DMGT as a developmental theory. In N. Colangelo & G. A. Davis (Eds.), *Handbook of gifted education* (3rd ed., pp. 60–74). Boston: Allyn & Bacon.

Gross, M. U. M. (1993). *Exceptionally gifted children*. New York: Routledge.

Hendricks, M. (1997). Yesterday's whiz kids: Where are they today? *Johns Hopkins Magazine, 49*(3), 30–36.

Lee, S.-Y., Matthews, M. S., & Olszewski-Kubilius, P. (2008). A national picture of talent search and talent search educational programs. *Gifted Child Quarterly, 52,* 55–69.

Neihart, M., Reis, S. M., Robinson, N. M., & Moon, S. M. (Eds.). (2002). *The social and emotional development of gifted children: What do we know?* Waco, TX: Prufrock Press.

Olszewski-Kubilius, P. (2005). The Center for Talent Development at Northwestern University: An example of replication and reformation. *High Ability Studies, 16*(1), 55–69.

Olszewski-Kubilius, P. (2007). The role of summer programs in developing the talents of gifted students. In J. VanTassel-Baska (Ed.), *Serving gifted learners beyond the traditional classroom: A guide to alternative programs and services* (pp. 13–32). Waco, TX: Prufrock Press.

Putallaz, M., Baldwin, J., & Selph, H. (2005). The Duke University Talent Identification Program. *High Ability Studies, 16*(1), 41–54.

Rigby, K. (2005). Rocky Mountain Talent Search at the University of Denver. *High Ability Studies, 16*(1), 71–75.

Robinson, H. B. (1983). A case for radical acceleration. In C. P. Benbow & J. C. Stanley (Eds.), *Academic precocity: Aspects of its development* (pp. 139–159). Baltimore: Johns Hopkins University Press.

Simonton, D. K. (2008). Childhood giftedness and adult genius. *Gifted Child Quarterly, 52,* 243–255.

Stanley, J. C. (1977). Rationale of the Study of Mathematically Precocious Youth (SMPY) during its first five years of promoting educational acceleration. In J. C. Stanley, W. C. George, & C. H. Solano (Eds.), *The gifted and creative* (pp. 75–112). Baltimore: Johns Hopkins University Press.

Stanley, J. C. (1989). Guiding gifted students in their educational planning. In J. VanTassel-Baska & P. Olszewski-Kubilius (Eds.), *Patterns of influence on gifted learners: The home, the self, and the school* (pp. 192–200). New York: Teachers College Press.

Stanley, J. C. (2005). A quiet revolution: Finding boys and girls who reason extremely well mathematically and/or verbally and helping them get the supplemental educational opportunities they need. *High Ability Studies, 16*(1), 5–14.

Stanley, J. C., & Benbow, C. P. (1986). Youths who reason exceptionally well mathematically. In R. J. Sternberg & J. E. Davidson (Eds.), *Conceptions of giftedness* (pp. 361–387). Cambridge: Cambridge University Press.

Stanley, J. C., & Brody, L. E. (2001). History and philosophy of the talent search model. *Gifted and Talented International, 16*(2), 94–96.

Stanley, J. C., & George, W. C. (1980). SMPY's ever-increasing D4. *Gifted Child Quarterly, 24*, 41–48.

Stanley, J. C., Keating, D. P., & Fox, L. H. (Eds.). (1974). *Mathematical talent: Discovery, description, and development.* Baltimore: Johns Hopkins University Press.

Terman, L. M. (1925). *Mental and physical traits of a thousand gifted children. Genetic studies of genius, Vol. I.* Stanford, CA: Stanford University Press.

VanTassel-Baska, J. (1989). Counseling the gifted. In J. Feldhusen, J. VanTassel-Baska, & K. Seeley (Eds.), *Excellence in educating the gifted* (pp. 299–314). Denver, CO: Love.

VanTassel-Baska, J. (1996). Contributions of the talent-search concept to gifted education. In C. P. Benbow & D. Lubinski (Eds.), *Intellectual talent: Psychometric and social issues* (pp. 236–245). Baltimore: Johns Hopkins University Press.

VanTassel-Baska, J. (Ed.). (2007). *Serving gifted learners beyond the traditional classroom: A guide to alternative programs and services.* Waco, TX: Prufrock Press.

CHAPTER 9

DEVELOPING TALENTS AND GIFTED BEHAVIORS IN CHILDREN

by

SALLY
M. REIS

AND

JOSEPH
S. RENZULLI

The best moments usually occur when a person's body or mind is stretched to its limits in a voluntary effort to accomplish something difficult and worthwhile.

—Mihaly Csikszentmihalyi

INTRODUCTION

The process of talent development across specific domains in both children and adults has fascinated parents, educators, and psychologists over the last century. Why, for example, do some extremely smart children fail to realize their promise and potential (Reis & McCoach, 2000; Renzulli & Park, 2000)? Why is it that some prodigies grow up to be average performers in the very fields in which they showed such promise when they were children (Feldman & Goldsmith, 1991)? Why do other traits, described by Renzulli (2002) as co-cognitive traits, appear to be so important in the process of talent development?

RESEARCH ON TALENT DEVELOPMENT

Inherent value exists in using retrospective research to better understand gifted and creatively productive individuals. These studies, such as those conducted by Bloom (1985);

Csikszentmihalyi, Rathunde, and Whalen (1993); Reis (1998); Renzulli (1978); and others examine the childhoods and backgrounds of highly accomplished individuals in different domains in order to identify common features in their backgrounds that contributed to their talent development. Retrospective studies suggest some of the factors that we should consider as we contemplate the process of talent development in children and young adults.

Talent development requires constant attention, nurturing, and sheer, focused effort and task commitment (Gruber, 1986; Renzulli, 1978). Whether or not a talent ultimately is developed depends on many factors including abilities, creativity, effort, motivation to achieve, societal support and appreciation of the talent area, environmental support and opportunities, and chance or luck (Bloom, 1985; Csikszentmihalyi et al., 1993; Renzulli, 1978, 1986; Tannenbaum, 1986). Supportive experiences at school, in the community, and at home also are critical forces in transforming potential into fully developed talents (Bloom, 1985; Csikszentmihalyi et al., 1993; Reis, 1998; Renzulli, 1978). For example, Csikszentmihalyi and his colleagues studied talented teens, identifying a variety of factors that contribute to the development of their talents, including enjoyment of classes and activities, having adults help them establish both short- and long-term goals, and encouraging student engagement and commitment to their talent areas during critical periods of development, such as adolescence.

Out-of-school and extracurricular activities have been consistently cited in the research as being critical to the process of talent development, as they contribute to the motivation that talented children must develop to work more diligently in their area of talent (Reis, 1998; Renzulli, 1978; Sternberg, 1985). Other retrospective studies of eminent individuals (Bloom, 1985; Reis, 1998; Roe, 1953) indicate that out-of-school learning, mentors, identification of interests, organized activities, and parental enrichment and teaching often play a much more important role in talent development than school-based programs. Research also has verified that the psychological development of outstanding talent is developed by the individual over a long period of time and is influenced by a variety of factors, such as the personal characteristics of the talented person and strong support systems of the individual (Bloom, 1985; Csikszentmihalyi et al., 1993).

Researchers who study the process of talent development often try to identify positive or negative environmental factors that focus on childhood, family, and school experiences of those who achieve eminence. Roe (1953), for example, studied 64 leading American scientists in the fields of biology, physics, and the social sciences, many of whom were Nobel Prize winners. She found that as children, the scientists typically began their collection of objects, experimentation, and theory building as young as the age of 7. Roe's classic research, published in a book entitled *The Making of a Scientist* (1953), examined different social and personal forces of 64 eminent scientists. She found that teachers had little or no influence on the vocational choice of the scientists, particularly at the elementary and secondary level. The only important classroom activity mentioned by some of the scientists as influential was the in-depth project work they did independently in school to learn information for themselves. Roe explained, "The important thing is that they learned that they could satisfy their curiosity by their own efforts" (p. 238).

Zuckerman (1977), surveying American Nobel laureates, reported that most had been students of previous laureates, and that these laureates had mentored the most talented students who appeared to be most likely to carry on their line of work. The American Nobel laureates sought guidance from these older mentors and recognized their greatness. The previous laureates were most helpful about the identification of scientific problems with future potential for discovery. Two additional important studies of talent development across domains also shed insight into this process, and are further summarized in the following sections: Bloom (1985) and Csikszentmihalyi et al. (1993).

Bloom's Study of Talent Development

Bloom (1985), in collaboration with several colleagues, studied musicians, athletes, and scholars who achieved high-level public recognition, focusing on the significant factors in the development of talent and the contributions of home and school. In interviews with more than 120 persons who excelled in an area before the age of 35, the researchers found that schools were, quite simply, not places where exceptional talent was identified or developed. The researchers sought to identify factors that contributed to the development of talent, and specifically, to determine how home and school contributed to an international level of accomplishment by individuals in three areas: the artistic (concert pianists and sculptors); the psychomotor (Olympic swimmers and tennis players); and the cognitive (research mathematicians and neurologists). In the majority of cases, Bloom found that a positive family environment existed with parents or other family members who had a personal interest in the talent field and provided strong support, encouragement, and rewards for developing the talent. In fact, family members assumed and took for granted that a child's talent would be identified and developed as part of the family's lifestyle, especially between the ages of 3 and 7.

Bloom and his colleagues found the home to be important during the early years of talent development—providing support and resources, monitoring practice sessions and correcting the child's work, and helping in the consideration of future options. Parents found numerous public arenas outside the home that provided opportunities for their children to express their talent, including recitals, contests, and concerts. These events motivated children by providing important rewards and approval. Competitions also were meaningful in providing an external goal for training, identifying benchmarks of a child's progress, and establishing a context in which a group of individuals who share a special interest can form a community. Bloom found that when working in the talent field, children became fully engaged, but that schools rarely (if ever) enabled students to become fully involved in any one part of the curriculum. Bloom concluded that talent development and schooling seldom enhanced each other.

When Bloom and his colleagues studied the talent development process, they found that talented individuals across the fields of music, art, athletics, mathematics, and science demonstrated the following qualities: a strong interest and emotional commitment to a particular talent field; a desire to reach a high level of attainment in the talent field; a willingness to put in the great amounts of time; and the effort needed to reach very high levels of achievement in the talent field. The psychological development of outstanding talent occurred in these young people over a long time period and was influenced by a variety of individuals and factors, including personal characteristics of the talented person, the need for a strong support system, and the instilled value of working hard.

Developing Talented Teens: Csikszentmihalyi, Rathunde, and Whalen

Csikszentmihalyi et al. (1993) conducted a 5-year longitudinal study to investigate the process by which 200 talented teenagers in athletics, art, music, and science became committed to the development of their talent, and why others with similar potential were disengaged from their talent areas. This study sought to identify similarities and differences between teens who developed and used their talents in adulthood, as opposed to those who drifted away from their talents to pursue work that required only average skills. The researchers described the need for talented teenagers to acquire a set of "metaskills" that allowed them to work with intense concentration and curiosity to develop their talents. Talent, these researchers learned, was developmental and affected by contextual factors in the environment. Talent was nurtured by the acquisition of knowledge of the domain, motivation provided by the family and persons in the specialized field of talent, and discipline created by a set of habits resulting in long-term concentrated study and superior performance.

The talented teenagers studied had certain personal characteristics, including the ability to concentrate, leading to both achievement and endurance, and an awareness of experience, enhancing understanding. Their personal goals sought both expressive and instrumental rewards, with students describing experiences of flow, an earlier area of Csikszentmihalyi's research, when engaged in their talent area. Csikszentmihalyi (1990) defined flow as "the state in which people are so involved in an activity that nothing else seems to matter; the experience itself is so enjoyable that people will do it even at great cost, for the sheer sake of doing it" (p. 4). The high school students studied experienced "flow" as they became totally engaged in their talent, which only occurred when they were consistently provided with challenges and emotional support. When immersed in pleasurable work, these teenagers pursued work as a reward in itself. Csikszentmihalyi also demonstrated that enjoyment plays a crucial role in inspiring students to become interested in a particular area and staying immersed in it.

These talented teens were aware of the conflict between giving in to peer pressure and maintaining productive work in their areas of talent. Many of them felt different from their peers and accepted this feeling because they knew they were different. They reacted to negative peer pressure in a variety of ways: changing groups of friends, adopting different personas in different groups, becoming more solitary, or deciding to attend specialized schooling to pursue their talents in a more supportive environment. Csikszentmihalyi and his colleagues also found that teens with little family support spent large amounts of time with peers instead of working on their talents, and subsequently failed to develop their abilities, suggesting the need for careful parental monitoring of talent development. Interestingly, the team also found that adolescents from disadvantaged backgrounds had higher levels of enthusiasm and optimism than those from affluent backgrounds. All teenagers' perceptions about work also were carefully examined and findings suggested that they had unrealistic expectations about the type of career they would have and how much money they would be expected to earn. Csikszentmihalyi et al. (1993) attributed this finding to the changing nature of adult jobs and to lack of exposure to real work experiences.

This research led to the identification of eight factors that influenced talent development in the teens who participated in this study (Csikszentmihalyi et al., 1993). First, the researchers found that children must initially be recognized as talented in order to develop a talent, and therefore they must have skills that are considered useful in their culture. Second, talented students had to have personality traits conducive to concentration, such as achievement orientation and endurance, as well as traits that enabled them to be open to experience, such as awareness and understanding. Third, talent development was easier for teens who developed habits that were conducive to cultivating talent (e.g., spending time in challenging pursuits with friends instead of hanging out, the modulation of attention, spending more time alone). Fourth, talented teens were more conservative in their sexual attitudes and aware of the possible conflict between productive work and peer relations. Fifth, families who provided both support and challenge enhanced the development of talent. Sixth, talented teenagers liked teachers best who were supportive and modeled enjoyable involvement in a field. Seventh, talent development was found to be a process that requires both expressive, positive feelings and instrumental goals that are useful to future rewards. Last, talents can be developed if the process produces optimal, enjoyable experiences, and the memories of peak moments that continue to motivate students.

Developing Talents in Gifted Females

Reis (1987, 1995, 1998) studied the paths leading to female talent realization in women. She studied 22 American women who gained eminence in diverse fields. Qualitative case study methodology was used including interviews, questionnaires, document review, and in-depth interviews to probe perceptions of both work and personal lives (Miles & Huberman, 1994; Yin, 1994). Each eminent woman was recognized as a major contributor in her field, and several achieved the distinction of being the first or one of the first women in her respective domain.

Using data from this and past research, Reis (1987, 1996, 1998, 2002, 2005) developed a theory of talent development in women. The theory includes abilities (intelligence and special talents), personality traits, environmental factors, and personal perceptions, such as the social importance of the use of one's talents to make a positive difference in the world. Underlying this theory is the belief that talent can be developed in women of high potential through systematic work, active choices, and individual, sustained effort (Dweck, 1999; Moon, 2003; Renzulli, 1978, 1986).

These women developed their talents over time. Each woman displayed a careful patience about the development of her gifts, with some waiting years to have the opportunity to invest considerable blocks of time to her work, while others were able to work steadily over the years. Rather than early recognition, the women in this study demonstrated persistent production, evolving into higher forms of talent. The sheer volume of output, what appeared to be "learned creativity," and intense love for work is what led the women in this study to exceptional achievement. The personality traits of these women included determination, motivation, creativity, patience, and the ability to take, and in some cases thrive on, risks. Each woman exhibited determination, reflected by an ability to strive for success and to continue to persevere, often under adverse conditions and sometimes without the love and support of one's family and/or partner. Each displayed a type of creativity rooted in the love of work, interests, and the way time was found for other essential aspects of life, such as family and relationships. In addition, each displayed a willingness to attempt tasks that they believed others would not have the courage or the interest to pursue.

The eminent women in this study had an intensity about work characterized by energy, passionate interest, and enjoyment. Several indicated that they would rather be doing their work than anything else. However, they reported experiencing guilt when they felt this way, and confessed their attempts to do more for their partners or children to assuage their guilt.

Importantly, although these women felt a drive to pursue their talents, not all were sure that doing so made them happier or more fulfilled. When questioned about their perceptions of their success and happiness, many chose to compare their own lives with the paths and life choices of equally talented contemporaries who did not achieve at similar levels. Most participants in this study perceived that their less successful, equally talented peers lived calmer, and in some cases, happier lives. They understood that the path to eminence involved sacrifices, and in some cases, harbored regrets about paths not taken and personal choices not made. Coexisting with these feelings, however, was pride in their accomplishments.

VanTassel-Baska (1995) studied the lives of Brontë and Woolf to investigate whether the path of a talented female writer is different from a male writer and identified similarities in the lives and work of Brontë and Woolf over the life span. She found three major influences on females writers: adversity (obstacles that the women had to overcome in order to realize their potential); autodidactism (dependence on self-learning due to limited or absent formal educational opportunities); and emotional support (need to have mentors to help these gifted women attain their potential). These areas also surface in other research related to women and the creative process across domains.

A review of studies related to talent development suggests several commonalities that emerge from research summarized in this chapter relating to this complicated process. Most important is the recognition that there is no common path that enables the development of talent to occur, but some factors contribute to the process, such as the right environment, family support, strong teachers, and the desire to work to develop one's talent (Bloom, 1985; Csikszentmihalyi et al., 1993; Reis, 1998). Some research suggests that children must be recognized as talented in order to develop a talent (Csikszentmihalyi et al., 1993) and also must have talents and gifts that are considered useful in their culture. Certain personality traits seem to accompany talent development such as concentration, endurance, and traits such as being open to experience, and abilities to focus attention (Bloom, 1985; Csikszentmihalyi et al., 1993; Reis, 1998). These, when coupled with instruction from teachers in the talent field, both at home and in an instructional setting that is more individualized and personalized, seem to enable talent development to occur if the process results in optimal experiences (Csikszentmihalyi et al., 1993). Memories of peak, exciting experiences such as starring in a drama production or publishing a story or book, can help to motivate students to continue to work to replicate the same intense experience again (Csikszentmihalyi et al., 1993; Reis, 1998). The importance of a supportive environment and parental presence also was a major key in the development of talent (Bloom, 1985; Csikszentmihalyi et al., 1993).

THE SCHOOLWIDE ENRICHMENT MODEL AND TALENT DEVELOPMENT

The Schoolwide Enrichment Model (SEM; Renzulli & Reis, 1985, 1997) is based on 30 years of research and field-testing and was designed to meet the needs of gifted and talented and academically advanced students, as well as to engage and enrich learning for all children. The SEM is based on Renzulli's (1977) Enrichment Triad and has been implemented in more than 2,500 schools across the country and has continued to expand internationally. The SEM provides enriched learning experiences and higher learning standards for all children through three goals: developing talents in all children, providing a broad range of advanced-level enrichment experiences for all students, and follow-up advanced learning for children based on interests. The SEM emphasizes engagement and the use of enjoyable and challenging learning experiences that are constructed around students' interests, learning styles, and product preferences.

Overview of the SEM
The SEM (Renzulli & Reis, 1985, 1997) has three major goals that are designed to challenge and meet all of the needs of high-potential, high-ability, and gifted students, and at the same time, provide challenging learning experiences for all students. In the SEM, a talent pool of 10–15% of above-average ability/high-potential students is identified through a variety of measures including achievement tests,

teacher nominations, assessment of potential for creativity and task commitment, as well as alternative pathways of entrance (self-nomination, parent nomination, etc.). High achievement test scores and/or IQ test scores automatically include a student in the talent pool, enabling those students who are underachieving in their academic schoolwork to be considered.

The SEM has three components of services for students: the Total Talent Portfolio, Curriculum Modification and Differentiation, and Enrichment. These three services are delivered across the regular curriculum, a continuum of services, and a series of enrichment clusters. Once students are identified for the talent pool, they are eligible for these services. First, interest and learning style assessments are used with talent pool students, through the development of a total talent portfolio for each student. Style preferences include projects, independent study, teaching games, simulations, peer teaching, programmed instruction, lecture, drill and recitation, and discussion.

Second, curriculum compacting and other forms of modification are provided to all eligible students for whom the regular curriculum must be adjusted. This elimination or streamlining of curriculum enables above-average students to avoid repetition of previously mastered work and guarantees mastery while simultaneously finding time for more appropriately challenging activities. A form, called the Compactor, is used to document which content areas have been compacted and what alternative work has been substituted.

Third, a series of enrichment opportunities organized around the Enrichment Triad Model offers three types of enrichment experiences through various forms of delivery, including enrichment clusters. Type I, II, and III enrichment are offered to all students; however, Type III enrichment usually is more appropriate for students with higher levels of ability, interest, and task commitment.

In the SEM, teachers are encouraged to work with student to help them better understand the three dimensions of their own learning: their abilities, interests, and learning styles. This information, focusing on their strengths rather than deficits, is compiled into a Total Talent Portfolio that can be subsequently used to make decisions about talent development opportunities in regular classes, enrichment clusters, and/or in the continuum of special services. The ultimate goal of learning that is guided by these principles and the SEM is to replace dependent and passive learning with independence and engaged learning. The three service delivery components of the SEM (Total Talent Portfolio, curriculum compacting, and enrichment teaching and learning) are applied to the regular curriculum, a continuum of services, and a series of enrichment opportunities for all students.

Longitudinal Research on the SEM Related to Talent Development

Delcourt (1988), Hébert (1993), Westberg (1999), and Starko (1986) investigated the long-term effects of SEM school and childhood experiences on creative productivity and talent development. Delcourt studied characteristics related to talent development of Type III products completed in or out of school. Results related to family, school, and individual students' talent development revealed that students exhibited characteristics similar to those of creative/productive adults and that they could produce high-quality work. Delcourt also found, as did Csikszentmihalyi et al. (1993), that students performed better when their talents were better understood by themselves, their parents, and their teachers.

Starko (1986) also examined the effects of the Enrichment Triad Model on student creative productivity. Students who participated in SEM programs for at least 4 years were compared with students who qualified for such programs but received no services. Questionnaires were used to determine the number of creative products produced by both groups, within school programs and within independent activities outside of school. Information about attitudes and skills associated with creative productivity also was gathered through a questionnaire. Results indicated that students who became involved in independent study projects in the SEM more often initiated their own creative products both *in and outside of school* than did students in the comparison group. The group in the enrichment program reported more than twice as many creative projects per student as the comparison group. The group that participated in the enrichment program also reported doing more than twice as many creative products outside of school on their own time than the comparison group. Additionally, students who participated in the enrichment program showed greater diversity in projects and more sophistication in both the creative products attempted and in their description of goals.

In an examination of students who participated in an Enrichment Triad program for almost a decade, Hébert (1993) found several benefits of program involvement. The students selected for the study were chosen because of the number and quality of the Type III products they completed during their elementary TAG program experience. The interviews with the students about their Type III experiences were transcribed and analyzed for themes, finding that Type III interests of students affected their postsecondary plans and that students missed the chance for more creative outlets in high school. He also found that the Type III process serves as an important training for later productivity in college and in adult life. Moreover, many students' Type III interests in school influenced their subsequent careers and work.

Westberg (1999) had similar results in a longitudinal study of students in Enrichment Triad programs, finding that they maintained interests and were still involved in both interests and creative productive work after they finished college and graduate school. Moon, Feldhusen, and Dillon (1994) also conducted a retrospective study investigating the effects of an elementary pull-out program gifted program based on the Purdue Three-Stage Model, which has similar components to the SEM program. Their results were similar, finding that students and their families believed that the program had a long-term positive impact on the cognitive, affective, and social development of most participating students.

CONCLUSION

Recent years have shown an increasing interest in and research about talent development (Olszewski-Kubilius & Lee, 2004a, 2004b, 2004c). The work of Joyce VanTassel-Baska has added to the volume of knowledge with both the biographical research cited in this chapter (VanTassel-Baska, 1995) as well as content-based curriculum (VanTassel-Baska, Bass, Ries, Poland, & Avery, 1998; VanTassel-Baska, Zuo, Avery, & Little, 2002) that results in talent development opportunities. Her extensive work on developing curriculum units to enrich curriculum for gifted students has extended basic curricular concepts within units that integrate advanced content and processes. Her model units across content areas have resulted in opportunities for accelerated work, problem-based learning, and issue-based student inquiry models. Longitudinal research should continue to examine the impact of her work, and this type of research should continue about all research-based approaches in gifted education. There is no more important research than understanding the process by which students can develop their gifts and talents.

REFERENCES

Bloom, B. S. (Ed.). (1985). *Developing talent in young people.* New York: Ballantine Books.

Csikszentmihalyi, M. (1990). *Flow: The psychology of optimal experience.* New York: Harper & Row.

Csikszentmihalyi, M., Rathunde, K., & Whalen, S. (1993). *Talented teenagers: The roots of success and failure.* Cambridge, England: Cambridge University Press.

Delcourt, M. A. B. (1988). *Characteristics related to high levels of creative/productive behavior in secondary school students: A multi-case study.* Unpublished doctoral dissertation, The University of Connecticut, Storrs.

Dweck, C. S. (1999). *Self-theories: Their role in motivation, personality, and development.* Philadelphia: Psychology Press.

Feldman, D. H., & Goldsmith, L. T. (1991). *Nature's gambit: Child prodigies and the development of human potential.* New York: Teachers College Press.

Gruber, H. E. (1986). The self-construction of the extraordinary. In R. J. Sternberg & J. E. Davidson (Eds.), *Conceptions of giftedness* (pp. 247–263). New York: Cambridge University Press.

Hébert, T. P. (1993). Reflections at graduation: The long-term impact of elementary school experiences in creative productivity. *Roeper Review, 16,* 22–28.

Miles, M. B., & Huberman, A. M. (1994). *Qualitative data analysis* (2nd ed.). Thousand Oaks, CA: Sage.

Moon, S. M. (2003). Personal talent. *High Ability Studies,* 14(1), 5–21.

Moon, S. M., Feldhusen, J. F., & Dillon, D. R. (1994). Long-term effects of an enrichment program based on the Purdue three-stage model. *Gifted Child Quarterly, 38*(1), 38–48.

Olszewski-Kubilius, P., & Lee, S.-Y. (2004a). The role of participation in in-school and outside-of-school activities in the talent development of gifted students. *Journal of Secondary Gifted Education, 15,* 107–123.

Olszewski-Kubilius, P., & Lee, S.-Y. (2004b). Gifted adolescents' talent development through distance learning. *Journal for the Education of the Gifted, 28,* 7–35.

Olszewski-Kubilius, P., & Lee, S.-Y. (2004c). Parent perceptions of the effects of the Saturday enrichment program on gifted students' talent development. *Roeper Review, 26,* 156–165.

Reis, S. M. (1987). We can't change what we don't recognize: Understanding the special needs of gifted females. *Gifted Child Quarterly, 31,* 83–88.

Reis, S. M. (1995). Talent ignored, talent diverted: The cultural context underlying giftedness in females. *Gifted Child Quarterly, 39,* 162–170.

Reis, S. M. (1996). Older women's reflections on eminence: Obstacles and opportunities. In K. D. Arnold, K. D. Noble, & R. F. Subotnik (Eds.), *Remarkable women: Perspectives on female talent development* (pp. 149–168). Cresskill, NJ: Hampton.

Reis, S. M. (1998). *Work left undone.* Mansfield Center, CT: Creative Learning Press.

Reis, S. M. (2002). Toward a theory of creativity in diverse creative women. *Creativity Research Journal, 14,* 305–316.

Reis, S. M. (2005). Feminist perspectives on talent development: A research-based conception of giftedness in women. In R. J. Sternberg & J. E. Davidson (Eds.), *Conceptions of giftedness* (pp. 217–245). New York: Cambridge University Press.

Reis, S. M., & McCoach, D. B. (2000). The underachievement of gifted students: What do we know and where do we go? *Gifted Child Quarterly, 44,* 152–170.

Renzulli, J. S. (1977). *The Enrichment Triad Model: A guide for developing defensible programs for the gifted.* Mansfield Center, CT: Creative Learning Press.

Renzulli, J. S. (1978). What makes giftedness? Re-examining a definition. *Phi Delta Kappan, 60,* 180–184, 261.

Renzulli, J. S. (1986). The three-ring conception of giftedness: A developmental model for creative productivity. In R. J. Sternberg & J. E. Davidson (Eds.), *Conceptions of giftedness* (pp. 53–92). New York: Cambridge University Press.

Renzulli, J. S. (2002). Expanding the conception of giftedness to include co-cognitive traits and to promote social capital. *Phi Delta Kappan, 84,* 33–40, 57–58.

Renzulli, J. S., & Park, S. (2000). Gifted dropouts: The who and the why. *Gifted Child Quarterly, 44,* 261–271.

Renzulli, J. S., & Reis, S. M. (1985). *The Schoolwide Enrichment Model: A comprehensive plan for educational excellence.* Mansfield Center, CT: Creative Learning Press.

Renzulli, J. S., & Reis, S. M. (1997). *The Schoolwide Enrichment Model: A guide for developing defensible programs for the gifted and talented.* Mansfield Center, CT: Creative Learning Press.

Roe, A. (1953). *The making of a scientist.* New York: Dodd, Mead, and Company.

Starko, A. J. (1986). *The effects of the revolving door identification model on creative productivity and self-efficacy.* Unpublished doctoral dissertation, University of Connecticut, Storrs.

Sternberg, R. J. (1985). *Beyond IQ: A triarchic theory of human intelligence.* New York: Cambridge University Press.

Tannenbaum, A. J. (1986). Giftedness: A psychosocial approach. In R. J. Sternberg & J. E. Davidson (Eds.), *Conceptions of giftedness* (pp. 21–52). New York: Cambridge University Press.

VanTassel-Baska, J. (1995). A study of life themes in Charlotte Brontë and Virginia Wolf. *Roeper Review, 13*(3), 14–19.

VanTassel-Baska, J., Bass, G. M., Ries, R. R., Poland, D. L., & Avery, L. D. (1998). A national pilot study of science curriculum effectiveness for high ability students. *Gifted Child Quarterly, 42,* 200–211.

VanTassel-Baska, J., Zuo, L., Avery, L. D., & Little, C. A. (2002). A curriculum study of gifted student learning in the language arts. *Gifted Child Quarterly, 46,* 30–44.

Westberg, K. L. (1999, Summer). What happens to young, creative producers? *NAGC: Creativity and Curriculum Divisions' Newsletter,* pp. 3, 13–16.

Yin, R. (1994). *Case study research: Design and methods* (2nd ed.). Beverly Hills, CA: Sage.

Zuckerman, H. (1977). *Scientific elite: Nobel Laureates in the United States.* New York: The Free Press.

CHAPTER 10

HIGHLY GIFTED CHILDREN AND ADOLESCENTS

by

MIRACA
U. M. GROSS

Acceleration and grouping are the lightning rod issues that test the level of acceptance that gifted programs enjoy in a local school district. The greater the commitment to serving gifted students, the greater the acceptance of advancing and grouping them appropriately.

—Joyce Van Tassel-Baska (1992, p. 68)

In the quote above, Joyce Van Tassel-Baska has, as so often before, hit the nail precisely but elegantly, "on the head." Acceleration and grouping are, indeed, the "lightning rod" issues that signal the degree of tolerance with which a school, a school district, or an educational system regards the education of academically gifted children and adolescents.

Most teachers and school administrators today would agree that schools have the responsibility to identify their highly able students and respond with some degree of curriculum modification. Some would qualify their agreement with the provision that the identification procedures should be culture-fair (with which I agree strongly), that they should not be too time-consuming (caution: it can mean "over in a day"), and that the curriculum modification should be "fair to the other students" (caution again: it can imply that gifted students should not be given work that is visibly more challenging than could be mastered by their classmates); but, even with those qualifications, there is generally a degree of acceptance that academically gifted students have special learning needs that the school should respect and meet through a certain degree of curriculum differentiation.

All too often, however, this agreement comes with an implicit proviso that the curriculum differentiation must take place in the regular classroom and should not involve gifted students being "set apart," "singled out," or "segregated" from their age peers; ability grouping is generally a "no-go" area. (A strange proviso given the reluctance, referred to above, to *visibly* differentiate the curriculum for gifted learners in terms of academic rigor; surely the nature and extent of the differentiation are most visible when it occurs in the regular classroom?) Similarly, gifted students should not be "pushed *ahead*," "jumped *ahead*," or "skipped *ahead*"; surely as powerful a metaphor as "no child left *behind*"! Schools are extremely wary of suggestions that gifted students could benefit from educational placements that require them to spend the majority of their time with ability peers or with older students.

Yet, what we know, from research, about the cognitive and affective characteristics of intellectually gifted students, and particularly the highly gifted, makes it clear that these students resemble older children much more than they resemble their age peers. Ability grouping and acceleration do not *segregate* gifted students; rather they are mechanisms through which students with certain developmental similarities (*developmental* peers) can be more appropriately *congregated* (grouped) for instruction than they generally are in the mixed-ability classroom.

The term *highly gifted* serves as an umbrella terminology for a group of students—a larger group than we sometimes appreciate—who differ significantly from more moderately gifted age peers not only in the way they think but also in the way they feel. This includes the metacognitive strategies they use; the *way* they think about *how* they think; and the way they respond, emotionally, to their own awareness of their socioaffective differences; in other words, the *way* they feel about *how* they feel.

WHO ARE THE HIGHLY GIFTED?

The term *highly gifted*, when it refers to intellectual giftedness, generally denotes intellectually gifted children or adolescents who score three or more standard deviations above the mean on a test of cognitive ability. This has come to mean (ignoring the variation in standard deviations among different IQ tests) young people with an IQ of 145 or greater. Within this population, however, are two subsets: exceptionally gifted (IQ 160–179) and profoundly gifted (IQ 180+) students.

The further one travels from the mean on any quantitative measure of human variability—height and weight are only two examples—the greater the variability encountered as one moves toward the tails of the distribution. Intellectual ability is no exception. If we set the standard deviation at 15 IQ points, we find a range of four standard deviations between an IQ of 70 and an IQ of 130, representing the 2nd and the 98th percentiles respectively. However, Goldstein, Stocking, and Godfrey (1999) pointed out that the range of scores of children in the top 1% of the population on IQ (from 135 to more than 200) is actually as broad as the range of scores from the 2nd percentile to the 98th! Indeed, in terms of intellectual capacity alone, the profoundly gifted child of IQ 190 differs from moderately gifted classmates of IQ 130 to the same degree that the latter differ from intellectually disabled children of IQ 70. The sheer extent of the variability *among* the gifted requires that we should think of intellectually gifted students not as a homogenous group but rather as a subpopulation of students distinguished by unusually high intelligence whose members can differ quite remarkably from each other.

WHAT DO WE KNOW ABOUT HIGHLY GIFTED CHILDREN?

Early Development of Communication and Reading Skills

Highly gifted children, and especially exceptionally and profoundly gifted children, often demonstrate quite remarkable achievement in the very early years. The precocious development of speech and reading are powerful indicators of possible giftedness and when these skills develop at extremely early ages, they generally are linked to unusually advanced intellectual development. Individual case studies set in many different countries provide some fascinating examples of early speech. Hollingworth (1926) reported on "David" who at the age of 8 months exclaimed, "Little boy!" when his shadow appeared on a wall and who was talking in sentences at the age of 11 months.

The facility for reading appears early in many gifted children and the love of reading stays with most of them through life. Joyce VanTassel-Baska, in an early study of the 1982 Midwest Talent Search finalists, found that reading was listed as the favorite leisure-time activity by the majority of her adolescent correspondents (VanTassel-Baska, 1983). Similarly, a survey of the children in my own longitudinal study found that reading was by far the most popular leisure activity, outranking sport, watching TV, computer use, playing, and socializing with friends (Gross, 1993). The love of reading generally continues into adulthood (Holahan & Sears, 1995; Terman & Oden, 1959).

COGNITIVE PROCESSING IN HIGHLY GIFTED STUDENTS

When considering the cognitive characteristics of gifted children, one must bear in mind . . . that characteristics may reveal themselves only when students are engaged in an area of interest and aptitude.

—VanTassel-Baska (1998a, p. 180)

Intellectually gifted children tend to differ from age peers of average ability in the cognitive processing strategies they utilize to solve structural problems. Gifted students use higher order (meta-componental) information processing strategies more frequently and more effectively than do average-ability age peers. These include forethoughtful deliberation (even in the early years of school the gifted child is likely to generate a thoughtful, deliberate, and highly structured development of a series of steps toward the resolution of a problem before setting out to solve it, whereas age peers of average ability will use a "hit-or-miss" technique); the systematic monitoring of progress and solutions (analyzing what worked, what failed, and the possible reasons for this); and the representation of information through structures more usually employed by an expert in the field (Kanevsky, 1994).

This preference for a thoughtful, analytical approach to problem solving may help to explain why, even in the early childhood years, highly gifted children may prefer to work on problem-solving activities by themselves rather than with another student or in a small group. Six-year-old Paul (IQ 152) recently tried to explain to me the frustration he experienced working with other children in his grade 1 class. "They don't understand that if something doesn't work that way today, it's not going to work that way tomorrow. You have to try *another* way. It's not magic." Paul was long past the "magical thinking" stage of believing that success or failure come by chance; he understood that success came through the following of a logical, structured series of actions while failure came through not doing so and he could become intensely irritated when his classmates could not accept this.

SOME ISSUES IN SOCIOAFFECTIVE DEVELOPMENT

Another persistent myth is that the superior cognitive functioning of gifted children is totally separate from their affective functioning, an argument frequently used to hold gifted students in place with their age-mates. Luthar, Zigler, and Goldstein (1992) found that intellectually gifted adolescents were more comparable to older adolescents with similar cognitive skills and psychological adjustment than they were to their age-mates, suggesting higher levels of affective functioning.

—VanTassel-Baska (1998b, p. 490)

Motivational Orientation

A number of studies have noted differences in motivational orientation between intellectually gifted students and average ability age peers, with the gifted students presenting as much more intrinsically motivated (Gottfried, Gottfried, Bathurst, & Guerin, 1994; Kanevsky, 1994). Case studies of exceptionally and profoundly gifted children often identify, as a dominant affective characteristic, a passionate desire to learn more, and improve, in the child's talent field. Sally Huang, a member of Gross's longitudinal study, planned her own program of radical acceleration through elementary and secondary school over a period of 5 years and, from the age of 8, personally negotiated each grade advancement with her teachers and school principals (Gross, 1993, 2004). Sally's maturity and deeply intrinsic motivation impressed her teachers, who were aware of her desire to move ahead to test herself against increasingly rigorous standards and become all she could become. In highly gifted children, this tendency toward intrinsic motivation may be linked to a preference for working independently rather than within a group. Terman was convinced that this preference for working independently reflected a natural cognitive orientation (Burks, Jensen, & Terman, 1930).

Significantly higher levels of intrinsic motivation were found among gifted students than among age peers (Gross, 1997). The study also examined a third group, highly gifted students in a full-time accelerated ability grouped setting, and revealed that these students were significantly more intrinsically motivated than even the moderately gifted group. Because the assessment of motivational orientation was made in the first few days of the program, it is probable that their unusual degree of intrinsic motivation predated their enrollment in the program for the gifted (Gross, 1997).

As the program progressed, several of the teachers who worked with this highly gifted class commented on the "cohort effect" of peer bonding, affectionate guidance, and mutual encouragement that swiftly developed among this group of students who were similar in their abilities and interests, were intrinsically rather than extrinsically motivated, and had been presented with a common but intellectually challenging goal (Gross, 1997). Yet, many of these children stated that in elementary school, in the mixed-ability classroom, they had much preferred to work independently. Collaborative work became a delight, rather than an imposition, when the students with whom they were grouped were intellectual peers rather than simply age-mates.

Friendship Choices Among Highly Gifted Students

> *Loneliness does not come from having no people about one, but from being unable to communicate to others the things that seem important to oneself, or from holding certain views which others find inadmissible . . . If a man knows more than others, he becomes lonely.*
>
> —Jung (1989, p. 356)

Research studies over many years have shown us that children tend to choose friends on the basis of similarities in mental age, rather than chronological age. When intellectually gifted children look for friends, they tend to gravitate either toward other gifted children of approximately their own age, or toward older children who are of well-above-average ability. As Jung (1989, p. 356) acknowledged, they are seeking children with whom they can talk about "the things that seem important to oneself." The interests—indeed the passions—of gifted children can sometimes seem quite inexplicable to their age peers.

Previous international studies (e.g., Selman, 1981) have found that children's conceptions of friendship develop in hierarchical stages that are strongly age-related. Children in the first few years of school tend to have rather egocentric views of friendship; a friend is seen as someone who meets *their* needs. The capacity to move beyond one's own needs and perceptions, and see one's friend as an individual with his or her own needs and values, does not develop in most children until around the age of 9, while the understanding of friendship as an intimate and mutually rewarding relationship that allows friends to draw strength from each other and contribute to each other's emotional growth does not, in general, develop until around age 12. There are, however, gender differences. Boys and girls in the preadolescent years tend to have different expectations of friendship, with girls reporting higher levels of intimacy, trust, and loyalty than do boys in same-sex best-friendships.

However, these studies of children's conceptions of friendship were conducted largely with children of average intellectual ability. The researchers did not investigate whether intellectually gifted children pass through the stages of friendship conception at the same ages, or at the same speed, as children of average ability or whether gifted girls or boys differed in their expectations of friendship from their same-sex age peers.

In a study of the conceptions of friendship held by children of average intellectual ability, moderately gifted children, and highly gifted children, results confirmed that children's conceptions of friendship do indeed form a developmental hierarchy of age-related stages, with expectations of friendship, and beliefs about friendship, becoming more sophisticated and complex with age (Gross, 2002). The five stages appear in order as follows, from the lowest to the highest level in terms of age and conceptual complexity.

- *Stage 1: "Play partner":* In the earliest stage of friendship, the relationship is based on "play partnership." A friend is seen as someone who engages the child in play and permits the child to use or borrow her playthings.
- *Stage 2: "People to chat to":* The sharing of interests becomes an important element in friendship choice. Conversations between friends are no longer related simply to the game or activity in which the children are directly engaged.
- *Stage 3: "Help and encouragement":* At this stage the friend is seen as someone who will offer help, support, or encouragement. However, the advantages of friendship flow in one direction; the child does not yet see himself as having the obligation to provide help or support in return.
- *Stage 4: "Intimacy/empathy":* The child now realizes that in friendship the need and obligation to give comfort and support flows both ways and, indeed, the giving of affection, as well as receiving it, becomes an important element in the relationship. This stage sees a deepening of intimacy; an emotional sharing and bonding.
- *Stage 5: "The sure shelter."* The title comes from a passage in one of the apocryphal books of the Old Testament: "A faithful friend is a sure shelter:

whoever finds one has found a rare treasure" (Ecclesiastics 6:14). At this stage, friendship is perceived as a deep and lasting relationship of trust, fidelity, and unconditional acceptance. A 12-year-old boy in my longitudinal study of children of IQ 160+ (Gross, 2004) told me: "A friend is a place you go to when you need to take off the masks. You can take off your camouflage with a friend and still feel safe."

In this study, I was able to compare the friendship conceptions of children of average intellectual ability, moderately gifted children, and children of IQ 160+. The study demonstrated strongly that what children look for in friends is dictated not so much by chronological age as by mental age. A strong relationship was found between children's levels of intellectual ability and their conceptions of friendship. In general, intellectually gifted children were found to be substantially further along the hierarchy of stages of friendship than were their age peers of average ability. Gifted children were beginning to look for friends with whom they could develop close and trusting relationships, at ages when their age peers of average ability were looking for play partners. The differences between gifted children and their average ability age peers were much larger in the primary school years, and in the early years of elementary school, than in the later years. This study suggests that intellectually gifted children may not only be seeking the intellectual compatibility of mental age peers; they also may be looking for children whose conceptions and expectations of friendship are similar to their own.

Hollingworth (1936) believed that the social isolation experienced by many highly gifted children was most acute between the ages of 4 and 9. My own findings strongly support this. Children of IQ 160+ tend to begin the search for "the sure shelter"—friendships of complete trust, honesty, and fidelity—4 or 5 years before their age peers even enter this stage. Indeed, in the friendship study, exceptionally and profoundly gifted girls aged 6 and 7 already displayed conceptions of friendship which do not develop in children of average ability until age 11 or 12. No wonder these children encounter difficulties with socialization. There is little common ground between a 6-year-old who is seeking the sure shelter and an age peer who is looking for a play partner.

As might have been expected, substantial gender differences were noticed. At all levels of ability, and at all ages, girls were, on average, significantly further along the developmental scale of friendship conceptions than boys. Exceptionally gifted boys who begin the search for intimacy at unusually early ages may be at even greater risk of social isolation than girls of similar ability as they will appear so dramatically different from the majority of boys of their age. This may explain why, in the early years of school, highly gifted boys sometimes prefer the company of girls.

Another characteristic of exceptionally and profoundly gifted children is that they seem to prefer the company of a few close friends rather than large, looser groups. This also is a characteristic of children who are introverts rather than extroverts. Highly gifted children who are introverts may have a double need for a few closer relationships rather than many more surface relationships.

It is ironic that schools in the United States and Australia so seldom develop ability grouped programs for gifted students in the early years of school and that teachers are so reluctant to allow young gifted children to grade advance. This study suggests that it is in the earlier grades, rather than the upper grades, that placement with chronological peers, without regard to intellectual ability or emotional maturity, is more likely to result in the gifted child experiencing loneliness or social isolation.

Ability grouping and acceleration can be of invaluable assistance in the early years of school to young gifted children whose accelerated conceptions of friendship are urging them to seek the sure shelter of a relationship of trust, fidelity, and authenticity, at ages when their age peers are seeking playmates or casual conversation. In the case of exceptionally and profoundly gifted children, it is difficult to justify, either educationally or socially, the inclusion of these children in classes comprised of age peers whose conceptions of friendship are so radically different from theirs.

THE "LIGHTNING ROD ISSUES": ACCELERATION AND GROUPING

It is a tragic irony that the two interventions that are most essential for, and so successful with, highly gifted students—acceleration and ability grouping—are those that educators are most reluctant to employ.

Acceleration simply means allowing students who are developmentally ready, in terms of their intellectual, academic, emotional, and social maturity, to enter school and/or progress through school at a faster pace than would be appropriate for their age peers of average ability. There are at least 18 distinct types of acceleration, each with its own research base (Colangelo, Assouline, & Gross, 2004). There is a wealth of research supporting its use and documenting its effectiveness, yet schools are extraordinarily reluctant to use it. Because it is so rarely used, teachers lack familiarity with it and therefore, understandably, are not confident that it will work. A vicious circle of wariness, nonuse, and therefore ongoing nonfamiliarity is established. Furthermore, acceleration is equated with *pushing* children—*hastening* them into an inappropriate grade placement—and the instinctive response of many teachers is to say, "Slow down; let the child find her own pace." However, acceleration is intended to respond to the child's natural, *accelerated* pace of learning and her *advanced* emotional and social development that are more like those of older students.

Ability grouping is placing children together, for the purposes of instruction, with children with whom they have certain commonalities of learning *status* (the stage they have reached in their acquisition of knowledge and skills within a given field or in terms of general capacity to learn) and learning *style* (e.g., speed of learning, degree of abstractness preferred in material presented, or a preference for learning with other able students). Grouping may be subject-specific or covering all academic areas; it may be short-term as in pull-out programs or long-term as with special classes or schools for the gifted.

All too often, ability grouping is criticized as establishing an educational elite; students who are viewed (and may come to view themselves) as innately superior to their age peers. It is noticeable, however, that the arguments that are employed to discourage acceleration and ability grouping of *intellectually* gifted students are seldom used to discourage these interventions with other forms of high ability. It is common for schools to employ, with pupils talented in athletics and the performing arts, many of the interventions and encouragements that they neglect or refuse to use with academically gifted pupils.

- ► *Ability grouping.* Sports teams and musical ensembles are generally formed on the basis of a certain homogeneity of ability and/or achievement. In general, the higher the level of expertise, the greater the homogeneity of the group that is formed in response.
- ► *Opportunity for social comparison.* Sports teams are matched with each other on the basis of ability and achievement, allowing a facilitative level of healthy competition and social comparison. Music festivals allow talented young musicians and singers to match themselves against others of similar ability. Festinger (1954) showed that realistic self-evaluation is only possible when we are allowed to compare our performance against that of other people whose abilities are similar to ours.
- ► *Acceleration.* Talented young musicians and athletes are permitted to progress at their own pace, training and performing with older pupils when this is appropriate. The repertoire that talented young musicians prepare and perform is chosen on the basis of the performer's maturity and readiness, rather than like his or her chronological age.
- ► *Mentorships.* Highly talented young athletes often are taken under the wing of an older player who will coach them on strategy. Talented young musicians may have the opportunity to take master classes.
- ► *Sustained and rigorous practice.* It is accepted that a structured and rigorous regime of practice, setting ever more demanding goals, is essential if gifted young musicians or athletes are to develop as talented. These pupils' friends understand and support them in this. By contrast, academically talented pupils who passionately commit themselves to developing their talents are often derided as "swots," "geeks," or "brainiacs"—the names vary from year to year and country to country but the social connotation (uncool) is unmistakable.
- ► *Pride in achievement.* Talented musicians and athletes are encouraged to feel pride in their gifts and strive to develop them. However, pride in academic success often is confused with conceit and covertly, or sometimes overtly, discouraged.
- ► Ironically, the arguments employed to dissuade educators from ability grouping arise mainly from sociopolitical, rather than educational, concerns such as the following illustrates. (1) Ability grouping is elitist and

adversely effects the self-esteem of those not in the top group. (2) Life experiences do not occur in homogeneous settings, and high-ability pupils must learn to work with a wide range of people. (3) Gifted pupils should be left in the regular classroom as models and mentors for pupils of lesser ability. (4) Ability grouping segregates pupils along ethnic and socioeconomic status (SES) lines. (5) Ability grouping makes children conceited about their academic ability. (6) Ability grouping damages gifted pupils' self-esteem. (It is difficult to see how both 5 and 6 can be valid!)

▶ The objections to acceleration are equally unfounded but equally emotive (Colangelo et al., 2004). (1) Gifted children may be academically advanced but emotionally they are just like their age peers. Acceleration will harm them. (2) We shouldn't push children to go faster than their natural pace. (3) The child will not make friends in the grade above. (4) The other children will be uncomfortable with a younger child in the room. (5) The younger child will hold the other children back. (6) There will be gaps in the child's knowledge. (7) The younger child will be disadvantaged in sport and games. (8) Why should one child get something that isn't offered to the other children?

Decisions regarding pupil placements have, all too often, been based not on educational and psychological principles, but on political expediency and administrative convenience, or on a concern for "equity," which confuses equal opportunity with equal outcomes. In special education, we seek to place the pupil with special needs in the least restrictive environment. For the gifted pupil, the "inclusion" classroom may not be the least restrictive environment, and for the highly gifted it is arguably the most restrictive environment we could devise. As educators, we need to be guided by empirical research, particularly that which is replicated over different eras and in different countries, rather than be dictated to by sociopolitical concerns that vary and veer with the winds of social and political change.

RESEARCH-BASED ADVANTAGES OF GROUPING BY ABILITY

1. The academic achievement of gifted pupils in ability-grouped settings is consistently and significantly higher than that of ability peers educated in the inclusion classroom. When gifted students are grouped by ability *and* the curriculum is differentiated in response to their ability, they perform significantly better on later measures of school achievement than do equally able students learning in mixed-ability settings. Measurable academic gains are noted for gifted students across all subject areas, particularly when the grouping is full time (Kulik, 1992). Goldring's (1990) meta-analysis of studies on various forms of grouping found that gifted students in special classes experienced significant gains in achievement over ability peers retained in the regular classroom, particularly in science and social studies, while Berge (1990) confirmed that high-ability students achieved at significantly higher levels in science instruction using computers when working in small groups of like ability than when they were working individually.

2. *The quality of gifted pupils' academic achievement is related not only to their access to ability grouping, but to its intensity and duration.* Researchers have noted the different effects of various forms of grouping on academic achievement. A longitudinal study (Delcourt, Loys, Cornell, & Goldberg, 1994) examined a range of academic and socioaffective variables for more than 1,000 academically gifted pupils in a range of educational settings: special schools for gifted pupils, full-time classes, pull-out programs, and small groups of individual students who received a differentiated curriculum within the inclusion classroom. Gifted pupils in special programs performed consistently better than did equally gifted pupils educated entirely in the regular classroom. Furthermore, gifted pupils in full-time ability-grouped settings (special schools and classes) performed significantly better than did equally gifted pupils who were ability grouped for only part of the week.

3. *Gifted students in ability-grouped settings have more positive attitudes toward learning, and more realistic attitudes toward their own abilities, than do ability peers in inclusion settings.* Students are much more motivated to learn when the level and pace at which the curriculum is pitched is slightly beyond their current level of achievement: Vygotsky's (1976) "zone of proximal development." Students in ability-grouped settings are more intrinsically motivated to achieve (Gross, 1997) and are more interested in sharing and comparing their work with other students. Delcourt et al. (1994) found that gifted students in special schools had more positive attitudes toward learning, and were more likely to feel confident about their judgments on issues related to school and learning than ability peers in any other ability-grouped or ungrouped setting. Interestingly, gifted students in mixed-ability classes and part-time grouping had higher perceptions of their own academic abilities than did equally gifted pupils in full-time grouped settings. Contrary to the belief that ability grouping makes gifted pupils conceited, it may be gifted pupils in the inclusion classroom who, having no opportunity to measure themselves against a valid comparison group, have inflated opinions of their own abilities.

RESEARCH-BASED ADVANTAGES OF ACCELERATION

In the 2 years during which we were writing *A Nation Deceived: How Schools Hold Back America's Brightest Students*, Nicholas Colangelo, Susan Assouline, and I, assisted by some of the world's leading scholars in gifted education, evaluated more than 80 years of educational and psychological research on the academic and social-emotional outcomes of 18 forms of acceleration. I will discuss here the main findings and refer you to Volume 2 of the report itself (accessible in full on its Web site http://www.accelerationinstitute.org/Nation_Deceived) for specific details of the studies from which these findings evolved.

Acceleration is, quite simply, the most effective curriculum intervention for gifted children and adolescents. It permits gifted students to learn at something closer to their natural speed of learning than is normally possible. As gifted students tend to be more emotionally and socially mature than their age peers, it places them with students with whom they share greater commonalities of socioaffective development, and those social and emotional benefits continue as the child grows and develops. By contrast, when gifted students are presented only with material developed for use with age peers of average ability, they can become bored and switched off from learning.

The 18 types of acceleration described in *A Nation Deceived* fall into two broad categories: grade-based acceleration, which shortens the amount of time a gifted student must spend in the school system; and subject-based acceleration, which allows for a gifted student to experience advanced content in a specific subject area earlier than is customary.

Students entering college early experience both short- and long-term academic success that leads to long-term occupational success and personal satisfaction. Alternatives to early enrollment in college include dual enrollment in high school and college-level courses, distance education, and summer programs. "The key question for educators is not *whether* to accelerate a gifted learner but rather *how*" (Colangelo et al. 2004, p. 2).

The Optimal Match of Student and Placement

Earlier in this chapter we discussed some of the cognitive and socioaffective characteristics of highly gifted children and adolescents. These characteristics make for an uneasy fit, academically and socially, with age peers; put simply, intellectually gifted students resemble older children much more than they resemble children of their own age. They pass through the developmental stages of speech and reading earlier and faster than their age peers. They are early and passionate readers and the books they like are very different to those preferred by their classmates. For most, reading is a lifelong passion.

The cognitive processing strategies used by highly gifted students are more like those that characterize children some years older; they remember more than their age peers and they remember it more effectively. They already may have outgrown, by the early years of school, the "magical thinking" approach to problem solving that still characterizes their classmates. They may have a strongly intrinsic motivational orientation and may, indeed, be disturbed by competitiveness; they are likely to find the successful completion of a task more inherently satisfying than being "the first to finish." This may lead to a strong preference for working independently rather than within a group; however, being grouped with other gifted children who are similarly intrinsically motivated can be a source of deep intellectual and emotional satisfaction.

As discussed earlier, gifted children have conceptions of friendship that can differ significantly from those of their age peers. They may be looking for friendships that include a strong element of mutual emotional support and the sharing of confidences at a stage where their age peers are seeking friends as play partners. Grade advancement or ability grouping can allow contact with children whose conceptions and expectations of friendship are more akin to their own.

Responding to the Highly Gifted: A New Direction Through the Influence of Teacher Training

To ensure equity and systematic talent search and programming, it is essential that teachers are educated in the relevant theory, research, pedagogy, and management techniques important to developing and sustaining classroom-based opportunities to learn for these students.
                                              —VanTassel-Baska and Johnsen (2007, p. 182)

Effective teacher training and in-service is critical to the development of more positive teacher attitudes toward gifted and talented students. Studies in England, Scotland, and Australia (Geake & Gross, 2008; Gross, 1994) have shown how powerfully teacher attitudes toward these students can change after even a single day of professional development training.

In 1991, the Gifted Education Research, Resource and Information Centre (GERRIC) within the University of New South Wales (UNSW) in Sydney, Australia, offered, for the first time, its Postgraduate Certificate of Gifted Education (COGE)—a course comprising 80 contact hours of lectures and seminars held across three consecutive school vacations within an 18-month timeframe. Dr. Joyce VanTassel-Baska is one of the international leaders in gifted education who teaches regularly in the curriculum and programming strands of COGE.

More than 1,500 teachers have graduated from this program in the 18 years since its commencement. Attitudinal surveys undertaken at the commencement of COGE regularly reveal that although these teachers, who are giving up a substantial proportion of their school vacation to train in gifted education, have a generally positive view of gifted students, they are very wary indeed about the use of ability grouping and acceleration. Interviews with the teachers at this stage reveal all of the uncertainties and all of the wariness uncovered by Colangelo et al. (2004) and discussed above (Gross, 1994).

By the end of the 80-hour program, these teachers' attitudes toward grouping and acceleration are much more positive and, by the end of the course, several of their schools have already accelerated gifted students and/or have established some degree of ability grouping.

During the mid-1990s, the School of Education at UNSW was the first university to introduce a gifted education course as a *mandatory* element of teacher training. In our case, this was a logical correlate of our decision to require all education students to take a mandatory course in special education—and to our delight a number of other Australian universities have followed suit.

Interviews with the educational administrators responsible for gifted education in several Australian state, church-affiliated, and independent (private) school systems have established that the growing teacher awareness of the academic and social needs of gifted students has been a powerful factor in the inclusion in their system's gifted education policy of recommendations that the mixed-ability classroom, with age peers, is not necessarily the only setting in which academically gifted students can be educated!

WHERE TO FROM HERE?

We know *so much* about acceleration. We know a substantial amount about its long-term effects through longitudinal studies such as those of Terman and the Study of Mathematically Precocious Youth (SMPY) team. Terman found that 20% of his subjects of IQ 135+ were permitted to skip all or part of first grade and, by the time they graduated from high school, 10% had skipped two grades and a further 23% had skipped one (Terman & Oden, 1947). A full third of Terman's subjects graduated from high school at least one year early with no significantly negative effects either in the short-term or in the long-term. The SMPY studies offer additional evidence for the effectiveness of acceleration, and the exceptionally gifted young people in my own longitudinal study who have accelerated cannot speak highly enough of it. "Where differences are found, they favor the accelerands over non-accelerands irrespective of the mode of acceleration. And Terman's data indicated that this is true even 50 years after the acceleration occurred" (Cronbach, 1996, p. 188).

However, we know much less about the long-term effects of ability grouping of highly gifted children and adolescents. Do they experience the "big-fish-in-the-little-pond effect" (BFLPE) of decreased self-esteem as Marsh and Parker (1984) predicted, and if so, when? My own research (Gross, 1997) established that the BFLPE was not a significant problem for gifted students in their first year of full-time ability grouping—but does it become an issue in later years of the program? That certainly would be interesting to investigate. Additionally, what happens when the highly gifted student who has been ability grouped with other highly gifted students for several years moves to on to college (which is still ability grouping but much less homogeneous)? What happens when he or she moves into the workforce? At some time, these highly gifted students have to return to heterogeneity; how does this affect them in terms of intellectual ability or in terms of socializing? This surely would be a fruitful field for enquiry.

One thing is certain: The work of Joyce VanTassel-Baska will inform thinking in our field for many years to come. Her work in curriculum, learning theory, ability grouping, acceleration, teacher standards, and so much else has been an inspiration and will continue to be so. Thank you, Joyce, with all my heart.

References

Berge, Z. L. (1990). Effects of group size, gender, and ability grouping on learning science process skills using microcomputers. *Journal of Research in Science Teaching, 27,* 923–954.

Burks, B. S., Jensen, D. W., & Terman, L. M. (1930). *Genetic studies of genius: Volume 3: The promise of youth.* Stanford, CA: Stanford University Press.

Colangelo, N., Assouline, S. G., & Gross, M. U. M. (2004). *A nation deceived: How schools hold back America's brightest students* (Vol. 1). Iowa City: The University of Iowa, The Connie Belin & Jacqueline N. Blank International Center for Gifted Education and Talent Development.

Cronbach. L. J. (1996). Acceleration among the Terman males: Correlates in mid-life and after. In C. P. Benbow & D. Lubinski (Ed.) *Intellectual talent: Psychometric and social issues* (pp. 179–191). Baltimore: Johns Hopkins University Press.

Delcourt, M. A. B., Loys, B. H., Cornell, D. G., & Goldberg, M. D. (1994) *Evaluation of the effects of programming arrangements on student learning outcomes.* Charlottesville, VA: National Research Center on the Gifted and Talented.

Festinger, L. (1954). A theory of social comparison process. *Human Relations, 7,* 117–140.

Geake, J., & Gross, M. U. M. (2008). Teachers' negative affect towards academically gifted students: An evolutionary psychological study. *Gifted Child Quarterly, 52,* 217–231.

Goldring, E. B. (1990). Assessing the status of information on classroom organizational frameworks for gifted pupils. *Journal of Educational Research, 83,* 313–326.

Goldstein, D., Stocking, V. B., & Godfrey, J. J. (1999). What we've learned from talent search research. In N. Colangelo & S. G. Assouline (Eds.), *Talent Development 111: Proceedings from the 1995 Henry B. and Jocelyn Wallace National Research Symposium on Talent Development* (pp. 143–152). Scottsdale, AZ: Great Potential Press.

Gottfried, W., Gottfried, A. E., Bathurst, K., & Guerin, D. W. (1994). *Gifted IQ: Early developmental aspects: The Fullerton longitudinal study.* New York: Plenum Press.

Gross, M. U. M. (1993). *Exceptionally gifted children.* London: Routledge.

Gross, M. U. M. (1994). Changing teacher attitudes towards gifted students through inservice training. *Gifted and Talented International, 8*(2), 15–21.

Gross, M. U. M. (1997). How ability grouping turns big fish into little fish—or does it? Of optical illusions and optimal environments. *Australasian Journal of Gifted Education, 6*(2), 18–30.

Gross, M. U. M. (2002). Gifted children and the gift of friendship. *Understanding Our Gifted, 14*(3), 27–29.

Gross, M. U. M. (2004). *Exceptionally gifted children* (2nd ed.). London: Routledge-Falmer.

Holahan, C. K., & Sears, R. S. (1995). *The gifted group in later maturity.* Stanford, CA: Stanford University Press.

Hollingworth, L. S. (1926). *Gifted children: Their nature and nurture.* New York: Macmillan.

Hollingworth, L. S. (1936). The development of personality in highly intelligent children. *National Elementary Principal, 15,* 272–281.

Jung, C. G. (1989). *Memories, dreams, reflections* (Rev. ed.; R. Winston & C. Winston, Trans.). New York: Vintage Books.

Kanevsky, L. K. (1994). A comparative study of children's learning in the zone of proximal development. *European Journal of High Ability, 5,* 163–175.

Kulik, J. A. (1992). *An analysis of the research on ability grouping: Historical and contemporary perspectives* (RDBM 9204). Storrs: University of Connecticut, The National Research Center on the Gifted and Talented.

Luthar, S. S., Zigler, E., & Goldstein, D. (1992). Psychological adjustment among intellectually gifted adolescents: The role of cognitive-developmental and experiential factors. *Journal of Child Psychology and Psychiatry and Allied Disciplines, 33,* 361–373.

Marsh, H. W., & Parker, J. W. (1984). Determinants of self-concept: Is it better to be a relatively large fish in a small pond even if you don't learn to swim as well? *Journal of Personality and Social Psychology, 47,* 213–231.

Selman, R. L. (1981). The child as a friendship philosopher. In S. R. Asher & J. M. Gottman (Eds.), *The development of children's friendships* (pp. 242–272). Cambridge, UK: Cambridge University Press.

Terman, L. M., & Oden, M. H. (1947). *Genetic studies of genius: Volume 4: The gifted child grows up.* Stanford, CA: Stanford University Press.

Terman, L. M., & Oden, M. H. (1959). *Genetic studies of genius: Volume 5: The gifted group at midlife.* Stanford, CA: Stanford University Press.

VanTassel-Baska, J. (1983). Profiles of precocity: The 1982 Midwest Talent Search finalists. *Gifted Child Quarterly, 27,* 139–144.

VanTassel-Baska, J. (1992). Educational decision-making on acceleration and ability-grouping. *Gifted Child Quarterly, 36,* 68–72.

VanTassel-Baska, J. (1998a). Characteristics and needs of talented learners. In J. VanTassel-Baska (Ed.), *Excellence in educating gifted and talented learners* (3rd ed., pp. 173–192). Denver, CO: Love.

VanTassel-Baska, J. (1998b). Counseling talented learners. In J. VanTassel-Baska (Ed.), *Excellence in educating gifted and talented learners* (3rd ed., pp. 489–509). Denver, CO: Love.

VanTassel-Baska, J., & Johnsen, S. K. (2007). Teacher education standards for the field of gifted education: A vision of coherence for personnel preparation in the 21st century. *Gifted Child Quarterly, 51,* 182–205.

Vygotsky, L S. (1976). *Thought and language.* Boston: MIT Press.

CHAPTER 11

PROMISING STUDENTS OF POVERTY:

Pathways and Perils to Success

by

TAMRA
STAMBAUGH

Making a difference in the lives of these learners will require the personal involvement of many people over time as well as the policy levers of government to target resources to this area of social need.

—Joyce Van Tassel-Baska

It is well known that Dr. Joyce Van Tassel-Baska has long emphasized the need for quality services and equitable identification measures for students of poverty. Her passion and interest in this area has been evidenced throughout her career. For example, she served as a teacher and coordinator of gifted students in an inner-city school district in Ohio; instituted programs for students of poverty at Northwestern University; published two monographs about the current state of talented students of poverty—one for the National Research Center on the Gifted and Talented (Van-Tassel-Baska, 2003) and another for the National Association for Gifted Children (Van Tassel-Baska & Stambaugh, 2007); conducted two large-scale research intervention studies in Title I schools while at The College of William and Mary's Center for Gifted Education; initiated the first National Leadership Conference on Low-Income Promising Learners, which encouraged diverse groups from across the nation to converse about ways to conduct research and craft policies for students of poverty; focused on this special group as a major platform during her term as president of the National Association for Gifted Children; and initiated and shaped significant statewide policies in South Carolina that have enhanced appropriate services and equitable identification protocols for minority and disadvantaged students.

It is with great pleasure that I write this chapter. I have had the privilege of working directly with Dr. VanTassel-Baska during her NAGC presidency, the inception and implementation of the National Leadership Conference on Low-Income Promising Learners, and as a grant team member and later, director of two Javits grants focusing on curriculum innovation in Title I schools. Her passion for students of poverty is central to her work and has positively influenced the field of gifted education and brought about a growing national awareness. As you read this chapter, you will discover that much of what we know about students of poverty, especially in terms of curriculum interventions, identification, and directions for the field, comes from the pioneering work of Dr. Joyce VanTassel-Baska. Although there is still much that needs to be understood and researched, there is much we do know.

THE LANDSCAPE OF POVERTY

The United States is listed as the richest nation per capita but ironically reports the highest percentage of students living in poverty when compared to other developed nations (Luxembourg Income Study, 2000). The National Center for Education Statistics (NCES; 2004) reported that 16.7% of school-age children are living in poverty, as defined by free/reduced lunch standards. Of the almost 17% of school-age students in poverty, approximately one third are Black, another third are Hispanic, and another third are White, Asian, or other. Although many assume that the overwhelming majority of students of poverty are from urban areas, approximately 41% of students are from rural areas and of that group, the majority are White (NCES, 2005). Poverty occurs in all races and geographic areas of this country.

Students who are born into poverty are at a greater risk for underachieving in school and contributing to the poverty cycle as adults unless appropriate educational services are available at earlier ages (usually during the preschool years) to equalize the opportunities of each group (Hodgkinson, 2003). Many students of poverty begin school with little exposure to the academic skills needed for success in a school system (Slocumb & Payne, 2000). These students have not had the same opportunities as their middle-class counterparts, yet they are expected to adapt to a different value system and are measured on the same scale as students from middle-class families. These students must function without the necessary exposure and access to enriched environments. To complicate the problem, schools in high-poverty geographic areas spend less money per student, employ less-experienced teachers who may have teaching assignments outside their area of expertise, and pay teachers substantially less than school districts with a wealthier clientele (NCES, 2005).

Although more money may be needed for students of poverty or to invest in the schools they attend, money alone will not fix the situation of poverty, as it is more complex than financial means. Burney (2008) reviewed the literature on the relationship between poverty and academic achievement. She cites research by Newberg (2006) in which the author reported the progress of 112 sixth-grade inner-city students of poverty who were promised free tuition from philanthropists if they would attend college. As Burney (2008) relays, "And, despite the unlimited remediation, counseling, and other support services, far fewer actually matriculated and graduated from college than was expected. Poverty proved to be a burden simply too heavy to shoulder for most" (pp. 296–297).

Not only are school personnel less equipped to work with students of poverty, the parents of students of poverty usually are less educated than their middle-class counterparts and, consequently, provide fewer enrichment opportunities to enhance learning and prepare a child for the demands of school—creating an unevenness in access before a child even begins his school career. This is especially true in early language development and critical thinking. Rothstein (2004) wrote:

> When working-class [those in poverty] parents read aloud, they are more likely to tell children to pay attention without interruptions or to sound out words or name letters. When they ask children about a story, questions are more likely to be factual, asking for names of objects or memory of events. Parents who are more literate are more likely to ask questions that are creative, interpretive or connective, like "what do you think will happen next?" "Does that remind you of what we did yesterday? Middle-class parents are more likely to read aloud, to have fun, to start conversations, as an entrée to the world outside. (p. 4)

Rothstein (2004) also suggested that middle-class parents model problem solving, involve their children in conversation, and exude a strong self-efficacy, which is mimicked by their children. Parents of poverty, on the other hand, expect children to be "seen and not heard," allow fewer opportunities for negotiation, problem solving, conversations, and enrichment—skills necessary for success in school and later in life.

It is no surprise then, that there is a wide achievement gap between students of poverty and their nonpoverty counterparts. Students of poverty score significantly lower on national and state achievement assessments in all core academic areas than their higher socioeconomic peers (NCES, 2004). In fact, although the achievement gap is closing between White and minority students, the gap remains wide between students of poverty and those of more financial means (NCES, 2004), regardless of ethnicity.

CHILDREN OF POVERTY AND GIFTEDNESS

Children of poverty are less likely to be identified as gifted or provided appropriate services and access to gifted programs, and they are more likely to be identified as special needs or having a learning disability (Donovan & Cross, 2002; Ford, 1995; U.S. Department of Education [USDOE], 1993). Specifically, 47% of identified gifted students are in the top 20% of the income levels whereas 9% of identified gifted students are in the lowest 20% of reported income levels (USDOE, 1993). If students of poverty are identified as gifted, serving these students in traditional gifted programs causes several issues of concern if the curriculum is not adjusted to provide remediation and resources to fill the missing gaps of a poverty lifestyle that may lack access to appropriate services, middle-class dialogue, and enrichment (Slocumb & Payne, 2000). Moreover, these students of poverty, even if they are identified, are less likely to attend schools that have advanced math and science courses (Gamoran, 2000), or to enroll in college preparatory and other advanced classes (Bill and Melinda Gates Foundation, 2003).

Students of poverty, especially those who also display the unique characteristics of giftedness, often are misunderstood by their teachers (Ford & Harris, 1999) and may be blocked from appropriate programming opportunities because their unique gifts go unnoticed, are unappreciated, or are viewed as inappropriate or defiant (Donovan & Cross, 2002; Peterson, 1999). Payne (1995) outlined the following characteristics of students of poverty: (1) disorganized, (2) don't do homework, (3) like to entertain, (4) do only parts of an assignment, (5) are great storytellers, (6) possess a unique sense of humor, (7) learn by discussion and hands-on activities, (8) provide creative responses, (9) laugh at inappropriate times or at inappropriate situations, (10) prefer verbal/physical assault over reasoning through a situation, (11) dislike authority, (12) talk back to authority figures, (13) may or may not do assigned work—but are more likely to do work if they like the teacher, (14) lack procedural self-talk to get started or continue on an assignment, (15) may appear to be rude, (16) show very independent skills, (17) need more "space" and opportunity for creativity, (18) speak their mind freely, and (19) prefer to live in the moment and have difficulty setting goals. These characteristics are very similar to creative or twice-exceptional gifted students and because of this, many students of poverty, who also are promising, may struggle in school more than their non-gifted or nonpoverty counterparts, as all are underidentified groups by traditional identification measures.

Even if gifted students of poverty are noticed and provided services, they may feel that they do not fit within these special programs, especially if the majority of students in the gifted program are wealthy or of a majority ethnic group (Ford & Harris, 1999). This perpetuates a cycle that further promotes inequity between those of poverty and those of financial means. In extreme cases, not only do promising students of poverty drop out of gifted programs, but they are at a greater risk of dropping out of school. This author conducted an action-research study of high school dropouts in 10 rural, high-poverty school districts in southeast Ohio.

Approximately 17% of all dropouts had test scores that would have qualified them for gifted education services; the majority of those students were of poverty. In a more formalized study of gifted dropouts, Renzulli and Park (2000) also found that the majority of gifted dropouts were from low income or minority groups, had less educated parents, and few goals for educational attainment. Pregnancy among females also was a contributor.

IDENTIFICATION OF PROMISING STUDENTS OF POVERTY

Identifying gifted students in general is still an act of controversy and disagreement in the field without the added complication of poverty. To accurately identify students of poverty who also are gifted, educators must understand the unique characteristics of these students and provide appropriate mechanisms for discovering their abilities. Two policy studies specific to gifted education and poverty suggest that although 38 states have policies related to the identification and service of economically disadvantaged populations (Coleman & Gallagher, 1995), few states translate these policies into funding structures commensurate with the needs of these students (Patton, Prillaman, & VanTassel-Baska, 1990).

General findings from studies on identification outline two main considerations when identifying disadvantaged students of poverty: (1) begin the identification process earlier in a child's school career and allow for ongoing monitoring and multiple chances to access gifted services (Callahan, 2005; Hodgkinson, 2003); and (2) use nontraditional measures of assessment in conjunction with more traditional measures (Callahan, 2005; Ford & Trotman, 2001; Gallagher, 2006; VanTassel-Baska, Bracken, Feng, & Brown, in press; VanTassel-Baska, Johnson, & Avery, 2002; VanTassel-Baska & Stambaugh, 2008a). Nontraditional classroom assessments include product and performance-based options that allow student choice in sharing the information acquired through drama, art, song, or other modes of expression besides writing. When teachers include a variety of options in the classroom, it encourages student interest and allows the teacher to observe a wider range of abilities for students of poverty (Ford & Trotman, 2001; VanTassel-Baska, 2003).

Performance-based assessments allow opportunities for teachers to view student growth and could serve as an alternative means of identifying promising learners for special programs (Callahan, 2005; Gallagher, 2006). VanTassel-Baska and her colleagues at The College of William and Mary have led several successful curriculum intervention and identification projects focused on students in Title I schools. Project Athena was a language arts-based intervention study focused on alternate identification procedures and innovative interventions for promising learners in Title I schools. Project assessment measures included standardized baseline assessments and performance-based pre- and posttesting to measure gains in literary analysis and persuasive writing. After 3 years of curriculum implementation, significant results were found with students in the treatment group on the performance-based assessments in both literary analysis and persuasive writing (VanTassel-Baska et al., in press).

Similarly, Project Clarion, another Javits-funded grant focused on students in Title I schools, incorporated performance-based assessments matched to specific science curriculum content, advanced concepts, and scientific investigation skills (VanTassel-Baska & Stambaugh, 2008a). Like Project Athena, important and significant gains were detected in all performance-based measured areas as students were exposed to high-powered curriculum. This suggests not only that the assessment should match the curriculum, but that technically adequate, performance-based measures are able to detect significant changes in student growth due to alternate ways of measuring and applying learned content (Gallagher, 2006).

Perhaps the most influential study to date on the identification of disadvantaged gifted students comes from a statewide initiative, Project Star, in South Carolina, led by VanTassel-Baska and her colleagues. The researchers were charged with creating performance-based assessments to identify more minority and students of poverty in the state. Performance-based measures were created and piloted for technical adequacy. The performance-based tasks included a combination of nonverbal, creative, and verbal tasks with preteaching opportunities that modeled the desired behaviors for students who may not have had prior experience or exposure to the thinking skill or task demand. When using these specially designed performance-based measures, approximately 17% more students from minority and low socioeconomic backgrounds were identified as gifted, as compared to more formal measures of identification (VanTassel-Baska et al., 2002). Success of this project has led to statewide policy changes in identification and follow-up case studies of the success of these disadvantaged students served in gifted programs.

INTERVENTIONS FOR PROMISING STUDENTS OF POVERTY

Due to a lack of home and external resources, students of poverty may need scaffolding in order to bridge gaps from informal to formal speech and to have appropriate behaviors and academic conversations modeled for them (Rothstein, 2004; Slocumb & Payne, 2000). Scaffolding of skills in the context of high-powered curriculum is critical to the success of promising students of poverty.

A curriculum intervention program, edited by VanTassel-Baska and Stambaugh (2009), incorporates the concept of scaffolding reading instruction from lower level to higher level thinking skills through the use and deliberate teaching of critical reading strategies. This program, entitled the *Jacob's Ladder Reading Comprehension Program,* has been shown to be successful in Title I schools. A curriculum intervention study using the program was conducted in two rural school districts of poverty in the Midwest. Results from this quasi-experimental study suggest that when compared to students who used only a basal reading series, the students in the treatment group showed statistically significant and important gains in reading comprehension and critical thinking (Stambaugh, 2008). This study also suggests that when students of poverty have exposure to an advanced curriculum through scaffolding, they can achieve at higher levels than expected or provided by the typical on-grade level curriculum.

Empirical data also suggest that mentoring relationships for promising students of poverty and their families are key to successful educational endeavors and access to higher academic endeavors (Olszewski-Kubilius, 2007). Hébert (2002) conducted a qualitative study of three gifted students of poverty and found that a major catalyst was a mentoring relationship with a significant adult who could provide guidance and expertise. Although the role of the significant adult varied in the mentor relationship, guidance counselors who provided care and active involvement were most instrumental in guiding these students toward advanced courses and more rigorous college options (Cross & Burney, 2005).

Students of poverty may not learn the same way as middle-class students (Ewing & Yong, 1993). Many times students of poverty prefer group work to discuss and share ideas instead of working in isolation or memorizing facts they believe to be unnecessary (Webb, 1998). Interdisciplinary units that allow student choice, options for studying various cultural groups, and the incorporation of different perspectives is one way to accommodate these differences (Banks, 1993; Sleeter, 1990; VanTassel-Baska, 2003) and recognize similarities across different groups (Gomez, 1991; VanTassel-Baska, 2003). Moreover, alternative services such as afterschool and extracurricular options that provide mentoring, access to accelerated and rigorous curriculum, and family education have been shown to aid gifted students of poverty in enrolling in advanced academic courses during the school day, attending premier universities after high school, and curbing underachievement (Hébert, 2002; Olszewski-Kubilius, 2007).

Two quasi-experimental studies, one in science and one in language arts, examined the impact of rigorous curriculum on students of poverty in Title I schools. The William and Mary language arts curriculum study focused on the impact of critical thinking and reading comprehension of fourth- through sixth-grade students in Title I schools and found significant differences favoring the experimental group in critical thinking and reading comprehension after 2 years of implementation (VanTassel-Baska et al., in press). In science, there were significant and important gains in the experimental group's level of critical thinking and content acquisition when compared to other students who did not have access to the curriculum (VanTassel-Baska & Stambaugh, 2008b).

In a separate study, the William and Mary science and language arts curriculum models were used with gifted students of poverty or of nonmajority ethnic groups (Swanson, 2006). Similarly, the results of this study showed that experimental students who were exposed to the curriculum models made significant gains in applicable content-based standardized assessments. These studies suggest that rigorous, content-based curriculum can be just as effective with students of poverty as with those who are more financially advantaged.

Other experimental design curriculum intervention studies, funded through the United Stated Department of Education Javits grants in reading and in math (Coleman, Gavin, Johnson, Reis, & Stambaugh, 2008), have shown significant differences in content acquisition of both gifted and nongifted students in Title I schools, favoring the experimental group. Commonalities among many of the curricula employed include the use of metacognition, the inclusion of the family in engaging in student learning, rich content-based instruction, and the incorporation of critical thinking skills in a curriculum or strategy-focused intervention. Professional development also was a critical factor in aiding teachers and families in how best to teach accelerated and advanced content.

FACTORS OF SCHOOL AND HOME

School and teachers have not been viewed as key factors in the talent development process of promising students (Bloom, 1985). Many times educators are unaware of the unique needs of gifted students in general, let alone those promising students who also are of poverty. Lyman and Villani (2002), in a study of faculty members who prepare teachers, asked 408 faculty members about their understanding of students of poverty and how the issue is addressed in their classes. Of that group, 37% felt that a deeper understanding of issues of poverty was important. Less than 13% considered students of poverty when planning lectures. Less than 20% included poverty or diversity as a topic in any of their education courses. The researchers concluded that more must to be done in teacher preparation programs to help educators understand the special needs of students of poverty and how these needs can be addressed.

Faculty members and teachers need to become aware of their own understandings and beliefs regarding students of poverty and incorporate additional opportunities for cross-cultural awareness in teacher education programs (Ford & Harris, 1999). When teachers consider the cultural differences of students, and are trained to do so, there is a greater chance that student performance will be positively affected (Frasier & Passow, 1994). Moreover, in each of the curriculum studies mentioned above, ongoing professional development and monitoring were key components to the success of the interventions.

Finally, regardless of the intervention previously discussed, the role of the family is important in the lives of students of poverty. When families are educated and engaged in the academic goals of their children, they are more likely to support their child's endeavors (Burney & Cross, 2006; Olszewski-Kubilius, 2007). A Javits research grant conducted by Coleman (Coleman et al., 2008) studied science identification protocols for students in Title I schools and learned that a contributing factor to science success was the family. Coleman incorporated science take-home activities and materials and also held family nights to engage and educate the families of students of poverty in the support of science initiatives.

Internal Motivators

There are a few studies that have examined internal motivators for gifted students of poverty, but additional research is needed in this area. VanTassel-Baska, Olszewski-Kubilius, and Kulieke (1994) compared the self-concept and social support networks of advantaged and disadvantaged adolescents and found that disadvantaged students reported lower academic and social self-concepts than did their more advantaged peers. The internal characteristic of resiliency in students of poverty has been found to be developed through external factors such as mentoring relationships, self-efficacy, cultural awareness and linkages (Kitano & Lewis, 2005), and rigorous coursework opportunities (Reis, Colbert, & Hébert, 2005).

Dai, Moon, and Feldhusen (1998, as cited in Burney, 2008) found that achievement motivation of high-ability students may rely solely on these students' personal beliefs about their competence. Likewise, Renzulli (1986) included task commitment in a specific interest area as a key component in his three-ring conception of giftedness, suggesting that high ability alone is not enough, but that internal factors play a part in high performance as well. These studies, while scant, underscore the relationship and importance of internal influences as part of the total picture of support for gifted students of poverty.

New Directions for Working With Gifted Students of Poverty

In summary, the literature suggests the following factors as essential for providing services to promising students of poverty:

- *Access.* Gifted students of poverty need access to: (a) fair and equitable identification measures matched to provided services; (b) high-powered curriculum and instructional strategies; (c) alternative programs such as pre-collegiate opportunities or remediation opportunities that provide students with the necessary scaffolding to compete with other gifted students, regardless of socioeconomic status; and (d) access to societal groups and norms of middle- and upper class value systems.
- *Relationships.* Students of poverty, both gifted and nongifted, place high value on meaningful relationships and require adults as role models in their lives. These relationships include family and student relationships and mentoring relationships among gifted students of poverty and a content expert or guidance counselor that provides exposure to college access and life. In addition, the importance of the role and support mechanisms of the family may be critical to the success of these individuals.
- *Psychological Factors.* The internal factors such as beliefs about one's cognitive abilities, accomplishments, resiliency, task commitment, interest, and efficacy impact student performance just as student performance impacts the students' beliefs. For example, if a student of poverty is provided

access to a program without the appropriate preparedness or relationship opportunities with like peers or a mentor, loss of self-esteem and efficacy may hinder student achievement and cause them to drop out of programs or courses.

Each of these factors influences and is influenced by the other and none can stand alone. The filter of intelligence or potential of students of poverty is impacted by the interplay between program access, psychological factors, and important relationships during critical developmental stages, which then impact the extent to which a student of poverty will become successful in a given field. It is not appropriate for schools to offer high-level courses to students of poverty without support structures in place, just as it is not appropriate to provide self-esteem counseling and mentoring devoid of appropriate placement or access to advanced courses and opportunities. Future researchers should build upon the work accomplished to continue the creation of high-powered curriculum, appropriate and equitable identification protocols, and to understand better how psychological factors influence promising students of poverty. The foundation has been laid but there is much more to be learned and acted upon if these students are to be appropriately served.

REFERENCES

Banks, J. A. (1993). Multicultural education: Development, dimensions, and challenges. *Phi Delta Kappan, 75*, 22–28.

Bill and Melinda Gates Foundation. (2003). *Closing the graduation gap: Toward high schools that prepare all students for college, work, and citizenship.* Seattle, WA: Author.

Bloom, B. S. (1985). *Developing talent in young people.* New York: Ballantine Books.

Burney, V. H. (2008). The constraints of poverty on high achievement. *Journal of Advanced Academics, 31*, 295–321.

Burney, V. H., & Cross, T. L. (2006). Impoverished students with academic promise in rural settings: 10 lessons from Project Aspire. *Gifted Child Today, 29*(2), 14–21.

Callahan, C. (2005). Identifying gifted students from underrepresented populations. *Theory Into Practice, 44*, 98–105.

Coleman, M. R., & Gallagher, J. (1995). State identification policies: Gifted students from special populations. *Roeper Review, 17*, 268–275.

Coleman, M. R., Gavin, K., Johnson, P., Reis, S., & Stambaugh, T. (2008, October). *The subject matters: Content-rich Javits projects and their implications for the field.* Featured panel presentation presented at the annual National Association for Gifted Children conference, Tampa, FL.

Cross, T. L., & Burney, V. H. (2005). High ability, rural, and poor: Lessons from Project Aspire and implications for school counselors. *Journal of Secondary Gifted Education, 16*, 148–156.

Dai, D. Y., Moon, S. M., & Feldhusen, J. F. (1998). Achievement motivation and gifted students: A social cognitive perspective. *Educational Psychologist, 33*(2/3), 45–63.

Donovan, M. S., & Cross, C.T. (Eds.). (2002). *Minority students in special and gifted education.* Washington, DC: National Academy of Sciences.

Ewing, N. J., & Yong, F. L. (1993). Learning style preferences of gifted minority students. *Gifted Education International, 9,* 40–44.

Ford, D. Y. (1995). *A study of achievement and underachievement among gifted, potentially gifted, and average African-American students* (Research Monograph No. 95128). Storrs: University of Connecticut, The National Research Center of the Gifted and Talented.

Ford, D. Y., & Harris, J. J. (1999). *Multicultural gifted education.* New York: Teachers College Press.

Ford, D. Y., & Trotman, M. F. (2001). Teachers of gifted students: Suggested multicultural characteristics and competencies. *Roeper Review, 23,* 235–239.

Frasier, M. M., & Passow, A. H. (1994). *Toward a new paradigm for identifying talent potential* (Research Monograph No. 9412). Storrs: University of Connecticut, The National Research Center on the Gifted and Talented.

Gallagher, J. (2006). How to shoot oneself in the foot with program evaluation. *Roeper Review, 28,* 122–124.

Gamoran, A. (2000). High standards: A strategy for equalizing opportunities to learn? In R. D. Kahlenberg (Ed), *A notion at risk: Preserving public education as an engine for social mobility* (pp. 93–126). New York: Century Foundation.

Gomez, R. A. (1991). *Teaching with a multicultural perspective.* Urbana, IL: ERIC Clearinghouse on Elementary and Early Childhood Education. (ERIC Document Reproduction Service No. ED339548)

Hébert, T. (2002). Educating gifted children from low socioeconomic backgrounds: Creating visions of a hopeful future. *Exceptionality, 10,* 127–138.

Hodgkinson, H. (2003). Leaving too many children behind. In J. VanTassel-Baska & T. Stambaugh (Eds.), *Overlooked gems: A national perspective on low-income promising learners.* Washington, DC: National Association for Gifted Children.

Kitano, M. K., & Lewis, R. B. (2005). Resilience and coping: Implications for gifted children and youth at risk. *Roeper Review, 27,* 200–205.

Luxembourg Income Study. (2000). *Key figures.* Retrieved from http://www.lisproject.org/keyfigures.htm

Lyman, L. L., & Villani, C. J. (2002). The complexity of poverty: A missing component of educational leadership programs. *Journal of School Leadership, 12,* 246–280.

National Center for Education Statistics. (2004). *The nation's report card: Reading highlights 2003.* Washington, DC: Institute of Education Sciences, U.S. Department of Education.

National Center for Educational Statistics. (2005). *Participation in education: Concentration of enrollment by race/ethnicity and poverty.* Retrieved from http://nces.ed.gov/programs/coe/2006/section1/table.asp?tableID=440

Newberg, N. (2006). *The gifted of education: How a tuition guarantee program changed the lives of inner-city youth.* New York: State University of New York Press.

Olszewski-Kubilius, P. (2007). The role of summer programs in developing the talents of gifted students (pp. 13–32). In J. VanTassel-Baska (Ed.), *Serving gifted learners beyond the traditional classroom: A guide to alternative programs and services.* Waco, TX: Prufrock Press.

Patton, J., Prillaman, D., & VanTassel-Baska, J. (1990). A state study on programs and services to the disadvantaged gifted. *Gifted Child Quarterly, 34,* 94–96.

Payne, R. (1995). *A framework: Understanding and working with students and adults from poverty.* Baytown, TX: RFT.

Peterson, J. S. (1999). Gifted through whose cultural lens? An application of the postpositivistic model of inquiry. *Journal for the Education of the Gifted, 22,* 354–383.

Reis, S. M., Colbert, R. D., & Hébert, T. P. (2005). Understanding resilience in diverse, talented students in an urban high school. *Roeper Review, 27,* 110–120.

Renzulli, J. (1986). The three-ring conception of giftedness: A developmental model for creative productivity. In R. J. Sternberg & J. E. Davidson (Eds.), *Conceptions of giftedness* (pp. 53–92). New York: Cambridge University Press.

Renzulli, J., & Park, S. (2000). Gifted dropouts: The who and the why. *Gifted Child Quarterly, 44,* 261–272.

Rothstein, R. (2004). *Even the best schools can't close the race achievement gap.* Washington, DC: Poverty and Race Research Action Council.

Sleeter, C. E. (1990). Staff development for desegregated schooling. *Phi Delta Kappan, 72,* 33–40.

Slocumb, P. D., & Payne, R. K. (2000). *Removing the mask: Giftedness in poverty.* Highlands, TX: aha! Process.

Stambaugh, T. (2008). *The effects of the Jacob's Ladder Reading Comprehension on reading comprehension and critical thinking.* Manuscript submitted for publication.

Swanson, J. (2006). Breaking through assumptions about low-income, minority gifted students. *Gifted Child Quarterly, 50,* 11–24.

U.S. Department of Education, Office of Educational Research and Improvement. (1993). *National excellence: A case for developing America's talent.* Washington, DC: U.S. Government Printing Office.

VanTassel-Baska, J. (2003). *Content-based curriculum for low income and minority gifted learners* (Research Monograph No. 03180). Storrs: University of Connecticut, The National Research Center on Gifted and Talented.

VanTassel-Baska, J., Bracken, B., Feng, A., & Brown, E. (in press). A longitudinal study of low-income minority students in Title I schools. *Journal of the Education of the Gifted.*

VanTassel-Baska, J., Johnson, D., & Avery, L. D. (2002). Using performance tasks in the identification of economically disadvantaged and minority gifted learners: Findings from Project STAR. *Gifted Child Quarterly, 46,* 110–123.

VanTassel-Baska, J., Olszewski-Kubilius, P., & Kulieke, M. (1994). A study of self-concept and social support in advantaged and disadvantaged seventh and eighth grade gifted students. *Roeper Review, 16,* 186–191.

VanTassel-Baska, J., & Stambaugh, T. (2007). *Overlooked gems: A national perspective on low-income promising learners.* Washington, DC: National Association for Gifted Children.

VanTassel-Baska, J., & Stambaugh, T. (2008a). *What works: 20 years of curriculum development and research for advanced learners.* Waco, TX: Prufrock Press.

VanTassel-Baska, J., & Stambaugh, T. (2008b, November). *Project Clarion: Research-based implications and lessons learned from a science Javits project.* Presentation at the annual National Association for Gifted Children conference, Tampa, FL.

VanTassel-Baska, J., & Stambaugh, T. (Eds.). (2009). *Jacob's ladder reading comprehension program.* Waco, TX: Prufrock Press.

Webb, M. (1998). Culture: A view toward the unexplored frontier. In M.E. Dilworth (Ed.), *Being responsive to cultural differences: How teachers learn.* (pp. 61–77). Thousand Oaks, CA: Corwin Press.

CHAPTER 12

PROVIDING GIFTED AND TALENTED EDUCATION TO UNDERREPRESENTED MINORITY YOUTH:

One Legacy of Joyce VanTassel-Baska

by

FRANK
C. WORRELL

For students of color, the issue of out-of-school programs appears to be inextricably linked to issues of ethnic identity and peer group affiliations. Although research has shown that these students' success in life is inextricably linked to pursuing academic activities, it is equally true that they need to develop strong ethnic identities that promote skills of bicultural competence.

—Joyce VanTassel-Baska (2007, p. 242)

INTRODUCTION

It is a truism to note that African American, American Indian, and Latino youth are underrepresented in gifted and talented education (GATE) programs relative to their percentage in the population of school-age children. Increasing the representation of youth from these racial and ethnic backgrounds has been an ongoing issue for researchers (Baldwin, 1985; Ford, 1998; Worrell, 2003) who study GATE programs. If you use *minority* as a keyword in a search alongside the author, *Joyce VanTassel-Baska*, PsycINFO and ERIC databases yield 12 results. Searches of this scholar's name with African American, Hispanic, Latino, American Indian, and Native American as keywords produce even fewer articles. The number of references obtained in these searches is ironic and misleading, as Dr. VanTassel-Baska's work has done more than most to bring gifted and talented education to minority youth for whom these programs have been inaccessible.

In the following pages, I briefly describe the issue of minority representation in GATE programs and the explanations that have been put forward on this topic. Next, I highlight some of the recent work that is focused on increasing the achievement of minority students. Finally, I situate the important and unique contributions of Joyce VanTassel-Baska's scholarship to the issue of underrepresentation. I use African Americans as the primary example in this paper for two reasons. First, there is a considerably larger body of scholarship about African American underachievement than there is about other ethnic groups. Second, I am more familiar with the literature on African Americans. Nonetheless, much of the scholarship in this area also is applicable to other underrepresented minority groups, and citations include studies on Latinos and American Indians wherever applicable.

MINORITY UNDERREPRESENTATION IN GATE AND THE ACHIEVEMENT GAP

As noted above, one way of describing minority underrepresentation in gifted and talented education is based on the assumption that the proportion of students in GATE programs should reflect the proportion of students in the school district they attend or the school-aged population. This interpretation of overrepresentation, which often is used in the literature (e.g., Kitano & DiJiosia, 2002), is exemplified in Ford (1998):

> In 1992, African American students represented 21.1% of the school population but 12% of gifted education—an underrepresentation of 41%. Further, Hispanic American students were underrepresented by 42%, and American Indians were underrepresented by 50%. Conversely, Asian American students were overrepresented by 43% and White students were overrepresented by 17%. (p. 6)

Although not made explicit, the concept of proportional representation also is based on another assumption: that students of all ethnic groups are achieving at the same levels. From this point of view, the underrepresentation of minority students is one of bias or discrimination, and the problem can be remedied by changing identification practices, implementing retention programs for minority students once enrolled, instituting multicultural education, and increasing the cultural competence of teachers and other school personnel (Harris, Brown, Ford, & Richardson, 2004; Harris & Ford, 1999). In other words, we need to provide the training and models for individuals to do the *right* thing.

All of the aforementioned strategies are important for a variety of reasons (e.g., increasing the accuracy and relevance of curricula), and can result in increases in the proportion of minority students that are identified (Kitano & DiJiosia, 2002).

However, these strategies will not make substantial inroads in decreasing under-representation because they are predicated on two incorrect assumptions—that is, that students from different racial and ethnic backgrounds have comparable rates of achievement and that identification procedures are inherently biased. However, the literature and data on the achievement gap are quite clear. Students from the minority groups that are underrepresented in GATE programs are not only doing less well than their overrepresented counterparts on IQ tests, often a key aspect of identification for GATE placement, but they also are performing less well in reading, mathematics, science, and other academic subjects (Lee, 2002; Lopez, Lopez, Suarez-Morales, & Castro, 2005; Powers, 2005; Worrell, 2005), resulting in distributions of achievement scores that are substantially lower than their coun-terparts from kindergarten through college. Thus, to the extent that most gifted and talented program use academic achievement and IQ to determine placement, students from groups with lower scores in both of these areas will be underrep-resented in GATE. Moreover, the lower distribution of scores is one reason why the underrepresentation of these students in GATE programs is mirrored by their overrepresentation in the special education category of mental retardation, for which academic achievement is a major part of the diagnostic criteria (McCray, Webb-Johnson, & Neal, 2003).

Given the different distributions of academic achievement, it may not be possible to increase the representation of minority students in GATE programs without increasing the achievement levels of underrepresented students more gen-erally. However, achieving this goal will not be an easy task because interventions that increase the performance of lower achieving groups often also increase the performance of the higher achieving groups, resulting in no lessening of the gap in achievement (Ceci & Papierno, 2005).

Two of the most common reasons put forward for underrepresentation in GATE include heredity and socioeconomic status (SES). The former is tied to IQ (e.g., Rushton & Jensen, 2005) and its prominence in identification, and the latter is generally cited in relation to the greater percentages of underrepresented minority students living in poverty (Lopez et al., 2005; Marks & Coll, 2007; Wor-rell, 2005), which is correlated with both IQ and academic achievement. Both of these variables are difficult to change. However, there is increasing evidence suggesting that (a) the heritability of IQ varies across SES groups (Turkheimer, Haley, Waldron, D'Onofrio, & Gottesman, 2003), (b) educational opportunities influence IQ (Brody, 1997; Ceci & Williams, 1997; Neisser et al., 1996), and (c) teacher effectiveness has a much larger effect on student achievement than race or SES (Sanders & Horn, 1998; Sanders & Rivers, 1996). These findings suggest that although one cannot ignore the contributions of SES and IQ to the achievement gap, there are probably other variables at work.

PERSPECTIVES ON MINORITY UNDERACHIEVEMENT

Three explanations of underachievement—and concomitantly, underrepresentation—include teacher expectation effects, cultural ecological theory (Ogbu, 1978, 2004; Ogbu & Simons, 1998), and stereotype threat (Aronson, 2002; Aronson & Steele, 2005; Steele, 1997, 2003; Steele & Aronson, 1998). All three perspectives highlight the role that the interaction of minority students' personal and social identities has on their achievement-related behaviors and motivation. Although each of these areas is reviewed separately below, it should become evident that they are intimately related.

Teacher Expectation Effects

The seminal study on teacher expectations, *Pygmalion in the Classroom* (Rosenthal & Jacobson, 1968), catapulted the potential impact of teachers' beliefs on student achievement into national prominence and generated a lively and sometimes acrimonious debate in the educational and psychological literatures. No replication of the study resulted in the substantial effects reported in the original study, and the current consensus is that teacher expectation effects do occur but are generally small (Jussim & Harber, 2005). Of particular importance to this paper, however, is Jussim and Harber's conclusion that "powerful self-fulfilling prophecies may selectively occur among students from stigmatized social groups" (p. 131).

Rhona Weinstein and several colleagues have conducted a substantial amount of research in this area over the past three decades (Brattesani, Weinstein, & Marshall, 1984; Kuklinski & Weinstein, 2001; Weinstein, 2002; Weinstein, Marshall, Sharp, & Botkin, 1987; Weinstein & Middlestadt, 1979). These researchers have reported that children from as early as first grade can distinguish on the basis of teacher behaviors which students are considered high versus low achievers. Children also report that the children who are high achievers are given more opportunities and choice in the classroom whereas low achievers receive more negative feedback and are more often *told* what to do (Weinstein, 2002). Thus, despite their best intentions, some teachers are communicating to some students that they *can* achieve at the same time that they are communicating to other students that they *cannot*. In many cases, these messages are tied to students' minority status, because there are pervasive stereotypes about the low intelligence of certain minority groups (Steele, 1997; Steele & Aronson, 1995).

In a recent study, McKown and Weinstein (2008) quantified the differences in classrooms with low and high levels of differential teacher treatment and estimated that these teacher expectancy effects accounted for differences in year-end achievement of about one third of a standard deviation. Similarly, Perry, Donohue, and Weinstein (2007) showed that first graders in classrooms of teachers who provided more instructional and social-emotional supports had greater gains in mathematics and behavior, as well as more positive views of their academic abilities, after controlling for characteristics of the children upon entry to school.

Although this work was not done with GATE programs in mind, the outcomes speak to setting academic trajectories that can affect whether students are classified at some later date. Based on these findings, Marshall and Weinstein (1984; see also McKown & Weinstein, 2008) proposed several classroom strategies that teachers can use to avoid communicating low expectations, including paying attention to (a) class structure, (b) the types of groupings used, (c) the nature of feedback and evaluation, (d) types of motivational strategies employed, (e) sharing responsibility for learning evaluation with students, and (f) monitoring teacher-student relationships. They argued that considering these variables together increases their impact on student performance.

Cultural Ecological Theory

Cultural ecological theory (CET; Ogbu, 1978, 2004) has been part of the educational literature for at least three decades, and most often is described in terms of and vilified about the "acting White" syndrome (Fordham & Ogbu, 1986). CET postulates that the achievement of minority groups in the U.S. can be understood in terms of the interplay between the larger systemic contexts (i.e., educational policies, rewards for educational accomplishment, and the treatment of minorities in schools) and the group's beliefs about schooling (i.e., instrumental beliefs about schooling, trust in school and the purpose of schooling, and the symbolic relationship of education to loss of minority cultural and linguistic identities; see Ogbu & Simons, 1998).

This interplay takes place in the context of a minority group's history of incorporation into the U.S. and how the group views itself as doing relative to other groups. CET defines minorities not only in numerical terms, but also in terms of being in subordinate positions of power in society, and categorizes minorities in the U.S. into four groups: autonomous minorities, voluntary (or immigrant) minorities, refugees and guest workers, and involuntary (or nonimmigrant) minorities (Ogbu & Simons, 1998). Autonomous minorities in the U.S. are White groups that may be discriminated against on occasion (e.g., Amish, Jews, Mormons), but are not totally subordinated or oppressed and who never reject mainstream America or its institutions.

Voluntary minorities include groups that "willingly moved to the U.S. because they expect better opportunities" (Ogbu & Simons, 1998, p. 164). These groups, which include immigrants from Africa, China, Japan, India, Mexico, and the Caribbean, use their countries of origin as points of comparison. Their lack of personal history with American discrimination, their improved status relative to their situation in their native country, the dual lens (America versus country of origin) through which they view their world, and their belief that they were not forced to be in America make it easier for voluntary minorities to transcend the psychological assaults associated with racism and maltreatment and to embrace the dream of America as the land of opportunity with education as the doorway to that dream. Refugees and migrant workers, who see themselves in America involuntarily but on a temporary basis, adopt a "tourist attitude" (Ogbu & Simons, 1998, p. 165) and also are able to see America as an opportunity, despite the negative things like racism that may come with their time in this country.

Involuntary minorities (i.e., African Americans, American Indians, early Mexican Americans, Native Hawaiians, and Puerto Ricans) "are people who have been conquered, colonized, or enslaved. Unlike immigrant minorities, the nonimmigrants have been made to be a part of the U.S. society permanently *against their will*," and "usually interpret their presence in the United States as forced on them by White people" (Ogbu & Simons, 1998, p. 165). CET postulates that involuntary minority groups' history in the U.S.—ongoing and systemic discrimination against group members in housing, employment, and wages—leads many members of these groups to be ambivalent about being American and to doubt that the American dream of meritocracy will ever apply to them. Thus, for some members of these groups, investing in education is seen as a betrayal of their group heritage because it requires transcending the cultural and language barriers that make them *different* from their oppressors, and some members of involuntary minority groups perceive doing well in school as acting White. Consequently, they downplay the importance of education and engage in behaviors that are incompatible with school success. Again, the implications of this interpretation of academic achievement clearly militate against the probability of being identified for GATE or for accepting the placement even if identified.

Although the notion of acting White has been criticized by several researchers (e.g., Cook & Ludwig, 1998; Irving & Wakefield, 2003), there are only two studies of this phenomenon using students classified as gifted and talented. In 2005, Ford reported on a study of 928 students (912 African American, 46% classified as gifted and talented) in grades 4 to 12 from school districts in Georgia, Illinois, Ohio, and Pennsylvania. Eight percent of the students were enrolled in Advanced Placement classes and 23% were in Honors classes. Ford (2005) asked them (a) how much effort they exerted (low versus high) and (b) if they had heard the phrases "acting White" and "acting Black." Students who responded that they knew either of the two phrases also were asked what the phrase meant.

Ford (2005) reported that 35% of the students classified as gifted reported exerting low effort as opposed to 25% of the students not classified as gifted. Forty percent reported being teased or ridiculed for high achievement, 65% knew someone who had been teased, 86% had heard of acting White, and 81% had heard of acting Black. Acting White was described as being "intelligent" and "achievement oriented"; speaking "standard English"; having "White friends"; and being "uppity" and "stuck-up"; and acting Black was described as being "Ghetto, "dumb," and "stupid"; speaking "non-standard English"; and dressing in "urban gear." These results also are discussed in Ford, Grantham, and Whiting (2008). Putting aside other criticisms of CET, Ford's (2005; Ford et al., 2008) study provides solid evidence for Ogbu's (2004) claims about some high-achieving African American students' ambivalence towards educational achievement.

Stereotype Threat

Steele's (1997, 2003) notion of stereotype threat (ST) is another theory that relates academic achievement to group identity. Steele and Aronson (1995) contended that stereotyping other groups is a common social psychological process, and that there are stereotypes of many groups in society (e.g., women, Asian Americans, old people). They further argued that if these stereotypes are negative, they could lead to decreased performance in the area of the stereotype. With regard to African Americans, the basic hypothesis of ST is that the negative stereotypes of African Americans' intelligence can have an impact on African American students' performance in academic situations where the stereotype is invoked (Steele, 1997; Steele & Aronson, 1998). In 1995, Steele and Aronson randomly assigned White and Black students who were taking a verbal test to one of three conditions. In the diagnostic (threat) condition, participants were told that the test involved "performance on problems requiring reading and *verbal reasoning abilities*" (Steele & Aronson, 1995, p. 799; emphasis added). In the two nondiagnostic (control) conditions, participants were told that the tests would help the researchers understand the "psychological factors involved in verbal problem solving" (p. 299), and reasoning abilities were not mentioned.

The results were stark. African Americans in the diagnostic condition obtained significantly lower scores than Whites in all conditions and African Americans in the nondiagnostic conditions. The priming of ability affected African Americans but not Whites. This finding has been repeated in many studies with medium to large effect sizes, and ST has been shown to depress mathematics scores in females (e.g., Shih, Pittinsky, & Ambady, 1999), academic achievement in individuals from low-SES backgrounds (Croizet & Claire, 1998), and academic achievement in African American and Latino elementary school students (McKown & Weinstein, 2003). Cohen, Steele, and Ross (1999) showed that unbuffered critical feedback about an academic task undermined the task motivation of Black college students and increased their perception of instructor bias, but had no such effects on White students. However, when the criticism was accompanied by comments about the students' capabilities to do the task and the instructor's interest in high standards, Black students' responses matched those of White students.

Extensions of this line of research have yielded further findings with implications for increasing the probability of being identified as gifted for negatively stereotyped minorities. In a meta-analytic review of ST studies, Walton and Cohen (2003) found that ST resulted in a boost in performance—termed *stereotype lift*—in members of the nonstereotyped group. This finding is supported by the absence of stereotype lift in situations where the negative stereotype is absent or invalidated. In other words, when negative stereotypes are made salient, ST depresses performance in the stereotyped group and boosts performance in their nonstereotyped peers. Finally, Walton (2008), in another meta-analytic study, showed that when one removes the effect of ST on the performance of the stereotyped group, the distribution of scores for this group is comparable or slightly higher than the distribution of scores for Whites, suggesting that ST can explain enough variance in the achievement of stereotyped minority groups to result in equal opportunities to be identified for GATE programs on the basis of achievement scores.

Motivation and Academic Achievement

There are many theories of motivation with implications for achievement. One that has particular relevance for minority populations, given the findings based on CET and ST reviewed above, is Dweck's (1999, 2001, 2002) theories of intelligence framework. Dweck has argued that students can adopt either an entity theory of intelligence (i.e., intelligence is a fixed trait that cannot be changed) or an incremental view of intelligence (i.e., intelligence is malleable and can be increased by effort and learning). Students with an entity theory "want to look smart and avoid looking dumb" (Good & Dweck, 2006, p. 40) and thus choose easy tasks that require little effort, whereas students with an incremental view want to improve their competence, and will choose challenging tasks, even when failure is a possibility.

Entity views of intelligence are developed in environments that promote messages about ability being fixed. If acting Black means that one is stupid and dumb (Ford, 2005), and the pervasive stereotype about African Americans in society is one of low intelligence (Steele & Aronson, 1995), it is probable that many African American students will have entity views of intelligence. The low effort toward academic achievement reported by researchers (Ford, 2005; Fordham & Ogbu, 1986), the fear of confirming negative stereotypes that underlies the ST response, and the lack of a sense of belonging in academic environments reported by many marginalized minority students (Walton & Cohen, 2007) all provide support for entity views in these groups of students.

JOYCE VANTASSEL-BASKA'S LEGACY

Given cultural ecological theory, stereotype threat, and entity views of intelligence, what can we do to make a meaningful difference in minority students' academic performance? As previously stated, effective teaching is a better predictor of student achievement than race or SES (Sanders & Horn, 1998; Sanders & Rivers, 1996). The importance of teachers is echoed in Weinstein's (2002) work and the intervention work on ST (Cohen et al., 1999). And, the arena of good teaching is one of VanTassel-Baska's greatest legacies to the field of gifted education. To do justice to this legacy (e.g., Project Star, Project Clarion, Project Athena, the Integrated Curriculum Model) requires far more pages and time than are available to this writer. VanTassel-Baska's work on improving teaching has been based on the assessment/instruction cycle, incorporating extensive curriculum development, evaluation of the curricula developed, professional development with teachers implementing the curricula, assessing teacher practices in the classroom, assessing the curricula's impact on student learning, refining curriculum units, and beginning the cycle all over again. She has developed units ranging from language arts to science and social studies.

In keeping with the theme of this paper, VanTassel-Baska has included a strong focus on bringing gifted and talented education to minority and low-income students. She has worked assiduously on the issue of alternative identification. However, recognizing the limitations of merely identifying students, she has demonstrated that carefully designed and implemented curriculum for the gifted and talented works well with students from underrepresented groups and in Title I schools. VanTassel-Baska has many other legacies, including promoting the use of systematic evaluation of programs, translating research for policy makers, and advocating tirelessly for services for gifted and talented learners.

CONCLUSION

It is not an exaggeration to say that VanTassel-Baska's voice is one of the most potent forces in service of all members of the gifted and talented community, from students to teachers, administrators, and researchers. Her passion, vision, and scholarship put her at the pinnacle of our field, and many of us will have done an excellent job if we could accomplish a fraction of what she has. It is fitting and not surprising that the last paragraph in her most recent article in *Gifted Child Quarterly* (at the time this is being written) begins with the phrase, "More research is needed" (VanTassel-Baska et al., 2008, p. 307). But, it is her passion for those whom we serve that will always be her greatest legacy:

> It is time that we woke up to the realities that talent development will not happen if it is left to chance, to the accident of birth or the serendipity of a caring teacher at a critical point in life. It will only happen if we have the will to work together and the insight to work smarter so that our efforts truly benefit the society and the high-potential individuals within it that we all care so deeply about. (VanTassel-Baska, 2007, p. 256)

REFERENCES

Aronson, J. (2002). Stereotype threat: Contending and coping with unnerving expectations. In J. Aronson (Ed.), *Improving academic achievement: Impact of psychological factors on education* (pp. 279–301). San Francisco: Elsevier Science.

Aronson, J., & Steele, C. M. (2005). Stereotypes and the fragility of academic competence, motivation, and self-concept. In A. J. Elliot & C. S. Dweck (Eds.), *Handbook of competence and motivation* (pp. 436–456). New York: Guilford Press.

Baldwin, A. Y. (1985). Programs for the gifted and talented: Issues concerning minority populations. In F. D. Horowitz & M. O'Brien (Eds.), *The gifted and talented: Developmental perspectives* (pp. 223–249). Washington, DC: American Psychological Association.

Brattesani, K. A., Weinstein, R. S., & Marshall, H. H. (1984). Student perceptions of differential teacher treatment as moderators of teacher expectation effects. *Journal of Educational Psychology, 76,* 236–247.

Brody, N. (1997). Intelligence, schooling, and society. *American Psychologist, 52,* 1046–1050.

Ceci, S. J., & Papierno, P. B. (2005). The rhetoric and reality of gap closing: When the "have-nots" gain but the "haves" gain even more. *American Psychologist, 60,* 149–160.

Ceci, S. J., & Williams, W. M. (1997). Schooling, intelligence, and income. *American Psychologist, 52,* 1051–1058.

Cohen, G. L., Steele, C. M., & Ross, L. D. (1999). The mentor's dilemma: Providing critical feedback across the racial divide. *Personality and Social Psychology Bulletin, 25,* 1302–1318.

Cook, P. J., & Ludwig, J. (1998). The burden of "acting White": Do Black adolescents disparage academic achievement? In C. Jencks & M. Phillips (Eds.), *The Black-White test score gap* (pp. 375–400). Washington, DC: Brookings Institution Press.

Croizet, J., & Claire, T. (1998). Extending the concept of stereotype threat to social class: The intellectual underperformance of students from low socioeconomic backgrounds. *Personality and Social Psychology Bulletin, 24,* 588–594.

Dweck, C. S. (1999). *Self-theories and goals: Their role in motivation, personality, and development.* Philadelphia: Taylor and Francis.

Dweck, C. S. (2001). The development of ability conceptions. In A. Wigfield & J. Eccles (Eds.), *The development of achievement motivation* (pp. 37–60). San Francisco: Academic Press.

Dweck, C. S. (2002). Messages that motivate: How praise molds students' beliefs, motivation, and performance (in surprising ways). In J. Aronson (Ed.), *Improving academic achievement: Impact of psychological factors on education* (pp. 37–60). San Francisco: Academic Press.

Ford, D. Y. (1998). The underrepresentation of minority students in gifted education: Problems and promises in recruitment and retention. *The Journal of Special Education, 32,* 4–14.

Ford, D. Y. (2005, November). *African American students' perceptions of barriers to education: A clarion call to gifted education.* Paper presented at the annual meeting of the National Association for Gifted Children, Louisville, Kentucky.

Ford, D. Y., Grantham, T. C., & Whiting, G. W. (2008). Another look at the achievement gap: Learning from the experiences of gifted Black students. *Urban Education, 43,* 216–239.

Fordham, S., & Ogbu, J. U. (1986). Black students' school success: Coping with the "burden of acting White." *Urban Review, 18,* 176–206.

Good, C., & Dweck, C. S. (2006). A motivational approach to reasoning, resilience, and responsibility. In R. J. Sternberg & R. F. Subotnik (Eds.), *Optimizing student success in school with the other three Rs: Reasoning, resilience, and responsibility* (pp. 39–56). Greenwich, CT: Information Age Publishing.

Harris, J. J., III, Brown, E. L., Ford, D. Y., & Richardson, J. W. (2004). African Americans and multicultural education: A proposed remedy for disproportionate special education placement and underinclusion in gifted education. *Education and Urban Society, 36,* 304–341.

Harris, J. J., III, & Ford, D. Y. (1999). Hope deferred again: Minority students underrepresented in gifted programs. *Education and Urban Society, 31,* 225–237.

Irving, A. A., & Wakefield, W. D. (Chairs). (2003, April). *Cultural identification, resistance, oppositional identity, perceived discrimination, and school achievement: African American and Latino experiences.* Symposium conducted at the annual meeting of the American Educational Research Association, Chicago, IL.

Jussim, L., & Harber, K. D. (2005). Teacher expectations and self-fulfilling prophecies: Knowns and unknowns, resolved and unresolved controversies. *Personality and Social Psychology Review, 9,* 131–155.

Kitano, M. K., & DiJiosia, M. (2002). Are Asian and Pacific Americans overrepresented in programs for the gifted? *Roeper Review, 24,* 76–80.

Kuklinski, M. R., & Weinstein, R. S. (2001). Classroom and developmental differences in a path model of teacher expectancy effects. *Child Development, 72,* 1554–1578.

Lee, J. (2002). Racial and ethnic achievement gap trends: Reversing the progress toward equity? *Educational Researcher, 31,* 3–12.

Lopez, C., Lopez, L., Suarez-Morales, L., & Castro, F. G. (2005). Cultural variation within Hispanic American families. In C. L. Frisby & C. R. Reynolds (Eds.), *Comprehensive handbook of multicultural school psychology* (pp. 234–264). Hoboken, NJ: Wiley.

Marks, A. K., & Coll, C. G. (2007). Psychological and demographic correlates of early academic skill development among American Indian and Alaska Native youth: A growth modeling study. *Developmental Psychology, 43,* 663–674.

Marshall, H. H., & Weinstein, R. S. (1984). Classroom factors affecting students' self-evaluations: An interactional model. *Review of Educational Research, 54,* 301–325.

McCray, A. D., Webb-Johnson, G., & Neal, L. I. (2003). The disproportionality of African Americans in special education: An enduring threat to equality and opportunity. In C. C. Yeakey & R. D. Henderson (Eds.), *Surmounting all odds: Education, opportunity, and society in the new millennium* (Vol. 2; pp. 455–485). Greenwich, CT: Information Age Publishing.

McKown, C., & Weinstein, R. S. (2003). The development and consequences of stereotype consciousness in middle childhood. *Child Development, 74,* 498–515.

McKown, C., & Weinstein, R. S. (2008). Teacher expectations, classroom context, and the achievement gap. *Journal of School Psychology, 46,* 235–261.

Neisser, U., Boodoo, G., Bouchard, T. J., Jr., Boykin, A. W., Brody, N., Ceci, S. J., et al. (1996). Intelligence: Knowns and unknowns. *American Psychologist, 51,* 77–101.

Ogbu, J. U. (1978). *Minority education and caste: The American education system in cross-cultural perspective.* New York: Academic Press.

Ogbu, J. U. (2004). Collective identity and the burden of "acting White" in Black history, community, and education. *The Urban Review, 36,* 1–35.

Ogbu, J. U., & Simons, H. D. (1998). Voluntary and involuntary minorities: A cultural-ecological theory of school performance with some implications for education. *Anthropology and Education Quarterly, 29,* 155–188.

Perry, K. E., Donohue, K. M., & Weinstein, R. S. (2007). Teaching practices and the promotion of achievement and adjustment in first grade. *Journal of School Psychology, 45,* 269–292.

Powers, K. (2005). Promoting school achievement among American Indian students throughout the school years. *Childhood Education, 81,* 338–342.

Rosenthal, R., & Jacobson, L. (1968). *Pygmalion in the classroom: Teacher expectation and pupils' intellectual development.* New York: Holt, Rinehart & Winston.

Rushton, J. P., & Jensen, A. R. (2005). Thirty years of research on race differences in cognitive ability. *Psychology, Public Policy, and Law, 11,* 235–294.

Sanders, W. L., & Horn, S. P. (1998). Research findings from the Tennessee Value-Added Assessment System (TVAAS) database: Implications for educational evaluation and research. *Journal of Personnel Evaluation in Education 12,* 247–256.

Sanders, W. L., & Rivers, J. C. (1996). *Cumulative and residual effects of teachers on future student academic achievement: Research progress report.* Knoxville: University of Tennessee Value-Added Research and Assessment Center.

Shih, M., Pittinsky, T. L., & Ambady, N. (1999). Stereotype susceptibility: Identity salience and shifts in quantitative performance. *Psychological Science, 10,* 80–83.

Steele, C. M. (1997). A threat in the air: How stereotypes shape intellectual identity and performance. *American Psychologist, 52,* 613–629.

Steele, C. M. (2003). Stereotype threat and African-American student achievement. In T. Perry, C. Steele, & A. G. Hilliard, III (Eds.), *Young, gifted, and Black: Promoting high achievement among African-American students* (pp. 109–130). Boston: Beacon Press.

Steele, C. M., & Aronson, J. (1995). Stereotype threat and the intellectual test performance of African Americans. *Journal of Personality and Social Psychology, 69,* 797–811.

Steele, C. M., & Aronson, J. (1998). Stereotype threat and the test performance of academically successful African Americans. In C. Jencks & M. Phillips (Eds.), *The Black-White test score gap* (pp. 401–427). Washington, DC: Brookings Institution.

Turkheimer, E., Haley, A., Waldron, M., D'Onofrio, B., & Gottesman, I. I. (2003). Socioeconomic status modifies heritability of IQ in young children. *Psychological Science, 14,* 623–628.

VanTassel-Baska, J. (Ed.). (2007). *Serving gifted learners beyond the traditional classroom: A guide to programs and services.* Waco, TX: Prufrock.

VanTassel-Baska, J., Feng, A. X., Brown, E., Bracken, B., Stambaugh, T., French, H., et al. (2008). A study of differentiated instructional change over 3 years. *Gifted Child Quarterly, 52,* 297–312.

Walton, G. M. (2008, October). *Latent ability: Evidence that grades and test scores systematically underestimate the intellectual ability of negatively stereotyped students.* Paper presented at the Institute of Personality and Social Research Colloquium, University of California, Berkeley, CA.

Walton, G. M., & Cohen, G. L. (2003). Stereotype lift. *Journal of Experimental Social Psychology, 39,* 456–467.

Walton, G. M., & Cohen, G. L. (2007). A question of belonging: Race, social fit, and achievement. *Journal of Personality and Social Psychology, 92,* 82–96.

Weinstein, R. S. (2002). *Reaching higher: The power of expectations in schooling.* Cambridge, MA: Harvard University Press.

Weinstein, R. S., Marshall, H. H., Sharp, L., & Botkin, M. (1987). Pygmalion and the student: Age and classroom differences in children's awareness of teacher expectations. *Child Development, 58,* 1079–1093.

Weinstein, R. S., & Middlestadt, S. E. (1979). Student perceptions of teacher interactions with male high and low achievers. *Journal of Educational Psychology, 71,* 421–431.

Worrell, F. C. (2003). Why are there so few African Americans in gifted programs? In C. C Yeakey & R. D. Henderson (Eds.), *Surmounting the odds: Education, opportunity, and society in the new millennium* (pp. 423–454). Greenwich, CT: Information Age.

Worrell, F. C. (2005). Cultural variation within American families of African descent. In C. L. Frisby & C. R. Reynolds (Eds.), *Comprehensive handbook of multicultural school psychology* (pp. 137–172). Hoboken, NJ: Wiley.

CHAPTER 13

EXALTING OUR CHILDREN:

The Role of Families in the Achievement of Low-Income African American Gifted Learners

by

JOY
L. DAVIS

Just as gold is an ore with rich possibilities, so too is the presence of culturally diverse gifted students in our midst. They may be difficult to identify as gifted students and even harder to convert through nurturing programs and services into creative producers in our society, but the end result cannot be denied. It is glorious to behold! Such students become the exemplars for their culture and for ours.

—Joyce VanTassel-Baska

More than 20 years ago, Joyce VanTassel-Baska embarked on a course that would later shape much of her work in the field of gifted education. This course of examination and program development would lead to a broader understanding of giftedness within a group of learners that heretofore had been underrepresented, underserved, and overlooked (VanTassel-Baska, Patton, & Prillaman, 1989). VanTassel-Baska's groundbreaking work began with an examination of talent development constructs within the homes and communities of economically disadvantaged and culturally diverse students. Although some of her contemporaries (Baldwin, 1987; Frasier, 1989) empowered the field through recommendations for the development of unique protocols for identifying giftedness among underrepresented populations, VanTassel-Baska (1989) was one of the first to direct our attention to the home environment of these same students. By doing so, her work opened doors to other researchers in gifted education who may have been curious about the most intimate origins of giftedness within these populations, but did not yet venture to design and implement studies to more closely examine the phenomenon of giftedness in economically depressed communities.

In addition to her examination of family influences in the lives of disadvantaged gifted learners, VanTassel-Baska and colleagues at William and Mary published the first national study of programs and services specifically designed to meet the needs of at-risk gifted learners (VanTassel-Baska, Patton, & Prillaman, 1991). This study later became the basis for one of the first federally funded research and demonstration grants focused on designing services for gifted learners at risk because of economic disadvantagement, disabling conditions, and/or being members of cultural minorities traditionally underrepresented in gifted programs.

More recently, Dr. VanTassel-Baska led the initiation of a national conference inviting some of the best minds across the nation to discuss and examine research and contemporary projects and programs related to the holistic development of talent in underrepresented populations. Among these "overlooked gems" are those economically disadvantaged and culturally diverse gifted learners whose needs remain unmet in a very comprehensive way because of lack of information, commitment, and support across varied stakeholders, including educators, policymakers, and in some cases, communities (VanTassel-Baska & Stambaugh, 2007).

THE ROLE OF FAMILIES

In an examination of the literature regarding family involvement and student achievement, there are studies that begin to shed light on the elusive phenomenon of nonmainstream families and the impact of their involvement in the success of their high-achieving children. Although there is much diversity within any single group, and there may be a tendency to overgeneralize, some researchers have found patterns within families of high-risk, high-potential populations that may illuminate why some students are more successful than others.

Talent development studies consistently have mentioned that one person, usually a parent, grandparent, or mentor, can be identified in the life of a successful gifted person to have had the greatest impact on his or her success (Sampson, 2002; Sloane, 1985). When these individuals' lives are examined more closely, there are expressions of encouragement and praise that the child can remember as being of great support to him or her during his or her developmental years (Davis, 2007). Parents of gifted learners, in particular, those who are traditionally underrepresented in gifted programs nationwide, will find that they often may be the child's sole source of praise and encouragement. Educators and other child development practitioners generally agree that parent and family involvement lend crucial support to the success of children in schools (Epstein, 2001). Epstein suggested that it is within the home context that students first begin to express behaviors associated with school achievement and success.

In my own experience as an African American gifted learner from a low-income environment, it was my parents, extended family members, and other adults in the neighborhood who encouraged me to do well in school so that I could have a better life than their generations. Our community always professed to believe that education was a "way out" of current oppressive life in the low-income setting. For generations we also were encouraged to believe that education was one of the most important mechanisms by which our race could be placed on a more equal footing with the dominant culture. With my family's early recognition of my special gifts came the offer of additional support for special programs, emotional support, and constant encouragement. A brief review of research related to family nurturance of giftedness within the African American community is provided here.

BRIEF REVIEW OF THE LITERATURE

In 1983, Clark's seminal study examining low socioeconomic Black students' achievement and underachievement in the family context provided new insight into this complex issue. The researcher concluded that Black parents of achieving students were forthright in their efforts to be involved with their children's school experiences; perceived themselves as having the ability to effectively cope with varied circumstances; held positive achievement orientations; set clear expectations for their children; and had positive parent-child relations. Clark's study was further supported by VanTassel-Baska (1989), who specifically examined low socioeconomic and minority families of gifted students. VanTassel-Baska presented evidence of the home's positive influence on achievement; in particular, the strength of relationships between disadvantaged gifted learners and significant others in their environment.

It was special education researchers who later noted that educational research has been negligent in failing to take on the challenge of studying the "adaptive processes" that African American and other oppressed families have used over time to protect and nurture their children in the midst of challenging circumstances. They specifically noted that:

> The absence of such insight from the literature on families reflects not only the deficit perspective of the research community as a whole, but also the lack of interest in research methodologies that can capture the dynamic, interpersonal aspects of family life. (Harry, Klingner, & Hart, 2005, p. 103)

Family values research provides additional insight into the complex social and psychological composition of African American families and communities. Several values of Black families are delineated across multiple studies spanning almost two decades. Among these values were the importance of religion and spirituality; the importance of the extended family and kinship networks; flexible roles of family members; achievement motivation; and the family's role in teaching self-resiliency in the face of adversity (Billingsley, 1992; Gibbs, 1989; Kitano & Lewis, 2005; Littlejohn-Blake & Darling, 1993; Majoribanks, 1992; McAdoo, 1991; Wilson & Tolson, 1990). Included among these also are studies that examined the influential and supportive role of mothers, grandmothers, fathers, and other family members as they provided the students' encouragement and nurturance toward success in academic endeavors.

In an analysis of data from a national educational longitudinal study, Yan (1999) captured four interactive social capital constructs: (1) parent-teen interactions, (2) parent-school interactions, (3) interactions with other parents, and (4) family norms across European and African American families. Yan borrowed the construct of social capital from earlier research by Coleman (1988), who suggested that social capital refers to social resources that generally are provided by parents and families to supervise, monitor, advise, and provide leadership for youth. The analysis provided evidence that African American parents' social capital in the area of home discussion and school contact were significantly higher than those of European American students' families. In the category of family norms, African American families were found to have higher levels of family rules than White families. After a complete analysis of all data, the researcher reported that despite their disadvantaged status, academically successful Black high school students have higher levels of social capital when compared to successful White students, as well as to their nonsuccessful equally disadvantaged Black peers.

Emergent themes across other studies included substantial parent involvement, support from external caregivers, an emphasis on the importance of education, emphasis on achievement, respect for others, spirituality, self-reliance, coping skills, self-respect, racial pride, and connection with family. Patton and Baytops (1995) recommended that practitioners draw on the strengths of these families to improve relationships between families, communities, and the educational system.

The extended family as a source of social capital has long been noted as valued within the African American community (Davis, 2007; Gibbs, 1989; Hatchett, Cochran, & Jackson, 1991; McAdoo, 1991; Wilson & Tolson, 1990). Four of five cases in an examination of families of high-achieving African American gifted students described the support of extended family members (Davis, 2007). In two cases, aunts were mentioned as support and models of success for students. One aunt was a regular visitor in the home, sharing, supporting, checking up on the student, and providing financial assistance when needed. The student referred to her aunt as "a second mother" and the mother referred to her sister as her "backbone." The student expressed her appreciation for the aunt who was "always there" watching over them, indicating a sense of security provided by the aunt's presence in their lives. Hatchett et al. (1991) also cited this type of financial and psychological support provided by an extended family member.

This distinctive support role of the extended family is clear. In 1990, Wilson and Tolson estimated a 25–85% incidence rate of extended family networks in the African American community. In her study of family influence in the lives of disadvantaged gifted learners, VanTassel-Baska (1989) described the role of the grandmother as significant in the development of youth from these backgrounds. Within the extended family network are persons of diverse classes and achievement levels (Prom-Jackson, Johnson, & Wallace, 1987; Wilson & Tolson, 1990). Baytops (1994) also noted that the African American extended family and the Black church have historically provided substantial support to their students in the educational and socialization processes. Multiple support systems have been shown to be advantageous to culturally diverse, low-income gifted learners within the family context. Such support also has been noted as an important survival mechanism for these learners.

Resiliency as a trait of at-risk high-ability and gifted students emerges in the research as a notable character trait (Floyd, 1996; Fordham, 1988; Kitano & Lewis, 2005; Reis, Colbert, & Hébert, 2005). Fordham (1988) suggested that such character traits first receive nurturing and encouragement within the home environment. In their study of resilience in urban high school students of diverse backgrounds, Reis et al. (2005) concluded that one protective factor contributing to the study participants' resilience in difficult settings was the support of at least one parent. This parent was important in providing at least minimal levels of economic and family support.

The role of at least one supportive adult in the talent development of gifted learners is cited in the research as positive and important to their success (Floyd, 1996; Gagné, 2000; Reis et al., 2005). In an earlier study, research noted that parents' expectations for their students' future success was positively correlated with student achievement scores (Halle, Kurtz-Costes, & Mahoney, 1997). The role of the African American mother as the primary source of affection, aspirations, and assistance with children's educational plans also was noted as important to students' development of resilience, despite adverse circumstances (Shade, 1983, as cited by Floyd, 1996). In addition to the support of mothers and fathers, students have reported the support of an extended family member and a "church family."

In a 4-year ethnographic, naturalistic study of the socialization, beliefs, and practices in a Baptist church and its impact on African American children, Haight (2002) found that the church's involvement with children helped to nurture competencies related to strengthening social, emotional, and intellectual skills. This study examined relationships between children and various church leaders, Sunday school teachers, choir directors, pastors, and youth ministry leaders and cited specific instances of conversations and interactions during which children and adults interacted in ways that lead children to develop their individual strengths. Church leaders are seen as an extension of the supportive family available to its youth. To adults, the children are seen as valued members of the church family as a whole, whose spirit and trusting behaviors are indicative of a higher understanding. It is within the church that children are provided a special nurturance that supports their confidence-building during their developmental years. This study supports similar conclusions found in the earlier work of Billingsley (1992) in his rich examination of the role of the church in the African American community.

According to Bloom (1985), families play a very important role in the realization of promise and potential (as cited in Olszewski-Kubilius, 2002). In his talent development model, Gagné (2000) theorized that families are among a set of environmental catalysts that may exert influence (positive or negative) on the development of specific gifts over time during the talent development process. Nurturance, support, and stimulation of gifts by motivation, developmental processes, and environmental catalysts are critical to the manifestation of talent in Gagné's theory. Among these catalysts noted in Gagné's model are the students' geographic, demographic, and sociological environments as well as parents, family parenting styles, and socioeconomic status.

Home influences on talent development are further described through a discussion of family values and parents' direct role as initiators of instruction in an area of talent development (Sloane, 1985). Interview responses from parents and other family members describe and define how parents of gifted and talented students share their values, work ethic, and modeling of behaviors that eventually lead to success in their children's area of talent. As described in this analysis, parents and family members deliberately and consistently organize their time to ensure maximum productivity and accomplishment of priority goals. The role of parents in early initiation of instruction (either as provider of funds/support, coach, or direct instruction) also is described as critical to full development of student potential.

Recently, Davis (2007) found that family members, in particular, parents, were influential in the success of high-achieving African American gifted learners from low-income environments. Mothers interviewed in this ethnographic study described how they guided and nurtured their children from early childhood into secondary school. In descriptions of their nurturance, the mothers discussed family conversations, the amount of time spent together, family traditions, and emphasis within the household on school achievement and future success. Although the mothers spoke often about rules and family norms, they also shared the important role as the child's motivator and encourager. Students interviewed also very candidly spoke of their parents' support and understanding. One student compared the support to having your own "cheering squad." Three students considered their mother their best friend. One student described the mother as her "idol." When asked for details, one mother shared her sense of responsibility to "exalt" her own son to let him know that he is special and capable of doing well in school and in life.

SYNTHESIS

The research examined reveals thematic concepts that have potential for expanding our understanding of the origins of learning and achievement of African American learners from varied backgrounds. At a time when a deficit perspective of the abilities, personal attributes, and home experiences of economically disadvantaged African American learners was pervasive in the field of gifted education, Joyce VanTassel-Baska was among a select set of pioneers who believed differently about these learners and set out to provide empirical evidence to the field that would enable the development of program services to more fully develop their gifts and talents.

As an educator who has spent more than 20 years in this field, I am deeply indebted to Dr. Joyce VanTassel-Baska's continued leadership and commitment to bring the field's attention back to an issue that has not yet been completely resolved. There is much work yet to do in gifted education, as children awake each day to difficult life settings, children who may have the potential to lead this nation and our world to a new prosperity.

REFERENCES

Baldwin, A. Y. (1987). Undiscovered diamonds: The minority gifted child. *Journal for the Education of the Gifted, 10,* 271–285.

Baytops, J. L. (1994). At-risk African American gifted learners: Enhancing their education. In J. S. Stanfield (Ed.), *Research in social policy* (Vol. 3, pp. 1–32). Greenwich, CT: JAI Press.

Billingsley, A. (1992). *Climbing Jacob's Ladder: The enduring legacy of African-American families.* New York: Simon & Schuster.

Clark, R. (1983). *Family life and school achievement: Why poor Black children succeed or fail.* Chicago: University of Chicago Press.

Coleman, J. (1988). Social capital in the creation of human capital [Supplement]. *American Journal of Sociology, 94,* 95–120.

Davis, J. L. (2007). *An exploration of the impact of family on the achievement of African American gifted learners originating from low-income environments.* Unpublished doctoral dissertation, The College of William and Mary, Williamsburg, VA.

Epstein, J. L. (2001). *School, family, and community partnerships: Preparing educators and improving schools.* Boulder, CO: Westview Press.

Floyd, C. (1996). Achieving despite the odds: A study of resilience among a group of Black high school seniors. *The Journal of Negro Education, 65,* 181–189.

Fordham, S. (1988). Racelessness as a factor in Black students' success: Pragmatic strategy or Pyrrhic victory? *Harvard Educational Review, 58*(1), 54–84.

Frasier, M. F. (1989). Identification of gifted Black students: Developing new perspectives. In J. Maker & S. W. Schiever (Eds.), *Critical issues in gifted education: Volume II* (pp. 213–225). Austin, TX: Pro-Ed.

Gagné, F. (2000). *A differentiated model of giftedness and talent (DMGT).* Retrieved from http://www.curriculumsupport.education.nsw.gov/au/policies/gats/assets/pdf

Gibbs, J. T. (1989). Black American adolescents. In J. T. Gibbs & L. N. Huang (Eds.), *Children of color: Psychological interventions with culturally diverse youth* (pp. 179–223). San Francisco: Jossey-Bass.

Haight, W. L. (2002). *African American children in church: A sociocultural perspective.* New York: Cambridge University Press.

Halle, T. G., Kurtz-Costes, B. E., & Mahoney, J. L. (1997). Family influences on school achievement of low-income African-American children. *Journal of Educational Psychology, 89,* 527–537.

Harry, B., Klingner, J., & Hart J. (2005). African American families under fire: Ethnographic views of family strengths. *Remedial and Special Education, 26,* 101–112.

Hatchett, S. J., Cochran, D. L., & Jackson, J. S. (1991). Family life. In J. S. Jackson (Ed.), *Life in Black America,* (pp. 46–83). Newbury Park, CA: Sage.

Kitano, M. K., & Lewis, R. B. (2005). Resilience and coping: Implications for gifted children and youth at risk. *Roeper Review, 27,* 200–205.

Littlejohn-Blake, S. M., & Darling, C. A. (1993). Understanding the strengths of African American families. *Journal of Black Studies, 23,* 460–471.

Majoribanks, K. (1992). Family capital, children's individual attributes and academic achievement. *The Journal of Psychology, 126,* 529–538.

McAdoo, H. P. (1991). Family values and outcomes for children. *Journal of Negro Education, 60,* 361–365.

Olszewski-Kubilius, P. (2002). A summary of research regarding early entrance to college. *Roeper Review, 24,* 152–158.

Patton, J. M., & Baytops, J. L. (1995). Identifying and transforming the potential of young gifted African Americans: A clarion call for action. In B. Ford, J. M Patton, & F. Obiakor (Eds.), *Effective education of African-American exceptional learners: New perspectives* (pp. 27–67). Austin, TX: Pro-Ed.

Prom-Jackson, S., Johnson, S. T., & Wallace, M. B. (1987). Home environment, talented minority youth, and school achievement. *Journal of Negro Education, 56*(1), 111–121.

Reis, S. M., Colbert, R. D., & Hébert. T. P. (2005). Understanding resilience in diverse, talented students in an urban high school. *Roeper Review, 27,* 110–121.

Sampson, W. A. (2002). *Black student achievement: How much do family and school really matter?* Lanham, MD: Scarecrow Press.

Sloane, K. (1985). Home influences on talent development. In B. Bloom (Ed.), *Developing talent in young people* (pp. 439–476). New York: Ballantine Books.

VanTassel-Baska, J. (1989). The role of the family in the success of disadvantaged gifted learners. In J. VanTassel-Baska & P. Olszewski-Kubilius (Eds.), *Patterns of influence on gifted learners: The home, the self, and the school* (pp. 60–80). New York: Teachers College Press.

VanTassel-Baska, J., Patton, J. M., & Prillaman, D. (1989). Disadvantaged gifted learners at-risk for educational attention. *Focus on Exceptional Children, 22*(3), 1–15.

VanTassel-Baska, J., Patton, J., & Prillaman, D. (1991). *Gifted youth at risk.* Reston, VA: Council for Exceptional Children.

VanTassel-Baska, J., & Stambaugh, T. (2007). *Overlooked gems: A national perspective on low-income promising learners.* Washington, DC: The National Association for Gifted Children.

Wilson, M. N., & Tolson, R. F. (1990). Familial support in the Black community. *Journal of Clinical Child Psychology, 19,* 347–355.

Yan, W. (1999). Successful Black students: The role of parental involvement. *The Journal of Negro Education, 68,* 5–22.

CHAPTER 14

SEARCHING FOR ASYNCHRONY:

A New Perspective on Twice-Exceptional Children

by

LINDA KREGER SILVERMAN

The majority of gifted people have uneven abilities; what matters is how they are taught to use their strengths in the talent development process.

—Joyce VanTassel-Baska

The first time I heard Joyce VanTassel-Baska deliver a keynote address at a National Association for Gifted Children (NAGC) conference, I was enthralled by her amazing mind and her depth of knowledge. I met Lee Baska at the same time and told him that his wife was brilliant. Of course, he already knew that. Everyone who knows Joyce is aware of her brilliance—everyone, that is, except Joyce. Why? Because she's not strong in math or related areas.

Like all asynchronous individuals, Joyce is haunted by what she cannot do well, instead of being filled with awe, like the rest of us are, at what she does brilliantly. This is the plight of individuals who have great disparities between their strengths and weaknesses. Society's deficit-based models of assessment and education, as well as its glorification of the "golden mean," rob too many of their hard-earned sense of pride. It is time to view individual differences through a more uplifting lens.

ASYNCHRONOUS DEVELOPMENT

The construct of asynchronous development is a fundamental principle of *Counseling the Gifted & Talented* (Silverman, 1993), a Keystone Consortium book Joyce talked me into writing. In a short time, asynchrony has become a staple in gifted education, especially in describing twice-exceptional (2e) children (e.g., Singer, 2008). Instead of viewing gifted children as achievers, producers, or potential stars, this definition focuses on the qualitatively different experience of being gifted. Advanced reasoning abilities and heightened intensity are partners in this experience. Asynchrony essentially means uneven development, as well as feeling out-of-sync with age-mates. All gifted children develop unevenly, because their mental growth is at a faster pace than their physical development (Silverman, 1995).

The most asynchronous children are twice-exceptional. They have enormous disparities between their strengths and their weaknesses, and they remain underrepresented in gifted programs (Karnes, Shaunessy, & Bisland, 2004; Morrison & Rizza, 2007; Olenchak & Reis, 2002). "Unevenness tends to be the rule rather than the exception. Thus, many children, due to a deficit in some aspect of development, are excluded from gifted programming—something many of them desperately need" (Little, 2001, p. 46).

Apparently, there is support for the concept of asynchronous development in brain research.

> A major cause of behavior problems in gifted and twice-exceptional students is asynchronous development (AD), or unevenness in the rate at which sensory, emotional, physical, and executive function skills develop. Children experiencing this uneven development have some skills that seem superior and others that lag behind. (Beljan, 2005, p. 1)

Whether twice-exceptional children learn to appreciate their strengths and forgive their weaknesses depends, a great deal, on how they are perceived by others. To find gifted children with learning disabilities, one continuously must search for signs of asynchrony and take their strengths as seriously as their weaknesses.

INCREASING INTEREST IN TWICE-EXCEPTIONAL CHILDREN

Recognition of the potential coexistence of gifts and disabilities has been in the literature from the inception of the field (Hollingworth, 1923). However, very little was written about this intersection of strengths and weaknesses until Maker's book, *Providing Programs for the Gifted Handicapped*, appeared in 1977. A flurry of interest in dual exceptionality appeared in the 1980s, demonstrated by the publication of a succession of books on this topic by Fox, Brody, and Tobin

(1983); Daniels (1983); Dixon (1983); and Whitmore and Maker (1985); as well as dozens of articles in professional journals. Since that time, there has been steady increase in awareness of twice-exceptional learners worldwide. In the last several years, a series of excellent books on this topic have become available, including *Uniquely Gifted* (Kay, 2000), *Different Minds* (Lovecky, 2004), and *The Mislabeled Child* (Eide & Eide, 2006). And, in October 2003, a new publication was born, *2e: Twice-Exceptional Newsletter*.

A great deal also has been written in recent years about the need for special programs for twice-exceptional children (e.g., Weinfeld, Barnes-Robinson, Jeweler, & Shevitz, 2002); characteristics of this group (e.g., Kim & Ko, 2007; Little, 2001; Zentall, Moon, Hall, & Grskovic, 2001); case studies (e.g., Cooper, Ness, & Smith, 2004; hannah & Shore, 2008); the lack of methods of identification in the schools (e.g., Baum, 2008; Cline & Hegeman, 2001; Karnes et al., 2004; Mann, 2005; Neihart, 2008); appropriate instructional modifications (e.g., Jeweler, Barnes-Robinson, Shevitz, & Weinfeld, 2008; Montgomery, 2004; Nielsen, Higgins, Wilkinson, & Webb, 1994; Olenchak & Reis, 2002); compensation strategies (e.g., Reis, McGuire, & Neu, 2000); and curricular interventions (e.g., Baum & Owen, 2003; also see Hughes in this volume). However, specific guidance has not been offered on how to assess this elusive population. As this has been the focus of my work for the last 30 years, the remainder of this chapter will address new methods of assessing twice-exceptional learners.

THE DEMISE OF FULL SCALE IQ SCORES

A continuing concern in identifying twice-exceptional children has been the pervasive use of Full Scale IQ scores to determine program placement (Baum, 2008; Morrison & Rizza, 2007). Joyce has played a significant role in broadening policies for the selection of students for gifted programs. Her recent book, *Alternative Assessments With Gifted and Talented Students* (VanTassel-Baska, 2008), provides expert guidance on the use of traditional and nontraditional measures, such as portfolio, product, and performance-based assessment. In addition, during her NAGC presidency, at the request of Sylvia Rimm, Joyce had the foresight to create a task force to study various interpretations and scoring methods of the Wechsler Intelligence Scale for Children, Fourth Edition (WISC-IV). One purpose of the task force was to design a position statement for NAGC on the effective use of the WISC-IV in identifying the gifted and the second was to discover how best to identify profoundly gifted students. To obtain data on which to base the position statement, a study of the performance of gifted children from various sites on the WISC-IV was conducted.

Data collection on 334 gifted children confirmed that 70% of the group did not qualify for a reporting of the full scale score due to significant discrepancies found among composite scores. The mean variance in index scores for the group was 21 points. The Verbal Comprehension Index (VCI) provided the best estimate of giftedness of these children, followed by the Perceptual Reasoning Index (PRI). Working Memory (WMI) was superior; however, Processing Speed (PSI) was only high average. These scores are similar to those of previous samples of gifted children (Rimm, Gilman, & Silverman, 2008; Silverman, Gilman, & Falk, 2004).

Fortunately, the test publisher had created another method of scoring that enabled far more twice-exceptional children to be identified: the General Ability Index (GAI). As the emphasis on Working Memory and Processing Speed had doubled on the WISC-IV in comparison to earlier versions of the WISC, the Full Scale IQ score failed to capture the true intellectual abilities of a vast number of children. The GAI solved the problem. It ignored Working Memory and Processing Speed, and generated a measure of intelligence based on the child's reasoning abilities, which are best represented by the Verbal Comprehension Index and the Perceptual Reasoning Index. These two indices have the highest loadings on general intelligence (*g*; Rimm et al., 2008). The handbooks used for interpreting the WISC-IV advocate the use of the GAI in place of the Full Scale IQ when it represents the best summary of a student's overall intelligence (Flanagan & Kaufman, 2004; Prifitera, Saklofske, & Weiss, 2005; Weiss, Saklofske, Prifitera, & Holdnack, 2006).

The official Position Statement of NAGC on "The Use of WISC-IV Scores for Gifted Identification," was Board-adopted in November 2007 and posted to the NAGC Web site in January 2008. It clearly focuses on the needs of twice-exceptional learners, as seen from this excerpt (NAGC, 2008):

> Also, for twice exceptional children, the WISC-IV plays an important role in documenting the child's giftedness and learning deficits, as well as revealing the giftedness of children with expressive, physical, or other disabilities. . . . It is recommended practice to derive the General Ability Index (GAI) when there are large disparities among the Composite/ Index scores. . . .
>
> When the WISC-IV is used for the identification of gifted students, either the General Ability Index (GAI), which emphasizes reasoning ability, or the Full Scale IQ Score (FSIQ), should be acceptable for selection to gifted programs. . . .
>
> The Verbal Comprehension Index (VCI) and the Perceptual Reasoning Index (PRI) are also independently appropriate for selection to programs for the gifted, especially for culturally diverse, bilingual, twice exceptional students or visual-spatial learners. It is important that a good match be made between the strengths of the child and the attributes of the program. (para. 1, 4–5)

The NAGC Position Statement represents an important step forward for twice-exceptional children. If it is heeded by school psychologists, it will provide an opportunity for more 2e students to gain access to gifted programs—access that was formerly denied.

Profoundly Gifted Children With Learning Disabilities

An even more startling breakthrough occurred in the testing industry. The data from the NAGC Task Force Study were submitted to the publisher as a basis for higher ceilings. The test constructors were totally unaware that children this bright actually existed; it opened their eyes to the need for extended norms. They worked for months to create a table of extended norms for highly, exceptionally, and profoundly gifted children. Their results were included in *WISC-IV Technical Report #7* (Zhu, Cayton, Weiss, & Gabel, 2008).

For the first time in the history of the Wechsler scales, raw score points beyond 19 can be counted in the IQ scores, and composite scores beyond 160 are now possible. The maximum Verbal Comprehension (VCI) and Perceptual Reasoning (PRI) composite scores were originally 155, the maximum Working Memory (WMI) and Processing Speed (PSI) composites were 150, and the maximum Full Scale IQ score (FSIQ) was 160. Now, scores can be generated as high as 210. The maximum subtest scaled score was raised from 19 to 28. Subtest scores of 18 or 19 may qualify for extended norms.

These extended norms allow the full strength of the discrepancies of profoundly gifted twice-exceptional learners to be documented. One child attained an incredible 35 points beyond the subtest ceilings of the WISC-IV; however, her eye-hand coordination was in the low average range:

Subtest	Scaled Score	Extended Norms
Similarities	19 + 8	24
Vocabulary	19 + 19	28
Comprehension	19 + 3	22
Matrix Reasoning	19 + 3	23
Digit Span	19 + 2	21
Picture Concepts	18	19
Coding	7	

As the extended norms are deviation IQ scores, on the same metric as all other WISC-IV scores, meaningful comparisons can be made between her strengths and her weaknesses. Her vocabulary, at the highest level of the extended norms (28), is a conservative estimate, because her raw score was 19 points beyond the ceiling. The discrepancy between her Vocabulary score of 28 and her Coding score (eye-hand coordination and speed) is 21 points—*seven standard deviations*! The extended norms clearly demonstrate how difficult it is for hands to keep up with minds.

The NAGC Position Statement and the Extended Norms were the immediate outcome of the work, but the NAGC study also opened doors for ongoing communication between NAGC and the National Association of School Psychologists (NASP), as well as with IQ test constructors.

What Place Do IQ Tests Have?

Comprehensive individual assessment of twice-exceptional children is needed to determine both their strengths (giftedness) and their weaknesses (disabilities); it becomes a basis for programming. In *Counseling the Gifted & Talented,* Joyce and Lee wrote an excellent chapter describing how to turn IQ and achievement test scores into Individual Instructional Plans (VanTassel-Baska & Baska, 1993). Individual IQ tests provide a more defensible basis for high-stakes decision making than group tests or teacher observations (Rimm et al., 2008). However, many advocates of the gifted vehemently oppose IQ testing.

> Common criticisms of testing and popular antitest reactions are often directed at the misuses of tests in the hands of inadequately qualified users. These misuses stem from a desire for quick answers and simple solutions to complex, real-life problems, and *too often the decision-making responsibility is shifted to the test when this is only a tool to be used judiciously.* (VanTassel-Baska & Baska, 1993, p. 193; italics added)

Uninformed users often allow test scores to negate their own experience and judgment.

The medical community relies on various types of tests to detect illnesses that might otherwise never have been discovered and treated in time. But, good doctors realize that tests are only part of the information that they have access to for diagnoses. They take family histories. They ask if these symptoms ever appeared in the past (not just in the last 3 years). They are aware that most tests are designed to guard against false positives, and that they are very likely to produce false negatives. For example, if a child has a seizure in the doctor's office, but the EEG reveals no seizure activity, does the doctor believe the EEG over her own experience? The doctor's experience and knowledge is informed by the test results, but test results do not override clinical judgment. Clinical judgment is just as important in psychological testing.

There is no perfect method of finding gifted children that locates all of them. Just like medical tests, IQ tests guard against false positives at the expense of false negatives. This means that many people are much smarter than their IQ scores. Does this render IQ tests useless? No. EEGs miss a lot of folks with seizure disorder, but when the EEG does detect it, you can count on it being real. IQ tests detect giftedness that may not be apparent in the classroom. It is impossible to fake abstract reasoning. However, because they miss many truly gifted children, alternative methods of assessment are needed (Feng & VanTassel-Baska, 2008).

In the current school climate, IQ testing has come under question. This severely compromises the identification of twice-exceptional learners. By the magnitude of their discrepancies shall they be known, but the educational community has turned a blind eye to discrepancies. Under Response to Intervention (RTI), if a child does not profit from regular classroom instruction, a method of intervention that is empirically based should be tried. Children who "succeed" in regular classroom instruction or through an intervention are not recognized as disabled. Success is measured by the ability to perform at the average level—the golden mean. Many schools have adopted the philosophy that they are only responsible for bringing children up to grade-level expectations, not beyond. How, then, can twice-exceptional children ever hope to reach their potential?

An Intrapersonal Model of Assessment for the Twice-Exceptional

Normative testing is the norm in all fields. Diagnosticians in audiology, optometry, speech and language therapy, occupational therapy, and psychology are all trained to ask the same question: "How does this child's performance compare to the norms?" If the child's scores fall within the norms, no difficulty is detected. The child's performance is "adequate." Perhaps it is adequate if the child is similar to the norm sample, but if the child is twice-exceptional, "adequate" may be quite inadequate.

The search for asynchrony requires that diagnosticians, educators, and parents ask an entirely different question: "To what extent does the discrepancy between this child's strengths and weaknesses cause frustration and interfere with the full development of the child's abilities?" This is an intrapersonal rather than normative view of test interpretation; it recognizes the uniqueness of each child and the importance of diagnosing the degree of asynchrony in the child's profile. When gifts and disabilities coexist, their interaction makes it difficult to detect either. The examiner must search for signs of giftedness and recognize how these mask disabilities. This attitude is imperative in order to locate gifted children with learning disabilities and support them.

To truly understand a twice-exceptional child, it is necessary to separate the high scores from the low scores. Scores in the superior range or above document the child's giftedness; scores three standard deviations lower document the disabilities—even if they are in the average range (Silverman, 1989). When high and low scores are averaged together to create composite scores, the strengths and weaknesses may cancel each other out, leaving the impression that the child is average.

If the child's weaknesses become apparent, the focus of instruction cannot be on simply remediating the deficits (Baum, 2008; Olenchak & Reis, 2002). Strengths need to be mobilized to help children overcome limitations. If the child's giftedness is developed, motivation will be fostered to succeed in spite of weaknesses; but if all the attention is placed on disabilities, a gifted child will quickly become disheartened (Renzulli, 2008).

Compensation also plays a role in disguising real needs. Gifted children can compensate for weaknesses by virtue of their abstract reasoning abilities. This may allow them to get by or to pass a course without anyone realizing that they are struggling. But, compensation cannot be counted on; it is vulnerable to fatigue, illness, discouragement, dieting (lack of proper nutrition), stress, age, new situations, and injury. It prevents accurate diagnoses of disabilities, as the child may use reasoning ability instead of modality strength during a visual or auditory examination, guessing correctly with only partial information. This masks the degree of the disability, sometimes bringing the child's scores up to the "adequate" range.

Some twice-exceptional children spend four times as long doing their homework because reading is so fatiguing and writing is painful. Their struggle is not acknowledged if the school's only concern is that they keep up with the others. As the demands of school become harder, their ability to compensate weakens, as does their motivation to succeed. Unless we recognize the existence of twice-exceptional children, assess their difficulties, develop their gifts, and provide accommodations to support them, we will soon see an alarming increase in the number of 2e students at-risk for delinquency, dropping out of school, or worse.

INTERPRETING THE WISC-IV FOR TWICE-EXCEPTIONAL CHILDREN

The Wechsler Intelligence Scale for Children, Fourth Edition (WISC-IV) is an excellent diagnostic tool for discovering gifts, learning disabilities, and their combination. It is important to understand the value of each of the subtests in determining giftedness and in detecting disabilities. High intelligence is revealed in those subtests with the richest g-loadings. Because Spearman's g is synonymous with abstract reasoning, and giftedness is advanced abstract reasoning, g could as easily stand for *giftedness* as for *general intelligence* (Silverman, in press). On the WISC-IV, Vocabulary (.82), Similarities (.79), and Comprehension (.70) have the highest g-loadings of all the core subtests (Flanagan & Kaufman, 2004). They make up the Verbal Comprehension Index (VCI). This makes the VCI an excellent predictor of success in a gifted program.

Many twice-exceptional children have higher scores in perceptual reasoning than in verbal reasoning (Bireley, 1991; Morrison & Rizza, 2007). They excel in visual-spatial abilities. The core subtests that make up the Perceptual Reasoning Index (PRI) are fair measures of g: Matrix Reasoning (.68), Block Design (.67), and Picture Concepts (.57). Children with high PRI scores and lower VCI scores may need more accommodations in the gifted program in order to succeed. They profit from visuals, hands-on activities, and opportunities to demonstrate knowledge in ways other than essay writing (e.g., PowerPoint presentations, poetry, photographic essays; Silverman, 2002).

Children with high GAI scores (the combination of VCI and PRI) are excellent candidates for gifted programs. They have facility with both left- and right-hemispheric abilities. Working Memory and Digit Span do not correlate well with giftedness; however, they are very useful in diagnosing learning disabilities. The two core subtests in the Working Memory Index, Letter-Number Sequencing (.60) and Digit Span (.51), have lower *g*-loadings than all of the subtests that make up the GAI. Twice-exceptional students may have difficulty with rote memorization, while excelling in abstract reasoning. They need to be educated at the level of their abstract reasoning, not their working memory.

Two subtest substitutions are allowed in the calculation of the Full Scale IQ. At the Gifted Development Center, we usually substitute Arithmetic (.74) for Letter-Number Sequencing (.60), unless the child hates mental math problems (Rimm et al., 2008). Arithmetic is a meaningful memory task, suggests mathematical talent, has the fourth highest *g*-loading, and was the second highest subtest for the gifted group in the *WISC-IV Technical Manual*. Alternatively, Flanagan (2005) recommends that Arithmetic be substituted for Digit Span (.51), which has a lower *g*-loading. This substitution can make a decided difference. One child missed the cut-off score for his district's gifted program by one point when the two core subtests, Digit Span and Letter-Number Sequencing, were employed in the calculation of his Full Scale IQ. The substitution of Arithmetic for Digit Span brought his Working Memory score from 120 to 129, and he qualified for the program.

Processing Speed subtests are the least useful for selecting students for gifted programs, and they may or may not assist diagnosis of disabilities in the gifted. One of the core subtests, Symbol Search (.58), is a fair measure of *g*, according to Flanagan and Kaufman (2004); however, Coding (.48) is considered a poor measure of *g*. The poorest indicator of *g*, Cancellation (.25), also is in the Processing Speed section.

Gifted children, even those without disabilities, are not fast processors (Kaufman, 1992; Reams, Chamrad, & Robinson, 1990). The gifted norm sample (*N* = 63) described in the *WISC-IV Technical Manual* (Wechsler, 2003) attained a mean score of 110.6 in Processing Speed. The mean score in Processing Speed for the Gifted Development Center sample (*N* = 103) was 104.3 (Silverman et al., 2004). Wasserman (2006) reports that more than 70% of the students applying for gifted placement have Processing Speed Index scores in the average range or below.

Given how low Processing Speed scores are for gifted children in general, it is absurd to allow these scores to disqualify qualified children for placement in gifted programs. Because Processing Speed is counted in the Full Scale IQ scores, Full Scale IQ scores may be a poor reflection of the abstract reasoning abilities of the student. The fluency (processing speed) sections of the Woodcock-Johnson–III Tests of Achievement suffer from the same defect and compromise Broad Reading, Broad Math, and Broad Language scores.

QUALITATIVE ASPECTS OF QUANTITATIVE ASSESSMENT

Individual IQ tests permit the skilled examiner to observe behaviors indicative of giftedness or learning disabilities. An elaborative thought process, an unusual perspective, precision, and imagination all can be noted as signs of giftedness. Children who frequently ask to have auditory items repeated, talk their way through visual items, can complete timed tasks perfectly after the time has lapsed, fail to recognize when a block has been placed in the right place, arrange the blocks at an angle, skip lines in Symbol Search, lose their place in Coding, consistently reverse numbers in Digit Span, rotate images in Matrix Reasoning, or respond impulsively on Picture Concepts, are demonstrating weaknesses, regardless of their scores.

Good diagnosticians put test scores in perspective. They look for patterns. They understand what is typical for gifted children and what may be a red flag. They review all the prior testing to see how the child has performed over time. Test scores for 2e children tend to be very erratic, so all prior tests must be taken into consideration (Silverman, 2003). They ask questions about the child's development and the family history. They listen to the child's use of language. They are talent scouts, always on the lookout for indicators that the child may be smarter than the scores presented. They are not just technicians trusting that the test scores tell the whole story.

A particular quality of the twice-exceptional learner is succeeding on more difficult items, while failing easier items (Silverman, 2002). Tests were not constructed with these children in mind. When average children fail three consecutive items in a subtest, they are usually unable to pass more difficult items. The test is stopped at that point to prevent frustration. However, twice-exceptional children have a longer attention span, and they often pass items beyond the discontinue criterion. More flexible use of discontinue criteria need to be employed when testing twice-exceptional learners.

We also have found that many gifted and 2e children, particularly those over age 10, pass items at the very highest level, but miss sufficient items along the way to depress their scores. Therefore, in our reports, we note the number of subtests in which the child did not reach the discontinue criterion. This suggests that the score is an underestimate, even if it is not particularly high. Children who miss easy items but pass harder ones rarely qualify for extended norms on the WISC-IV. Considerably more difficult items will need to be generated to capture their strengths on standardized tests.

CONCLUSION

To recognize giftedness in twice-exceptional children, we must always be on the lookout for strengths and take them seriously when they appear. Strengths give us a window into the child's abilities. This is the lens through which we should look at any child, but it is imperative in discovering gifted children with learning disabilities. The child's giftedness is documented by subtest scores in the superior range, high achievement scores in any area, or outstanding performance; disabilities are detected by analyzing the weakest subtest scores in relation to the strongest, as well as noting areas of struggle. The greater the discrepancies between strengths and weaknesses, the greater the frustration that the child experiences. Any demonstration of superior abilities should be recognized as a sign of giftedness and developed to the fullest extent possible, even if the child is less advanced in other areas. Joyce's work on alternative assessments confirms this.

Twice-exceptional learners who are perceived by others to be in constant need of remediation come to view themselves with shame and doubt. They are unable to value their gifts when the significant others in their lives are overly concerned with fixing them. They become victims of their disabilities. But, when those closest to them honor their strengths and believe in their ability to fulfill their dreams, they are able to mobilize their will to succeed against all odds. With the right support, they can become our most creative, productive innovators. Like Joyce, they become people who change the world.

REFERENCES

Baum, S. (2008). Bumps along the road. In M. W. Gosfield (Ed.), *Expert approaches to support gifted learners: Professional perspectives, best practices, and positive solutions* (pp. 199–204). Minneapolis, MN: Free Spirit.

Baum, S., & Owen, S. (2003). *To be gifted and learning disabled: Strategies for helping bright students with LD, ADHD, and more.* Mansfield Center, CT: Creative Learning Press.

Beljan, P. (2005). Behavioral management of gifted children: A neuropsychological approach. *2e Twice-Exceptional Newsletter, 2*(9), pp. 1, 16–18.

Bireley, M. (1991). The paradoxical needs of the disabled gifted. In M. Bireley & J. Genshaft (Eds.), *Understanding the gifted adolescent: Identification, developmental, and multicultural issues* (pp. 163–175). New York: Teachers College Press.

Cline, S., & Hegeman, K. (2001). Gifted children with disabilities. *Gifted Child Today, 24*(3), 16–24.

Cooper, E. E., Ness, M., & Smith, M. (2004). A case study of a child with dyslexia and spatial-temporal gifts. *Gifted Child Quarterly, 48,* 83–94.

Daniels, P. R. (1983). *Teaching the gifted/learning disabled child.* Rockville, MD: Aspen.

Dixon, J. P. (1983). *The spatial child.* Springfield, IL: Charles C. Thomas.

Eide, B., & Eide, F. (2006). *The mislabeled child.* New York: Hyperion.

Feng, A. X., & VanTassel-Baska, J. (2008). Identifying low-income and minority students for gifted programs: Academic and affective impact on performance-based assessment. In J. VanTassel-Baska (Ed.), *Alternative assessments with gifted and talented students* (pp. 129–146). Waco, TX: Prufrock Press.

Flanagan, D. P. (2005, August). *Use of the WISC-IV in the assessment of giftedness.* Paper presented at the meeting of the World Council for Gifted Children, New Orleans, LA.

Flanagan, D. P., & Kaufman, A. S. (2004). *Essentials of WISC-IV assessment.* Hoboken, NJ: John Wiley.

Fox, L. J., Brody, L., & Tobin, D. (Eds.). (1983). *Learning-disabled gifted children: Identification and programming.* Baltimore: University Park Press.

hannah, C. L., & Shore, B. M. (2008). Twice-exceptional students' use of metacognitive skills on a comprehension monitoring task. *Gifted Child Quarterly, 52,* 3–18.

Hollingworth, L. S. (1923). *Special talents and defects: Their significance for education.* New York: Macmillan.

Jeweler, S., Barnes-Robinson, L., Shevitz, B. R., & Weinfeld, R. (2008). A teaching tool for twice-exceptional students. *Gifted Child Today, 31*(2), 40–46.

Karnes, F. A., Shaunessy, E., & Bisland, A. (2004). Gifted students with disabilities: Are we finding them? *Gifted Child Today, 27*(4), 16–21.

Kaufman, A. S. (1992). Evaluation of the WISC-III and WPPSI-R for gifted children. *Roeper Review, 14,* 154–158.

Kay, K. (Ed.). (2000). *Uniquely gifted: Identifying and meeting the needs of the twice-exceptional student.* Gilsum, NH: Avocus.

Kim, J.-Y., & Ko, Y.-G. (2007). If gifted/learning disabled students have wisdom, they have all things! *Roeper Review, 29,* 249–258.

Little, C. (2001). A closer look at gifted children with disabilities. *Gifted Child Today, 24*(3), 46–53, 64.

Lovecky, D. V. (2004). *Different minds: Gifted children with AD/HD, Asperger Syndrome, and other learning deficits.* London: Jessica Kingsley.

Maker, C. J. (1977). *Providing programs for the gifted handicapped.* Reston, VA: Council for Exceptional Children.

Mann, R. L. (2005). Gifted students with spatial strengths and sequential weaknesses: An overlooked and underidentified population. *Roeper Review, 27,* 91–96.

Montgomery, D. (2004). Double exceptionality: Gifted children with special educational needs and what ordinary schools can do. *Gifted and Talented International, 19*(1), 29–35.

Morrison, W. F., & Rizza, M. G. (2007). Creating a toolkit for identifying twice-exceptional students. *Journal for the Education of the Gifted, 31,* 57–76.

National Association for Gifted Children. (2008). *Use of the WISC-IV for gifted identification.* Retrieved from http://www.nagc.org/index.aspx?id=375

Neihart, M. (2008). Identifying and providing services to twice exceptional children. In S. I. Pfeiffer (Ed.), *Handbook of giftedness in children: Psycho-educational theory, research, and best practices* (pp. 115–137). New York: Springer.

Nielsen, M. E., Higgins, L. D., Wilkinson, S. C., & Webb, K. W. (1994). Helping twice-exceptional students to succeed in high school. *Journal of Secondary Gifted Education, 5*(3), 35–39.

Olenchak, F. R., & Reis, S. M. (2002). Gifted children with learning disabilities. In M. Neihart, S. M. Reis, N. M. Robinson, & S. M. Moon (Eds.), *The social and emotional development of gifted children: What do we know?* (pp. 177–191). Waco, TX: Prufrock Press.

Prifitera, A., Saklofske, D. H., & Weiss, L. G. (Eds.). (2005). *WISC-IV clinical use and interpretation: Scientist-practitioner perspectives.* Burlington, MA: Elsevier Academic Press.

Reams, R., Chamrad, D., & Robinson, N. M. (1990). The race is not necessarily to the swift: Validity of the WISC-R bonus points for speed. *Gifted Child Quarterly, 34,* 108–110.

Reis, S. M., McGuire, J. M., & Neu, T. W. (2000). Compensation strategies used by high-ability students with learning disabilities who succeed in college. *Gifted Child Quarterly, 44,* 123–134.

Renzulli, S. (2008). The irony of "twice exceptional." In M. W. Gosfield (Ed.), *Expert approaches to support gifted learners: Professional perspectives, best practices, and positive solutions* (pp. 205–208). Minneapolis, MN: Free Spirit.

Rimm, S., Gilman, B. J., & Silverman, L. K. (2008). Non-traditional applications of traditional testing. In J. VanTassel-Baska (Ed.), *Alternative assessments with gifted and talented students* (pp. 175–202). Waco, TX: Prufrock Press.

Silverman, L. K. (1989). Invisible gifts, invisible handicaps. *Roeper Review, 12*(1), 37–42.

Silverman, L. K. (Ed.). (1993). *Counseling the gifted & talented.* Denver, CO: Love.

Silverman, L. K. (1995). The universal experience of being out-of-sync. In L. K. Silverman (Ed.), *Advanced development: A collection of works on giftedness in adults* (pp. 1–12). Denver, CO: Institute for the Study of Advanced Development.

Silverman, L. K. (2002). *Upside-down brilliance: The visual-spatial learner.* Denver, CO: DeLeon.

Silverman, L. K. (2003). Gifted children with learning disabilities. In N. Colangelo & G. Davis (Eds.), *Handbook of gifted education* (3rd ed., pp. 553–543). Boston: Allyn & Bacon.

Silverman, L. K. (in press). The measurement of giftedness. In L. Shavinina (Ed.), *The international handbook on giftedness.* Amsterdam: Springer Science.

Silverman, L. K., Gilman, B. J., & Falk, R. F. (2004, November). *Who are the gifted using the new WISC-IV?* Paper presented at the meeting of the National Association for Gifted Children, Salt Lake City, UT.

Singer, L. (2008). Twice exceptionality: Life in the asynchronous lane. In K. Kay, D. Robson, & J. F. Brenneman (Eds.), *High IQ kids; Collected insights, information, and personal stories from the experts* (pp. 71–74). Minneapolis, MN: Free Spirit.

VanTassel-Baska, J. (Ed.). (2008). *Alternative assessments with gifted and talented students.* Waco, TX: Prufrock Press.

VanTassel-Baska, J., & Baska, L. (1993). The role of educational personnel in counseling the gifted. In L. Silverman (Ed.), *Counseling the gifted & talented* (pp. 181–200). Denver, CO: Love.

Wasserman, J. (2006). *Tips for parents: Intellectual assessment of exceptionally and profoundly gifted children.* Retrieved from http://www.gt-cybersource.org/Record.aspx?NavID=2_0&rid=14107

Wechsler, D. (2003). *The WISC-IV technical and interpretive manual.* San Antonio, TX: The Psychological Corporation.

Weinfeld, R., Barnes-Robinson, L., Jeweler, S., & Shevitz, B. (2002). Academic programs for gifted and talented/learning disabled students. *Roeper Review, 24,* 226–233.

Weiss, L. G., Saklofske, D. H., Prifitera, A., & Holdnack, J. A. (2006). *WISC-IV advanced clinical interpretation.* Burlington, MA: Elsevier Academic Press.

Whitmore, J. R., & Maker, C. J. (1985). *Intellectual giftedness in disabled persons.* Rockville, MD: Aspen.

Zentall, S. S., Moon, S. S., Hall, A. M., & Grskovic, J. A. (2001). Learning and motivational characteristics of boys with AD/HD and/or giftedness. *Exceptional Children, 67,* 499–519.

Zhu, J., Cayton, T., Weiss, L., & Gabel, A. (2008). *Wechsler Intelligence Scale for Children–Fourth Edition: Technical report #7.* Upper Saddle River, NJ: Pearson Education.

CHAPTER 15

JANUSIAN GIFTED:

Twice-Exceptional Children and Two Worlds

by

CLAIRE
E. HUGHES

Twice-exceptional students have the ability to change the world but first they must break through their own limitations to find their strengths.

—Joyce Van Tassel-Baska

One of the first words I had to look up when I met Dr. Joyce Van Tassel-Baska was the word *Janusian* that she used in a conversation, meaning "In a manner to that of the god Janus—or looking in two directions at once." It was but the first of many times I had to use a dictionary when talking to Joyce. Her vocabulary is immense, and her use of explicit words to accurately define exact connotations of language is unparalleled. A master of language, Joyce selects her words to capture precisely the inferences to be made. Her use of that one word—Janusian—captured my imagination and gave an image to the conundrum apparent when working with gifted children with disabilities.

A JANUSIAN GRADUATE EXPERIENCE

I selected The College of William and Mary to attend my doctoral program with Joyce precisely because of her work with gifted children from diverse backgrounds. Joyce had several Javits grants funded at the time in the areas of language arts and science curriculum, and I would have the opportunity not only to extend my knowledge of gifted education and special education, but also address the practical issues related to my experiences as a teacher. I was driven by the question of "What do you do with twice-exceptional students on a day-to-day basis?"—a passion shared by Joyce for providing teachers with direct tools for use in classrooms.

Although Joyce is well-known for her work in curriculum (VanTassel-Baska, 2003) and program effectiveness (VanTassel-Baska, Avery, Little, & Hughes, 2000), it is important for others to know that her passion for practical teacher-based interventions is for the express purpose of meeting the needs of those students who have potential, but are constrained by other factors such as poverty or cultural differences—or disabilities. She has made significant inroads in the development and awareness of the needs of gifted students from poverty and diverse backgrounds (VanTassel-Baska, 2008; VanTassel-Baska & Stambaugh, 2007). Her publishing record is truly stunning, in many areas of education, but it is my honor to share how her work has far-reaching implications for the development of appropriate interventions for twice-exceptional children.

In this chapter, the term *twice-exceptional* will refer not to a given definition of either giftedness or disability, but to children who "exhibit remarkable strengths in some areas and disabling weaknesses in others" (Hughes, in press; Weinfeld, Barnes-Robinson, Jeweler, & Shevitz, 2002, p. 226). This article will particularly focus on the effects of Joyce's work on those children who exhibit learning and social difficulties, rather than physical or sensory impairments, primarily because they constitute the largest population of twice-exceptional students (National Education Association [NEA], 2006). There is a well-established body of research on gifted children with learning disabilities (Brody & Mills, 1997) and a growing body of literature focusing on gifted children with autism and Asperger's syndrome (Cash, 1999; Kalbfleisch & Iguchi, 2008).

JANUSIAN IDENTIFICATION: STRENGTHS WITHOUT WEAKNESSES

Perhaps the most significant issue in identifying twice-exceptional children is the very ability to identify them (Hughes, in press). "[T]he strengths and weaknesses often mask each other" (Silverman, 1993, p. 159) so that the high level of ability can hide the extreme difficulties that the child is exhibiting while conversely, the disability can impede the demonstration of the cognitive strengths. This "wobble" in test scores can impact a student's final composite score. If a student has unusual strengths and weaknesses, the final score may not, in fact, reflect a "true" picture of that child's ability (Silverman, 2002). Because so many programs depend on composite scores for services, children may neither get recognized for having strengths that need developing nor for the underlying disabilities that need assistance.

Another difficulty in identifying twice-exceptional students is the challenge that many teachers and schools face in recognizing different patterns of learning. In today's educational system of one-size-fits-all curriculum and standards, teachers often are constrained by a system that does not value atypical pacing and processes of learning. When students are "too different" and do not fit a standard mold, such as fitting into an acceptable label, school systems, teachers, and peers tend to "blame the victim" and reject the student and even the parents on a personal, hostile, basis (Nowak, 2000). Parents often find themselves in conflict with the very school system that is attempting to educate their child. Stories abound of parents "fighting the system" before finding teachers or programs sympathetic to their child's needs (Hughes, Coleman, Nielsen, Reis, & Friedman-Nimz, 2005; Nowak, 2000).

A third issue that leads to problems in identification is the "reverse hierarchy" of learning that so many twice-exceptional children experience. Trained teachers of twice-exceptional students often note that these students learn difficult, conceptually oriented information faster than they learn memory-based tasks, such as multiplication tables, dates, and other rote information. Silverman (1989) found that twice-exceptional students will score quite well on the upper levels of intelligence tests if allowed to continue past the cut-off points of the lower level material that they were unable to do. These are children who learn global information first, and then connect discrete facts to that larger global concept. For example, they may understand the concept of multiplication before they have the solid memory of addition facts (Tannenbaum & Baldwin, 1983). In her research, Silverman (2002) found that these students often are "all at once" learners (para. 3) who learn material in large chunks, rather than through a sequential process. However, few teachers and school programs will recommend a child who is failing basic math for advanced Algebra during middle school. Traditional programs teach in an upward, hierarchal method (Anderson et al., 2001), rather than a conceptually framed, "hard-ideas-first, basic-skills-second" organization. Thus, students who might have the ability to understand difficult, complex material may end up stifled in the lower level, simpler classes because of their inability to remember and perform "basic" skills and the lack of linkages to the global concepts at which they excel. Programs serving these unique learners often begin with large, relevant concepts, and then attach the specific, basic skills to these as a scaffold and purpose for learning (Montgomery County Public Schools, 2004; Silverman, 2002).

A final issue facing the identification of twice-exceptional children is the ability to qualify for special programming options. Recently, students may find themselves unable to qualify for special education because of the change in the definition of learning disabilities in the Individuals with Disabilities Education Improvement Act of 2004 (Council for Exceptional Children [CEC], 2007). In Response to Intervention (RTI), students are identified for learning disability services when their performance falls below a designated level, and they receive intensive, individually determined instruction to fill in any potential educational gaps (Vaughn, 2003). If they do not respond effectively to such short-term intervention but require longer term special education, they can be identified for learning disabilities.

Such an identification process might exclude students whose performance was not significantly below their age/grade peers. Such concerns of identification for intervention needs as they pertain to twice-exceptional students are directly noted by both the Council for Exceptional Children and the National Education Association, who warn that school districts must be aware of the potential to miss and the necessity to serve twice-exceptional students (CEC, 2007; NEA, 2006), because the potential to miss students who are not screened through IQ test scores nor identified by poor performance when compared to peers is present. Noting the concerns, the recent reauthorization of the federal IDEA law acknowledges the needs of twice-exceptional children for the first time ever (Colorado Department of Education, 2006). It added gifted and talented students who have disabilities to the groups of students whose needs have priority in U.S. Department of Education grants to guide research, personnel preparation, and technical assistance.

Not only do twice-exceptional students have a difficult time qualifying for special education, many students may not be able to qualify for gifted programs either if the programs require either a high-level IQ score, high achievement level, or high motivation. IQ scores can be impacted by the disability; in fact, Nielsen (2002) suggests that students with learning disabilities who have IQ scores at or above 120 should be viewed as potentially twice-exceptional. Because of the influence of the disability, academic performance can be significantly negatively impacted, and the gifted child's motivational level can be influenced by his or her frequent failure (Baum & Owen, 2003). Qualifying for, and being served in, gifted or special education programs is a challenge for twice-exceptional children. In order to determine appropriate programming and instruction, it is critically important to understand the characteristics and needs of gifted children.

Academically, twice-exceptional students often are referred to as "paradoxes." They may score far above their peers in one or more academic areas, and have extensive knowledge in specific areas. Yet, at the same time, they may experience problems in other areas. Artistic and spatial abilities often have been particularly noted as areas of strength, while writing, reading, and organization often are cited as common areas of challenge. Thus, twice-exceptional children may be extraordinarily knowledgeable in science, but have serious difficulty reading the textbook. Once knowledge is acquired, it often is manipulated in facile and unusual ways, but acquiring the information may be significantly challenging. Teachers in the various content areas can sound like they're describing quite different children; whereas one can sing the praises of the child who performs at a high level, the other can express frustration at the child who can verbalize, but cannot write nor read.

Although there are no clear-cut testing patterns that can be discerned across the twice-exceptional category, it is known that students with learning disabilities often exhibit significant problems in the areas of working memory. This inability to hold numerous pieces of information simultaneously demonstrates itself in global areas of skill that have not become automatized. Thus, reading can take longer to master; math skills can be slowed down by the lack of access to facts contained in memory; and writing can become a hodge-podge as students try to remember hand grasp, spelling skills, mechanical skills such as grammar, and composition skills all at the same time. This means that twice-exceptional students often can use information that is provided to them, but cannot access information from their memory banks.

Implications From VanTassel-Baska's Work in Assessment

Joyce's work in alternative assessment has significant implications for identification of twice-exceptional students. By decreasing the emphasis on a single set of test scores, and emphasizing the demonstration of critical thinking abilities in either general or content-specific arenas, there has been a greater ability to identify students from racially and economically diverse backgrounds (Feng & VanTassel-Baska, 2008). Because students with language disabilities and other memory challenges are similar to other students from diverse backgrounds in terms of their challenges on traditional testing measures, it is necessary to determine the ways in which twice-exceptional students can display their ability to manipulate information and expand upon their thoughts in creative modes.

Two alternative assessment activities in particular hold significant promise for twice-exceptional students. Performance-based measures, such as the ones identified in South Carolina's STAR program (Feng, VanTassel-Baska, Quek, & Struck, 2003), can serve as models for schools looking to identify students through a dynamic, content-focused approach that allows students to not be impeded by their disability but to exhibit their critical thinking abilities in specific areas of strength. Similarly, nonverbal measures that do not limit a child's ability to learn in general ways (Lohman & Lakin, 2008) can assist in identifying twice-exceptional students' more global learning abilities. Through the use of global reasoning and specific content-based assessments, schools have the ability to more fully identify twice-exceptional students' strengths while not being constrained by their areas of challenge, issues that have been faced and addressed by Joyce in her extensive work with gifted children from poverty and minority backgrounds.

JANUSIAN CHARACTERISTICS: TWO INTEGRATED ASPECTS

In practical terms, these are the children who are the "mountain peaks"— unusually high level and unusually low levels on test scores, behavioral patterns, peer and teacher acceptance, and self-awareness. On EEG tests, children with learning differences are more likely than other students to have "peaks" of brain activity during errors on a task that do not decrease over time, indicating that their level of awareness of their own learning is impacted (Groen et al., 2008). Similarly, twice-exceptional children tend to demonstrate a high degree of scatter on IQ tests; often, twice-exceptional students have higher scores in the Performance domain than the Verbal domain, and most notably, lowered scores in the Wechsler Intelligence Scales for Children Freedom from Distractibility subtests of Digit Span and Coding (Kalbfleisch & Iguchi, 2008). The author's own child demonstrated scores in the 99th percentile on the Picture Concepts subtest of the WISC-IV and the 25th percentile in Coding, and yet, scored consistently in all academic areas in the 70th and 80th percentiles on an achievement test. Often, neither the final composite test scores nor the overall achievement scores are high enough or low enough to warrant special attention for programming.

Twice-exceptional children are first and foremost gifted in their thinking, their levels of creativity, and their sensitivities. However, demonstration of the characteristics of their giftedness is affected by their area of disability (VanTassel-Baska & Baska, 2004). This impact of disability can be observed in academic, as well as social and emotional, areas and produce an overall paradoxical picture. Although twice-exceptional children have characteristics similar to other children with special needs, there is a very strong component of cognitive strengths. As Vail (1989) stated, they are "Smart kids with school problems." Like many other gifted children, they often have strong senses of humor, a high level of creativity, and unusual insights about the world around them. Research finds that twice-exceptional students have extraordinary strengths in either verbal or visual-spatial areas (Montgomery County Public Schools, 2004; Silverman, 2002) and are very strong at manipulating abstract, holistic tasks (Baum & Owen, 2004; Colorado Department of Education, 2005). However, they also experience significant difficulties in production of academic work and are less able in tasks involving sequencing and memorization (Baum & Owen, 2004; Montgomery County Public Schools, 2008). Perhaps it is most compelling to compare twice-exceptional children's academic areas where their strengths are so intertwined with their areas of disability, resulting in mixed and often confusing performances.

A case in point is in the area of reading, the most common academic area of challenge for twice-exceptional students (Baum & Owen, 2004). Reading typically requires an interlink of background knowledge, processing speed, and ability to translate sound/symbol relationships with attention, memory, language, and motivation (Snow, Burns, & Griffin, 1998). With its multiple cognitive demands, reading—and by close association, writing—are common areas of concern for these students (Birely, 1995; Reis & McCoach, 2000; Silverman, 1989). Language processing issues are extraordinarily common among students with disabilities (Vaughn, 2003), and this also is the case among twice-exceptional students. However, unlike students with learning disabilities, twice-exceptional students do not often have an issue with reading comprehension, but rather with the more specific skills-oriented areas of basic automaticity such as graphomotor speed, perceptual scanning, sequencing, organization, and study skills (Barton & Starnes, 1989). Once the material is decoded and integrated into their understanding, they tend to have an excellent level of comprehension and the ability to synthesize and create new ideas (Baum & Owens, 2004).

JANUSIAN CURRICULUM:
ENRICHING AND REMEDIATING

One of the challenges facing teachers and parents of twice-exceptional children is that the fields of gifted education and special education emphasize significantly different aspects of learning. Gifted education tends to be fast-paced, wide in breadth, and conceptually oriented, and emphasizes creativity and critical thinking skills (VanTassel-Baska, 2003). In contrast, special education tends to be highly structured, skills-oriented, and emphasize specific metacognitive learning strategies, direct instruction, and development of automaticity through a diagnostic-prescriptive approach (Graham & Harris, 2003).

The ultimate goal of instruction is to allow the student to develop in her area of ability without being negatively impacted by disability and to take control of life and the learning process. To that end, curriculum specialists warn of the distinction between "empowering" strategies that allow the student to increase control over her own life while accommodating a disability, and "enabling" strategies that encourage dependence upon others for feedback and reduce self-efficacy (Kalafat, 2004). There are a number of practice-developed strategies effective for twice-exceptional students. These can be examined in three areas: (1) social-emotional and behavioral strategies, (2) general academic strategies in global areas of challenge, and (3) strengths-based instructional accommodations and integrative strategies (Hughes, in press).

The literature continually refers to the need of a twice-exceptional child to perceive herself as a gifted child with challenges, rather than as a child who is a failure and cannot succeed (Baum & Owen, 2004; Birely, 1995; Silverman, 2002). Strategies designed to assist the twice-exceptional child must then focus on identifying the student's area of strength and involve the student in talent development activities as well as suggestions for academic compensations. Often, time and encouragement of creative products allows the student to grow and identify herself as a successful producer rather than a frustrated underachiever. This process is called "de-mystification" by Levine (2008) and "takes place when a knowledgeable adult (outside of the immediate family) describes and interprets for a student her or his profile of strengths and weaknesses" (para. 2). Programming and content accommodation must be individual and allow the child an opportunity to demonstrate her own thinking abilities in the solution of personal problems.

General strategies emphasize the challenges faced by many twice-exceptional students in the areas of organization, memory, and metacognitive thinking skills. Because these skills are not necessarily directly content-related, they affect the demonstration of ability in most of the content areas. Because twice-exceptional students often exhibit challenges in these global areas, overall academic performance is impacted.

There are two approaches that integrate these two diverse aspects of twice-exceptional student makeup: (1) enriched remediation, in which twice-exceptional students are presented the complex background nature of the remediation that is being given to them, and (2) task-analyzed acceleration, in which information is presented to students in very discrete, specific steps at an advanced rate (Hughes, in press). In either case, strength-based accommodations include the concept that students are taught in a specific content area of strength using accommodations for their areas of disability or taught in a content area of challenge using their strengths to assist them. When children who have challenges in reading are asked to read their science books in order to acquire the content, a disability in science has just been created. To avoid this, instruction in science, social studies, and all content not directly related to an area of disability should focus less on the process of acquisition, and more on the content knowledge that can then be applied. Although reading across the content areas is a worthwhile goal, twice-exceptional children can have their strong abilities muted by their disability. VanTassel-Baska and Baska (2004) noted that the ability of a twice-exceptional child to demonstrate his gifted characteristics has to be filtered through the disability.

Implications From Joyce's Work in Curriculum

Gifted students with disabilities have been assisted by Joyce's efforts in curriculum through (a) the use of explicit models that specifically target metacognition—thinking skills that often elude students with disabilities, (b) the use of critical thinking to analyze content—skills that twice-exceptional students can apply to content of which they may not have a strong grasp, and (c) the use of targeted content skills that contribute to the broader understanding of a content area, such as the infusion of grammar and persuasive writing into the larger arena of language arts. Such content adaptations, while part of appropriate instructional strategies, allow twice-exceptional students access to content and higher order thinking skills that often are not accessible to them in typical special education settings and yet provide specific guided instructional metacognitive activities not often provided to them in gifted education programs.

Joyce's work in science, for example, exemplifies strategies that are recommended for use with twice-exceptional students. "Systems" as an overarching concept allows students to link specific content to a more global concept—a strategy that allows twice-exceptional students to link concepts to memory-challenging content such as the differences between acids and bases. The use of problem-based learning (PBL) allows students with language challenges but visual abilities to more directly relate to abstract content. And finally, the use of the scientific method allows students to critically analyze content and manipulate it through metacognitive scaffolding.

Such structures are clearly present in the language arts and social studies units as well, in which students' metacognitive thinking is structured through a visual representation, specific content is linked to overarching concepts that frame the unit, and an experiential, visual aspect of learning is emphasized. Little wonder, then, that so many of Joyce's curriculum units have been found to be highly effective with so many students (VanTassel-Baska et al., 2000; VanTassel-Baska, Bass, Reis, Poland & Avery, 1998; VanTassel-Baska, Johnson, Hughes, & Boyce, 1996)!

A MULTIFACETED LEGACY:
CONCLUSIONS AND IMPLICATIONS

Joyce leaves a tremendous legacy in the area of twice-exceptional learners through her significant work in the areas of assessment and curriculum development. In order to serve students appropriately, one must first be able to assess their areas of strength and challenge. Through Joyce's work in alternative assessment, curriculum development, and program evaluation, so many children from diverse backgrounds have benefited. Twice-exceptional children, in particular, have benefited from teachers and administrators who have learned to make the implicit explicit, who have learned how to assess in ways that do not allow disabilities to impact the measurement of abilities, and who have realized that the population of gifted children is far larger than the group traditionally identified and served. Although I as a doctoral student, as a professor, and as a person have benefited from knowing Joyce, it is with the children around the world where she truly leaves her legacy. Joyce's impact is more than Janusian—it is a multifaceted diamond shining brightly.

REFERENCES

Anderson, L. W., Krathwohl, D. R., Airasian, P. W., Cruikshank, K. A., Mayer, R. E., Pintrich, P. R., et al. (2001). *A taxonomy for learning, teaching, and assessing: A revision of Bloom's taxonomy of educational objectives.* New York: Longman.

Barton, J. M., & Starnes, W. T. (1989). Identifying distinguishing characteristics of gifted and talented/learning disabled students. *Roeper Review, 12,* 23–29.

Baum, S., & Owen, S. (2004). *To be gifted and learning disabled: Strategies for helping bright students with LD, ADHD, and more.* Mansfield, CT: Creative Learning Press.

Birely, M. (1995). *A sourcebook for helping children who are gifted and learning disabled* (2nd ed.). Reston, VA: Council for Exceptional Children.

Brody, L. E., & Mills, C. J. (1997). Gifted children with learning disabilities: A review of the issues. *Journal of Learning Disabilities, 30,* 282–297.

Cash, A. B. (1999). A profile of gifted individuals with autism: The twice-exceptional learner. *Roeper Review,* 22(1), 22–27.

Colorado Department of Education. (2006). *Twice-exceptional students, gifted students with disabilities: An introductory resource book.* Denver, CO: Author

Council for Exceptional Children. (2007). *Position on response to intervention (RTI): The unique role of special education and special educators.* Retrieved from http://www.cec.sped.org/AM/Template.cfm?Section=CEC_Professional_Policies&Template=/CM/ContentDisplay.cfm&ContentID=9213

Feng, A. X., & VanTassel-Baska, J. (2008). Identifying low-income and minority students for gifted programs: Academic and affective impact of performance-based assessment. In J. VanTassel-Baska (Ed.), *Alternative assessments with gifted and talented students* (pp. 129–146). Waco, TX: Prufrock Press.

Feng, A. X., VanTassel-Baska, J., Quek, C., & Struck, J. (2003). *A report of Project Star follow-up study*. Williamsburg, VA: The College of William and Mary, The Center for Gifted Education.

Graham, S., & Harris, K. R. (2003). Students with learning disabilities and the process of writing: A meta-analysis with SRSD studies. In H. L. Swanson, K. R. Harris, & S. Graham (Eds.), *Handbook of learning disabilities* (pp. 323–344). New York: Guilford Press.

Groen, Y., Wijers, A., Mulder, L., Waggeveld, B., Minderaa, R., & Althus, M. (2008). Error and feedback processing in children with ADHD and children with Autistic Spectrum Disorder: An EEG event-related potential study. *Clinical Neurophysiology, 119*, 2476–2493.

Hughes, C. E. (in press). Twice-exceptional learners: Twice the strengths, twice the challenges. In J. Castellano (Ed.), *A kaleidoscope of special populations in gifted education: Considerations, connections, and meeting the needs of our most able diverse gifted students*. Waco, TX: Prufrock Press.

Hughes, C. E., Coleman, M. R., Nielsen, M. E., Reis, S., & Friedman-Nimz, R. (2005, November). *Living the research: Parenting twice-exceptional girls*. Paper presented at the annual National Association for Gifted Children conference, Louisville, KY

Kalafat, J. (2004). Enabling and empowering practices of Kentucky's school-based family resource centers: A multiple case study. *Evaluation and Program Planning, 27*(1), 65.

Kalbfleisch, M. L., & Iguchi, C. M. (2008). Twice exceptional learners. In J. A. Plucker & C. M. Callahan (Eds.), *Critical issues and practices in gifted education: What the research says*. (pp. 707–719). Waco, TX: Prufrock Press.

Levine, M. (2008). *Demystification: Taking the mystery out of disappointing mastery*. Retrieved from http://www.allkindsofminds.org/articleDisplay.Aspx?articleID=16

Lohman, D. F., & Lakin, J. (2008). Nonverbal test scores as one component of an identification system: Integrating ability, achievement and teacher ratings. In J. VanTassel-Baska (Ed.), *Alternative assessments with gifted and talented students* (pp. 41–66). Waco, TX: Prufrock Press.

Montgomery County Public Schools. (2004). *A guidebook for twice-exceptional students*. Rockville, MD: Author.

Montgomery County Public Schools. (2008). *Twice-exceptional students at a glance*. Rockville, MD: Author.

National Educational Association. (2006). *The twice-exceptional dilemma*. Washington, DC: Author.

Nielsen, M. (2002). Gifted students with learning disabilities: Recommendations for identification and programming. *Exceptionality, 10*(2), 93–111.

Nowak, M. (2000). Pain, waste, and the hope for a better future: "Invisible disabilities" in the educational system. In K. Kay (Ed.), *Uniquely gifted: Identifying and meeting the needs of the twice-exceptional student* (pp. 50–57). Gilsum, NH: Avocus.

Reis, S. M., & McCoach, D. B. (2000). The underachievement of gifted students: What do we know and where do we go? *Gifted Child Quarterly, 44*, 152–170.

Silverman, L. K. (1989). Invisible gifts, invisible handicaps. *Roeper Review, 12*, 37–42.

Silverman, L. K. (1993). *Counseling the gifted and talented*. Denver, CO: Love.

Silverman, L. K. (2002). *Upside-down brilliance: The visual-spatial learner*. Denver, CO: DeLeon.

Snow, C. E., Burns, M. N., & Griffin, P. (1998). *Preventing reading difficulties in young children*. Washington, DC: National Academies Press.

Tannenbaum, A. I., & Baldwin, L. J. (1983). Giftedness and learning disability: A paradoxical combination. In L. H. Fox, L. Brody, & D. Tobin (Eds.), *Learning-disabled/gifted children: Identification and programming* (pp. 11–36). Baltimore: University Park Press.

Vail, P. L. (1989). *Smart kids with school problems: Things to know and ways to help.* New York: Penguin Books.

VanTassel-Baska, J. (2003). *Curriculum planning and instructional design for gifted learners.* Denver, CO: Love.

VanTassel-Baska, J. (2008). Using performance-based assessment to document authentic learning. In J. VanTassel-Baska (Ed.), *Alternative assessments with gifted and talented students* (pp. 285–308). Waco, TX: Prufrock Press.

VanTassel-Baska, J., Avery, L. D., Little, C. A., & Hughes, C. E. (2000). An evaluation of the implementation of curriculum innovation: The impact of the William and Mary units on schools. *Journal for the Education of the Gifted, 23,* 244–273.

VanTassel-Baska, J., & Baska, A. (2004). Working with gifted students with special needs: A curriculum and program challenge. *Gifted Education Communicator, 35*(2), 4–7, 27.

VanTassel-Baska, J., Bass, G., Ries, R., Poland, D., & Avery, L. D. (1998). A national study of science curriculum effectiveness with high ability students. *Gifted Child Quarterly, 50,* 199–215.

VanTassel-Baska, J., Johnson, D. T., Hughes, C. E., & Boyce, L. N. (1996). A study of language arts curriculum effectiveness. *Journal for the Education of the Gifted, 19,* 461–481.

VanTassel-Baska, J., & Stambaugh, T. (Eds.). (2007). *Overlooked gems: A national perspective on low-income promising learners.* Washington DC: National Association for Gifted Children.

Vaughn, S. (2003, December). *How many tiers are needed for response to intervention to achieve acceptable prevention outcomes?* Paper presented at the Responsiveness-to-Intervention Symposium, Kansas City, MO. Retrieved from http://www.nrcld.org/symposium2003/vaughn/vaughn.pdf

Weinfeld, R., Barnes-Robinson, L., Jeweler, S., & Shevitz, B. (2002). Academic programs for gifted and talented/learning disabled students. *Roeper Review, 24,* 226–233.

CHAPTER 16

ISSUES RELATED TO THE UNDERACHIEVEMENT OF GIFTED STUDENTS

by

DEL
SIEGLE

AND

D. BETSY
MCCOACH

The greater danger for most of us lies not in setting our aim too high and falling short; but in setting our aim too low, and achieving our mark.

—Michelangelo

INTRODUCTION

When gifted students fail to achieve at levels commensurate with their abilities, educators and parents lament the waste of such potential. The underachievement of gifted students is not only a resource loss for the nation, but also a personal loss of self-fulfillment for the underachieving individual. When the National Research Center on the Gifted and Talented conducted a national needs assessment in 1990 (Renzulli, Reid, & Gubbins, 1991), the number one issue concerning the field of gifted education was the underachievement of gifted students. Almost 20 years later, the underachievement of gifted students continues to plague educators and parents.

Determining the extent of gifted underachievement is difficult for two reasons. First, no universally accepted definition of giftedness exists. Further, disagreement surrounds how to define underachievement. Most definitions of underachievement involve a discrepancy between ability or potential (expected performance) and achievement (actual performances; Baum, Renzulli, & Hébert, 1995a; Dowdall & Colangelo, 1982; Emerick, 1992; Reis & McCoach, 2000; Rimm, 1997; Supplee, 1990; Whitmore, 1980). However, researchers and scholars differ in terms of how they operationalize the discrepancy between potential and performance. For instance, Emerick (1988) suggested this discrepancy might include any of the following combinations: high IQ score and low achievement test scores; high IQ score and low grades; high achievement test scores and low grades; high indicators of intellectual, creative potential and low creative productivity; or high indicators of potential and limited presence of appropriate opportunity for intellectual and creative development. However, the subpopulations of students identified using these different discrepancy definitions are likely to be radically different. This example helps to illustrate the difficulties surrounding the multiple definitions and operationalizations of giftedness and underachievement.

Reis and McCoach published an extensive review of literature on gifted underachievers in 2000. In that review, they proposed an operational definition of underachievement that has been adopted in several empirical studies (Matthews & McBee, 2007; McCoach & Siegle, 2003; Siegle, Reis, & McCoach, 2006). They posited that:

> Underachievers are students who exhibit a severe discrepancy between *expected achievement* (as measured by standardized achievement test scores or cognitive or intellectual ability assessments) and *actual achievement* (as measured by class grades and teacher evaluations). To be classified as an underachiever, the discrepancy between expected and actual achieve-ment must not be the direct result of a diagnosed learning disability and must persist over an extended period of time. Gifted underachievers are underachievers who exhibit superior scores on measures of expected achievement (i.e., standardized achievement test scores or cognitive or intellectual ability assessments). (Reis & McCoach, 2000, p. 157)

The severity of the discrepancy required to label someone as a gifted under-achiever also is a crucial component of any operationalization of the construct. Given the phenomenon of regression to the mean, we would not expect the achieve-ment levels of those with the highest measured ability to be equally extreme. In addition, most people probably perform somewhat below their capacity or ability. Thus, the discrepancy between a student's ability and his or her achievement must be severe enough to warrant substantial concern. Operationalizing this degree of discrepancy is critical for research on gifted underachievers.

Although grades are less reliable than standardized measures of academic achievement, they do provide an indication of a student's current level of achieve-ment within a classroom environment. In addition, to some extent, grades also reflect student motivation. Conversely, students with high ability and low standard-ized achievement test scores may be underachievers, or they may have undiagnosed learning disabilities. Therefore, Moon and Hall (1998) recommended that gifted students with low standardized achievement test scores should be screened for undiagnosed learning disabilities prior to treating them as underachievers.

Without a commonly accepted definition of giftedness or a common definition of underachievement, it is impossible to determine how prevalent underachievement is among gifted students. Speculation ranges from 10% to more than 50% (Hoffman, Wasson, & Christianson, 1985; Richert, 1991). The issue is further confused when considering underachievement in academics versus underachievement in nonacademic areas, which often are essential for original contributions to a field (Richert, 1991). Therefore, as McCoach and Siegle (2008) noted, any estimation of the number of gifted underachievers is speculation at best.

When parents and teachers are asked to identify underachievers, they predominately identify males. Across a number of studies of underachievers, the ratio of male underachievers to female underachievers appears to be at least 2:1 (Baker, Bridger, & Evans, 1998; Matthews & McBee, 2007; McCoach, 2002; Peterson & Colangelo, 1996; Richert, 1991; Siegle, Reis, McCoach, Mann, et al., 2006). However, Richert suggested that although twice as many males as females underachieve academically in school, "over an individual's lifetime, females as a group are the greater underachievers" (p. 145). This is because women are far more likely to abandon or compromise their careers to take care of family obligations such as children.

EMPIRICAL LITERATURE

Underachievement tends to appear in middle school and often continues into high school (Peterson & Colangelo, 1996). Peterson and Colangelo examined the school records of 153 gifted students and analyzed trends in their achievement throughout their secondary school careers. In their study, 45% of the students who were underachieving in grade 7 continued to underachieve throughout junior high and high school. Peterson (2000) later conducted a follow-up study of these achievers and underachievers 4 years after high school graduation. High school and college academic achievement were strongly related ($r = .64$). All of the achievers in her study attended college, and 83% of the achievers finished 4 years of college. In contrast, 87% of underachievers attended college; only 52% finished 4 years.

In the largest longitudinal study of underachievers conducted to date, McCall, Evahn, and Kratzer (1992) found that 13 years after high school, the educational and occupational status of high school underachievers paralleled their grades in high school, rather than their abilities. They also found that underachievers were less likely to complete college and remain in their jobs.

Underachievement can occur when gifted students do not receive the support and educational services they require to develop their talent. Gifted students of poverty and students from underserved groups are particularly vulnerable. Students who are not given adequate opportunities to develop their talents often become "involuntary underachievers." Forty-four percent of lower income students who enter first grade in the top 10% will not score in the top 10% by the time they reach fifth grade (Wyner, Bridgeland, & DiIulio, 2007). Gifted students from higher income homes progress twice as fast as their gifted peers from lower income homes. "In elementary and high school, lower-income students neither maintain their status as high achievers nor rise into the ranks of high achievers as frequently as higher-income students" (Wyner et al., 2007, p. 5). High-achieving lower income students drop out of high school or do not graduate on time at a rate twice that of their higher income peers. They are less likely to graduate from college than their higher income peers (59% versus 77%) and less likely to attend the most selective colleges (19% versus 29%). Limited resources in their schools, communities, and families factor into the involuntary underachievement of many students from underserved populations.

Research suggests that quality of schooling (Anderson & Keith, 1997; Baker et al., 1998) and completion of academic coursework (Anderson & Keith, 1997) appear to be significant predictors of achievement for at-risk high school students. The completion of each additional academic course results in an increase of one eighth of a standard deviation in predicted academic achievement test scores (Anderson & Keith, 1997).

Underachievers are a fairly heterogeneous group. Although some underachievers may display low levels of characteristics associated with underachievement, other underachievers score high on measures of these same characteristics. Therefore, checklists of characteristics of underachievers have limited value. Moreover, the variability of motivational and attitudinal measures within samples of underachievers tends to be higher than the variability for comparison groups of average or high achievers (McCoach & Siegle, 2003). The large amount of variability suggests that although underachievers may share some common characteristics, they are not a homogeneous population of students. Each student may underachieve for a somewhat unique combination of reasons; therefore, it is possible that gifted underachievers may be low on only one or two of the many characteristics commonly ascribed to underachievers and may be average or even high in all other areas. Given the variability among underachievers, several researchers in the area of underachievement have proposed specific subtypes of underachievers (e.g., Heacox, 1991; Mandel & Marcus, 1995; Rimm, 1995, 1997; Siegle & McCoach, 2005).

MAJOR THEMES FOR THE FIELD OF GIFTED EDUCATION

The research literature generally suggests six possible causes of underachievement: an initiating situation, excessive power, inconsistency and opposition, inappropriate classroom environment, competition, and value conflicts. Sometimes events in students' lives alter their achievement patterns. This might be a move to a new school or a change in the family structure. Parents and educators who are aware of these potential pitfalls can prevent or lessen their impact (Rimm, 1995).

Young people who experience excessive power at home sometimes have difficulty adjusting to a school environment where they have limited choices. Bestowing adult status on a child at too young an age may contribute to the development of underachievement (Rimm & Lowe, 1988).

Gifted students who receive conflicting messages from parents, conflicting messages from parents and teachers, or conflicting messages from gifted specialists and classroom teachers may find reasons not to achieve. Rimm and Lowe (1988) studied the family environments of 22 underachieving gifted students. In 95% of the families, one parent emerged as the disciplinarian, while the other parent acted as a protector. Often, opposition between parents increased as the challenger became more authoritarian and the rescuer became increasingly protective. Parents of underachievers also tend to be either overly lenient or overly strict (Pendarvis, Howley, & Howley, 1990; Weiner, 1992) or may vacillate between lenient and strict.

Classrooms do not always provide intellectually stimulating environments for gifted and talented students to thrive. Many gifted students underachieve by default; they simply do not receive the academic content or instruction necessary to reach their potential. Regular classroom time often is unproductive for gifted learners. Many gifted elementary school students already know 40–50% of the material to be covered in their current grade prior to the start of the school year (Reis et al., 1993). The majority of gifted students spend 80% of their time in regular education settings instead of in specialized programs designed to meet their unique needs (Westberg, Archambault, Dobyns, & Salvin, 1993), yet 61% of classroom teachers have not received training in meeting the needs of advanced students (Robinson, Shore, & Enersen, 2007).

Students must learn to function within a competitive society; at the same time, overly competitive situations also can be detrimental. Gifted students with a fixed theory of intelligence may not wish to risk their "giftedness" by performing poorly in competitive situations. For them, not performing is less risky than performing and failing.

> . . . holding a fixed theory of intelligence appears to turn students toward concerns about performing and looking smart. Holding a malleable theory appears to turn students toward concerns about learning new things and getting smarter. We have also seen that entity theorists' concerns about looking smart can prevent them from seeking learning opportunities, even ones that could be critical to performing well in the future. (Dweck, 2000, p. 23)

Finally, value conflicts between family, peers, and the school environment can limit student achievement. Negative peer attitudes often relate to underachievement (Clasen & Clasen, 1995; Weiner, 1992). Underachieving students frequently report peer influence as the strongest force impeding their achievement. In one study, 66% of high-ability students named peer pressure or the attitude of the other kids and friends as the primary force against getting good grades (Clasen & Clasen,

1995). In a national longitudinal study of secondary students (NELS:88), students with friends who cared about learning demonstrated better educational outcomes than those in less educationally oriented peer groups (Chen, 1997). Berndt (1999) measured students' grades and behavior in the fall and spring of one academic year. Berndt found that students seemed to more closely resemble their friends at the end of the school year than they did at the beginning of the school year; students' grades decreased between fall and spring if their friends had lower grades in the fall. On the other hand, Reis, Hébert, Diaz, Maxfield, and Ratley (1995) found that high-achieving peers had a positive influence on gifted students who began to underachieve in high school and those peers contributed to some students' reversal of their underachievement. As McCoach and Siegle (2008) noted in their review of literature on gifted underachievers, although peer achievement levels do relate to students' academic achievement, it is unclear whether the choice to associate with other nonachievers is a cause or a result of gifted students' underachievement.

TRENDS AND DIRECTIONS

Although some gifted students underachieve because they have not had opportunities to develop their potential, others choose not to develop their potential. Siegle and McCoach (2002) suggested that students who underachieve may espouse one of three problematic beliefs: They do not believe they have the skills to do well and are afraid to try and fail; they do not see the work they are being asked to do as meaningful; or they believe the "deck is stacked against them" and that any effort they put forth will be thwarted. When any one of these beliefs exists, students tend not to perform well.

Students must believe they have the skills to perform a task before they will attempt it. For example, students must believe they are capable in mathematics before they will attempt a difficult math problem. If they believe that mathematics is too difficult, they are unlikely to put forth appropriate effort. Motivated students believe that they have the skills to do well in school. It also is imperative that students recognize their own role in developing these skills (Siegle, 2008). Students who believe that their abilities are not innate but have been developed are more likely to attempt challenging tasks. Gifted students are at risk for believing that their abilities are simply innate, particularly if others in their lives have not discussed their giftedness with them. Parents and teachers often are reluctant to talk with children about their giftedness. It is important for gifted children to recognize that the talents they possess are acquired, that they have something to do with acquiring them, and that they are capable of further developing these talents and even acquiring new ones. Wu (2005) noted that Chinese culture de-emphasizes giftedness as an innate ability and emphasizes the concept of talent performance. Therefore, gifted children need to take responsibility for developing their gifts.

For many students, school is not meaningful. Eccles' general expectancy-value model of motivation posits a value of self-regulated learning. This includes goals and beliefs about the importance and interest of the task (Pintrich & De Groot, 1990). With this model, achievement values include the perceived enjoyment, importance, and potential usefulness of a task (Wigfield & Karpathian, 1991). When students value the goals of school, they are more likely to engage in academics, expend more effort on their schoolwork, and do better academically (Pintrich & De Groot, 1990; Wigfield, 1994). In a study of university freshman honors students, Siegle, Condon, and Romey (2007) found that in 15 different talent areas (from leadership and musical to mathematics and writing) there was always a significant, positive relationship between students' interest in a talent area and their assessment of their skill in that area. Students who reported being interested in an area tended to do well; those with lower interest also had lower self-reported achievement.

Brophy (2008) suggested that some content is not important and educators must do a better job of sharing why other content is pertinent. "[M]uch of the school curriculum . . . does have potential value, but we have lost sight of the reasons for including it. We need to rediscover and articulate the life-application bases for retaining this content and teach it accordingly" (p. 137).

Kaplan (2006) proposed that educators can make learning meaningful by helping students develop an appreciation of learning. Accordingly, students can develop a personal value for learning by reflecting on how their lives will be different by learning, or not learning, given school content.

Students' perceptions of their environment play an important role in their achievement motivation. Students must expect to succeed and know that those around them will support their efforts. They must trust that their efforts will not be thwarted by external factors and that putting forth effort is not a waste of time and energy. Students who view their environment as friendly and reinforcing may be more likely to demonstrate motivated behavior. Phrases such as, "My teachers does not like me" or "I cannot learn the way he teaches" may be signs that students do not view their environment as friendly or that they have developed a belief that their efforts do not affect outcomes (Rathvon, 1996).

Some environmental factors are within an individual's control, others are not. Ogbu (1978) noted that people put their effort into areas where they believe they can be successful and in environments where they believe they are supported. Worrell (2007) noted that the relationship between ethnic identity exploration/affirmation and academic achievement was moderated by the environment for African American students. Thus, perceptions of the environment factor significantly in achievement motivation.

Although each of the three attitudes discussed above is important, it is their interaction that results in engagement and performance. Motivated students feel good about their abilities, find the tasks in which they are engaged meaningful, and feel supported and appreciated in their environment. When these three areas are measured, the lowest scoring one of them often is the single best predictor of achievement and satisfaction levels (McCoach, in press; Siegle & McCoach, 2009). In other words, those who are motivated and achieve tend to believe they have the skills to do well (self-efficacy), tend to find the work meaningful (goal valuation), and tend to view their environment as supportive (environmental perceptions). The intensity of the attitudes in the three areas need not be the equally strong; however, attitudes must be positive in each area. Ultimately, the three attitudes direct a resultant behavior (self-regulation) that results in achievement. According to this model, if any one of the three components is low, regardless of the strength of the others, motivation is hindered.

UNRESOLVED ISSUES, QUESTIONS, AND SUGGESTIONS

Although much of the research on underachievement has focused on characteristics of underachievers, the most important unresolved issue is how to reverse the underachievement of gifted students. Most interventions designed to reverse underachievement fall into two general categories: counseling and instructional interventions (Butler-Por, 1993; Dowdall & Colangelo, 1982). Unfortunately, there is no magic solution to the problem of underachievement, and a combination of counseling and instructional interventions appears to currently be the most promising option. The best-known interventions involve part-time or full-time special classrooms (e.g., Supplee, 1990; Whitmore, 1980). These interventions usually involve smaller student/teacher ratios, student choice, and less conventional teaching and learning activities. Baum, Renzulli, and Hébert (1995b) and Emerick (1992) demonstrated that using students' strengths and interests can reverse the underachieving cycle.

No one type of intervention appears to be effective for the full range of underachieving gifted students. Because the factors influencing the development and manifestation of underachievement vary, a continuum of strategies and services may be necessary if we are to systematically address this problem. Different types of underachievers may require different combinations of counseling and instructional or curricular modifications. Successful interventions should incorporate both proactive and preventative counseling and innovative instructional interventions. Future researchers in this field should posit coherent, complete models of gifted underachievement and design interventions in accordance with their proposed models.

First, researchers should begin to explore the relationship between classroom practices and academic underachievement. Research exploring the impact of differentiation, acceleration, enrichment, and other curricular modifications on patterns of achievement and underachievement could provide important information for educators. Reis (1998) observed a relationship between unchallenging or inappropriate curriculum in elementary school and underachievement in middle or high school. If unchallenging scholastic environments produce underachieving gifted students, then providing intellectual challenge and stimulation at all grade levels should decrease underachievement. VanTassel-Baska's curriculum development work at The College of William and Mary is a good example of creating intellectually challenging curriculum in a variety of content areas (VanTassel-Baska & Stambaugh, 2007b). Whether using the William and Mary curriculum with underachievers can help to reverse their underachievement behaviors would be an interesting line of future inquiry.

Second, the long-term effects of interventions aimed at reversing underachievement behaviors remain underexplored. Do underachievement interventions have enduring effects on student motivation and achievement? What happens when the student is once again faced with nonstimulating schoolwork? Are there critical periods in which the interventions appear to sustain more positive long-term effects? These and many other questions remain unanswered.

Third, research should examine the effectiveness of family oriented interventions, such as family counseling and home and school partnerships. The Focusing on the Future event designed by VanTassel-Baska at The College of William and Mary exposes high-ability learners to career opportunities related to the arts, humanities, mathematics, and sciences; and informs parents of considerations and guidelines for effective career and academic planning. Events such as this can encourage and promote long-term goal setting and subsequent academic achievement.

Finally, special attention needs to be paid to the underachievement of underrepresented groups. In 2006, VanTassel-Baska, with assistance of the Jack Kent Cooke Foundation and the National Association for Gifted Children, organized a conference on low-income promising learners. The proceedings of that conference resulted in the publication of *Overlooked Gems: A National Perspective on Low-Income Promising Learners*, which contained priorities for action in this area (VanTassel-Baska & Stambaugh, 2007a). This conference and the subsequent publication provide an agenda for promoting talent development among underserved groups.

As stated earlier, no single intervention will work with all gifted underachievers. Just as gifted achievers differ from gifted underachievers, gifted underachievers differ from each other. Researchers and practitioners need to discover how the factors discussed in this chapter interact with each other and the extent to which they impact the achievement of gifted students. Motivation research has only begun to explore the role giftedness plays on achievement motivation. We look forward to the work future researchers will conduct in this arena.

REFERENCES

Anderson, E. S., & Keith, T. Z. (1997). A longitudinal test of a model of academic success for at-risk high school students. *The Journal of Educational Research, 90,* 259–268.

Baker, J. A., Bridger, R., & Evans, K. (1998). Models of underachievement among gifted preadolescents: The role of personal, family, and school factors. *Gifted Child Quarterly, 42,* 5–14.

Baum, S. M., Renzulli, J. S., & Hébert, T. P. (1995a). *The prism metaphor: A new paradigm for reversing underachievement* (CRS95310). Storrs: University of Connecticut, The National Research Center on the Gifted and Talented.

Baum, S. M., Renzulli, J. S., & Hébert, T. P. (1995b). Reversing underachievement: Creative productivity as a systematic intervention. *Gifted Child Quarterly, 39*, 224–235.

Berndt, T. J. (1999). Friends' influence on students' adjustment to school. *Educational Psychologist, 34*, 15–28.

Brophy, J. (2008). Developing students' appreciation for what is taught in school. *Educational Psychologist, 43*, 132–141.

Butler-Por, N. (1993). Underachieving gifted students. In K. A. Heller, F. J. Mönks, & A. H. Passow (Eds.), *International handbook of research and development of giftedness and talent* (pp. 649–668). Oxford, UK: Pergamon.

Chen, X. (1997). *Students' peer groups in high school: The pattern and relationship to educational outcomes.* (NCES 97-055). Washington, DC: U.S. Department of Education.

Clasen, D. R., & Clasen, R. E. (1995). Underachievement of highly able students and the peer society. *Gifted and Talented International, 10*(2), 67–75.

Dowdall, C. B., & Colangelo, N. (1982). Underachieving gifted students: Review and implications. *Gifted Child Quarterly, 26*, 179–184.

Dweck, C. S. (2000). *Self-theories: Their role in motivation, personality, and development.* Philadelphia: Psychology Press.

Emerick, L. J. (1988). *Academic underachievement among the gifted: Students' perceptions of factors relating to the reversal of the academic underachievement pattern.* Unpublished doctoral dissertation, University of Connecticut, Storrs.

Emerick, L. J. (1992). Academic underachievement among the gifted: Students' perceptions of factors that reverse the pattern. *Gifted Child Quarterly, 36*, 140–146.

Heacox, D. (1991). *Up from underachievement.* Minneapolis, MN: Free Spirit Press.

Hoffman, J. L., Wasson, F. R., & Christianson, B. P. (1985). Personal development for the gifted underachiever. *Gifted Child Today, 8*(3), 12–14.

Kaplan, S. (2006, July). *Gifted students in a contemporary society: Implications for curriculum.* Keynote at the 29th Annual University of Connecticut Confratute, Storrs, CT.

Mandel, H. P., & Marcus, S. I. (1995). *Could do better.* New York: Wiley & Sons.

Matthews, M. S., & McBee, M. T. (2007). School factors and the underachievement of gifted students in a talent search summer program. *Gifted Child Quarterly, 51*, 167–181.

McCall, R. B., Evahn, C., & Kratzer, L. (1992). *High school underachievers: What do they achieve as adults?* Newbury Park, CA: Sage.

McCoach, D. B. (2002). A validity study of the School Attitude Assessment Survey (SAAS). *Measurement and Evaluation in Counseling and Development, 35*, 66–77.

McCoach, D. B. (in press). Commentary. In B. Thompson & R. F. Subotnik (Eds.), *Methodologies for conducting research on giftedness.* Washington, DC: American Psychological Association.

McCoach, D. B., & Siegle, D. (2003). The structure and function of academic self-concept in gifted and general education samples. *Roeper Review, 25*, 61–65.

McCoach, D. B., & Siegle, D. (2008). Underachievers. In J. A. Plucker & C. M. Callahan (Eds.), *Critical issues and practices in gifted education: What the research says* (pp. 721–734). Waco, TX: Prufrock Press.

Moon, S. M., & Hall, A. S. (1998). Family therapy with intellectually and creatively gifted children. *Journal of Marital and Family Therapy, 24*, 59–80.

Ogbu, J. U. (1978). *Minority education and caste.* New York: Academic Press.

Pendarvis, E. D., Howley, A. A., & Howley, C. B. (1990). *The abilities of gifted children.* Englewood Cliffs, NJ: Prentice Hall.

Peterson, J. S. (2000). A follow-up study of one group of achievers and underachievers four years after high school graduation. *Roeper Review, 22,* 217–225.

Peterson, J. S., & Colangelo, N. (1996). Gifted achievers and underachievers: A comparison of patterns found in school files. *Journal of Counseling and Development, 74,* 399–406.

Pintrich, P. R., & De Groot, E. V. (1990). Motivational and self-regulated learning components of classroom academic performance. *Journal of Educational Psychology, 82,* 33–40.

Rathvon, N. (1996). *The unmotivated child: Helping your underachiever become a successful student.* New York: Simon and Schuster.

Reis, S. M. (1998). Underachievement for some—Dropping out with dignity for others. *Communicator, 29*(1), 1, 19–24.

Reis, S. M., & McCoach, D. B. (2000). The underachievement of gifted students: What do we know and where do we go? *Gifted Child Quarterly, 44,* 158–170.

Reis, S. M., Hébert, T. P., Diaz, E. P., Maxfield, L. R., & Ratley, M. E. (1995). *Case studies of talented students who achieve and underachieve in an urban high school* (Research Monograph No. 95120). Storrs: University of Connecticut, The National Research Center for the Gifted and Talented.

Reis, S. M., Westberg, K. L., Kulikowich, J., Caillard, F., Hébert, T., Plucker, J., et al. (1993). *Why not let high ability students start school in January? The curriculum compacting study* (Research Monograph No. 93106). Storrs: University of Connecticut, The National Research Center for the Gifted and Talented.

Renzulli, J. S., Reid, B. D., & Gubbins, E. J. (1991). *Setting an agenda: Research priorities for the gifted and talented through the year 2000.* Storrs: University of Connecticut, The National Research Center for the Gifted and Talented.

Richert, E. S. (1991). Patterns of underachievement among gifted students. In J. H. Borland (Series Ed.), M. Bireley, & J. Genshaft (Vol. Eds.), *Understanding the gifted adolescent* (pp. 139–162). New York: Teacher College Press.

Rimm, S. (1995). *Why bright kids get poor grades and what you can do about it.* New York: Crown Trade Paperbacks.

Rimm, S. (1997). Underachievement syndrome: A national epidemic. In N. Colangelo & G. A. Davis (Eds.), *Handbook of gifted education* (2nd ed., pp. 416–435). Boston: Allyn & Bacon.

Rimm, S., & Lowe, B. (1988). Family environments of underachieving gifted students. *Gifted Child Quarterly, 32,* 353–358.

Robinson, A., Shore, B. M., & Enersen, D. L. (2007). *Best practices in gifted education: An evidence-based guide.* Waco, TX: Prufrock Press.

Siegle, D. (2008). The time is now to stand up for gifted education: 2007 NAGC Presidential Address. *Gifted Child Quarterly, 52,* 111–113.

Siegle, D., Condon, E., & Romey, E. (2007, April). *Role of interest, ability, and effort in developing talent in gifted students.* Paper presented at the annual meeting of the American Educational Research Association, Chicago.

Siegle, D., & McCoach, D. B. (2002). Promoting a positive achievement attitude with gifted and talented students. In M. Neihart, S. M. Reis, N. M. Robinson, & S. Moon (Eds.), *The social and emotional development of gifted children: What do we know?* (pp. 237–249). Waco, TX: Prufrock Press.

Siegle, D., & McCoach, D. B. (2005). *Motivating gifted students.* Waco, TX: Prufrock Press.

Siegle, D., & McCoach, D. B. (2009, April). *The application of the Achievement-Orientation Model to the job satisfaction of teachers of the gifted.* Paper presented at the annual convention of the American Educational Research Association, San Diego, CA.

Siegle, D., Reis, S. M., & McCoach, D. B. (2006, June). *A study to increase academic achievement among gifted underachievers.* Poster presented at the Institute of Education Sciences Research Conference, Washington, DC.

Siegle, D., Reis, S. M., McCoach, D. B., Mann, R. L., Greene, M., & Schreiber, F. (2006). [The National Research Center on the Gifted and Talented increasing academic achievement study]. Unpublished raw data.

Supplee, P. L. (1990). *Reaching the gifted underachiever.* New York: Teacher College Press.

VanTassel-Baska, J., & Stambaugh, T. (Eds.). (2007a). *Overlooked gems: A national perspective on low-income promising learners.* Washington, DC: National Association for Gifted Children.

VanTassel-Baska, J., & Stambaugh, T. (Eds.). (2007b). *What works: 20 years of curriculum development and research for advanced learners.* Retrieved from http://cfge.wm.edu/Documents/What%20Works.pdf

Weiner, I. B. (1992). *Psychological disturbance in adolescence* (2nd ed.). New York: John Wiley & Sons.

Westberg, K. L., Archambault, F. X., Jr., Dobyns, S. M., & Salvin, T. (1993). *An observational study of instructional and curricular practices used with gifted and talented students in regular classrooms* (Research Monograph No. 93104). Storrs: University of Connecticut, The National Research Center on the Gifted and Talented.

Whitmore, J. R. (1980). *Giftedness, conflict, and underachievement.* Boston: Allyn & Bacon.

Wigfield, A. (1994). The role of children's achievement values in the self-regulation of their learning outcomes. In D. H. Schunk & B. J. Zimmerman (Eds.), *Self-regulation of learning and performance: Issues and educational applications* (pp. 101–124). Mahwah, NJ: Erlbaum.

Wigfield, A., & Karpathian, M. (1991). Who am I and what can I do? Children's self-concept and motivation in achievement situations. *Educational Psychologist, 26,* 233–262.

Worrell, F. C. (2007). Ethnic identify, academic achievement, and global self-concept in four groups of academically talented adolescents. *Gifted Child Quarterly, 51,* 23–38.

Wu, E. H. (2005). Factors that contribute to talented performance: A theoretical model from a Chinese perspective. *Gifted Child Quarterly, 49,* 231–246.

Wyner, J. S., Bridgeland, J. M., & DiIulio, J. J., Jr. (2007). *Achievement trap: How America is failing millions of high-achieving students from lower-income families.* Retrieved from http://www.jkcf.org/assets/files/0000/0084/Achievement_Trap.pdf

AUTHORS' NOTE

Some of the material featured in this chapter was previously presented in McCoach, D. B., & Siegle, D. (2008). Underachievers. In J. A. Plucker & C. M. Callahan (Eds.), *Critical issues and practices in gifted education: What the research says* (pp. 721–734). Waco, TX: Prufrock Press.

CHAPTER 17

GIFTED EDUCATION'S LATEST CHALLENGE:

Social-Emotional Underachievement, a New Glimpse at an Old Problem

by

F. RICHARD
OLENCHAK,

JOHN
P. GAA,

AND

SUSAN
E. JACKSON

Things that matter most must never be at the mercy of things that matter least.
—Attributed to Johann Wolfgang von Goethe, 1749–1832

INTRODUCTION

Although perspectives about underachievement continue to be as heterogeneous as people themselves, there is general agreement among educators, counselors, and psychologists involved with gifted youth that underachievement represents a significant discrepancy between a student's school performance and some index of ability (Rimm, 1986). Typically, underachievement among school-aged youth is defined academically, but there is ample reason to believe that, in keeping with Rimm's widely accepted definition, youngsters demonstrate underachievement whenever they fail to operate at a level at least somewhat commensurate with indicators of superior ability *of any kind*. What if the discrepancy between performance and potential occurs in the affective domain? What if the indicators of superior ability are more of an affective, social-emotional type than of a cognitive, academic type?

There continues to be a pervasive belief in society, as well as among many educators, that spending time and money on noncognitive skills takes away from content learning and that affective education amounts to a frill (Bluestein, 2001). Certainly, the No Child Left Behind (2001) legislation and its attendant emphasis on achievement test performance as the predominant, if not sole, measure of educational success or failure has exacerbated the design and implementation of programming aimed at affective development. Although the notion of purposefully identifying and nurturing social and emotional talent in schools seems as far from reality as imaginable, recent attention to affective curriculum development (e.g., VanTassel-Baska, Cross, & Olenchak, 2009) provides some optimism that society may gradually expand the scope of what it means to be educated.

There is ample confirmation from neurological science that cognitive development is influenced to a great degree by affective development. In fact, it has been demonstrated that cognition is activated by emotional stimuli, and thinking, problem solving, and decision making are individually and collectively enhanced by positive emotions (Damasio, 1994; Isen, 2004). It is logical to conclude then that when schools and the larger society do not support educational efforts to develop critical social and emotional abilities, students are likely to be less than fully educated. For gifted students, who by definition present an array of unique psychosocial needs (Neihart, Reis, Robinson, & Moon, 2002), such an oversight prompts comparisons with students who underachieve—in this case, underachievement that is attributable to inadequate educational provisions in the social-emotional arena.

Gifted students, whether or not they have disabilities, are highly susceptible to the same pitfalls of underachievement that epitomize giftedness with disabilities; both groups represent statistical outliers from the dominant population and as such are susceptible to manifesting social and emotional issues (Baum & Olenchak, 2002). The concern for gifted students with disabilities is the same as the totality of gifted students: achievement that is not commensurate with ability. Moreover, opportunities for identifying and developing affective talent will be lost if educators and schools do not systematically address social and emotional potential.

CONCEPTUALIZING AFFECTIVE TALENT

Educators are traditionally oriented toward curriculum and instruction that are content-driven; the very notion of schooling is geared toward preparing young people for careers that also may include advanced and later-life training. With the advent of talent development in gifted education, there has been increasing interest in designing schools and programs that do more than simply provide a broad foundation of knowledge and skills on which gifted students can erect higher levels of learning. In spite of the assessment emphasis in general education, schools and programs in gifted education have emphasized development of individual talent. Spearheaded by VanTassel-Baska, the legacy of curriculum work aimed at maximizing gifted learners on an individual level of development is emblematic of efforts to hone content in ways likely to move gifted students well beyond rote learning—even sophisticated, high-level rote learning—toward integration of affect with cognition (VanTassel-Baska, 2001, 2009; VanTassel-Baska, Avery, Little, & Hughes, 2000; VanTassel-Baska, Cross, et al., 2009; VanTassel-Baska & Little, 2003).

The realization that curriculum and instruction in gifted education can be improved to evoke not only cognitive learning but also affective learning gives rise to the notion that developing student talent consists of both academic and social-emotional components. Whereas programming for academically gifted students seeks cognitive talent development, there is no parallel emphasis for affectively gifted students. Consequently, there is a population of gifted students who could most benefit from advanced work in the affective domain, yet because of a generalized lack of such curriculum and instruction, underachievement attributable to underdevelopment is highly likely.

UNDERACHIEVEMENT ENIGMA

Underachievement has been attributed to the inability of the underachiever to integrate self-regulation and affect, the latter of which includes the collection of social-emotional traits and skills (Borkowski & Thorpe, 1994). With the exception of studies in psychiatry targeting an array of serious mental health disorders such as schizophrenia (e.g., Ciompi, 1982, 1988, 1991, 1999), few theorists and researchers have examined underachievement in any way other than cognitively.

When one contemplates the recent neurobiological research referenced previously, it seems misguided to consider metacognition without also considering meta-affect. Although it is not the purpose here to examine the notion of meta-affect or the theoretical and research underpinnings of this construct, it is nonetheless useful to consider that meta-affect should be conceptualized as one of the foundations for human performance. The Bull's Eye Model for Affective Development (Olenchak, 2009), along with the attendant research from positive psychology on which the Bull's Eye is constructed, provides an uncomplicated means for grappling with the complexities of the cognitive-affective interaction. As a result, there is every reason to believe that underachievement is as much a social and emotional phenomenon as it is cognitive. Similarly, among gifted students, underachievement of the social-emotional type may be more critical in coming to terms with the situations gifted underachievers face in order to assist them.

Social-Emotional Underachievement Among Gifted Youth

When a broader conception of underachievement—one that allows for incongruent performance and ability to be demonstrated in a wide range of gifts and talents—is considered, the tidiness of previously held beliefs regarding identification of underachieving gifted students all but disappears. In the academic domain, typical identification systems compare student academic ability (usually IQ tests) with academic performance (usually standardized achievement tests); where significant discrepancies are noted, it has been felt that underachievement prevails despite the limitations of such a simplistic definition (Delisle, 1992). Although the root causes for such discrepancies remain undetermined, the key to the traditional identification process lies in academic test results that are almost explicitly cognitive in nature.

Yet, due to increasing research accentuation on the identification of and programming for a multiplicity of abilities including those in the affective domain (Olenchak, 2009; Sternberg, 1995, 2007), the diagnosis of underachievement is gradually becoming more complex than simply comparing intelligence with achievement test scores. To identify underachievement using test discrepancy formulae among students enrolled in a program designed for those with gifts in the artistic realm or for young people with talents in leadership would be as illegitimate as using IQ cut-scores for placement of students in such programs. In the few locations where schools have progressed to create programs aimed at gifts and talents camouflaged by disabilities, poverty, gender, or talents other than those that schools customarily emphasize, effort has been instigated to develop comprehensive microethnographic studies of pupils that attempt to capture a holistic picture of each student (Olenchak, 2009). Even in academic-only gifted programs, school attempts have increased in the collection of more detailed data than tests results alone, as diverse, qualitative—often affective—data have proven useful not only for identification of needs but also for personalized placement and programming.

Despite their utility, professionals are confronted with the unseemly task of making judgments based largely on behaviors and emotions, many of which can only be observed and cannot be measured empirically. The ultimate dilemma arises when professionals attempt to isolate behaviors and collections of behaviors in order to arrive at diagnoses. Simply put, although giftedness and superior talent potential tend to center around a set of identifying behaviors, underachievement does not look significantly different than a number of other disorders that cause young people to perform at levels below those which have been, in some way, preindicated.

For example, in a study completed by Kardaras (1996), a list of 18 social and emotional, 5 physical, and 10 academic characteristics was distributed to 285 teachers, counselors, and psychologists; participants were asked to attribute each characteristic to either ADHD, giftedness, both, or neither. It was found that a small number of characteristics (11 of 33) could be isolated and attributed *only* to ADHD or to giftedness or to neither. Two thirds of the characteristics were identified with *both* ADHD and giftedness, and she found no significant differences between professions in how they attributed characteristics. Most critically, *all* of the social and emotional characteristics fell in the grouping that professionals connected to *both* ADHD and giftedness.

If professionals have difficulty discerning affective characteristics of giftedness from those of ADHD, imagine the quandary when underachievement is introduced as yet another variable to be considered concomitantly with giftedness. Although Kardaras' (1996) study did not examine underachievement specifically, all of the 33 characteristics included in her survey have been previously ascribed to underachievers and particularly to underachievers who also are gifted (Rimm, 1986).

Consequently, underachievement among gifted students, like giftedness and underachievement separately, is not a clearly defined construct. Although research results have shown that various intervention approaches are successful for transforming underachievement into appropriate levels of performance, few generalizations can be drawn (Delisle, 1992; Emerick, 1989; Rimm, 1986; Whitmore,1980). One of the few that appears generalizable is rooted in the need for underachieving gifted youth to adjust their skepticism about their own abilities so that more optimistic, hopeful attitudes prevail (Silverman, 1997). Hence, the overarching issue is one that is affective and not cognitive.

The Emotional Toll of Underachievement

Similarities to Academic Giftedness

Although previous studies of the emotional traits of gifted individuals have been primarily restricted to those with academic giftedness, the efforts of Dabrowski (1938, 1964) and later of Piechowski (1997) expanded the conception of advanced emotional development. Dabrowski's "psychic overexcitabilities" have been described as heightened sensitivities in five contexts: psychomotor, sensual, intellectual, imaginational, and emotional. In and of themselves, each contextual overexcitability can be described as a "gift," but there has been conclusive evidence that individuals with academically oriented, IQ-delineated giftedness (that which is most frequently measured and served in schools) tend to have heightened overexcitabilities across all five contexts (Silverman, 1993). However, there also has been significant investigation revealing that emotional development in *other* types of giftedness—including affective giftedness—parallels the amplified sensitivities found in the academically gifted (Lind & Olenchak, 1995).

Previous research has determined that context-specific overexcitabilities must be integrated with all other overexcitabilities before there are influences on emotional development equating with characteristics of giftedness (Piechowski, Silverman, & Falk, 1985). Using Dabrowski's theory, the emotional development associated with academically gifted persons has been confirmed in individuals whose talent domains are not particularly scholastic: studies of artists (Piechowski & Cunningham, 1985), creative children (Gallagher, 1985; Schiever, 1985), and social reformers and leaders (Brennan & Piechowski, 1991; Grant, 1990). Hence, it appears that emotionality in gifted persons, whether academically or otherwise gifted, is parallel. Although distinctions certainly exist in the emotional characteristics of gifted individuals, persons of high ability of any type tend to develop pronounced sensitivities and, therefore, require specialized affective curriculum and instruction (VanTassel-Baska, Buckingham, & Baska, 2009).

Differences From Academic Giftedness

Although the internal emotional traits of gifted persons appear to be similar regardless of talent domain, distinctions exist demarcating those who have great ability in fields aside from the academic; these appear to be external to the individual. A wide array of exogenous variables—home, parents, peers, school, and social values, among others—have significant influence on the emotional development of individuals, gifted or not. These are described as among the World Context in the Bull's Eye Model for Affective Development (Olenchak, 2009). Due to the amplified sensitivities described above, these external variables likely have a heightened effect on gifted individuals' emotions, but a case can be made that they can have even greater significance on the emotions of those with nonscholastic gifts.

Many persons with great potential must learn to live in a society that fails to celebrate their gifts and often rejects them due to their superior abilities. Although academically gifted students often respond to social rejection by camouflaging their gifts, if specialized programs are at least available, they have some chance for adjusting their emotional development. In the absence of suitable school programming, these children are frequently forced not only to hide their abilities, but worse, they come to deny them (Kogan, 1995). Denial of one's abilities among gifted populations often leads to risk of underachievement, dropping out of school, delinquency, eating disorders, drug abuse, and other activities deemed not only unacceptable socially but also personally destructive. A review of literature over the past decade revealed that previous investigations of this group have largely been limited to three categories: (1) gifted students with concomitant disabilities; (2) those from poverty, minority, and/or overlooked cultures, or otherwise being at educational disadvantage; and (3) those who are underserved due to their gender and/or degree of giftedness. Although few studies were located that examined the emotional risks of students having significant talents aside from the academic, this group's strong similarities with those who have concomitant giftedness and disabilities place them equally in danger. Where talents—regardless of their type—remain either underserved or unserved in schools, students are placed at risk of developing serious affective problems (Kogan, 1995; Rimm, 1986).

IMPLICATIONS FOR INTERVENTION

Obviously, if professionals in education and psychology are aware that gifted youth with advanced abilities in areas other than academic are more socially and emotionally fragile than other gifted students, it would seem that preventive measures would be appropriate. Leta Hollingworth (1939) suggested that gifted students should be involved in "emotional education" (p. 585) to assist them in handling the special problems they were likely to encounter in school. Hollingworth felt that such emotional programming would help prevent potential maladjustment and enhance full development of their talents.

Hollingworth defined emotional education as a comprehensive program integrating all aspects of emotional, social, cognitive, and physical development. Such a program would incorporate sufficiently challenging curriculum and instruction appropriate to the individual interests and needs of each gifted student. Inherent in her emotional education plan is a general willingness in schools to equip gifted students with information and techniques useful and rewarding for handling stress. To prevent emotional maladjustment, personally rewarding curriculum and instruction, opportunities for interaction with others of similar ability and interests, and situations likely to teach how to relate to those with lesser abilities and differing interests are critical school components for all gifted youth (Hollingworth, 1942).

Examples of Interventions

Future problem solving. The Future Problem Solving Program (FPS) was originally designed by E. Paul Torrance (Torrance & Reynolds, 1978) as a means for teaching young people the Creative Problem Solving model and, concurrently, increasing student awareness and appreciation for the future. This futuristic orientation assists students in creating more accurate images of the future, their places in it, and their interaction with its development (Torrance, 1976; Torrance & Reynolds, 1978).

For socially emotionally underachieving gifted students, the importance of a healthy, futuristic outlook is linked very closely to pathways for reversing their underachievement condition. It is virtually impossible, for example, to ameliorate underachievement if the student perceives little opportunity in which to interact positively with the various aspects of personal life in the future. Moreover, by equipping underachieving students with a heuristic that is effective for both problem resolution and for assessing the future, it is likely such students will begin to feel a sense of control over their own destinies. For underachievers, most of whom feel as if life "just happens" to them, a strategy for seizing control over at least some aspect of one's life can be incredibly appealing. More importantly, teaching a strategy that works amounts to handing those who feel both helpless and hopeless a tool that helps them develop optimism.

Designed to parallel most of the steps encompassed in Creative Problem Solving, the FPS heuristic most often is practiced through an interscholastic competition. Though competition may, at face value, appear improper for those already experiencing significant problems with achievement, Rimm and Olenchak (1991) found that FPS:

1. serves to change both self-expectations and expectations of others about the underachiever,
2. provides role models for achievement;
3. teaches *how* to compete in a safe environment,
4. serves to form teacher-student alliances, and
5. provides sanctuary to the underachieving gifted student who often can find no peer group.

Its most important application—to personal dilemmas—is the aspect that counselors and teachers must demonstrate *themselves* through modeling, so that gifted underachievers can see the real-world utility of the process beyond the game-like sessions of the competitive team program.

Role-playing. Counseling activities should be designed to assist gifted students in self-discovery: understanding themselves, their abilities and how they are manifested, problems they encounter, values of society and family, motives supporting actions, and interests of self and others (Davis & Rimm, 1989; Silverman, 1993). Further, it is strongly recommended that counseling activities for gifted students should be based on the fact that many such young people are simply in need of an adult whom they can trust, with whom they feel relaxed, and with whom they can develop open lines of communication (Delisle, 1992). Few counseling strategies better integrate this array of recommendations for working with gifted youth than role-playing.

The stages of the role-playing strategy delineate the various means through which students are likely to come to greater self-awareness by removing themselves from situations empathically and analytically even though they are performing a part in simulating those same situations. Moreover, the opportunity to forge a bond with an adult becomes authenticated because role-playing in individual counseling requires openness in communication, with the student and therapist working as coequals in "staging the play."

Use of role-playing with students—especially those who are gifted underachievers and who often have become masters of manipulation—demands the counselor to be highly creative, willing to take risks, and at least moderately charismatic. Even if the student should move the role-play in a direction that was not predictable, it must *always* appear to the student that the adult knows precisely what is happening and why (Kipper, 1986). Although high-quality role-playing must afford students latitude to exercise some creativity themselves, the counselor must have careful control of the overall events in a way that facilitates emergence of students' authentic emotions and behaviors. Consequently, role-playing requires the counselor to be clearly in charge but not to the degree that it arrests student responses.

PESSIMISM BEGETS HOPELESSNESS; OPTIMISM BEGETS HOPE

Although academic underachievement is one issue that confronts the gifted student population, it appears more significant that educational and psychological scholars and practitioners begin to recognize the potential for underachievement in each gifted student's domain of talent, with particular attention to its implications on social-emotional development. Although academic underachievement is of concern to teachers and parents of any child, there must be growing consciousness that scholastic success alone is unlikely to nurture in gifted students the élan, commitment to task, ability, and creativity upon which gifted-like performances are founded and on which contentment and self-actualization can be constructed. If anything, an entrenched school system and social climate, often supporting appropriate programs only for academic and/or athletic gifts while ignoring many others, runs the risk of so alienating these young people that they may never fully realize their potential. Worse, their overall affective development could be delayed if not stifled altogether.

Although there has been effort to alert the field to the needs of gifted students whose differences lie in socioeconomics, race and culture, gender, and concomitant disabilities, there has been little attention paid to students whose talents are significant yet are in no way reflected in school gifted programs. Those young people with the predisposition for high levels of affective talent, such as that embodied in altruists, are especially disenfranchised. Underachievement of any kind and the resultant affective dilemmas are the same for each of these populations of gifted students; hence, gifted students, because of inadequate services, are *all* placed in social-emotional jeopardy.

If we are to extend the spirit of equality of opportunity to persons without distinction, it is crucial that all gifted students be included and that when educators speak of talent development, nurturing abilities in the affective domain receives emphasis. A cornerstone of the American dream is the prospect for each individual to succeed. If we continue to underaddress the social-emotional needs of gifted students, thereby promoting underachievement for all of them, their individual sense of optimism is likely to become damaged to the extent that hopelessness may well consume them. Our next great leaders cannot possibly emerge from hopelessness; the upcoming generation of inventions will be masked by hopelessness; the beauty of the arts will become ugly in hopelessness; and dreams imagined are likely to become nightmares mired in hopelessness. The time has come to activate affective services for gifted and talented youth with all kinds of abilities, or we will surely lose many of them.

A Final Comment

Joyce VanTassel-Baska's assiduousness coupled with her sincere devotion to gifted and talented children is what led me to seek her guidance and steady hand in completing the recent *Social-Emotional Curriculum With Gifted and Talented Students* (VanTassel-Baska, Cross, et al., 2009). That volume is the result of an idea I had in 2003 when I served as NAGC President-Elect, and although I had assembled a fine team of authors to construct the book, its publication would likely still be delayed because of a series of health and personal obstacles with which I had to contend. Once Joyce had agreed to shepherd the project in my behalf, bringing Tracy Cross on board as a most capable third coeditor, the book swiftly and smoothly was brought to life. And, while Joyce was ardent in her adherence to timelines, I was able to count on her not only with regard to the book's completion, but more importantly, I came quickly to rely on her as an insightful and compassionate friend. In fact, given that psychosocial development of gifted persons has increasingly become the steering rudder for my research, I can think of only a few other examples of someone in our own field of gifted education and psychology whom I feel has attained her "Personal Niche" as described in the Bull's Eye Model for Affective Development (Olenchak, 2009). She has become one of my most prized friends not simply because of her excellent scholarship or her astute leadership but because I can rely on her when life seems to hand me challenges that seem insurmountable. She has stood by me, she has braced me, and she has consistently lent me her assistance. I only hope that I one day can return the many favors she has granted me. This chapter addressing trends in social-emotional development of gifted young people is but a tiny first installment in recompense.

REFERENCES

Baum, S. M., & Olenchak, F. R. (2002). The alphabet children: GT, AD/HD, and more. *Exceptionality, 10*(2), 77–91.

Bluestein, J. (2001). *Creating emotionally safe schools: A guide for educators and parents.* Deerfield Beach, FL: Health Communications.

Borkowski, J. G., & Thorpe, P. K. (1994). Self-regulation and motivation: A life-span perspective on underachievement In D. H. Schunk & B. J. Zimmerman (Eds.), *Self-regulation of learning and performance: Issues and educational applications* (pp. 45–74). Hillsdale, NJ: Lawrence Erlbaum.

Brennan, T. P., & Piechowski, M. M. (1991). The developmental framework for self-actualization: Evidence from case studies. *Journal of Humanistic Psychology, 31*(3), 43–64.

Ciompi, L. (1982). *Affektlogik [Affect Logic].* Stuttgart, Germany: Klett-Cotta.

Ciompi, L. (1988). *Psyche and schizophrenia: The bond between affect and logic.* Cambridge, MA: Harvard University Press.

Ciompi, L. (1991). Affects as central organising and integrating factors: A new psychosocial/biological model of the psyche. *British Journal of Psychiatry, 159,* 97–105.

Ciompi, L. (1999). *Die emotionalen grundlagen des denkens [The emotional bases of thinking].* Göttingen, Germany: Vandenhoeck & Ruprecht.

Dabrowski, K. (1938). Typy wzmozonej pobudliwosci: psychicnej [Types of increased psychic excitability]. *Biul. Inst. Hig. Psychicznej, 1*(3–4), 3–26.

Dabrowski, K. (1964). *Positive disintegration.* Boston: Little-Brown.

Damasio, A. R. (1994). *Descartes' error: Emotion, reason, and the human brain.* New York: Grosset/Putnam.

Davis, G. A., & Rimm, S. B. (1989). *Education of the gifted and talented* (2nd ed.). Englewood Cliffs, NJ: Prentice Hall.

Delisle, J. R. (1992). *Guiding the social and emotional development of gifted youth: A practical guide for educators and counselors.* New York: Longman.

Emerick, L. J. (1989). Student interests: A key to reversing the underachievement pattern. *Understanding Our Gifted, 2*(1), 1, 10–12.

Gallagher, S. A. (1985). A comparison of the concept of overexcitabilities with measures of creativity and school achievement in sixth grade students. *Roeper Review, 8,* 115–119.

Grant, B. (1990). Moral development: Theories and lives. *Advanced Development, 2,* 85–91.

Hollingworth, L. S. (1939). What we know about the early selection and training of leaders. *Teachers College Record, 40,* 575–592.

Hollingworth, L. S. (1942). *Children above 180 IQ Stanford-Binet: Origin and development.* Yonkers-on-Hudson, NY: World Book.

Isen, A. M. (2004). Some perspectives on positive feelings and emotions: Positive affect facilitates thinking and problem solving. In A. S. R. Manstead, N. Frijda, & A. Fischer (Eds.), *Feelings and emotions: The Amsterdam Symposium* (pp. 263–281). Cambridge, UK: Cambridge University Press.

Kardaras, K. (1996). *Teacher perceptions of negative characteristics and their attributions to giftedness and/or Attention Deficit Hyperactivity Disorder.* Unpublished doctoral dissertation, Adler School of Psychology, Chicago, IL.

Kipper, D. A. (1986). *Psychotherapy through clinical role playing.* New York: Brunner/Mazel.

Kogan, N. (1995, September). *Motivational and personality patterns in performing artists.* Paper presented at the Esther Katz Rosen Symposium on the Psychological Development of Gifted Children, Lawrence, KS.

Lind, S., & Olenchak, F. R. (1995, March). *ADD/ADHD and giftedness: What should educators do?* Paper presented at the annual conference of the Association for the Education of Gifted Underachieving Students, Birmingham, AL.

Neihart, M., Reis, S. M., Robinson, N. M., & Moon, S. M. (Eds.). (2002). *The social and emotional development of gifted children: What do we know?* Waco, TX: Prufrock Press.

No Child Left Behind Act, 20 U.S.C. §6301 (2001).

Olenchak, F. R. (2009). Creating a life: Orchestrating a symphony of self, a work always in progress. In J. VanTassel-Baska, T. L. Cross, & F. R. Olenchak (Eds.), *Social-emotional curriculum with gifted and talented students* (pp. 41–78). Waco, TX: Prufrock Press.

Piechowski, M. M. (1997). Emotional giftedness: The measure of intrapersonal intelligence. In N. Colangelo & G. A. Davis (Eds.), *Handbook of gifted education* (pp. 366–381). Boston: Allyn & Bacon.

Piechowski, M. M., & Cunningham, K. (1985). Patterns of overexcitability in a group of artists. *Journal of Creative Behavior, 19,* 153–174.

Piechowski, M. M., Silverman, L. K., & Falk, R. F. (1985). Comparison of intellectually and artistically gifted on five dimensions of mental functioning. *Perceptual and Motor Skills, 60,* 539–549.

Rimm, S. B. (1986). *Underachievement syndrome: Causes and cures.* Watertown, WI: Apple.

Rimm, S., & Olenchak, F. R. (1991). How future problem solving helps underachieving gifted students. *Gifted Child Today, 14*(2), 19–22.

Schiever, S. W. (1985). Creative personality characteristics and dimensions of mental functioning in gifted adolescents. *Roeper Review, 7,* 223–226.

Silverman, L. K. (1993). The gifted individual. In L. K. Silverman (Ed.), *Counseling the gifted and talented* (pp. 3–28). Denver, CO: Love.

Silverman, L. K. (1997). Family counseling with the gifted. In N. Colangelo & G. A. Davis (Eds.), *Handbook of gifted education* (2nd ed., pp. 382–397). Needham Heights, MA: Allyn & Bacon.

Sternberg, R. J. (1995). *A triarchic approach to giftedness.* Storrs: University of Connecticut, The National Research Center on the Gifted and Talented.

Sternberg, R. J. (2007). *Wisdom, intelligence, and creativity synthesized.* New York: Cambridge University Press

Torrance, E. P. (1976, October). *Career education of the gifted and talented: Images of the future*. Paper presented at the Western Symposium on Learning, Bellingham, WA.

Torrance, E. P., & Reynolds, C. R. (1978). Images of the future of gifted adolescents: Effects of alienation and specialized cerebral functioning. *Gifted Child Quarterly, 22,* 40–54.

VanTassel-Baska, J. (2001). The talent development process: What we know and what we don't know. *Gifted Education International, 16,* 20–28.

VanTassel-Baska, J. (2009). Affective curriculum for gifted and talented learners. In J. VanTassel-Baska, T. L. Cross, & F. R. Olenchak (Eds.), *Social-emotional curriculum with gifted and talented students* (pp. 113–132). Waco, TX: Prufrock Press.

VanTassel-Baska, J., Avery, L. D., Little, C., & Hughes, C. (2000). An evaluation of curriculum innovation: The impact of the William and Mary units on schools. *Journal for the Education of the Gifted, 23,* 244–270.

VanTassel-Baska, J., Buckingham, B. L. E., & Baska, A. (2009). The role of the arts in the socioemotional development of the gifted. In J. VanTassel-Baska, T. L. Cross, & F. R. Olenchak (Eds.), *Social-emotional curriculum with gifted and talented students* (pp. 227–257). Waco, TX: Prufrock Press.

VanTassel-Baska, J., Cross, T. L., & Olenchak, F. R. (2009). *Social-emotional curriculum with gifted and talented students*. Waco, TX: Prufrock Press.

VanTassel-Baska, J., & Little, C. (2003). *Content-based curriculum for high-ability learners*. Waco, TX: Prufrock Press.

Whitmore, J. R. (1980). *Giftedness, conflict, and underachievement*. Boston: Allyn & Bacon.

CHAPTER 18

EQUITABLE ASSESSMENT:

Social Justice in Practice

by

BRUCE BRACKEN

Developing effective and reliable assessment is not an easy task, and to create meaningful assessment for gifted students is even harder, given the nature of the learner and the nature of the expectations in the program.

—Joyce VanTassel-Baska (2008)

INTRODUCTION

Psychologists and educators have long sought equitable methods for assessing the cognitive abilities of examinees who lack the cultural foundation or manifest language to demonstrate their latent abilities. This lofty goal has been sought for students across the ability range (e.g., Bracken & McCallum, 1998; Bracken & Naglieri, 2003; Bracken, VanTassel-Baska, Brown, & Feng, 2007; McCallum, Bracken, & Wasserman, 2001) and the ages (e.g., Arthur & Woodrow, 1919; Itard, 1932; Seguin, 1907), and has highlighted the issue of social justice for people of poverty, people of color, English Language Learners, and individuals with linguistic-limiting exceptionalities (e.g., elective/selective mute, verbal learning disabled). Equitable assessment within gifted education is an especially important focus because the field often has been criticized for an elitist orientation and exclusionary practices that may deny opportunities to the less fortunate, which strikes at the heart of social justice concerns.

The French clinician, Jean Itard, was among the first to address the problem of assessing and remediating the cognitive abilities of language-challenged individuals. Itard was presented with Victor, a mute feral youth, since referred to as "The Wild Boy of Aveyron" (Carrey, 1995; Itard, 1932). In addition to Itard's well-publicized assessment and instructional efforts with Victor, other clinicians are noteworthy for similar efforts. Seguin (1907), for example, is acknowledged for having developed one of the first nonverbal tests of cognitive ability, the Seguin Form Board. The Seguin Form Board, as well as many modifications of the original instrument, requires examinees to place geometric pieces into cutouts of the same size and shape. The nonverbal form board approach to intellectual assessment still can be seen on current instruments and set the stage for a long history of nonverbal assessment practices—practices that chronologically parallel the history of verbally oriented assessment approaches.

During World War I, the Committee on the Psychological Examination of Recruits was created and charged with developing procedures to assess the cognitive abilities of new recruits in this country (Thorndike & Lohman, 1990). As a result of the committee's efforts, two forms of the exam were created—the standard English language form, Army Alpha, and a second nonverbal form, Army Beta, to assess the abilities of recruits who either were illiterate and couldn't respond reliably to a written test or whose English language mastery was insufficient for a valid assessment on the Army Alpha examination.

The Army Beta included several performance-type tasks, which were to be most prominently associated in later years with the various forms of the Wechsler Scales of Intelligence. The Army Beta, and later the Wechsler subtests, employed novel puzzle completion tasks, cube constructions, speeded copying of digit symbol pairs, maze completions, picture completions, and picture arrangements. Experimental work devoted to the assessment of linguistically different and illiterate individuals during this era resulted in a host of pioneer instruments, including instruments such as the Kohs Cubes (Kohs, 1919), Porteus Mazes (Porteus, 1915), and the Arthur Point Scale (Arthur & Woodrow, 1919). The Point Scale is especially noteworthy because it was a civilian effort that combined a variety of extant performance tests, including a revision of the Knox Cube Test (Knox, 1914), Sequin Form Board, Porteus Mazes, and an adaptation of the Healy Picture Completion Test (Healy, 1914, 1918, 1921) into a single nonverbal battery.

Arthur's goal for the Point Scale was to create a nonverbal battery of cognitive tests that would collectively "furnish an IQ comparable to that obtained with the Binet scales" (Arthur, 1947, p. 1). A variety of nonverbal and "culture fair" tests were later developed during subsequent decades, but most were met with only limited success or were co-opted into standard intelligence batteries as performance subtests with verbal directions. Because of rapidly changing demographic characteristics of the United States, there has been a resurgence of interest in nonverbal test development (Bracken & McCallum, 1998).

LINGUISTIC AND CULTURAL DIVERSITY

U.S. demographics continue to change at a rapid pace, resulting in an increasingly diverse overall American population and an ever-increasing bilingual population. Population diversity means not only that educators and psychologists must accommodate clients and students from different cultural backgrounds and nations of origin, but with increasing frequency they will find themselves working with students who either speak English as a second language or not at all.

Newspaper articles published at the end of the previous century highlighted the growing number of languages spoken by students in public schools throughout the country, regardless of region of the U.S. As an extreme example, Chicago public school students collectively speak more languages than any other school system—200 in all (Pasko, 1994).

Linguistic diversity is not restricted to a single dominant "second" language (e.g., Spanish in the Southwestern U.S.) or to major megalopolises such as Chicago, Los Angeles, or New York City. Virtually all villages, towns, cities, states, and regions of the country face incredibly diverse local student populations—populations that require new approaches to the delivery of educational and psychological services, including gifted education.

In addition to the cultural and linguistic diversity that has been brought about by historic legal and illegal immigration to the United States, it should be recognized that considerable cultural and linguistic diversity also exists among aboriginal North Americans and many long-term residents of the United States. For example, some Native Americans, especially those who live in the Western U.S. (e.g., Navaho) and Alaska, as well as long-standing residents (e.g., African American slave descendents in isolated areas) either speak English as a second language or speak nonstandard or unique forms of English blended with a second language (e.g., Gullah). In all of these instances, it has been assumed historically and incorrectly that the use of verbally oriented intelligence tests to assess cognitive functioning is both fair and reasonable; an assumption that warrants renewed examination by those concerned about social justice.

What is the common denominator among all of these otherwise disparate groups of people? All of these individuals, for many different reasons, may be seriously disadvantaged when their cognitive functioning is assessed by any of the available traditional language-loaded intelligence batteries (e.g., Stanford-Binet, Wechsler Scales, Woodcock-Johnson). Examinees' disadvantages in these cases lie in the linguistic and/or cultural demands that are placed on them by traditional language-loaded intelligence tests; language and cultural demands that are not essential to the process of assessing intelligence.

Not only are the ubiquitous linguistic and cultural demands of traditional intelligence tests often unnecessary, sometimes they are blatantly unfair and socially unjust. It is important to recall that the measurement of any construct (e.g., general intelligence) results in two sources of score variability: reliable variance and error variance. Any extraneous variable (e.g., linguistic or cultural demands of an intelligence test) that contributes to error variance by definition is "construct irrelevant." When clients' personal language, culture, or other noncognitive attributes cause them to perform less than optimally on a measure of general intelligence, such interference produces construct irrelevant variance. Although verbally and socially relevant intellectual factors can be an important part of a standard intellectual assessment (e.g., to assess verbal development, social awareness), the underlying assumption has been that all examinees have been similarly exposed to the culture and language represented by the test. This assumption is invalid for many within the U.S. population.

There have been a number of approaches employed to render the assessment process fairer for the many individuals for whom a language-loaded intelligence test is inappropriate. The previous "solutions" have included the use of performance tests, translated tests, and unidimensional "nonverbal" tests. These approaches have met with various levels of success, as well as having created unique problems.

Performance Tests

In a variety of test use surveys (e.g., Chattin & Bracken, 1989), the Wechsler Scales continue to be the dominant tests employed to assess children's and adults' intelligence. Psychologists are so comfortable with and have relied so heavily on the Wechsler instruments that they resort to these tests even when they are patently inappropriate. For example, the Wechsler Performance Scales have been used as "nonverbal" measures in instances where examinees speak English as a second language, are deaf or hard of hearing, or when children have language-related disabilities that detrimentally influence their intelligence test performance.

In such instances, psychologists have correctly reasoned that the *language-reduced* Performance Scale is a better choice than the Verbal Scale; however, they have incorrectly reasoned that a *better choice* is the most appropriate action to take. Psychologists often assume that examinees understand the verbal directions spoken by the examiner and therefore they understand the task demands for Performance subtests. This assumption is not valid in many cases—how would a monolingual Spanish-speaking examinee possibly understand the lengthy and convoluted directions for Block Design or the subtle corrections and admonishments vocalized by the examiner when the examinee rotates a block design during construction? Each of the Wechsler Performance subtests has test directions that are heavily laden with wordy verbal instructions, including language concepts that are beyond the developmental levels of many English dominant examinees (Bracken, 1986; Kaufman, 1990, 1994).

Performance subtests such as Picture Arrangement not only have verbal directions but the item content is based in Western culture and requires an understanding of specific cultural events. In both Block Design and Picture Arrangement, unnecessary verbal and cultural item content presents unnecessary hurdles for *many* examinees. Although the Wechsler Performance Scale may be fairer for many individuals than the Verbal Scale, it is still grossly unfair to many examinees.

Translated Tests

Historically, popular and useful tests have been translated for use with individuals who speak languages other than English. Although the effort to assess individuals' intelligence in their native language is commendable, there are many problems associated with the practice. Even though quality test translations are both possible and available (e.g., Bracken et al., 1990; Bracken & Fouad, 1987; Munoz-Sandoval, Cummins, Alvarado, & Ruef, 1998), "state-of-the-art" test translations are rare due to the inordinate expense and difficulty associated with the translation and validation process. Unfortunately, most translated tests, regardless of the quality of their translation, are not normed or properly validated on the population with which they are employed.

Even in an "ideal world" in which publishers would produce a translated test for every language spoken in the United States, there would still be an irreconcilable shortage of bilingual psychologists or educators who are available to administer the more than 200 translated tests that would be necessary. Given the relative unavailability of quality translated tests and the very limited number of bilingual psychologists, the most reasonable alternative to testing children in their native language is to remove language as a confounding variable and use nonverbal tests in the assessment process (Frisby, 1999).

Unidimensional Nonverbal Tests

Of the various nonverbal tests that are available there are two basic types. There are nonverbal tests that assess a narrow aspect of intelligence primarily through the use of progressive matrices, and there are the comprehensive tests of intelligence that assess multiple facets of children's intelligence. Unfortunately, these limited samples of intelligent behavior tend to be what most educators think of when asked about nonverbal tests. There is a plethora of progressive matrix tests available, but there are only two comprehensive nonverbal tests of intelligence (i.e., Leiter International Performance Scale–Revised, Roid & Miller, 1997; Universal Nonverbal Intelligence Test, Bracken & McCallum, 1998).

Tests of the matrix solution type include the Comprehensive Test of Nonverbal Intelligence (C-TONI; Hammill, Pearson, & Wiederholt, 1996); Test of Nonverbal Intelligence, Third Edition (TONI-3; Brown, Sherbenou, & Johnsen, 1997); Matrix Analogies Test (MAT; Naglieri, 1985); Naglieri Nonverbal Ability Test (N-NAT; Naglieri, 1996); General Ability Measure for Adults (GAMA; Naglieri & Bardos, 1997); and, the Raven's Progressive Matrices (Raven, Raven, & Court, 1998). Each of these measures is useful for individual and, in some instances, group (e.g., NNAT, GAMA) screening purposes.

These unidimensional nonverbal tests offer efficient assessment as a trade-off for comprehensive assessment. In general, unidimensional tests have some advantages over comprehensive measures of intelligence (e.g., cost-effectiveness, ease of administration, testing efficiency); however, currently available comprehensive nonverbal scales also provide screening batteries, comprised of a limited number of subtests.

The benefits of unidimensional nonverbal tests are offset in many cases by limitations. Several of the unidimensional nonverbal tests rely on brief verbal directions. Collectively, these tests assess a narrow and limited aspect of intelligence (i.e., spatial/figural relations) through a matrix-completion testing format. Typically, these measures do not employ adaptive testing procedures, which permit items to be administered within an examinee's ability level. And, unidimensional tests do not sample a broad range of important cognitive dimensions such as memory that are elements of most major theories of intelligence.

Given the narrow focus of the unidimensional matrix analogy type tests and the fact that many of these tests employ verbal directions, these instruments are best suited for "low stakes" applications (e.g., group screening). When psycho-educational assessments are conducted for "high stakes" placement, eligibility, or diagnostic decision-making reasons, broader, more comprehensive measures of intelligence (e.g., Leiter-R, UNIT) would appear to be more appropriate and show strong technical adequacy (see Leiter-R, Roid & Miller, 1997; UNIT, Bracken & McCallum, 1998).

SOCIAL JUSTICE IN GIFTED IDENTIFICATION: AN EXAMPLE

Project Athena was a federally funded Jacob K. Javits grant administered through the U.S. Department of Education, for which I was a coprincipal investigator with Dr. Joyce VanTassel-Baska. The project was a demonstration intervention study, designed in part to scale up a nationally validated language arts curriculum designed for high-ability learners. As a curriculum intervention study, Project Athena employed a quasi-experimental research design that randomized the assignment of classrooms of students and teachers in grades 3–5 to comparison and experimental instructional conditions. The project was implemented in 15 schools, in 7 school districts across 3 states (i.e., Maryland, South Carolina, Virginia).

Several studies were embedded within the overall project framework, including the issue of conducting equitable assessments. Objective 1 of Project Athena was to develop and implement instrumentation sensitive to low socioeconomic learners for the purposes of identification and assessment of learning (i.e., equitable assessment and identification).

During a 3-year implementation cycle (2003–2006), a total of 2,771 students participated in Project Athena. The racial/ethnic composition of the sample was diverse, with 43% White, 27.5% African American, 18 % Hispanic, and 2.4% Asian American students participating. The remaining students (9.1%) were identified as Pacific Islander, American Indian, or Other. Ethnic or racial minority students comprised 53.5% of the Project Athena student sample. Gender was approximately evenly divided within and across groups.

Instruments

Two tests were of particular interest in this study and were used as a means of identifying more students of poverty as intellectually gifted. The two tests included the Cognitive Abilities Test (CogAT; Lohman & Hagen, 2001) and the Universal Nonverbal Intelligence Test (UNIT; Bracken & McCallum, 1998). The CogAT and UNIT were used to identify students as intellectually gifted, in addition to the extant identification procedures employed in each of the three school districts.

The CogAT is a well-known and established group-administered test of verbal, spatial reasoning, and quantitative ability. Because the focus of Project Athena was on language arts, only the CogAT verbal and nonverbal scales were administered (i.e., quantitative reasoning was not germane to the project). Each section of the CogAT requires approximately 30 minutes for administration, for an approximate administration time of one hour. The CogAT technical manual indicates strong evidence for the instrument's validity, internal consistency, and stability. Levels B, C, and D of the CogAT Form 6 were group administered to students in the third, fourth, and fifth grade, respectively.

The UNIT is a popular individual, nonverbally administered test of intelligence. A two-subtest UNIT Abbreviated Battery was administered for this study. Considerable UNIT technical adequacy and fairness evidence is presented in the examiner's manual, with estimates of reliability posted by gender, race/ethnicity, exceptional/clinical students, and for important decision-making points (i.e., MR and gifted levels of cognitive functioning). The UNIT examiner's manual also presents an array of construct, criterion-related, and content validity evidence, with considerable fairness evidence presented as well.

Results

As a result of using two varied measures of intelligence, Project Athena identified nearly twice as many Title One students as gifted as compared to the school districts' identification procedures. Of 253 students identified as intellectually gifted with an IQ $\geq$ 120, 94 had been identified by the school districts and 159 were identified through the Project Athena assessments. Using a cut-score of 130 or greater, a total of 64 students were identified as gifted, with 29 identified by the districts and 35 identified by Project Athena. Importantly, for those students with IQs at 120 or above, 17.9% of the group was African American when assessed by the UNIT (11.9% were African American when the CogAT Nonverbal was used). With IQs at 130 or above, 14.7% were African American when assessed by the UNIT and 8.7% were African American when assessed by the CogAT Nonverbal scale. A total of 10.1% and 5.4% of the sample were African American at the 120 and 130 IQ levels, respectively, when the CogAT Verbal scale was used.

This multiyear curriculum and assessment intervention study showcased an equitable assessment practice in which the Project Athena identification measures nearly doubled the number of Title I students identified as intellectually gifted. By including verbal and nonverbal tests of intelligence or general ability in the assessment process, the project identified representative numbers of African

American students as would be anticipated in a normal distribution and given the demographic base of the project's school populations. This project underscored the importance of using multiple measures, including standardized tests, to identify low-income students who are gifted, and highlights the importance of recognizing that different tests will identify different students as gifted even when the tests purport to assess the same construct (see Bracken, 1988, for a more detailed explanation of why similar tests produce dissimilar outcomes).

SUMMARY

The United States continues to serve the world as a "melting pot," with immigrants settling farther and farther from their U.S. ports of entry. Because it is impossible to translate and validate intelligence tests for a population that collectively speaks more than 200 languages, and intelligence tests continue to carry significant weight in determining the opportunities and outcomes that are important parts of people's lives, it is apparent that the traditional, language-loaded intelligence tests used at the turn of the 21st century are just as unfair to many individuals as the English language tests administered to immigrants who processed through Ellis Island during the turn of the 20th century. Attempts to produce language-free tests have been renewed with better success and greater acceptance in recent years. There now are many unidimensional and short forms of comprehensive nonverbal tests available for intellectual screening, and there are comprehensive nonverbal intelligence tests that psychologists can use whenever a traditional language-loaded intelligence test is inappropriate for either screening or eligibility decision making.

What is most important in terms of progress in social justice is that educators and psychologists broaden their assessment repertoire and begin to use nonverbal tests of intelligence when students' manifest language skills inhibit the assessment of their latent cognitive abilities and combine verbal and nonverbal measures in general screening activities to provide a fairer assessment or identification procedure for all students, regardless of ability or disability.

CONCLUDING COMMENTS

It was an honor to contribute to Joyce VanTassel-Baska's Festschrift, in large part because I know that Joyce shares my dedication to equity and social justice. Joyce and I also share many other core values—values that have formed the basis of our strong personal and working relationship. My 8-year involvement with the Center for Gifted Education has been the highlight of my work at The College of William and Mary. I have found during that period that the Center's energy flows from, and is directed by Joyce, a truly talented leader.

Among Joyce's characteristics that I admire most as a colleague and friend, is her exceptional work ethic. She sets an expectation for doctoral students that academia is not a 10:00 to 2:00, 3 day-a-week *job*; it's a 365 day-a-year *career* that includes long days of scholarship, service, and mentoring. She knows what work is and has never shied from it. She has superb intellect and epitomizes the popular educational term, *authentic*—she is a dedicated blue-collar scholar. Joyce also has a strong personality, confident when working with other talented colleagues and creative in her ideas, always open to daring new proposals. She holds high expectations of others, balanced by good interpersonal skills, earned trust, and respect. Importantly, she is appropriately introspective when criticized or challenged and responds maturely. May her many former students carry her academic tradition, work ethic, sense of social justice, and ethics forward in her absence.

REFERENCES

Arthur, G. (1947). *A Point Scale of Performance Tests: Clinical manual.* New York: The Commonwealth Fund.

Arthur, G., & Woodrow, H. (1919). An absolute intelligence scale: A study in method. *Journal of Applied Psychology, 3,* 118–137.

Bracken, B. A. (1986). Incidence of basic concepts in the directions of five commonly used American tests of intelligence. *School Psychology International, 7,* 1–10.

Bracken, B. A. (1988). Ten psychometric reasons why similar tests produce dissimilar results. *Journal of School Psychology, 26,* 155–166.

Bracken, B. A., Barona, A., Bauermeister, J. J., Howell, K. K., Poggioli, L., & Puente, A. (1990). Multinational validation of the Spanish Bracken Basic Concept Scale for cross-cultural assessment. *Journal of School Psychology, 28,* 325–341.

Bracken, B. A., & Fouad, N. (1987). Spanish translation and validation of the Bracken Basic Concept Scale. *School Psychology Review, 16,* 94–102.

Bracken, B. A., & McCallum, R. S. (1998). *Examiner's manual for the Universal Nonverbal Intelligence Test.* Itasca, IL: Riverside.

Bracken, B. A., & Naglieri, J. A. (2003). Assessing diverse populations with nonverbal tests of general intelligence. In C. R. Reynolds & R. W. Kamphaus (Eds.), *Handbook of psychological and educational assessment of children* (2nd ed., pp. 243–274). New York: Guilford.

Bracken, B. A., VanTassel-Baska, J., Brown, E. F., & Feng, A. (2007). Project Athena: A tale of two studies. In J. VanTassel-Baska & T. Stambaugh (Eds.) *Overlooked gems: A national perspective on low-income promising learners* (pp. 63–67). Washington, DC: National Association for Gifted Children.

Brown, L., Sherbenou, R. J., & Johnsen, S. K. (1997). *Test of Nonverbal Intelligence, 3rd Edition.* Austin, TX: PRO-ED.

Carrey, N. J. (1995). Itard's 1828 memoire on "mutism caused by a lesion of the intellectual functions": A historical analysis. *Journal of the American Academy of Child and Adolescent Psychiatry, 341,* 655–661.

Chattin, S. H., & Bracken, B. A. (1989). School psychologists' evaluation of the K-ABC, McCarthy Scales, Stanford-Binet IV, and WISC-R. *Journal of Psychoeducational Assessment, 7,* 112–130.

Frisby, C. L. (1999). Straight talk about cognitive assessment and diversity. *School Psychology Quarterly, 14,* 195–207.

Hammill, D. D., Pearson, N. A., & Wiederholt, J. L. (1996). *Comprehensive Test of Nonverbal Intelligence*. Austin, TX: PRO-ED.

Healy, W. L. (1914). A pictorial completion test. *The Psychological Review, 20,* 189–203.

Healy, W. L. (1918). *Pictorial Completion Test II*. Chicago: C.H. Stoelting.

Healy, W. L. (1921). Pictorial Completion Test II. *Journal of Applied Psychology, 5,* 232–233.

Itard, J. M. G. (1932). *The wild boy of Aveyron*. New York: Appleton-Century-Crofts.

Kaufman, A. S. (1990). *Assessing adolescent and adult intelligence*. Boston: Allyn & Bacon.

Kaufman, A. S. (1994*). Intelligent testing with the WISC-III*. New York: Wiley.

Knox, H. A. (1914). A scale based on the work at Ellis Island for estimating mental defect. *Journal of the American Medical Association, 62,* 741–747.

Kohs, S. C. (1919). *Intelligence measurement*. New York: Macmillan.

Lohman, D. F., & Hagen, E. P. (2001). *Cognitive Abilities Test (CogAt), Form 6*. Itasca, IL: Riverside.

McCallum, R. S., Bracken, B. A., & Wasserman, J. (2001). *Essentials of nonverbal assessment*. New York: Wiley.

Munoz-Sandoval, A. E., Cummins, J., Alvarado, C. G., & Ruef, M. L. (1998). *Bilingual Verbal Ability Tests*. Itasca, IL: Riverside.

Naglieri, J. A. (1985). *Matrix Analogies Test–Expanded Form*. San Antonio, TX: The Psychological Corporation.

Naglieri, J. A.(1996). An examination of the relationship between intelligence and reading achievement using the MAT-SF and MAST. *Journal of Psychoeducational Assessment 14*(1), 65–69.

Naglieri, J. A., & Bardos, A. N. (1997). *General Ability Measure for Adults*. Minneapolis, MN: NCS Assessments.

Pasko, J. R. (1994). Chicago—Don't miss it. *Communique, 23*(4), 2.

Porteus, S. D. (1915). Mental tests for the feebleminded: A new series. *Journal of Psycho Asthenics, 19,* 200–213.

Raven, J., Raven, J. C., & Court, J. H. (1998). *Manual for Raven's Progressive Matrices and Vocabulary Scales*. Oxford, UK: Oxford University Press.

Roid, G. H., & Miller, L. J. (1997). *Leiter International Performance Scale–Revised*. Wood Dale, IL: Stoelting.

Seguin, E. (1907). *Idiocy and its treatment by the physiological method*. New York: Teachers College, Columbia University.

Thorndike, R. M., & Lohman, D. F. (1990). *A century of ability testing*. Chicago: Riverside.

VanTassel-Baska, J. (2008). Using performance-based assessment to document authentic learning. In J. Van-Tassel-Baska (Ed.) *Alternative assessments with gifted and talented students* (pp. 285–308). Waco, TX: Prufrock Press.

CHAPTER 19

THE CONTEXTUAL ASSESSMENT OF TALENT

by

DAVID
F. LOHMAN

There are many reasons for the intractable problems associated with identification of the gifted. One of them is related to the concept of absolute versus relative notions of giftedness.
—Joyce VanTassel-Baska

INTRODUCTION

Joyce VanTassel-Baska has been one of the most prolific and thoughtful contributors to the field of gifted education. Although some of her most impressive contributions have been in the development and evaluation of innovative curriculum for gifted students, she has an uncanny ability to understand and summarize developments in virtually all aspects of our field. In a remarkable paper published 8 years ago (VanTassel-Baska, 2000), she provided probably the best summary of the major controversies, misunderstandings, and dilemmas in and future directions for the assessment of talent. Of the many issues that make identification difficult, she argues, two of the most important are the transition from absolute to relative notions of giftedness and the ongoing concern that underrepresented groups are not adequately being assessed.

My primary goal in this paper is to expand on the first issue and to show how it is linked to the second. A relative notion of giftedness refers to the argument that judgments about giftedness depend on "the context of the school, the nature of the student's background, and the demands of the program" (VanTassel-Baska, 2000, p. 39). In other words, talent is best understood as relative to the context of its development and use. Thus, the assessment of talent also must be contextual.

The Contextual Assessment of Talent

There are three distinguishably different aspects of context in assessment. The first and most obvious concerns the context in which the assessment takes place. If rating scales are used, are the observations made in the home or in the classroom? If tests are used, are they administered individually in an unfamiliar setting by a professionally trained examiner or in a familiar environment by the classroom teacher? How do the children feel about the assessment? Are they afraid of making mistakes? Are they tired or distracted? Are they giving their best effort? These and many other factors can impair performance. Both trained examiners and observant teachers can observe and document events or behavior that might influence test performance. Indeed, those who administer standardized tests should always make notes during testing—notes that later may prove helpful in interpreting or responding to unexpected results.

The context of interpretation is equally important. These are the aspects of context that VanTassel-Baska (2000) referred to as "the context of the school" and "the nature of the student's background." Although critical for inferences about talent, the role of interpretive context often is ignored, especially for ability testing. The only interpretive context commonly used is the one provided by the norms that accompany the test.

The third context is the context of use. This is the aspect of context reflected in "the demands of the program" (VanTassel-Baska, 2000). The claim here is that aptitude for learning depends not only on what the student brings to the situation, but also on the demands and affordances of the learning situation itself.

Intelligence, Talent, and Aptitude

Although the move away from the concept of *giftedness* toward a more heterogeneous notion of *talent* has undoubtedly been a productive one, *talent* also can mislead: While there are many different talents, each talent is understood as a single trait or potential. This interpretation misleads efforts to identify talent, however, because the development of competence in any domain requires different constellations of aptitudes—some cognitive, some psychomotor, some affective, and some conative (Corno et al., 2002). For example, the development of mathematical talent requires the ability to reason with quantitative symbols and concepts, together with an interest in or even an enthusiasm for mathematics that leads a student to persist in learning about mathematics. But interest, enthusiasm, and persistence do not occur in a vacuum. Rather, they represent ways of responding to, interacting with, selecting, or altering an environment. Thus, more than possessing needed cognitive, affective, and conative resources, *aptitude* requires an attunement to or resonance with the demands and affordances of the learning environment. Bright children who do not resonate well with traditionally structured schools will have a hard time displaying and developing their talents in that environment. Thus, defining the treatment or learning context is an integral part of defining *aptitude* (Snow & Lohman, 1984).

Opportunity to Learn

We infer that someone has aptitude or talent for something in two ways. First, and most unambiguously, we infer that a person has talent for something when that person learns quickly what other persons learn less rapidly. Because it incorporates the specific mix of cognitive, psychomotor, affective, and conative resources required for learning, the *speed of learning* a task or skill itself often is the best indicator of aptitude for that task or skill.

The second route for inferring aptitude is from superior performance on other tasks or dimensions known to be required for and therefore predictive of success in the target domain. For example, we infer that the individual who scores well on an ability test has the aptitude to succeed academically because reasoning abilities are known to be required for academic learning; but learning anything of nontrivial complexity requires much more than having the requisite cognitive resources. Aptitude includes interest, motivation, and strategies for persisting in the pursuit of excellence in learning. Not recognizing the multidimensional nature of aptitude often results in the unwarranted assumption that cognitive resources are sufficient for talent development. Discrepancies between achievement and ability are then interpreted as evidence of underachievement. However, as Thorndike (1963) concluded, the problem is better understood as *underprediction*. That is, the conceptual or statistical model for predicting achievement that includes only ability is insufficiently complex. An analogy to physical skills may help: Although height is an aptitude for basketball, some tall people do not play basketball well. One does not call them "basketball underachievers." In fact, these tall people may lack interest in the sport, coordination, aggressiveness, or any one of the many other personal resources required for developing basketball skills; or may have all the requisite resources but lack the opportunity to develop them.

Whether aptitude is inferred from performance of the task itself or from performance on other variables that predict that performance, the proper comparison is always with other people who have had roughly similar opportunities to acquire those abilities or develop the characteristics that we are assessing. Depending on the norm group or standard, the same performance can indicate remarkable aptitude or remarkable inaptitude. When nationally normed ability and achievement tests are used, comparisons can be made to a wide range of individuals grouped by age, grade, or both age and grade. Typically, one only compares performance to the examinee's age or grade group, although other comparisons also can be helpful. When acceleration is considered, for example, if the test used contains content that is appropriate for children of different grades, one can ask not only how a score compares with the scores of other students in the child's current grade, but also with the scores of students in the target grade. Local norms provide the most direct evidence for such decisions.

Alternative Assessments or Alternative Norms?

When children's experiences in a domain differ significantly from those of children in the normative sample, one can either use tests that attempt to sample from domains of common experience or instead use the same aptitude tests used for other children but create a new, more appropriate reference group. The first approach is exemplified by administering nonverbal ability tests to bilingual children. This allows one to use common, national norms for all children. However, one cannot assume that nonverbal tests level the playing field for bilingual children (Lohman, Gambrell, & Lakin, 2008). Further, nonverbal ability tests underrepresent the ability construct of interest and thus do not predict as well as more comprehensive assessments the academic success of both majority and minority children. Therefore, I have argued that those who have been assigned the responsibility of identifying talent also should consider how they might move beyond national norms, especially when looking for talent in groups whose experiences differ from the norm (Lohman & Lakin, 2007). This is made difficult, though, by the belief that ability tests provide an absolute or gold standard of giftedness.

Beyond Absolute Notions of Giftedness

The belief that IQ scores provide an absolute standard for determining intellectual giftedness is ancient but erroneous. Performance on IQ tests has been improving ever since ability tests were first introduced. Flynn (2007) estimated an increase of about three IQ points per decade between 1948 and 2002, with the largest increase occurring on figural reasoning tests such as the Progressive Matrices Test (Raven, Court, & Raven, 1996). The mean IQ score remains 100 only because intelligence tests are renormed every few years; therefore, old norms are invariably too lenient. For example, the most recent edition of the Progressive Matrices test uses normative data collected in the 1970s and 1980s. A comparison of these normative scores with two more recently normed tests showed that scores on the Raven were approximately 11 IQ-like points ($.67$ SD) too high (Lohman et al., 2008).

Therefore, those who assume that national norms on ability or achievement tests represent fixed standards are sorely mistaken. Changing the context of assessment, for example, by reducing anxiety or by administering a different collection of test tasks also changes the score that a child obtains. Changing the context of interpretation from old norms to new norms, from one national norming sample to another, from age-based to grade-based comparisons, or from national to local norms also changes the interpretation of a score. Scores that are unusual in one normative context often are not unusual in another normative context.

Furthermore, even if old norms could be used with impunity, a rule that limits the talent pool to the subset of students who reason well across cognitive domains excludes more academically talented students than it admits. The problem posed by uneven profiles of abilities is exacerbated at the extremes of the score distributions. An uneven profile with significant or extreme score discrepancies is as common among the most-able students as a relatively flat profile. Yet, the students with uneven profiles are excluded when only a single composite score is used (Lohman et al., 2008).

Beyond Standards-Based Assessment

Dissatisfaction with the relativity of normative interpretations of test scores led many educators to advocate for criterion- or standards-based assessments. The goal was to describe what students know and can do—seemingly an absolute standard—rather than their rank within a normative population. Statements about competence were made either in reference to some domain of tasks or to a set of judgmental standards about proficiency. Although always helpful in guiding instruction (e.g., for a child being considered for academic acceleration), such information generally is *not* helpful for making inferences about exceptionality *unless the standards are interpreted normatively*. By definition, performance is exceptional relative to a normative group. As one wit put it, "Behind every criterion there lurks a norm."

Variation and the Need for Measurement

Variation thus is inherent in the concept of exceptionality. If there is no variation in a characteristic, then there can be no exceptionally high or low instances of that characteristic. Further, variation presumes measurement. We cannot defend the proposition that people or events vary along some dimension unless we have some dependable means for measuring that dimension. Assessment then is at the very core of the concept of *talent* and of efforts to identify students who display it.

Unfortunately, like most educators, those who have the responsibility for identifying talented students generally have little formal training in educational and psychological measurement. Unlike classroom teachers—who might know little about assessment but who can learn enough to explain score reports from an achievement test during parent-teacher conferences—the persons responsible for developing and implementing a talent identification program must know considerably more. If they do not, they will select (or be sold) ineffective tests and rating scales or often will use in inappropriate ways the information that the assessments provide. When this happens, those responsible for the program might be aware that something is amiss but would not be able to identify the psychological, psychometric, and statistical issues that have derailed the talent-identification system.

Even those educators with some background in measurement often are unprepared for the special problems that can bedevil efforts to identify exceptionality. Problems that are a minor nuisance near the mean of a score distribution can be real headaches when one is dealing with extreme scores. For example, errors of measurement at the extremes of a score distribution often are many times larger than errors of measurement at the mean (Feldt & Brennan, 1989). Regression to the mean—which, by definition, is nonexistent at the mean—increases as scores depart from the mean. Difficulties in establishing normative scores also increase at the extremes of the distribution. Finally, different methods for scaling test scores can dramatically expand or restrict the range of scores that can be observed on the test. For example, the frequency of extremely high scores was substantially reduced after the scaling methodology used on the Stanford-Binet Form L-M was replaced with the more robust scaling methods used on recent editions of the test (Ruf, 2003). Those educators who do not understand how the methodology changed can easily misinterpret the lower scores that are now reported.

A Primer on Developing Norms

Norms establish the context for inferences about accomplishment or talent. Understanding how norms are developed can help users judge the quality of the norms that provide the interpretive context for test scores and can inform efforts to develop local norms.

From Raw to Scale Scores

Responses on any test must first be scored in some way. The process can be as easy as applying a scoring key or as difficult as rating open-ended responses to moral dilemmas or essay prompts. Raw scores are then transformed to scale scores. Although the process of mapping raw scores onto scale scores can be complex, the result is straightforward. Number correct scores are mapped onto a new scale on which differences between adjacent raw scores are compressed or expanded, much like a rubber band that is selectively stretched or compressed at different points. The greatest expansion typically occurs at the extremes of the score scale, especially on fixed-length ability and achievement tests. This can be critical for the assessment of giftedness because the standard error of measurement for such scores is proportional to the amount by which the scale is stretched. Larger errors of measurement mean not only that the scores are likely to change on retest, but also that the change is most likely to be back toward the mean. The amount of regression always increases as scores depart further from the mean.

National Norms

Although scale scores have many desirable properties—especially for modeling growth—they usually are not directly interpreted. Rather, the test developer or user first administers the test to a sample of persons and determines the distributions of scale scores for subgroups of students classified by grade or age. This allows statements about the frequency with which different scale scores were observed in the norming sample. The norming sample can be broadly or narrowly defined. A national norm for children 6 years of age is an example of the former; a local norm for English-language learners (ELL) is an example of the latter. Both kinds of normative comparisons are useful, but for different kinds of inferences.

Unless otherwise indicated, percentile rank (PR) or IQ-like scores use national norms. Good national norms offer a way to compare the scores of students to a common standard. This is important in regional and national talent searches. National norms also provide a convenient way to compare scores for different cohorts (e.g., "Is this year's applicant pool less able than last year's?") and to make statements about the level and profile of ability for individuals and groups that usually are more dependable than can be made from the test user's data. National norms also are more carefully constructed than local norms. It is difficult to appreciate the differences between national and local norms without some understanding of how good national norms are developed.

The normative sample. The first step is to define a sampling strategy that will make the norming sample representative of the target population. Herein lies one of the most important differences between individual and group ability tests. Individual ability tests try to represent the national population; group tests aim to represent that portion of the population that attends school and can take, perhaps with accommodations, the group-administered test. Because of these restrictions, IQ-like scores on group tests often are lower than corresponding scores on individual tests. The differences typically are quite small in the primary grades but can be substantial at higher grades as the rate of dropping out of school increases. Because less-able students are more likely than more-able students to drop out, the school-attending portion of the population tends to be more able. Therefore, a student's rank in the full population will be somewhat higher than his or her rank in the school-attending sample.

The sampling plan for the norming study defines the target population. The population of interest is stratified along demographic characteristics known to moderate test performance. For individual and group tests, commonly used demographic variables include region of the country, socioeconomic status, ethnicity, and urban versus rural community. For group tests, school district size and public versus private schools also are used. Lists of individuals or schools within each cell of this design are assembled, and some number proportional to the size of the cell in the sampling design is randomly identified and asked to participate in the study. However, some schools or individuals refuse to participate, even in government-mandated assessments such as the National Assessment of Educational Progress (NAEP). To make the obtained sample better represent the demographic characteristics of the target sample, cases typically are reweighted. Thus, when norms are computed, scores for some individuals are counted more and scores for others, less. (In the case of group tests, this method would be applied to entire schools.) In the test manual, professionals look for descriptions of the demographic characteristics of both the original, unweighted sample and the final, weighted sample. Comparing these two samples shows how much the data were weighted. Large differences on the dimensions most strongly related to test performance make the norms suspect. Unfortunately, some test manuals report only the characteristics of the final, weighted sample.

Weighting is performed so that the normative sample on average better represents the target population. However, weighting can markedly alter the demographic characteristics of the small portion of the sample of students who obtain extreme scores. For example, the government statisticians who oversee large longitudinal data sets such as the National Education Longitudinal Study (NELS) provide weights that attempt to make the data representative of the U.S. population. However, sampling occurs not only at the initial testing, but at every retesting as participants drop out. The resulting weights for individual cases can exceed 100. Therefore, analyses of the scores for gifted students in these data sets are probably better made from the unweighted data than from the weighted data.

Creating norms. Once the weighted set of scale scores has been obtained, the norming process can be started. The first step is to divide the sample into smaller groups of test-takers who are similar in age (or grade). Most age-normed tests group children in 3- or 6-month intervals. For example, on Form 6 of CogAT, 55 three-month age groups were created beginning at 57 months (less than 5 years of age) and extending through 219 months (greater than 18 years). The distribution of scale scores within each of these 55 age groups was then obtained.

The scale scores corresponding to the same percentile rank should increase smoothly from one age group to the next. But, sampling errors in each distribution make scores vary less predictably. Norm tables derived from these distributions would show considerable irregularity. Sometimes adding 3 months to a child's age and moving to the next age group would result in a large increase in the scale score and other times would result in no increase or perhaps even a decrease. Further, the amount of jumping about would be greatest where the data are relatively sparse (i.e., at the extremes of the distribution). Therefore, the within-age group score distributions must first be smoothed.

Although many methods have been devised for smoothing score distributions, one of the best uses bootstrapping. This procedure provides a way to estimate sampling errors in each of the 55 score distributions. Estimates of these sampling errors are then incorporated into the smoothing process. If the scale score that corresponds to a particular PR on a distribution is estimated to have little sampling error, then the smooth curve that attempts to connect this scale score with the scale scores for the same PR on the previous and subsequent age groups is allowed only a little wiggle room. However, if the scale score corresponds to a point on the distribution that is estimated to have considerable noise, say, at the 99th PR, then the smooth curve that connects the scale score for this 99th PR with the scale scores for the 99th PRs of the previous and subsequent age groups is allowed much wiggle room.

But, how can we estimate the sampling error at each point from only one distribution of scores? This is where the bootstrapping procedure comes in. Literally, we pull ourselves up by our bootstraps by repeatedly resampling from the obtained score distribution and then estimating how much change we observe. Suppose that there are 100 students in the age group centered at 6 years 0 months. We create a new sample that also has 100 students by drawing *with replacement* from the initial set of 100 students. Further, the probability that a student will be selected in each draw is determined by the weight attached to that student's data. Because the sampling was done with replacement, each of the 100 students could be selected more than once (or not at all). Further, because the scores were weighted, the new sample of 100 cases generally would be more representative of the population than the initial, unweighted set of scores.

Then, we repeat the sampling process hundreds of times. Each time we determine the scale scores that are associated with fixed percentiles of the new distribution of scale scores. The variability of these scale scores for each PR provides the estimated sampling error at that PR. For the 2005 CogAT norms, we used the 21 PR values associated with SAS scores of 50, 55, 60, . . . 140, 145, 150. We resampled 500 times at each of the 55 age groups. Therefore, we were able to estimate the amount of sampling error at 21 separate locations in each of the 55 score distributions. The final step was to use the sampling error around each scale score to fit a smooth curve across the 55 age groups, separately for each of the 21 PR levels. The plots of these curves were then inspected and adjusted as necessary to remove inconsistencies. This entire process was performed for each of the three CogAT scores (Verbal [V], Quantitative [Q], and Nonverbal [N]), the three partial composite scores (VQ, VN, and QN), and the three-battery (VQN) composite score.

The process outlined here also has been used on individually administered ability tests such as the Woodcock-Johnson III (McGrew, Dailey, & Schrank, 2007). However, national norms for some tests are obtained much more haphazardly. For the Progressive Matrices Test and the Culture Fair Intelligence Test, the sampling plan was omitted and norms were assembled from user data. On one recently normed test, the distributions were simply assumed to have the same variability at all test levels and the norms were computed directly from the initial, unsmoothed distributions of scale scores (see Lohman et al., 2008). Unsurprisingly, the normative scores on this test showed systematic biases.

Local Norms

Because it usually is expensive and always time consuming to test children one at a time, national norms are the only norms offered on tests that must be administered individually. Local norms, on the other hand, can be obtained from most test publishers when a group ability or achievement test is administered to all children in a grade in a particular school, school district, or state. Local norms are created directly from the distribution of scores in the sample. Local norms also can be estimated from the test data by anyone who can use a spreadsheet application such as Microsoft Excel. Norms for subgroups (e.g., grade 3 ELL children) can be computed in the same way.

Local norms can be helpful in several ways. Decisions about the need for special services at the school level often are best made using school norms (Renzulli,

2005). The need for special services depends primarily on the discrepancy between the child's development in a domain and that of his or her *local* classmates. Further, many programs have resources that allow them to serve only a certain number of students. Local norms make it easy to identify a given number of students because there are always, say, 5% of the students in a school in the top 5% of that school's score distribution. This allows school administrators to focus on finding methods that best identify those students who need services rather than on reweighting nationally normed test scores or searching for new tests whose national norms will identify the desired number of students. In spite of their usefulness, however, many school-based programs rely exclusively on national norms. This is in part the legacy of an earlier era in which giftedness was defined by IQ scores and IQs were thought to be fixed.

Local norms for age-based scores. For achievement tests, scores are normed by week or month in grade. If all students take the achievement test at approximately the same time, then year and month of grade is held constant. Distributions of scale scores for classes or subgroups give the desired local norms. For ability tests, however, scores are normed by the year and month of the student's age. Students in a class who are tested at the same time will differ widely in age. Unless the sample is very large, it would be difficult to approximate age norms using the methods used to construct national age norms. However, the IQ-like scores reported on nationally normed ability tests already are adjusted for the effects of age. Therefore, distributions of these scores for students within a grade who are tested at approximately the same time controls for both the effects of age and grade.

Percentile ranks versus ranks. Sometimes only the best students in the local group or subgroup need to be identified. An easier (and less precise) method is simply to rank order the scores and then identify the number of students who can be served by starting at the top of the list and working down. The primary difference between rank orders and percentile ranks is that rank-ordering the data discards information about the magnitude of the differences in performance between students with adjacent ranks. Percentile ranks—whether national or local—preserve this information.

As this summary shows, the precision and dependability of the normative score declines as one moves from national PR to local PR to subgroup ranks. However, the extent to which one has contextualized the score for making inferences about talent increases to the extent that an examinee's experiences differ from those of the typical student in the national norming sample and align with those of other students in the local group or subgroup. For such students, then, there is a tradeoff between getting a *more precise but less valid* estimate of the student's talent by using an inappropriate national norm group and getting *a less precise but more valid* estimate by using a more appropriate local or subgroup norm. All three perspectives— national, local, and subgroup—can be helpful, and each is better suited to different kinds of inferences.

Multiple Measures

A cardinal rule of identification is to use multiple measures for every trait that is assessed. Scores from tests that measure the same trait should be weighted approximately by their reliability and then summed or averaged. Scores from tests that measure different traits (e.g., verbal abilities versus quantitative abilities) should not be averaged. Both tests identify students who are talented but in different domains. Finally, scores from rating scales, classroom observations, and assessments with questionable validity (e.g., tests of creativity) should be used to provide opportunities but never to deny them. It is difficult to defend a decision to deny services to a student with low scores on the rating scale but high ability or achievement test scores. But, this is what happens whenever all measures are assigned point totals and summed. For every student admitted because of high ratings, another student with equally high scores on other measures but lower ratings is rejected. A simple scheme for combining multiple measures of ability and achievement with teacher ratings that avoids this pitfall is described in Lohman and Lakin (2007).

Problems With Contextual Assessment

Moving from the security of an absolute to a relative frame of reference always is unsettling. Indeed some have argued that it requires a style of thinking or level of conceptual development that most adults find uncomfortable and some find inaccessible (Hofer & Pintrich, 1997). One moves from the security of *yes* or *no* to the fuzzy world of *maybe* and *it depends*. In the social sciences, this is seen in the transition from objectivism to phenomenology. Whereas objectivists believe that they can stand *outside the system* and still understand it, phenomenologists believe that true understanding comes only if the observer can see the world as it appears from *inside the system*. As in theories of adolescent cognitive development, the danger with achieving a relativist point of view is getting lost in it. Although context matters, generalization still is possible. Indeed, the better equalized the contexts of administration and interpretation, the more valid the individual differences that are measured.

Contextual assessment is surely not without problems or controversy. The major problem with contextual norms is that they can mask important differences in levels of performance. For example, boys score higher than girls on spatial tests that require three-dimensional rotation. The differences are quite large—sometimes a full standard deviation. Separate norms for girls and boys mask real differences in spatial ability. Similarly, the ELL child who scores at the 95th PR when compared to other ELL children may score only at the 50th PR when compared to non-ELL children. Although we may be able to support the inference that the ELL child has displayed talent, there is little justification for placing her in the same instructional situation as her higher scoring classmates. Always, instruction should start at the child's current level of achievement or development. However, she may be expected to learn faster and more deeply than her non-ELL classmates who show a similar level of achievement. This means that contextually sensitive assessment of talent must be coupled with developmentally appropriate instruction.

In statistics, the problem of relativity is sometimes discussed under the concept of *exchangeability*. When reporting the mean of a group, we assume that individuals are exchangeable members of that group. However, as Novick (1982) pointed out:

> Our success as scientists can be measured by our skill in identifying variables that can be used to find relevant, exchangeable subpopulations. To the extent that we make global statements that are true only on average for a global population when we could be making more precise statements for more precisely defined populations, we fail in our role as scientists. It is even worse when we knowingly use the wrong reference population. (p. 6)

Nevertheless, the search for the best set of relevant subpopulations is fraught with difficulties. Sometimes the relative gain in precision is small. Further, as Cronbach (1975) lamented, it is like entering a hall of mirrors. If familiarity with the language matters, then why not also consider the similarity of the first language to English or the level of parental education? Thus, there is an understandable reluctance to open the door that would entertain the possibility of contextual interpretations of test scores.

For ability tests, however, the door has already been opened. The WISC-IV Spanish (Wechsler, 2004) now provides scores that attempt to take into account opportunity to learn for bilingual, Spanish-speaking children attending U.S. schools. Specifically, three scores can be reported: an ability score that compares the child to all other children in the U.S., a percentile rank that compares the child to other Spanish-speaking bilingual children with similar exposure to U.S. schools, and a percentile rank that controls for both exposure to U.S. schools and parental education. Those educators who want a simple answer to how smart the child is will find this ambiguity unsettling.

CONCLUSION

In some respects, each person is like all other people, like some other people, and like no other person (Kluckholm & Murray, 1953). Theories of ability, personality, motivation, and interests posit a vast array of ways in which people differ. However, the only subdivision captured in most of the test norms that measure these traits is that of age or its surrogate, grade. The measurement of talent among children whose opportunities to learn differ markedly from their age-mates requires that we learn to do more.

References

Corno, L., Cronbach, L. J., Kupermintz, H., Lohman, D. F., Mandinach, E. B., Porteus, A. W., et al. (2002). *Remaking the concept of aptitude: Extending the legacy of Richard E. Snow.* Hillsdale, NJ: Erlbaum.

Cronbach, L. J. (1975). Beyond the two disciplines of scientific psychology. *American Psychologist, 30,* 116–127.

Feldt, L. S., & Brennan, R. L. (1989). Reliability. In R. L. Linn (Ed.), *Educational measurement* (3rd ed., pp. 105–146). New York: Macmillan.

Flynn, J. R. (2007). *What is intelligence?* New York: Cambridge University Press.

Hofer, B. K., & Pintrich, P. R. (1997). The development of epistemological theories: Beliefs about knowledge and knowing and their relation to learning. *Review of Educational Research, 67,* 88–140.

Kluckholm, C., & Murray, H. A. (1953). *Personality in nature, society, and culture.* New York: Knopf.

Lohman, D. F., Gambrell, J., & Lakin, J. (2008). The commonality of extreme discrepancies in the ability profiles of academically gifted students. *Psychology Science Quarterly, 50,* 269–282.

Lohman, D. F., & Lakin, J. (2007). Nonverbal test scores as one component of an identification system: Integrating ability, achievement, and teacher ratings. In J. VanTassel-Baska (Ed.), *Alternative assessments for identifying gifted and talented students* (pp. 41–66). Waco, TX: Prufrock Press.

McGrew, K. S., Dailey, D. E. H., & Schrank, F. A. (2007). *Woodcock-Johnson III/Woodcock-Johnson III Normative Update score differences: What the user can expect and why* (Woodcock-Johnson III Assessment Service Bulletin No. 9). Rolling Meadows, IL: Riverside.

Novick, M. R. (1982). Educational testing: Inferences in relevant subpopulations. *Educational Researcher, 11,* 4, 6–10, 28.

Raven, J. C., Court, J. H., & Raven, J. (1996). *Manual for Raven's Progressive Matrices and Vocabulary Scales: Section 3. Standard Progressive Matrices.* Oxford, UK: Oxford Psychologists Press.

Renzulli, J. S. (2005). *Equity, excellence, and economy in a system for identifying students in gifted education: A guidebook* (Research Monograph No. 05208). Storrs: University of Connecticut, The National Research Center on the Gifted and Talented.

Ruf, D. L. (2003). *Use of the SB5 in the assessment of high abilities* (Stanford-Binet Intelligence Scales, Fifth Edition, Assessment Service Bulletin No. 3). Itasca, IL: Riverside.

Snow, R. E., & Lohman, D. F. (1984). Toward a theory of aptitude for learning from instruction. *Journal of Educational Psychology, 76,* 347–376.

Thorndike, R. L. (1963). *The concepts of over- and underachievement.* New York: Columbia University, Teachers College, Bureau of Publications.

VanTassel-Baska, J. (2000). The on-going dilemma of identification practices in gifted education. *The Communicator, 31,* 39–41

Wechsler, D. (2004). *WISC-IV Spanish.* San Antonio, TX: Pearson.

CHAPTER 20

TRADITIONAL AND ALTERNATIVE ASSESSMENT OF INTELLECTUAL AND ACADEMIC APTITUDE

by

NANCY
M. ROBINSON

Assessment is a critical tool for ongoing curriculum planning. Assessment data provide information about how well the planning and teaching of learning outcomes have fared.
—Joyce VanTassel-Baska (2003)

In the field of gifted education, rife as it is with controversies, none is more impassioned or politically overcharged than that surrounding the use of psychological assessment tools for identifying gifted children and for guiding program admission. Although the first intellectual measures devised by Binet and Simon (1905) were developed to protect students of average ability from erroneous placement in classes for mentally retarded children, issues of program placement are still with us. The issues have to do with both retarded and gifted students, and continue to cloud understanding of such measures by professionals and the public alike.

INTRODUCTION

Assessment measures of cognitive and academic ability have been derived for a number of purposes. Group aptitude tests like the Cognitive Abilities Test, the SAT and the ACT, and group achievement tests like the Metropolitan,

California, Stanford, or Iowa Tests of Basic Skills have generally functioned as admission or program placement guides, as in the military, originally, and then in school contexts for admission to special programs or selective colleges. Sometimes they also are used to track the progress of groups of students, as in No Child Left Behind (NCLB) or in comparative international studies. Group-administered measures like these have been criticized the most. Those administered individually, like the various Wechsler tests or the Woodcock-Johnson Tests of Achievement, usually serve more clinical purposes, in the quest of understanding why a student might not be doing as well as expected, and to guide educational planning for specific students.

CONCERNS ABOUT TESTING

Public mistrust of traditional assessment instruments stems from several sources. First, it must be admitted that, in the past (much less often today), there have been blatant misuses of the instruments, with far too many victims seriously impacted. Among these: Early in the 20th century, English-language tests of intelligence were used to exclude perfectly capable non-English-speaking immigrants trying to enter the United States. In the hope of speeding up the slow course of evolution, tests were touted by adherents of the eugenics movement as tools to guide selective reproduction. Intelligence tests were used with frightened young children traumatized by the breakup of their families to decide whether to place them in foster/adoptive homes or in institutions for children with retardation. Developmental tests with little predictive power during infancy were used inappropriately, not to screen for major problems but in misguided attempts to improve a match with adoptive families. One can make no apologies for such errors except to acknowledge that, for the most part, well-meaning people had been misled by overhyped promises of a powerful x-ray into human potential and disability.

Objectivity and fairness were the two major goals for developing assessment instruments. Never intended to be used in isolation from other information about the individuals involved, it was hoped that carefully standardized measures could overcome the effects of personal misjudgment as, for example, when a child from a low-income family or a child with unappealing appearance or behavior was being considered for admission to a special class. A test like the SAT was supposed to treat everyone fairly in college admissions, no matter whether they came from a top-ranked or a low-ranked high school, or, nowadays, a homeschool setting. This goal of fairness continues to underlie to a large extent the use of ability and achievement tests in public school districts seeking to be equitable in offering special services and to depoliticize the admissions process. Alas, political issues do not disappear that readily.

Specifically with regard to the current use of ability and achievement tests to find and select students of high ability for special programs or selective colleges, doubts and criticisms abound today among some (not all) segments of the gifted-ness community as well as the public. Individual tests are less controversial but so expensive that their use would consume the entire budgets for the programs themselves. In certain circumstances, in fact, the traditional measures are actu-ally quite well accepted, as in the use of the SAT and ACT in the regional talent searches in which upwards of 150,000 bright young adolescents participate every year. There also is no objection to those occasional welcome surprises when group tests identify students with previously unsuspected high talent.

By and large, the discomfort with the use of nationally standardized instru-ments stems from a single issue: *the racial, ethnic, and socioeconomic dispropor-tionality in the groups identified as gifted when the measures are used.* Advocates for underrepresented groups tend to expect that equal proportions of all groups should emerge from these situations, and that when they do not, there must be bias in the tests themselves. (Bias in tests does not refer to group differences in performance, but rather, whether a given score has a different meaning or predictive power depending on one's group membership.) Programs typically are under considerable pressure to do something about the disproportionality—a situation that can only be changed by significant modifications in society itself. The effects of unequal life opportunities cannot be erased by the use of "objective" measures. All we know about child development points to the powerful influence on development of environmental factors from the moment of conception on (Robinson, 2003). Rather than blaming the messenger (i.e., the tests), we must address children's unequal experiences and opportunities, doing our best as a society to assure each the best chance possible for optimal development. To the extent we are successful, I believe, racial and cultural differences in school status likely will disappear. But, by the time children reach school age, especially in districts that ignore gifted children until third grade or so, too much irreplaceable time has gone by, and the job is ever so much harder.

WHY HAVE SPECIAL PROGRAMS FOR GIFTED STUDENTS?

Perhaps at this point it is wise to review the reasons for and the contexts in which programs for gifted students are developed. In most K–12 schools, the majority of the instructional day is devoted to verbal- and mathematical-based sub-jects such as reading and understanding literature, social studies, expository writing, mathematics, and science. This is what the community demands and, therefore, to the virtual exclusion of anything else including the fine arts, it is these subjects which we emphasize for 13 years of public school, at least 6 hours per day and at least 180 days per year. Whole-class instruction is directed to about the middle attainment level of the class, although classes are typified by a wide range of talent and accomplishment. In the current NCLB climate, when teachers have a bit of extra time, they are likely to spend it with the students who are struggling.

Children who have already mastered the material and whose reasoning is more mature than most of their classmates are ill served in such settings—indeed, to a large extent not served at all—and in desperate need of rescue, challenge, academic rigor, and opportunity to acquire new ideas and skills and, perhaps most important, the opportunity to master the difficult, to persevere when the material is not immediately obvious. They also need the company of classmates who speak their language, both literally and figuratively (Neihart, Reis, Robinson, & Moon, 2002). Programs that are appropriate for them must make demands for achievement and cognitive maturity significantly more difficult than the ordinary age-calibrated fare.

THE SYNERGY BETWEEN TESTS AND PROGRAMS

Traditional tests do a reasonably good job of identifying such children and describing their knowledge and skills, when taken in the context of their school performance, when testing conditions are reasonably optimal, and when the selection procedures facilitate the match (e.g., math-talented children admitted to math-oriented programs; Lohman, this volume; Robinson, 2005, 2008). The traditional approach generally yields an effective match *for most gifted children* between their academic development and the programs being offered. Furthermore, over the years, existing programs have conformed more and more closely to the successive populations of children selected for them, a circular, synergistic system that improves the match but does nothing to improve the proportional enrollment of children from underserved backgrounds.

WHAT MIGHT BE WRONG?

The synergy in the system is not perfect. In part, this is because no assessment instrument is perfect. In practice, furthermore, some children in need of the programs are missed because of anxiety, illness, or undetected learning disabilities that interfere with their best responses, especially during group tests. Some children who are inexperienced with tests either take too long with items that intrigue them, or are reluctant to guess unless they are absolutely sure (two maladies more likely to strike bright children who are somewhat perfectionistic). Some children tested in English are still learning the language. Sometimes, nonverbal or spatial components of standard measures can be used to identify these children, but these issues are not entirely straightforward, either, especially because the content of programs is so highly verbal (see Bracken and Lohman chapters, this volume). In part, too, the match is imperfect because of developmental asynchronies such that children are not equally advanced in all areas represented in the programs to which they are admitted, so that the match is imperfect.

But, there is an additional possibility: The system may be missing children who actually have the wherewithal to succeed in existing or slightly modified programs, but who fail to be noticed because teachers and parents do not recognize them, because the existing measures do not do them justice, or because their academic talents are not in the "traditional" mode tapped effectively by the test. Examples of these abilities might be practical and/or creative modalities such as those Sternberg and Grigorenko include in their Rainbow and Aurora projects (Chart, Grigorenko, & Sternberg, 2008).

Moreover, it is suspected that a disproportionate number of the children being missed by the existing system, and typically affected by the factors mentioned in the preceding paragraph, are from marginalized backgrounds. These children may be highly capable in meeting the demands and expectations of their own homes and neighborhoods but not necessarily successful according to the rules of the traditional educational enterprise. Furthermore, there is some evidence (Aronson & Steele, 2005) that the performance of children from minority backgrounds may be unduly suppressed by what is known as *stereotype threat*, the tendency to do less well on evaluative measures than one otherwise might when one belongs to a group that suffers a negative stereotype in that area of endeavor. This effect has been demonstrated with highly competent students in selective universities; with women on math tests; with African Americans on tests of ability; with the elderly; and with members of many other groups about whom negative images are held, whether there is any truth to the images or not.

To the extent that children are able to rise to the challenge and rigor of what programs for highly capable, high-achieving students have to offer, it would be criminal to exclude them because we doggedly stick to the narrow confines of traditional tests, which may in some instances underestimate their abilities and accomplishments. On the other hand, it would be equally unwise to discard in a wholesale fashion all standardized tests of ability and achievement, because in many instances these assessments are in the right ballpark and facilitate appropriate education for able students.

Note that this author is *not* referring here to children whose talents lie outside the boundaries of school curricula, such as those with abilities in the arts. The typical school severely limits instruction in these areas, and encouragement of such talents—when it occurs—must take place outside of school and may not occur at all for children whose families do not have the means to seek extra help. Unfair to the children and costly to our society as is this state of affairs, it is outside the purview of this chapter. There is one lesson to be learned from the way we approach these talents, however: We do not "test" for them in the usual way. Rather, we use samples of learning and performance to detect and assess children's talents (i.e., *performance measures*). It is this sort of approach that VanTassel-Baska has effectively added to the assessment picture for academically gifted children.

NEW TRENDS AND DIRECTIONS
IN ALTERNATIVE ASSESSMENT

Although issues of assessment clearly have not constituted VanTassel-Baska's major professional focus in the same way curriculum issues have, she never has been one to leave a significant problem or controversy in the field of giftedness unattended, certainly not one with which she could be helpful. Indeed, two very different approaches to assessment issues—both highly related to selection proce-dures—serve as bookends to her illustrious career (so far). The first, much earlier in her trajectory, had to do with the nontraditional use of traditional measures, namely the use of the SAT with young teenagers, a reasoning measure ordinarily used with high school juniors and seniors for college admission (VanTassel-Baska, 1984). Her establishment of the Center for Talent Development at Northwestern University in the 1970s, following the leadership of Professor Julian Stanley, was clearly a courageous act that paid off handsomely (see the chapters by Brody and Olszewski-Kubilius in this volume for discussion of this approach, which modifies the age of administration, not the paper-and-pencil measures themselves).

Another highly influential contribution to this field by VanTassel-Baska (2008a) is her recently published edited volume that summarizes the current tra-ditional and nontraditional approaches to assessment with gifted students, with the emphasis on alternative assessments such as nonverbal measures, off-level testing, portfolio assessment (typically, examples of class work or creative work), product assessment (typically, the end product of a special project undertaken as part of an enrichment program), measures of abilities often overlooked such as creative and practical reasoning abilities, and performance-based assessment. Another approach, dynamic assessment (Feuerstein, 1986), which consists of an initial assessment fol-lowed by intervention/teaching and reassessment, is mentioned but not discussed. Bringing these resources together in a single, highly readable volume for the first time enables practitioners to consider and evaluate a number of possibilities most appropriate to their local situations and their goals.

The nontraditional method VanTassel-Baska has chosen to evaluate is perfor-mance-based assessment, which she defines as focusing "on challenging open-ended problems [that] put an emphasis on the process the student uses to come to an answer rather than whether or not the student can quickly find the right answer" (VanTassel-Baska, Feng, & de Brux, 2007, pp. 10–11). Performance-based mea-sures might include, for example, writing a title and descriptive paragraph about a picture, designing a simple scientific experiment, reasoning with numbers to discover or create a pattern, and the like.

The maturity and reasoning shown by the student are key, although largely verbal in nature within the measures VanTassel-Baska has developed. These mea-sures are designed to capture potential strengths of any students, but particularly, economically disadvantaged and minority students, tapping reasoning power that might be suppressed in time-limited situations, preference for creative responses and synthetic thinking, hands-on strategies to solve problems, real-world skills that show fluid intelligence but are not necessarily classroom-typical, and preference for modes of learning that allow for metacognitive reflection based on practice. In addition, when performance-based assessment is conducted, students are given pretest exposure to the kinds of tasks, and/or prior dynamic assessment, because their relevant experience may be limited. Successful responses show fluency, complexity, multiple solutions, and higher level thinking (see VanTassel-Baska, 2008b, p. 290).

Not content to stay on the sidelines of educational assessment application, Professor VanTassel-Baska and her colleagues have put into place a strong research effort to see how, in fact, performance-based measures might work in the real world. Putting such measures into operation system-wide in the state of South Carolina was a daunting undertaking, one she planned and executed with characteristic care, control, collaborative skill, and energy. The effort was carefully designed to yield, over time, not only a look at the effect on proportionality of adding such measures to a menu of possible paths of choosing students for special programming (the state providing mainly pull-out programs rather than full-time programs), but the subsequent academic performance over time of children entering by various pathways, the social-emotional impact of participation by various groups of students, teacher perceptions of the comparative strengths of the students, and an estimate of the impact of the participation of these students on the nature and rigor of the programs themselves. The details of the research have been described in several publications (Van Tassel-Baska, Feng, & de Brux, 2007; Van Tassel-Baska, Johnson, & Avery, 2002).

Using a substantive database of 22,671 students accepted by traditional criteria and 7,855 by criteria that included performance-based tasks from 2000–2006, four pathways were developed, two traditional (A and B) and two including performance-based tasks (C and D): (A) 96th percentile or higher on a test of cognitive ability; (B) 90th percentile or higher on a test of cognitive ability plus 94th percentile or higher on the reading or math portion of a test of academic achievement; (C) 90th percentile or higher on a test of cognitive ability, achievement below 94th percentile, 80th percentile or higher on performance tasks; (D) aptitude below 90th percentile, achievement above 94th percentile, and 80th percentile or higher on performance tasks. The groups were designated as A, A + B, and A + C or B + C, where A refers to aptitude, B refers to achievement, and C refers to performance tasks. Note that the B set of criteria are somewhat lower than many school districts require. Important findings included:

- The addition of the performance-based tasks significantly increased enrollment of African American students (14% vs. 11.8%) but only in districts in which the overall population included a substantial number of African American students; in districts with low African American enrollment, the reverse was actually found.
- The proportion of low-SES children (free or reduced lunch) increased even more (23.0% vs. 18.6%) when performance-based tasks were included.
- Female enrollment increased (54.2% vs. 47.6%).

- Most students who qualified by traditional criteria showed strength in both verbal and nonverbal domains (nearly 80%), while the same was true of only about 60% of those who qualified by performance-based criteria. Of the remainder, most showed strength in the nonverbal domain (80% of the 20% of traditionally qualifying [A or A + B] and 73% of the 40% of those qualifying by A + C or B + C). This finding has particular relevance for the type of programming in the special classes, which in South Carolina, as in most places, are highly verbal in nature.
- Teachers modified the program to some extent to accommodate both the nonverbal strengths of the students and the somewhat lower level of their performance on cognitive and achievement criteria.
- Teacher perceptions of the nontraditional students—assessed for only a limited number—tended to view these students as somewhat less motivated and less focused than the others.
- A small sample of students assessed by interview cited the program as a confidence-builder and seemed to have had little trouble making friends, although the African American students in particular were interested in maintaining their social networks outside the class and were more often perceived as loners.
- Longitudinal results of yearly achievement testing on the state's Palmetto Achievement Challenge Test (PACT) were disappointing for the group as a whole. The test covers English and Math. Scores were all converted to a common set of standard scores across grade levels. Students qualifying by Criterion A scored highest (with the mean about the 86th percentile most years in English and 87th percentile in math), those qualifying by A + B scoring on average about the 80th–81st percentile in both, those qualifying with A + C about the 73rd percentile, and those qualifying by B + C at roughly the 77th percentile. Clearly, those qualifying by traditional criteria achieved on this traditional achievement test at a somewhat higher level. It should be recalled, however, that the programs are primarily pull-out in nature and much of the core teaching probably occurs in the regular classroom.

These are, in fact, an impressive set of findings, and suggest that, on the whole, adding the performance-based tasks to the mix can effectively increase the enrollment of students from lower income families and, to some extent, those from African American families. Although the academic performance of those qualifying by performance-based criteria did not quite equal that of those qualifying by the A + B criteria, this finding is hard to evaluate for two reasons: First, much of the teaching of subjects represented on the PACT probably occurs in regular classrooms rather than gifted classrooms, so this finding is irrelevant to special-class placement except that students in the pull-out programs have *less* time for academic mastery of standard subjects in their regular classrooms, if they actually can profit from it (as might special-class students who did not score high on the academic achievement criteria). Second, there is little indication of the achievement of the various groups of children on those domains emphasized within the pull-out classes themselves, classes that tend to emphasize higher level reasoning and enrichment of the curriculum.

Some other questions remain as well:

▶ Special classes for gifted children are designed to rescue these children from classes that provide a poor match for their academic skills. Especially for those children who qualified on nonverbal rather than verbal criteria, just how bad was the match in the regular classroom—how great was their need for a more appropriate environment?

▶ For all children who qualify on nonverbal criteria, how can and should we modify curricula to capitalize on their strengths, while continuing to build up the verbal skills they need to succeed in school? What would such curricula look like, and how would they prepare students to succeed in postsecondary programs?

▶ How costly is the inclusion of performance-based testing? Does it tap into valuable thinking and problem-solving skills that typically are ignored by traditional tests? Should it be included in measures of achievement as all children proceed through school?

Whatever the answers to these and the many other questions that persist in the field of assessment with gifted students, it is clear that Professor VanTassel-Baska has, both in the beginning of her career and as she approaches what, we hope, will be not retirement but only a new phase of her leadership, made significant contributions to this field—always respectful of all sides of the controversies, eschewing polarization, and incorporating the best that all parties have to offer into something better than anything else that has existed so far.

References

Aronson, J., & Steele, C. M. (2005). Stereotypes and the fragility of human competence, motivation, and self-concept. In C. Dweck & E. Elliot (Eds.), *Handbook of competence and motivation*. New York: Guilford.

Binet, A., & Simon, T. (1905). New methods for the diagnosis of the intellectual level of subnormals. *L'Année Psychologique, 11*, 191–244.

Chart, H., Grigorenko, E. L., & Sternberg, R. J. (2008). Identification: The Aurora Battery. In J. A. Plucker & C. M. Callahan (Eds.), *Critical issues and practices in gifted education: What the research says* (pp. 281–301). Waco, TX: Prufrock Press.

Feuerstein, R. (1986). Learning to learn: Mediated learning experiences and instrumental enrichment. *Special Services in the Schools, 3*, 49–82.

Neihart, M., Reis, S. M., Robinson, N. M., & Moon, S. M. (Eds.). (2002). *The social and emotional development of gifted children: What do we know?* Waco, TX: Prufrock Press.

Robinson, N. M. (2003). Two wrongs do not make a right: Sacrificing the needs of academically talented students does not solve society's unsolved problems. *Journal for the Education of the Gifted, 26,* 321–328.

Robinson, N. M. (2005). In defense of a psychometric approach to the definition of academic giftedness: A conservative view from a die-hard liberal. In R. J. Sternberg & J. E. Davidson (Eds.), *Conceptions of giftedness* (2nd ed, pp. 280–294). New York: Cambridge University Press.

Robinson, N. M. (2008). The value of traditional assessments as approaches to identifying academically gifted students. In J. Van Tassel-Baska (Ed.), *Alternative assessments with gifted and talented students* (pp. 157–174). Waco, TX: Prufrock Press.

Sternberg, R. (2003). Giftedness according to the theory of successful intelligence. In N. Colangelo & G. A. Davis (Eds.), *Handbook of gifted education* (3rd ed., pp. 88–90). Boston: Allyn & Bacon.

Van Tassel-Baska, J. (1984). The talent search as an identification model. *Gifted Child Quarterly, 28,* 172–176.

Van Tassel-Baska, J. (Ed.). (2008a). *Alternative assessments with gifted and talented students.* Waco, TX: Prufrock Press.

Van Tassel-Baska, J. (2008b). Using performance-based assessment to document authentic learning. In J. Van Tassel-Baska (Ed.), *Alternative assessments with gifted and talented students* (pp. 285–308). Waco, TX: Prufrock Press.

Van Tassel-Baska J., Feng, A. X., & de Brux, E. (2007). A study of identification and achievement profiles of performance task-identified gifted students over 6 years. *Journal for the Education of the Gifted, 31,* 7–34.

Van Tassel-Baska, J., Johnson, D., & Avery, L. D. (2002). Using performance tasks in the identification of economically disadvantaged and minority gifted learners: Findings from Project STAR. *Gifted Child Quarterly, 46,* 110–123.

CHAPTER 21

THE POTENTIAL IMPACT OF REGULATORY FOCUS RESEARCH ON THE USE OF ALTERNATIVE ASSESSMENTS

by

BRANDY
L. E.
BUCKINGHAM

Alternative assessment provides an important way of gauging gifted student potential in domain-specific areas of learning. It is hardly a panacea to solve all the problems of identification, however.

—Joyce VanTassel-Baska

In recent years, researchers and practitioners alike have recognized the need to move beyond traditional forms of assessment in the identification of gifted learners. Although traditional measures such as standardized achievement and ability tests have well-established records of reliability and validity and are important tools in identifying many gifted learners, they may not identify equally well for all populations. For example, these measures may miss some learners who would benefit from gifted programming who are members of minority populations, whose first language is not English, who have learning disabilities that may mask potentially high performance, or who have talents in areas not tested by these measures (VanTassel-Baska, 2008a).

Because of this, a variety of alternative forms of assessment have been developed in order to more readily identify all learners who would benefit from placement in a gifted program, and current best practices in the field call for the use of multiple forms of assessment in the identification procedures for any gifted program. The National Association for Gifted

Children's (NAGC) Standards for Student Identification reflect this multiple-criteria approach (NAGC, 2000), which includes both traditional and alternative forms of identification. These alternative assessments often are grounded in other theories of ability or designed to address specific shortcomings of traditional tests, and include measures such as nonverbal ability tests, portfolios, performance tasks, dynamic assessments, and behavioral inventories or checklists (VanTassel-Baska, Feng, & Evans, 2007). Much work has been and is currently being done to determine the reliability, validity, and predictive power of these alternative assessments (e.g., Callahan, Hunsaker, Adams, Moore, & Bland, 1995; Cunningham, Callahan, Plucker, Roberson, & Rapkin, 1998; VanTassel-Baska et al., 2007).

Because many of these methods are fairly new (especially compared to IQ tests, which boast more than 100 years of development and research), there still are many open questions with regards to the factors that may affect learners' performance and identification. The aim of this chapter is to examine research coming from social psychology that may point to one factor that could have an impact on students' performance on these assessments, independent of the abilities, talents, or potential of the student: regulatory focus.

WHAT IS REGULATORY FOCUS?

Regulatory focus can be defined as the tendency to pursue either *promotion-focused* or *prevention-focused* goals. Promotion-focused goals are those that involve pursuing the presence of positive outcomes while avoiding the absence of positive outcomes, and prevention-focused goals are those that involve pursuing the absence of negative outcomes or avoiding the presence of negative outcomes (Higgins, 1997). Regulatory focus at first seems similar to the idea of approach versus avoidance goals, but the two concepts are orthogonal. Both promotion-focused and prevention-focused individuals pursue both approach and avoidance goals; the difference lies in the types of outcomes they are approaching or avoiding. Individuals tend to have a chronic regulatory focus, but it also can be situationally induced. That is, most individuals tend toward pursuing one of the two types of goals as a general pattern in their everyday lives, but cues in a particular environment can cause a normally promotion-focused individual to focus on prevention goals or vice versa. There currently is no evidence that either type of chronic regulatory focus is more correlated with high ability than the other—most studies on regulatory focus have been conducted on students at major research universities, and both chronic foci have been found in that population. Therefore, if regulatory focus were to affect performance on ability assessments, it is very likely that this effect would be independent of the student's true ability.

The presence of one type of focus or the other (whether chronic or situationally induced) has been linked to differences in a number of experimental outcomes. For example, Freitas, Liberman, Salovey, and Higgins (2002) found that regulatory focus affects task initiation; participants with a prevention focus (whether chronic or induced) tended to prefer to initiate tasks sooner than those with a promotion focus and that, in general, people will complete prevention-framed tasks before promotion-framed tasks. Along similar lines, individuals with a prevention focus tend to focus on accuracy on tasks at the expense of speed, whereas those with a promotion focus complete tasks quickly but less accurately (Forster, Higgins, & Bianco, 2003). In another vein, Liberman, Molden, Idson, and Higgins (2001) showed that regulatory focus can affect the number of hypotheses an experimental participant generates; such an effect could affect the results of some types of assessments.

It is important to note that situationally inducing a regulatory focus is not a difficult process; in fact, many of the techniques used in these psychological experiences could happen unintentionally in everyday life. In some experiments (Forster, Higgins, & Idson, 1998), participants were simply asked to either push on the table (as if pushing away negative things) or pull on the table (as if pulling good things toward them), and this was enough to create a statistically significant difference in the performance of the two groups. In other studies, the task itself was slightly reworded to imply either promotion or prevention; for example, Forster et al. (2003) told participants that they would either be paid an extra dollar for achieving a score above 60 on a task (promotion focus) or that they would be paid a dollar less for scoring below 60 on the task (prevention focus). In most of the regulatory focus research, the differences found are statistically significant but would likely not result in practical differences in an assessment; however, these small differences are the result of small inducement procedures, such as the pushing/pulling protocol. Larger influences, such as being urgently told by a teacher or parent "Make sure you don't fail this test" (a prevention-focused suggestion) versus "Work hard on this test so you'll qualify for the program," (a promotion-focused suggestion) may result in larger differences in performance.

BEHAVIORAL SCALES AND PERFORMANCE TASKS

Although there are many types of alternative assessments currently available (including portfolios, nonverbal intelligence tests, and dynamic assessments), two are particularly relevant for our purposes: behavioral scales and performance tasks. Some of the earliest suggestions for the use of alternative assessments in identifying minority students were behavioral checklists created by Hilliard (as cited in Baldwin, 1987) and Torrance (Torrance, 1977). The theory behind these is that gifted students do not simply learn faster and score higher on tests than other students; their behavior as a whole is qualitatively different from other learners. This is backed up by findings that gifted individuals have emotional characteristics and needs that are different from the general population (Silverman, 1993; VanTassel-Baska, 2008a). These checklists can serve to standardize the traditional teacher nomination process in order to prevent biases from affecting the nominations. There are now multiple behavioral scales and checklists that have been found to be valid and reliable, such as the Scales for Rating the Behavioral Characteristics of Superior Students (Renzulli et al., 2004) and the Purdue Academic Rating Scales (Feldhusen, 2001).

Performance tasks differ from traditional standardized tests in that they are more open-ended; there may be many correct answers, or no "right or wrong" answers. They focus on assessing problem-solving ability and the articulation of students' thinking process rather than the student's ability to find the correct answer (VanTassel-Baska, Johnson, & Avery, 2002), and measure fluid rather than crystallized ability (Mills & Tissot, 1995). For example, one performance-based assessment of mathematical reasoning gives students a short list of numbers and asks students to find as many ways as possible to use the numbers, with multiple mathematical operations, to get an answer of eight (VanTassel-Baska, 2008b). Although students do need basic arithmetic skills, the open-ended nature of the task allows for a wide variety of approaches to the problem. Some students may decide to quickly find as many of the most basic ways to complete the task as possible, while others may look for more interesting and creative solutions that will take more time. Both of these valid approaches would give valuable information as to the student's abilities.

In a recent review of the literature on performance-based assessments, Van-Tassel-Baska (2008b) points out six specific ways in which the features of these tasks are especially well-suited for characteristics of economically disadvantaged and minority gifted learners. In fact, the addition of performance tasks to state identification procedures has been successful in increasing the number of minority and low-SES students identified as gifted; what's more, although these students initially scored lower than traditionally identified students on achievement tests, after a year in the gifted program their achievement scores had significantly improved, giving support to the identification of these students as ones who would benefit from placement (VanTassel-Baska et al., 2007).

The many ways that regulatory focus impacts our behavior and decision-making processes may have an effect on student performance on a variety of assessments. For the purposes of this chapter, I will focus on the common methods of behavioral scales and performance tasks; however, research is needed across the range of identification techniques.

Regulatory Focus Effects on Behavioral Scales

A promotion-based regulatory focus is associated with a tendency to try to maximize gains even when it might mean increasing false positives, and avoiding errors of omission. In contrast, a prevention-based focus is associated with minimizing losses even when it means increasing false negatives, avoiding errors of commission (Crowe & Higgins, 1997). This can lead to higher rates of risk-taking behavior in promotion-focused individuals, who are willing to risk errors in order to gain the most positive outcomes while prevention-focused individuals take a more cautious approach to avoid negative outcomes.

This differential level of risk-acceptance has a variety of consequences; of interest here is its effect on idea generation. Friedman and Forster (2001) used a pencil-

and-paper maze task to situationally cue either a promotion (the maze involved the act of *getting to* a reward) or prevention focus (the maze involved the act of *running away from* a threat). Individuals cued with a promotion focus were able to generate more creative uses for a brick than those cued with a prevention focus. Similarly, Liberman et al. (2001) found that both chronic and situational regulatory focus can affect an individual's ability to generate hypotheses about the identity of an ambiguous photograph. As in the Friedman and Forster study, those individuals with a promotion focus (whether chronic or induced via a reward scheme) were able to generate more hypotheses than those with a prevention focus.

It is possible that, given these results, chronic regulatory focus could affect a student's behavior in such a way that it would affect scores on a behavioral scale, possibly masking his or her potential. The following are relevant example items from a subtest of the Scales for Rating Behavioral Characteristics of Superior Students (Renzulli et al., 2001, as reprinted by Davis, 2003):

> 2. Generates a large number of ideas or solutions to problems and questions; often offers unusual ("way out"), unique, clever responses.
> 4. Is a high risk taker; is adventurous and speculative. (p. 316)

It seems that items such as these may favor students with a chronic promotion focus, while those students who are intelligent but more reserved and cautious due to a chronic prevention focus could be overlooked in the identification process. Creative behaviors such as these certainly can be considered valid aspects of giftedness and should be assessed if they may be relevant to success in a given gifted program. However, it is possible that prevention-focused gifted children may be capable of such behaviors yet only display them in particular situations that prime a promotion focus, making it possible that a teacher will not see the behavior on a day-to-day basis.

Potential Effects of Regulatory Focus on Performance Task Use

The same risk-acceptance behaviors and greater hypothesis generation in promotion-focused individuals may give these children an advantage on performance tasks as well. Because these tasks are given in a more controlled setting, however, it should be possible to situationally induce an appropriate regulatory focus in order to ensure that all students are performing at their peak ability during the task.

One example of such a performance task is the Diet Cola Test, in which students are asked to design a way to determine whether or not bees are attracted to diet cola. Although this task has been used in individual assessments, Callahan et al. (1995) determined that its reliability, although high (.76), was not quite sufficient for use as an individual measure, only as a group evaluation measure. Because a student's ability to generate hypotheses and ways to test them could be affected by regulatory focus, I propose that controlling the regulatory focus of students who are participating in the Diet Cola Test could lead to greater reliability, thus making it a more useful identification tool.

Another assessment tool currently in use is DISCOVER, which is made up primarily of performance tasks to assess various aspects of intelligence (Sarouphim, 1999). Although hypothesis generation is a part of some of these tasks, the story-telling task presents the possibility of another regulatory focus effect. In this task, students in grades 3–8 are given an array of toys (which differs according to grade level) and are asked to list descriptors of single items and of groups of multiple items. The students then are asked to tell a story involving some or all of the items, which are rated according to criteria such as plot, quality of words used, sequencing of events, and use of dialogues.

Zhu and Myers-Levy (2007) have found an effect of regulatory focus that could impact performance on this type of task. They found that individuals with a promotion focus are more likely to engage in relational processing, in which they attend more to relationships among items and higher level abstractions, whereas individuals with a prevention focus are more likely to engage in item-specific processing, in which they elaborate on the characteristics of individual items and encode more context-specific associations to each item. When students partici-pating in the DISCOVER assessment are asked to elaborate on individual items, those with a prevention focus may have the advantage. However, it seems that promotion-focused students will have an advantage in relating the items through story creation; higher rates of risk-taking and hypothesis generation also may prove to be an advantage in this task. It seems likely that inducing a promotion focus will lead to better performance on the storytelling task, while inducing a prevention focus will lead to better performance on the item-elaboration task.

FUTURE DIRECTIONS

No research has yet been conducted to directly test the effects of regulatory focus on the results of these types of assessments; the connections suggested here are only theoretical, based on the results of experiments whose tasks bear similarities to tasks commonly used in alternative assessment procedures. Because most (if not all) of the current research on regulatory focus has been conducted on adult college students (Molden & Miele, in press), a first step would be to replicate previous findings with elementary school aged children in order to confirm that children of this age display regulatory focus, and that it has effects similar to those seen in adults. Chronic regulatory focus often is measured by asking participants about things that they "ought" to do in their life versus things that they would "ideally" do in life; these lists may not be as meaningful for children, and so different pro-tocols may need to be devised to determine whether children have a stable chronic regulatory focus. In addition, it is important to determine whether the small effects found using subtle situational cues would scale up given stronger cues. This type of research would be necessary in order to determine the types of cues that would be necessary if regulatory focus were to be controlled during assessment procedures.

If all of this basic research suggests that chronic and/or situationally induced regulatory focus can affect the results of identification procedures, then ways to control for this during identification will need to be created. In the case of assessments that are conducted in a controlled setting, such as nonverbal tests, performance tasks, or possibly even traditional IQ tests, it may be possible to cue every student being assessed with the regulatory focus that will maximize performance on each test. Behavioral scales or other assessments that are completed by teachers cannot be controlled in this manner, but it may be possible to add assessments of students' chronic regulatory focus and augment the results accordingly.

CONCLUSION

One of the most important goals in research and practice in gifted education is ensuring that all students who would benefit from a program are identified and placed in that program. The use of multiple identification procedures, including both traditional and alternative assessments, helps to ensure that all such students are identified. The purpose of this chapter was to call attention to research coming out of social psychology that may point to a factor that could affect student performance and thus placement, regulatory focus. There currently is no research investigating the possible impact of regulatory focus on these assessments, but the psychological research shows that it can have an impact on tasks very similar to those used in common assessment procedures. Therefore, both basic and applied research is needed to ensure that students' regulatory focus does not limit their performance when they are being identified for gifted programs.

THE LEGACY

Although the Center for Gifted Education she founded at The College of William and Mary is most well-known for research on and development of curriculum units, Joyce VanTassel-Baska also has been instrumental in advocating for the use of alternative assessments in the identification and learning of gifted students. Through Project STAR, she ensured that performance tasks were put in place as a standard identification method across the state of South Carolina (VanTassel-Baska et al., 2007). This project also helped to bolster the validity of these assessments in identifying disadvantaged and minority students. More recently, she edited the volume *Alternative Assessments With Gifted and Talented Students* (VanTassel-Baska, 2008a, 2008b), the National Association for Gifted Children's official guide to the topic, consolidating the most recent research on the full spectrum of alternative assessment types and uses. She has helped to show that these types of assessments are a vital part of finding and serving underidentified populations, and that they deserve as much research attention as traditional assessments have received. Hopefully, future generations of researchers will follow this legacy to ensure that all students who would benefit from services are identified.

REFERENCES

Baldwin, A. Y. (1987). I'm Black, but look at me, I am also gifted. *Gifted Child Quarterly, 31,* 180–185.

Callahan, C. M., Hunsaker, S. L., Adams, C. M., Moore, S. D., & Bland, L. C. (1995). *Instruments used in the identification of gifted and talented students* (Research Monograph No. 95130). Storrs: University of Connecticut, The National Research Center on the Gifted and Talented.

Crowe, E., & Higgins, E. T. (1997). Regulatory focus and strategic inclinations: Promotion and prevention in decision-making. *Organizational Behavior and Human Decision Processes, 69,* 117–132.

Cunningham, C. M., Callahan, C. M., Plucker, J. A., Roberson, S. C., & Rapkin, A. (1998). Identifying Hispanic students of outstanding talent: Psychometric integrity of a peer nomination form. *Exceptional Children, 64,* 197–209.

Davis, G. A. (2003). Identifying creative students, teaching for creative growth. In N. Colangelo & G. A. Davis (Eds.), *Handbook of gifted education* (3rd ed., pp. 311–324). Boston: Allyn & Bacon.

Feldhusen, J. F. (2001). *Talent development in gifted education.* (ERIC Digest #EDO-EC-01-5)

Forster, J., Higgins, E., & Bianco, A. T. (2003). Speed/accuracy decisions in task performance: Built-in trade-off or separate strategic concerns? *Organizational Behavior and Human Decision Processes, 90,* 148–164.

Forster, J., Higgins, E. T., & Idson, L. C. (1998). Approach and avoidance strength during goal attainment: Regulatory focus and the "goal looms larger" effect. *Journal of Personality and Social Psychology, 75,* 1115–1131.

Freitas, A. L., Liberman, N., Salovey, P., & Higgins, E. T. (2002). When to begin? Regulatory focus and initiating goal pursuit. *Personality and Social Psychology Bulletin, 28,* 121–130.

Friedman, R. S., & Forster, J. (2001). The effects of promotion and prevention cues on creativity. *Journal of Personality and Social Psychology, 81,* 1001–1013.

Higgins, E. T. (1997). Beyond pleasure and pain. *American Psychologist, 52,* 1280–1300.

Liberman, N., Molden, D. C., Idson, L. C., & Higgins, E. T. (2001). Promotion and prevention focus on alternative hypotheses: Implications for attributional functions. *Journal of Personality and Social Psychology, 80,* 5–18.

Mills, C., & Tissot, S. (1995). Identifying academic potential in students from underrepresented populations: Is using the Ravens Progressive Matrices a good idea? *Gifted Child Quarterly, 39,* 209–217.

Molden, D. C., & Miele, D. B. (in press). The origins and influences of promotion-focused and prevention-focused achievement motivations. In M. Maher, S. Karabenick, & T. Urdan (Eds.), *Advances in motivation and achievement* (Vol. 15). New York: Elsevier.

National Association for Gifted Children. (2000). *Pre-K to grade 12 gifted program standards.* Retrieved from http://www.nagc.org/index.aspx?id=546&terms=Pre-K+to+Grade+12+Gifted+Program+Standards

Renzulli, J. S., Smith, L. H., White, A. J., Callahan, C. M., Hartman, R. K., Westberg, K. L., et al. (2004). *Scales for Rating the Behavioral Characteristics of Superior Students: Technical and administration manual* (Rev. ed.). Mansfield Center, CT: Creative Learning Press.

Sarouphim, K. M. (1999). DISCOVER: A promising alternative assessment for the identification of gifted minorities. *Gifted Child Quarterly, 43,* 244–251.

Silverman, L. K. (1993). The gifted individual. In L. K. Silverman (Ed.), *Counseling the gifted & talented* (pp. 3–28). Denver, CO: Love.

Torrance, E. P. (1977). *Discovery and nurturance of giftedness in the culturally different* (ERIC Clearinghouse #EC102563). Reston, VA: ERIC Clearinghouse for Handicapped and Gifted Children.

VanTassel-Baska, J. (2008a). An overview of alternative assessment measures for gifted learners and the issues that surround their use. In J. VanTassel-Baska (Ed.), *Alternative assessments with gifted and talented students* (pp. 1–16). Waco, TX: Prufrock Press.

VanTassel-Baska, J. (2008b). Using performance-based assessment to document authentic learning. In J. VanTassel-Baska (Ed.), *Alternative assessments with gifted and talented students* (pp. 285–308). Waco, TX: Prufrock Press.

VanTassel-Baska, J., Feng, A. X., & Evans, B. L. (2007). Patterns of identification and performance among gifted students identified through performance tasks: A three-year analysis. *Gifted Child Quarterly, 51,* 218–231.

VanTassel-Baska, J., Johnson, D., & Avery, L. D. (2002). Using performance tasks in the identification of economically disadvantaged and minority gifted learners: Findings from Project STAR. *Gifted Child Quarterly, 46,* 110–123.

Zhu, R., & Meyers-Levy, J. (2007). Exploring the cognitive mechanism that underlies regulatory focus effects. *Journal of Consumer Research, 34,* 89–96.

CHAPTER 22

WHAT WE NOW KNOW ABOUT APPROPRIATE CURRICULUM AND INSTRUCTION FOR GIFTED LEARNERS

by

KAREN
B. ROGERS

Curriculum designed for the gifted must provide students a rigorous, high-quality experience that readies them to successfully traverse the next level of educational challenge in a selective university as well as ground them in self-learning and social learning of the moment.

—Joyce VanTassel-Baska (2003)

S everal years ago, I conducted a database search on the 29 curriculum and instruction models used in gifted education to differentiate the learning of students with gifts and talents. I dutifully entered the name of each model: "Enrichment Triad Model," "Bloom's Taxonomy of Cognitive Objectives," "Taba's Inquiry Model," and so on. What printed out was a scant dozen articles, only four of which were actual research studies documenting the efficacy of the implemented model. As one can imagine, I was aghast. Were we a field that promoted and disseminated great ideas for learning experiences without bothering to find out what effects these models actually produced on gifted learners?

I then took a different tack on the issue, hoping against hope that we did have research to back up our school-based practices. I used Maker's (1983) menu of content, process, and product modifications to see if the actual strategies these 29 models use had been studied in a systematic way when used with gifted learners (Rogers, 2007). Many more studies emerged from this search, so my worst fears were calmed. Shortly after this, I happened to be on a bus with Joyce and told her of my findings. She looked puzzled and concerned, commenting, "But, how does one actually research the effects of a curriculum development model? What should one look for as effects?" We spent most of the rest of that bus trip together brainstorming ways one could measure the impact of an implemented curriculum model on gifted learners. When one looks at the remarkable body of research that currently supports the Integrated Curriculum Model (ICM) that undergirds The College of William and Mary curriculum units in language arts, social studies, science, and mathematics, it is clear that my initial concern has been well laid to rest.

There are two issues in play here. First, when one looks at the structure of a curriculum model, do its elements or components utilize research-based "best practices"? And second, does the curriculum model, when implemented, produce the expected effects promised by previous research? Joyce and her colleagues at The College of William and Mary have amply proven the second to be the case (VanTassel-Baska & Stambaugh, 2006).

MODIFICATIONS OF CONTENT THAT ARE RESEARCH-BASED

There are seven modifications that are supported as providing significant academic benefits for gifted learners (Rogers, 2002). These include: (1) *abstraction*: using abstract concepts, principles, generalizations (Hanley, Whitla, Moo, & Walker, 1970); (2) *complexity*: making the content more intricate and detailed as well as more complex through a variety of means such as across time, other perspectives, and language of the discipline (Kaplan & Cannon, 2001); (3) *multidisciplinary*: uniting different disciplines via a theme or concept (VanTassel-Baska & Little, 2003); (4) *organization*: changing the sequence of the content presented (Scruggs & Mastropieri, 1988); (5) *study of people*: relating content to the humans and social issues involved (Parke, 1983); (6) *methods of inquiry*: relating content to the ways things are done by practicing professionals (Treffinger, 1986); and (7) *subject acceleration*: providing content that is beyond grade or age expectations (Nikolova & Taylor, 2003).

Modifications of the ways learners think and learn and the ways teachers teach for this also have been supported by the research as significant for academic achievement in gifted learners. These include: (1) *higher order thinking*: providing opportunities to analyze, reflect, evaluate, and synthesize (Nasca & Davis, 1981); (2) *open-ended thinking*: offering questions and tasks for which there is no right or wrong answer and for which multiple perspectives or original thinking are required (Parke, 1983); (3) *proof and reasoning*: requiring learners to support their arguments with evidence (Bishop, 1999); (4) *discovery/inquiry-based/problem-based learning*: providing structured experiences in which the learners must "find" the idea, solution, procedure to follow (Gallagher, Stepien, & Rosenthal, 1992);

(5) *group production*: structuring small-group experiences for which all learners recognize the superiority of the group process and product over individual work (Burns & Mason, 2002); and (6) *freedom of choice*: provision of opportunities for individual study on some aspect of the content under study according to readiness, interest, or style preference (Pentelbury, 2000).

Product modifications have a less strong research backing for significant differences for gifted learners. They do show positive academic benefits but those seem to be present for regular learners as well. These modifications include: (1) *real-world problems*: providing assessment as well as learning tasks that are related to the learner's current world rather than focused on the "schoolhouse problem," which appears to be academic in nature only (Bishop, 1999); (2) *real audiences*: accessing product evaluators who have the expertise to judge and provide feedback on real-world ideas and solutions (Bishop, 1999); and (3) *transformations*: requiring products and performances that use what has been learned in some genuine, yet nontraditional, medium rather than just summarizing what has been learned (Nikolova & Taylor, 2003).

If one looks at the structure of The College of William and Mary curriculum units that have been developed, the match with research-based differentiation practices is made quite clear. Table 22.1 displays these matches. As can be seen, all units are particularly strong in content and process differentiation with product differentiation perhaps being a bit more traditional in nature. Considering that the research itself is not particularly differentiated for gifted learners with product differentiation, it is clear the ICM model more than meets the academic and intellectual needs of gifted learners and promises the achievement effect sizes that have been reported for these units in recent years (e.g., Little, Feng, VanTassel-Baska, Rogers, & Avery, 2007; VanTassel-Baska, Bass, Ries, Poland, & Avery, 1998; VanTassel-Baska, Johnson, Hughes, & Boyce, 1996; VanTassel-Baska, Zuo, Avery, & Little, 2002).

In looking over the field of gifted education in general, how central to this field is the curriculum and instruction we disseminate? Does it hold greater import than finding the learners to whom it will be offered, or than providing training to the teachers who will work on a daily basis with our "found" learners? How long lasting in the ultimate development of a gifted or talented learner are the outcomes attained in a differentiated unit of instruction? As a product of gifted programs while growing up in California, I can certainly answer this question from my own perspective. The reader of this chapter will have to determine if he or she agrees with my response or not.

THE IMPORTANCE OF BEING FOUND

Being identified as gifted had a profound effect on my self-efficacy and my motivation to do well in school. I was tested at age 8 by a psychologist from Stanford (Maud Merrill, I believe) over the course of 2 days, being given two forms of the Stanford-Binet: the older 1937 version and the newer one that ultimately was

Table 22.1

ICM MATCHES WITH RESEARCH-BASED DIFFERENTIATION PRACTICES IN THE FIELD

Modification	Language Arts Units	Social Studies Units	Science Units	Mathematics Units
Content Differentiation				
Abstraction	H	H	M	H
Complexity	M	M	H	M
Multidisciplinary	H	H	M	M
Organization	H	H	H	M
Study of People	M	H	M	L
Methods of Inquiry	M	M	H	H
Subject Acceleration	M	M	M	M
Process Differentiation				
Higher Order Thinking	H	H	H	H
Open-Ended Thinking	H	M	H	M
Proof and Reasoning	H	M	H	H
Discovery/Inquiry/PBL	M	M	H	M
Group Production	H	H	H	M
Freedom of Choice	M	M	M	M
Product Differentiation				
Real-World Problems	L	L	H	M
Real Audiences	L	L	M	L
Transformations	M	M	H	L

Note. H = high focus; M = moderate focus; L = low focus.

published in 1960. I remember the excitement of those problems: challenging and thought-provoking and just plain fun to try to answer. Then, to find out I was "gifted" and be provided with special services in my small rural school were an added bonus. There is no question that the process of being "found" had great impact on my ultimate development. I certainly didn't know my actual score at the time but was led to believe it was quite high and that I should plan on "doing something important with [my] life." School took on an added zing and zip, one that continued all the way through university and graduate school. I have often wondered if I would have gone as far without that basic knowledge of my potential capability.

THE IMPORTANCE OF HAVING THE RIGHT TEACHERS

Mrs. Hanson and Mr. Tarentino remain vivid in my memories of school because of the remarkable things they allowed me to do in their classes. Mrs.

Hanson was the teacher who had me tested in the first place and her course of action upon hearing the results was to begin me on a program of reading that has continued throughout my life. She would set out a list of novels for me to read: I remember *Call of the Wild*, *The Old Man and the Sea*, *The Old Man and the Boy*, and Bullfinch's *Greek Mythology*. Each week my independent reading assignments were provided and off I would go into my own literary world while she worked with all of the other children in our class. Once or twice during the week she would spend a few minutes with me, asking me about what I was reading and moving me ahead. After reading 2–3 novels she would assign some sort of synthesis project, usually open-ended, that allowed me to apply what I was reading about in some way. I remember writing plays, which the others in my class would perform (I was director!) and which ultimately were performed at schoolwide assemblies. I ran candy sales, conducted numerous independent studies in science, and just had a remarkably happy time *learning* in school, all due to the tasks designed by this wonderful and supportive teacher.

Mr. Tarentino, a high school German teacher, fell into this category of wonderful teacher as well. He allowed me to complete 4 years of German in one full year (school year plus 6 weeks of summer school) by moving at my own pace through the texts and carrying on individual "conversations" with me "auf Deutsch" when moments could be spared from his regular classes of students. The feeling of accomplishment was utterly fulfilling, not to mention the underlying self-efficacy that emerged that I was "good" at learning languages but it was more than just the access to learning that he provided. He spent much time counseling me about where I needed to go to college and what I should be studying. He let me into his own life so that I met his family: his wife was very gifted in languages herself and was learning Sanskrit at the time. Both of these teachers, and many more along the way, had a remarkable influence on my adult development. Without them I would not be the person I am today.

But now, we come to the question that began this section of the chapter. How central to the field is the curriculum we disseminate? My personal reflections bring me back to argue that *the curriculum is the most central thing*. Yes, it was good to know I was bright and that helped me. Yes, it was good to have flexible and supportive teachers—that helped me. But, it was the actual "stuff" I learned that sticks with me to this day. I could never get enough of the content, the knowledge. I wanted to learn everything there was to learn (and still do). I was strongly influenced by accelerated content (e.g., studied algebra in sixth grade, completed three levels of Latin in one school year, four levels of German in one school year). The idea of learning ahead was inspiring and motivating. To have been relegated to just learning the outcomes provided for a given year in each subject area would have been stifling and I know I would not have developed into the lifelong student I am today if that had been the case.

But, there also were subjects in school that have stuck over the years: the big ideas of science and mathematics, the great philosophies of the world, the literary canon—when aspects of these were open for learning in school, they opened new worlds for me. If these subjects had not been offered, I am not sure I would have fully developed into my current state of being.

Hence, I must answer this question about curriculum as a resounding "yes." It is central to the development of talent in learners with high potential. It is the nutritious part of their upbringing and the part that stays with them long after their memories of a favorite teacher have faded. The curriculum we are speaking about includes the content piece, as well as the conceptual piece. It also contains the process and skill development piece. It is the whole jigsaw puzzle as Joyce so aptly visualizes it with ICM. This is what Joyce's legacy to the field will be: that she has provided a solid model for developing the ideological food that nurtures gifted development. Thank you, Joyce, for a job well done.

REFERENCES

Bishop, K. (1999). *Authentic learning and the research process of gifted students.* Paper presented at the 3rd International Forum on Research in School Librarianship, Birmingham, AL. (ERIC Document Reproduction Service No. ED437056)

Burns, R. B., & Mason, D. A. (2002). Class composition and student achievement in elementary schools. *American Educational Research Journal, 39,* 207–233.

Gallagher, S., Stepien, W., & Rosenthal, H. (1992). The effects of problem-based learning on problem solving. *Gifted Child Quarterly, 36,* 195–200.

Hanley, J. P., Whitla, D. K., Moo, E. W., & Walter, A. (1970). *Man: A course of study: An evaluation.* Cambridge, MA: Educational Development Center.

Kaplan, S., & Cannon, M. W. (2001). *Curriculum starter cards: Developing differentiated lessons for gifted students.* Waco, TX: Prufrock Press.

Little, C. A., Feng, A. X., VanTassel-Baska, J., Rogers, K. B., & Avery, L. D. (2007). A study of curriculum effectiveness in social studies. *Gifted Child Quarterly, 51,* 272–284.

Maker, C. J. (1983). *Teaching models in education of the gifted.* Rockville, MD: Aspen.

Nasca, D., & Davis, H. B. (1981). *Verbal behaviors of teachers of the gifted.* Unpublished manuscript. (ERIC Document Reproduction Service No. ED216478)

Nikolova, O. R., & Taylor, G. (2003). The impact of a language learning task on instructional outcomes in two student populations: High ability and average ability students. *Journal of Secondary Gifted Education, 14,* 205–227.

Parke, B. N. (1983). Use of self-instructional materials with gifted primary-aged students. *Gifted Child Quarterly, 27,* 29–34.

Pentelbury, R. (2000). The independent learner program. In Centre for Gifted Education (Ed.), *The quest for giftedness: Proceedings of the annual conference of the Society for the Advancement of Gifted Education.* Calgary, Alberta, Canada: Centre for Gifted Education. (ERIC Document Reproduction Service No. ED466055)

Rogers, K. B. (2002). *Re-forming gifted education: Matching the program to the child.* Scottsdale, AZ: Great Potential Press.

Rogers, K. B. (2007). Lessons learned about educating the gifted and talented: A synthesis of the research on educational practice. *Gifted Child Quarterly, 51,* 382–396.

Scruggs, T., & Mastropieri, M. (1988). Acquisition and transfer of learning strategies by gifted and nongifted students. *Journal of Special Education, 22,* 153–166.

Treffinger, D. J. (1986). *Blending gifted education with the total school program.* Buffalo, NY: DOK Publishers.

VanTassel-Baska, J., Bass, G. M., Ries, R. R., Poland, D. L., & Avery, L. D. (1998). A national pilot study of science curriculum effectiveness for high-ability students. *Gifted Child Quarterly, 42,* 200–221.

VanTassel-Baska, J., Johnson, D. T., Hughes, C., & Boyce, L. N. (1996). A study of language arts curriculum effectiveness with gifted learners. *Journal for the Education of the Gifted, 19,* 461–480.

VanTassel-Baska, J., & Little, C. A. (2003). *Content-based curriculum for high-ability learners.* Waco, TX: Prufrock Press.

VanTassel-Baska, J., & Stambaugh, T. (2006). Project Athena: A pathway to advanced literacy development for children in poverty. *Gifted Child Today, 29*(2), 58–63.

VanTassel-Baska, J., Zuo, L., Avery, L. D., & Little, C. A. (2002). A curriculum study of gifted student learning in the language arts. *Gifted Child Quarterly, 46,* 30–44.

CHAPTER 23

THE INTEGRATED CURRICULUM MODEL

by

CATHERINE
A. LITTLE

The ICM provides educators a way to integrate high-level learning experiences for the gifted, using both accelerative and enriched modes in a complementary way.

—Joyce VanTassel-Baska

The Integrated Curriculum Model (ICM) is a comprehensive framework for curriculum that combines key elements of good curricular design in general with consideration of significant learning characteristics of gifted and talented learners. The ICM, which emerged from careful study of existing curricular models in gifted and general education (VanTassel-Baska, 1986), integrates a strong content emphasis reflecting the habits of mind of a discipline under study with conceptual and critical thinking skills that enhance the rigor and relevance of the learning experience for students. Under the guidance of Joyce VanTassel-Baska, the Center for Gifted Education at The College of William and Mary has conducted extensive curriculum development work using the ICM, resulting in several series of curriculum units in language arts, science, and social studies, as well as supplementary materials in these areas and in mathematics. A systematic development process, including field-testing with extensive data collection from teachers and students, has led to the refinement of these materials and their use in classrooms around the United States and beyond (VanTassel-

Baska & Stambaugh, 2008). Moreover, the model itself has been influential in other curriculum development efforts through its use in school district initiatives and graduate courses in gifted education.

The ICM draws upon gifted education traditions of accelerating and advancing content, engaging students in direct study and application of thinking skills, encouraging research with culminating products for real audiences, and promoting greater depth and complexity in student learning through a focus on abstract concepts. Curriculum developed with the ICM is intended to respond to gifted students' salient characteristics of precocity, intensity, and complexity in thinking, while also providing sufficient flexibility to allow for differentiation across a range of learners (VanTassel-Baska, 2003). Evidence from studies of classroom implementation supports the applicability of the model in a variety of settings.

OVERVIEW OF THE INTEGRATED CURRICULUM MODEL

In the mid-1980s, VanTassel-Baska (1986) reviewed the existing research on curriculum for the gifted and talented. She examined approaches that had traditionally been used in gifted programs and explored the rationale for providing specific curriculum targeting gifted students (e.g., Gallagher, 1985; Ward, 1961, 1981). She proposed the ICM as a synthesis of curricular dimensions that had shown effectiveness with gifted students and that aligned conceptually with several important learning characteristics of this population. The ICM also is influenced by Vygotsky's (1978) theory of the zone of proximal development, emphasizing the importance of learning experiences above students' mastery level, and by his recommendations for engaging learners in making meaning for themselves individually and through interaction with others.

The key dimensions of the ICM are the *advanced content dimension,* the *process/ product dimension,* and the *issues/themes dimension,* and they are linked to the key learner characteristics of *precocity, intensity,* and *complexity.* The dimensions are interrelated, and they may serve as the foundation for curriculum in any discipline. None of the dimensions takes primacy or priority over the others; they are essentially inextricable within a curriculum unit, and the integrity of the total ICM is grounded in the connections across dimensions. Each dimension is described in more detail below, with an explanation of the major influences that led to this dimension as well as key aspects of how it is applied in curriculum development.

Advanced Content Dimension

The advanced content dimension of the ICM is grounded in the strong literature base in gifted education on the effectiveness of acceleration as an intervention to respond to the needs of gifted learners (Colangelo, Assouline, & Gross, 2004). Throughout the history of gifted education, scholars have advocated attention to modification and advancement of content for gifted learners, emphasizing the need to introduce content to these learners earlier and/or at a faster pace than to their age peers, because of the key learner characteristic of *precocity* (e.g., Gallagher, 1985; Maker, 1982; Stanley, Keating, & Fox, 1974). Various content acceleration approaches, such as rapid progress through advanced coursework (as in the Talent Search model) and curriculum compacting, have been found to result in academic gains for gifted students (Lubinski & Benbow, 1994; Olszewski-Kubilius, 2005; Reis, Westberg, Kulikowich, & Purcell, 1998; Swiatek, 2002). Each of these accelerative models relies upon careful use of assessment, in a diagnostic-prescriptive approach, to document student readiness for advanced work, with elimination of previously learned material in the curriculum and reduction of repetition.

In conjunction with this emphasis on advancing content, the ICM also relies upon ensuring that the content under study is substantive and worthwhile. The model reflects attention in the wider educational field to strengthening the rigor and authenticity of disciplinary content provided in schools. The ICM was emerging and being developed into curricular materials during the period of the national standards projects in the late 1980s and early 1990s, and throughout its history, curriculum developers have worked to align curriculum developed under the ICM with standards on and above grade level in the content areas (Little & Ellis, 2003). Furthermore, each major curriculum development initiative with the ICM has relied not only on alignment with standards, but also on collaboration between education specialists and content-area experts. Such collaboration has allowed the content of the curriculum to emphasize important topics, concepts, and habits of mind of the disciplines, as well as to incorporate high-quality materials that will provide challenge and effective representation of the discipline.

Thus, with the combined emphases on substantive and advanced content, the application of the advanced content dimension within curricular materials occurs through a variety of methods. First, the goals and objectives addressing the specific content area under study are at once authentic to the discipline and advanced compared to the normal curriculum for a given grade level. Second, in order to target instruction appropriately to the students participating in the curriculum, units developed under the ICM rely on a diagnostic-prescriptive approach to inform instructional planning, including not only efforts to eliminate and compact content as appropriate, but also supporting decisions to be made about grouping and specific activities and materials. Third, both the assessment and the instruction rely on off-level materials to promote deeper and more advanced understanding of the content as well as to provide challenge. Finally, the development of all of these pieces is guided by collaborative work between educators and content-area specialists who work to give students opportunities to interact with materials and ideas that are authentic and central to the discipline under study.

Process/Product Dimension

The process/product dimension of the ICM is grounded in a tradition in gifted education of giving specific attention to the development of thinking skills, as well as the emphasis of intensive focus on product development and independent pursuit of areas of interest (VanTassel-Baska & Stambaugh, 2006). Examples of process/product integration in gifted education have included Type II and Type III activities in the Schoolwide Enrichment Model (Renzulli & Reis, 1985), which engage students in learning specific thinking skills to support inquiry and then applying these skills to an area of interest in the development of a research product. Another example may be found in the application of problem-based learning to elementary and secondary education, with student engagement in actual or simulated real-world, ill-structured problems (Boyce, VanTassel-Baska, Burruss, Sher, & Johnson, 1997; Gallagher & Stepien, 1996).

The integrated nature of the ICM is intended to ensure linkage between such process skills and content, reflecting research that has demonstrated the importance of context- and content-bound thinking skills (Perkins & Salomon, 1989; Wineburg, 2001), as well as findings and recommendations that support teaching more generalized thinking skills in conjunction with deep content knowledge and opportunities for content applications (Haskell, 2001). Therefore, the process dimension of the ICM is inextricably tied to the content area under study, and is designed to encourage students to develop skills for inquiry related to the content area.

The process/product dimension responds to the learner characteristic of *intensity*. It reflects the understanding that when engaged at an appropriate level of challenge in an area of interest and talent, advanced learners have a stronger capacity for working at an intensive and extended level than other students might have (Csikszentmihalyi, Rathunde, & Whalen, 1993; VanTassel-Baska, 2003). Therefore, the ICM is designed to promote engagement at this advanced level, while also providing scaffolding and support that guide the student in the process of making meaning for themselves as they experience the curriculum. In addition, students are guided to understand and evaluate their thinking through an emphasis on metacognitive skills.

The process/product dimension echoes the emphasis of the advanced content dimension on reflecting authentic practices of the disciplines and engaging students in authentic experiences. Students engaged in ICM curriculum are intended to develop products for real audiences as a result of the processes with which they engage, and as a result of their developing understanding of advanced content. Like the advanced content itself, the goal of an authentic product for an audience is intended to be engaging and motivational, thus encouraging the students to respond to learning tasks with the intensity of which they are capable. In addition, the emphasis on integrating processes with products and with content promotes attention in the curriculum to problems that are existing and significant in the "real world," thereby promoting student development of responsibility for understanding diverse perspectives and taking social action to make the world a better place (Banks, 1994; Ford & Harris, 1999).

The application of the ICM process/product dimension emerges both in direct teaching of the intended skills and as an embedded component throughout lessons and activities. For example, a unit might include lessons that directly teach a reasoning model (e.g., Paul, 1992) as well as lessons that embed the model within discussion of a particular reading or situation. ICM units also incorporate goals and learner outcomes specifically related to the intended process emphases and product development components. Unit elements such as journal prompts and self-assessment forms also promote metacognition related to the cognitive processes being explored.

Issues/Themes Dimension

The issues/themes or epistemological concept dimension of the ICM reflects a perspective that curriculum should be organized around deeper ideas and philosophies that help learners understand the nature and structure of knowledge and the connections that bind people and cultures across space and time. Thus, this dimension allows ICM curriculum to be built around central interdisciplinary themes that are fundamental to the discipline under study, but also across disciplines, and that help to deepen students' understanding of the world around them. The concept dimension does not *introduce* concepts so much as *reveal* them; it draws upon students' existing experiences of universal ideas such as change, cause and effect, and power, and then guides students through a process of structuring and further building their understandings of these concepts as they apply within and across content areas (Avery & Little, 2003).

Scholars in gifted education have long advised a conceptual orientation to curriculum (e.g., Maker, 1982; Ward, 1961, 1981), as have many from the larger general education field. Among curricular programs and courses that emphasize this approach are Man: A Course of Study, Philosophy for Children, and the Junior Great Books program, as well as many Advanced Placement courses. In addition, the International Baccalaureate program is organized around an epistemological core. The current widespread emphasis on backward design and on developing essential understandings, as recommended through the Understanding by Design curriculum framework, also highlights the importance of conceptual understanding (Wiggins & McTighe, 1998); this also has been highlighted in gifted education within the Parallel Curriculum Model (Tomlinson et al., 2002).

Such programs and frameworks, with their emphasis on depth in understanding ideas, reflect both a longstanding philosophy of conceptually oriented curriculum as well as more recent recommendations on the importance of learning fewer concepts more deeply. For example, the American Association for the Advancement of Science (1990) recommended that science curriculum be centered around only about six major concepts in grades K–12; recommendations in other content areas have similarly called for greater attention to depth over broad coverage (e.g., National Council of Teachers of Mathematics, 2000).

The concept dimension responds most directly to the learner characteristic of *complexity,* addressing the gifted learner's higher capacities for abstraction, complexity, and depth of understanding. Because advanced learners tend to have greater capacity for managing multiple ideas and variables at the same time than their age peers might, the conceptual dimension invites them to grapple with this complexity within the discipline under study.

This dimension is enacted through direct attention to concept teaching as well as through embedded attention to the concept throughout curriculum units. Within a unit, at least one major learning goal and set of outcomes should be focused on a central concept, which should be a major idea within the discipline under study as well as one that applies across disciplines. For example, the study of mathematics includes a strong emphasis on the concept of *patterns;* this concept also applies more broadly across disciplines, and thus could frame a mathematics ICM unit and allow multiple interdisciplinary applications. Such a unit would center around building understanding of patterns and their relevance within mathematics and using problem solving and related processes to clarify students' understanding of content and concept. At the same time, the unit would use a series of generalizations about the concept of patterns to make connections to other disciplines. The central concept of a unit initially is explored directly through concept development activities that encourage students to develop deeper understandings of what they already know about a concept (Seiger-Ehrenberg, 2001; Taba, 1962). The concept then is addressed through applications within the content area through questioning, Socratic discussions, interdisciplinary connections, and other concept application activities (Avery & Little, 2003).

Ultimately, the goal of the concept dimension is to help students understand the ideas that underscore the human condition and the world in which we live. A focus on an overarching, abstract idea gives depth and complexity to curriculum because it requires students to make connections between discrete content elements that they study and the bigger ideas that make the content significant (VanTassel-Baska, 1998). In a world in which information is ever more accessible, education must become less about conveying information and more about facilitating meaning-making; therefore, conceptual emphases in the curriculum are critical.

The Realization of ICM Dimensions in Curricular Documents and Classroom Practice

All three ICM dimensions are critically important in developing curricular materials, because ultimately each enriches and strengthens the others. Although particular learning outcomes and lessons might emphasize one dimension more prominently than the others, all three must be addressed simultaneously in the planning and design of a unit. Elements that are essential for student learning, however, stem from the reiterated use of specific teaching models, the use of high-quality materials as content stimuli, and questioning approaches.

Teaching Models

The ICM in practice has centered around a core set of teaching models that may be applied in multiple contexts within the same unit, both to help students make meaning for themselves and to provide them with tools they may use in the future as they approach similar tasks. As each major curriculum development project evolved at the Center for Gifted Education, core teaching models were adopted, adapted, or developed to guide implementation of the curriculum. Several examples of these teaching models are described below.

In language arts, curriculum developers applied several specific teaching models to provide structure for student analysis of literature and of language (Center for Gifted Education, 1999). The Literature Web is a model that guides discussion by asking students to note the key words, feelings, ideas, images and symbols, and structure of a given literature selection; students respond to these five areas individually and then engage in discussion, thereby contributing their own understanding to the group's overall analysis. This model encourages students to bring their own perspectives and feelings to a piece of literature while also promoting key content understanding by highlighting the abstract themes and structural elements. Similarly, the Vocabulary Web guides students to understand the stems that make up words and how these stems are building blocks of many words in the language. Each of these webs is fairly simple in structure; therefore, practice with them allows students to gain confidence and skill in asking themselves questions as they work to understand a new piece of literature or a new word.

In social studies, a model for analyzing sources was developed to reflect key questions that drive historical analysis of both source and context. This model aligns with standards and recommendations in the social studies literature (e.g., National Center for History in the Schools [NCHS], 1996) while also reflecting more general critical thinking concepts. Paul's (1992) model, including elements of thought and standards of reasoning, was linked with emphases such as contextualizing, corroborating, and ensuring authenticity and representativeness of primary sources in the development of this model. In addition, Paul's model informed a framework for reasoning about a situation to help students examine multiple perspectives and understand that events of history were not inevitable, but depended on the perspectives and assumptions of people involved.

In science, the central role of the scientific method is highlighted through extensive application of experimental design and opportunities for students to develop and carry out their own experiments. This emphasis on the scientific process occurs within a problem-based learning (PBL) model that frames the science units along with the ICM. PBL presents students with ill-structured problems and places them in the role of stakeholders to engage them in inquiry as they seek to respond to the problem situation. The specific unit content and the scientific design process are embedded within components of the problem, and students develop understanding of the organizing concept of systems as they engage with the problem as well.

Each of these examples demonstrates how the teaching models support the relationships among the ICM dimensions. Each model is grounded both in general principles of critical and conceptual thinking and in the processes and habits of mind that are specific to the content areas. In addition, each model lends itself well to use with advanced content, but also may be applied with less advanced content with a wider range of students. Therefore, the models stand as scaffolds for making meaning, and the content stimuli to which they are applied provide the varied levels of challenge to make them appropriate for groups of learners.

High-Quality Stimulus Materials

A second important aspect of building ICM units and preparing them for classroom use is the integration of high-quality materials as the invitation to the content. Materials for curriculum units are carefully selected with attention to how they represent the core understandings of the content area, how they reflect the concept being studied, how they represent diverse perspectives and contexts, and how students will be able to relate to them. As noted previously, ideal use of the ICM relies upon collaboration between content-area experts and curriculum designers, so that the content-area experts may recommend materials along with key understandings and habits of mind that educational experts then can structure into experiences reflecting best pedagogical practices. In language arts, the selection of literature that is challenging, high-quality, and engaging for students and that represents diversity in authorship and perspective is a key factor in building a strong unit. In social studies, the primary and secondary sources with which students engage are central to the learning experience, and therefore rely upon careful selection and authentication. Moreover, modeling for students of the practices of the discipline requires that their study of primary sources provide opportunities for corroboration and for exploring multiple perspectives (NCHS, 1996).

Beyond the reading materials for a unit, other resources also are critical for building a strong unit under the ICM. Technology resources, for example, can enrich a student's understanding of the content by providing virtual access to places and people from far away and long ago; they also can give students power for computing and for organizing and presenting data as they develop their products. Effective teaching of experimental design in science depends on students' opportunity to carry out experiments using hands-on resources. In addition, hands-on materials for the classroom and technology sources, including bookmarked Web sites, can provide important extensions that allow students to pursue areas of interest.

Questioning

Units developed under the ICM also rely on the development of guiding questions to support the overall instructional process. Preplanned questions help to ensure that questioning and discussion maintain a high level of challenge and complexity, and that key objectives are addressed through the dialogue between teachers and students and among students. This is not to discount the types of questions that emerge from discussion in "teachable moments" and in the general flow of conversation; however, preparation of questions in advance should be combined with these questions of the moment to ensure that lessons are directed toward the key learning outcomes of the particular activity and the overall unit. The questions used in ICM units have been carefully developed using the scaffold of the Paul (1992) model of reasoning and the Junior Great Books inquiry-based approach, among others, to ensure high-level and interpretive questions. Within existing

ICM units, lessons generally include questions that support progress within each of the dimensions of the model. For example, in the language arts units developed at the Center for Gifted Education, prepared questions address the categories of "Literary Analysis and Interpretation," "Reasoning," and "Change," representing, respectively, the content, process, and concept dimensions of the unit. In the social studies units, journal prompts across the unit directly address concept, process, or content dimensions. In the science units, questions for discussion and for written response help to clarify understanding of the central problem throughout a unit, and also encourage reflection on the scientific process and the inferences to be made from experimental data. Throughout all of these examples, questions form a critical scaffolding system for promoting students' understanding of the content under study and of their own thinking processes.

PROFESSIONAL DEVELOPMENT

Even the very best curricular materials are not given life and meaning without the voice of a teacher who translates design into reality in the classroom, and such translation occurs most effectively with good professional development opportunities for teachers. The ICM as a design framework has complex components that result in complex curricular materials. Moreover, any curriculum that is rigorous for students and engages them in challenging study of complex ideas and questions also will be challenging for a teacher to implement, because of the need for deep understanding as well as flexibility in thinking to respond to the questions and discussions that arise from students. Therefore, teachers who are going to use materials developed under this model need professional development opportunities and support to build and strengthen their understanding of the materials and how best to translate them into classroom practice.

In addition, several research studies have demonstrated the importance of professional development about gifted students and their needs for the teachers who are going to work with them (e.g., Hansen & Feldhusen, 1994). Especially given the limited differentiation that occurs for gifted students in regular classrooms (Westberg, Archambault, Dobyns, & Salvin, 1993; Westberg & Daoust, 2003), this attention to teacher preparation to work with gifted students is particularly important. Therefore, professional development related to ICM curriculum must incorporate characteristics of gifted learners and differentiation principles and strategies along with specific information about the curriculum to be implemented.

With each major curriculum development initiative at the Center for Gifted Education, a professional development model was simultaneously developed and refined to provide the strongest possible introductory and follow-up experiences for teachers intending to implement the materials in the classroom. These professional development programs have centered around modeling and practice with the teaching models, with deliberate connections made back to the ICM at the foundation of the models. Teachers have the opportunity to play the student role as they participate in each model, but then replace their teacher "hat" and ask and discuss questions about how to make the models work most effectively. Such initial learning experiences for teachers should be coupled with support during the teaching of the unit to promote fidelity of implementation and, thus, the full intended learning experience for students.

RESEARCH EFFORTS

Under Joyce VanTassel-Baska's direction, the Center for Gifted Education at The College of William and Mary has conducted extensive curriculum development work over the last two decades (VanTassel-Baska & Stambaugh, 2008). Curriculum development projects, frequently conducted with support from the Jacob K. Javits program, have investigated the effects on student achievement of curriculum materials developed under the ICM as compared to existing materials and programs in the content areas examined. These studies have explored effects of the curriculum on gifted students, on students of high potential from disadvantaged backgrounds, and on learners not identified in either of these groups. Studies also have explored the influence of the units on teaching practice and on the school community in various sites. Key findings from the research in each of the major content areas studied are discussed below.

The language arts units developed under the ICM have been the most thoroughly researched, with several large-scale studies occurring over the course of more than a decade. The first two large-scale studies of student achievement with these units focused on comparing pre- and posttest results on performance-based measures of literary analysis and interpretation and persuasive writing for students in similar treatment and comparison classes (VanTassel-Baska, Johnson, Hughes, & Boyce, 1996; VanTassel-Baska, Zuo, Avery, & Little, 2002). The results showed significant student gains and significant differences between the treatment and comparison groups in each study; in the later, larger study, effect sizes were calculated across four units, with a very high effect size for persuasive writing ($d = 2.42$) and a high effect size for literary analysis ($d = .70$; VanTassel-Baska et al., 2002). In addition, results demonstrated gains for students from lower and higher SES schools, for students of both sexes, and for students in a variety of class settings; students who engaged in multiple units across years also showed gains in each year of exposure.

More recently, a large 3-year longitudinal study was conducted on implementation of language arts units with more than 1,300 students in 28 elementary classrooms in Title I schools, using an experimental design with random assignment of classrooms to treatment and control conditions. Instruments for this study included the original performance-based measures from the earlier studies and also the reading comprehension section of the Iowa Tests of Basic Skills (ITBS) and the investigator-developed Test of Critical Thinking (TCT; Bracken et al., 2003). Results showed gains for treatment and control group students on the ITBS and on the TCT, with significant differences favoring the treatment group on the TCT. Significant differences also were observed between groups on the performance-based measures, again favoring the treatment group; these results were apparent across ability groups, supporting differentiated implementation of the units in heterogeneous classrooms (VanTassel-Baska, Bracken, Feng, & Brown, in press).

A quasi-experimental study of implementation of problem-based science units developed under the ICM examined student performance on a test of integrated science process skills (Fowler, 1990). The study found significant and important treatment effects, comparing groups across 62 classrooms in grades 2–7 (VanTassel-Baska, Bass, Ries, Poland, & Avery, 1998). Another study examined students who participated in multiple units across 3 years in grades 3–5, finding significant gains for students in each year they participated (Feng, VanTassel-Baska, Quek, Bai, & O'Neill, 2005).

Social studies units developed under the ICM were implemented with 1,200 students at grades 2, 4, and 7 in 6 schools. Student performance on tests of conceptual thinking, critical thinking, and content learning were compared across treatment and comparison classes. Results demonstrated significant differences favoring the treatment group on the test of content learning (Little, Feng, VanTassel-Baska, Rogers, & Avery, 2007).

In addition to these findings regarding student learning gains, studies of the ICM units across content areas also have examined results for teachers and for schools more broadly. An evaluation study in schools implementing science and language arts units found that the curriculum was a factor in promoting positive school change (VanTassel-Baska, Avery, Little, & Hughes, 2000). Results from classroom observations conducted during the social studies curriculum study showed significant gains for treatment group teachers in their use of critical thinking strategies based on their use of the units (Little et al., 2007). Similarly, teachers participating in the most recent large-scale language arts study showed significant gains from using the units in their use of critical thinking and other strategies important for differentiation (VanTassel-Baska et al., in press).

Overall, research has demonstrated positive effects of the ICM units on students and on their teachers across subject areas. These effects have been observed for students from a variety of backgrounds and in a variety of settings.

Future Directions and Questions

As more and more gifted programs move toward service delivery options that find gifted students in heterogeneous classrooms or in self-contained settings, and as the field calls for greater attention to gifted students' needs throughout the school day rather than in partial pullout experiences, the significance of curriculum that responds to the needs of gifted learners continues to escalate (VanTassel-Baska, 2003; VanTassel-Baska & Wood, in press). VanTassel-Baska's ICM provides a basis for curriculum that responds to the needs of gifted learners in a variety of settings, and the units that have been developed within this framework provide strong models of such curriculum. Many of these units have been recognized by the National Association for Gifted Children's Curriculum Studies Division with awards for excellence in curriculum. The ICM draws attention to the characteristics of high-ability learners and their concomitant learning needs, while also emphasizing the importance of high expectations for all students and authenticity to the disciplines, as well as deep conceptual learning.

Joyce VanTassel-Baska's work in gifted education has spanned four decades and has addressed myriad challenges and issues in the field. The Integrated Curriculum Model is one of her most significant and lasting contributions, as it has permeated so many classrooms and affected the learning experiences of thousands of students and their teachers. The model has brought attention to the learning needs and capabilities of gifted learners from a wide range of backgrounds by giving students the opportunity to interact with complex material that honors their strengths and helps them take early steps toward expertise in their disciplines. Through VanTassel-Baska's leadership, the model has continued to demonstrate the power of targeted curriculum to optimize gifted students' learning experiences.

REFERENCES

American Association for the Advancement of Science. (1990). *Science for all Americans.* New York: Oxford University Press.

Avery, L. D., & Little, C. A. (2003). Concept development and learning. In J. VanTassel-Baska & C. A. Little (Eds.), *Content-based curriculum for high-ability learners* (pp. 101–124). Waco, TX: Prufrock Press.

Banks, J. (1994). *An introduction to multicultural education.* Boston: Allyn & Bacon.

Boyce, L. N., VanTassel-Baska, J., Burruss, J., Sher, B. T., & Johnson, D. T. (1997). A problem-based curriculum: Parallel learning opportunities for students and teachers. *Journal for the Education of the Gifted, 20,* 363–379.

Bracken, B. A., Bai, W., Fithian, E., Lamprecht, S., Little, C., & Quek, C. (2003). *Test of critical thinking.* Williamsburg, VA: The College of William and Mary, Center for Gifted Education.

Center for Gifted Education. (1999). *Guide to teaching a language arts curriculum for high-ability learners.* Dubuque, IA: Kendall/Hunt.

Colangelo, N., Assouline, S. G., & Gross, M. U. M. (2004). *A nation deceived: How schools hold back America's brightest students* (Vol. 1). Iowa City: The University of Iowa, The Connie Belin & Jacqueline N. Blank International Center for Gifted Education and Talent Development.

Csikszentmihalyi, M., Rathunde, K., & Whalen, S. (1993). *Talented teenagers: The roots of success and failure.* New York: Cambridge University Press.

Feng, A. X., VanTassel-Baska, J., Quek, C., Bai, W., & O'Neill, B. (2005). A longitudinal assessment of gifted students' learning using the Integrated Curriculum Model (ICM): Impacts and perceptions of the William and Mary language arts and science curriculum. *Roeper Review, 27,* 78–83.

Ford, D. Y., & Harris, J. J. (1999). *Multicultural gifted education.* New York: Teachers College Press.

Fowler, M. (1990). The diet cola test. *Science Scope, 13*(4), 32–34.

Gallagher, J. (1985). *Teaching the gifted child* (3rd ed.). Boston: Allyn & Bacon.

Gallagher, S. A., & Stepien, W. J. (1996). Content acquisition in problem-based learning: Depth versus breadth in American studies. *Journal for the Education of the Gifted, 19,* 257–275.

Hansen, J., & Feldhusen, J. (1994). Comparison of trained and untrained teachers of the gifted. *Gifted Child Quarterly, 38,* 115–123.

Haskell, R. E. (2001). *Transfer of learning: Cognition, instruction, and reasoning.* San Diego, CA: Academic Press.

Little, C. A., & Ellis, W. T. (2003). Aligning curricula for the gifted with content standards and exemplary secondary programs. In J. VanTassel-Baska & C. A. Little (Eds.), *Content-based curriculum for high-ability learners* (pp. 327–354). Waco, TX: Prufrock Press.

Little, C. A., Feng, A. X., VanTassel-Baska, J., Rogers, K. B., & Avery, L. D. (2007). Study of curriculum effectiveness in social studies. *Gifted Child Quarterly, 51,* 272–284.

Lubinski, D., & Benbow, C. P. (1994). The study of mathematically precocious youth: The first three decades of a planned 50-year study of intellectual talent. In R. Subotnik & K. D. Arnold (Eds.), *Beyond Terman: Contemporary longitudinal studies of giftedness and talent* (pp. 375–400). Norwood, NJ: Ablex.

Maker, C. J. (1982). *Curriculum development for the gifted.* Rockville, MD: Aspen.

National Center for History in the Schools. (1996). *National standards for history.* Los Angeles: Author.

National Council of Teachers of Mathematics. (2000). *Principles and standards for school mathematics.* Reston, VA: Author.

Olszewski-Kubilius, P. (2005). The Center for Talent Development at Northwestern University: An example of replication and reformation. *High Ability Studies, 16*(1), 55–69.

Paul, R. (1992). *Critical thinking: What every person needs to survive in a rapidly changing world.* Rohnert Park, CA: Foundation for Critical Thinking.

Perkins, D., & Salomon, G. (1989). Are cognitive skills context bound? *Educational Research, 18*(1), 16–25.

Reis, S. M., Westberg, K. L., Kulikowich, J. M., & Purcell, J. H. (1998). Curriculum compacting and achievement test scores: What does the research say? *Gifted Child Quarterly, 42,* 123–129.

Renzulli, J. S., & Reis, S. M. (1985). *The Schoolwide Enrichment Model: A comprehensive plan for educational excellence.* Mansfield Center, CT: Creative Learning Press.

Seiger-Ehrenberg, S. (2001). Concept development. In A. L. Costa (Ed.), *Developing minds: A resource book for teaching thinking* (3rd ed., pp. 437–441). Alexandria, VA: ASCD.

Stanley, J., Keating, D., & Fox, L. (1974). *Mathematical talent.* Baltimore: Johns Hopkins University Press.

Swiatek, M. A. (2002). A decade of longitudinal research on academic acceleration through the Study of Mathematically Precocious Youth. *Roeper Review, 24,* 141–144.

Taba, H. (1962). *Curriculum development, theory and practice.* New York: Harcourt, Brace & World.

Tomlinson, C. A., Kaplan S. N., Purcell, J., Renzulli, J., Leppien, J., & Burns, D. (2002). *The parallel curriculum: A design to develop high potential and challenge high-ability learners.* Thousand Oaks, CA: Corwin Press.

VanTassel-Baska, J. (1986). Effective curriculum and instructional models for talented students. *Gifted Child Quarterly, 30,* 164–169.

VanTassel-Baska, J. (Ed.). (1998). *Excellence in educating gifted & talented learners* (3rd ed.). Denver, CO: Love.

VanTassel-Baska, J. (2003). Content-based curriculum for high-ability learners: An introduction. In J. VanTassel-Baska & C. A. Little (Eds.), *Content-based curriculum for high-ability learners* (pp. 1–24). Waco, TX: Prufrock Press.

VanTassel-Baska, J., Avery, L. D., Little, C. A., & Hughes, C. E. (2000). An evaluation of the implementation: The impact of the William and Mary units on schools. *Journal for the Education of the Gifted, 23,* 244–272.

VanTassel-Baska, J., Bass, G. M., Ries, R. R., Poland, D. L., & Avery, L. D. (1998). A national study of science curriculum effectiveness with high ability students. *Gifted Child Quarterly, 42,* 200–211.

VanTassel-Baska, J., & Bracken, B. (2008). *Project Athena evaluation report.* Williamsburg, VA: The College of William and Mary, Center for Gifted Education.

VanTassel-Baska, J., Bracken, B., Feng, A. & Brown, E. (in press). A longitudinal study of reading comprehension and reasoning ability of students in elementary Title I schools. *Journal for the Education of the Gifted.*

VanTassel-Baska, J., Johnson, D. T., Hughes, C. E., & Boyce, L. N. (1996). A study of language arts curriculum effectiveness with gifted learners. *Journal for the Education of the Gifted, 19,* 461–480.

VanTassel-Baska, J., & Stambaugh, T. (Eds.). (2006). *Comprehensive curriculum for gifted learners* (3rd ed.). Boston: Allyn & Bacon.

VanTassel-Baska, J., & Stambaugh, T. (Eds.). (2008). *What works: 20 years of curriculum development and research.* Waco, TX: Prufrock Press

VanTassel-Baska, J., & Wood, S. (in press). *The Integrated Curriculum Model.* In J. S. Renzulli, E. J. Gubbins, K. McMillen, R. D. Eckert, & C. A. Little (Eds.), *Systems and models for developing programs for the gifted and talented* (2nd ed.). Mansfield Center, CT: Creative Learning Press.

VanTassel-Baska, J., Zuo, L., Avery, L. D., & Little, C. A. (2002). A curriculum study of gifted student learning in the language arts. *Gifted Child Quarterly, 46,* 30–44.

Vygotsky, L. S. (1978). *Mind in society: The development of higher psychological processes.* Cambridge, MA: Harvard University Press.

Ward, V. (1961). *An axiomatic approach to educating the gifted.* Columbus, OH: Merrill.

Ward, V. (1981). *Educating the gifted: An axiomatic approach.* Ventura County, CA: Leadership Training Institute on Gifted and Talented.

Westberg, K. L., Archambault, F. X., Jr., Dobyns, S. M., & Salvin, T. J. (1993). An observational study of classroom practices used with third- and fourth-grade students. *Journal for the Education of the Gifted, 16,* 120–146.

Westberg, K. L., & Daoust, M. E. (2003, Fall). The results of the classroom practices survey replication in two states. *The National Research Center on the Gifted and Talented Newsletter,* 3–8.

Wiggins, G., & McTighe, J. (1998). *Understanding by design.* Alexandria, VA: ASCD.

Wineburg, S. S. (Ed.). (2001). *Historical thinking and other unnatural acts: Charting the future of teaching the past.* Philadelphia: Temple University Press.

CHAPTER 24

SCIENCE EDUCATION FOR GIFTED LEARNERS

by

JANICE
I. ROBBINS

The most exciting phrase to hear in science, the one that heralds the most discoveries, is not "Eureka!" (I found it), but "That's funny . . ."

—Isaac Asimov

Guiding the education of future scientists is a critical task. Given our current national focus on major issues in energy, climate, health, and the environment, as well as our nation's voracious appetite for new and better technologies, we Americans expect scientists to be our problem finders and our problem solvers. Learning to think like scientists is particularly critical for high-ability students who are ready for and drawn to advanced studies in science. Today's aspiring scientists are the discoverers and inventors who will support new ways of living and working in an environment that is overused, polluted, and often disrespectful of its resources, living and nonliving.

Too often, students who are gifted in science are confronted on a daily basis by science instruction, restricted by classroom conditions and state standards. The standards-based effort to ensure that all children become literate in science (American Association for the Advancement of Science, 1989; National Research Council, 1996), although a laudable goal, is an acknowledged deterrent to the advanced learning of gifted students who, rather than being held back, should actually be accelerated in their studies (Colangelo, Assouline, & Gross, 2004; Rogers, 1999). Curriculum and instruction that measures success by meeting state standards, and restricts student access to higher level content and processes in science is doomed to fail gifted students. Rogers (1999) indicated that American teachers aim content instruction toward the 19th percentile rather than stretching gifted learners toward the 99th.

One example of a noted scientist who experienced restricted opportunities was Linus Pauling, one of the most influential chemists of the 20th century. Pauling began his lifelong interest in chemistry as a boy, intrigued by a friend's experimentation with a chemistry set. Pauling started conducting his own experiments, using materials he found at an abandoned steel mill. As a 15-year-old high school senior, he had sufficient credits for graduation, but lacked two required history courses. His request of the school to allow him to take these courses concurrently during his spring semester was rejected, and so he left school without graduating. Forty-five years and two Nobel Prizes later, Pauling was finally awarded his diploma. Fortunately, Pauling found his way to college and advanced studies without high school graduation, but, unfortunately, many talented students in science lose their drive and passion for science when not provided with work that is challenging for them in school.

State standards, many by their very content, constrain students' advanced learning in science. A 2005 review of all K–12 state standards in science, conducted by the Fordham Foundation (Cross et al., 2005), reported that more than half of the states were given a grade of C or lower and 15 states received a grade of F for the quality and rigor of their standards. Two areas identified as among the weakest across state standards in the Fordham report are of particular concern in relation to the education of gifted students in science. First, many of the state standards are overwhelming in size and content, such that educators find it impossible to "cover" all the material. Second, an imbalance exists between process skills and real science content (e.g., astronomy, biology, chemistry, ecology, physics), with the process skills tipping the balance. This shallow presentation of scientific information and the imbalance of content and process found in many of the state standards offer a weak foundation for effective differentiation of curriculum and instruction for students gifted in science.

At the classroom level, teachers often seem overwhelmed as they attempt to plan for the educational needs of gifted learners in science. Given the complex demands of teaching and limited time for general science instruction, teachers find differentiation of science for high-ability students a daunting task. At the elementary level, the instructional focus is primarily on English/language arts and mathematics. Even in high school, many students are required to take only two years of science, thus limiting their exposure to the more interesting and concentrated science topics at the higher levels. Elementary teachers often feel inadequate in science, having had limited coursework in this content area. Secondary science teachers, while significantly more competent in the content, often are inadequately trained in modifying curriculum and expectations for gifted students. It is no surprise, then, that highly able students often find themselves in learning environments that diminish rather than extend their curiosity, interest, and motivation to gain new knowledge and explore new ideas in science.

THE NATURE OF SCIENCE AND SCIENTISTS' WAYS OF KNOWING

Science by its very nature is a process that seeks to explain the natural world. Scientists are seekers of knowledge, looking for patterns in things and events, using their intellectual tools of observation, logical thinking, and experimentation. Scientists engage in ongoing studies, seeking to improve and refine current knowledge based on new observations and interpretations.

The very nature of a scientist's work is a clear match to the nature and needs of gifted students. Studies of common characteristics of eminent scientists (Proctor & Capaldi, 2006; Simonton, 1988, 1992; Thagard, 2004) reveal characteristics similar to those evidenced by gifted learners. Such characteristics include high intellectual ability, curiosity, personal drive and persistence, creativity, and strong analytical skills. These similarities reinforce the need for high-ability learners to be exposed to quality science, enabling them to use their talents and gifts to gain new knowledge and develop new skills. Simonton (1988) reported that students who have the opportunity to work with eminent scientists have a greater chance of becoming renowned scientists and making significant contributions to the field.

Researchers (Brandwein, 1986, 1995; Brandwein & Passow, 1988; Franks & Dolan, 1982; Mintzes, Wandersee, & Novak, 2005) have pinpointed specific characteristics of gifted learners in the area of science. These characteristics, although quite similar to the more generalized lists of characteristics of gifted students, do include an expanded focus on specific interest in science, a strong ability to recognize patterns in seemingly unrelated things, and a propensity for work with a quantitative approach. Metacognitive strengths also have received recognition. Mintzes et al. (2005) found that, "Learners who excel in the natural sciences habitually employ a set of metacognitive strategies enabling them to plan, monitor, regulate, and control their own learning" (p. 76). Looking at the evolution of science talent, Brandwein (1995) suggested that

> science proneness begins in a base of a general giftedness and develops its component skills in verbal, mathematical, and in time, the nonentrenched tasks of problem seeking, finding, and solving in specialized science fields. Eventually, given favorable ecologies, science proneness can shift to an expression in a work showing science talent. (p. 104)

The strengths gifted students display in science reinforce their readiness for investigation, experimentation, and the depth of knowledge in their particular areas of interest in science and have significant implications for curricular modifications.

In general, students who are high achievers in science can be found by observing certain behaviors in their science work (Brandwein, 1995; Mintzes et al., 2005). They are likely to:

- make careful and thorough observations,
- show strong interest in problem solving,
- ask many questions,
- experiment with ideas,
- maintain interest in a problem over time,
- express a passion for science,
- show persistence,
- demonstrate inventiveness,
- express extreme curiosity,
- enjoy reading books on science and science fiction,
- conduct self-initiated science activities,
- show an interest in numbers and magnitudes, and
- notice simple and complex patterns.

Brandwein (1995) suggested that educators look for student talent within meaningful science experiences offered in school. He stated, "The structure of curriculum and the mode of instruction in classroom and laboratory serve to identify science proneness, an understanding that suggests a significant way to increase the science talent pool" (p. xviii). Because students express their talents in different ways, depending on their prior knowledge, cultural and socioeconomic background, motivation, and other pertinent factors, offering engaging science instruction at schools and looking for high-level student behaviors may, indeed, support the recognition of otherwise unseen gifted students in science.

SCIENCE CURRICULUM FOR GIFTED STUDENTS

As a corollary to the expressed characteristics of gifted students, Van Tassel-Baska (1986, 2003) developed the Integrated Curriculum Model (ICM) to guide curriculum responsive to the nature and needs of advanced learners. The ICM employs overarching, interdisciplinary concepts, issues, and themes; advanced content; and higher level process and product development.

As applied to science units of study developed at the Center for Gifted Education at The College of William and Mary, the ICM incorporates:

- An overarching concept developed throughout the unit. Examples of concepts, sometimes called themes, include change, systems, and patterns.
- Advanced content developed through the use of expanded resources, in-depth topics, advanced reading, use of primary sources, and the development of related skills such as measurement and use of technology.

> ▶ Scientific processes including scientific investigation and reasoning, as well as specific research skills and models of real-world applications such as problem-based learning.

These three areas of advanced development are the foundation of an excellent instructional program for high-ability learners in science. Once certain students are identified as advanced learners, responsible educators must accept their obligation to capitalize on students' innate aptitudes, traits, and behaviors by providing a challenging curriculum.

Research evidence on the effectiveness of the William and Mary science units when used with gifted students was recently reported (VanTassel-Baska & Stambaugh, 2008):

> ▶ Primary students exposed to the William and Mary science units performed better on a standardized achievement test than control students (VanTassel-Baska, Bracken, Stambaugh, & Feng, 2007).
>
> ▶ Primary students exposed to the William and Mary units showed significant growth in critical thinking compared to those students who used the regular science curriculum (VanTassel-Baska et al, 2007).
>
> ▶ Continued use of problem-based science curriculum over a 3-year period resulted in continued academic growth for gifted students (Feng, VanTassel-Baska, Quek, O'Neill, & Bai, 2005).

Scientific Concept Development

The Atlas of Science Literacy (2007) highlights the importance of themes or overarching concepts that cross disciplines in science and also guide students to understanding how science is centered in universal ideas. As students apply their understanding of an overarching concept to their current and developing knowledge, they begin to articulate and internalize generalizations that can be associated with each concept, connecting them to future work in multiple disciplines. Overarching concepts incorporated into William and Mary science units include change, systems, patterns, and cause and effect.

Students with advanced potential in science need to develop deep knowledge of the specific science content through strong and focused concept development, wide reading, and the interconnection of ideas. Pfundt and Duit (1994), reporting on more than 20 years of research and more than 3,500 studies on students' understanding of science concepts, proposed several knowledge claims that are widely supported by cognitive scientists. One claim, especially pertinent to gifted students' development of advanced content, suggests that individuals with highly integrated, well-developed knowledge frameworks in a specific domain are able to solve problems in real-world settings by attending to and reflecting on related objects and/or events.

Novak and Gowin (1984) supported this notion with a claim based on their own work. They found that successful science learners possessed a strongly hierarchical, cohesive framework of related concepts. Successful students were able to represent those concepts at a deep level, making meaning by restructuring their existing knowledge frameworks using subsumptions, superordination, integration, and differentiation.

Concept Mapping

To reinforce students' advanced work in science, Novak and Gowin (1984) promoted the use of concept mapping as a powerful strategy for assisting students with the development of their personal knowledge frameworks. According to Novak (1998), concept maps help students to see the relationship between concepts as they exist in their minds, to isolate and visually express those concepts and relationships. The use of concept maps for pretesting, learning activities, and posttesting has been successfully used in the William and Mary Project Clarion science units for primary grades, leading students to higher levels of meaningful learning.

Scientific Inquiry

All scientists work to improve our knowledge and understanding of the world. In the process of scientific inquiry, they connect evidence with logical reasoning and imagination. Recognizing this important aspect of scientists' work, the National Science Education Standards (National Research Council, 1996) specifically address inquiry as a critical component of all students' science learning. The primary-grade science units developed at the Center for Gifted Education at The College of William and Mary (2005) incorporate a clear focus on scientific investigation and reasoning, emphasizing the important actions scientists take when engaging in a scientific inquiry. Using methods generally employed in the scientific world, students learn the importance of observation, questioning, reviewing related bodies of scientific knowledge, designing and conducting experiments, analyzing data and creating meaning from experimental findings, and communicating with others to share new knowledge. The students learn to work collaboratively and recognize the importance of building upon the work of others. Students come to understand what kinds of questions can be answered through scientific methodology and which cannot. They come to recognize the importance of knowledge, skills, and critical and creative thinking in science.

NINE ESSENTIALS FOR SUPPORTING SCIENCE TALENT

Nine essentials that address the specific strengths of gifted students with advanced abilities in science are listed below. If implemented, these essentials will provide strong support for gifted students' advancement in science.

1. Gifted students have an advanced ability to construct meaning. Ensure strong, challenging content that promotes understanding.

Students often receive instruction from teachers who do not possess strong background knowledge in their science area. Because the extent of a teacher's knowledge in science greatly impacts the students' opportunities to learn science, teachers must possess a solid background in the particular science discipline they teach. Recent national emphasis on teacher quality may begin to make a difference in this area. Standards for Science Teacher Preparation, adopted by the National Science Teachers Association (2003), call for teachers to "develop a broad knowledge of science content in addition to some in-depth experiences in at least one science subject" (p. 60). A recent publication, *Using the National Gifted Education Standards for PreK–12 Professional Development* (Kitano, Montgomery, VanTassel-Baska, & Johnsen, 2008), is aimed at strengthening professional development for teachers, using the National Association for Gifted Children (NAGC) gifted education standards as a foundation. Teachers of the gifted in science should be familiar with these standards and be held accountable for their expected outcomes. How teachers present the content also is critical. Meaningful learning should be the primary goal rather than rote learning. Students should be guided to strengthen their own conceptual frameworks, engaging in inner logic in which experience is translated into language. Bruner's (1963) focus on the "structure of the discipline" is the essence of this type of content teaching.

2. Gifted students exude intellectual curiosity. Engage students in real-life situations that pique their curiosity.

When high-ability students approach the study of science, they readily draw upon their inner curiosity to question things around them. They want answers or want to figure out how to get the answer. Teachers support the student's inner curiosity by acknowledging it, valuing it, and encouraging student investigations. Gifted students are particularly drawn to the resolution of real-world problems (Williams, Papierno, Makel, & Ceci, 2004). Rogers (1999) reported that the general literature in gifted education supports real-world problem solving and, coupled with realistic, corrective feedback, this approach has been shown to have significant positive effects for gifted students. It is clear that students who actually make direct contributions to real-world experiments in science enhance their motivation and self-efficacy.

3. Gifted students have high abstract reasoning ability. Teach reasoning skills directly.

Without effective reasoning skills, gifted students are apt to remain impulsive and satisfied with their first views. These students often are recognized for the speed of their reactions and the general "correctness" of their responses. Students need to learn the hard work and the logic of scientific thinking. Paul and Elder (2006) promoted the direct teaching of reasoning, indicating that "scientists make judgments about the physical world based on observations and experimentation. These judgments lead to systematized knowledge, theories, and principles helpful in explaining and understanding the world" (p. 28).

4. Gifted students emotionally and creatively gravitate to abstract concepts. Embrace creativity as part of science teaching and learning.

One form of creative thinking frequently used by science teachers in helping students grasp abstract concepts and by scientists in interpreting findings is metaphorical thinking. Hoffmann (2006) indicated that, although scientists frequently use metaphors, they don't admit it until they meet the challenge of explaining what they know to nonscientists. Metaphorical thinking helps students connect prior knowledge to new situations. In a study of teacher education students, researchers (Clement, 1993; Ritchie, Bellocchi, Polt, & Wearmouth, 2006; Wong, 1993) found that students showed significant improvement in the quality of their explanations, the complexity of their thinking, and their unusual connections when they developed their own analogies.

In addition to the encouragement of metaphorical thinking, gifted students would benefit greatly from opportunities in science to develop the creative thinking skills of fluency, flexibility, originality, and elaboration.

5. Gifted students have a real interest in precision and quantitative approaches. Engage students in the use of real instruments and tools of scientists, incorporating a focus on the quantitative side of science.

Teachers should be encouraged to use sophisticated equipment in science instruction. Often they are concerned that these instruments are too fragile and expensive as well as too time-consuming to set up. However, the use of quantitative measures becomes important in science investigations. Students begin to recognize the importance of questions such as "how much?", "how many?", "how often?", and "how large or small?", learning that numbers are powerful and numeracy is an important foundation for scientific investigation. Gifted students need to learn precision in data collection methods and the value of careful records. Data collection experiences should build upon each other, teaching students the ways in which scientists persistently pursue clear findings.

6. Gifted students need to experience scientific collegiality. Guide students to use collaborative methods and establish ways of communicating results to an interested audience.

Roald Hoffmann (2006), Nobel Prize winner in chemistry, stated that, "a commitment to telling others what you have done is essential to the functioning of science. The primary medium of communication in the profession is the peer-reviewed article" (p. 1). Although young students of science may not be ready for formal writing for science journals, they are able to work with others to establish a research agenda of interest to them, complete and record a scientific investigation, and identify ways to present their findings to an interested audience. Gifted students often are motivated to complete the experimental phase of scientific study, particularly if they have a vested interest in the problem, but they often fall short when it comes to drawing conclusions and communicating their results. Through more formal investigations with planned reporting, students engage in the behaviors of real scientists, develop deeper interest in their own work and the work of others, and strengthen their communications skills. Brandwein (1995) shared the extra benefits of student-selected research:

> The experience of originative research in high school may motivate a decision to pursue a career in science and thus qualify students for continued research in their undergraduate years. Originative inquiry can lead to early expression of science talent in the young; it therefore is a worthy practice in the quest of the young scientist-to-be. (p. 84)

7. Gifted students are exposed to sophisticated technology in their daily lives. Provide opportunities for students to experience the scientist's technological world.

Very powerful uses of technology in science include precision instruments, databases to retrieve and/or contribute to, virtual labs that allow the use of materials and specimens that are not available in the classroom, multimedia presentations, and electronic communications. These technologies are readily available and used in the professional world of scientists. The tools help students engage in real science activities where the investigation is not about finding the correct answer as in a prescribed "lab," but rather going where the initial results seem to lead, asking questions about what happened in the experiment, and then considering what might be done differently, thus continuing the process.

The ease of teaching and learning using tools of technology and the use of simulations and virtual laboratories engages students in feedback and discussion about new ideas and hypotheses rather than on the procedures themselves. This ease is of great benefit to students with disabilities and/or different learning styles.

8. Support students' motivation for and interest in science.

Gifted students need the support of adults who recognize and nurture their talents. Students, left on their own and/or confronted with less than challenging science, often lose interest in science. From the earliest years, recognition of science talent is essential. At the college level, studies (Barlow & Villarejo, 2004; Clewell, 2006; Russell, Hancock, & McCullough, 2007) indicate that students who have early opportunities in college to engage in the work of scientists, conducting research or internships, were more likely to stay in or switch to science and engineering majors and to pursue science and engineering graduate education. A quote from Rachel Carson, noted environmentalist, is quite appropriate here.

If a child is to keep alive his inborn sense of wonder without any such gift from the fairies, he needs the companionship of at least one adult who can share it, rediscovering with him the joy, excitement, and mystery of the world we live in. (Lewis, n.d.)

9. Gifted students need multiple and varied opportunities to learn science. Schools should consider the many and varied alternative instructional delivery models.

Appropriate instructional delivery models in science are dependent upon multiple factors, including the student population to be served, required curriculum standards, the availability of resources, the preparedness of the teaching staff, and general school district policies. Options selected should be ones that match program goals and expected student outcomes. Delivery models may include instructional groups of gifted students assigned to specific course sections or classroom cluster groups, or heterogeneous instruction with modifications in pace, depth, and complexity. Advanced courses such as honors, Advanced Placement, or International Baccalaureate may be offered at the secondary level. Some schools are able to provide course options in cooperation with community colleges or universities. In addition to the modification of standard curriculum options, cocurricular activities, competitions, and exhibitions promote challenging science inquiry. Mentorships and internships with practicing scientists may be made available, enabling gifted students to learn about actual real-world challenges in science. Whatever delivery models are in place, gifted students should experience learning that offers the pacing, richness, and complexity that are the hallmarks of advanced learning.

THOUGHTS FOR THE FUTURE

To further the education of high-ability students in science, educators need more personalized training in models for effective curriculum, instruction, assessment, and the practice of science in the real world. Such models should incorporate depth and breadth of content, real-world experiences in scientific inquiry, and a broadened view of the connections between science and the other disciplines. Gifted students need teachers well-prepared to provide them with advanced content, meaningful inquiry, and opportunities to expand their conceptual framework within the areas of science that are interesting to them as well as in the broader context of science and the other disciplines.

Early recognition of science interest and talent is essential in promoting the education of young students who will embrace science as a profession and continually grow in their passion for learning more. Further studies should be completed on what works with students gifted in science so that they can be more readily nurtured. Longitudinal studies of identified gifted students can bring insight into the effect of advanced curriculum and acceleration opportunities on students' postsecondary education and career outcomes.

Gifted students are ready for advanced experiences in science that engage them in the ways of knowing and learning that are the hallmark of outstanding scientists. These advanced experiences as outlined in this chapter align well with the Committee on Science Learning's (National Research Council, 2007) four fundamental strands of learning. Students should:

- know, use, and interpret scientific explanations;
- generate and evaluate scientific evidence and explanations;
- understand the nature and development of scientific knowledge; and
- participate productively in scientific practices and discourse.

Effective science education for gifted learners is dependent upon many factors, including proper recognition of talents, purposeful development of appropriate curriculum, instruction from highly qualified teachers, assessment that recognizes and supports advanced learning, and nurturing from adult mentors. As Brandwein (1995) stated: "To achieve fully, to realize their gifts, children require the support of a gifted environment of resources and people" (p. 9). It is up to leaders in education to find the way to create such environments.

Many years ago, in the early stages of my career as an educator of gifted students, I became very focused on how to help my students think more deeply, reason more clearly, and become more creative. This satisfied me for a while, but as I began to look more closely at my students and their learning, I became aware that something was missing. It took just one reading of Joyce's work to realize that she had uncovered the missing pieces of my puzzle! Her Integrated Curriculum Model enlightened me, helping me recognize that *what* students learn is equally as important as *how* they process it. From that time, Joyce's work has inspired me to promote curriculum development that is grounded in the conceptual framework of each discipline and illuminated by a clear view of how gifted students can learn the approach to thinking and knowing that is at the heart of the discipline. The ICM truly was a catalyst for meaningful curriculum work.

REFERENCES

American Association for the Advancement of Science. (1989). Educational foundations for tomorrow's information scientists. *Bulletin of the American Society for Information Science, 15*(5), 21.

Atlas of Science Literacy. (2007). *Project 2061.* Washington, DC: American Association for the Advancement of Science.

Barlow, A., & Villarejo, M. (2004). Making a difference for minorities: Evaluation of an educational enrichment program. *Journal of Research in Science Teaching, 41,* 861–881.

Brandwein, P. (1986). A portrait of gifted young science talent. *Roeper Review, 8,* 235–243.

Brandwein, P. (1995). *Science talent in the young expressed within ecologies of achievement* (RBDM 9510). Storrs: University of Connecticut, The National Research Center on the Gifted and Talented.

Brandwein, P., & Passow, A. H. (Eds.). (1988). *Gifted young in science: Potential through performance.* Washington, DC: National Science Teachers Association.

Bruner, J. (1963). *The process of education.* New York: Vintage Books.

Center for Gifted Education, The College of William and Mary. (2005). *Project Clarion science units.* Williamsburg, VA: Author.

Clement, J. (1993). Using bridging analogies and anchoring institutions to deal with students' preconceptions in physics. *Journal of Research in Science Teaching, 30,* 1241–1257.

Clewell, B. (2006). *Revitalizing the nation's talent pool in STEM: Science, technology, engineering and mathematics.* Washington, DC: The Urban Institute.

Colangelo, N., Assouline, S. G., & Gross, M. U. M. (2004). *A nation deceived: How schools hold back America's brightest students* (Vol. 1). Iowa City: The University of Iowa, The Connie Belin & Jacqueline N. Blank International Center for Gifted Education and Talent Development.

Cross, P., Goodenough, U., Lerner, L., Haack, S., Schwartz, M., Schwartz, R., et al. (2005). *The state of the state science standards 2005.* Washington, DC: Thomas B. Fordham Institute.

Feng, A., VanTassel-Baska, J., Quek, C., O'Neill, B., & Bai, W. (2005). A longitudinal assessment of gifted students' learning using the Integrated Curriculum Model: Impacts and perceptions of the William and Mary language arts and science curriculum. *Roeper Review, 27,* 78–83.

Franks, B., & Dolan, L. (1982). Affective characteristics of gifted children: Educational implications. *Gifted Child Quarterly, 26,* 172–178.

Hoffmann, R. (2006. The metaphor, unchained. *American Scientist, 94,* 406. Retrieved from http://www.americanscientist.org/issues/pub/the-metaphor-unchained/1

Kitano, M., Montgomery, D., VanTassel-Baska, J., & Johnsen, S. K. (2008). *Using the national gifted education standards for preK–12 professional development.* Thousand Oaks, CA: Corwin Press.

Mintzes, J. J., Wandersee, J. H., & Novak, J. (2005). *Teaching science for understanding.* San Diego, CA: Academic Press.

Lewis, J. J. (n.d.). *Rachel Carson quotes.* Retrieved October 23, 2008, from http://womenshistory.about.com/od/quotes/a/rachel_carson.htm

National Research Council, Committee on Science Learning, Kindergarten Through Eighth Grade. (2007). *Taking science to school: Learning and teaching science in grades K–8.* Washington, DC: National Academies Press.

National Research Council, National Committee on Science Education Standards and Assessment, Center for Science, Mathematics, and Engineering Education. (1996). *National science education standards.* Washington, DC: National Academies Press.

National Science Teachers Association. (2003). *Standards for science teacher preparation.* Retrieved from http://www.nsta.org

Novak, J. D. (1998). *Learning, creating, and using knowledge.* New York: Lawrence Erlbaum.

Novak, J. D., & Gowin, D. B. (1984). *Learning how to learn.* New York: Cambridge University Press.

Paul, R., & Elder, L. (2006). *A miniature guide for students and faculty to scientific thinking.* Dillon Beach, CA: Foundation for Critical Thinking.

Pfundt, H., & Duit, R. (1994*). Bibliography: Students' alternative frameworks and science education* (4th ed.). Kiel, Federal Republic of Germany: Institute for Science Education.

Proctor, R., & Capaldi, E. (2006). *Why science matters: Understanding the methods of psychological research.* Malden, MA: Blackwell.

Ritchie, S. M., Bellocchi, A., Polt, H., & Wearmouth, M. (2006). Metaphors and analogies in transition. In P. J. Aubusson, A. G. Harrison, & S. M. Ritchie (Eds.), *Metaphor and analogy in science education* (pp. 143–154). Dordrecht, The Netherlands: Kluwer.

Rogers, K. (1999). *Research synthesis on gifted provisions.* Retrieved from http://austega.com/gifted/articles/Rogers_researchsynthesis.htm

Russell, S. H., Hancock, M. P., & McCullough, J. (2007). Benefits of undergraduate. research experiences. *Science, 316,* 548–549.

Simonton, D. K. (1988). *Scientific genius: A psychology of science.* New York: Cambridge University Press.

Simonton, D. K. (1992). The social context of career success and course for 2,026 scientists and inventors. *Personality and Social Psychology Bulletin, 18,* 452–463.

Thagard, P. (2004). How to be a successful scientist. In M. E. Gorman, R. D. Tweney, D. C. Gooding, & A. P. Kincannon (Eds.), *Scientific and technological thinking* (pp. 159–171). Mahwah, NJ: Lawrence Erlbaum.

VanTassel-Baska, J. (1986). Effective curriculum and instructional models for talented students. *Gifted Child Quarterly, 30,* 164–169.

VanTassel-Baska, J. (2003). Content-based curriculum for high-ability learners: An introduction. In J. VanTassel-Baska & C. A. Little (Eds.), *Content-based curriculum for high-ability learners* (pp. 1–23). Waco, TX: Prufrock Press.

VanTassel-Baska, J., Bracken, B. A., Stambaugh, T., & Feng, A. (2007, September). *Findings from Project Clarion.* Presentation to the United States Department of Education Expert Panel, Storrs, CT.

VanTassel-Baska, J., & Stambaugh, T. (Eds.). (2008). *What works: 20 years of curriculum development and research for advanced learners.* Waco, TX: Prufrock Press.

Williams, W. M., Papierno, P. B., Makel, M. C., & Ceci, S. J. (2004). Thinking like a scientist about real-world problems: The Cornell Institute for Research on Children Science Education Program. *Applied Developmental Psychology, 25,* 107–126.

Wong, E. D. (1993). Understanding the generative capacity of analogies as a tool for explanation. *Journal of Research in Science Teaching, 30,* 1259–1272.

CHAPTER 25

GLOBAL LEARNING:

Teaching World Languages to Gifted Learners

by

BRONWYN
MACFARLANE

Learning a second language provides a mirror to another culture, reflecting on beliefs, values, the arts, and an alternative vision of reality.

—Joyce VanTassel-Baska

The study of world languages has long been a valued component of a high-quality liberal arts education. Founders of American democracy were steeped in the study of classic Latin and Greek as well as various romance languages. Illustrious alumni of The College of William and Mary such as Thomas Jefferson, the fourth U.S. President; John James Beckley, the first Librarian of Congress; and U.S. Supreme Court Chief Justice John Marshall were tutored in the elements of language acquisition, production, and fluency. The development of skillful language use with sophistication of thought and competencies in composition across reading, writing, and rhetoric are essential skills for success in schooling and society. Language development and study always has been a foundational cornerstone of a comprehensive curriculum.

The development of second language skills with a sophisticated level of thought also lies at the heart of the curriculum work and leadership modeled by Dr. Joyce VanTassel-Baska. To examine world language education and the gifted learner is to return to her dissertation study with a group of high-ability learners studying Latin in an afterschool program in Ohio that provided the foundation of the career honored with this festschrift volume. Working with verbally precocious junior high school students enrolled in a fast-paced Latin class in an English class focused on the study of Greek and Latin roots, and in another English class focused on creative writing, achievement results indicated a significant gain in English grammar and vocabulary among students enrolled in Latin study in contrast to those enrolled in the English-dominant courses comparison group. Based on these student gains, VanTassel-Baska (1982, 1987) concluded that Latin study had real transfer to English language achievement by enhancing student linguistic competency and vocabulary development. Indeed, studies consistently find a positive correlation between a student's world language education and overall educational achievement across content areas, standardized exam performance, and college enrollment and success (Cooper, 1987; Olsen & Brown, 1992; Wiley, 1985). Children who study foreign languages statistically outperform non-second-language learning students in language, math, science, and social studies (Shaw, Grbic, & Franklin, 2004).

WORLD LANGUAGE EDUCATION AND GIFTED EDUCATION

Becoming bilingual is a lifestyle change. As an individual struggles to acquire a second language, her whole being is impacted as she reaches beyond the boundaries of her native language and into a new dimension of language and culture. The learning of another language involves a complex process, with a seemingly infinite number of variables impacting language production. Understanding this intricate web of variables is essential to appreciating what impacts successful acquisition of a second language among learners and recognizing how these variables can be impacted through world language teaching and instruction to maximize learning.

World language learning and teaching have changed substantially over the past 25 years. From a paradigm that once focused almost exclusively on grammar, translation, and the memorization of dialogues, the profession has largely embraced teaching for communicative competence (Candlin & Widdowson, 1987; Rifkin, 2006). Scholars in world language education focus their attention on program organization, curriculum, and instruction, addressing questions related to (a) diversity and equity in K–12 schools, (b) articulation between levels and between secondary and postsecondary instruction, (c) standardization of teaching and testing practices, (d) syllabus and curriculum design, and (e) program administration and models of teacher preparation (Kramsch, 2000). These elements of curriculum and instruction are linked to constructivist and social constructivist learning theories, which are consistent with the communicative approach to world language teaching and learning (Met, 1999). World language teachers share many constructivist beliefs about learning and instruction with teachers in other content areas including the active engagement of students in constructing knowledge, the role of prior learning, the power of social interaction, the use of real-life tasks, and more performance-based approaches to assessment that reflect complex behaviors.

Eight language teaching methods in practice today embody these beliefs including (1) the Grammar-Translation Method, (2) the Direct Method, (3) the Audio-Lingual Method, (4) the Silent Way, (5) Suggestopedia, (6) Community Language Learning, (7) the Total Physical Response Method, and (8) the Communicative Approach. However, no comparative study has consistently demonstrated the superiority of one method over another for all teachers, all students, and all settings (College Board, 1986; Snow, 1994). Indeed, how a method is manifested in a classroom depends heavily on an individual teacher's interpretation of it. Moreover, some teachers may prefer to practice one method to the exclusion of others while other teachers may prefer to pick and choose among the methodological options that exist, creating their own unique blend (Snow, 1994).

These teaching methodologies are in line with the development of the language skills: listening, speaking, reading, and writing. The great variety of programs for teaching novice language learners can be divided into four general categories, although what happens in classrooms is often a mix of strategies: (1) direct instruction of the target language, (2) specially designed target language instruction with primary language support, (3) "sheltered immersion"—special instruction in the target language, or (4) no special services (Amselle, 1997). These four modes of teaching world languages may produce variability across language classrooms impacting student acquisition. Specific instruction appears to play a significant role in language accuracy (Elliot, 1995).

RESEARCH ON BEST PRACTICE INSTRUCTION IN WORLD LANGUAGE EDUCATION

World language literature guides professionals on how learners acquire new languages and the conditions under which language acquisition is most likely to occur. The prevailing view among world language educators today is that the goal of instruction is to prepare students to function effectively in the real-life situations they are likely to encounter (American Council on the Teaching of Foreign Languages [ACTFL], 2006; Met, 1999; Shaw et al., 2004). This goal has generated the prevailing terminology of "proficiency-orientated instruction" and "communicative language teaching."

The research base for communicative language instructional practices is both direct and indirect. Some evidence directly supports practices associated with the communicative approach; however, other practices may be inferred from research on cognition, information, processing, and sociocultural theory. Although the research on emerging practices may be limited or indirect, the body of research to support past approaches to world language teaching, such as the grammar-based approach, also is limited (Met, 1999).

It is ironic that world language education has been late to join the realm of interdisciplinary curriculum development with the other content areas, because by its very nature world language education is concerned with bridging disciplines. The integration of second language education into the core curriculum will be enhanced as practitioners develop skills to do so (Reagan & Osborn, 2002).

Specific instructional strategies found to be effective in second language learning include (1) extensive exposure to the target language at an early age with continuing instruction; (2) opportunities to hear and use the language comprehensibly with others; (3) frequent opportunities to apply the language in purposeful, real-life tasks; (4) integration of cultural instruction in making meaning for socioculturally appropriate functioning; (5) explicit instruction in learning strategies for developing skills in the target language and learner autonomy; (6) explicit instruction in listening, reading, and writing for meaning with grammatical competence; (7) opportunities to use technological resources to enhance language learning and practice; and (8) appropriate assessment to measure student progress in producing a second language and identification of instructional needs for continued growth (Fares & Zinke, 2008; Met, 1999; Mulhair, 2008).

Determining which type of foreign language instruction is best depends on a number of variables: the learner's age, aptitude, and motivation; the amount of time available for instruction; and the difference between the native and the foreign language (American Educational Research Association [AERA], 2006). Cognitive processes are affected by differential sources of input, instruction, and one's particular attitudes and levels of awareness (Oxford, 1990). In a study comparing the instructional practices in honors and nonhonors French and Spanish classes at a Midwestern high school, Morris (2005) found a significant relationship between the type of class and the type of activity: Honors classes had more communicative activities while nonhonors classes focused on mastering the discrete parts of language. Teacher respondents reported that the honors students had a higher level of motivation for language learning and generally accepted communicative approaches more readily than students in the nonhonors classes. However, Chela-Flores (2001) suggested activities for sustained dialogue and paragraph-utterances could be incorporated naturally throughout the instructional sequence of beginning through advanced. Specific world language instructional strategies that have been crowned with the moniker "best practice" are somewhat limited by the literature base ranging from second language acquisition to applied linguistics to world language education.

World Language Assessment

To appropriately educate a gifted learner at any level, her readiness level must be assessed for initial placement, followed by ongoing evaluation for adapting to her educational needs (VanTassel-Baska, 2004). With the use of standardized foreign language aptitude assessments, students can be placed at the appropriate challenge level commensurate to their current skill level. Furthermore, with the use of ongoing assessment, gifted students can accelerate through the average world language curriculum at a speed commensurate to their learning pace and at a greater level of depth and complexity with the content. By purposefully applying standardized, reliable, and valid instruments, world language program practices at each level can be revised and improved, and schools can maximize available programming options both in the classroom, with computer programs, with alternative interventions, and online.

In assessing whether students are achieving at a particular proficiency level in a target language, schools can reference the nationally defined levels of proficiency in second language learning for teachers to differentiate their use of appropriate instruction and learning activities at each level. Instead of describing language learners as first-year or second-year students, they can be described as students who have acquired novice, intermediate, or advanced levels of proficiency, which is a nationally shared terminology (ACTFL, 1985). With this change in terminology, not only will a student's proficiency level be clarified but his potential for acceleration through a district's articulated language program can be streamlined.

THE GOOD LANGUAGE LEARNER

Some researchers have explored what constitutes "good language learning" by emphasizing cognitive strategies, personality or "talent" factors (neurocognitive abilities), and proficiency in the first/native language (Bialystok, 1994; Hulstijn & Bossers, 1992; Schmidt, 1992). These areas have focused on discovering particular traits or strategies that might predictably lead to high levels of second language attainment. Additional dimensions from sociocultural perspectives have expanded the discussion to the impact of context, community, and the individual learner's communicative and social intentions as also being key to understanding how second language competence develops (Lantolf, 2000; Norton Pierce & Toohey, 2001; Pavlenko & Lantolf, 2000). Ultimate attainment studies, however, consistently focus on the age factor, rather than on specific talents, contextual factors, or orientations to the task (Bialystok, 1997; Bialystok & Hakuta, 1999; Birdsong, 2002). As with any type of learning, a student's individual characteristics have an impact on how well each one grasps a subject. In world language learning, an individual's aptitude and motivation can be key components in their individual trajectory of language acquisition (AERA, 2006).

The search to adequately describe the gifted language learner has motivated research on style and skill pertaining to language learning aptitude, short- and long-term memory capacity, deductive reasoning skills (analysis and hypothesis information based on available input), and degree of conscious attention or focus. However, some researchers posit that second language acquisition utilizes the same processes and mechanisms as first language acquisition regarding abstract concept learning and decoding and encoding strategies (C. Brown, 1993; H. Brown, 2000) and that therefore aptitude presents no significant influence as languages are acquired with parallel processes. This finding clearly is contradictory to studies in gifted education showing that students precocious in language ability can master a foreign language in half the time of other learners (Olszewski-Kubilius, 2007; VanTassel-Baska, 2004).

World Language Programming

Although the acceptance of brain-research findings about the positive influence of early exposure to a second language on cognitive development has brought about an increased interest in elementary world language programs, and policies have been put in place to create such programs, there is great variance across programs and outcomes. Indeed, the majority of world language education in the United States remains formally conducted at the secondary school level. However, there is not consensus within empirical research to say how talents and abilities are affected by maturation, and whether a lack of certain talents may be overridden by other factors, such as motivation (Moyer, 2004). Yet, McLaughlin (1990) concluded that expert multiple language learners use more systematic and useful problem-solving and comprehension strategies and show greater plasticity in restructuring their internal representations of the rules governing linguistic input. It is the expertise acquisition processes of good language learners that researchers have yet to thoroughly study (Nation & McLaughlin, 1986). Why? Markham (1997) provided a succinct summation of the situation: "The good learners go largely ignored, for the sake of pondering the failure of the majority" (p. 12).

Lack of instructional time necessary for acquiring a second language not only impacts student performance and self-efficacy but teacher performance and individual expectations for their students, thereby creating a cyclical effect as the students enter world language teacher preparation programs and proceed to the classroom with their perceptions of past learning experiences. The typical student who begins studying a world language in grade 7 or 9 is exposed only to a fraction of the contact hours required to achieve a high level of proficiency in a second language (Goranson & Howland, 1999). In Teaching English to Speakers of Other Languages (TESOL) research, students usually receive only a few hundred hours of instruction, spread over several years, and only students who are exceptionally gifted or motivated or who have out-of-school exposure acquire the ability to use the language effectively (Lightbrown, 2001). This situation often leads world language teachers to focus more on students who clearly struggle to reach proficiency rather than on differentiating for those who can learn the language faster and more readily.

World Language Teacher Preparation

World language education research provides research-based and practical guidance regarding classroom instructional strategies. However, specific strategies with proven efficacy for high-ability language learners are excluded from the literature base. In a study examining how world language teachers are trained, Wilbur (2007) found that the methods of teaching used in world language methods courses vary extensively based on the instructors' background, syllabi, and evaluation techniques. The most salient research outcome was the discovery that teacher methods ranged vastly across teacher training institutions. Wilbur suggested that the profession identify a more systematic means of providing relevant instructional practices for new teacher candidates. Furthermore, she recommended identifying effective instructional practices through the lens of what best enhances student comprehension and retention.

Advanced course offerings are the face of gifted education at the secondary level, and although gifted students are attracted to Advanced Placement (AP) options, teacher training by the College Board course facilitators does not include specific differentiation practices for gifted learners within the AP World Language classroom. Moreover, the majority of AP teachers have received little, if any, explicit training on working with gifted students (Hertberg-Davis, Callahan, & Kyburg, 2006; Westberg, 1994). To improve the delivery of differentiated instruction in the Advanced Placement classroom, AP teacher training and continuing professional development is needed to assist teachers in developing a greater understanding of differentiated instruction.

In a study examining AP World Language teachers' perceptions of high-ability language students and differentiated instructional approaches (MacFarlane, 2008), findings indicated that teachers held somewhat positive attitudes toward providing support for the needs of gifted students and the social value of the gifted in society. Teachers held ambivalent attitudes toward the instructional practice of ability grouping, the rejection of gifted students by others, and the practice of advocating on behalf of gifted learners. Teachers reported somewhat negative attitudes toward the appropriate acceleration of gifted students. Findings further revealed limited teacher use of differentiated strategies in the AP classroom, and limited teacher training in gifted pedagogy. The implications for practice from this study focus on the need to train AP World Language teachers on relevant knowledge and skills in working with the gifted including (1) differentiated instruction for the gifted that remodels AP curricula to meet high-ability student needs, and (2) advanced teacher-training practices that focus on effective delivery and classroom management techniques.

NEW TRENDS AND DIRECTIONS

Although the case has been made for the value of world language education in a school curriculum and the value of second language study for gifted students, programmatic trends show concern among language education programs. Throughout the 20th century, world languages historically have been elective courses at the high school level, attracting college-bound students. Across the years, world language offerings in the K–12 sequence have varied, and enrollment has fluctuated. According to Welles (2002), world language enrollment at universities nationwide has continued to fall from 16% in 1960 to 8% in 2002. This decline can be attributed to a variety of influences including the current accountability movement that has taken focus away from electives in the K–12 arena and focused the attention of educators and policy makers on the core content areas of language arts, mathematics, science, and social studies.

Although foreign language study is an effective challenge for high-ability students, few studies exist in the educational literature that isolate the best instructional practices in language education for all, let alone practices in teaching gifted students rapid acquisition of foreign language skills. To enhance the literature base in this realm, interventions using the teaching tools that are effective with gifted learners in other content areas must be applied. World language curriculum and programs can be purposefully designed to match the theoretical dimensions of the Integrated Curriculum Model (ICM), a proven model for curriculum design for advanced learners (VanTassel-Baska & Brown, 2007). In addition to applying the ICM to world language curriculum development, the application of the William and Mary teaching models also should be used in world language teaching to foster critical thinking skills. Language production goes beyond just knowing a second language. Translation involves a much more complex process of code-switching across cultures, requiring advanced metacognitive processing skills. Teaching models such as the reasoning model and the vocabulary web may assist students in such processes.

Summary:
The Case for Globalizing Language Learning

The benefits of language proficiency are known to extend well beyond linguistics. The skills students develop while learning a language can directly affect their performance in other subjects as well. Yet, schools have cut or eliminated language programs to focus on the core subject areas being assessed in response to No Child Left Behind (Shaw et al., 2004). As language programs are cut and expectations of language proficiency remain in conflict with the time allocated for learning, the opportunity for language study may be at risk!

Yet, world language education presents educators with a clear structure for fostering natural interdisciplinary connections across content domains. Although the gifted education literature has expanded as more research has been conducted on effective differentiation in curriculum, the literature on gifted and world language education is sparse (Robinson, Shore, & Enersen, 2007). World language teachers need more training on best practices in teaching their subject area and in differentiating for the gifted learners that inhabit their classrooms (MacFarlane, 2008). To increase critical and higher order thinking in gifted language learners, key elements of a challenging world language curriculum must be identified, programmatically placed, and practiced regularly in schools. In the ever-changing global society and increasingly smaller world that students are developing within, it is time again for world language education to be fully recognized and valued as an integral curricular component of a high quality educational program.

CLOSING COMMENTARY

Meeting Dr. Joyce VanTassel-Baska occurred at a critical point in my talent development. As a school practitioner responsible for rural district programs in gifted education and French, I sought an advanced level of training and a mentor who would provide the right challenge at the right time in my development. As it happened, I met Dr. Joyce VanTassel-Baska as a result of receiving the Eleanor Roosevelt Teacher Fellowship from the American Association of University Women. I chose to use my grant to attend my first National Association for Gifted Children (NAGC) conference in Indianapolis where I met gifted education graduate student representatives at the William and Mary exhibit booth. At the conclusion of my first NAGC conference, I was so energized that I could have practically propelled myself home to Missouri on my enthusiasm alone. For a full year I considered whether I could change my life to move across the country to Virginia. I decided to go back to NAGC to see if it was a fluke or if I would still feel the same way toward the William and Mary program. In Salt Lake City, in November 2004, I approached Dr. VanTassel-Baska following her session and talked to her about the program and my ideas for educational media. Her empowering response to me was a crystallizing moment in my life. In such an affirmative and direct way, Joyce conveyed to me the value of my ideas and that achieving these goals are within my reach. I knew she was the mentor and teacher I was seeking and that I had found the doctoral home where I belonged. Upon receiving notification of my appointment as her graduate assistant at the Center for Gifted Education, I pulled up stakes and set off on the great American doctoral adventure.

Joyce is an amazing force in action. She models consistent strength, immeasurable knowledge and insight, a whirlwind of high-quality productivity, humility, consummate ethical professionalism, and maintains a steady eye in preparing and planning for the future as an ongoing, positive change agent. She is a master teacher and leader in every sense. Joyce was easy for me to connect with on many levels; we shared common backgrounds in teaching world language; gifted education; coaching high school teams (she with the girls' basketball team, and I with the boys' golf team); connections to the Midwest, Ohio, and Colorado; and shared interest and passion for international travel, photography, culinary delights, ballroom dancing, leadership, policy, and most importantly, family.

For 3 special years, I had the ultimate professional development learning experience and the privilege of unique and amazing opportunities made possible by Joyce, the Center for Gifted Education, and The College of William and Mary in Virginia. Passionate to experience all I could, I enthusiastically pursued every learning option that presented itself. In addition to challenging coursework and a bouquet of meaningful project work at the Center, I ran full tilt into experiencing fully the opportunities that came, such as writing for publication; attending AERA, NAGC, and the Virginia Association for the Gifted (VAG) annually; serving an internship as Academic Dean of a residential program for secondary gifted students at Princeton University; delivering workshops and speaking to a variety of audiences; and an exciting cornucopia of postgraduation job opportunities. Through it all, Joyce continually offered steady guidance and critical input and feedback. As a student, I envisioned an exciting journey ahead in which I would be able to apply my professional skills and areas of specialization as an educational researcher and instructional leader to benefit gifted children. As assistant professor of gifted education in the educational leadership department at the University of Arkansas, I am living that vision today. The possibilities are boundless—as Joyce told me the day of our first meeting, "Good idea, go for it!"

References

American Council on the Teaching of Foreign Languages. (1985). *ACTFL proficiency guidelines.* Hastings-on-Hudson, NY: ACTFL Materials Center.

American Council on the Teaching of Foreign Languages. (2006). *Standards for foreign language learning: Preparing for the 21st century.* Yonkers, NY: Author.

American Educational Research Association. (2006). Foreign language instruction: Implementing the best teaching methods. *Research Points: Essential Information for Education Policy, 4*(1), 1–4.

Amselle, J. (1997, November). Adios, bilingual ed. *Policy Review.* Retrieved from http://www.hoover.org/publications/policyreview/3572952.html

Bialystok, E. (1994). Analysis and control in the development of second language proficiency. *Studies in Second Language Acquisition, 16,* 157–168.

Bialystok, E. (1997). The structure of age: In search of barriers to second language acquisition. *Studies in Second Language Acquisition, 13,* 116–137.

Bialystok, E., & Hakuta, K. (1999). Confounded age: Linguistic and cognitive factors in age differences for second language acquisition. In D. Birdsong (Ed.), *Second language acquisition and the critical period hypothesis* (pp. 161–181). Mahwah, NJ: Lawrence Erlbaum.

Birdsong, D. (2002, February). *Age and the end state of second language acquisition.* Paper presented at the Applied Linguistics Distinguished Speaker Series, University of Maryland, College Park.

Brown, C. (1993). The role of the L1 grammar in the L2 acquisition of segmental structure. *McGill Working Papers in Linguistics, 9,* 180–210.

Brown, H. (2000). *Principles of language learning and teaching* (4th ed). White Plains, NY: Longman.

Candlin, C., & Widdowson, H. (Series Eds.). (1987). *On language teaching: A scheme for teacher education.* Oxford, UK: Oxford University Press.

Chela-Flores, B. (2001). Pronunciation and language learning: An integrative approach. *International Review of Applied Linguistics, 39,* 85–101.

College Board. (1986, October). The SAT and statewide assessment. *Vital Speeches of the Day, 52*(24), 765.

Cooper, T. C. (1987). Foreign language study and SAT-Verbal scores. *Modern Language Journal, 71,* 381–387.

Elliot, A. (1995). Foreign language phonology: Field independence, attitude, and the success of formal instruction in Spanish pronunciation. *Modern Language Journal, 79,* 530–542.

Fares, G., & Zinke, L. (2008). *AP Spanish language teacher's guide.* Retrieved from http://apcentral.collegeboard.com/apc/public/repository/spanish_lang_teachers_guide.pdf

Goranson, D., & Howland, M. (1999). *A guide to K–12 program development in world languages.* (ERIC Document Reproductive Service No. ED462005)

Hertberg-Davis, H., Callahan, C. M., & Kyburg, R. M. (2006). *Advanced Placement and International Baccalaureate programs: A "fit" for gifted learners?* (Research Monograph No. 06222). Storrs: University of Connecticut, The National Research Center on the Gifted and Talented.

Hulstijn, J., & Bossers, B. (1992). Individual differences in L2 proficiency as a function of L1 proficiency. *European Journal of Cognitive Psychology, 4,* 341–353.

Kramsch, C. (2000). Second language acquisition, applied linguistics, and the teaching of foreign languages. *Modern Language Journal, 84,* 311–326.

Lantolf, J. P. (Ed.) (2000). *Sociocultural theory and second language learning.* Oxford, UK: Oxford University Press.

Lightbrown, P. (2001). L2 instruction: Time to teach. *TESOL Quarterly, 35,* 598–599.

MacFarlane, B. (2008). *Advanced Placement world language teacher perceptions of high ability students and differentiated instruction.* Unpublished doctoral dissertation, The College of William and Mary, Williamsburg, VA.

Markham, D. (1997). *Phonetic imitation, accent, and the learner.* Lund, Sweden: Lund University Press.

McLaughlin, B. (1990). The relationship between first and second languages: Language proficiency and language aptitude. In B. Harley, P. Allen, J. Cummings, & M. Swain (Eds.), *The development of second language proficiency* (pp. 158–174). Cambridge, UK: Cambridge University Press.

Met, M. (1999). Research in foreign language curriculum. In G. Cawelti (Ed.), *Handbook of research on improving student achievement* (2nd ed., pp. 86–111). Arlington, VA: Educational Research Service.

Morris, M. (2005). Two sides of the communicative coin: Honors and nonhonors French and Spanish classes in a Midwestern high school. *Foreign Language Annals, 38,* 236–249.

Moyer, A. (2004). *Age, accent, and experience in second language acquisition: An integrated approach to critical period inquiry.* Buffalo, NY: Cromwell Press.

Mulhair, M. (2008). *AP French language teacher's guide.* Retrieved from http://apcentral.collegeboard.com/apc/public/repository/AP_French_Language_Teacher_Guide.pdf

Nation, R., & McLaughlin, B. (1986). Experts and novices: An information-processing approach to the "good language learner" problem. *Applied Psycholinguistics, 7,* 41–56.

Norton Pierce, B., & Toohey, K. (2001). Changing perspectives on good language learners. *TESOL Quarterly, 35,* 307–322.

Olsen, S. A., & Brown, L. K. (1992). The relation between high school study of foreign languages and ACT English and mathematics performance. *Association of Departments of Foreign Language Bulletin, 23*(3).

Olszewski-Kubilius, P. (2007). The role of summer programs in developing the talents of gifted students. In J. VanTassel-Baska (Ed.), *Serving gifted learners beyond the traditional classroom: A guide to alternative programs and services* (pp. 13–32). Waco, TX: Prufrock Press.

Oxford, R. (1990). *Language learning strategies: What every teacher should know.* Rowley, MA: Newbury House.

Pavlenko, A., & Lantolf, J. (2000). Second language learning as participation and the reconstruction of selves. In J. Lantolf (Ed.), *Sociocultural theory and second language learning* (pp. 155–177). Oxford, UK: Oxford University Press.

Reagan, T. G., & Osborn, T. A. (2002). *The foreign language educator in society: Toward a critical pedagogy.* Mahwah, NJ: Lawrence Erlbaum.

Rifkin, B. (2006). Studying a foreign language at the postsecondary level. *The Language Educator, 2,* 48–51.

Robinson, A., Shore, B. M., & Enersen, D. L. (2007). *Best practices in gifted education: An evidence-based guide.* Waco, TX: Prufrock Press.

Schmidt, R. (1992). Psychological mechanisms underlying second language fluency. *Studies in Second Language Acquisition, 14,* 357–385.

Shaw, S., Grbic, N., & Franklin, K. (2004). Applying language skills to interpretation: Student perspectives from signed and spoken language programs. *Interpreting, 6*(1), 69–100.

Snow, R. (1994). Abilities in academic tasks. In R. Sternberg & R. Wagner (Eds.), *Mind in context: Interactionist perspectives on human intelligence* (pp. 3–37). New York: Cambridge University Press.

VanTassel-Baska, J. (1982). Results of a Latin-based experimental study of the verbally precocious. *Roeper Review, 4,* 35–37.

VanTassel-Baska, J. (1987). A case for the teaching of Latin to the verbally talented. *Roeper Review, 9,* 159–161.

VanTassel-Baska, J. (2004). Quo vadis? Laboring in the classical vineyards: An optimal challenge for gifted secondary students. *Journal of Secondary Gifted Education, 15,* 56–60.

VanTassel-Baska, J., & Brown, E. F. (2007). Toward best practice: An analysis of the efficacy of curriculum models in gifted education. *Gifted Child Quarterly, 51,* 342–358.

Welles, E. (2002, Fall). Foreign language enrollments in United States institutions of higher education. *Profession, 26,* 128–153.

Westberg, K. L. (1994). Teachers who are good with the gifted. *Instructor, 104*(2), 65.

Wilbur, M. (2007). How foreign language teachers get taught: Methods of teaching the methods course. *Foreign Language Annals, 40*(1), 79–101.

Wiley, P. D. (1985). High school foreign language study and college academic performance. *Classical Outlook, 62*(2), 33–36.

CHAPTER 26

CARPE DIEM!

World Language Study and the Teaching of Latin

by

FRANCES
R. SPIELHAGEN

Learning Latin provides an important antidote to the anti-intellectual climate of American society through its disciplined analytic rigor, its universal ideas that have been applied to contemporary life, and its rich cultural history that allows us to know Western civilization.

—Joyce VanTassel-Baska

INTRODUCTION

E*xegi monumentum aere perennius* (Horace, Odes, III, 30)—"I have built a monument more lasting than bronze," wrote the Roman poet, Horace, in the first century. Amidst a complex and pragmatic society replete with wealth and ostentatious display of power, Horace wisely noted that bronze monuments fade away or fall into disrepair. However, he confidently proclaimed that his life's work, a compendium of Latin poetry and satires, would survive and continue to inform the generations that would follow. More than 2,000 years later, the words of Horace resonate to a world hungry for enduring and meaningful knowledge.

Joyce VanTassel-Baska began her career as a teacher of Latin and English. Her work with students of high verbal ability inspired her to explore the ways that teachers might design curriculum to meet those needs. This early experience was a logical prequel to her long and prolific career, during which she not only designed curriculum for gifted learners, she also researched extensively the ways in which these students learn and might best be served and created avenues for teachers to learn how to use the results of her efforts. The work of Dr. Joyce VanTassel-Baska has withstood the test of time and is, indeed, *aere perennius.* Moreover, the study of Latin in addition to other world languages continues to be a strong and viable option for verbally able students.

THE STUDY OF LATIN IN AMERICAN EDUCATION

There was a time when any well-educated individual would be fluent in Latin language and literature. In the earliest days of education in the United States, students who advanced beyond the common school automatically studied Latin in the first high schools—the academies—that enrolled primarily White male students. The advent of the modern comprehensive high school in the early days of the 20th century changed the landscape of secondary education. Although it provided greater access to secondary education, the new high school paradigm removed from prominence the importance of classical studies. Until the late 1920s, at least half of all public school students studied Latin and the language was included in the required tests of the College Entrance Examinations (Sparks, Fluharty, Ganshow, & Little, 1995/1996). However, the blanket assumption that Latin was beneficial to students' intellectual growth came under fire in the 1920s. Relevance and pragmatism held sway among some Progressive educators, who conducted "classic transfer studies" (Thorndike & Ruger, 1923). These theorists used their studies to repudiate successfully the widely accepted benefits of studying Latin. As a result, schools began to remove Latin from the standard curriculum and discouraged students from taking Latin courses. Fifty years later, studies of positive transfer effect (LeBovit, 1973; Mavrogenes, 1977; Sussman, 1978) clearly showed the correlation between the study of Latin and facility in English, but the damage to Latin's position of prominence in the curriculum was already accomplished.

In the latter half of the 20th century, the demand for relevance in course offerings and a pragmatic emphasis on scientific study and modern languages combined to further diminish the importance of Latin for all students, and enrollments in Latin classes declined significantly. LaFleur (1986) chronicled the decline of language enrollment that characterized the age of relevance in American education. He optimistically suggested that the tide of relevance was turning even though there was an "increasingly critical shortage of foreign language teachers" (p. 77). That shortage continues today, despite a program sponsored by the National Endowment for the Humanities in the 1980s to encourage college-age students to study Latin and enter the teaching profession. However, as the pipeline of high school students taking Latin courses declined, so did the pool of potential teacher-candidates to carry on Latin programs in high schools. As Latin teachers retired or left the profession, school districts experienced difficulty in filling the vacancies they left. The American Classical League initiated and continues to administer a database of teaching jobs and candidates to attempt to address this problem.

In the last years of the 20th century, despite these declines, Latin remained a viable option for serious students, that is, those who were capable of studying the language and reading the literature. The study of Latin became a logical pursuit for students now considered gifted, because it reinforces logical thinking and increases English vocabulary. In her study of verbally precocious junior high school students enrolled in either a fast-paced Latin class or a creative writing class, VanTassel-Baska (1982) found a significant ($p < 0.01$) increase in English grammar and vocabulary among the students in the Latin class. She later concluded, "Research suggests that if vocabulary development and linguistic competence in English are desirable gifted program objectives, then Latin would be a logical language choice" (VanTassel-Baska, 1987). The most recent report from the American Council on the Teaching of Foreign Languages (2000) indicated that although only 1.3% of high school students were taking Latin at that time, the College Board's Advanced Placement program reported a 95% increase in students taking the AP Latin exam for credit (VanTassel-Baska, 2004). Clearly, Latin has maintained its place as an option for verbally gifted students, however few their number. The challenge now becomes how to incorporate Latin into the current school environment and make it possible for verbally precocious students across the grades to benefit from the study of world languages in general and Latin in particular. The benefits of language study abound for verbally gifted students, starting in the elementary grades and continuing throughout their academic careers.

LATIN FOR YOUNGER STUDENTS

Although enrollment in high school Latin classes continued to decline drastically over the last three decades of the 20th century, several researchers examined Latin programs in the intermediate and middle school grades. These studies supported the importance of the study of Latin for younger students across all populations. They are worth examining because they not only support Latin for students in the general population, they also support advocating for the study of Latin among students identified as verbally highly able or gifted.

Hoffenburg (1971) analyzed the effect of one year of daily Latin instruction (15–20 minute lessons) on academic achievement as measured by the vocabulary section of the Iowa Tests of Basic Skills (ITBS). Using a quasi-experimental design, Hoffenburg and his colleagues compared the scores of 34 fifth- and sixth-grade students enrolled in the Latin program with scores of a matched control group, with a limitation that socioeconomic factors were controlled only by neighborhood matching and not be individual characteristics of the students. The results of this study indicated that the fifth-grade students in the experimental Latin program were functioning on grade level on the ITBS English vocabulary measure, while the control group scored one grade below grade level. The authors concluded that Latin instruction was effective in building English vocabulary of the students in the experimental Latin group.

In that same year (1971), the Washington, DC, public schools conducted a study of the effect of Latin instruction on the English reading skills of sixth-grade students. This study also employed quasi-experimental design and compared students receiving instruction in Latin with a control group that had no foreign language instruction. Data included the average achievement of each group of more than 1,100 students on pretests and posttests in three specific languages arts areas: vocabulary, comprehension, and total reading skills. The results indicated a significant difference between the reading achievement scores of the two groups, with the Latin group scoring higher on all measures.

In a 3-year project in Indianapolis, Sheridan (1976) explored the hypothesis that English language skills and control of syntactic structures would be improved through student participation in a Latin Foreign Language in the Elementary Schools (FLES) program that focused on Latin roots. This project sought to assess whether the study of Latin and classical civilization would expand the verbal functioning of selected sixth-grade students ($N = 400$) who received a daily 30-minute lesson taught by a Latin specialist. Evaluation of the program showed overall gains on the Metropolitan Achievement Test in word knowledge, reading, and spelling after the first year and gains in spelling and reading in the second and third years of the program.

As a teacher and administrator for foreign language study in the Philadelphia area, Rudolph Masciantonio organized an innovative "Language Arts Through Latin Program" for teaching Latin and Greco-Roman culture to inner-city youths. In the 1970s, this Latin program allowed every Philadelphia student to learn some Latin. Masciantonio (1977) examined eight educational projects in middle grades in which an experimental group of students taking Latin were compared to a control group not taking Latin on pretests and posttests of English verbal skills. In each case, the Latin students showed significant gains over the control group. He furthered explored other studies of middle school Latin programs to promote the pedagogical implications of offering Latin to improve language skills.

HIGH SCHOOL AND BEYOND

The study of world languages in general offers significant benefits for verbally capable students as they progress through school. Timpe (1979) examined the effect of foreign language study on ACT scores of students ($N = 7,460$) at Southern Illinois University to assess the extent to which foreign language study correlated with their ACT scores. To control for intelligence, students were divided into a "more gifted" group (based on GPA of at least 3.0, top quartile of their high school class, college preparatory courses) and another group not meeting these requirements. The authors stated that students in the "gifted" group were more likely to take foreign languages, but that for each group, years of language study correlated with higher ACT scores, with the highest effect on English language scores. More than a decade later, when Olsen and Brown (1992) analyzed the ACT scores of 17,451 students applying for college admission between 1981 and 1985, they found that those who had studied a foreign language consistently scored higher on ACT English and mathematics components than those students who did not study a foreign language.

Other studies support the correlation between foreign language study and success in both secondary and postsecondary environments. Eddy (1981) analyzed the SAT-Verbal scores of students in three Montgomery County, MD, high schools to determine the effect of foreign language study on those scores. Results suggested that when verbal ability is controlled, students who study foreign language for longer periods of time will do better on the SAT-Verbal test than those who have less foreign language experience. Similarly, Cooper (1987) compared the SAT-Verbal and California Achievement Test scores of high school students in two groups, those who had or had not taken at least one year of foreign language. His results supported the conclusion that length of foreign language study correlated positively with high SAT scores. Furthermore, Wiley (1985) examined the correlation between high school language study and success at nine colleges in Tennessee. Her findings suggested that those who studied Latin, French, German, or Spanish in high school may be expected to fare better in college than students of equal academic capacity who do not study a foreign language.

Although 60% of common English vocabulary derives from Latin roots, that percentage increases with the complexity of the words in an individual's personal lexicon. Latin offers an interesting and exciting way for gifted students to develop a rich understanding of language in general. The assumed benefit of greater vocabulary proficiency might seem to gain support from a recent report by the National Committee for Latin and Greek (2002) that showed a correlation between studying Latin and higher Verbal SAT mean scores. The mean Verbal score for all students in 2002 was 504, while those students who had studied Latin scored a mean of 666, followed by scores of students who had studied other languages (French, 637; German, 622; Spanish, 581.) Correlation of Verbal SAT scores to Latin suggest a strong connection between the study of Latin and verbal facility. At the very least, these correlations indicate the chicken-egg symbiosis that results when highly capable students engage in advanced and rigorous study. It's a win-win situation.

MAJOR THEMES FOR THE FIELD OF GIFTED EDUCATION

In the current era of accountability and adequate yearly progress for all students, verbally precocious students often soldier along in classrooms that are stultifying at best. Most often they are victims of the benign neglect of teachers overburdened by the mandate to bring all students "up to standard." Ceilings on state tests preclude any real understanding of the actual proficiency levels or learning needs of those already at standard or beyond. Although it is easy to blame the current situation on

No Child Left Behind (NCLB; 2001), this reality existed well before the current federal emphasis on "one-size-fits-all" education. Westberg, Archambault, Dobyns, and Salvin (1993) found that intermediate grade students experienced no differentiation in 84% of their classroom activities across all content areas, and the little differentiation that was in place focused on mathematics skills. The study of Latin in intermediate grades can provide curriculum differentiation that enhances the literacy skills of students already reading at grade level. Latin can further enrich these students' understanding of world cultures.

Early literature in gifted education supports the role of language study for verbally precocious students. Ward (1961), a pioneer in current theories of gifted education, emphasized the integral relationship between language study and understanding of thought and behavior, essential and important goals for gifted students. Arnold (1962) advocated the informal teaching of linguistics, while Dale and Rozik (1963) focused on vocabulary development as a critically important focus for gifted students. Gallagher (1975) recommended that verbally gifted students would benefit from readings in world literature that foster discussion of values and grappling with complex ideas. Study of a second world language and the literature of other cultures support this recommendation.

Learning a second language offers immediate and long-term benefits for gifted students. Matthews (2006) listed these benefits into three categories: personal, academic, and professional. Personal benefits include a greater awareness of humanity through understanding of world cultures. Latin further provides academic benefits in the long-acknowledged capacity for reading comprehension facility with the roots of words in complex academic content areas like math and science. These academic benefits lead logically to professional benefits in careers that require advanced degrees, like law, medicine, and academe. Latin has long been regarded as the core of the liberal arts basis for these advanced careers.

Studying Latin provides other related benefits in the competitive environment of college admissions. In a recent survey administered by the Texas Classical Association (2002), college and university admissions personnel responded to the question, "When you see Latin on a transcript, what impression of the student does that give you?" Their responses were universally positive, ranging from "Students taking Latin are typically scholarly" to "This student is likely to be disciplined, have a strong basis for further learning, be a little more creative toward intellectual pursuits than most." Some admissions counselors further admitted that they value the study of Latin (and other world languages) highly, even adding "extra weight" to the student's application.

For students capable of complex thought and rigorous analytical activity, Latin provides several additional benefits (Van Tassel-Baska, 2004). The study of Latin develops intellectual habits of mind and teaches deep analysis of thought and speech. In fact, very often students learn English grammar from their study of Latin (Van Tassel-Baska, 1987) and gain greater facility with additional language study, typically in Spanish and French (Prager, 2000). Moreover, because gifted students benefit especially well from complex discourse in interdisciplinary studies, they profit from the study of Latin, which combines history, philosophy, literature, and art to provide a comprehensive way of examining world culture. Finally, Latin offers practice in a complex abstract symbol system (Wilhelm & Wilhelm, 1991), while encouraging higher level thinking through constant analysis and comparison of contemporary ideas with ancient culture. Given the reality that emphasis on basic skills instruction in the general education classroom has diminished time spent on social studies subject matter (National Center for Education Statistics, 2002), the study of Latin and Roman culture can provide a welcome oasis for the gifted student who can see more deeply into universal human concerns and conditions.

NEW TRENDS AND DIRECTIONS

The stage has been set for an innovative marriage of renewed interest in the study of Latin with differentiation in language study for verbally capable students. This creates a dual challenge. First, proponents of the study of Latin must overcome general unfamiliarity with its benefits and reluctance stemming from feasibility issues. If we agree that Latin is beneficial for verbally gifted students, then how can we best provide instruction for them in the language? VanTassel-Baska (2004) outlined a model program that is a template for initiating the study of Latin in the fifth grade and culminating in the 11th grade. Moreover, her plan involves inherently accelerated instruction because, like mathematics, foreign languages enjoy a "cumulative organizational pattern where incrementalization is essential to learning the subject(s) deeply and well" (VanTassel-Baska, 2004, p. 57). Therefore, acceleration for gifted students in these subjects is possible. Hence, educators face the second challenge: the reluctance of schools to accelerate students in any subject (Colangelo, Assouline, & Gross, 2004). However, a willingness to meet the needs of verbally gifted youngsters should move educators to seek solutions to these challenges so that they do not impede the implementation of Latin programs.

Admittedly, finding qualified teachers for Latin classes at any level remains a significant challenge, but one obvious solution promises to enable willing educators to overcome this potential obstacle. Online language learning sites offer a facile and potentially efficient way to provide Latin instruction either *in toto* or as an ancillary resource for teachers. A simple Google search for "online Latin courses" yielded almost 400,000 links. Obviously, any search requires discretion and judgment when pursuing responses. However, the first three output pages alone yielded links to established courses in Latin like the esteemed Cambridge Latin program (http://www.cambridgescp.com), and the long-revered Latin textbook by Allen and Grenough (http://community.middlebury.edu/~harris/AG_1.html).

Several free online Latin courses are available for creative teachers in intermediate grades through high school to access as resources for their highly able students to engage in independent study. One general site for self-directed learning includes the study of Latin (http://www.learnlangs.com/latin.htm). Even more inviting is Linney's Latin Class, a Web site created by a renowned Latin scholar who promises "to make Latin available, accessible, and affordable for everyone who wishes to learn" (http://www.gettingstartedwithlatin.com). The course includes free MP3 downloads of Latin lectures.

Another solution can be found through online university courses that have long provided an intellectual respite for gifted students. In the last few decades, distance learning has gained prominence as a way to provide enrichment or alternate course offerings for students willing and able to move beyond the traditional curriculum, especially when the numbers of those students in individual schools is small and there are no qualified teachers in the local environment. The University of Missouri offers several online courses, including Latin levels I and II, which may be offered through traditional high schools (http://www.cdis.missouri.edu/gifted-courses.aspx). Ohio Wesleyan University also provides online courses in various languages, including basic through advanced Latin (http://humanities.owu.edu/courses_latin.html). For those students who seek completely nontraditional school environments or who are homeschooled, Stanford University also offers a course in Latin II through its Education Program for Gifted Youth Online High School, a 3-year fully accredited alternate high school for gifted students (http://epgy.stanford.edu).

In spite of dire predictions about the demise of Latin, in the first decade of the 21st century, several organizations and veteran educators continue to promote the study of Latin and provide resources for teachers and parents. The Association for Latin Teaching (http://www.arlt.co.uk/dhtml/index.php), based in the United Kingdom, regularly chronicles the ways in which teachers in the U.S. and UK use Latin in novel ways to involve their gifted students. In Texas, one teacher of the gifted, Cathy Earle, assigns Latin sentences to her gifted students to translate into both English and Spanish. This provides a level playing field for her gifted Latino students and an opportunity for all of her students to examine the cognate status of Spanish and English. What an exciting way to address the needs of diverse student populations!

The American Classical League (ACL) continues to provide resources for Latin teachers, including a link that connects schools with potential teacher candidates. The ACL site (http://www.aclclassics.org) also contains links for general teaching materials, as well as an list of links to materials and activities for the teaching of Latin in grades K–9. The National Committee for Latin and Greek (http://www.promotelatin.org) provides informational brochures that can be downloaded free, including one called "Why Latin in the Middle School?" This document provides cogent reasons for implementing Latin programs in the grades in which student achievement in general declines and gifted students may face the most acute challenge to their progress in verbal development. It is a powerful tool for educators advocating the creation of Latin classes in their schools.

Finally, several organizations devoted to the study of classical languages have united to expand Latin classes. To this end, the American Classical League, the American Philological Association, and several state and local organizations have collaborated to institute National Latin Teacher Recruitment Week (NLTRW), which takes place in March of each year, traditionally "foreign language week." Publicized through a communal Web site (http://www.promotelatin.org/nltrw.htm), this annual event encourages as many educators as possible across the nation (and beyond) to find *one day* to devote to talking to their students about becoming secondary Latin teachers. NLTRW was created to address the Latin teacher shortage that the field of education is facing in this country. The demand for Latin continues to grow, in great measure due to our own best efforts to raise awareness of the importance and richness of the study of Latin. Now that we've created the demand, it's time to create the teachers.

If Latin is delivered to gifted students, either by traditional means or through alternate online avenues, one of the obvious outcomes might certainly be an increase in students who pursue Latin in college and then advance to teaching Latin in the K–12 environment. One of Joyce's most significant legacies is the fact that her daughter Ariel, to whom she introduced Latin at an early age, earned a bachelor of arts in Latin. She now is a successful, certified, and tenured Latin teacher in northern Virginia and has just begun her graduate studies in gifted education. As Virgil would have said, *Mirabile dictu!* (Wonderful to relate!)

UNRESOLVED ISSUES AND QUESTIONS

Latin remains an important possibility for verbally gifted students who can appreciate and benefit from the richness of the language itself, its links to modern vocabulary and instruction, and its connection to logic and reasoning, as well as to the roots of Western civilization. However, several unresolved issues remain for educators seeking to maintain or reintroduce this language into the array of possibilities for their students. The dilemma of finding and training teachers, despite the optimistic efforts of the classical organizations, is a critical issue that will not be resolved unless Latin instruction increases. If gifted students are to be afforded the benefit of studying Latin, some of them must pursue the study long enough to be able to convey it to other gifted students. This issue, incidentally, also is true of any world language. In the United States, the study of a second language is regarded as a nonessential pursuit and ever declining numbers are enrolled in any world language in college. Moreover, among those who do study a second language in college, very few go on to preparing for teaching careers in world language.

Another unresolved issue is the reluctance of public school teachers and guidance counselors to encourage students, even the most capable, to pursue advanced language study in high school. However, despite this general lack of support, the number of students taking Advanced Placement Latin exams has nearly doubled from 4,700 to 8,700 students, including an increase from 1,744 to 3,771 on the Latin Literature exam, which is widely regarded as more difficult (Little, 2008). Unfortunately, these statistics did not prevent the announcement in the spring of 2008, by the College Board that it would no longer administer the AP Latin Literature, as well as AP French Literature and AP Computer Science AB courses.

(The AP Italian Language and Culture course also is scheduled to be discontinued but may get a 3-year extension if external partners come forth to supplement the College Board's investment in the Italian exam. No such extension was offered to Latin and French.)

The irony that the AP Latin Literature course includes study of the works of Horace would not be lost on the poet himself. It also should come as no surprise that the American Classical League and other language organizations have entered into full assault on the decision of the College Board, because elimination of the advanced exams creates a ceiling on the levels of Latin that will be offered to students in public schools. The battle continues! As Julius Caesar proclaimed as he crossed the Rubicon, *Alea iacta est!* (The die is cast!) Educators and researchers in the field of gifted education must join the fight, not only by initiating new Latin classes, but by uniting to engage systematic study of Latin instruction in contemporary classrooms and program implementation. This constructive work will inform the practice of educators and provide research-based evidence for further implementation efforts. The recently published volume *Critical Issues and Practices in Gifted Education* (Plucker & Callahan, 2008) contains 50 chapters and 785 pages, but not one study pertains to world language study or Latin. The time is ripe to fill that gap.

The ultimate unresolved question surrounding the role of Latin and other world languages in the education of verbally advanced students is that which permeates all discussions of gifted education and how to provide options for those who can learn more quickly and more deeply. To what extent does the American educational environment support genuine intellectual pursuits? Unfortunately, the answer is discouraging at best. Educators of gifted students understand fully the struggle to provide advanced learning opportunities in all facets of the educational arena. Not surprisingly, mathematics and science courses have long been accepted as appropriate courses for advanced study. Therefore, an additional question emerges: How might educators implement and encourage advanced language study? This question underlies the discussion of Latin in elementary and middle school and permeates decisions made about language offerings in high school and college.

Now, more than ever, the study of world languages in general and Latin in particular are essential for the intellectual growth of verbally advanced students, starting in the middle school. In a contemporary society plagued by massive illiteracy and pop culture, the classics and the study of Latin offers a gold standard of "disciplined rigor, universal ideas, and rich cultural history" (Van Tassel-Baska, 2004, p. 60). After the decline and fall of the Roman Empire, when Western Civilization finally emerged from the Dark Ages, the study of Latin was the means of educating the population. The anti-intellectual environment that pervades American education is a call to action to create a new Renaissance of learning and culture that will feed the curiosity of gifted youngsters and develop their cognitive capabilities. Therefore, educators must strive to introduce the study of Latin, particularly in the middle school, where students are most likely to engage in the study freely and with enthusiasm. From such beginnings, further Latin study will ensue, if the commitment to provide rigor and challenge is allowed to take root.

CONCLUSION

An ancient Chinese proverb admonishes that any long journey begins with the first step. The esteemed poet Horace also aptly captured the importance of our first steps in offering Latin, by whatever means possible, to young verbally precocious students. When he admonished, *Dimidium facti qui coepit habet!* ("He who has begun, has the work half done"), he might well have been referring to the task laid out to us by Joyce VanTassel-Baska. As we celebrate her career and legacy, our mandate is clear. Joyce has begun the work of providing appropriate experiences for gifted students. She has explained how and why educators must provide rigorous curriculum that not only meets the needs of gifted students but also extends the horizons for the general population. She also has clearly delineated the reasons why verbally gifted students should study Latin and how teachers and schools might implement Latin instruction. Now more than ever, young educators must take up the baton and continue the fight to return Latin to its deserved place in the curriculum for gifted students.

REFERENCES

Arnold, J. E. (1962). Useful creative techniques. In S. J. Parnes & H. F. Harding (Eds.), *A source book for creative thinking* (pp. 255–257). New York: Charles Scribner and Sons.

Colangelo, N., Assouline, S. G., & Gross, M. U. M. (2004). *A nation deceived: How schools hold back America's brightest students* (Vol. 1). Iowa City: The University of Iowa, The Connie Belin & Jacqueline N. Blank International Center for Gifted Education and Talent Development.

Cooper, T. C. (1987). Foreign language study and SAT–Verbal scores. *Modern Language Journal, 71*(4), 381–387.

Dale, E., & Rozik, T. (1963). *Bibliography of vocabulary studies.* Columbus: Ohio State University Bureau of Educational Research and Service.

Eddy, P. A. (1981). *The effect of foreign language study in high school on verbal ability as measured by the Scholastic Aptitude Test—Verbal: Final report.* Washington, DC: Center for Applied Linguistics. (ERIC Document Reproduction Service No. ED196312)

Gallagher, J. (1975). *Teaching the gifted child* (2nd ed.). Boston: Allyn & Bacon.

Hoffenberg, R. M. (1971). *Evaluation of the elementary school (FLES) Latin program, 1970–71.* Washington DC: American Council on the Teaching of Foreign Languages.

LaFleur, R. (1986). The study of Latin in American schools: Success and crisis. In T. B. Fryer & F. W. Medley, Jr. (Eds.), *Perspectives on proficiency: Curriculum & instruction. Dimension: Language '84–'85,* (pp. 73–82). Washington, DC: U.S. Department of Education.

LeBovit, J. (1976). *The teaching of Latin in the elementary and secondary school: A handbook for educators and administrators.* Washington, DC: National Endowment for the Humanities.

Little, S. (2008). *ACL responds to the College Board.* Retrieved from http://www.aclclassics.org/pdf/CollegeBoardletter.pdf

Masciantonio, R. (1977). Tangible benefits of the study of Latin: A review of research. *Foreign Language Annals, 10,* 375–382.

Matthews, M. (2006). Second-language learning. *Duke Gifted Letter, 6*(2). Retrieved from http://www.dukegiftedletter.com/articles/vol6no2_article.html

Mavrogenes, N. (1977). The effect of Latin on language arts performance. *Elementary School Journal, 77,* 268–273.

National Center for Education Statistics. (2002). *The nation's report card: U.S. history 2001* (NCES 2002-483). Washington, DC: U.S. Department of Education, Office of Educational Research and Improvement.

National Committee for Latin and Greek. (2002). *Why study Latin?* Retrieved from http://www.promotelatin.org/WhyStudyLatin2003.pdf

Olsen, S. A., & Brown, L. K. (1992). The relation between high school study of foreign languages and ACT English and mathematics performance. *Association of Departments of Foreign Language Bulletin, 23*(3), 47–50.

Plucker, J., & Callahan, C. (Eds.). (2008). *Critical issues and practices in gifted education: What the research says.* Waco, TX: Prufrock Press.

Prager, R. (2000). Introductory language: Opening new doors. *Middle School Journal, 31*(4), 29–33.

Sheridan, R. (1976). *Augmenting reading skills through language learning transfer. FLES Latin Program Evaluation Reports, 1973–74, 1974–75, 1975–76* (ERIC Document Reproductive Service No. ED135218)

Sparks, R., Fluharty, K., Ganshow, L., & Little, S. (1995/1996). An exploratory study on the effects of Latin on the native language skills and foreign language aptitude of students with and without learning disabilities. *The Classical Journal, 91,* 165–194.

Sussman, L. (1978). The decline of basic skills. *The Classical Journal, 73,* 346–352.

Texas Classical Association. (2002). *College & university personnel respond to Latin.* Retrieved from http://aclclassics.org

Thorndike, E. L., & Ruger, C. (1923). The effect of first-year Latin upon knowledge of English words of Latin derivation. *School and Society, 81,* 268–270.

Timpe, E. (1979). The effect of foreign language study on ACT scores. *Association of Departments of Foreign Language Bulletin, 11*(2), 10–11.

VanTassel-Baska, J. (1982). An experimental study on the teaching of Latin to the verbally precocious. *Roeper Review, 4*(3), 35–37.

VanTassel-Baska, J. (1987). A case for the teaching of Latin to the verbally talented. *Roeper Review, 9,* 159–161.

VanTassel-Baska, J. (2004). Quo vadis? Laboring in the classical vineyards: An optimal challenge for gifted secondary students. *Journal of Secondary Gifted Education, 15,* 56–60.

Ward, V. (1961). *Educating the gifted: An axiomatic approach.* Columbus, OH: Charles E. Merrill.

Washington D.C. Public Schools. (1971). *Evaluation of the FLES Latin Program in the Washington D.C. Public schools, 1970–71.* Washington, DC: Author. (ERIC Document Reproductive Service No. ED060695)

Westberg, K. L., Archambault, F. X., Jr., Dobyns, S. M., & Salvin, T. J. (1993). *An observational study of instructional and curricular practices used with gifted and talented students in regular classrooms* (Research Monograph No. 93104). Storrs: University of Connecticut, The National Research Center on the Gifted and Talented

Wiley, P. D. (1985). High school foreign language study and college academic performance. *Classical Outlook, 62*(2), 33–36.

Wilhelm, M. P., & Wilhelm, R. M. (1991). Bringing the classics to life. *Humanities, 12*(1), 13–16.

CHAPTER 27

APPROPRIATE CURRICULUM AND INSTRUCTIONAL APPROACHES FOR THE GIFTED

by

WILLIAM ORTON

Clearly, the task of curriculum-making is complex and arduous, but it is the most important area of work to be done in the field of gifted education.

—Joyce VanTassel-Baska

Perhaps no strand of work more succinctly defines gifted education than the two related areas of curriculum and instruction. This is particularly true when we examine applications of the field to school-based practices. For it is at the individual classroom level, within all service-delivery models, that the implementation of a gifted program manifests itself. Research, policy-making, and program frameworks are pursued and advanced to the end point of delivering effective instruction to each gifted learner.

As in the past, today we face many challenges in creating, advancing, and delivering effective educational programming for gifted learners. There are new catalysts, new barriers, and endless possibilities in how we respond to emergent issues and themes in these areas of gifted education. Fortunately, today, as in our past, we have exceptional, forward-thinking leaders in our field who help to define and sharpen our perspective of the task and motivate us to find solutions. Understanding and building on the past, analyzing the present, and anticipating and preparing for the future is the model that advances a field. Central to that model is insightful research and examination of best practices. Where we are today has been greatly influenced by Dr. Joyce VanTassel-Baska.

She consistently has been in the forefront in curriculum efforts, making a major impact at all levels of gifted education. Her efforts to elevate curriculum development to a science have made a major impact nationally and internationally, as she has called for, and consistently demonstrated in her own curriculum efforts, rigorous standards and reflection in crucial areas of planning, development, research, and evaluation. Those high standards have allowed VanTassel-Baska's curriculum products and models to be among the most effective in gifted education, and represent an important legacy she has left to those who follow her in the field.

Curriculum Foundations

The origins of curriculum and instruction in the field of gifted education are based in a response to the cognitive and affective characteristics of gifted learners (VanTassel-Baska, 1998). Terman (1925) and Hollingworth (1926) identified many of the behavioral characteristics that we associate with gifted learners today. Commonly recognized critical characteristics include the ability to handle abstraction, the power of concentration, and the ability to learn rapidly. On the affective side, gifted learners exhibit perfectionism, humor, and altruism, among other characteristics.

Specific features of effective curriculum accommodating those characteristics include provisions for acceleration, complexity, depth, challenge, creativity, and abstraction (VanTassel-Baska & Stambaugh, 2006). Various models of curriculum have been developed to address those specific learning needs of gifted learners. VanTassel-Baska & Stambaugh (2006) made five underlying assumptions regarding the need of differentiated curriculum for gifted learners. They are based on the optimal match between learning characteristics and needs of gifted students, as well as the appropriateness of the existing general education curriculum provided in the regular classroom. These assumptions are: (1) the regular school curriculum is insufficient and at times inappropriate for gifted learners; (2) reorganization of the general education curriculum is an appropriate modification; (3) appropriate curriculum development for the gifted should be based on research, adapting existing curriculum, and developing new curriculum; (4) gifted curriculum needs to be written and distributed across the school system; and (5) all students at a school can benefit from curriculum designed for gifted learners.

Curriculum Approaches

VanTassel-Baska (1998) advocated for inclusion of multiple approaches to curriculum development for the gifted. The development of the Integrated Curriculum Model (ICM) was her attempt to take the research base of the field and to create a more holistic response to how curriculum might be organized. The emphasis on advanced content linked to higher order processes and the generation of products linked then to the world of intellectual ideas through issues, themes, and concepts provided such a synergistic organization for the work done over the past 20 years.

Of fundamental learning philosophies, those rooted in constructivism have offered learning platforms that have been widely accepted in gifted education as a foundation for important instructional approaches. Considerable instructional time immersed in in-depth study is essential for gifted learners to cognitively construct personal meaning (Wheatley, 1989). That in-depth study often is organized around major emergent concepts or themes. Themes, generalizations, and domain-specific concepts are useful structures by which learners organize and make sense of issues and phenomena. VanTassel-Baska identified nine universal themes and generalizations as appropriate conceptual frameworks for understanding across disciplines (VanTassel-Baska & Stambaugh, 2006). These are change, conflict, exploration, force, relationships, power, patterns, structure, and order and chaos.

INFLUENCE OF LEARNING THEORY RESEARCH

Current learning theory research applicable to school-based practice supports models with a constructivist organization and approach, and has direct and specific implications for both curriculum and instructional design. Learning theory research suggests that knowledge is acquired by construction (Resnick, 1987), and involves restructuring (Carey, 2000). This implies active participation and motivation on the part of the learner engaged in a learning task of appropriate depth and complexity. There also must be a heightened level of abstraction that presents a significant cognitive task demand for the learner. Content must be at an advanced level and ideally organized conceptually to facilitate the desired restructuring and construction task on the part of the learner. Research further suggests that knowledge is acquired in a domain-specific manner (Hirschfeld & Gelman, 1994), which demands a comprehensive and articulated curriculum, well-designed, and focused specifically on the underlying principals and structure of each discipline. Prior knowledge and sociocultural influences also may constrain knowledge acquisition (Rogoff, 1998), which speaks directly to early years education that includes significant engagement and active learning environments for all children, particularly those with limited educational opportunities.

Richness and depth of curriculum must be present in curriculum design and presentation to permit an ideal balance of personal skill level and challenge for each learner (Csikszentmihalyi, 2000). If the gifted learner is to engage in the curriculum experience with personal investment, there must be an optimal match between the present state of the learner and the curriculum. This infers obvious learning management skills of the teacher in the classroom, as well as sensitivity toward individual engagement. This may or may not be the reality in most classrooms where the level of instruction is admittedly geared to minimum standards.

Unfortunately, a constructivist approach often is the exception today rather than the rule in general education. This dichotomy has at times resulted in tension over the perceived learning needs of gifted learners in the regular classroom by the general education teacher. Various curricular and instructional responses and service delivery models have been created and implemented in an attempt to infuse into the gifted learner's education a more appropriate curriculum and instructional approach matched to their unique learning needs.

Ultimately, effective curriculum integrates a number of specific qualities from each available learning model (VanTassel-Baska & Stambaugh, 2006). VanTassel-Baska believes that curriculum should reflect a combination of philosophies of curriculum such as cognitive processes, technology, personal relevance, and social perspective. Additionally, it should address the philosophy of academic rationalism, and provide an appropriate process or pathway to a professional career. A resultant well-designed, articulated, and personally challenging curriculum is essential to effective learning for the gifted learner.

Technology can supplement curriculum development when used in meaningful ways in the classroom (VanTassel-Baska & Stambaugh, 2006). Like other curricula, however, its inherent quality dictates its appropriateness for gifted learners. It must present advanced content, demonstrate sufficient depth and complexity to engage higher order thought and processing, and ideally should cause the gifted learner to reorganize and construct meaning. Web-based instruction that can be effective include simulations, WebQuests from San Diego State University, virtual field trips, telementoring, and distance learning options. Due to the many Web-based curriculum options available, significant time needs to be invested in previewing and selecting those that best match the learning needs of the gifted learner. With technology becoming more available in our schools, it can become a strong asset to our students as a curriculum and instructional option.

INSTRUCTIONAL STRATEGIES

Translation of curriculum into teaching at the classroom level should respond to four main factors: learner characteristics, teaching/learning models and activities, resources and materials, and instructional strategies (VanTassel-Baska & Stambaugh, 2006). Fundamental to that translation is the underlying issue of what one wants the gifted learner to gain from the curriculum experience. Instructional strategies are a large contribution to the learning environment, dictating the manner in which the gifted learner will encounter and process the desired learning. It is the relationship between quality curriculum and instructional strategies that ensures effective actualization of the curriculum to the learner.

Although the concept of overexcitabilities (OE's) has been used to understand the socioemotional needs of the gifted child and related counseling needs (Piechowski,

1979), the relationship of overexcitabilities to teaching and learning is potentially invaluable to framing a learning environment that the gifted find engaging and satisfying. Deliberate construction and maintenance of a learning environment that honors an individual's overexcitability profiles is a significant modification that can differentiate learning for the gifted student. If the dimensions of process and product can be organized and framed in a manner that also accommodates learners' OEs, full engagement and significant motivation is likely for all gifted learners in the classroom. Differentiation along the three dimensions, viewed through the lens of overexcitabilities, has potential to significantly impact learning.

Grouping as a differentiation strategy is one of the easiest options available in the regular classroom. Research findings have strongly supported ability grouping coupled with differentiated curriculum and/or instructional strategies (Kulik & Kulik, 1987), while ability grouping without differentiation has no effect for any learners (Slavin, 1986). The beneficial use of ability grouping for enhanced achievement has been demonstrated at all school levels (VanTassel-Baska, 1998). Groupings may be formed and reformed by content area or specific tasks according to the nature of individual learners. Ultimately, differentiated instructional plans must employ ability grouping to be effective.

Acceleration is a commonly used strategy for differentiation for gifted learners. It is the practice of allowing level of competence to determine appropriate learning options rather than chronological age (Benbow, 1998). There are many forms of acceleration that can be utilized, including early entrance to the next level of education, content acceleration, and telescoping.

Current research indicates that higher level strategies used in conjunction with appropriately complex curriculum results in high level behaviors of students in the classroom (VanTassel-Baska, Quek, & Feng, 2007). Those strategies, however, must match the learning and processing styles of the learners, their ability, and the purpose of the instruction. For that reason, then, the use of multiple strategies has been recommended (Troxclair, 2000).

Many researchers have encouraged the use of instruction that employs complex thinking strategies when the curriculum engages the learner in real-world problems and issues. Problem-based learning is one such strategy that requires complex reasoning and the use advanced intellectual skills to find resolution to complex issues and problems (Gallagher, 1998; VanTassel-Baska, 2003). Likewise, creative problem solving makes similar intellectual and processing demands on the learner, requiring complex thinking skills (Treffinger, Isakson, & Dorval, 2000).

VanTassel-Baska (2003) suggested a model for application of strategies that addresses several dimensions: foundational skills and concepts; creative and critical thinking; and problem solving, decision-making, and policy development. Metacognitive processes drive the application and use of any given strategy used. Within those dimensions, she encourages the specific instructional strategies of question asking, discussion, project work, reading, and homework. The nature of each strategy depends on the learning outcome desired.

CURRICULUM AND INSTRUCTIONAL DELIVERY

The provision of effective curriculum and instruction and our ability to appropriately serve gifted students is partly dependent upon the service delivery model that we utilize. There are several models that have been historically employed in our country that form a continuum of service. At the elementary level, these services range from consultation provided to the regular classroom teacher, to pull-out models, part-time, and ultimately full-time placement in a specialty school designed specifically for gifted learners. The type of service delivery model can dictate the nature and extent of both curriculum as well as instructional services. Political climate, support, resources, number of students identified as gifted, parental pressure, as well as the very nature of the gifted program, all play a role in determining the specific model chosen. Elementary programs, for various reasons, often look quite different from those at the secondary level. The amount of direct student contact time, philosophical alignment between the gifted program and the general education program, and influence of the gifted program upon the school where the program is based, all impact on the level and degree of control and influence over instruction and curriculum.

Meta-analyses of various strategies and service delivery models indicate wide-ranging effect sizes of interventions, dependent on subject area, nature of student grouping, grade skipping, and curriculum compacting (Rogers, 1999). Unfortunately, intervention effect sizes are not always employed in educational decision-making with gifted students. A combination of effective strategies that meets the needs of individual students is advisable. Content extension within a pull-out group coupled with curriculum compacting may be one feasible manner in which to achieve desired educational goals in a pull-out program: Compacting provides the benefits of access to more advanced content, while curriculum connections can provide appropriate instructional strategies for at least a portion of the day. Linkage with the standard curriculum also may allow for more productive content, process, and product modifications. It also encourages "bridging" across to the regular education classroom where gifted students may continue to pursue independently, or with other identified students, further aspects or learning demands of the content. Full-time placement, of course, has the potential to employ multiple strategies to match specific needs of individual students.

SCHOOL-BASED REALITY TODAY: CURRENT SITUATION AND CHALLENGES

The realities of school and classroom practices and beliefs, in large part, determine the nature, extent, and appropriateness of educational services gifted students receive. VanTassel-Baska believes that effective curriculum for gifted learners must be sensitive to three major issues: organizational structures of schools; contemporary K–12 curriculum needs of gifted learners; and recommendations for change being advocated (VanTassel-Baska & Stambaugh, 2006). Each of these issues take place within a shifting political landscape, and manifest themselves within different educational paradigms. The impact of these issues is instrumental in shaping the nature of the educational environment in which gifted education is delivered today.

The current realities that impact on effective curriculum for the gifted are framed and administered through two primary educational stakeholders: the administrative organization of the school system and building, and the instructional staff at the school. How the curriculum is organized for the gifted learner and what instructional approach is utilized by the teacher have become functions increasingly removed from the authority and responsibility of the gifted program director. In the current era of state standards and testing, school administrators have increasingly taken on the mantle of instructional leadership (Lambert, 1998, 2003). At the same time, an emerging administrative level has appeared that has taken on greater responsibility and decision-making authority for student testing and instruction (Seeley, 1994). Translated into school-based instructional practices and accountability, the nature and quality of educational services and instruction for the gifted rely then on several critical factors that may well lay outside the impact of the formal gifted program (VanTassel-Baska & Stambaugh, 2006).

The first of these is the translation of state standards into curriculum at the school system level. Of the two fundamental facets of standards—content and intent—content often becomes the dominant basis for curriculum development at the expense of the fundamental intent of the standards. This is particularly true when those making the translation come from a behaviorist learning orientation. The content standards become the essential learning foundation for the curriculum, as they define the learning outcomes, often dictating the most efficient instructional approach. The need for differentiation in the classroom also becomes dubious when the learning outcomes are content defined by grade level and the dominant and seemingly appropriate instructional approach is didactic.

If, however, one adheres to a constructivist philosophy, and believes that students develop understanding through experiences and personal exploration of a discipline, the intent of the standards becomes the crucial foundation for curriculum development. Each student must encounter and process the curriculum at a personal, meaningful level, defined by the learner herself. Curriculum defined in this manner necessitates and implies depth and complexity, which is integral to understanding and is an appropriate response to the learning characteristics of the gifted learner. Problem-, inquiry-, and issue-based learning all provide appropriate responses to curriculum with a foundation in the philosophy of standards, and differentiation becomes essential for individual encounters with the curriculum. Mastery of the curriculum, when defined in the process dimensions of the standards, is learner-dependent and easily individualized based on interest, ability, and motivation.

Curriculum designed along the process dimensions of state standards also permits reorganization of curriculum for gifted learners within specific disciplines, as well as across disciplines in integrated units of study. In addition to providing better use of instructional time to extend learning, it also may provide a richer, deeper exposure to curriculum, thus allowing needed accelerative learning opportunities. When content is not owned by a particular grade level, access to more complex and advanced learning is facilitated in pursuit of deeper understanding of concepts or processes. Integrated units also encourage the use of multiple resources that are beneficial to all learners, as they present opportunities for authentic use of community resources—both material as well as human. Exposure to experts in various fields brings to light habits of mind of practicing professionals, as well as providing important mentoring to gifted learners.

In the event that a school system does frame its curriculum approach around the intent or process standards of its state, the level of understanding or expertise of the teacher along multiple dimensions has the potential of limiting effective delivery of learning opportunities for gifted students. The best intentions of curriculum design are ineffective if the classroom teacher is unable or unwilling to implement appropriate instructional approaches, or lacks the skills as an instructional manager in the classroom to allow the needed complex dynamics to accommodate various learners. A fundamental constructivist orientation may be highly beneficial to effective implementation of a process-driven curricular approach, and thus more effectively bringing the gifted student to the desired curriculum. Preservice training may equip a teacher with the requisite skills, but it is often up to the school or system to provide appropriate in-service experiences that encourage professional development to that end. The fundamental question facing the gifted program then is how to ensure that teachers have the requisite knowledge and skills to implement a curriculum that is aimed at helping gifted learners construct their own meaning working on real-world issues and problems.

WHERE WE ARE GOING

Emerging technologies have the potential to positively impact the learning environment, but must be accompanied by critical teacher training and support of the instructional decision-makers. Technology, training, and support all come with a price. At a time when school finances are already strained, investments in technology must further well-designed and thought-out curricular and instructional approaches. Policy and decision-makers must be able to see the relationship of resources spent to student achievement. Sophisticated technology without a purpose is of little help to any learners, not just the gifted. Thoughtful use of technology to integrate advanced content and resources with a meaningful instructional approach may be highly beneficial to the delivery of effective educational experiences to gifted learners in the classroom in the coming years.

This is particularly true when the learning experiences are crafted around the intent, or process dimensions, of the state standards. For the most part, as reflections of standards developed by national-level discipline organizations, all of our states have common ground within those process dimensions, making well-developed integrated units meaningful and usable by multiple audiences from many diverse areas. Technology that permits student access to appropriate instructional approaches, quality resources, and diverse student dynamics have the ability to significantly improve gifted students' educational experiences, particularly in light of the interactive nature of technologies available to schools today. Simultaneous video, together with a shared, common workspace, allow students to engage together in pursuit of well-designed and provocative instructional units, accompanied by specific meaningful, well-developed assessments of learning. Schools or classrooms may enter into consortiums of institutions with similar motivations and needs. Appropriate instructional design may be modeled by the embedded dynamic, thus delivering the elements of effective instruction such as challenging questioning and probing, and providing the catalyst for further student investigation and analysis of common issues and problems facing students across the country and world.

Learning delivered through interactive technology has the potential to impact on instructional strategies and practices of classroom teachers. If there is a built-in dynamic of collaboration and interactivity between practitioners, students, and resources, significant modeling can be designed within that dynamic. This is particularly if there is a strong teacher training component contingent upon participation in the collaboration (optimally delivered through videoconferencing). Multiple networks of teachers can be created to include "mentor" teachers, with strong command of appropriate strategies, and "partner" teachers who may gain professional development opportunities through the relationship. When the curriculum is based in a constructivist philosophy and the content is organized conceptually, the model teacher can employ (and demonstrate) appropriate instructional strategies within their role in the dynamic. The partner teacher can respond in like manner with her own students in a "shared classroom space" where there is a degree of professional accountability. Feedback from the model teacher would provide development potential, especially if simultaneous video between classrooms is regularly employed.

The organizational structure at the state and regional level, together with fairly extensive networks already in place, provides an opportunity for educational improvement. States with similar standards and curriculum could develop additional networks regionally or nationally. International networks would be a logical extension to further expand the learning community. Collaborative classrooms linked through interactive technology also provide a wider array of grouping possibilities. Gifted learners from partner classes can be grouped together and given differentiated learning objectives with appropriate task demand, communicating through various mediums such as discussion groups, blogs, e-mail, video messages, and videoconferencing. Interaction and evaluations with multiple teachers and resource personnel can be conducted in the same fashion, with written or visual evidence available for instructional or evaluative use. Shared resources would be an additional benefit of the networked relationships. Quality curriculum that is developed, field-tested, and improved through such networks also could become an excellent resource for school systems across the nation.

LEADERSHIP

VanTassel-Baska has provided tremendous leadership to the field of gifted education within many domains. In a field with several, at times, competing camps, she has gained the respect and admiration of all by demonstrating respect, thoughtfulness, and inclusion. She has developed and nurtured collaboration and constructive relationships between diverse groups and individuals to the benefit of all.

Her impact on curriculum, instruction, and leadership has been remarkably strengthened and enhanced by the development of the Center for Gifted Education at The College of William and Mary in Virginia in 1988. Curriculum development efforts at the Center are overwhelmingly successful and delivered to gifted learners. The National Curriculum Network Conference, founded by the Center, brings together multiple audiences, researchers, students, and practitioners. William and Mary units are disseminated and dissected by participants and staff, and relationships and alliances have been created and nurtured over the years.

Many levels of gifted education have been fortunate to have had the chance to receive the support and assistance of Dr. VanTassel-Baska. She has been the keynote speaker at countless conferences, always providing insightful, provocative, and timely perspectives. VanTassel-Baska has never shied away from directly confronting issues and problems, although always with tact and with precise information and data. She has performed many consultation services to states, programs, school systems, and individual schools. As in all endeavors, she attains a deep knowledge of underlying issues, politics, and problems, and guides the stakeholders through an exacting process of discovery, problem-solving, consensus, and solution.

Joyce VanTassel-Baska's greatest contribution to leadership in the field of gifted education perhaps came from the development of the gifted education courses at William and Mary, culminating with the education leadership doctoral program with specific emphasis in gifted education. The program has been producing leaders in teaching, curriculum, research, higher education, and an array of gifted education policy-makers that will impact on the field for years to come. VanTassel-Baska's passion, extraordinarily high standards of excellence, mentorship, friendship, and support have been passed on to countless individuals who have had the extreme good fortune to know her. Joyce has made an indelible mark on all of us.

REFERENCES

Benbow, C. P. (1998). Acceleration as a method for meeting the academic needs of intellectually talented children. In J. VanTassel-Baska (Ed.), *Excellence in educating gifted* (3rd ed., pp. 279–294). Denver, CO: Love.

Carey, S. (2000). The origins of concepts. *Journal of Cognition and Development, 1,* 37–41.

Csikszentmihalyi, M. (2000). The contribution of flow to positive psychology: Scientific essays in honor of Martin E. P. Seligman. In J. E. Gillham (Ed.), *The science of optimism and hope* (pp. 387–395). Philadelphia: Templeton Foundation Press.

Gallagher, S. A. (1998). The road to critical thinking: The Perry scheme and meaningful differentiation. *NASSP Bulletin, 82*(595), 12–20.

Hirschfeld, L. A., & Gelman, S. A. (Eds.). (1994). *Mapping the mind: Domain specificity in cognition and culture.* New York: Cambridge University Press.

Hollingworth, L. (1926). *Gifted children: Their nature and nurture.* New York: World Book.

Kulik, J. A., & Kulik, C. C. (1987). Effects of ability grouping on student achievement. *Equity & Excellence, 23*(1–2), 22–30.

Lambert, L. (1998). *Building leadership capacity in schools.* Alexandria, VA: ASCD.

Lambert, L. (2003). *Leadership capacity for lasting school improvement.* Alexandria, VA: ASCD.

Piechowski, M. M. (1979). Developmental potential. In N. Colangelo & R. T. Zaffrann (Eds.), *New voices in counseling the gifted* (pp. 25–27). Dubuque, IA: Kendall/Hunt.

Resnick, L. B. (1987). Constructing knowledge in school. In L. S. Liben (Ed.), *Development and learning: Conflict or congruence?* (pp. 19–50). Hillsdale, NJ: Lawrence Erlbaum.

Rogers, K. (1999). *Research synthesis on gifted provisions.* Retrieved from http://www.austega.com/gifted/articles/Rogers_researchsynthesis.htm

Rogoff, B. (1998). Cognition as a collaborative process. In D. Kuhn & R. S. Siegler (Eds.), *Handbook of child psychology: Vol. 2. Cognition, perception, and language* (5th ed., pp. 679–744). New York: Wiley.

Seeley, K. (1994). Arts curriculum for the gifted. In J. VanTassel-Baska (Ed.), *Comprehensive curriculum for gifted learners* (pp. 282–300). Boston: Allyn & Bacon.

Slavin, R. W. (1986). Best-evidence synthesis: An alternative to meta-analytic and traditional reviews. *Educational Researcher, 15*(9), 5–11.

Terman, L. M. (1925). *Mental and physical traits of a thousand gifted children. Genetic studies of genius, Vol. 1.* Stanford, CA: Stanford University Press.

Treffinger, D. J., Isakson, S. G., & Dorval, K. B. (2000). *Creative problem solving: An introduction.* Waco, TX: Prufrock Press.

Troxclair, D. (2000). Differentiating instruction for gifted students in regular education social studies classes. *Roeper Review, 22,* 195–198.

VanTassel-Baska, J. (Ed.). (1998). *Excellence in educating gifted and talented learners* (3rd ed.) Denver, CO: Love.

VanTassel-Baska, J. (2003). *Curriculum planning and instructional design for gifted learners.* Denver, CO: Love.

VanTassel-Baska, J., Quek, C., & Feng, A. X. (2007). The development and use of a structured teacher observation scale to assess differentiated best practice. *Roeper Review, 24,* 84–92.

VanTassel-Baska, J., & Stambaugh, T. (2006). *Comprehensive curriculum for gifted learners* (3rd ed.). Boston: Allyn & Bacon.

Wheatley, G. H. (1989). Instructional methods for the gifted. In J. Feldhusen, J. VanTassel-Baska, & K. Seeley (Eds.), *Excellence in educating the gifted* (pp. 261–275). Denver, CO: Love.

CHAPTER 28

WHAT DO YOU NEED TO KNOW?

Becoming an Effective PBL Teacher

by

SHELAGH
A. GALLAGHER

Problem-based learning puts gifted students in charge—a welcome respite from the impositional role of many teachers.
—Joyce VanTassel-Baska

INTRODUCTION

A true story: About a year ago I was sitting on an airplane, scribbling notes for a presentation on Advanced Placement when I slowly realized that the woman next to me was looking over my shoulder. She looked friendly enough, so I smiled and she started talking, "My kids were in AP and IB." "Really?" I asked, "When was that? "Oh, a long time ago. They're both in college now." "Were they in gifted programs all the way through school?" "Oh yes!" she said, suddenly quite animated. "They were in a great program. I remember when my oldest was in fourth grade her class had to figure out how to get the lights on in a town because there had been a storm . . ."

Could there be a better testament to a 4-week unit than a positive parent report—almost 10 years after the fact? More than 15 years have passed since *Electricity City* (Center for Gifted Education, 2007b) and the other William and Mary science units were pilot tested in Virginia schools. The units have become such as standard in the field that it's easy to forget how groundbreaking they were: Among the first widely distributed curriculum from a Javits grant, the first formally published curriculum from the Center for Gifted Education, the science units also were—and still are—among the few fully articulated problem-based learning (PBL) units. The project was shaped by VanTassel-Baska's initial vision of what would later evolve into the Integrated Curriculum Model (ICM) and that curricula would result from a collaboration of experts in content, curriculum, and classroom delivery, but I don't think even Joyce imagined the synergy of the development team. The science units have stood the tests of time and research; they will remain, to my mind, a significant part of the legacy she leaves to the field. We can add to that legacy by ensuring that the units are used as intended—adding the framework of PBL instruction to the ill-structured problem.

Instruction in the PBL Classroom

Problem-based learning never was intended to be just a curriculum model. From the outset, it was designed to create simultaneous change in curriculum *and* instruction (Barrows, 1988; Barrows & Tamblyn, 1980). As is often true, the whole is greater than the sum of its parts. Ironically, most K–12 writing about PBL emphasizes creation of the problem and the first day of instruction, leaving teachers without a sense of what to do after the first day, a situation bound to discourage many in this era of accountability.

The progression of a PBL problem has been described in detail elsewhere (Gallagher, 2008a, 2008b; Stepien & Pyke, 1997), so it is only described briefly here. A PBL unit starts when students are presented with an ill-structured problem, or problem engagement. The problem engagement sets the scene and provides students with a stakeholder role, someone who has responsibility for solving some aspect of the problem. Students use a Learning Issues Board (Need to Know Board for younger students) to record questions about their problem. Hooked both by the storyline and their own questions, students begin to research and reassess the problem in light of new information. Once they understand the situation better, they define the problem and begin to think about possible resolutions. After comparing different options, they choose one using criteria formed from critical elements of the problem. After they present their solution, the teacher and students debrief the problem to review the content and processes they learned and to reflect on how to improve performance in their next PBL experience. Fortunately, research into PBL instruction can help provide guidelines on how to ensure success throughout a PBL unit.

The Ill-Structured Problem: Foundation for Instruction

The first step in becoming an effective PBL teacher is to ensure that the problem will lead students to required content. A PBL problem is designed to be ill-structured from the students' point of view, yet should reliably lead to predictable content, skills, and ideas (Barrows & Tamblyn, 1980; Gallagher, 2008a; Ross, 1997; Stepien & Pyke, 1997).

PBL Instruction: Scaffolding Self-Directed Learning

A well-constructed ill-structured problem allows teachers freedom from didactic content delivery because content emerges as students find answers to their questions. Thus, liberated teachers can focus on helping students become self-directed learners by promoting metacognitive reasoning, independent thinking, independent action, and collaboration.

Promoting metacognition. Knowing how to conduct an analysis is only useful if you know when an analysis is needed and whether the analysis is accurate or useful. Metacognition is the practice of being self-aware while planning, executing, and evaluating any activity, a kind of ongoing self-assessment. Skilled independent performance is impossible without metacognitive awareness. The questions on the Learning Issues Board are a student's first exposure to metacognition; "What do I know?" "What do I need to learn?" and "How can I find out?" are classic metacognitive questions. Teachers continue to build students' metacognitive awareness by modeling questions such as "How can I do better next time?" "Why aren't we making progress right now?" "What should I do to get this information organized?" as well as providing journal prompts and encouraging students' analysis of their stakeholder role.

Cultivating independent thought. Independent thinkers have a toolkit of analytical skills that they select from as necessary. PBL teachers help students fill their toolkits and show them how to choose the proper tool for any given task—sometimes helping students to invent a tool as well. The tools include generic skills in research, critical thinking, problem solving, and ethics as well as discipline-specific skills like the experimental design process incorporated into the William and Mary science units (Center for Gifted Education, 2007a, 2007b). Mini-lessons, or "embedded instruction," provide some tools on an as-needed basis so students are immediately motivated to put the tool to work. Other tools, like conceptual reasoning, are presented to introduce students to advanced ways of looking at the problem.

Cultivating independent action. Independent action comprises all the activities involved while solving a problem, creating a learning agenda, scheduling research time, selecting homework assignments, leading discussions, setting timelines and deadlines, contacting speakers, and facilitating group discussion. In typical classrooms, teachers make many of these decisions; in PBL, students take on as many as possible as they become more independent. Needless to say, this looks different in different classrooms: Third graders may practice holding their own class discussion, while in a 10th grade history class students may take responsibility scheduling guest speakers and updating the Learning Issues Board each day. With practice, students should be able to run a discussion at the Learning Issues Board, divide research responsibilities, share research results, analyze information, and consider solutions with only occasional assistance.

Fostering collaboration. Students in PBL spend a substantial amount of time in group work; the group is where they begin to apply their growing skills in self-directed learning. In medical school, students are placed in small tutorial groups; in the K–12 classroom, students move in and out of groups to conduct research, analyze information, and create and compare solutions (Gallagher, 2008a). Typical collaborative groups can wander off task, but PBL groups tend to be productive. An analysis of discourse during group time revealed that 80% of talk-time was both on-task and productive (Visschers-Pleijers, Dolmans, Wolfhagen, & Van Der Vleuten, 2004). Others have found that students in PBL tutorials spend more time engaged than students in other kinds of tutorials (Wun, Tse, Lam, & Lam, 2007). Successful PBL groups become increasingly self-regulated, taking responsibility to study and prepare for discussion. As they discuss, they build their critical thinking skills to explain ideas to others, build concepts together, or take a moment to think things through on their own (Cooper, Cox, Nammouz, Case & Stevens, 2008). It should be no surprise that student achievement is higher when PBL groups are effective (Van den Hurk, 2006).

Multiple levels of support. The job of a PBL teacher is to create a structure that allows the problem to flow as intended, ensuring that students acquire requisite content, skills, and ideas. The structure includes establishing a classroom framework that supports PBL, selecting a workable problem and creating a plan for instruction, working with students to managing classroom activity, and helping students conduct skillful analysis of the problem. This is quite an agenda; is all of it really necessary? What does each part add to the students' experience? Research investigating different aspects of PBL instruction helps identify what aspects of classroom practice are particularly important.

Research on Best Practice in PBL

PBL is arguably the most researched model in education; the PubMed Web site has a list of 250 articles published in 2008—and these don't include research on PBL in other fields. Research in K–12 is sparse but growing, thanks in part to the Center for Gifted Education. Much of the research is designed to test the efficacy of PBL. A growing number of studies show either equal or greater content acquisition in PBL when compared to traditional instruction (Dods, 1997; Gallagher, 2001; Gallagher & Stepien, 1996; Geban, Sungar, & Ceren, 2006; Hmelo-Silver, 2004; VanTassel-Baska et al., 2008; Verhoeven et al., 1998). Adding lectures to PBL does not increase student achievement (Van Berkel & Schmidt, 2005).

PBL also is successful in cultivating specific process skills. When embedded into a PBL unit, students learn to use rules of argumentation (Belland, Glazewski, & Richardson, 2008), experimental method (Feng, VanTassel-Baska, Quek, Bai, & O'Neill, 2005), problem finding (Gallagher, Stepien, & Rosenthal, 1992), and analysis (VanTassel-Baska, Bass, Ries, Poland, & Avery, 1998; VanTassel-Baska et al., 2008). As early as first grade, students can learn peer tutoring and metacognitive reasoning through PBL (Shamir, Zion, & Spector-Levi 2008).

The evidence that PBL evokes positive attitudes toward learning is so consistent that in a summary of the research Vernon and Blake (1993) claimed, "no sample was found in which the students' attitudes did not favor PBL to some degree" (p. 554). Even though medical students sometimes complain about the increased workload, they seem more engaged and motivated in class (Canavan,

2008). Improved attitudes also are documented in K–12 classrooms (Feng et al., 2005; Hmelo & Ferrari, 1997; VanTassel-Baska et al., 1998).

Meta-analyses of PBL research yield inconsistent results. Albanese & Mitchell (1993) found no effect for content knowledge based on training but superior diagnostic skills among PBL students. Similarly, Dochy, Segers, Van den Bossche, and Gijbels (2003) found that PBL students were not better than traditional students on traditional knowledge tests, but sustained a moderate effect size favoring PBL when assessments focused on application of knowledge.

Longitudinal studies of PBL medical school graduates have provided some assurance that they are as competent as their traditionally trained colleagues (Norman, Wenghofer, & Klass, 2008). In another carefully controlled synthesis of research studies comparing PBL and traditionally trained doctors, PBL doctors were superior in diagnostic skills, communication, coping with ambiguity, responsibility, appreciation of ethical and legal issues, and appreciation for cultural aspects of health care, with no differences in content knowledge (Choon-Huat Koh, Khoo, Wong, & Koh, 2008). The only longitudinal study of PBL in K–12 to date is the 3-year analysis conducted by VanTassel-Baska, Feng, Quek, and Struck (2004). They found continued growth with ongoing experience in PBL among elementary school students.

Overall, PBL students seem to learn just as much as traditionally instructed students, with the added advantage of enhanced engagement in learning, better skill development, and heightened awareness of ethical issues. Building instructional skills is a clear way of ensuring that students in any PBL class fare at least this well. However, this research leaves unanswered the question of which elements of PBL instruction are important. A second set of research studies attempt to make these causal links.

The focused ill-structured problem. Do classroom problems really need focus? Davis, Nairn, Paine, Anderson, and Oh (1994) compared new and experienced PBL teachers and found no achievement differences if the problem was aligned to curriculum goals, a connection found by others as well (Goodnough & Cashion, 2003). Predictable content coverage should be a benefit of aligning a problem to curriculum goals. Dolmans, Gijselaers, Schmidt, and van der Meer (1993) found that students across 12 sections of the same PBL course identified 85% of the course goals. The same students were less consistent in identifying objectives for specific problems, a finding also reported by Mpofu, Das, Murdoch, and Lanphear (1997). In both studies this variability was attributed to differences in the quality of individual problems in the course. There was little to no agreement on vague problems and excessive agreement—nearly 100%—on well-structured problems. Student and teacher experience also contributed to the variability.

Expertise in problem content. Students are more likely to achieve when the PBL curriculum is aligned to goals. Do teachers have to be content experts in the problem, or is it sufficient to understand the goals? Does expertise tempt teachers to revert to lecturing? Eagle, Harasym, and Mandin (1992) found that students whose teachers had content expertise identified twice as many learning issues in the first discussion of the problem, and went on to spend twice as much time in self-directed study compared to students whose teachers were not content experts. Another study found that teachers without content expertise could not reliably predict whether their students had learned required content. The teachers' uncertainty affected student assessment (Kaufman & Hansell, 1997), an unfortunate finding as corrective feedback contributes to student success in PBL (Norman & Schmidt, 1992). Looking a little deeper, Schmidt and Moust (1995) studied the questioning patterns of new and experienced PBL teachers. They found that experienced teachers asked more insightful questions about the problem, helping students identify both central issues and interesting or controversial topics for investigation. They attributed this difference to the experienced teacher's deeper knowledge of the problem. Davis et al. (1994) found that students performed better in PBL classes led by tutors with an active interest in the area, and speculated that interest led to a broader content base as well as enthusiasm.

Sometimes teachers with content expertise stray away from best practice. Silver and Wilkerson (1991) found teachers with problem expertise were more directive, spoke more, and spoke longer than teachers without expertise. They also found that classes led by content experts had more teacher-student interactions than student-student interactions. Still other studies found little or no effect based on content expertise. de Grave, de Volder, Gijselaers, and Damoiseaux (1990) found that level of expertise was unimportant when predicting student achievement. Some groups don't need a tutor at all, operating perfectly well and covering necessary outcomes without the presence of one (Wilkerson, 1996).

Schmidt (1994) dug a little deeper to identify conditions where expertise was a helpful to addition to the PBL classroom. He found that content expertise was helpful when the problem was vague or when students had little prior knowledge. Under these conditions the students needed extra help identifying central learning issues. On the other hand, teacher expertise was not essential when the problem had cues that prompted student questions, when students had encountered similar problems before, or when they had prior knowledge about the problem. Once again, findings emphasize the importance of working with a focused ill-structured problem.

Overall, the weight of the evidence suggests that students learn more in PBL when their teacher is knowledgeable about the problem. This knowledge is most effective when used to ask insightful questions, guiding students to a deeper understanding of the problem.

PBL instructional skills. Research on effective PBL instruction is a bit more consistent than the research on expertise. Students are clear that they prefer PBL teachers who helped the group set learning issues by asking provoking questions; stimulated discussion when necessary; engaged students in insightful analysis of ideas; provided helpful, specific feedback; listened to students and allowed them to fumble; contributed knowledge and experience when necessary; supported a pleasant and productive learning environment; and balanced student direction with assistance (Barrows, 1988; Wilkerson, 1996). This list, at one level, simply describes an effective teacher (Shavelson & Stern, 1981); however, it is noteworthy that students seemed to like the open-ended nature of PBL and sought opportunities for higher order thinking. A better sense of what instructional skills are needed for PBL comes from the finding that student satisfaction is enhanced when students feel supported in their efforts toward self-directed learning (Greening, 1998). Because achievement increases as PBL students become more independently self-directed (Van den Hurk, 2006), the balance between support and independence is particularly important.

A synthesis of skills. PBL is a dynamic combination of the problem, constructivist instruction, and independent student work. A more sophisticated analysis is required to identify how the different elements contribute to achievement. Van Berkel and Dolmans (2006) undertook this description in a path analysis by investigating the ways in which constructivist instruction, self-directed learning, collaborative learning, student perception of the problem, and group behavior contributed to student achievement. The causal paths created in the analysis showed that student satisfaction with the problem, constructivist instruction, a well-functioning group, and supported self-directed learning are *all* important contributors to student achievement in PBL.

Helpful scaffolds. Anticipating using PBL for the first time, Vardis and Ciccarelli (2008) took a closer look at classroom practice. Through a review of the literature they identified the most common problems in PBL classes: dysfunctional student groups where some students are unprepared or do not participate in discussions and activities; conflicts among students because of unclear expectations; prior knowledge or research is presented that is not related to the problem; unclear, vague learning questions; spending research time on resources or investigating issues that don't advance understanding of the problem; lack of depth; unproductive group meetings (caused by many of the above); and emphasis on research rather than substantial thinking about the problem and its ramifications. Recognizing that many of these problems resulted from inadequate student support, the authors created structures that provided more concrete guidance: a list of online resources that supplemented student research, rules of discussion were made explicit, student preparation was recorded (not graded), assessments were criterion referenced, and class started with a warm-up of key conceptual questions that students could discuss quietly before the larger discussion began. Having an established set of procedures and clear expectations contributed to a more comfortable first attempt for both teachers and students.

Hmelo-Silver, Duncan, and Chinn (2007) also discussed scaffolding, but focused on cognition instead of procedures. They presented a number of cognitive scaffolds that support student learning in PBL including (1) techniques that make disciplinary thinking and strategies explicit (each problem should expose students to tools and thinking strategies used by real professionals in their stakeholder role); (2) providing students with various forms of expert guidance (allowing students to watch how experts approach problem solving); (3) methods that help students organize complex tasks or reduce cognitive load of the overall environment (this includes everything from research organizers to classroom routines that help students become comfortable in the "flow" of PBL); and (4) methods that enhance complexity. Table 28.1 presents the combined set of scaffolds with examples of each.

The list may seem overwhelming but a close look will reveal that several scaffolds are part of standard teaching practices transferred to the PBL environment. These scaffolds are not limited to embedded instruction; they can be posters on the wall, resources provided for research, or problem log entries. Students will find scaffolds everywhere they turn in a well-prepared PBL classroom. Far from being restrictive, the scaffolds form a safety net that keeps the students within their zone of proximal development—challenged but not overwhelmed.

From Research to Practice

Taken together, findings from the research literature create a picture of what a teacher needs to do to maximize her likelihood of success in using PBL. Preparation includes learning about the problem, thinking about what scaffolds students will need most, and continuing to build skills in constructivist instruction. Familiarity with the problem is crucial to going beyond the problem engagement to antici- pate the full path of the unit. PBL problems have a story-like quality. They set the scene, providing an outline of the problem and indicating the students' stakeholder role. The initial problem engagement of a focused ill-structured problem tells the first chapter of the story; a well-prepared PBL teacher can imagine the remaining chapters, predicting what students will need to learn and do to solve the problem. Teachers who can write a narrative or create a flexible coaching plan for the unit (Gallagher, 2008a) are helping to maintain the general focus of the problem, while allowing some flexibility for unanticipated student ideas. In combination, the scaf- folds presented by Vardis and Ciccarelli (2008) and Hmelo et al. (2007) create a set of structures to support independent thought and action.

Ongoing professional development. Neither students nor teachers can be expected to excel if thrown into PBL without support. Teachers need scaffolds, too! Administrators who want PBL in their schools can help by providing training in PBL that includes both content and teaching processes. PBL pulls on virtually every teaching tool there is— except lecturing. Operating a PBL classroom requires knowledge of group dynamics, collaborative learning, self-directed learning, questioning skills, higher order thinking, conceptual reasoning, thinking tools like graphic organizers, and authentic assessment. Teachers can succeed in PBL without being masters of all these skills but their efforts at PBL will improve as their skills improve. Everyone will benefit if classroom observation forms can be adapted to reflect best practice in PBL as well.

WHAT ARE MAJOR THEMES AND IMPLICATIONS FOR THE FIELD OF GIFTED EDUCATION?

Problem-based learning should be a common feature in the education of gifted students. It is inherently geared toward their natural inclinations for inquiry and open-endedness and uses their skill at knowledge acquisition and analysis (Gallagher, 2009a). This may be because so many medical school students (and their teachers) also are gifted—and it incorporates a majority of the core recommendations. In

Table 28.1

CLASSROOM SCAFFOLDS FOR PBL

Process Scaffolds That . . .	Type of Scaffold	Example
Communicate Expectations	Orientation	Discussion with students before class informing them of different expectations
	Rubrics describing performance expectations	Classroom Engagement Rubric*
	Classroom structures	Discussion guidelines Procedures for leaving the classroom
Support Independent Action	Outside contacts	Guidelines for contacting Guest speakers E-mail mentors
	Communication skills	Organizers to prepare written and oral presentations
	Interactions	Procedures to resolve disputes
Support Effective, Independent Investigation	Balance between student-discovered research and assigned articles	WebQuests Assigned articles
	Helping students connect research to the problem	Note-taking structure requiring explicit connection to the problem Clear, specific, researchable Learning Issues Questions

Cognitive Scaffolds That . . .	Type of Scaffold	Example
Make Disciplinary Thinking and Strategies Explicit	Pushing students to explain their thinking	Discussion questions Student syntheses of research Metacognitive reflections about the discipline in Problem Log
	Prompts to use specific reasoning strategies	Four question experimental design** Historical analysis Conceptual reasoning with icons* Practice diagnostic skills
	Filling in argument diagrams	Graphic organizers incorporated into daily activities and Problem Log
	Templates for domain-specific explanations	Policy* Experimental Results Guide**
	Models of expert performance	Videos of experts in action, Field trips to observe experts Modeling expert thinking
Embed Expert Guidance	Time with experts	Guest speakers, e-mail mentors, telephone interviews
	Mini lectures	Brief explanations of content to clarify issues when necessary
	Modeling good reasoning	Provide models to help students analyze data and find implications for the problem.
Structure Complex Tasks or Reduce Complexity	Charts showing thinking processes	Chart depicting the Flow of the Problem*
	Building student reasoning	Protected time for analysis and synthesis of data, discussion of conflicting information, and other advanced reasoning
	Graphic organizers	Thinking maps
	Automization	Use computers and calculators for routine tasks
	Classroom routine	Begin and end class with a review of the Learning Issues Board
	Assessment	Use criterion-referenced assessments Provide performance expectations in advance
Enhance Complexity	Increase depth, complexity, or range of the problem	Conflicting data Twists in storyline Conceptual analysis Advanced metacognitive reflection

* See Gallagher (2008b) for samples.
**See Center for Gifted Education (2007a, 2007b) for samples.

fact, it shares a core set of qualities common to most models of gifted curriculum: abstraction, real-world problem solving, self-awareness, higher order thinking, independent research, and apprenticeship in disciplinary thinking and practice (VanTassel-Baska et al. 2008). Moreover, it is evidence-based, raising the likelihood that advanced training can coexist with standards-driven education. Similarly, the forms of instruction described here are commonly recommended for classrooms of gifted students (Maker, 1982).

The challenge for teachers of gifted students will be to remember that PBL is not inherently gifted curriculum. PBL works well with students of all ability levels; if used in the regular classroom, teachers will have to incorporate differentiated experiences for some students. In some ways, this is easier in the PBL environment because student questions tend to be developmentally appropriate, but care should be taken to ensure that gifted students receive appropriate challenges to push their thinking forward (Gallagher, 2009b).

WHAT ARE THE NEW TRENDS OR DIRECTIONS?

More PBL curriculum is becoming available at more grade levels, and hopefully this trend will continue from many different sources. Not only will this make PBL available to more teachers and students, it also will allow for greater balance between discussions of the problem and instruction. Pushing the field ahead will involve more research and also experimenting with alternate modes of delivering PBL, including distance education and Web-based formats.

Also intriguing will be the investigation of what it means to be advanced in PBL. To date, traditional forms of increasing levels of depth and complexity have dominated the discussion; however, the emphasis placed in PBL on disciplinary thinking and metacognition introduce new and intriguing possibilities. Paul (1992) presented standards of good thinking, but Nelson (1989) noted that fields also have advanced standards to judge the quality of ideas, such as fecundity and parsimony. Introducing these standards to gifted students may constitute one form of differentiated disciplinary thinking. In a similar vein, metacognition seems inherently advanced because it is by definition abstract, yet expert performers provide compelling reminders that optimum performance requires reflection that goes beyond metacognition and into mindfulness that brings attention to the psychological barriers, physical reactions, and feelings that cause us to block our own performance (Waitzkin, 2007).

UNRESOLVED ISSUES AND QUESTIONS

Although research on the William and Mary science units has provided helpful evidence of effectiveness, far more is needed. A challenge to all research on classroom practice in gifted education is that it is commonly conducted on new programs. Certainly in the case of PBL, much of the research has been in class-rooms where students and teachers are new to PBL, and likely to return to "regular curriculum" at the end of a single PBL unit. Research across Javits projects demonstrates that it takes 3–5 years for any innovation to take hold, yet decisions about efficacy often are made before then. Canavan (2008) cautions that it is also impossible to get the full effect of PBL without the process of reflecting on what happened during one problem in preparation for improved performance in the next.

Until there is more systematic implementation, many questions will remain unanswered. What is the impact of experiencing a sequence of PBL problems? How do students' impressions of PBL change over time? How much of the initial enthusiasm over PBL is simply the Hawthorne effect? Can we create a meaningful scope and sequence for self-directed learning? At what point, if any, do students reach saturation in PBL?

CONCLUSION

Contemplating "what could be" can shadow appreciation of "what is." Because of Joyce's commitment to disciplinary-rich curricula, we have the units, evidence of efficacy, and a model for producing more. That may just be the tip of the iceberg, but it's a pretty substantial tip. At least the woman next to me on the plane thought so.

If nothing else happens in PBL for gifted students—and that's not likely—what we have is a significant set of high-quality curricula, appropriate for the gifted but adaptable for all. They are valuable for what they contribute and for paving the way for other curriculum that follow. They are a landmark in the field, and with ongoing attention to implementation, they should be around long enough to move gracefully from being innovative to becoming classic.

REFERENCES

Albanese, M., & Mitchell S. (1993). Problem-based learning: A review of the literature on its outcomes and implementation issues. *Academic Medicine, 68,* 52–81.

Barrows, H. (1988). *The tutorial process.* Springfield: Southern Illinois University School of Medicine.

Barrows, H. S., & Tamblyn, R. M. (1980). *Problem-based learning: An approach to medical education.* New York: Springer.

Belland, B., Glazewski, K., & Richardson, J. (2008). A scaffolding framework to support the construction of evidence-based arguments among middle school students. *Educational Technology Research & Development, 56,* 401–422.

Canavan, B. (2008). A summary of the findings from an evaluation of problem-based learning carried out at three UK universities. *International Journal of Electrical Engineering Education, 45,* 175–354.

Center for Gifted Education. (2007a). *Acid, acid everywhere.* Dubuque, IA: Kendall Hunt.

Center for Gifted Education. (2007b). *Electricity city.* Dubuque, IA: Kendall Hunt

Choon-Huat Koh, G., Khoo, H., Wong, M., & Koh, D. (2008). The effects of problem-based learning during medical school on physician competency: A systematic review. *Canadian Medical Association Journal, 178*(1), 34–41.

Cooper, M. M., Cox, C. T., Jr., Nammouz, M., Case, E., & Stevens, R. (2008). An assessment of the effect of collaborative groups on students' problem-solving strategies and abilities. *Journal of Chemical Education, 85,* 866–872.

Davis, W. K., Nairn, R., Paine, M. E., Anderson, R. M., & Oh, M. S. (1994). Influences of a highly focused case on the effect of small-group facilitators' content expertise on students' learning and satisfaction. *Academic Medicine, 69,* 663–669.

Dochy, F., Segers, M., Van den Bossche, P., & Gijbels, D. (2003). Effects of problem-based learning: A meta-analysis. *Learning & Instruction, 13*(5), 533–568.

Dods, R. F. (1997). An action research study of the effectiveness of problem-based learning in promoting the acquisition and retention of knowledge. *Journal for the Education of the Gifted, 20,* 423–437.

Dolmans, D. H. J. M., Gijselaers, W. H., Schmidt, H. G., & van der Meer, S. B. (1993). Problem effectiveness in a course using problem-based learning. *Academic Medicine, 68,* 207–213.

Eagle, C. J., Harasym, P. H., & Mandin, H. (1992). Effects of tutors with case expertise on problem-based learning issues. *Academic Medicine, 67,* 465–469.

Feng, A., VanTassel-Baska, J., Quek, C., Bai, W., & O'Neill, B. (2005). A longitudinal assessment of gifted students' learning using the integrated curriculum model (ICM): Impacts and perceptions of the William and Mary language arts and science curriculum. *Roeper Review, 27,* 78–83.

Gallagher, S. A. (2001). But does it work? Testing the efficacy of problem-based learning: A review of the literature and research agenda for educators of the gifted. In N. Colangelo & S. G. Assouline (Eds.), *Talent development IV: Proceedings from the 1998 Henry B. and Jocelyn Wallace National Research Symposium on Talent Development* (pp. 179–204). Scottsdale, AZ: Great Potential Press.

Gallagher, S. A. (2008a). Problem-based learning. In J. Renzulli & J. Gubbins (Eds.), *Systems and models for developing programs for the gifted and talented* (2nd ed.). Storrs, CT: Creative Learning Press.

Gallagher, S. A. (2008b). *All work and no play: Child labor in the Progressive Era.* Unionville, NY: Royal Fireworks Press.

Gallagher, S. (2009a). Adapting problem-based learning for gifted students. In F. A. Karnes & S. M. Bean (Eds.), *Methods and materials for teaching the gifted* (3rd ed., pp. 301–330). Waco, TX: Prufrock Press.

Gallagher, S. (2009b). Designed to fit: Educational implications of gifted adolescents' cognitive development. In F. A. Dixon (Ed.), *Programs and services for gifted secondary students: A guide to recommended practices* (pp. 3–20). Waco, TX: Prufrock Press.

Gallagher, S. A., & Stepien, W. (1996). Content acquisition in problem-based learning: Depth versus breadth in American studies. *Journal for the Education of the Gifted, 19,* 257–275.

Gallagher, S. A., Stepien, W. J., & Rosenthal, H. (1992). The effects of problem-based learning on problem solving. *Gifted Child Quarterly, 36,* 195–200.

Geban, O., Sungar, S., & Ceren, T. (2006). Improving achievement through problem-based learning. *Journal of Biological Education, 40,* 155–160.

Goodnough, K., & Cashion, M. (2003). Fostering inquiry through problem-based learning. *The Science Teacher, 70*(9), 21–25.

de Grave, W. S., de Volder, M. L., Gijselaers, W. H., & Damoiseaux, V. (1990). Peer teaching and problem-based learning: Tutor characteristics, group functioning and student achievement. In Z. Nooman, H. G. Schmidt, & E. Ezzat (Eds.), *Innovation in medical education: An evaluation of its present status* (pp. 123–134). New York: Springer.

Greening, T. (1998). Scaffolding for success in PBL. *Medication Education Online, 3*(4). Retrieved from http://www.med-ed-online.org

Hmelo, C. E., & Ferrari, M. (1997). The problem-based learning tutorial: Cultivating higher order thinking skills. *Journal for the Education of the Gifted, 20,* 401–422.

Hmelo-Silver, C. (2004). Problem-based learning: What and how do students learn? *Educational Psychology Review, 16,* 235–266.

Hmelo-Silver, C. E., Duncan, R. G., & Chinn, C. A. (2007). Scaffolding and achievement in problem-based and inquiry learning: A response to Kirschner, Sweller, and Clark. *Educational Psychologist, 42,* 99–107.

Kaufman, D. M., & Hansell, M. M. (1997). Can non-expert PBL tutors predict their students' achievement? An exploratory study. *Academic Medicine, 72*(10), 16–18.

Maker, C. J. (1982). *Teaching models in the education of the gifted.* Rockville, MD: Aspen.

Mpofu, D. J. S., Das, M., Murdoch, J. C., & Lanphear, J. H. (1997). Effectiveness of problems used in problem-based learning. *Medical Education, 31,* 330–334.

Nelson, C. E. (1989). Skewered on the unicorn's horn: The illusion of the tragic tradeoff between content and critical thinking in the teaching of science. In L. W. Crow (Ed.), *Enhancing critical thinking in the sciences* (pp. 17–27). Washington, DC: National Science Teachers Association.

Norman, G. R., & Schmidt, H. G. (1992). The psychological basis of problem-based learning: A review of the evidence. *Academic Medicine, 67,* 557–565.

Norman, G., Wenghofer, E., & Klass, D. (2008). Predicting doctor performance outcomes of curriculum interventions: problem-based learning and continuing competence. *Medical Education, 42,* 794–799.

Paul, R. (1992). *Critical thinking: What every person needs to survive in a rapidly changing world.* Santa Rosa, CA: The Foundation for Critical Thinking.

Ross, B. (1997). Towards a framework for problem-based curricula. In D. Boud & G. Feletti (Eds.), *The challenge of problem based learning* (pp. 34–41). New York: St. Martin's Press.

Shamir, A., Zion, M., & Spector-Levi, O. (2008). Peer tutoring, metacognitive processes and multimedia problem-based learning: The effect of mediation training on critical thinking. *Journal of Science Education & Technology, 17,* 384–398.

Schmidt, H. G. (1994). Resolving inconsistencies in tutor expertise research: Does lack of structure cause students to seek tutor guidance? *Academic Medicine, 69,* 656–662.

Schmidt, H. G., & Moust, J. H. (1995). What makes a tutor effective? A structural-equations modeling approach to learning in problem-based curricula. *Academic Medicine, 70,* 708–714.

Shavelson, R. J., & Stern, P. (1981). Research on teachers' pedagogical thoughts, judgments, decisions and behavior. *Review of Educational Research, 51,* 455–498.

Silver, M., & Wilkerson, L. (1991). Effects of tutors with subject expertise on the problem-based tutorial process. *Academic Medicine, 66,* 298–300.

Stepien, W. J., & Pyke, S. (1997). Designing problem-based learning units. *Journal for the Education of the Gifted, 20,* 380–400.

Van Berkel, H. J. M. (2006). The influence of tutoring competencies on problems, group functioning, and student achievement in problem-based learning. *Medical Education, 40,* 730–736.

Van Berkel, H. J. M., & Dolmans, D. (2006). The influence of tutoring competencies on problems, group functioning, and student achievement in problem-based learning. *Medical Education, 40,* 730–736.

Van Berkel, H. J. M., & Schmidt, H. G. (2005). On the additional values of lectures in a problem-based curriculum. *Education Health, 18,* 45–61.

Van den Hurk, M. (2006). The relation between self-regulated strategies and individual study time, prepared participation and achievement in a problem-based curriculum. *Active Learning in Higher Education, 7,* 155–169.

VanTassel-Baska, J., Bass, G. M., Ries, R. R., Poland, D. L., & Avery, L. D. (1998). A national pilot study of science curriculum effectiveness for high ability students. *Gifted Child Quarterly, 42,* 200–211.

VanTassel-Baska, J., Feng, A. X., Brown, E., Bracken, B., Stambaugh, T., French, H., et al. (2008). A study of differentiated instructional change over three years. *Gifted Child Quarterly, 52,* 297–312.

VanTassel-Baska, J., Feng, A., Quek, C., & Struck, J. (2004). A study of educators' and students' perceptions of academic success for underrepresented populations identified for gifted programs. *Psychology Science, 46,* 363–378.

Vardis, I., & Ciccarelli, M. (2008). Overcoming problems in problem-based learning: A trial of strategies in an undergraduate unit. *Innovations in Education & Teaching International, 45,* 345–354.

Verhoeven, B. H., Verwijnen, G. M., Scherpbier, A. J., Holdrinet, R. S., Oeseburg, B., Bulte, J. A., et al. (1998). An analysis of progress test results of PBL and non-PBL students. *Medical Teacher, 20,* 310–316.

Vernon, D. T. A., & Blake, R. L. (1993). Does problem-based learning work? A meta-analysis of evaluative research. *Academic Medicine, 68,* 550–563.

Visschers-Pleijers, A., Dolmans, D., Wolfhagen, I., & Van Der Vleuten, C. (2004). Exploration of a method to analyze group interactions in problem-based learning. *Medical Teacher, 26,* 471–478.

Waitzkin, J. (2007). *The art of learning: An inner journey to optimal performance.* New York: Free Press.

Wilkerson, L. (1996). Tutors and small groups in problem-based learning: Lessons from the literature. *New Directions for Teaching and Learning, 68,* 23–22.

Wun, Y. T., Tse, E. Y. Y., Lam, T. P., & Lam, C, L. K. (2007). PBL curriculum improves medical students' participation in small-group tutorials. *Medical Teacher, 29,* 198–203.

CHAPTER 29

CURRICULUM DIFFERENTIATION

by

HEATHER
M. FRENCH

Differentiation of curriculum for gifted learners requires attention to the strongest characteristics that separate these students from their age peers—precocity and complexity.

—Joyce VanTassel-Baska

Curriculum differentiation is not a new concept. Virgil Ward, pioneer in the field of gifted education, first coined the phrase "differential education" in his book entitled *Education for the Gifted: An Axiomatic Approach* (Ward, 1961). In this published work, Ward advocated differentiating process, product, and content to provide gifted students with the necessary knowledge to apply to both current and future problem situations. Since Ward first raised the important issue of adequately providing for the education of our gifted and talented students, researchers, educators, curriculum developers, administrators, parents, and students have been refining approaches to differentiation that work in real-world classrooms.

WHAT IS CURRICULUM DIFFERENTIATION?

Educators have addressed differentiation from a number of different perspectives, each choosing to focus on a different element. For example, Tomlinson (1999) focused on the differentiated classroom, maintaining that differentiation is not just something that happens during instructional time, but it is pervasive throughout all classroom experiences. Tomlinson and Allan (2000) also addressed the role of instructional leaders in making differentiated classrooms a success through understanding the concept of differentiation; being optimistic about its success; providing optimal conditions for differentiation to occur; providing relevant staff development for teachers; and communicating with parents about what they should expect from their children's classroom experiences. More recently, Tomlinson (2001) identified what differentiation is and is not, noting that differentiated instruction is proactive; qualitative rather than quantitative; rooted in assessment; provides multiple approaches to content, process, and product; is student centered; is a blend of whole-class, small-group, and individual instruction; and is organic, meaning it is something that naturally evolves from within the classroom rather than being something that happens to the classroom.

On the other hand, Gregory and Kuzmich (2004) focused on using quantitative data for student growth and achievement to inform when, how, and why differentiation occurs; their focus is on making differentiation work within the current standards movement. This focus also is evident in the curriculum and research efforts of the Center for Gifted Education at The College of William and Mary (VanTassel-Baska, 2003a, 2003b).

Nordlund (2003) has focused primarily on using differentiated instruction to meet the needs of students who qualify for special education due to cognitive impairments, attention deficits, learning difficulties, low English proficiency, and being at risk for school failure. He firmly believes that teachers and other educational personnel should view "diversified learning" as a positive experience for all involved, that variety among students in the classroom enhances the "learning climate" for students, and teachers should encourage students to view the entire school as their classroom where learning can take place anywhere at any time (p. 5).

Other researchers like Phillips (2008) focus on specific strategies such as acceleration to provide differentiated experiences for the highest achieving students. Phillips argues instructional practices such as continuous progress, subject acceleration, and Advanced Placement should be used more frequently to address the unique educational needs of gifted students and to maintain an educational pace commensurate with their abilities. Phillips states that acceleration is a differentiation strategy supported by more than 50 years of research as reiterated in the publication of *A Nation Deceived: How Schools Hold Back America's Brightest Students* (Colangelo, Assouline, & Gross, 2004).

Academic competitions also have been the focus of recent claims made by Ozturk and Debelak (2008). These authors state that within the current standards movement, the focus of education is on all students reaching proficiency, not on furthering the academic experiences of gifted students. They assert that, by entering academic competitions, gifted students are given the opportunity to experience differentiated content, process, product, and environment. Content is differentiated by expanding both depth and breadth by engaging in activities such as primary document research and interviewing experts in a given field. Process is differentiated by "immersing children in the essential structure of the discipline" (Ozturk & Debelak, 2008, p. 47). Students are expected to acquire a certain level of working knowledge and then collect, analyze, synthesize, apply, and evaluate data in the relevant field. Product is differentiated by exposing students to work completed by their intellectual equals and revealing a much higher level of expectations than those to which most gifted students have previously been held. Gifted individuals often are accustomed to completing schoolwork without feeling challenged and without having to put forth much effort to receive the highest grade in the class. At academic competitions, many gifted students come face-to-face, for the first time, with work that far exceeds their own accomplishments. Finally, the environment is differentiated by providing gifted individuals with a forum for collaborating, communing, and commiserating with like-minded individuals. These talented learners discover that there is a place where it is "cool" to like school, to be passionate about knowledge, and to have intellectual aspirations.

In a similar attempt to provide challenging educational experiences for gifted learners in mixed-ability classrooms in the midst of the standards movement, Powers (2008) argues that independent study is an excellent alternative, particularly for underachieving gifted learners and/or gifted individuals who refuse to adhere to the traditional educational setting and requirements. Powers' study focuses on middle school gifted students in Arlington, VA. She primarily explores the roles that student choice, independent study, and connections to real-world experiences played in students' responsiveness to social studies, concluding that self-efficacy, in-depth learning, and critical thinking were the outcomes of import.

Clark (2002) provided a guide for differentiating for gifted learners by acceleration, adding complexity and depth, providing novelty, supporting idealism, and acknowledging intensity. For each of these areas of differentiation, she provided specific characteristics of gifted individuals that match each differentiating technique, ideas for opportunities required to meet students' needs using the technique, and details regarding the teacher's role in each technique.

VanTassel-Baska (2005) listed differentiated curriculum, instruction, materials, and assessment among the "nonnegotiables" of gifted services. She stated that differentiation must occur within the "context of providing acceleration and grouping as basic policy provisions in gifted programs—within which a curriculum base that is advanced, in-depth, complex, creative, and challenging may be offered" (VanTassel-Baska, 2005, p. 90). The nonnegotiable, research-supported policies that VanTassel-Baska (2005) stated should be in place for all gifted learners include accelerated study; content acceleration; grade-level acceleration; telecommunications options; flexible grouping; differentiated curriculum providing experiences "sufficiently different from the norm" (p. 93); differentiated curriculum resources that move beyond a single textbook; instructional differentiation including problem-based learning and higher level questioning; assessment differentiation in the form of high-level standardized assessments such as Advanced Placement (AP) exams and performance-based assessment with rubrics to guide student work; requirements that schools match gifted learners with those teachers who are passionate lifelong learners, good thinkers, and who have a deep understanding of their content area; and finally, access to advanced opportunities outside of school through enrichment programs at local universities to internships within professional fields.

VanTassel-Baska (2003b) also advocated differentiating at the level of educational standards rather than just classroom instruction and materials. She asserted that each curriculum standard must be evaluated for appropriateness when being used with gifted learners and, as a whole, the standards should incorporate all five elements of differentiation: acceleration, complexity, depth, challenge, and creativity. VanTassel-Baska (2003b) recommended teachers follow six strategies for ensuring standards are appropriately differentiated for gifted learners: (1) recognize that many standards already focus on higher level thinking skills; (2) discern the scope and intent of each standard; (3) create a rubric to assess learning in each standard using the "essence" of the standard; (4) organize standards by higher order thinking skills and employ interdisciplinary teaching across subjects; (5) accelerate after careful pretesting of students' prior knowledge; and (6) select materials that relate to the intent of the standard and not just the literal content.

VanTassel-Baska and Little (2003) discussed differentiation in terms of content-based curriculum development for high-ability learners. Using the same criteria established by VanTassel-Baska (2003a, 2003b), they espoused that differentiation approaches should apply to the content of curriculum within which students are working, the process through which students learn, and the products that result from student learning. The content, process, and product must be matched to a student's need for advancement, depth, and complexity at any given stage of his or her development. The research conducted at the Center for Gifted Education at The College of William and Mary on the use of differentiated units of study in language arts, science, and social studies (Little, Feng, VanTassel-Baska, Rogers, & Avery, 2007; VanTassel-Baska, Bass, Ries, Poland, & Avery, 1998; VanTassel-Baska, Zuo, Avery, & Little, 2002) demonstrates the viability of having carefully designed units as the basis for curriculum delivery to high-ability learners.

The research on the use of such curriculum in science found that students using the William and Mary curriculum scored higher on standardized achievement tests; demonstrated an improved ability to plan a scientific experiment, think critically, and understand higher order concepts; and were more engaged in the problem-based learning approach employed than in more typical science instruction (VanTassel-Baska, 1998; VanTassel-Baska, Bracken, Stambaugh, & Feng, 2007).

Similarly, research on the use of the William and Mary language arts curriculum units showed significant gains for students in reading comprehension, critical thinking, literary analysis, and persuasive writing (Bracken, VanTassel-Baska, Brown, & Feng, 2007; VanTassel-Baska et al., 2008; VanTassel-Baska et al., 2002). Interestingly, these effects were found for students of all ability levels, not just those identified as gifted learners, demonstrating the far-reaching, powerful effect of curriculum designed specifically to capitalize on the elements of differentiation.

In the content area of social studies, researchers at William and Mary found similar effects to those in science and language arts. Students in classrooms where teachers were implementing the William and Mary differentiated curriculum demonstrated significant academic progress in conceptual thinking, content learning, and critical thinking (Little et al., 2007). Again, these gains were not limited to gifted learners, but extended to all learners exposed to the curriculum. These studies clearly illustrate across three different content areas the effectiveness of differentiated curriculum units designed using the elements of accelerated pace, complexity, depth, challenge, and creativity as espoused by VanTassel-Baska.

A Definition for Differentiation in Gifted Education

With so many different conceptions of differentiation in the educational literature, the establishment of an operational definition within the field of gifted education is imperative. However, it quickly becomes apparent that a consensus cannot be reached within the field. In gifted education literature, differentiation is defined in nearly as many ways as in the general education literature. Feldhusen and Moon (1995) defined differentiation as "providing enriched and accelerated curricula, classroom experiences that are challenging and open to discussion, opportunities to work with talented peers and project activity with high-level expectations, and a striving for excellence" (pp. 105–106). Parke (1995) also included the important element of including, or subsuming, the regular curriculum within the differentiation curriculum for gifted students. Ehlers and Montgomery (1999), drawing from Maker's (1982) *Curriculum Development for the Gifted*, emphasized the necessity of "qualitative differences from the general education curriculum in content, process, product, and learning environment" (p. 96). Dinnocenti (1998) used Renzulli's (1997) Five Dimensions of Differentiation to include differentiated instructional strategies, essentially a differentiated teacher, to the list of content, process, product, and classroom environment. She stated, "Educators of the gifted and talented have the task of developing and utilizing the five dimensions of differentiation in a consistent and progressive manner to truly address the needs of highly able learners and direct them into choices that challenge their potential" (p. 11).

Many educators in the field of gifted education recognize differentiation is a necessity for meeting the needs of these unique students. However, they cannot agree on a standard, operational definition of differentiation. In a qualitative study conducted by Tomlinson (1995) with middle school teachers, the teachers were quoted as stating, "Nobody knows what differentiation means'" (p. 79). According to Tomlinson (1999), a differentiated classroom is one in which teachers begin where students are, where teachers provide "specific ways for each individual to learn as deeply as possible and as quickly as possible, without assuming one student's road map for learning is identical to anyone else's," where teachers use time flexibly with a range of instructional strategies, and where teachers have a clear understanding of what powerful curriculum and instruction look like (p. 2).

VanTassel-Baska (2003a) noted that there are no specific strategies that are differentiated only for gifted learners. She wrote, rather, that "strategy use is inextricably tied to the nature and level of the curriculum being addressed" (VanTassel-Baska, 2003a, p. 3). In other words, strategies that are effective with gifted learners—questioning for high-level discussion, open-ended activities, and problem-based learning, for example—must be used in conjunction with advanced curriculum in order to be effective with this unique population of learners.

The research on differentiation practices for gifted learners in the regular classroom is scarce and suggests that little is happening for these learners. In 1992, researchers conducted a national study of third- and fourth-grade teachers regarding the instructional and curricular methods they used with their gifted and talented learners. The major findings of the study revealed that teachers were making only minor modifications in curriculum and instruction to meet the needs of their gifted learners. Of those teachers who did provide differentiation for gifted students, the most common modifications were advanced reading, independent projects, enrichment worksheets, and assigning various types of reports. None of these modifications reached the level of depth, complexity, and challenge recommended for gifted learners. Only a very few teachers compacted the curriculum, provided opportunities for acceleration, asked for gifted students' input on curricular modifications, or exposed students to higher level thinking skills (Archambault et al., 1993; Westberg, Archambault, & Brown, 1997).

Based on the results of this study, several follow-up studies have been conducted by The National Center for Research on the Gifted and Talented. The Classroom Practices Observation Study (Westberg, Archambault, Dobyns, & Salvin, 1993) was designed to examine, through classroom observations, the instructional and curricular practices being used with gifted learners in regular elementary classrooms. Across all subject areas, students were heterogeneously grouped for 79% of instructional time. In addition, the majority of instructional time was spent on passive activities, with 84% of the activities containing no differentiation for gifted and talented students (Westberg et al., 1993). A recent follow-up study conducted by Westberg and Daoust (2003) found no greater use of differentiated strategies than was true 10 years prior, suggesting that differentiation for gifted learners in the regular classroom may not be a viable approach to ensuring services.

However, many gifted learners remain in the regular classroom being served ineffectively. As a field, we must address this dilemma. Perhaps the most realistic option is a tiered service delivery model that flexibly utilizes proven grouping strategies that include pull-out options, resource room opportunities, special classes, and cluster grouping, all well-supported by research (Kulik & Kulik, 1992, 1997; Rogers, 1998). In addition, gifted specialists also must be provided with opportunities to model differentiated lessons for regular classroom teachers (Westberg et al., 1993). Professional development focused on differentiation for gifted learners should provide teachers with more choices in materials, resources, and products to meet their students' interest and needs; should aid teachers in recognizing a variety of learning styles and abilities; should help teachers grow personally and professionally as they reflectively examine their instructional philosophies and practices; and should encourage teachers to raise their expectations for student work (Gubbins, 2002).

In a related 3-year study on teachers' instructional behavior and how it changed through the implementation of high-level, research-based differentiated curriculum, VanTassel-Baska et al. (2008) discovered that multiple years of ongoing professional development is required for teachers to incorporate differentiation into their instructional practices. Throughout a 3-year study, experimental teachers received 3 days of training prior to the beginning of each school year in a summer institute and one day of training at the beginning of the second semester in a midwinter institute. The training for each summer and midwinter institute focused on specific differentiation strategies for implementing the language arts curriculum to be used with third through fifth graders in the experimental classrooms. During implementation of the curriculum, experimental and comparison teachers were each observed twice using the Classroom Observation Scales, Revised (COS-R), which measures observed teacher behavior against best practices in the areas of curriculum planning and delivery; accommodating for individual differences; problem solving; critical thinking; creative thinking; and research. VanTassel-Baska et al. (2008) found that at the end of the 3-year study, experimental teachers who had been receiving ongoing professional development in differentiation strategies and used the differentiated curriculum "demonstrated higher levels of differentiated instructional practices than comparison teachers in all behavioral categories across both observations" (p. 306). Moreover, veteran experimental teachers, those teachers who participated in all 3 years of the study and participated in professional development 4 days each year, showed a "consistently stable and high level of instructional practice, suggesting maturity in using both general and differentiated instructional strategies" (VanTassel-Baska et al., 2008, p. 306). In addition, the students in these classrooms also demonstrated responses at higher levels, reflecting what the researchers found in teachers' instructional patterns. This study clearly shows the need for long-term professional development rather than one-day workshops, as well as the need for monitoring classroom implementation of differentiation strategies through well-designed, high-level curriculum.

FUTURE DIRECTIONS

Clearly, the idea of differentiating instruction to meet the needs of individual learners is not new. Teachers, administrators, and policy makers have been trying for decades to implement such strategies. As evidenced by the literature and empirical research discussed, differentiation is not a "plug and play" concept for teachers. VanTassel-Baska et al. (2008) have strong evidence to show effective implementation of differentiated strategies requires at least 2 years of professional development incorporated with ongoing observations and monitoring of implementation. However, many teachers are already overtaxed with preparations for state standardized testing and the unrealistic expectations of all students reaching the same level of proficiency on the same time schedule. If gifted students are going to receive the quality education they deserve, more focused efforts must be made to train teachers in the use of differentiated strategies.

There are many viable techniques to choose from in the literature. What matters most is that districts choose a differentiation method; develop strong, effective, long-term professional development to train teachers in its implementation; follow through with teacher training, making it mandatory for all teachers; match teacher quality with student characteristics; and follow up with monitoring of classroom implementation to ensure fidelity of treatment. As espoused by VanTassel-Baska et al. (2008), "teachers persisted in the project because they believed that their students were benefiting, a frequently voiced sentiment bolstered by evidence of annual student growth" (p. 307). If teachers believe they are giving each of their students what he or she needs, and they are given the necessary training and support, they will persist in finding ways to make differentiation a daily occurrence in their classrooms.

Dr. VanTassel-Baska's contributions, particularly in the area of curriculum differentiation, have had a significant impact on the field of gifted education internationally. Her conceptualization of differentiation within the structure of her Integrated Curriculum Model has helped scholars, researchers, and teachers gain a better understanding of how to meet the academic needs of their most promising learners. Dr. VanTassel-Baska's dedication to developing well-designed differentiated curriculum across the content areas has facilitated the delivery of high-level, high-powered instruction for numerous teachers and countless students across the world. To work with Dr. VanTassel-Baska on curriculum development has been an honor. To see students of all ability levels, backgrounds, genders, and socioeconomic status excel while delightfully engaged in the curriculum conceived by her is inspiring.

REFERENCES

Archambault, F. X., Jr., Westberg, K. L., Brown, S. W., Hallmark, B. W., Emmons, C. L., & Zhang, W. (1993). *Regular classroom practices with gifted students: Results of a national survey of classroom teachers* (Research Monograph No. 93102). Storrs: University of Connecticut, The National Research Center on the Gifted and Talented.

Bracken, B. A., VanTassel-Baska, J., Brown, E. F., & Feng, A. (2007). Project Athena: A tale of two studies. In J. VanTassel-Baska & T. Stambaugh (Eds.), *Overlooked gems: A national perspective on promising students of poverty* (pp. 63–67). Washington, DC: National Association for Gifted Children.

Clark, B. (2002). *Growing up gifted* (6th ed.). Columbus, OH: Merrill Prentice Hall.

Colangelo, N., Assouline, S. G., & Gross, M. U. M. (2004). *A nation deceived: How schools hold back America's brightest students* (Vol. 1). Iowa City: The University of Iowa, The Connie Belin & Jacqueline N. Blank International Center for Gifted Education and Talent Development.

Dinnocenti, S. T. (1998, Spring). Differentiation: Definition and description for gifted and talented. *The National Research Center on the Gifted and Talented Newsletter,* 10–11. (ERIC Document Reproduction Service No. ED436909)

Ehlers, K., & Montgomery, D. (1999). *Teachers' perceptions of curriculum modifications for students who are gifted.* Paper presented at the meeting of American Council on Rural Special Education, Albuquerque, NM. (ERIC Document Reproduction Service No. ED429750)

Feldhusen, J. F., & Moon, S. M. (1995). The educational continuum and delivery of services. In J. L. Genshaft, M. Bireley, & C. L. Hollinger (Eds.), *Serving gifted and talented students: A resource for school personnel* (pp. 103–121). Austin, TX: Pro-Ed.

Gregory, G. H., & Kuzmich, L. (2004). *Data driven differentiation in the standards-based classroom.* Thousand Oaks, CA: Corwin Press.

Gubbins, E. J. (2002). *Implementing a professional development model using gifted education strategies with all students* (Research Monograph No. 02172). Storrs: University of Connecticut, The National Research Center on the Gifted and Talented.

Kulik, C., & Kulik, J. (1997). Ability grouping and gifted students. In N. Colangelo & G. A. Davis (Eds.), *Handbook of gifted education* (pp. 178–196). Boston: Allyn & Bacon.

Kulik, J. A., & Kulik, C. C. (1992). Meta-analytic findings on grouping programs. *Gifted Child Quarterly, 36,* 73–77.

Little, C. A., Feng, A. X., VanTassel-Baska, J., Rogers, K. B., & Avery, L. D. (2007). A study of curriculum effectiveness in social studies. *Gifted Child Quarterly, 51,* 272–284.

Maker, C. J. (1982). *Curriculum development for the gifted.* Rockville, MD: Aspen.

Nordlund, M. (2003). *Differentiated instruction: Meeting the educational needs of all students in your classroom.* Lanham, MD: Scarecrow Education.

Ozturk, M. A., & Debelak, C. (2008). Academic competitions as tools for differentiation in middle school [Electronic version]. *Gifted Child Today, 31*(3), 47–54.

Parke, B. N. (1995). Developing curricular interventions for the gifted. In J. L. Genshaft, M. Bireley, & C. L. Hollinger (Eds.), *Serving gifted and talented students: A resource for school personnel* (pp. 123–134). Austin, TX: Pro-Ed.

Phillips, S. (2008). Are we holding back our students that possess the potential to excel? *Education, 129*(1), 50–55.

Powers, E. (2008). The use of independent study as a viable differentiation technique for gifted learners in the regular classroom [Electronic version]. *Gifted Child Today, 31*(3), 57–66.

Renzulli, J. S. (1997). The Multiple Menu Model: A successful marriage for integrating content and process. *NASSP Bulletin, 81*(587), 51–58.

Rogers, K. B. (1998). Using current research to make "good" decisions about grouping. *NASSP Bulletin, 82,* 38–46.

Tomlinson, C. A. (1995). Deciding to differentiate instruction in middle school: One school's journey. *Gifted Child Quarterly, 39,* 77–87

Tomlinson, C. A. (1999). *The differentiated classroom: Responding to the needs of all learners.* Alexandria, VA: Association for Supervision and Curriculum Development.

Tomlinson, C. A. (2001). *How to differentiate instruction in mixed-ability classrooms* (2nd ed.). Alexandria, VA: Association for Supervision and Curriculum Development.

Tomlinson, C. A., & Allan, S. D. (2000). *Leadership for differentiating schools and classrooms.* Alexandria, VA: Association for Supervision and Curriculum Development.

VanTassel-Baska, J. (1998). Characteristics and needs of talented learners. In J. VanTassel-Baska (Ed.), *Excellence in educating gifted and talented learners* (3rd ed., pp. 173–191). Denver, Co: Love.

VanTassel-Baska, J. (2003a). Content-based curriculum for high-ability learners: An introduction. In J. VanTassel-Baska & C. A. Little (Eds.), *Content-based curriculum for high-ability learners* (pp. 1–24). Waco, TX: Prufrock Press.

VanTassel-Baska, J. (2003b). *Curriculum planning and instructional design for gifted learners.* Denver, CO: Love.

VanTassel-Baska, J. (2005). Gifted programs and services: What are the nonnegotiables? *Theory Into Practice, 44,* 90–97.

VanTassel-Baska, J., Bass, G., Ries, R., Poland, D., & Avery, L. (1998). A national pilot study of science curriculum effectiveness for high ability students. *Gifted Child Quarterly, 42,* 200–211.

VanTassel-Baska, J., Bracken, B. A., Stambaugh, T., & Feng, A. (2007, September). *Findings from Project Clarion.* Presentation to the United States Department of Education Expert Panel, Storrs, CT.

VanTassel-Baska, J., Feng, A. X., Brown, E., Bracken, B., Stambaugh, T., French, H., et al. (2008). A study of differentiated instruction change over 3 years. *Gifted Child Quarterly, 52,* 297–312.

VanTassel-Baska, J., & Little, C. A. (Eds.). (2003). *Content-based curriculum for high ability learners.* Waco, TX: Prufrock Press.

VanTassel-Baska, J., Zuo, L., Avery, L., & Little, C. (2002). A curriculum study of gifted-student learning in the language arts. *Gifted Child Quarterly, 46,* 30–43.

Ward, V. (1961). *Education for the gifted: An axiomatic approach.* Columbus, OH: Charles E. Merrill.

Westberg, K. L., Archambault, F. X., Jr., & Brown, S. W. (1997). A survey of classroom practices with third and fourth grade students in the United States. *Gifted Education International, 12,* 29–33.

Westberg, K. L., Archambault, F. X., Jr., Dobyns, S. M., & Salvin, T. (1993). *An observational study of instructional and curricular practices used with gifted and talented students in regular classrooms* (Research Monograph No. 93104). Storrs: University of Connecticut, The National Research Center on the Gifted and Talented.

Westberg, K. L., & Daoust, M. E. (2003, Fall). The results of the replication of the classroom practices survey replication in two states. *The National Research Center on the Gifted and Talented Newsletter,* 1–8.

CHAPTER 30

THE "WISE FRIEND":

Joyce VanTassel-Baska's Contribution to School Counseling

by

SUSANNAH
M. WOOD

Honoring the affective development of the gifted is integral to a comprehensive balanced curriculum.

—Joyce VanTassel-Baska

Prior studies have indicated that although gifted children, as a group, show mostly positive emotional adjustment, some gifted students may encounter emotional and behavior concerns (Keiley, 2002; Robinson, 2002). Others suggest that the very nature of giftedness may mean that this population is predisposed to certain vulnerabilities based on gifted students' asynchronous development when compared to nongifted peers, gifted students' ability to manage and regulate their emotional responses, and gifted students' membership in groups with special needs (culturally diverse backgrounds, rural populations, GLBTQ, and gifted students with disabilities; Keiley, 2002; Robinson, 2002). Gifted students also encounter concerns and challenges that their nongifted peers experience such as moving, illness, separation, divorce and remarriages within the family, death or loss, peer conflicts, abuse and neglect, and substance abuse (Peterson, 2006). But, their gifted traits and characteristics can make these incidences harder to cope with and cause them to be experienced differently than their nongifted peers (Peterson, 2006).

Hence, there is a need for counseling gifted students around issues that arise along the normal developmental trajectory, but which are compounded by the additional task of being gifted and navigating the traditional developmental milestones of childhood and adolescence from that unique experience (Blackburn & Erickson, 1986; Colangelo, 2003; Peterson, 2006). Counseling has been suggested from the earliest research in gifted education as a primary method of meeting the social-emotional needs of this population in addition to helping the gifted student identify, hone, and nurture his or her special talents and gifts.

Traditionally, the teacher of the gifted child has served as the primary contact for counseling; however, meeting the academic, career, and social-emotional needs of all students in the schools has been the province of the school counselor. The professional school counselor is in a unique position to address the counseling concerns gifted students may have, but little is known about what work actually is being done by school counselors in reference to their gifted students.

The purpose of this chapter is twofold: first, to expand upon the literature regarding school counseling in gifted education, specifically what is known about school counselors and their work with gifted students; and second, to highlight Joyce VanTassel-Baska's many contributions to the research and literature pertaining to school counseling and the gifted.

A HISTORICAL CONTEXT FOR COUNSELING THE GIFTED

The terms counseling and guidance will refer to the processes employed to help gifted students develop as whole persons within the context of the school setting. In that sense, then, both affective and cognitive concerns require the assistance of a "wise friend."

—VanTassel-Baska (1983, p. 2)

Building upon Karen St. Clair's (1989) timeline, in 2006 Assouline and Colangelo provided an updated historical review of the progress in the understanding of and service to social and emotional needs of gifted students. The work of Terman and Hollingworth in the early 1900s highlighted unique social and emotional needs of gifted children that might require attention through counseling.

Although the Terman studies dispelled common myths about gifted children, such as the gifted being puny, weak, and physically ill, they perpetuated others (Colangelo, 2003; Myers & Pace, 1986; Sajjadi, 2000). Specifically, Terman found that gifted children were *more* socially stable than average children, from which arose the myth that gifted children were "all well adjusted and [could] get by without specialized psychological or educational services" (Myers & Pace, 1986, p. 548). However, Hollingworth, in her research at Columbia University, discovered that the social-emotional development of the gifted student was subtly more complex

(Colangelo, 2003; Myers & Pace, 1986). In essence, Hollingworth believed that the gifted child's social-emotional development corresponded directly with the educational environment in which he resided such that, "the greater the gift, the greater the need for what she called 'emotional education'" (Colangelo & Davis, 2003, p. 7). Although the early longitudinal studies were powerful and informative in establishing the learning environment as a critical component in the development of the gifted learner, their opposing findings generated the two conflicting views.

Neihart and Robinson (2001) in the *Task Force on Social-Emotional Issues for Gifted Student* stated the argument succinctly: Either gifted students are just as well adjusted as the average population and that they need no differentiated services for their social-emotional development, or the fact that they are gifted means that these students by their very nature have unique interpersonal and intrapersonal needs from that of the general population (Colangelo, 2003; Grossberg & Cornell, 1988). This conflict continues through research within the field of education, although currently there is no consensus as to whether gifted students have greater or fewer counseling needs than their nongifted peers (Gallagher, 2003; Peterson, 2008; Robinson, 2002). Colangelo (2003, p. 373) and Robinson (2002) suggested a middle view: that most gifted students will experience positive adjustment, but there will be a "sizable minority" that may be at risk for specific kinds of social and emotional challenges and who will require counseling as an interventive factor to meet their needs. Thus, counselors need to be aware of these needs and knowledgeable enough to work with them effectively.

In 1983, Joyce VanTassel-Baska called for school personnel working with the gifted to act as a "wise friend," helping gifted students navigate the challenges faced both in terms of normal development and in relation to their gift. But, what kind of friend and guide do gifted students need?

Traditionally, it has been the teacher who has acted as the wise friend and nurturer of talent for the gifted student because he or she has the appropriate level of training in gifted psychology and education (VanTassel-Baska, 1998). Recently, the school counseling profession has drawn attention to and highlighted the school counselor's involvement with gifted students (Milsom & Peterson, 2006; Peterson, 2006). Professional school counselors are leaders, advocates, and specialists in delivering comprehensive developmental guidance and counseling curricula that provides an array of services and collaborative partnerships and whose effectiveness and impact on both student achievement and school culture can be measured (American School Counselor Association [ASCA], 2003a). The professional school counselor is a key person in the support of individual talent development of gifted students (ASCA, 2003b).

SCHOOL COUNSELORS' ROLES
AND RESPONSIBILITIES

As in so many areas of social need, however, the schools must take responsibility for the total education and guidance of children with whom they are entrusted, including the gifted. To do less is to jeopardize the healthy development of children whose parents cannot afford outside counseling assistance.

—VanTassel-Baska (1990, p. 40)

St. Clair (1989) suggested that the 1960s marked the beginning of counseling the gifted in schools, emphasizing the role of the school counselor, and the 1970s focused on counseling programs. Between the 1970s and 1980s several texts, monographs, and articles were published, designed to help educators and counselors meet the needs of gifted students. One of these was Joyce VanTassel-Baska's 1983 (updated in 1990) edited volume, *A Practical Guide to Counseling the Gifted in a School Setting*.

VanTassel-Baska and authors discussed affective issues, counseling, counseling models, collaboration, and strategies designed to meet the needs of gifted students. She began the text by stipulating that counseling and guidance is necessary for gifted students to fulfill their potential, and that these services should be delivered by personnel and professionals who are aware and knowledgeable of the characteristics and needs of gifted students (1983, pp. 1–2). Although the monograph was designed to "speak" to teachers of the gifted and program coordinators, the volume's voice carried a strong and singular message to school counselors as well: School counselors were not exempt from being aware of issues and needs of the gifted students, knowledgeable of their characteristics and avenues for appropriate learning, or having the skill sets to provide effective services and programs.

This text also elaborated on the many different roles and responsibilities school counselors could assume when working with and serving gifted students. According to VanTassel-Baska (1983), school counselors should be aware of issues pertaining to the gifted, initiate the identification process, act as an advocate and information clearinghouse, provide counseling services, develop programs, and act as a collaborator and partner with parents and educators.

It was not until 1988 that the American School Counselor Association developed a position statement (subsequently revised) on the school counselor's involvement with gifted students. This position statement articulated the roles and responsibilities school counselors can assume in working with the gifted in their building. These roles included the following: (a) identification of gifted students; (b) advocacy for counseling activities which address the academic, career and personal/social needs of the gifted through individual and group guidance; (c) the provision of resources and materials; (d) raising awareness of gifted issues such as those discussed above; and (e) engaging in professional development activities in order to facilitate their continuing education of the psychology and development of gifted students (ASCA, 2003b).

Currently, the American School Counselor Association's National Model (2003a) provides the foundation for school counselors to advocate for all students, including gifted students, and identify systems issues that may impede gifted students' academic, personal/social, or career development, and gives the school counselor the vocabulary and professional stance that lends itself naturally to leadership positions that can promote changes that benefit gifted students in their schools. However, to begin, school counselors must be familiar not only with gifted students' unique characteristics, development, and learning needs, but also be aware of their own beliefs pertaining to gifted students and their education.

TRENDS IN TRAINING AND RESEARCH

One reason counseling tends to be ignored in the education of the gifted is the lack of trained personnel who feel they are adequately prepared to counsel gifted children. Trained counselors are in short supply in most educational institutions. . . . In addition, few counselors have been trained in the special characteristics and needs of the gifted population, and therefore may not perceive the necessity of providing special services to this group. All of these reasons obviate against the likelihood that gifted students will receive appropriate counseling intervention from counseling specialists in schools.

—VanTassel-Baska and Baska (1993)

Written more than 15 years ago, VanTassel-Baska offered an astute observation and an urgent warning. School counselors need to have adequate training in the needs and nature of gifted students. Currently, few school counselors receive more than one 2-hour class period in understanding gifted students. In fact, Peterson and Wachter (in press) found that, of the school counseling training programs participating in their study that were accredited by the Council for Accreditation of Counseling and Related Educational Programs (CACREP), only 62% included counseling issues pertaining to students of high ability or gifted learners, and 47% dedicated 3 or fewer contact hours with those populations.

What few studies in the literature do exist pertaining to school counselors and the gifted, focus on school counselors' attitudes, knowledge, and skills regarding gifted students have reported that school counselors' preparation, perceptions, experience, and training all impact their service to gifted students. First, although school counselors may feel that they are more effective when differentiating their counseling in terms of pace, depth, novelty, and complexity to match their gifted students' developmental level, they also may feel ill prepared to meet the needs of these students (Earle, 1998). Second, although school counselors with more years of experience are more likely to report that they have more knowledge about gifted students via in-service workshops, high school counselors have the least amount of involvement with these students (Carlson, 2004). However, school counselors who have a gifted program or a gifted specialist in their building are more likely to be knowledgeable about gifted and talented students and more involved with them (Carlson, 2004). Third, in general, perceptions of and knowledge about gifted students, including identification knowledge, can be linked to school counselors' involvement with gifted students in areas of advocacy (Carlson, 2004). School counselors in specialized high schools for the gifted do not necessarily perceive that their gifted students are any different from any other adolescents and thus believe they are not in need of differentiated counseling (Dockery, 2005).

Anecdotal evidence supports the idea that gifted teens believe that school counselors are available and appropriate for others, but not for them as a gifted students (Peterson, 2003). These findings suggest that school counselors then may encounter difficulties in serving gifted students if they do not feel they have the adequate knowledge or skills (Peterson, 2006). Silverman (1993) argued that a prepared and effective counselor of the gifted needed to have a repertoire of counseling skills interwoven with the understanding of the characteristics and needs of the gifted students. Her suggestion of counselor knowledge and skill when working with gifted students resonates with what is known as the knowledge, skills, and awareness approach to multicultural counseling (Pederson, 1994), a paradigm of counseling with which counselors should be familiar with from their master's-level training. This paradigm has three unique aspects: awareness, knowledge, and skills.

First, Pederson (1994) advocated for counselor examination of personal biases, stereotypes, and faulty assumptions and the development of personal awareness related to sociopolitical issues that challenge culturally different clients. Second, counselors require information about culturally different groups including demographic information, social and historical experiences of oppressed groups, and educational and cultural values. Last, counselors should be able to integrate their developing awareness with the newly gained knowledge into effective and ethical counseling skills when working with diverse client populations.

Levy and Plucker (2008) apply this paradigm for counselors working with the gifted student. The authors write that:

> As a school counselor, one must realize that by entering into a counseling relationship with a client, one has essentially become a potentially significant part of the client's environment. Thus, in working with gifted and talented clients, it is crucial for counselors to develop an awareness of their assumptions, values, biases, and beliefs about giftedness and the gifted in general, as well as their assumptions about giftedness in culturally diverse children. (p. 8)

Levy and Plucker (2008) suggest that counselors should gain awareness of their attitudes toward gifted and talented children, note the similarities and differences between gifted students, and acknowledge their need for referral, supervision, and consultation when working with them. However, awareness of gifted concerns and issues and knowledge about gifted psychology and talent development are not required in most school counseling preparation programs (Moon, 2002). School counselors and other school personnel may not have considered reflecting upon and examining their beliefs about gifted students nor may have a starting place in which to do so.

Cross (2002) and Delisle and Galbraith (2002) offer several myths, assumptions, and stereotypical beliefs that can impact the thinking of counselors who work with the gifted. Additional basic beliefs stem from VanTassel-Baska's work. Although the following assumptions were originally offered by VanTassel-Baska (2004) in her chapter discussing curricular diversity and the gifted student as a rationale for providing a specialized curricula for the gifted, these assumptions could be used as statements to be reflected upon when school counselors and other personnel wish to examine their thinking as it pertains to providing counseling services or affective curricula to the gifted. A few key assumptions (VanTassel-Baska, 2004) include the following: (1) all children can learn, but in different ways at different times in different contexts; (2) some children learn more quickly than others; (3) gifted children differ from each other as to what curricular areas they find easy to learn and therefore the rate at which they can learn them; and (4) gifted students also vary considerably amongst themselves.

Without wise friends who are aware of their own beliefs, understand the special needs and challenges gifted students face, as well as their amazing talent and future contributions, society stands to lose countless bright minds and remarkable talent. But, discrete skill sets and roles and responsibilities are not the most advantageous assemblage of services. What is truly necessary is the collaborative development of a counseling curriculum.

School Counselors and Affective Curriculum

Addressing affective issues should be a major way to reach gifted adolescents, help them create meaning in their lives, relieve their anxieties about being gifted, and contribute to the development of strong peer networks for them. What could be more important . . .?

—VanTassel-Baska (2006, pp. 500–501)

Joyce VanTassel-Baska has been a persistent, unshakable, and influential force behind the development, implementation, and evaluation of appropriate curriculum for gifted learners. Beginning in the 1980s and continuing to the present, VanTassel-Baska has contributed an enormous amount of wisdom and guidance to field of gifted education with regard to curriculum development. For this wise friend to educators and school counselors, appropriate curriculum for gifted learners always incorporates a social-emotional (1993), counseling (1998), or affective (2006) element.

In her latest contributions, VanTassel-Baska (2006; VanTassel-Baska & Stambaugh, 2006) addressed the development of a preventive affective curriculum for gifted students. She begins by providing a powerful series of points to structure a rationale based on the known characteristics and needs of gifted students including the cognitive characteristics, asynchronous development, students' rapid learning rate and complex thought processes that may cause disequilibrium in social contexts, and other characteristics that may lead to possible vulnerabilities during the talent development process (VanTassel-Baska & Stambaugh, 2006). A rigorous affective curriculum needs to be deliberate, planned, preventive, and developmental. In addition, clear linkages need to be drawn between the cognitive and the emotional arenas in both skill sets and product.

Built on the Integrated Curriculum Model (ICM), affective curricula need to be challenging and involve both higher order thinking and problem solving, as well as an emphasis on abstract concepts, issues, and problems. These areas combine to produce a curricula that addresses developing affective skill sets, decision-making and critical thinking, affective regulation, and identity exploration. ICM as it is applied to an affective curricula "begins with being able to perceive, appraise, and express emotion in a variety of contexts, then moves to using emotions to facilitate thinking and on to applying emotional knowledge. The last component of the framework emphasizes the regulation of emotion" (VanTassel-Baska, 2006, p. 486). Her suggested strategies included writing about emotions; Socratic seminars; shared inquiry using the literature/arts web; self-assessment; developing a talent development plan and philosophy of life; understanding; analyzing and employing emotional knowledge; bibliotherapy; and problem-based learning. An additional and vital piece is the role of academic planning within the delivery of the curriculum.

VanTassel-Baska (1993, 1998) suggested that academic planning is vital piece in the development of gifted students and addresses not only issues of scheduling, personalized education, and the assurance of necessary challenge and rigor in coursework, but also facilities student exploration of careers and lends itself to individual counseling. VanTassel-Baska (1993, 1998) recommended the use of academic "blueprints" that allow students plan a flexible program of study reflecting their abilities and interests and which aids in the provision of a individualized educational plan. The concept of flexible academic planning was a practical and useful contribution to both gifted education and counseling. Instead of conceptualizing 4-year plans for high school as finite and set in stone, VanTassel-Baska challenged counselors and teachers to see planning as way of exploring resource options and student choice in order to match the student with classes to create an optimum balance of support and rigor.

Although many school counselors have backgrounds in teaching and education, some may not know how to develop programs or curricula for gifted students. School counselors can easily apply VanTassel-Baska's suggestions and strategies when developing curricula for gifted students specifically or differentiating an already developed curriculum. Or, they may opt to partner with educators and coordinators of the gifted to either develop affective curricula or to collaborate on activities and strategies for individual or groups of gifted students.

BUILDING POWERFUL PARTNERSHIPS

Modifying and adapting current practice is always easier than instituting a new job. Thus teachers and counselors can cooperatively structure new opportunities for affective growth of gifted students, secure in the knowledge that such a program can be implemented without major trauma.

—VanTassel-Baska (1990, p. 52)

Educators of the gifted have the skills and resources to provide interventive skills and techniques such as modeling, bibliotherapy, discussion groups, special projects, career exploration, tutorials, and role-playing that can be facilitated inside the classroom (VanTassel-Baska & Baska, 1993). The teacher also is in the position to act as an advocate for gifted students' needs within the school environment, an "assurance" to parents who might be confused about how best to help their child, an active listener, and an informal advisor on a variety of topics because the teacher knows the gifted student (VanTassel-Baska & Baska, 1993).

School counselors, however, are responsible for assisting all students in the buildings they are placed and are trained to provide consultative and collaborative services toward that end. School counselors must contend with establishing a results-based school counseling program that facilitates the achievement of all students and encompasses services to all students, their parents, the school building, and community (ASCA, 2003a). Counselors also are largely responsible for delivering the traditional individual counseling and planning, small-group counseling, and classroom guidance units, as well as a plethora of noncounseling related duties. School counselors understand the need for consulting with other educators and professionals and are trained to do so through their counselor preparation programs (ASCA, 2003a). Their training also allows counselors to be specialists in human relationships, a broker of resources and services, and a promoter of both positive student outcomes and team building (Allen, 1994, as cited in Murphy, DeEsch, & Strein, 1998)

Both the counselor and educator can encounter pressure to meet a diverse group of needs from their consumers, and with limited resources. Some schools may not able to provide comprehensive programs and services for gifted students specifically (Hobbs & Collison, 1995), especially if it means risking cutting resources for other student groups. Hence, there is an increased need for collaborative efforts in order to serve diverse student groups with diverse needs (Hobbs & Collison, 1995). From their given expertise and shared stakeholder group, that of gifted students and their families, it would seem reasonable to assume that these educators would work effectively together to serve this population and in so doing offer greater wrap-around services and decrease frustration, overwhelming feelings of responsibility, and stress. However, this seems not to be the case. In fact, very little is known about how these two groups work collegially on behalf of gifted students.

In the updated 1990 version of a *Practical Guide* text, VanTassel-Baska highlighted the need for school counselors and teachers to work together. In fact in her chapter "Collaboration of Teachers and Counselors," she provided a table that articulated strategies school counselors and teachers could implement together to match an array of gifted social and emotional needs. In a chapter on academic counseling, VanTassel-Baska (1993) revisited this issue of partnerships and expanded on additional roles and activities such as the provision of mentorships, internships, seminars, field trips, and annual academic planning conferences. Both the 1990 and 1993 contributions discussed the necessary training and skill sets school counselors needed to have to work with the gifted such as basic counseling techniques; knowledge of psychopathology; and student development, program development, and test interpretation. The logical conclusion was that these skills would compliment those of the teacher of the gifted who would be knowledgeable about the nature and cognitive and affective needs of the gifted. Together, these educators could partner to provide wrap-around guidance and counseling services for gifted students that included the provision of mentorships and internships; teaching decision-making and metacognition, and test-taking skills; and facilitating individual's plans of study.

Collaborative work between gifted educators and school counselors would appear to be both beneficial and effective; however, there is little research to support how, if at all, these two professionals form relationships to serve the group they most have in common, that is, gifted students and their families. Effective services can be increased to this population if the fields of gifted education and school counseling had a better understanding of what a positive, effective, and collaborative relationship between these professional groups might look like.

Conclusions

In 1996, Joyce VanTassel-Baska contributed a rather remarkable chapter on the talent development of Charlotte Brontë and Virginia Woolf. In it, she wrote that these influential authors ". . . used the solitary pursuit of writing as a way to create meaning and make sense of their lives, thus bringing their talent to its optimal development" (VanTassel-Baska, 1996, p. 312). Gifted students need not feel isolated or solitary as they pursue their own gifts and dreams. The professional school counselor, through his or her awareness of gifted needs, knowledge of gifted psychology, and development in the academic, career, and personal/social arenas, can skillfully provide the programs and services the gifted student needs. However, much more needs to be done. Much more research in the areas of school counseling and gifted education is needed.

Current training methods need to be assessed and the effectiveness of master's-level training of counselors and professional development opportunities pertaining to gifted students needs to be investigated. Qualitative work should be conducted to examine more closely counselor beliefs, their work with gifted students and their parents, as well as the gifted students' perspectives of the same counseling work. Last, both gifted education and school counseling are in dire need of longitudinal research documenting student counseling needs and counseling services over time.

Joyce VanTassel-Baska has initiated a long and loving call for support of gifted students through intentional academic planning, the development of affective curricula, and collaborative partnerships between school counselors and gifted educators. Bridging the two fields, Joyce VanTassel-Baska (1990, p. 2) has urged the wise friends of gifted students to present students with "opportunities for informed choice in all aspects of their lives [which is] at the crux of the conception of counseling and guidance."

REFERENCES

American School Counselor Association. (2003a). *The ASCA National Model: A framework for school counseling programs*. Fairfax, VA: Author.

American School Counselor Association. (2003b). *Position statement: Gifted programs*. Retrieved from http://www.schoolcounselor.org/content.asp?contentid=209

Assouline, S. G., & Colangelo, N. (2006). Social-emotional development of gifted adolescents. In F. A. Dixon & S. M. Moon (Eds.), *The handbook of secondary gifted education* (pp. 65–85). Waco, TX: Prufrock Press.

Blackburn, A. C., & Erickson, D. B. (1986). Predictable crises of the gifted student. *Journal of Counseling and Development, 64,* 556–557.

Carlson, N. (2004). School counselors' knowledge, perceptions, and involvement concerning gifted and talented students. (Doctoral dissertation, University of Maryland College Park, 2004). ProQuest Dissertation and Theses: AAT3128875.

Colangelo, N. (2003). Counseling gifted students. In N. Colangelo & G. A. Davis (Eds.), *The handbook of gifted education* (3rd ed., pp. 373–387). Boston: Allyn & Bacon.

Colangelo, N., & Davis, G. (2003). Introduction and overview. In N. Colangelo & G. A. Davis (Eds.), *Handbook of gifted education* (3rd ed., pp. 3–10). Boston: Allyn & Bacon.

Cross, T. (2002). Competing myths about the social and emotional development of gifted students. *Gifted Child Today, 25*(3), 44–48.

Delisle, J., & Galbraith, J. (2002). *When gifted kids don't have all the answers: How to meet their social and emotional needs*. Minneapolis, MN: Free Spirit.

Dockery, D. J. (2005). *Ways in which counseling programs at specialized high schools respond to social and emotional needs of gifted adolescents* (Doctoral dissertation, University of Virginia, 2004). ProQuest Dissertations and Theses: AAT3161256.

Earle, S. (1998). *A critical incident study of the school guidance counselor's interactions with gifted students*. (Doctoral dissertation, Kent State University, 1999). ProQuest Dissertation and Theses: AAT9842490.

Gallagher, J. (2003). Issues and challenges in the education of gifted students. In N. Colangelo & G. A. Davis (Eds.), *Handbook of gifted education* (3rd ed., pp. 11–23). Boston: Allyn & Bacon.

Grossberg, I. N., & Cornell, D. G. (1988). Relationship between personality adjustment and high intelligence: Terman versus Hollingworth. *Exceptional Children, 55,* 266–272.

Hobbs, B. B., & Collison, B. B. (1995). School-community agency collaboration: Implications for the school counselor. *School Counselor, 43*(1), 58–64.

Keiley, M. K. (2002). Affect regulation and the gifted. In M. Neihart, S. M. Reis, N. M. Robinson, & S. M. Moon (Eds.), *The social and emotional development of gifted children: What do we know?* (pp. 41–50). Waco, TX: Prufrock Press.

Levy, J. L., & Plucker, J. A. (2008). A multicultural competence model for counseling gifted and talented children. *Journal of School Counseling, 6*(4). Retrieved from http://www.jsc.montana.edu/articles/v6n4.pdf

Milsom, A., & Peterson, J. (2006). Introduction to special issue: Examining disability and giftedness in schools. *Professional School Counseling, 10*(1), 1–2.

Moon, S. M. (2002). Counseling needs and strategies. In M. Neihart, S. M. Reis, N. M. Robinson, & S. M. Moon (Eds.), *The social and emotional development of gifted children: What do we know?* (pp. 213–222). Waco, TX: Prufrock Press.

Murphy, J. P., DeEsch, J. B., & Strein, W. O. (1998). School counselors and school psychologists: Partners in student services. *Professional School Counseling, 2*(2), 85–88.

Myers, R. S., & Pace, T. M. (1986). Counseling gifted and talented students: Historical perspectives and contemporary issues. *Journal of Counseling and Development, 64,* 556–557.

Neihart, M., & Robinson, N. M. (2001). *Task force on social-emotional issues for gifted students.* Washington, DC: National Association for Gifted Children.

Pederson, P. (1994). *A handbook for developing multicultural awareness* (2nd ed.). Alexandria, Virginia: American Counseling Association.

Peterson, J. S. (2003). An argument for proactive attention to affective concerns of gifted adolescents. *Journal of Secondary Gifted Education, 14,* 62–70.

Peterson, J. S. (2006). Addressing counseling needs of gifted students. *Professional School Counseling, 10*(1), 43–51.

Peterson, J. S. (2008). Counseling. In C. M. Callahan & J. A. Plucker (Eds.), *Critical issues and practices in gifted education: What the research says* (pp. 119–138) Waco, TX: Prufrock Press.

Peterson, J. S., & Wachter, C. A. (in press). Understanding and responding to concerns related to giftedness: A study of CACREP-accredited programs. *Journal for the Education of the Gifted.*

Robinson, N. M. (2002). Introduction. In M. Neihart, S. M. Reis, N. M. Robinson, & S. M. Moon (Eds.), *The social and emotional development of gifted children: What do we know?* (pp. xi–xxiv). Waco, TX: Prufrock Press.

Sajjadi, S. H. (2000). Counseling gifted students: Past research, future directions. *Gifted Education International, 15,* 111–121.

Silverman, L. (1993). Techniques for preventive counseling. In L. Silverman (Ed.), *Counseling the gifted and talented* (pp. 81–100). Denver, CO: Love.

St. Clair, K. (1989). Counseling gifted students: A historical review. *Roeper Review, 12,* 98–102.

VanTassel-Baska, J. (1983). Introduction. In J. VanTassel-Baska (Ed.), *A practical guide to counseling the gifted in a school setting* (pp. 1–5). Reston, VA: Council for Exceptional Children.

VanTassel-Baska, J. (Ed.). (1990). *A practical guide to counseling the gifted in a school setting.* Reston, VA: Council for Exceptional Children.

VanTassel-Baska, J. (1993). Academic counseling for the gifted. In L. Silverman (Ed.), *Counseling the gifted and talented* (pp. 201–214). Denver, CO: Love.

VanTassel-Baska, J. (1996). The talent development process in women writers: A study of Charlotte Brontë and Virginia Woolf. In K. D. Arnold, K. D. Noble, & R. F. Subotnik (Eds.), *Remarkable women: Perspectives on female talent development* (pp. 295–316). Cresskill, NJ: Hampton Press.

VanTassel-Baska, J. (1998). Counseling talented learners. In J. VanTassel-Baska (Ed.), *Excellence in educating gifted and talented learners* (pp. 489–509). Denver, CO: Love.

VanTassel-Baska, J. (2004). Curricular diversity and the gifted. In D. Boothe & J. C. Stanley (Eds.), *In the eyes of the beholder: Critical issues for diversity in gifted education* (pp. 167–178). Waco, TX: Prufrock Press.

VanTassel-Baska, J. (2006). Secondary affective curriculum and instruction for gifted learners. In F. A. Dixon & S. M. Moon (Eds.), *The handbook of secondary gifted education* (pp. 481–503). Waco, TX: Prufrock Press.

VanTassel-Baska, J., & Baska, L. (1993). The roles of educational personnel in counseling the gifted. In L. Silverman (Ed.), *Counseling the gifted and talented.* (pp. 181–200). Denver, CO: Love.

VanTassel-Baska, J., & Stambaugh, T. (2006). Affective curriculum and instruction for gifted learners. In J. VanTassel-Baska & T. Stambaugh (Eds.), *Comprehensive curriculum for gifted learners* (3rd ed., pp. 211–226). Boston: Allyn & Bacon.

CHAPTER 31

THE IMPACT OF JOYCE VANTASSEL-BASKA'S WORK ON NATIONAL TEACHER EDUCATION STANDARDS

by

SUSAN
K. JOHNSEN

AND

MARGIE
K. KITANO

Program standards in gifted education are a necessary feature of ensuring that the highly able learners in our society are adequately identified and nurtured in the context of school settings.
—Joyce VanTassel-Baska (2006)

INTRODUCTION AND HISTORY

Joyce VanTassel-Baska's work has had a long-lasting impact on establishing national teacher standards that ultimately affect the quality of teachers in gifted education. This chapter will highlight her work in the standards-setting process and her spirit of determination that brought two national organizations together. We identify themes and trends based on her collaborative leadership and the standards themselves as well as issues whose resolution will move the field forward.

Purpose and History of Standards

Teacher education standards are a set of requirements that offer many advantages to professionals in gifted education. First and foremost, they define the essential knowledge (e.g., research, inquiry, theory, wisdom of practice) and skills (i.e., use of the knowledge) that teachers need to know to be effective in teaching gifted and talented students in diverse classroom settings (National Council for Accreditation of Teacher Education [NCATE], 2008). Second, they help in gaining consensus among educators who prepare future teachers and who provide professional development for in-service teachers. This consistency ensures educational quality across school districts and educational institutions so that equal access to talent searches and programming is available for each gifted and talented student. Third, they offer a coherent structure that allows professionals to commit to common values and rules. This structure presents a model that educators may use for improving their professional competencies. Fourth, they provide a curriculum template for the design of teacher education courses, professional development workshops, and other resources that have the potential for improving teaching and ultimately deepening learning for gifted and talented students. Fifth, the standards give educators benchmarks for providing pre-K–12 students and candidates in higher education with meaningful outcomes to work toward, criteria for selecting problems and finding solutions, and a focus and direction for new research efforts. Finally, they legitimize gifted education not only in the area of teacher preparation but also as a separate field of study at the higher education level that is based on a strong foundation of research (Darling-Hammond, Wise, & Klein, 1999; Johnsen, VanTassel-Baska, & Robinson, 2008; Kitano, Montgomery, VanTassel-Baska, & Johnsen, 2008; VanTassel-Baska, 2004).

Because of the importance of standards, they have been a part of the educational landscape for almost a century. The standards movement can be traced to 1922 when the International Council for the Education of Exceptional Children (now the Council for Exceptional Children [CEC]) declared the establishment of professional standards as a fundamental aim (CEC, 2003). In 1927, the American Association of Teachers Colleges was organized to develop standards and accreditation procedures to ensure that graduates of accredited programs could teach (Kraft, 2001). In 1955, the National Council for Accreditation of Teacher Education (NCATE) was founded as an affiliation of professional and public organizations (Kitano, 2008). NCATE now accredits more than 650 colleges of education that meet national standards, has affiliations with 33 member organizations, and has partnerships with all 50 states.

The Challenge in Gifted Education

Interest in establishing standards in gifted education can be traced to the early 1980s (Robinson & Kolloff, 2006). The standard development efforts of the Council for Exceptional Children's The Association for the Gifted (CEC-TAG) and the National Association for Gifted Children (NAGC) paralleled one another (Kitano, 2008). During the 1980s, NAGC held Professional Training Institutes and created a Professional Development Division, which resulted in the NAGC Standards for Graduate Programs in Gifted Education that were published ultimately in *Gifted Child Quarterly* (Parker, 1996). NAGC also developed and adopted the PreK–Grade 12 Gifted Program Standards in 1998 to assist school districts in developing higher quality programs. During the same time period, CEC formed a partnership with NCATE with each Division, including TAG, developing standards for its particular field within a common core of 10 overarching standards. Using this framework, TAG established NCATE standards in 1989 to encourage higher quality of the growing number of programs in gifted education.

Although these efforts focused the field's attention toward the importance of standards, the two national organizations (e.g., NAGC and CEC-TAG) were not in agreement as to the quality and number of indicators. In 2002, there were 137 knowledge and skill statements for preparation of teachers in gifted education that served as NCATE's national standards for university programs that prepare teachers of the gifted. Professional criticisms of the standards related to the (a) special education tone of the language, which didn't reflect the field of gifted education, (b) limited involvement of one of the national organizations, (c) lack of relevance to practice in the field, and (d) limited research support. Joint committee work between the two national organizations over a 10-year period had led to growing frustration and even consideration of the development of two different sets of standards (e.g., NAGC joined NCATE as an affiliate in the fall of 2002).

The Emergence of a Shared Vision

In April of 2003, CEC's Professional Standards and Practices Standing Committee and Knowledge and Skills Subcommittee asked each of their divisions to revalidate their specific field's standards using newly developed research guidelines. The Association for the Gifted agreed to complete the revalidation of their standards by 2006, using the following eight-step process established by CEC (2003):

- *Step 1.* The Professional Standards and Practices Standing Committee (PSPSC) determines knowledge and skill sets that need to be developed and/or revalidated and identifies a set group facilitator (SF) to guide the process.
- *Step 2.* The Knowledge and Skills Subcommittee (KSS) Chair and the set group facilitator establish a small work group.
- *Step 3.* The work group identifies possible items for validation, documents the professional literature that supports each proposed knowledge and skill statement, summarizes the literature base, formats the items, and submits this information to the KSS.
- *Step 4.* The KSS reviews the work of the group to ensure readiness of the standards for survey.
- *Step 5.* The Professional Standards and Practices Unit conducts the survey of members using a targeted stratified random sample and submits the results to the KSS Chair and the set group facilitator.
- *Step 6.* A select group of experts, selected by the PSPSC Chair in consultation with the set group facilitator, reviews the standards and the survey data.
- *Step 7.* The KSS reviews and approves the revalidated or validated set of Knowledge and Skills.

▸ *Step 8.* The PSPSC oversees the process, makes a determination regarding the KSS recommendations, and submits its decision to the CEC Board of Directors.

This revalidation process opened a new opportunity for collaboration between the two national gifted associations. Stepping toward this challenge was NAGC's new president-elect, Joyce VanTassel-Baska. By fall of 2003, after a joint meeting with CEC-TAG and NAGC leadership, the standards revalidation work group was formed and ready to move forward. Susan Johnsen, Margie Kitano, and Diane Montgomery represented CEC-TAG, and Rick Olenchak, Karen Rogers, and Joyce VanTassel-Baska represented NAGC.

The first meeting to examine the NCATE standards in gifted education was held in the spring of 2004 at CEC's annual meeting in New Orleans. Stakeholders representing diverse cultural and geographic backgrounds and a variety of roles (e.g., administrators, teachers, higher education faculty, state education agency gifted education directors) attended this meeting to review the current standards and their relevance to practice in the field, their appropriateness of vocabulary for gifted educators, and their research support. Joyce made an impressive presentation that (a) outlined the purpose for the collaboration, (b) the realities of teacher preparation in gifted education, (c) resources available for the development of the standards, (d) major components of a conceptual framework in gifted education, (e) initial teacher competencies, (f) advanced teacher competencies, (g) field experiences, and (h) issues in creating standards for gifted and talented education. By the end of the day, the higher education work group, emboldened by Joyce's presentation, had reduced the 67 knowledge statements to 32, and the 70 skills statements to 38. This reduction in the number of standards did not eliminate any of the 10 CEC Content Standards, but removed redundancies, combined similar standards, and added standards that were specific to the field of gifted education. Moreover, the standards explicitly addressed diversity. Given the continuing and significant underrepresentation of specific groups receiving educational services for the gifted and talented, it was critical that the standards stress the preparation of teachers who support the learning of all gifted students and not privilege some groups over others (The Association for the Gifted, 2001).

To update other higher education institutions, Joyce reinstituted the University Network and called a May meeting in Washington, DC, to review a synthesis of the New Orleans work. Along with Arthur Wise, President of NCATE, members of both organizations presented. Separate work groups were formed to review the revised draft of the initial standards, the scope and sequence, and the conceptual framework. The momentum garnered at this meeting moved the standards discussion forward. By the end of the fall of 2004, NAGC had sent a survey to all higher education faculty to review a draft of the initial standards, the joint work group had revised the standards, and both the CEC-TAG and the NAGC Boards had approved the new initial set of standards. Given the previous impasse, this *one-year* development span and approval process was unprecedented. An obvious, important factor was Joyce's outstanding leadership.

Empirical Literature

Following the approval of the standards, the work group began the critical task of identifying the underlying research base for each knowledge and skill indicator within the 10 content standards. CEC's Knowledge and Skills Subcommittee (2003) had organized research into three categories:

1. *Literature/Theory-Based.* Knowledge or skills that are based on theories or philosophical reasoning. They include knowledge and skills derived from sources such as position papers, policy analyses, and descriptive reviews of the literature.

2. *Research-Based.* Knowledge or skills that are based on peer-reviewed studies that use appropriate research methodologies to address questions of cause and effect, and that researchers have independently replicated and found to be effective.

3. *Practice-Based.* Knowledge and skills that are derived from a number of sources. Decisions based on a small number of studies or nomination procedures, such as promising practices, are usually practice-based. Practice-based knowledge or skills also include those derived primarily from model and lighthouse programs. Practice-based knowledge and skills include professional wisdom. These practices have been used so widely with practical evidence of effectiveness that there is an implicit professional assumption that the practice is effective. Practice-based knowledge and skills also include "emerging practice," practices that arise from teachers' classroom experiences validated through some degree of action research.

Joyce immediately involved the University Network at the NAGC's 2004 conference in Salt Lake City, UT, instituting an annual meeting of Institutions of Higher Education. Using Karen Rogers' literature review, the institutions of higher education were allowed to make additions and deletions to the initial compilation of research that was aligned to each standard. The work group then divided the standards among themselves to review the suggested research literature and develop an annotation for each reference. As usual, Joyce assumed responsibility for the majority of the standards. By the next meeting at CEC's 2005 annual conference in Baltimore, MD, the work group was able to review more than 250 pages of annotations that were aligned with each of the 10 content standards. Joyce encouraged the delineation of the following criteria to be used in identifying the inclusion of specific research studies in a final draft:

1. Works published in the last 10 years would be cited with the exception of seminal works and research for Standard 1, which requires the inclusion of the historical research literature.

2. References would be made to major texts on gifted education, including individual chapters, where appropriate.
3. References would be used if they appeared suitable for a course in gifted education or as a source for the Praxis or a state licensure test.
4. No doctoral dissertations, professional position papers, or presentations at professional meetings would be used.
5. No references would be used more than twice among the subsections of a single standard.
6. Citations would address the key aspects of each knowledge and skill standard.
7. The annotation would be limited to 50–100 words and include research questions, sample, instrumentation, method, and findings.
8. Annotations would be cited if obtained from the ERIC database, a journal, or the author.

Using these criteria, the work group reviewed all of the drafts of the evidence-based reports, ultimately winnowing the number to around 400 by the end of the 2005 summer. At NAGC's 2005 annual meeting in Louisville, KY, the work group distributed CDs to the University Network with a draft of the initial standards and research validation. Joyce also made sure that special sessions were available to present the new standards to different constituency groups (e.g., universities, coordinators of gifted programs, teachers). The presenters represented both of the national organizations and honored the work group's efforts.

Final Steps

The initial standards in gifted education were now ready to complete the final steps in CEC's validation process. They were reviewed by CEC's Knowledge and Skills Subcommittee in January 2006 for format and overlaps. They then were sent to a sample of individuals that included all individuals who had been previously involved and a stratified random sample of individuals from administrator and teachers positions from NAGC and CEC-TAG memberships who rated each of the initial standards as "essential," "desirable but not essential," and "other." After the results were reviewed by the work group and the KSS at CEC's 2006 annual meeting in Salt Lake City, UT, one standard was omitted, which left 70 standards in the final document. These ultimately were approved by CEC's PSPSC. The two national associations now had a common set of standards!

We did have one last hurdle—approval of the standards by NCATE. Joyce and Susan Johnsen presented the standards to NCATE's Specialty Areas Studies Board in the fall of 2006 for final approval. They were approved with commendations regarding the research base and the collaboration between the two national associations. Universities would now be able to use them for accreditation.

Dissemination

However, this success was not sufficient for Joyce. She wanted to make sure that the standards were disseminated. She reconvened the University Network following the April 2006 meeting to share the final standards and the status of using them for accreditation. She then arranged a meeting with the leadership of both national organizations, which included presidents, past presidents, president-elects, executive directors, and political advocates to develop a 3-year action plan that included the dissemination of the standards. Finally, she reconvened the work group during the summer to outline and develop two guidebooks—one for universities and one for school districts—that could be used in implementing the standards. The guidebooks were subsequently published in April 2008 and launched at CEC's annual convention in Boston, MA.

Throughout the standard-setting process, Joyce provided leadership for developing a set of initial standards, establishing a strong research base, involving all constituency groups, disseminating the standards, developing a long-range plan, and ending a 10-year impasse between the national organizations in gifted education. Professionals in gifted education now had a set of research-based standards that distinguished them from other professional educators and from laypersons.

Implications of the Standards

Joyce's leadership and collaborative process in developing and disseminating the new standards for preparing teachers of gifted and talented students will have long-range influence. Recent reviews of research on teacher preparation (Robinson, Shore, & Enersen, 2007; Starko, 2008) acknowledge the importance of the standards for pre- and in-service teacher development. The national standards establish themes and identify new directions that have promise for improving the lives of all children and youth who are gifted and talented. The standards also raise issues whose resolution will further advance work in the field.

Major Themes

The teacher preparation standards have a documented research and literature base derived from gifted education and cognitive psychology. In addition, the standards reflect several themes consciously considered by the work group but not necessarily explicit in the standards themselves. Some of these themes derive from Kraft's (2001) critical analysis of standards for preparation of general education teachers. Kraft identified a number of criteria by which standards might be assessed:

- ► Do the standards endorse the status quo or support reform?
- ► Are they superficial or substantive?
- ► Are they piecemeal or systematic?
- ► Are they biased or inclusive in their assumptions, definition of good teaching, development, and outcomes? Do they privilege some groups?

- ▶ Do they encourage/invite individuals of color to the field?
- ▶ Are they realistic for a range of contexts?
- ▶ Are they viewed as a means to an end rather than as end in themselves?

The standards support reform in school programs and teacher development by identifying research-supported knowledge and skills not necessarily widespread in gifted education practice today. For example, Standard 6, Language and Communication, requires that educators "match their communication methods to an individual's language proficiency and cultural and linguistic differences" and "use communication strategies and resources to facilitate understanding of subject matter for individuals with gifts and talents who are English language learners." Preparing teachers of the gifted to work effectively with gifted students who have primary languages other than English should improve identification and services to this unique group whose members currently are underrepresented and underserved. As noted above, field review of the draft standards eliminated only one item, also in Standard 6: Promote multilingualism among individuals with gifts and talents. The intent of including this skill had been to reframe the bilingual potential of gifted English learners as a strength and encourage bilingual and multilingual competence for all gifted students in a global society.

The new standards also emphasize educators' use of information and assistive technologies to meet exceptional learning (4S7) and communication (6S2) needs, support instructional planning and individualized instruction (7), and evaluate learning (8S4). Inclusion of knowledge and skills in new areas for gifted education has the potential to support positive changes in teacher preparation and school services.

The standards are substantive and systematic in emphasizing integrated approaches to differentiation. For example, the standards cohesively support iterative diagnostic-prescriptive assessment, requiring preassessment, planning based on resulting data, implementing the planned instruction, and evaluating progress:

- ▶ Standard 4, Instructional Strategies (Skill 4): Pre-assess learning needs in various domains and adjust instruction based on continual assessment.
- ▶ Standard 7, Instructional Planning: Learning plans are modified based on ongoing assessment of the individual's progress.
- ▶ Standard 8, Assessment (Skill 3): Develop differentiated curriculum-based assessments for use in instructional planning and delivery.

The standards comprehensively address diversity in recognition of needs for more inclusive identification, more effective instruction, and increased numbers of teachers of color in gifted education. Of the 32 knowledge and 38 skill standards, 27 explicitly address diversity (VanTassel-Baska & Johnsen, 2007).

To assure meaningfulness and utility across contexts, development and vetting of the current standards involved participation of two national organizations, pre-K–12 professionals, state directors, university teacher preparation faculty, and researchers. NCATE will use the standards in accrediting higher education preparation programs. Yet the standards have clear, and perhaps, greater applicability to pre-K–12 contexts, where education of gifted students takes place. The standards identify what the field agrees entry-level teachers of the gifted should know and be able to do and can inform hiring, selection, and professional development decisions.

During their development, refinement, and adoption, Joyce led the joint task force in envisioning national standards as a means, and not as an end in themselves. The standards serve as a systemic strategy for advancing differentiation in serving gifted and talented students and ultimately influencing student outcomes. As noted in the introductory quote, Joyce described standards as "ensuring that the highly able learners in our society are adequately identified and nurtured in the context of school settings."

New Directions

The new standards establish or reaffirm directions that will continue to enhance recognition of the field's legitimacy. Joyce and Susan Johnsen (VanTassel-Baska & Johnsen, 2007) identified several such trends, including emphasis on research-based teacher preparation and practice, diversity, and alignment with other standards. In addition, the new standards offer guidance on short- and long-term outcomes for gifted learners.

The research-, literature-, and practice-based studies supporting the new set of standards encourage continued growth of research and knowledge in the field. The research base "represents a major step forward in the development of scholarly consensus regarding the knowledge and skills necessary to teach highly able students" (Starko, 2008, p. 685).

The consensus process used in developing the standards ensures alignment with desired practice and an infrastructure for systematic implementation in teacher preparation. Joyce's leadership in this process was particularly critical with regard to retaining their emphasis on diversity. The original standards brought a strong diversity focus to expectations for teachers of the gifted, having been developed by CEC-TAG with invited review by CEC's diversity division. Representing only one organization, many university educators criticized the standards as not reflecting the field's thinking. The new standards streamline, clarify, and integrate the knowledge and skills critical to new teachers' understanding of the effects of culture and disability on identification and development, use of effective strategies for emotional and cognitive learning, and celebration of multiculturalism. Diversity—defined to include differences in race, culture, language, economic status, religion, sexual orientation, and ability/disability—continues to be central to each of the 10 standards. Joyce's influence on the joint task force, the higher education network, state directors' organization, and pre-K–12 schools nationally, fostered a collaborative approach to standards revision and development over time. Collaboration resulted in broad participation, ownership, and cohesion within the field to substantively address the needs of gifted students from diverse backgrounds through knowledge and skill standards based on relevant scholarship. Implementation of the new standards has potential for positively affecting identification and instructional practice through a paradigm shift in professional development programs. Preparing novice teachers of the gifted to address the cognitive, social, emotional, and family needs of culturally and linguistically diverse gifted students, gifted students from low-income environments, and twice-exceptional students will require comprehensive knowledge and skill development from the beginning (Starko, 2008) rather than through "add-on" courses and workshops.

The approval of new standards for teacher preparation also sets the stage for revising other, extant sets of standards affecting gifted and talented education. In framing the university and pre-K–12 guidebooks for standards implementation, Joyce urged the work group to address standards alignment. She expressed particular concern for the NAGC PreK–12 Gifted Program Standards, developed in 1998, because teacher preparation and program development are "hand in glove" operations that translate research into practice. The preK–12 program standards, prepared by NAGC alone, did not include a systematic validation process against a research base. Joyce's comparative analysis of the NCATE teacher preparation and NAGC program standards (VanTassel-Baska, 2008) identifies a clear need for revision in program design, professional development, and program evaluation, and for greater focus on technology and diversity in program standards.

One difficulty in evaluating the effects of teacher preparation on student outcomes, perhaps unique to gifted education, is the range of expected outcomes identified by different programs. Goals will vary based on developmental level of students, their talents and interests, and type of program. They range from mastery of advanced content, to skills for conducting independent research, to creative productivity in the visual and performing arts. The standards for teacher preparation offer some guidance regarding short- and long-term outcomes of appropriate education for gifted and talented students:

- Standard 3—Educators of the gifted plan instruction to provide "meaningful and challenging learning."
- Standard 4—Educators of the gifted "enhance self-awareness and self-efficacy for individuals with gifts and talents," "enhance the learning of critical and creative thinking, problem solving, and performance skills in specific domains," and "emphasize the development, practice, and transfer of advanced knowledge and skills across environments throughout the life span, leading to creative, productive careers in society for individuals with gifts and talents."
- Standard 5—Educators of the gifted "foster environments in which diversity is valued and individuals are taught to live harmoniously and productively in a culturally diverse world" and "encourage independence, motivation, and self-advocacy of individuals with gifts and talents."

In sum, the national standards support teacher preparation and development designed to enable gifted and talented students to engage in meaningful, challenging learning; develop self-awareness and self-efficacy; value diversity; think creatively and critically; acquire and apply advanced knowledge and skills; and become creatively productive adults.

Issues and Challenges

Joyce and the work group (Johnsen & VanTassel-Baska, 2008; Johnsen, Van-Tassel-Baska, Montgomery, & Kitano, 2008) identified several issues related to national implementation of the NCATE standards for preparation of teachers of the gifted. Most significant is the lack of consistent policies across states on the amount and nature of preparation required of teachers to work with gifted and talented students. Only 18 states mandate specific preparation of teachers in this area, and these states vary in the number of hours required for certification. Moreover, 18 states have no higher education institutions that prepare teachers to work with gifted learners. A related issue concerns the growing number of alternative preparation programs that do not address professional standards for teacher preparation. As a result, many school districts are faced with the task of hiring and assigning teachers who lack formal, standards-based preparation to serve gifted and talented students. These districts may offer professional development to their teachers without the advantage of standards-driven content and typically do not assess the impact of training on teacher or student behavior. Joyce continues to exercise leadership to bring together universities, state directors, and pre-K–12 schools to advocate for state policies and develop collaborations that implement standards-based teacher preparation and development.

Another challenge concerns the need for empirical validation of standards-based teacher preparation and development on teacher and student performance. Although the rationale and logic are well-established, the field has yet to establish with data the link between improved preparation and student performance (Starko, 2008). Joyce has been an outspoken advocate as well as a model for conducting research that examines the effects of teacher preparation on both teacher and student performance. In the higher education standards guidebook, she shares an effective, standards-based professional development model for pre-K–12 schools, made highly credible by data from her studies demonstrating positive effects of professional development on teacher behavior and student outcomes (e.g., Van-Tassel-Baska & Stambaugh, 2006).

Widespread adoption of the national standards in preparing, assigning, and developing teachers provides a powerful, systemic strategy for enhancing services to gifted students and supporting their short- and long-term needs. Joyce's leadership in bringing stakeholders together to collaborate and reach consensus on a set of research-based standards for teacher preparation will have significant impact on the field, on educators, and on gifted students and their families.

References

The Association for the Gifted. (2001). *Diversity and developing gifts and talents: A national action plan.* Reston, VA: Council for Exceptional Children.

Council for Exceptional Children. (2003). *What every special educator must know: Ethics, standards, and guidelines for special educators* (5th ed.). Arlington, VA: Author.

Council for Exceptional Children, Knowledge and Skills Subcommittee. (2003). *CEC professional standards and practices definitions.* Unpublished manuscript.

Darling-Hammond, L., Wise, A., & Klein, S. (1999). *A license to teach: Raising standards for teaching.* San Francisco: Jossey-Bass.

Johnsen, S. K., & VanTassel-Baska, J. (2008). Challenges. In S. K. Johnsen, J. VanTassel-Baska, & A. Robinson, *Using the national gifted education standards for university teacher preparation programs* (pp. 169–172). Thousand Oaks, CA: Corwin Press.

Johnsen, S. K., VanTassel-Baska, J., Montgomery, D., & Kitano, M. (2008). Challenges and prospects. In M. Kitano, D. Montgomery, J. VanTassel-Baska, & S. K. Johnsen, *Using the national gifted education standards for preK–12 professional development* (pp. 75–79). Thousand Oaks, CA: Corwin Press.

Johnsen, S. K., VanTassel-Baska, J., & Robinson, A. (2008). *Using the national gifted education standards for university teacher preparation programs.* Thousand Oaks, CA: Corwin Press.

Kitano, M. (2008). National standards for preparation of teachers of the gifted: Historical and implications for preK–12 schools. In M. Kitano, D. Montgomery, J. VanTassel-Baska, & S. K. Johnsen, *Using the national gifted education standards for preK–12 professional development* (pp. 1–5). Thousand Oaks, CA: Corwin Press.

Kitano, M., Montgomery, D., VanTassel-Baska, J., & Johnsen, S. K. (2008). *Using the national gifted education standards for preK–12 professional development.* Thousand Oaks, CA: Corwin Press.

Kraft, N. P. (2001, April). *Standards in teacher education: A critical analysis of NCATE, INTASC, and NBPTS.* Paper presented at the annual meeting of the American Educational Research Association, Seattle, WA.

National Council for Accreditation of Teacher Education. (2008). *NCATE glossary.* Retrieved from http://www.ncate.org/public/glossary.asp?ch=155

Parker, J. (1996). NAGC standards for personnel preparation in gifted education: A brief history. *Gifted Child Quarterly, 40,* 158–164.

Robinson, A., & Kolloff, P. B. (2006). Preparing teachers to work with high-ability youth at the secondary level: Issues and implications for licensure. In F. A. Dixon & S. M. Moon (Eds.), *The handbook of secondary gifted education* (pp. 581–610). Waco, TX: Prufrock Press.

Robinson, A., Shore, B. M., & Enersen, D. L. (2007). Professional development for teachers. In A. Robinson, B. M. Shore, & D. L. Enersen (Eds.), *Best practices in gifted education: An evidence-based guide* (pp. 263–271). Waco, TX: Prufrock Press.

Starko, A. J. (2008). Teacher preparation. In J. A. Plucker & C. M. Callahan (Eds.), *Critical issues and practices in gifted education: What the research says* (pp. 681–694). Waco, TX: Prufrock Press.

VanTassel-Baska, J. (2004). Metaevaluation findings: A call for gifted program quality. In J. VanTassel-Baska & A. X. Feng (Eds.), *Designing and utilizing evaluation for gifted program improvement* (pp. 227–245). Waco, TX: Prufrock Press.

VanTassel-Baska, J. (2006, October). *Brief introduction to the program standards.* Report to the Specialty Area Studies Board, National Council for Accreditation of Teacher Education, Washington, DC.

VanTassel-Baska, J. (2008). Alignment with NAGC preK–12 gifted program standards. In S. K. Johnsen, J. VanTassel-Baska, & A. Robinson, *Using the national gifted education standards for university teacher preparation programs* (pp. 157–162). Thousand Oaks, CA: Corwin Press.

VanTassel-Baska, J., & Johnsen, S. K. (2007). Teacher education standards for the field of gifted education: A vision of coherence for personnel preparation in the 21st century. *Gifted Child Quarterly, 51,* 182–205.

VanTassel-Baska, J., & Stambaugh, T. (2006). Project Athena: A pathway to advanced literacy development for children of poverty. *Gifted Child Today, 29*(2), 58–63.

CHAPTER 32

QUALITIES OF TALENTED TEACHERS:

Reflections and New Directions

by

JAMES
H. STRONGE,

CATHERINE
A. LITTLE,

AND

LESLIE
W. GRANT

While educators may not wish to assume the responsibility of creating eminent persons in the sense of a Dickinson or an Einstein, they are in the business of promoting the pursuit of excellence through constant utilization of potential.

—Joyce VanTassel-Baska (1989)

INTRODUCTION

Despite the extensive efforts to explain the elusive concept of effective teaching, particularly with students who are highly able or gifted, there are few clear answers to the question of how effective and ineffective teachers differ—and fewer clear directions about how effective teachers develop (Redfield, 2000). One question with a clear answer is whether gifted students need quality teachers and the answer is a resounding "yes." VanTassel-Baska (2005), in describing the nonnegotiables of gifted programs, specifically named quality teaching as a requirement for successful delivery of service. Among the descriptors of effective teachers are many qualities and behaviors that cannot necessarily be taught. Instead, they are personal characteristics or outcomes of unidentified practices and behaviors. For example, a descriptor that notes that the students of effective teachers are highly engaged does not explain how they came to be so or what actions the teacher took to promote that behavior (Allington & Johnston, 2000). Consequently, the next stage of research about effective teaching must go beyond describing the person or classroom, into a deeper understanding of how these traits and behaviors work together in the complex act of teaching and how the teacher deliberately manages that complexity. This chapter outlines the literature on effective teachers and highlights an international study on the effectiveness of talented teachers.

EMPIRICAL LITERATURE

Defining the effective teacher of the gifted is a complex task. Van Tassel-Baska and Feng (2004) noted that "the research base on the implementation of best instructional practice in classrooms serving gifted students is fairly scant" (p. 87). However, research and literature regarding what makes an effective teacher in the general education classroom is fairly replete with empirical studies. Looking across varied ways of defining effective teaching, Stronge (2007) synthesized findings into six domains encompassing key qualities and behaviors of effective teachers of high-ability learners. The authors of this chapter used the domains as a framework for exploring the practices of talented teachers (see Table 32.1).

The research and literature review resulting in these standards and frameworks provide the litmus test by which effective teaching may be viewed. In order to have an understanding of the practices of effective teachers, we interviewed national and international award-winning teachers from the United States, Australia, and New Zealand. We used the Framework of Effective Teaching (see Table 32.1; Stronge, 2007) in order to examine their practices. Although the framework of the six qualities influenced the interview data, what emerged were major themes for further exploration in the work of talented teachers that can inform the next steps in studying this phenomenon.

MAJOR THEMES OF EFFECTIVE TEACHING: RESULTS FROM A CROSS-CASE ANALYSIS

Based on the interview data, eight major themes were identified and further classified into four major categories. The categories, connections to the qualities of effective teaching framework, and key themes are listed in Table 32.2 and further discussed.

Category One: Educational Purpose and Place in Society

Two themes were identified that could be classified under a general category of the teachers' understanding of their purpose as teachers, the overall purpose of education, and the place of education in the larger society. Participants made comments that related to a sense of purpose in their work and discussed their awareness

Table 32.1
QUALITIES OF EFFECTIVE TEACHERS FRAMEWORK

Quality (Domain)	Examples of Key Descriptors and Literature Base
Teacher Background	• Verbal ability (Agne, 2001; Dubner, 1979; Silverman, 1995; VanTassel-Baska, 1993) • Subject matter expertise (Nelson & Prindle, 1992) • Training and expertise in needs of gifted students (Copenhaver & McIntyre, 1992; Feldhusen, 1991; Hansen & Feldhusen, 1994)
Personal Characteristics of the Teacher	• Enthusiasm for subject area (Csikszentmihalyi, Rathunde, & Whalen, 1993; Quek, 2005) • Personal, caring relationships with students (Bloom, 1985; Carper, 2002; Nikakis, 2002) • Sense of self-efficacy (Heath, 1997; Thomas & Montgomery, 1998)
Classroom Environment	• Adept management of students involved in different activities (Feldhusen, 1991) • Positive classroom environment (Hansen & Feldhusen, 1994) • Clear expectations of students with students involved in norm-setting (Maddux, Samples-Lachman, & Cummings, 1985; Nikakis, 2002)
Planning for Instruction	• Selection of appropriate high-level materials, matching complexities and individual skill (Csikszentmihalyi et al., 1993; Hansen & Feldhusen, 1994; Nelson & Prindle, 1992) • Connection of students with access to resources such as content area experts and mentors (Shore & Delcourt, 1996; Westberg & Archambault, 1997)
Implementing Instruction	• Skillful implementation of a range of instructional strategies, focusing on in-depth analysis (Hansen & Feldhusen, 1994; Renzulli, 1997; VanTassel-Baska & Little, 2003) • High-level student engagement (Ford & Trotman, 2001; Hansen & Feldhusen, 1994; Henderson, 1996)
Monitoring Learning and Responding to Student Differences	• Differentiation of instruction (Ford & Trotman, 2001; Nelson & Prindle, 1992) • Informational feedback provided that encourages experimentation (Csikszentmihalyi et al., 1993)

Note. Adapted from Stonge (2007).

of various larger systems and the influence of those systems on their own classroom practice. These elements relate to the teacher as a person in that the teacher has a positive attitude toward the teaching profession, engages in constant reflective practice, and seeks to understand her students as well as capitalize on the students' strengths (Stronge, 2007).

In reflecting upon their teaching practices, the teachers embedded comments demonstrating a sense of purpose in their work beyond the day-to-day objectives of teaching. None of the questions directly asked teachers to explain their motivation

Table 32.2

MAJOR CATEGORIES AND THEMES IN INTERVIEW RESULTS

Categories	Connection to Qualities of Effective Teachers Framework	Themes
Educational Purpose and Place in Society	Personal Characteristics of the Teacher	• Sense of purpose • Awareness of larger systems and their influence
Practices and Habits of Mind in Teaching	Planning for Instruction Implementing Instruction Monitoring Learning and Responding to Student Differences	• Pedagogical knowledge and skills • Content knowledge and content-specific pedagogy • Differentiation and attention to group and individual differences
Development as a Professional	Teacher Background Personal Characteristics of the Teacher	• Personal and professional growth and change • Use of reflection
Relationships	Personal Characteristics of the Teacher	• Relationships with students, parents, and other professionals

for teaching or their sense of purpose, yet this theme emerged in the comments of a number of teachers. For example, Diane commented, "It's not just about the content and the curriculum. It's about them [the students] as a whole person, and we want what is absolutely best for every single child that's in here." Janie wished to influence students with "just the kinds of things that don't have anything to do with necessarily the content but have to do with the idea that learning can be joyful, that learning makes us human and it gives us tools to be real people and enjoy our lives."

Discussions of purpose focused not only on student development, but also on professional development and linkages to larger systems. Matthew emphasized his sense of purpose within the profession, his responsibility for advocating for the development and better education of future teachers: "My challenge is figuring out ways to make our profession better . . . making sure that our colleges are preparing kids to come into the field adequately." Diane focused on a sense of purpose for practicing teachers as well: "We need to connect and remember—get rid of the amnesia—why we became educators to begin with. And have enough courage to put that out in front."

Category Two: Practices and Habits of Mind in Teaching

The category encompassing the greatest portion of the teachers' interview responses was one of practices and habits of mind of the teacher. Within this category the most extensive theme was one of pedagogical knowledge and skills. The two additional themes emphasized differentiation practices and content-specific knowledge and pedagogy.

The pedagogical knowledge and skills reflected in teachers' comments included: (a) a strong emphasis on planning, with clear connections to assessment; (b) attention to variation and flexibility in organizing instructional activities; (c) a focus on student engagement through environmental and instructional elements in the classroom, with consideration of authenticity in the learning context; and (d) the interaction of instruction and classroom management. Each of the teachers spoke of the detail involved in their instructional planning; most of them commented that because of their lengthy experience with their current grade level or content area, they no longer wrote meticulous plans for every lesson, but that they nevertheless relied on a combination of plans from earlier years and a mental planning process that linked familiar instruction from the past with the current class and context. To illustrate, one teacher stated:

> If I'm starting something new . . . I would develop a day-by-day, almost word-by-word lesson plan, unit, that would say anticipatory set I'm going to say this, this, this, and this, in the introduction I'm going to say this, this, this . . . I'm very detail-oriented when it comes to that. Then after I've done it 2 years in a row, I'll have in my mind what questions are that I think are appropriate, and what extensions I can do to that, so then I'll just be more generic in my daily lesson plan.

Formal and informal assessment data influenced planning for instruction across all of the teachers; several of them shared that their use of assessment in this way, as well as their purposefulness in planning and linkage of objectives and assessment, had developed over time as an area of skill they had carefully honed. Julia shared:

> I've recently become more interested in backwards planning . . . I have sort of forcibly changed my own lesson planning in the last 2 years, once I started reading *Understanding by Design* and thinking a lot more about it. I always have loved planning—it's possibly my favorite part. But I think now the planning's better, and the lessons are better, because I always, always now develop the assessment first.

Teachers also discussed their habits of flexibility and variation in classroom activities, both within their plans and as alterations to their plans. Several of the teachers commented specifically that with experience they had become more comfortable with allowing lessons to follow a different path than the one originally planned, because of the teachers' own confidence and comfort with the structure of the lesson and the possible variation within it. Timothy compared teaching to jazz music, in which a structure exists but extensive creativity is possible from the musicians within that structure. This flexibility also was reflected in teachers' comments on working for student engagement; each of the teachers spoke of working to connect students authentically and enjoyably to the learning, encouraging enthusiasm through modeling and through careful calibration of the learning experience to the students' level of development.

Another aspect of pedagogical knowledge and skill that emerged in teachers' comments was the role of the classroom environment and its connection to the teaching and learning process. Teachers spoke of developing the physical environment in ways that would interest and engage students, including practices such as displaying student work and changing displays on a frequent basis. Matthew described how from the beginning of each year, he makes the design and decoration of the classroom a responsibility and privilege of the students themselves, thus inspiring a sense of ownership and connecting students to their learning. Classroom management also formed a part of teachers' comments, with consideration of how the rules and procedures in the classroom help to minimize time spent on behavior and free up time for more instructional engagement.

A theme of content knowledge and content-specific pedagogy also emerged from the teachers' comments. Several of the teachers offered specific comments about the ways in which their particular content area should be taught. In reflecting on her own questioning skills, Julia discussed the different expectations for higher level questioning and thinking that characterize world language classes, arguing that the process of thinking and communicating in a different language is itself the higher level demand: "I think that that's where the real higher order thinking is coming in, just the existing, just the—when we do comparisons, but we're doing it only in [the other language], or just when we're telling a story or reading a book."

The teachers who commented frequently on content-specific pedagogy also focused on the importance of authenticity in learning experiences within a specific content area. Janie, referring to secondary English courses, emphasized that she makes a habit of "show[ing] them how good writers do use all of this stuff and give them examples of why it's important." Julia commented that in developing assessment situations, she strives for authenticity in both the language skills to be used and the simulated circumstances that form the context for language use. This emphasis on authenticity also fits within a focus on each teacher's own content knowledge, acknowledged by the teachers to be a critical part of their work and their credibility in the eyes of students.

Within their comments under the theme of pedagogical knowledge and skills, teachers commented on the importance of using varied methods of instruction and engagement to involve students in learning. In addition to this, the teachers commented more directly on using their understanding of the needs of particular students or groups of students to inform instruction and management; these comments were grouped as a subtheme of differentiation.

Comments about differentiation focused on understanding specific characteristics and needs of students, the types of modifications that teachers make to their plans and practices to support differentiation, and the need for attention to differentiation with regard to organization and management as well as instruction.

Teachers commented on knowing specific student characteristics, including learning preferences and modalities, the speed and format in which different students best learn, and the background knowledge students bring to each lesson and each year.

The teachers' comments on differentiation also included more technical and specific discussion of the ways in which student needs are assessed and the types of accommodations that are made. Teachers spoke of using preassessment and conversations with students and parents as ways of determining modifications and accommodations to be made for given students, including students with exceptionalities as well as across the entire group of students. Matthew mentioned neighborhoods of questioning as an important influence on his planning; several of the teachers made reference to multiple intelligences and multiple modalities. They also commented on collaborating with resource teachers for special education and gifted education to meet the needs of identified students and also to inform instruction for other students who might be struggling with a particular topic or skill at a particular time.

Category Three: Development as a Professional

A theme related to growth and change emerged within teachers' comments. Their comments about professional growth and change they had experienced included discussion of key influences on their practice, specific aspects of their teaching that had changed over the years, and the impact of their involvement in the field beyond the classroom. In a review of the literature, Stronge (2007) found that more effective teachers of high-ability learners had more training in working with the gifted, which entails the prerequisites of teaching. Several of the teachers identified specific instructors of their own who had influenced either their desire to become a teacher or their practices of teaching. Each teacher also commented on some structured educational opportunity that had been influential; however, none of the teachers specifically credited a teacher preparation program as having much influence on their success. Key professional development experiences among the teachers included:

- The National Board Certification process, which was mentioned by three teachers: "It made me much more analytical and reflective about what I do."
- Coursework in a child development program, which one teacher specifically noted to be separate from and more valuable than educational coursework: "There we really honed in on theory and the workings of a child and we got to begin to explore what makes a child tick, what kind of activities can you do."
- Opportunities for one teacher to work as a demonstration teacher in a professional development institute and to attend an annual conference in her field: "I could choose the sessions I needed at the time, and every year, as I got better at what I was doing or I knew what I wanted to learn, then I could sort of step up what I was choosing to do something different, and so it was absolutely tailored to my needs."

Each teacher spoke of ways in which developing experience had changed his or her work, frequently with reference to the beginning teacher's concern with "survival" versus the more experienced teacher's focus on finer details of professional practice. The teachers spoke of becoming more systematic in their planning, including making greater use of assessment as a tool for planning for each particular class, even as they built a repertoire of lessons and activities from year to year.

Each teacher also spoke of how he or she used reflection as a key part of planning and of growing as a professional. The theme of reflection included an emphasis on reviewing lessons for ways to improve, using self-evaluation and feedback, and selecting areas for improvement.

Each teacher commented on the practice of systematically looking back over lessons he or she had conducted for purposes of informing further planning, whether it was for future implementation of the same lessons or for subsequent lessons. Timothy spoke of a combination of daily reflection for ongoing planning with time spent on weekends to reflect more broadly, to:

> step back and say, "Am I going through this too slowly, or do I need to pick things up a little bit to still cover the things that are important, or is this really worth focusing on, should I adjust my long term plan . . .?"

Janie shared that her reflection is one of the habits she has changed and refined over time:

> It [used to be] just OK, I did a good job, I got through today, and now it's much more than that. Did I do a good enough job today? Did I explain it well enough? Did I make the right choices?"

The teachers commented several times on the value of both self-evaluation and feedback and of their own efforts to get feedback on their own practice and to use experiences with other teachers as ways of promoting self-evaluation.

Category Four: Relationships

The final theme was an emphasis on relationships and their importance in the work of a teacher and who the teacher is as a person. Teachers spoke of their relationships with other professionals, with parents, and most significantly with students. Several of the teachers incorporated comments about relationships with students and the importance of knowing and connecting with students as people into their responses to the majority of the questions, whether the question as written specifically emphasized relationships or not. Diane said, "I try to have meaningful connections with them. You know, I try to know them as people and to meet their individual needs and have an understanding of what's going on at home." The teachers also highlighted developing relationships and connecting with students on an emotional or personal level. Janie said,

I think where I've been successful in the classroom is that just about every single student in there knows that I like them. They know it and I always try to find something important about them and I try to personalize them. I try to use their names. I try to pay attention to what they care about and make sure that I say "Nice new piercing you got there" . . . or "Hey, you got some blue hair going on."

All of these teachers commented not only on developing relationships in general, but also on how teacher-student relationships were important in achieving desired results with students, in encouraging students to engage with the learning process and to behave appropriately in school. Janie commented, "I think knowing your students and making sure that they know that you care about them goes a thousand percent to getting results from them." Diane said, "I think that we have a deep sense of trust. My kids know that I believe in them and so they're willing to take risks." Julia, who sees her students over a period of years because of her role, spoke of relationships with regard to student behavior:

I feel such a bond with them because I have them for so long. . . . [H]aving them 3 years, by that point you get so close to them that you feel like if they do something wrong, it's out of their character in the relationship with you.

The teachers who highlighted relationships with students most thoroughly also were the ones who made the most comments about relationships with parents. Diane mentioned the necessity of strong home-school connections and understanding what is happening at home. Breanna spoke of her relationships with parents and with the students beyond the classroom with a broad sense of the community: "My relationship with the child is community based. It's not just I'm teaching you between 9 and 3, but it's my whole life, because that's vocation." Janie, although she did not speak specifically of her relationships with parents, referred to the larger set of influential student and parent relationships with this comment: "Every single child is so important to somebody. That's somebody's precious gift there and they need to be paid attention to."

Teachers also spoke of their relationships with other professionals, but these comments were much more limited than comments about connections with students or even with parents.

DISCUSSION

The study of the process of teaching is crucial to understanding what effective teachers do in the classroom. The interview questions that we used focused on the process of teaching, rather than the products, or outcomes, of teaching. Effective teaching also can be viewed in terms of outcomes, that is, are students making learning gains as a result of being a student in the teacher's classroom (Mendro, 1998; Nye, Konstantopoulos, & Hedges, 2004; Palardy & Rumberger, 2008; Sanders & Horn, 1995; Wright, Horn, & Sanders, 1997)? However, these studies use state assessment data that may not adequately assess learning gains of gifted students, given the ceiling effect (Avery & VanTassel-Baska, 2002). Therefore, in order to truly measure the value-added impact of teachers of gifted students, more authentic measures of student learning gains must be used (VanTassel-Baska, Quek, & Feng, 2007). However, by talking with effective teachers, we have information as to their beliefs and practices that make them effective in the classroom. These beliefs and practices can then be grounded in the existing literature and begin to build a composite sketch of the elusive effective teacher of gifted students.

Patterns that were evident across the group of case study teachers and across the categories and themes outlined included a strong habit of reflection about all aspects of the work of teaching and an emphasis on purposeful work at the "micro" level of daily classroom work as well as at the "macro" levels of the purposes of the profession at large. The teachers also assumed responsibility for their own professional growth and development, evaluating their past experiences for influential activities yet highlighting those that involved high levels of investment of their own time and energy.

CONCLUSION

As a profession we know a considerable amount about the desired—and, indeed, necessary—qualities of effective teachers for gifted and talented students. Consider the following illustrative set of findings relating teacher quality to effectiveness in working with gifted students:

- ▸ *Teacher background:* Effective teachers understand the nature and needs of gifted learners and have received training in appropriate instructional practices (Sternberg & Grigorenko, 2002).
- ▸ *Teacher dispositions and personal qualities:* Gifted students value teachers with whom they have a caring and positive relationship (Csikszentmihalyi et al., 1993; Quek, 2005).
- ▸ *Classroom management and organization:* Effective teachers of gifted students provide a rich array of instructional resources in the classroom (VanTassel-Baska & Little, 2003).
- ▸ *Planning for instruction:* Effective G/T teachers select appropriate high-level materials for their gifted learners (Shore & Delcourt, 1996).
- ▸ *Implementing instruction:* Teachers of high-ability students actively engage students through various instructional activities (Renzulli, 1997), including direct and indirect instruction (VanTassel-Baska & Little, 2003).
- ▸ *Monitoring student progress:* Effective teachers use diagnostic tools to identify student abilities and talents (VanTassel-Baska, 1998).

Despite these findings and myriad others, in actuality, we know far less than is needed regarding the connection between effective teachers and effective learning for high-ability students. Thus, in many respects, we are in the infancy of exploring teacher quality, especially for gifted students. Dr. Joyce Van Tassel-Baska has created a pathway for this research to continue through the development of the Classroom Observation Scales, Revised (VanTassel-Baska et al., 2003), a research-based instrument to measure observable, differentiated teacher behaviors in the areas of classroom planning and delivery, differentiation, creative thinking, problem solving, critical thinking, and issue-based research. Moreover, her work during the past 20 years has shown the connection among quality professional development focused on specific content areas and curriculum, teacher behaviors, and student achievement (see VanTassel-Baska & Stambaugh, 2008). Her pioneering work, coupled with emerging research, can provide new directions in the area of effective teaching of gifted students.

REFERENCES

Agne, K. J. (2001). Gifted: The lost minority. *Kappa Delta Pi Record, 37,* 168–172.

Allington, R. L., & Johnston, P. M. (2000). What do we know about effective fourth-grade teachers and their classrooms? *CELA Research Report, Report Series 13010.* Retrieved from http://cela.albany.edu/4thgrade/index.html

Avery, L. D., & VanTassel-Baska, J. (2002). The impact of gifted education evaluation at state and local levels: Translating results into action. *Journal for the Education of the Gifted 25,* 153–176.

Bloom, B. S. (Ed.). (1985). *Developing talent in young people.* New York: Ballantine Books.

Carper, A. (2002). *Bright students in a wasteland: The at-risk gifted: A qualitative study of fourteen gifted dropouts.* Unpublished doctoral dissertation, North Carolina State University, Raleigh.

Copenhaver, R. W., & McIntyre, D. J. (1992). Teachers' perception of gifted students. *Roeper Review, 14,* 151–153.

Csikszentmihalyi, M., Rathunde, K., & Whalen, S. (1993). *Talented teenagers: The roots of success and failure.* New York: Cambridge University Press.

Dubner, F. S. (1979). Thirteen ways of looking at a gifted teacher. *Journal for the Education of the Gifted, 3,* 143–146.

Feldhusen, J. F. (1991, September/October). Full-time classes for gifted youth. *Gifted Child Today,* 10–13.

Ford, D. Y., & Trotman, M. F. (2001). Teachers of gifted students: Suggested multicultural characteristics and competences. *Roeper Review, 23,* 235–239.

Hansen, J., & Feldhusen, J. F. (1994). Comparison of trained and untrained teachers of gifted students. *Gifted Child Quarterly, 38,* 115–123.

Heath, W. J. (1997). *What are the most effective characteristics of teachers of the gifted?* (ERIC Document Reproduction Service No. ED411665)

Henderson, J. (1996). Effective teaching in Advanced Placement classrooms. *Journal of Classroom Instruction, 31*(1), 29–35.

Maddux, C. D., Samples-Lachman, I., & Cummings, R. E. (1985). Preferences of gifted students for selected teacher characteristics. *Gifted Child Quarterly, 29,* 160–163.

Mendro, R. L. (1998). Student achievement and school and teacher accountability. *Journal of Personnel Evaluation in Education, 12,* 257–267.

Nelson, C., & Prindle, N. (1992). Gifted teacher competences: Ratings by rural principals and teachers compared. *Journal for the Education of the Gifted, 15,* 357–369.

Nikakis, S. (2002). What makes an expert teacher of the gifted? *Learning Matters, 7*(1), 42–44.

Nye, B., Konstantopoulos, S., & Hedges, L. V. (2004). How large are teacher effects? *Educational Evaluation and Policy Analysis, 26,* 237–257.

Palardy, G. J., & Rumberger, R. W. (2008). Teacher effectiveness in first grade: The importance of background qualifications, attitudes, and instructional practices for student learning. *Educational Evaluation and Policy Analysis, 30,* 111–140.

Quek, C. G. (2005). *A national study of scientific talent development in Singapore.* Unpublished doctoral dissertation, The College of William and Mary, Williamsburg, VA.

Redfield, D. (2000). *What makes effective teachers effective?* Unpublished manuscript.

Renzulli, J. S. (1997). The Multiple Menu Model: A successful marriage for integrating content and process. *NASSP Bulletin, 81*(587), 51–58.

Sanders, W. L., & Horn, S. P. (1995). The Tennessee Value-Added Assessment System (TVAAS): Mixed model methodology in educational assessment. In A. J. Shinkfield & D. L. Stufflebeam (Eds.), *Teacher evaluation: Guide to effective practice.* Boston: Kluwer.

Shore, B. M., & Delcourt, M. A. B. (1996). Effective curricular and program practices in gifted education and the interface with general education. *Journal for the Education of the Gifted, 20,* 138–154.

Silverman, L. (1995). How are gifted teachers different from other teachers [Abstract]? *The Kaleidoscope, 1,* 8–9.

Sternberg, R. J., & Grigorenko, E. L. (2002). The theory of successful intelligence as a basis for gifted education. *Gifted Child Quarterly, 46,* 265–277.

Stronge, J. H. (2007). *Qualities of effective teachers* (2nd ed.). Alexandria, VA: ASCD.

Thomas, J. A., & Montgomery, P. (1998). On becoming a good teacher: Reflective practice with regard to children's voices. *Journal of Teacher Education, 49,* 372–380.

VanTassel-Baska, J. (1993). Linking curriculum development for the gifted to school reform and restructuring. *Gifted Child Today, 16*(4), 34–37.

VanTassel-Baska, J. (1998). The development of academic talent: A mandate for educational best practice. *Phi Delta Kappan, 79,* 760–764.

VanTassel-Baska, J. (2005). Gifted programs and services: What are the nonnegotiables? *Theory Into Practice, 44,* 90–97.

VanTassel-Baska, J., Avery, L., Struck, J., Feng, A., Bracken, B., Drummond, D., & Stambaugh, T. (2003). *The William and Mary Classroom Observation Scales, Revised.* Williamsburg, VA: The College of William and Mary, The Center for Gifted Education.

VanTassel-Baska, J., & Feng, A. X. (2004). *Designing and utilizing evaluation for gifted program improvement.* Waco, TX: Prufrock Press.

VanTassel-Baska, J. & Little, C. (2003). *Content-based curriculum for high-ability learners.* Waco, TX: Prufrock Press.

VanTassel-Baska, J., Quek, C., & Feng, A. (2007). The development and use of a structured teacher observation scale to assess differentiated best practice. *Roeper Review, 29,* 84–92.

VanTassel-Baska, J., & Stambaugh, T. (2008). *What works: 20 years of curriculum development and research for advanced learners.* Waco, TX: Prufrock Press.

Westberg, K. L., & Archambault, F. X. (1997). A multi-site case study of successful classroom practices for high ability students. *Gifted Child Quarterly, 41,* 42–51.

Wright, S. P., Horn, S. P., & Sanders, W. L. (1997). Teacher and classroom context effects on student achievement: Implications for teacher evaluation. *Journal of Personnel Evaluation in Education, 11,* 57–67.

CHAPTER 33

CRITICAL THINKING AND PRESERVICE TEACHER EDUCATION

by

SᴜSAN
MᴄGOWAN

> . . . teachers must help students understand that real thinking is hard work, that it takes effort over time to improve, and that the products of good thinking may not yield short-term results.
>
> —Joyce VanTassel-Baska

Critical thinking often is referred to as a higher order thinking skill (Paul & Elder, 2001). This level of thinking is equivalent to Bloom's (1956) hierarchical levels known as evaluation, analysis, and synthesis, respectively, as well as the components of the revised taxonomy which added *creating* as a higher order thinking skill (Pohl, 2000). Scriven and Paul (2005) defined this complex process as the "intellectually disciplined process of actively and skillfully conceptualizing, applying, analyzing, synthesizing, and/or evaluating information gathered from, or generated by, observation, experience, reflection, reasoning, or communication, as a guide to belief and action" (p. 1).

Gifted education is particularly "recognized for advancing the introduction of innovative instructional practices into the classroom, such as inquiry learning, critical and creative thinking skills, higher order questioning strategies, [and] metacognition" (VanTassel-Baska, Quek, & Feng, 2005, p. 5) in response to gifted students' "capacity to perceive information and use it productively to a unusual degree" (Parks,

2005, p. 249). According to Cotton (1991), higher order thinking skills enhance academic achievement in such a way that over time thinking skills instruction accelerates student learning gains. Higher order thinking skills are habits that educators should desire to instill in their students.

Although educators have shown considerable interest in higher order thinking skills during the last decade, processes and principles of sound reasoning are seldom developed meaningfully in the classroom. "Virtually all informed commentators agree that schooling today does not foster the higher order thinking skills and abilities which represent the basics of the future" (Paul & Nosich, 2005, p. 1). For example, American students are adept at computing but not reasoning; they have mastered writing and correcting sentences but not the ability to prepare logical arguments (Paul & Nosich, 2005).

The key focus and area of concern in fostering the teaching of higher order thinking skills is the teacher (Hargrove, 2003) who must learn to design, analyze, and objectively evaluate assignments that require critical thinking skills (Paul & Elder, 2000). Furthermore, because "those we label gifted possess special charac-teristics that affect their ability to learn to a significant degree, and [because] they will not reach their full educational potential unless we modify their curricula substantially" (Borland, 1988, p. 2), teachers must themselves be competent criti-cal thinkers who can apply structured critical thinking frameworks to existing and reformed curriculum. In this effort, teachers can help students link different areas of knowledge and develop skills that "transfer across, apply to, and enhance any field of inquiry a student may encounter" (VanTassel-Baska, 1994, p. 4).

BRIEF REVIEW OF RESEARCH

Many gifted education scholars tout higher order thinking skills as necessary for the development of gifts. For example, Shore and Kanevsky (1993) declare that higher order thinking skills are thinking processes that are "an important compo-nent of a contemporary conception of giftedness and its development" (p. 133). Parks (2005) cited gifted students' capacity to "analyze information intuitively and efficiently" (p. 249) as the rationale for teaching these students to think critically and to measure their efforts appropriately.

Research in this area has shown that teachers' critical thinking abilities can improve through targeted instruction (Lang, 2001). In one recent study, a combi-nation of recurring professional development, teacher support through innovative curriculum, and clarity of goals contributed to strengthening teachers' critical thinking abilities (McGowan, 2007). It also has been demonstrated that student achievement can increase as a result of instruction in critical thinking strategies (Roberts, Ingram, & Harris, 1992). These research results are predicated on two notions: (1) through modeling metacognition, teachers demonstrate for students the dispositions of critical thinkers and (2) by creating cognitive dissonance in the classroom, gifted students' academic achievement increases. Creating cognitive dissonance links with the Piagetian concept that "when children's interactions with the world result in experiences that do not fit their current conceptions, their mental balance is disturbed" (Zohar & Aharon-Kravetsky, 2005, p. 829).

Evidence also exists that teachers are not adequately prepared to foster critical thinking skills in the classroom. A critical component of teacher competencies concerning critical thinking stems from the work of Paul and Elder (2001) who discovered through a case-by-case analysis that most university faculty have not carefully thought through a concept of critical thinking and therefore are unlikely to foster critical thinking in their students.

An examination of exceptional undergraduate teacher preparation programs, investigating common areas of study, yielded the following similar themes: a firm grounding in academic content, developing leadership roles for teachers, collegiality and community, current reform issues, research, and reflective practices (Darling-Hammond, 2000). Field experiences overwhelmingly took center stage in teacher preparation programs, with the bulk of preservice teacher time and effort being expended on classroom experiences. Only one college out of the four studied for excellence in teacher education considered analysis as an outcome of its education program, defining it as "clear think[ing] . . . fus[ing] experience, reason, and training into considered judgment" (Darling-Hammond, 2000, p. 19).

Initial findings of a current study being conducted support this perspective. Preservice teachers participating in the study generated high average scores on the Watson-Glaser Critical Thinking Assessment (Watson & Glaser, 2006), but admit that their skills remain largely underdeveloped through the lack of targeted instruction in critical thinking strategies. Preservice teachers overwhelmingly report that field experiences stretched over a 3-year period focus on factual recall rather than higher order thinking skills, rendering little, if any, opportunity to delve into the teaching of critical thinking strategies with students (McGowan & Powers, 2008).

Major Themes

Important themes that emerge from both empirical research and practice recounts on the issues of teacher preparation in critical thinking suggest: (1) the classroom teacher is the essential element in fostering critical thinking skills in the classroom, (2) targeted instruction in critical thinking improves both teacher and student achievement, and (3) teacher preparation programs largely neglect to teach cohesive strategies to foster critical thinking in the classroom. Taken as a whole, these themes indicate a breech between what educators know to be successful, what teacher education programs stress, and ultimately what is *not* being done in the classroom.

New Directions

Current research suggests that a common framework for teaching preservice teachers to apply critical thinking to field placement experiences is crucial (McGowan & Powers, 2008). Preservice teachers involved in this research score in the medium range on the Watson-Glaser Critical Thinking Assessment (Watson &

Glaser, 2006) and freely admit that their approach toward critical thinking relies heavily on intuition rather than on a formal critical thinking model. Paul's Critical Thinking Standards (Paul & Elder, 2001) were chosen for use with preservice teachers because they provide an elegant framework on which to ground the elements and traits of reasoning as teachers begin to work toward grappling with how to teach critical thinking strategies. The standards and suggested teacher applications are shown in Table 33.1.

After working with the critical thinking standards in sustained field placement experiences, preservice teachers report that not only do their students use critical thinking in core content areas but also in problem-solving situations in the classroom. Furthermore, teachers themselves provide more thoughtful written work and reflection about how they think about teaching as well as about instructional choices they make (McGowan & Powers, 2008).

Unresolved Issues

Although the history of critical thinking dates back to the time of Socrates (Paul & Elder, 2001) encompassing well more than 2,500 years, there exists neither a common language nor a commonly accepted definition for this construct. The importance of "a set of paradigmatic practices that underlie the particular concepts and argument types characteristic of a discipline" (Weinstein, 1995, p. 7) or a language of the discipline cannot be understated. Teachers naturally seek a common language when they use terms like "Bloom's Taxonomy" and "higher order thinking skills" in attempting to articulate their definition of and describe classroom practices involving critical thinking. Adoption of a universally common language of critical thinking, based upon the critical thinking standards, would allow both teachers and student learners to cognitively organize concepts with clarity and precision as well as to communicate those concepts to others in a highly effective manner. The common language should be taught throughout teacher preparation programs.

Once a means of effective communication is in place, teacher preparation and subsequent teacher professional development experiences must be targeted to reconceptualize teacher practices regarding critical thinking. Such experiences must be accomplished so that teachers can then move from relying solely on disseminating procedures and information to conveying meaning and helping students, particularly gifted students, make connections. Furthermore, teacher preparation experiences involving the development of critical thinking standards and encompassing topics such as designing instruction to foster critical thinking skills within the framework of the standards must be sustained over time and accompanied by adequate resources.

Teachers and students must be conversant in and have practice with the standards of reasoning across content areas before they approach understanding and application of critical thinking. In order to foster a nation of critical thinkers,

Table 33.1
CRITICAL THINKING STANDARDS CORRELATED TO STUDENT OUTCOMES

Standard	Teachers Can Help Students:
• Clarity involves elaboration and illustrative discussion both verbal and written. Requires examples from more than one facet of an issue so that the listener can make connections among disparate thoughts.	• Practice clarity in everyday speech. • Choose the most apt word from among a choice of words.
• Accuracy demands evidence garnered from multiple sources. • Conflicting evidence provides a basis from which to search out the truth. • Accurate statements reflect clarity and correctness.	• Be aware of and able to select from a variety of resources from which to gather information. • Distinguish reliable from unreliable or sensational information.
• Precision requires not only clear, accurate statements but also detailed facts.	• Learn to pick out details that help clarify both written and oral work. • Recognize ambiguous statements within text.
• Relevance links seemingly disjointed thought processes so the reader or listener acquires distinct appreciation for the significance of a thought to the issue.	• Help students recognize "goodness of fit." • Distinguish relevant statements from irrelevant ones.
• Depth examines complexities of an issue accounting for the most pervasive factors of a multifaceted problem.	• Consider the dualities of an issue, especially of a moral issue. • Think through the nuances of an issue or problem.
• Breadth considers more than one perspective or point of view.	• Examine conflicting theories. • Pinpoint both consistencies and inconsistencies. • Examine various perspectives and apply information gleaned to a wide variety of situations.
• Logic requires mutually supportive thoughts bolstered by data.	• Distinguish between logical and illogical thoughts. • Reflect on thinking through journal writing or oral discussion. • Model reflective processes.
• Significance involves discarding extraneous ideas in favor of central idea(s) of great importance.	• Focus on central problem. • Choose the most significant idea. • Support opposing viewpoints using central significant ideas.
• Fairness heightens individual biases and forces reasoning about stakeholder emotions.	• Consider different levels of objectivity through discussion of various issues. • Give rationale for taking a stance on a given issue.
• Completeness considers possibilities about what has been either omitted or overlooked.	• Identify omissions to ideas. • Discern potential path for investigation when solving a problem.

gifted students must be taught from their first days of school to question what they are learning from materials, classmates, and teachers, using the standards of clarity, accuracy, precision, relevance, depth, breadth, logic, significance, fairness, and completeness to judge it (Paul & Elder, 2001).

Thompson and Zeuli (1999) suggested that a combination of teacher strategies is necessary to optimize critical thinking in the classroom. In addition to teacher knowledge regarding connections that students must make among relevant topics and the background students bring to the classroom, these researchers advocate for a model of teaching as a process by which teachers provoke students to think through correctly choosing or designing problems to solve and allowing for extended engagement among students in order for such dialogue to take place. They suggest that in order for this to happen, a sufficiently high level of cognitive dissonance must be created in order for teachers' existing beliefs and practices to be questioned. This idea bolsters the argument that critical thinking instruction should consist of a focused framework for ease of transfer from classroom to classroom.

An additional implication concerns gifted curriculum, which should include the standards of critical thinking as well as creative teaching and learning so that these constructs are not overlooked in favor of covering content. Discussion of and overt practice with the standards of reasoning should be a part of curriculum. Curriculum development emphasizing the standards serves to connect metacognitive functioning with the content being studied, which would then enhance both teacher effectiveness and student production. Furthermore, because there is no guarantee that optimally developed curriculum will be properly implemented in the classroom setting, observable, measurable, and accountable indices of teacher behavior must be addressed through sustained professional development experiences.

Yet, that is not enough. Curriculum must be aligned to a universally accepted set of standards that foster the "capacity to think more clearly, more accurately, more precisely, more relevantly, more deeply, more broadly, and more logically" (Paul, 2000, p. 3). This implication for practice is aligned with Ball and Cohen (1999) who suggest that professional development could be improved by seeking ways to ground curriculum in the tasks, questions, and problems of practice" (p. 20). Such alignment will assist in educating intellectually responsible citizens capable of dealing efficiently with global challenges through the use of critical thinking.

CONCLUSION

At the time of this writing, the national mandate of the No Child Left Behind (2001) legislation has enjoyed almost 8 years of active implementation and is awaiting reform by a new federal administration. Because each state is responsible for implementation of this legislation and because achievement of a 70% pass rate holds meanings as diverse as this nation's regions, it is widely known and accepted that critical thinking has given way to factual recall and rote memorization, not to mention teaching to the test. Therefore, it is tantamount that teachers, particularly teachers of the gifted, offer their students manifold opportunities to learn to think and problem solve in real-world situations and scaffold these opportunities because the consequences are dire if they do not.

Students cannot be taught to be critical thinkers by teachers who are not practiced critical thinkers themselves. Therefore, "unless teacher education can prepare beginning teachers to learn to do much more thoughtful and challenging work and unless ways can be found through professional development to help teachers sustain such work, traditional instruction is likely to persist. . ." (Ball & Cohen, 1999, p. 7). Critical thinking must retake center stage in discussions involving teacher preparation and learning.

The results of working with Dr. VanTassel-Baska at the Center for Gifted Education as a graduate assistant not only provided a focus for my doctoral work in the area of critical thinking, but also has been applied to my work with preservice and practicing teachers as an assistant professor of education at Longwood University.

REFERENCES

Ball, D., & Cohen, D. (1999). Developing practice, developing practitioners: Toward a practice-based theory of professional education. In L. Darling-Hammond & G. Sykes (Eds.), *Teaching as the learning profession: Handbook of policy and practice* (pp. 3–32). San Francisco: Jossey-Bass.

Bloom, B. S. (Ed.). (1956). *Taxonomy of educational objectives: The classification of educational goals Handbook I: Cognitive domain.* New York: Longman.

Borland, J. H. (1988). Cognitive controls, cognitive styles, and divergent production in gifted preadolescents. *Journal for the Education of the Gifted, 11*(4), 57–82.

Cotton, K. (1991). Teaching thinking skills. *School Improvement Research Series.* Retrieved from http://www.nwrel.org/scpd/sirs/6/cu11.html

Darling-Hammond, L. (Ed.). (2000). *Studies of excellence in teacher preparation: Preparation in the undergraduate years.* New York: AACTE.

Finely, S. J. (2000). *Instructional coherence: The changing role of the teacher.* Retrieved from http://www.sedl.org/pubs/teaching99/changingrole.pdf

Hargrove, K. (2003). If you build it, they will come: Teaching higher order thinking skills. *Gifted Child Today, 26*(1), 30–32.

Lang, K. S. (2001). *Critical thinking dispositions of pre-service teachers in Singapore: A preliminary investigation.* Retrieved from http://www.aare.edu.au/01pap/kon01173.htm

McGowan, S. (2007). *An exploratory study of teachers' critical thinking in elementary language arts classrooms.* Unpublished doctoral dissertation, The College of William and Mary, Williamsburg, VA.

McGowan, S., & Powers, N. B. (2008). *Pre-service teachers' dispositions toward critical thinking.* Manuscript submitted for publication.

No Child Left Behind Act, 20 U.S.C. §6301 (2001).

Parks, S. (2005). Teaching analytical and critical thinking skills in gifted education. In F. A. Karnes & S. M. Bean (Eds.), *Methods and materials for teaching the gifted* (2nd ed.). Waco, TX: Prufrock Press.

Paul, R., & Elder, L. (2000). *The miniature guide to critical thinking: Concepts & tools.* Dillon Beach, CA: Foundation for Critical Thinking.

Paul, R., & Elder, L. (2001). *Study of 38 public universities and 28 private universities to determine faculty emphasis on critical thinking in instruction.* Dillon Beach: CA, Center for Critical Thinking.

Paul, R., & Nosich, G. M. (2005). *A model for the national assessment of higher order thinking.* Dillon Beach: CA, Center for Critical Thinking.

Pohl, M. (2000). *Learning to think, thinking to learn: Models and strategies to develop a classroom culture of thinking.* Cheltenham, Australia: Hawker Brownlow.

Roberts, C., Ingram, C., & Harris, C. (1992). The effect of special versus regular classroom programming on higher cognitive processes of intermediate elementary aged gifted and average ability students. *Journal for Education of the Gifted, 15,* 332–343.

Scriven, M., & Paul, R. (2005). *Defining critical thinking: A draft statement for the national council for excellence in critical thinking.* Retrieved from Nohttp://www.criticalthinking. org/University/univlibrary/library.nclk

Shore, B. M., & Kanevsky, L. S. (1993). Thinking processes: Being and becoming gifted. In K. A. Heller, F. J. Mönks, & A. H. Passow (Eds.), *International handbook of research and development of giftedness and talent* (pp. 133–147). Tarrytown, NY: Pergamon Press.

Thompson, C. L., & Zeuli, J. S. (1999). The frame and the tapestry: Standards-based reform and professional development. In L. Darling-Hammond & G. Sykes (Eds.), *Teaching as the learning profession: Handbook of policy and practice* (pp. 341–375). San Francisco: Jossey Bass.

VanTassel-Baska, J. (1994). A study of self-concept and social support in advantaged and disadvantaged seventh and eighth grade gifted students. *Roeper Review, 16,* 186–191.

VanTassel-Baska, J., Quek, C., & Feng, A. (2005). *Classroom Observation Scales, Revised: Preliminary user's manual.* Williamsburg, VA: The College of William and Mary, Center for Gifted Education,

Watson, G., & Glaser, E. M. (2006). *Watson-Glaser Critical Thinking Appraisal short form manual.* New York: Harcourt Assessment.

Weinstein, M. (1995). *Critical thinking: Expanding the paradigm.* Retrieved from http:// www.chss.montclair.edu/inquiry/fall95/weinste.html

Zohar, A., & Aharon-Kravetsky, S. (2005). Exploring the effects of cognitive conflict and direct teaching for students of different academic levels. *Journal of Research in Science Teaching, 42,* 829–855.

CHAPTER 34

TEACHER PERCEPTIONS OF SELF-EFFICACY AND DIFFERENTIATED STRATEGY USE IN WORKING WITH GIFTED LEARNERS IN TITLE I SCHOOLS

by

KIMBERLY
M. TYLER

Systematic differentiation in the field is nested in teacher under-standing of how to translate curriculum and instruction in appropriate ways with diverse gifted learners.
—Joyce VanTassel-Baska

For the past 25 years, the powerful role that teacher efficacy plays in student achievement has been the focus of many educational studies (Tschannen-Moran & Woolfolk Hoy, 2002). Research has shown that effective teachers demonstrate certain characteristics and behaviors that make them successful in most settings, and that those teachers really do make a great difference in their students' achievement (Marzano, Pickering, & Pollock, 2001; Stronge, 2002; Wright, Horn, & Sanders, 1997).

One important aspect of teacher efficacy pertains to the affective characteristics of teachers (National Board for Professional Teaching Standards [NBPTS] 2005; Stronge, 2002; Tucker & Stronge, 2005). Effective teachers really do care about their students; these teachers support their students by encouraging an open line of communication and listening and responding to what their students are saying in a positive and trustful way. In addition, the National Board for Professional Teaching Standards recognized that effective teachers treat all students with respect, fostering students' self-esteem, motivation, character, and civic responsibility, as well as their respect for individual, cultural, religious, and racial differences.

Effective teachers also demonstrate a real enthusiasm for the learning process and the subject matter they teach. Being able to reach students through various instructional methods when difficulties arise leads to greater feelings of success for the student, which can increase motivation level and lead to a greater willingness to work to higher levels of achievement (NBTS, 2005; Stronge, 2002; Tucker & Stronge, 2005).

However, there are additional teacher characteristics that are required to work effectively with gifted students. VanTassel-Baska (2003a) stated that teachers of the gifted need to be lifelong learners who value knowledge and the learning process as it applies to the classroom, effectively manipulating ideas at high levels with their students. Rogers (1999) conducted a research synthesis and discovered that effective teachers of the gifted need to exhibit the following characteristics: high degree of intelligence and intellectual honesty; expertise in a specific area of interest; passion for advanced knowledge; genuine interest in gifted learners; and a strong belief in individual differences. It also is critical that teachers of the gifted have insights into both cognitive and social and emotional needs of gifted learners (Feldhusen, 1991; Gross, 1994; Hansen & Feldhusen, 1994).

In addition to both cognitive and affective traits, there are specific instructional strategies that effective teachers of the gifted consistently implement with their students. Although it is important to ask basic recall questions to establish a knowledge base, it is critical that higher level questions be asked, as these types of questions generate a deeper understanding of the content being studied (Marzano et al., 2001; Stronge, 2002). High-level questions that require critical and creative thinking can be used to challenge students because it gives them the opportunity to make the connection between subject matter and real-world applications. This strategy is highly effective with students of all ability levels, but it is especially effective with gifted learners.

The use of graphic organizers also allows students to organize information and ideas on a given topic, allowing teachers to assess and promote student understanding more effectively (Marzano et al, 2001). The Center for Gifted Education at The College of William and Mary has strong research to support this strategy with gifted learners, and incorporates graphic organizers such as the Hamburger Model for Persuasive Writing in all of its curricular units (VanTassel-Baska & Stambaugh, 2005).

Effective teachers are persistent in "challenging and engaging students in all aspects of instruction" (Stronge, 2002, p. 49). This can be accomplished through student questioning, real-world problem solving, and positive reinforcement of desired behaviors. Problem solving also encourages student engagement as it solicits multiple ideas and solutions to given situations.

Using preassessment strategies allows teachers to plan more effectively for individual students, leading to greater achievement (Reis & Renzulli, 2003; Stronge, 2002; VanTassel-Baska, 2003b). Curriculum compacting is one model of preassessment that accommodates individual differences by giving students the option of taking a pretest to determine if they have already mastered the objectives or standards for a given unit. Students who show mastery should be provided accelerative instruction in the core area of learning.

A STUDY OF TEACHER SELF-EFFICACY AND USE OF DIFFERENTIATION

A study was conducted to determine the self-efficacy of teachers in Title I classrooms and to assess if their self-perceptions of behaviors matched the observed behaviors when implementing the important skills and strategies necessary for successfully teaching gifted students.

Context of the Study

This study was based on a larger quasi-experimental study that randomized teacher assignment to treatment conditions, conducted by the Center for Gifted Education at The College of William and Mary. One purpose of the larger study was to assess the learning outcomes of all students who were exposed to a curriculum designed for high-ability learners. Results suggested that all learners benefited from the intervention and that teachers exposed to both the curriculum and targeted professional development improved across 3 years in the use of differentiated strategies (VanTassel-Baska, Bracken, Feng, & Brown, in press).

Participants

A total of 67 elementary school teachers were asked to participate in this study. Forty of the teachers responded, for a response rate of 60%. Of these 40, 16 were experimental teachers and 24 were control. Of the teachers participating in this study, 6.3% were male and 93.8% were female. In the control group, 4.2% were male while 95.8% were female. Ethnicity differences were as follows: 6.3% of the experimental teachers were African American; 6.3%, Asian American; 81.3%, Caucasian; and 6.3% "Other." Control teachers were 7.2% African American and 91.7% Caucasian. Frequencies were run on the highest degree earned, and results revealed that 50% of the participants held a bachelor's degree, 45% held a master's degree, and 5% held "Other" advanced degrees.

Teaching experience ranged from 0–1 year of experience to more than 20 years of experience, with a mean range of 6–10 years. Experience working with gifted learners ranged from 0–1 year to more than 20 years, with a mean range of 2–5 years. Of the 40 participants, 10% hold a gifted endorsement and 90% did not. The majority of teachers participating in this study had fewer than 10 hours of professional development specific to gifted learners. Not including the Project Athena professional development seminars, 68.8% of the experimental and 75% of the control teachers reported fewer than 10 hours of training in gifted education.

Instrumentation

An investigator-developed questionnaire was organized to collect basic demographic data on the teachers and open-ended responses to their attitudes toward working with the gifted. In addition, two instruments were used to address the core study questions.

The Teachers' Sense of Efficacy Scale (short form; TSES), developed by Tschannen-Moran and Woolfolk Hoy (2001) at the Ohio State University, provided a measure of overall teacher efficacy. The short form has 12 questions that are rated on a 9-point continuum. The three subscales of this instrument include: Efficacy in Student Engagement, Efficacy in Instructional Strategies, and Efficacy in Classroom Management. The Teachers' Sense of Efficacy (short form) has a reliability of .98 and a content validity of .89 in Instructional Strategies, .84 in Classroom Management, and .87 in Student Engagement.

The Classroom Observation Scales, Revised (COS-R; VanTassel-Baska et al., 2003) is an instrument designed to analyze differentiated teaching behaviors. The scale is divided into six categories: Curriculum Planning and Delivery, Accommodations for Individual Differences, Problem Solving, Critical Thinking Strategies, Creative Thinking Strategies, and Research Strategies. Each category has between three and five underlying indicators. The content validity of the COS-R was found to be .97. The internal consistency for the COS-R was .91 with an inter-rater reliability of .89.

Treatment Fidelity

The experimental teachers received 5 days per year of professional development in unit implementation through the Center for Gifted Education, specifically targeted at the successful use of the curriculum. The comparison teachers had been using the recommended curriculum of their school districts and receiving no professional development through the Center for Gifted Education. All teachers were observed twice annually during the 3 years of grant implementation to assess both differentiated practice and fidelity of implementation of the William and Mary curriculum.

Procedures for the Study

Teachers were asked to complete the Teacher Questionnaire and both instruments. The COS-R also was used by external observers to collect data on actual demonstrated behaviors that were then compared to teacher self-perceptions of behaviors.

Data Analysis

Descriptive statistics were run to obtain demographic profiles of teachers and to analyze open-ended responses to structured questions. A t-test for independent means was run to determine whether there was a statistically significant difference in teachers' self-ratings on the Teachers' Sense of Efficacy Scale (short form). In order to study the relationships between teachers' self-perceptions and external observer scores on the COS-R, a paired sample t-test was run.

Limitations of the Study

There were several limitations of this study that must be considered when assessing the validity of the findings. The first limitation is the reaction of the experimental group, commonly referred to as the Hawthorne Effect. Those participating in the experimental population may have reacted to the novelty of participating in a study (Gall, Gall, & Borg, 2003), therefore leading to artificial inflation of self-rated scores of their abilities and an inflated sense of differentiation strategy use in the classroom. Conversely, the comparison teachers may have suffered from demoralization as a result of not receiving special materials or training. Diffusion of treatment also may have been a limitation. Because there were experimental teachers in the same schools as control teachers, discussions about teaching strategies and working with gifted students may have occurred between the two groups. Finally, the generalizability of findings from this study is limited by both the sample size and the random selection of intact groups of teachers working in low socioeconomic school settings. As a result, the findings may not necessarily be relevant to teachers working in non-Title I schools with students from other socioeconomic backgrounds.

FINDINGS

Results From the TSES

No significant differences were found between experimental and comparison groups on the scale. For the Student Engagement subscale, both experimental and control teachers rated themselves slightly lower than the norm population. For the Instructional Strategies subscale, experimental teachers rated themselves slightly lower than the norm population, while the control teachers rated themselves slightly higher. Finally, on the Classroom Management subscale, both experimental and control teachers rated themselves higher than the norm population. Differences were nonsignificant, however.

Results From Open-Ended Questions

Five open-ended questions were posed to the teachers on their sense of efficacy in working with gifted learners. The content of the teacher responses was analyzed using frequency counts and holistic coding to determine emerging themes. Question 1 on the Teacher Questionnaire asked, "Do you think gifted students will learn no matter what strategies you implement in the classroom?" Out of the 40 surveys, 22 teachers answered "yes," 14 answered "no," and 4 responded with answers indicating that both "yes" and "no" are equally valid answers. Comments made by those teachers who answered "yes" focused mainly on personal characteristics, such as curiosity, self-motivation, and a desire to excel, that allow gifted students to learn regardless of their environment. Comments of teachers who responded "no" focused mainly on external factors such as lack of differentiation and/or challenging curriculum that hinder gifted students' abilities to excel in the regular classroom.

Questions 2–4 focused specifically on perceptions of self-efficacy in working with gifted students. Question 2 asked, "What do you feel are your greatest strengths in working with gifted learners?" The responses clustered around the traits of flexibility, high expectations, understanding individual needs, ability to motivate, and patience. Question 3 asked, "How successful do you feel you are at planning for multiple ability levels, including gifted learners?" Out of the 40 surveys, 15 teachers answered that they felt successful differentiating for ability levels, 16 responded that they were somewhat successful, 7 teachers answered that they were not successful, 1 was undecided, and 1 did not answer the question. Comments made by teachers who felt they were successful at planning for multiple ability levels focused on experience and mastery knowledge. Those who did not feel successful focused mainly on a lack of time to differentiate appropriately and overloaded schedules. Question 4 asked, "How successful do you feel in keeping even the most unmotivated students engaged in language arts?" Out of the 40 surveys, 24 teachers answered that they felt successful keeping students engaged in language arts, 8 responded that they were somewhat successful, 5 teachers answered that they were not successful, 2 answered that the question was not applicable to them, and 1 did not answer the question. Some comments made by those who felt successful were, "I can keep students engaged in a guided reading group by choosing good literature"; and "I feel pretty successful as I have a lot of positive feelings towards reading and writing." Those who did not feel successful stated, "I would like to be more successful. I try to motivate students in a variety of ways, but I would definitely like to learn more strategies"; and "Not very. My lack of experience does not provide me with a lot of tried and proven strategies."

Question 5 asked, "What, if any, professional development sessions have been the most effective in increasing your confidence in working with gifted students? Be specific." Out of the 40 teachers surveyed, 15 stated that they had not received any specific professional development sessions in gifted education. Four stated that they had not received any additional training outside of Project Athena, and 13 mentioned they had received some form of additional training, including 2 who had taken some college coursework. Four of the teachers did not answer this question, and 4 stated that it was not applicable to them. Eleven participants mentioned participating in professional development as beneficial; however, they did not provide enough information for the researcher to develop definitive themes about which aspects of these opportunities were most helpful.

Results from the Classroom Observation Scales, Revised

Paired samples *t*-tests were run to determine if any statistically significant differences could be found between teacher self-ratings and the ratings of external observers. The range of self-rated scores for the experimental teachers was 1.88 to 2.88 and the range for the control teachers was 1.88 to 2.83. The mean of means for the experimental teachers was 2.45 and 2.42 for control teachers. The range of externally rated scores for the experimental teachers was 1.80 to 2.67 and the range

Table 34.1

RESULTS FROM PAIRED SAMPLES *T*-TEST OF TEACHER SELF-PERCEPTIONS AND EXTERNAL OBSERVER PERCEPTIONS ON THE COS-R: EXPERIMENTAL TEACHERS

n = 16	Self-Perception		External Observers			
	M	*SD*	*M*	*SD*	*t*	Sig. (2-tailed)
Curriculum Planning and Delivery	2.59	.27	2.24	.50	2.39	.031*
Accommodations for Individual Differences	2.59	.30	2.26	.68	1.57	.14
Problem Solving	2.52	.38	2.00	—	—	—
Critical Thinking Skills	2.41	.46	2.07	.81	1.59	.14
Creative Thinking Skills	2.55	.44	2.05	.69	2.78	.015*
Research Strategies	2.11	.45	2.00	—	-1.00	.50

* *p* ≤ .05

for the control teachers was 1.00 to 2.47. The mean of means for the experimental teachers was 2.25 compared to 1.81 for control teachers.

Based on the mean scores, external observers rated both experimental and control teachers lower than the teachers rated themselves. However, it should be noted that for the categories of Problem Solving and Research Strategies for both experimental and control groups, the number of external observers who witnessed these strategies taking place was much lower than the number of teachers who self-reported on these behaviors. In addition, this discrepancy between the number of behaviors witnessed by external observers and self-reports also existed for control teachers in the categories of Critical Thinking and Creative Thinking.

For experimental teachers, a paired samples *t*-test was run for each category of the COS-R to determine if a statistically significant difference existed between how the teachers rated themselves and how they were rated by external observers. A statistically significant difference was found in two of the six categories, Curriculum Planning and Delivery and Creative Thinking Skills, favoring self-assessment. Table 34.1 reflects the findings from these paired samples *t*-tests.

For control teachers, a paired samples *t*-test was run for each category of the COS-R to determine if a statistically significant difference existed between how the teachers rated themselves and how they were rated by external observers. A statistically significant difference was found in four of the six categories (i.e., Curriculum Planning and Delivery, Accommodations for Individual Differences, Critical Thinking Skills, and Creative Thinking Skills), favoring self-assessments. It is important to note that no determination of significance could be made for the

Table 34.2

RESULTS FROM PAIRED SAMPLES *T*-TEST OF TEACHER SELF-PERCEPTIONS AND EXTERNAL OBSERVER PERCEPTIONS ON THE COS-R: CONTROL TEACHERS

	Self-Perception		External Observers			
n = 24	*M*	*SD*	*M*	*SD*	*t*	Sig. (2-tailed)
Curriculum Planning and Delivery	2.65	.36	2.04	.78	3.62	.001*
Accommodations for Individual Differences	2.43	.41	2.08	.58	2.76	.012*
Problem Solving	2.53	.49	2.00	—	—	—
Critical Thinking Skills	2.42	.44	1.79	.67	2.49	.027*
Creative Thinking Skills	2.51	.44	1.64	.72	2.93	.015*
Research Strategies	2.04	.67	1.00	—	2.33	.258

* $p \leq .05$

category of Problem Solving because only one external observer noted witnessing behaviors in this category. Table 34.2 presents these findings.

DISCUSSION

In order to improve the implementation of differentiation skills with gifted learners, teachers must first be self-efficacious as well as trained in working with these unique learners. Through professional development sessions and academic coursework, teachers gain a greater understanding of the characteristics and special needs common to this population of students. With the majority of our schools organizing classes heterogeneously, teachers must work with students who demonstrate varying degrees of ability. Given that there were no significant differences on the self-efficacy scale, yet teachers self-reported concerns about their ability to work effectively with the gifted, it would seem that more professional development opportunities that are targeted to differentiated strategy use for these teachers may be appropriate to consider.

Professional Development

The first step in encouraging the implementation of effective teaching strategies is offering valuable professional development sessions to teachers. This is the "primary methodology through which teachers update their skills and new teachers are socialized to the priorities of a particular school and/or district" (VanTassel-Baska,

2002). Effective professional development should include the following essential elements: focus on content knowledge and content pedagogy; opportunities for active learning; continuous and ongoing with opportunities for follow-up; and coherence with other learning activities (Garet, Porter, Desimone, Birman, & Yoon, 2001; Guskey, 2000; Hawley & Valli, 1999).

The fact that so few teachers have received any training in working with gifted students is disappointing as all of the teachers participating in this study currently teach gifted students in their classroom. The accuracy of these teachers' attitudes and beliefs regarding gifted students may improve with strong professional development opportunities, leading to greater student achievement (Sanders & Horn, 1998; Sanders & Rivers, 1996; Stronge, 2002; Tucker & Stronge, 2005).

Another aspect of this study that supports the research on the need for professional development in gifted education is the teachers' comments about gifted students' ability to succeed without differentiation, which shows their lack of understanding about the needs of the gifted. More than half of the participating teachers felt that gifted students would learn no matter what strategies are implemented in the classroom. One experimental teacher stated that this is because gifted students are "inquisitive and creative," while another stated that "they are usually quicker learners and self-motivated." Although research does support these comments (Colangelo & Davis, 2003; Tomlinson, 1996; VanTassel-Baska, 2003b, 2005), research also suggests that gifted students will not always stay self-motivated and productive if their academic and social needs are not being met (Colangelo, Assouline, & Gross, 2004; Silverman, 2004; Winebrenner, 2001).

Perceived Self-Efficacy

Research shows that there is a strong positive effect on student achievement when teachers believe that they are positively influencing their students' learning (Bandura, 1994; Tschannen-Moran, Woolfolk Hoy, & Hoy, 1998). Those with low self-efficacy in a given area tend to fear failure, stopping them from even attempting to be successful. Individuals with a high sense of self-efficacy in a given area or on a specific task tend to be more task-oriented and demonstrate greater resilience when faced with difficult situations or failures (Bandura, 1994). This concept of self-efficacy is a powerful component in professional growth and in the improvement of educational opportunities for students.

This study found that on 10 out of the 12 questions on the Teachers' Sense of Efficacy Scale (short form), there was no statistically significant difference in how the experimental teachers rated themselves as compared to how the control teachers rated themselves. Because teachers were randomly assigned to treatment conditions, it is difficult to understand why the experimental group did not score higher, given their professional development experiences. It is possible that self-efficacy change requires a longer period of time to set in.

A statistically significant difference was found, however, in how experimental and control teachers rated themselves on questions pertaining to classroom management and instruction. The fact that the control teachers felt more efficacious in instructional strategies and in classroom management may be due to the fact that they have experienced more mastery teaching experiences than the experimental teachers, given more years of working with the gifted. These experiences, according to Bandura (1994), are the most effective way of developing and improving self-efficacy.

Perceptions of Differentiated Teaching Behaviors

As the *National Excellence* report noted, gifted students already know 35–50% of the curriculum before they begin the school year (U.S. Department of Education, 1993). With traditional schools in our country grouping students based on age and not ability, the continuum of knowledge in any given heterogeneous classroom is vast. When differentiation strategies are used effectively, however, the needs of most learners can be met better. How teachers perceive such strategy use in their classrooms is critical to the successful implementation of differentiated curriculum.

When it comes to how well teachers participating in this study perceived differentiated teaching behaviors in their classrooms, the external reviewers and the experimental teacher ratings were similar on the Classroom Observation Scales, Revised (COS-R). This comparable rating was most likely due to professional development, designed to help the experimental teachers recognize and effectively implement differentiation strategies with gifted students in their classrooms.

Control teachers rated themselves much higher on the COS-R than the external observers rated them, a finding consistent with earlier studies of regular untrained classroom teachers' perceptions of using differentiated behaviors (VanTassel-Baska, Zuo, Avery, & Little, 2002). The most obvious explanation for this discrepancy is that the control teachers have neither received targeted professional development on the differentiation strategies on the COS-R nor been given any feedback regarding the effective implementation of those strategies from outside observers.

IMPLICATIONS

As an exploratory study of teacher perceptions of self-efficacy and differentiated classroom behaviors in regular classrooms, this study presented few findings of statistical or educational significance. However, it does demonstrate the potential role of professional development in elevating teacher perceptions to a realistic level in respect to the practice of differentiation in the regular classroom. Moreover, it suggests that the COS-R is an instrument of utility for both self-assessment and observer use that could provide data for a needs-based approach to professional development.

Dr. Joyce VanTassel-Baska is an extraordinary talent whose lifelong work and dedication have led to remarkable changes in the field of gifted education. Dr. VanTassel-Baska's work in curriculum development holds teachers of the gifted to higher standards, therefore increasing the educational experiences of those students in classrooms where her findings are implemented. It has truly been an honor to work with such a remarkable woman, and I feel that I have learned from the very best.

REFERENCES

Bandura, A. (1994). Self-efficacy. In V. S. Ramachaudran (Ed.), *Encyclopedia of human behavior* (Vol. 4, pp. 71–81). New York: Academic Press.

Colangelo, N., & Davis, G. A. (2003). *Handbook of gifted education* (3rd ed.). Boston: Allyn & Bacon.

Colangelo, N., Assouline, S. G., & Gross, M. U. M. (2004). *A nation deceived: How schools hold back America's brightest students* (Vol. 1). Iowa City: The University of Iowa, The Connie Belin & Jacqueline N. Blank International Center for Gifted Education and Talent Development.

Feldhusen, J. F. (1991). Full-time classes for gifted youth. *Gifted Child Today, 14*(5), 10–13.

Gall, M. D., Gall, J. P., & Borg, W. R. (2003). *Educational research: An introduction.* Boston, MA: Allyn & Bacon.

Garet, M. S., Porter, A. C., Desimone, L., Birman, B. F., & Yoon, K. S. (2001). What makes professional development effective? Results from a national sample of teachers. *American Educational Research Journal, 38,* 915–945.

Gross, M. U. M. (1994). Changing teacher attitudes toward gifted students through inservice training. *Gifted and Talented International, 8*(2), 15–21.

Guskey, T. R. (2000). *Evaluating professional development.* Thousand Oaks, CA: Corwin Press.

Hansen, J. B., & Feldhusen, J. F. (1994). Comparison of trained and untrained teachers of gifted students. *Gifted Child Quarterly, 38,* 115–121.

Hawley, W. D., & Valli, L. (1999). The essentials of effective professional development: A new consensus. In L. Darling-Hammond & G. Sykes (Eds.), *Teaching as the learning profession: Handbook of policy and practice.* San Francisco: Jossey-Bass.

Marzano, R. J., Pickering, D. J., & Pollock, J. E. (2001). *Classroom instruction that works: Research-based strategies for increasing student achievement.* Alexandria, VA: ASCD.

National Board for Professional Teaching Standards. (2005). *What teachers should know and be able to do: The five core propositions of the national board.* Retrieved from http://www.nbpts.org/Userfiles/File/What_teachers.pdf

Reis, S. M., & Renzulli, J. S. (2003). *Curriculum compacting: A systematic procedure for modifying the curriculum for above average ability students.* Retrieved from http://www.gifted.uconn.edu/sem/semart08.html

Rogers, K. B. (1999). *Research synthesis on gifted provisions.* Retrieved from http://www.austega.com/gifted/articles/Rogers_researchsynthesis.htm

Sanders, W. L. & Horn, S. (1998). Research findings from the Tennessee Value Added Assessment System (TVAAS) database: Implications for educational evaluation and research. *Journal of Personnel Evaluation in Education, 12,* 247–256.

Sanders, W. L., & Rivers, J. C. (1996). *Cumulative and residual effects of teachers on future academic achievement.* Knoxville: University of Tennessee Value-Added Research and Assessment Center.

Silverman, L. K. (2004). *Do gifted students have special needs?* Retrieved from http://www.gifteddevelopment.net/xcart/product.php?productid=16234

Stronge, J. H. (2002). *Qualities of effective teachers.* Alexandria, VA: ASCD.

Tomlinson, C. A. (1996). Good teaching for one and all: Does gifted education have an instructional identity? *Journal for the Education of the Gifted, 20,* 155–174.

Tschannen-Moran, M., & Woolfolk Hoy, A. (2001). Teacher efficacy: Capturing an elusive construct. *Teaching and Teacher Education, 17,* 783–805

Tschannen-Moran, M., & Woolfolk Hoy, A. (2002, April). *The influence of resources and support on teachers' efficacy beliefs.* Paper presented at annual meeting of the American Educational Research Association, New Orleans, LA.

Tschannen-Moran, M., Woolfolk Hoy, A., & Hoy, W. K. (1998). Teacher efficacy: Its meaning and measure. *Review of Educational Research, 68,* 202–248.

Tucker, P. D., & Stronge, J. H. (2005). *Linking teaching evaluation and student learning.* Alexandria, VA: ASCD.

U.S. Department of Education, Office of Educational Research and Improvement. (1993). *National excellence: A case for developing America's talent.* Washington, DC: U.S. Government Printing Office.

VanTassel-Baska, J. (2002). Planning professional development experiences in gifted education. *Newsletter: Virginia Association for the Gifted, 24*(1), 1–4.

VanTassel-Baska, J. (2003a). *Basic educational options for gifted students in schools.* Retrieved from http://cfge.wm.edu/Gifted%20Educ%20Artices/Basic_Educational_Options.htm

VanTassel-Baska, J. (2003b). *Curriculum planning and instructional design for gifted learners.* Denver, CO: Love.

VanTassel-Baska, J. (2005, March). *Lessons learned in curriculum differentiation, instruction, and assessment.* Paper presented at the National Curriculum Network Conference, Williamsburg, VA.

VanTassel-Baska, J., Avery, L., Drummond, D., Struck, J., Feng A., & Stambaugh, T. (2003). *The Classroom Observation Scales, Revised.* Williamsburg, VA: The College of William and Mary, Center for Gifted Education.

VanTassel-Baska, J., Bracken, B., Feng, A., & Brown, E. (in press). A longitudinal study of reading comprehension and reasoning ability of students in elementary Title I schools. *Journal for the education of the Gifted.*

VanTassel-Baska, J., & Stambaugh, T. (2005). *Comprehensive curriculum for gifted learners* (3rd ed.). Boston: Allyn & Bacon.

VanTassel-Baska, J., Zuo, L., Avery, L. D., & Little, C. A. (2002). A curriculum study of gifted student learning in the language arts. *Gifted Child Quarterly, 46,* 30–45.

Winebrenner, S. (2001). *Teaching gifted kids in the regular classroom: Strategies and techniques every teacher can use to meet the academic needs of the gifted and talented.* Minneapolis, MN: Free Spirit.

Wright, S. P., Horn, S. P., & Sanders, W. L. (1997). Teacher and classroom context effects on student achievement: Implications for teacher evaluation. *Journal of Personnel Evaluation in Education, 11,* 57–67.

CHAPTER 35

LOOKING BACK AND MOVING AHEAD:

Quantitative Research in Gifted Education

by

CAROL
L. TIESO

The proper study of mankind has been said to be man. [But] . . . in large part, the proper study of mankind is the study of design.
—Henri Saint-Simon

INTRODUCTION

Those of us who conduct research in gifted education seem to be on the pointed end of the rhetoric that the scientific (and medical) community frequently fires at general and special education. Over the decades we, specifically in gifted education, have not had abundant retorts to these accusations; in fact, we have had a tendency to recommend practices and interventions that we *think* will succeed, but except for the long empirical research base behind acceleration and ability grouping, we haven't had much evidence to counter these attacks. My colleague (and friend) Dr. Joyce VanTassel-Baska recognized this problem years ago and has spent a long and esteemed career addressing it through her teaching, advocacy, policy work, and most importantly for our discussion, her tireless work to demonstrate that advanced content and powerful curriculum was the antidote to random acts of gifted education. Additionally, over the past 10 years, Joyce has demonstrated, not just to the field of gifted education but to the larger domain of education, that the curriculum for which she has devoted a career of advocacy also will help advance the achievement of students who do not come to school with the same advantages as others. It is her work, and that of the Center for Gifted Education (CFGE), that will serve as the centerpiece around which this discussion pivots.

In this chapter, I will discuss the past and future of quantitative research, and its role in the field of gifted education. It is an exciting time for quantitative research methods due to the new, more powerful techniques discussed in the literature, and the analytic and creative minds that are emerging in the field. These two phenomena together bode well for the future of empirical research in our field.

RESEARCH PARADIGMS

Qualitative

My colleague, Laurence Coleman, has expertly described the use of qualitative designs in gifted education in this volume. Although I have been known to be something of a post-positivist, I firmly believe that the "stories" we tell are incomplete without the vision of qualitative findings. I may be straddling the fence, but I believe there is a place in our research portfolio for mixed-methods designs. The richness derived from multiple methods and data sources may not be replicated with one method used in isolation.

Mixed Methods

Creswell and Clark (2007) described four types of mixed-methods designs: Triangulation Design, the Embedded Design, the Explanatory Design, and the Exploratory Design. The authors suggested that the purpose of the Triangulation Design is to collect different but mutually reinforcing data on the same topic at the same time. The key to this design is that quantitative and qualitative data are collected at the same time and are assigned equal weight. The Embedded Design is a mixed-methods design for which "one data set provides a supportive, secondary role in a study based primarily on the other data type" (Creswell & Clark, 2007, p. 67). In gifted education, for example, an experimental study may measure the effects of integrating technology into the William and Mary literature units; qualitative data may be collected during the professional development stage to describe the issues and difficulties teachers encounter when learning to integrate technology. The Explanatory Design is a two-phase design, the purpose of which is for qualitative data to help explain or build upon initial quantitative results. For example, a research study might consist of administering a survey regarding gifted students' perceptions of their class activities (Gentry & Gable, 2001), which may be supplemented by a short, semistructured interview as a follow-up. The fourth type of mixed methods design is the Exploratory Design, a two-phase design in which results from the first method (qualitative) help or inform the second method (quantitative). The authors suggest that there are several occasions that call for this kind of design: at times when "measures or instruments are not available, the variables are unknown, or there is no guiding framework or theory" (Creswell & Clark, 2007, p. 75). One example of this study was a year 4 follow-up study that emerged from Project Athena (VanTassel-Baska, Bracken, Brown, & Feng, 2005). In the first phase, researchers at the CFGE conducted focus group and semistructured interviews with teachers, coordinators, and administrators from the treatment schools. The qualitative data from these interviews were transcribed, coded, and analyzed for major themes. Then, several of us compiled these themes and quotes and developed a survey instrument, A Stakeholder's Perceptions of Reform Efforts (ASPIRE), which has been pilot-tested and found to have strong psychometric properties. Creswell and Clark (2007) have written a volume that clearly and concisely defines a structure for what in the past has been a haphazard approach to research design.

Quantitative

Rather than attempt to rewrite excellent texts on research design (cf. Creswell, 2002; Gall, Gall, & Borg, 2006), I will briefly outline a framework for a quantitative research study and delineate differences between research and evaluation, both activities in which the CFGE has excelled.

Research or evaluation? According to Gall et al. (2006), educational research is a process that helps inform practice, whereas evaluation is a process used to make judgments about the value or worth of educational programs. The authors suggested that educational research contributes four types of knowledge to a domain: description, prediction, improvement, and explanation. Quantitative researchers propose that they are examining phenomena in an objective, or value-free environment; however, the questions that researchers choose to address point to a bias on the part of that researcher. In that way, quantitative researchers may not be as honest as their qualitative brethren with respect to actual practice. This also tends to confuse the distinction between research and evaluation; but there are differences, however subtle.

Research and evaluation use many of the same tools, but may have distinctly different purposes. For example, in Project PROMISE, a Javits project that was recently evaluated by the CFGE, the purpose of the evaluation was to assess the impact of using the pedagogy of gifted education and the science curriculum of the CFGE with students in heterogeneous, Title I schools. Some of the methods used were quantitative in nature; for example, the evaluator examined standardized achievement data using typical statistical procedures. But, the purpose was not simply *to explain* what happened, but rather *to evaluate* the effectiveness of such practices in order to effect policy changes at the school, state, or federal level.

An additional difference between research and evaluation is the extent to which one can generalize the results. In Project PROMISE, there was no attempt made to generalize results to other settings or students, but to determine how well the program worked with this particular population. A researcher may have used a thorough description of the participants' characteristics to attempt to generalize the results to other participants.

A third major difference between these processes is that evaluation, by its definition, involves making judgments of the *value* of the intervention. Many states across the country are facing difficult decisions regarding funding educational programs. Some have adopted a *value added* approach (Wright, Horn, & Sanders, 1997) to assess how much value is added to students' achievement due to a program or intervention. Unfortunately, the nature of the outcome is typically student achievement scores, which are not readily responsive to interventions such as Creative Problem Solving (Treffinger, Isaksen, & Stead-Dorval, 2006) or writing models such as the Hamburger Model (Center for Gifted Education, 2004). It is important that those of us in gifted education not let our colleagues be swayed by evaluation techniques that may not match data collection to outcome.

Two other major differences include the level of rigor of the study and the role of stakeholders in the process. In quantitative educational research, the researcher tries to remain as detached and objective as possible and attempts to control other variables besides those manipulated or measured. In evaluation studies, the evaluator typically intrudes at certain points (formative evaluation) or at the conclusion of the study (summative evaluation) and there is no attempt to control study variables. An additional difference is that in educational evaluation, there are numerous stakeholders who are involved or may be interested in the outcome. It is important for the evaluator to explore the perceptions of these stakeholders and to report back to them when the study is complete.

Finally, in evaluation, the results will be examined in terms of four criteria: utility, feasibility, propriety, and accuracy (Gall et al., 2006), whereas in educational research, the results will be evaluated in terms of how well the researcher limited the threats to internal and external validity.

CONDUCTING A STUDY

Many novice researchers approach their research designs with a question, albeit the wrong one: I've got this survey I want to use; what can I do with it? A research question is important, but the real question is, "What do you want to know?" Once a researcher has decided on these questions, it is very simple to move to the next step, deciding whether qualitative, quantitative, or mixed-methods designs will best answer those questions. Finally, the researcher can then fashion research questions that are specific to the type of research she's planning to conduct. The following example will describe how this process has been used; first, an example from the past and second, an example from the present.

PAST STUDY EXAMPLE:
DIFFERENTIATION AND GROUPING

When I began my doctoral work at the University of Connecticut, while working as a graduate assistant for the National Research Center on the Gifted and Talented (NRC/GT), I became aware that school districts and educators throughout the region and the U.S. wanted someone from the NRC/GT to come out and "do" differentiation in the form of a professional development workshop. I immediately was concerned that, with the exception of the research on curriculum compacting (Reis et al., 1993), differentiation as an instructional strategy for gifted students was supported by a paucity of empirical research. At that moment, I knew that it was important for us as a field to advocate strategies that were supported by research. I wanted to know, "Does remodeled or differentiated curriculum lead to higher levels of student achievement than curriculum derived from a textbook?" I also wanted to know if differentiation would work better if accompanied by flexible grouping. Hence, we designed a study to test a model of differentiation combined with flexible grouping, specifically in mathematics.

Theoretical Framework and Research Design
The research design for this study emerged over the course of several months of collaboration with Dr. Deborah Burns and Dr. Robert Gable. The purpose of the study was to investigate the effects of different grouping practices (whole class, within class, and between class) and curricular adjustments (revised or differentiated, combined with flexible grouping) on intermediate students' mathematics achievement. The theoretical framework was based on Tomlinson's (1995, 1999) work with differentiation and Erickson's (2002) and VanTassel-Baska's (1986) work with concept-based, enhanced curriculum. After much deliberation, we decided on a quasi-experimental, repeated measures design to address these research questions:

1. To what extent do textbook-based or remodeled curriculum units explain differences in elementary students' post-unit achievement in mathematics, as measured by a curriculum-based assessment that addresses knowledge related to data representation and analysis?
2. To what extent do curriculum differentiation practices, combined with either between-class or within-class grouping practices, explain differences in elementary students' post-unit achievement in mathematics, as measured by a curriculum-based assessment that addresses knowledge related to data representation and analysis?

What began as a need to know whether or not what we advocated as best practices for gifted students truly were, ended as specific questions that would lead to specific data collection and analysis techniques.

Methods and Procedures

Participants. The participants consisted of 31 grade 4 or 5 teachers and their students (*N* = 686) from 4 New England school districts who had sought professional development assistance from researchers at the NRG/GT at the University of Connecticut. To address the issue of selection bias, I chose students from schools of diverse SES and type (rural or suburban). To control for grade-level differences in knowledge, I chose to control the effects of grade level by limiting the participants to students in grades 4 and 5.

Instrumentation. Because this was a short, 3-week intervention, it was necessary to develop a curriculum-based assessment (CBA) to measure students' achievement prior to and at the conclusion of the study. The CBA was developed using standard instrument development procedures, and found to have acceptable values for construct validity and reliability. Instrumentation is an often-overlooked aspect of a study; as a field, we should strive to use or create instruments that demonstrate strong content and construct validity (especially for the study's participants), as well as good reliability.

Procedures. Teachers and their students were randomly assigned to either the comparison or treatment group. Teachers administered the pretest version of the CBA approximately 4–6 weeks prior to the curriculum and grouping intervention. Teachers taught either the treatment curricula, remodeled with whole-class grouping or differentiated with flexible grouping, or their typical textbook curricula for 3 weeks. To assess treatment fidelity and to limit the threat of statistical conclusion validity (unreliability of treatment implementation; Shadish, Cook, & Campbell, 2002), teachers completed a daily log indicating which components of each lesson were completed. The identical CBA was administered at the end of treatment implementation to assess within- and between-group differences.

Data Analysis

The pretest results from treatment and comparison groups were compared to check for group differences. Data from both administrations of the CBA were analyzed for time and treatment group effects using repeated measures analysis of variance (ANOVA) and reporting effect sizes (Grissom & Kim, 2005).

Results

There were significant differences between treatment and comparison groups and over time. Effect sizes ranged from .48 to .81 for students in the treatment high-ability groups.

Conclusions and Implications

Students in all treatment groups had higher means than their respective peers in the comparison groups. These results suggested that students could be challenged in a differentiation classroom that used appropriate flexible, temporary ability groups. In examining the results, there was evidence of a threat due to statistical conclusion validity based on a restricted range of responses from the students. To avoid a ceiling effect for gifted students, the CBA utilized items from grades 4–8, which made the test very difficult for most nongifted students. This threat may have reduced the power of the test to detect differences and may in fact have underestimated potential gains due to the treatment. According to Shadish et al. (2002), this threat to the validity of test inferences has been ignored by most researchers and may help explain the results (or nonresults) of many quantitative studies.

PRESENT STUDY EXAMPLE: PROJECT ATHENA

One of the most important projects in the field during the past two decades was Project Athena, a Javits demonstration grant. This project exemplifies the dedication that Dr. Joyce VanTassel-Baska has had over the years in conducting the difficult work of assessing the effectiveness of curriculum interventions. This example also highlights an area that may represent fertile ground for future researchers in gifted education: secondary data analysis. After original data were analyzed using multivariate analyses of variance (MANOVA), we used secondary data analytic techniques to evaluate potential growth models. The purpose of this study was to conduct secondary, hierarchical analyses of data collected from Project Athena, a quasi-experimental intervention study of the effects of William and Mary language arts curriculum units in Title I schools. The researchers posed several questions about the relative contributions of various individual- and school-level variables to students' mean scores and learning rates:

1. How much variation in students' Test of Critical Thinking (TCT) and Iowa Test of Basic Skills (ITBS) scores is attributable to school membership?
2. To what extent do students' background and school characteristics affect mean scores and learning rates on the TCT and ITBS?

Procedures

To assess the efficacy of the language arts curriculum, the original study employed a pre-post quasi-experimental, longitudinal design with six data points over 3 years. At each participating site, researchers randomly assigned grades 3–5 classes into experimental or comparison conditions. Participating experimental teachers from across multiple states and sites were trained on the William and Mary language arts curriculum and provided the necessary materials for implementation. The original implementation used tests of critical thinking and achievement to assess possible student learning gains in literary analysis and persuasive writing. Teachers in the comparison groups were invited to participate based on similar characteristics. The studies focused explicitly on student application of literary analysis and interpretation, persuasive writing, and linguistic competency.

Data Collection and Analyses

Data collected over 3 years of the curriculum implementation included results from students in treatment and comparison groups on the Test of Critical Thinking

(Bracken et al., 2003) and the Iowa Tests of Basic Skills (Hoover, Dunbar, & Frisbie, 2001). Results from six data points were analyzed using HLM 6.0 (Raudenbush & Bryk, 2002) to model student growth. The advantage of using HLM to analyze linear growth curves is that HLM can accommodate missing data at Level 1 (individual over time) by using all available data to estimate individual growth curves. This is important in longitudinal studies as attrition is a pervasive problem.

Nested data. For this study, data were collected at three levels: within student (over time), between student, and between schools. It is inappropriate to analyze data using traditional methods of regression due to the violation of the independence assumption and the nested nature of the data. HLM was chosen as the data analytic technique due to the nonindependent, nested nature of the data: students are nested within schools. By using HLM with multilevel data (e.g., students over time, between students, between schools), the researcher can overcome the unit of analysis problem common to educational research studies and partition variance components into individual- and group-level components to suggest a richer analysis. An additional advantage of HLM is the provision for calculating the Intraclass Correlation Coefficient (ICC), which allows researchers to separate variation into between-student and between-school components.

Results

There was significant variation around and significant differences in students' mean TCT and ITBS scores at the midpoint of the study (for this analysis, time was centered at the midpoint of data collection). There was significant variation in individual learning rates and in individual mean TCT and ITBS scores based on school membership. There were significant differences in mean TCT and ITBS scores for experimental and control groups with the experimental group earning the higher mean scores. Finally, an examination of the ICC suggested that 19% and 17% of the variance in students' scores on the TCT and ITBS, respectively, was between schools.

Conclusions and Implications

A summary of the most important results suggests that there was a ceiling effect for gifted students on the ITBS, but not on the TCT. This may suggest that typical achievement tests may not appropriately measure gifted students' true growth. Additionally, although African American and Hispanic students had lower mean scores at the beginning of the study, they had steeper growth curves, which suggests that the curriculum intervention was extremely successful for students of color. Perhaps the gains were due to the high level of expectations placed on all of participants, but whatever the backdrop, these findings demonstrate why the work of the CFGE has so influenced the field of gifted education. Again, statistical conclusion validity is a threat due to the artifact of regression to the mean for gifted and struggling learners alike. This honesty in reporting effects and noneffects alike is another characteristic that distinguishes Joyce's work from that of others who may not always share her deep sense of responsibility and strong ethical values. For additional studies in the field that have utilized HLM, see McCoach, O'Connell, Reis, and Levitt (2006) and Preckel, Zeidner, Goetz, and Schleyer (2008).

CURRENT CUTTING EDGE STUDIES IN GIFTED EDUCATION

Finally, in addition to Joyce's willingness to address difficult research issues in curriculum effectiveness and her honesty and integrity in reporting results, she also is willing to adopt new statistical and data analytic techniques and work with those who advocate for them. Research coordinators and tenure-track faculty members at centers throughout the field have collaborated to introduce a new level of rigor and sophistication in research design and analysis. An additional factor propelling this innovation is the type of quantitative research training that is available to current graduate students, who represent the next generation of leaders in our field. Many of them have emerged, not surprisingly, from these gifted centers, which are proving to be the axes upon which the field turns. In conclusion, I would like to provide a tantalizing peek at several quantitative and statistical methods that may yet bring this field to the forefront of educational research.

Confirmatory Factor Analyses

My colleague at the University of Connecticut, D. Betsy McCoach, has had an integral role in encouraging graduate students to conduct confirmatory, rather than simply exploratory, factor analyses to assess the construct validity of inferences from new instruments. Two recent studies by her graduate students were accepted for inclusion in the annual AERA conference. New graduate students are inspired by these studies to take coursework or attend institutes on conducting confirmatory factor analyses or assessing structural equation models. Recent examples include the validation of the SAAS-R, an instrument to measure self-concept, self-motivation, self-regulation, attitude toward school, and peer attitudes (McCoach, 2002) and a validation of the structure of the Social Coping Questionnaire with an American sample (Rudasill, Foust, & Callahan, 2007).

Logistic Regression

Logistic regression analysis is a set of statistical techniques that have their roots in multiple regression analysis; the major differences lie in the type of dependent variables analyzed (dichotomous or categorical) and the form of the results achieved (odds ratios). This kind of analysis could be very useful in gifted education in analyzing the effects of various independent variables (IVs) on whether or not a student is identified for a gifted program. The researcher is assessing the regression weights of the IVs in terms of the dichotomous dependent variable (identified or not). A recent example was an examination of the long-term achievement loss during transition to high school (Smith, 2006).

Single Subject

Another area of research that is not new, but underutilized in gifted education, is the single-subject experimental design (Kennedy, 2004). These research designs could be especially useful in determining the effects of various interventions with small subsamples of gifted students, such as those with learning disabilities or those who may be underachieving. These designs require that the researcher collect baseline data, identify the point at which the intervention is introduced, and assess the effects of the intervention on some intended outcome. The use of these designs also may help our field earn more acceptance for our interventions in special education or other specialized fields.

Regression Discontinuity Design

Finally, the hot topic among federal grant evaluators is the regression discontinuity design (RD; Shadish et al., 2002). According to the authors, the RD design requires the researcher to assign participants to two or more treatment conditions based on a cutoff score on an assigned variable, such as an achievement test or unit pretest. The basic requirement for the assigned variable is that it must be measured prior to the intervention and on at least an ordinal scale; so, for example, gender or ethnicity could not be used as the assignment variable as they are both considered nominal variables. After participants have been assigned to a treatment group (or treatment and control), those scoring on one side or the other of the cutoff score will receive the treatment. In gifted education, for example, this design could be used to investigate the effectiveness of a new program for gifted underachievers, whereby gifted students who scored below a certain cutoff on an achievement test would receive an intervention consisting of self-regulation strategies, activities to boost self-esteem, and individual counseling. The researcher would then graph the results in the form of a scatterplot around a regression line and indicate, with a vertical line, the point at which the intervention was introduced. If a vertical displacement appears in the regression line (the discontinuity) when compared to the control, that would demonstrate that the treatment had an effect on the intended treatment group (cf., Shadish et al., 2002, pp. 210–211). According to the authors, the analysis has more statistical power if the researcher is able to choose the mean of the distribution as the cutoff score. These are just a few of the statistical and design tools available to the next generation of researchers in gifted education. One more example comes from Herbert Marsh (1998), who models the analysis in examining the benefits to students of enrollment in a gifted program.

CONCLUSION

Reading these examples and peaking at the *zeitgeist* in the field of research reminds us of critical issues in designing research, in this case, quantitative research. First, there are no fancy statistical methods that can compensate for a poor research design. I'm reminded of a dear friend who often counsels, "measure twice, cut once." This is as true in research as it is in sewing or construction. Second, one makes one's place in the field by demonstrating honesty and integrity in reporting findings, or more illustratively, no findings. When one has earned a reputation for "unethical" behavior, there is little she can do with the rest of her career to overcome that perception. Finally, always remember that, in the field of gifted education, the subjects of our research are not lab rats or specimen in a Petri dish, but children. My colleague and friend, Joyce VanTassel-Baska, has taught me many lessons, none more important than the last.

REFERENCES

Bracken, B. A., Bai, W., Fithian, E., Lamprecht, M. S., Little, C. A., & Quek, C. (2003). *Test of Critical Thinking.* Williamsburg, VA: The College of William and Mary, Center for Gifted Education.

Center for Gifted Education. (2004). *The Hamburger Model.* Williamsburg, VA: The College of William and Mary, Center for Gifted Education.

Creswell, J. W. (2002). *Research design: Qualitative, quantitative, and mixed methods approaches* (2nd ed.). Thousand Oaks, CA: Sage.

Creswell, J. W., & Clark, V. L. (2007). *Designing and conducting mixed methods research.* Thousand Oaks, CA: Sage.

Erickson, H. L. (2002). *Concept-based curriculum and instruction: Teaching beyond the facts.* Thousand Oaks, CA: Corwin Press.

Gall, M. D., Gall, J. P., & Borg, W. R. (2006). *Educational research: An introduction* (8th ed.). Boston: Allyn & Bacon.

Gentry, M., & Gable, R. K. (2001). From the students' perspective—My Class Activities: An instrument for use in research and evaluation. *Journal for the Education of the Gifted, 24,* 322–343.

Grissom, R. J., & Kim, J. J. (2005). *Effect sizes for research: A broad practical approach.* Mahwah, NJ: Lawrence Erlbaum.

Hoover, H. D., Dunbar, S. B., & Frisbie, D. A. (2001). *Iowa Tests of Basic Skills, Form A.* Rolling Meadows, IL: Riverside.

Kennedy, C. (2004). *Single case designs for educational research.* Boston: Allyn & Bacon.

Marsh, H. W. (1998). Simulation study of nonequivalent group-matching and regression-discontinuity designs: Evaluations of gifted and talented programs. *Journal of Experimental Education, 66,* 163–193.

McCoach, D. B. (2002). A validation study of the School Attitude Assessment Survey. *Measurement and Evaluation in Counseling and Development, 35,* 66–77.

McCoach, D. B., O'Connell, A. A., Reis, S. M., & Levitt, H. A. (2006). Growing readers: A hierarchical linear model of children's reading growth during the first 2 years of school. *Journal of Educational Psychology, 98,* 14–28.

Preckel, F., Zeidner, M., Goetz, T., & Schleyer, E. J. (2008). Female "big fish" swimming against the tide: The "big-fish-little-pond effect" and gender-ratio in special gifted classes. *Contemporary Educational Psychology, 33,* 78–96.

Raudenbush, S. W., & Bryk, A. S. (2002). *Hierarchical linear models: Applications and data analysis models* (2nd ed.). Thousand Oaks, CA: Sage.

Reis, S. M., Westberg, K. L., Kulikowich, J., Caillard, F., Hébert, T., Plucker, J., et al. (1993). *Why not let high ability students start school in January? The curriculum compacting study* (Research Monograph No. 93106). Storrs: University of Connecticut, The National Research Center on the Gifted and Talented.

Rudasill, K. M., Foust, R. C., & Callahan, C. M. (2007). The Social Coping Questionnaire: An examination of its structure with an American sample of gifted adolescents. *Journal for the Education of the Gifted, 30,* 353–371.

Shadish, W. R., Cook, T. D., & Campbell, D. T. (2002). *Experimental and quasi-experimental designs for generalized causal inference.* Boston: Houghton Mifflin.

Smith, J. S. (2006). Examining the long-term impact of achievement loss during the transition to high school. *Journal of Secondary Gifted Education, 17,* 211–221.

Tomlinson, C. A. (1995). *How to differentiate instruction in mixed-ability classrooms.* Alexandria, VA: ASCD.

Tomlinson, C. A. (1999). *The differentiated classroom: Responding to the needs of all learners.* Alexandria, VA: ASCD.

Treffinger, D. F., Isaksen, S. G., & Stead-Dorval, K. B. (2006). *Creative problem solving: An introduction* (4th ed.). Waco, TX: Prufrock Press.

VanTassel-Baska, J. (1986). Effective curriculum and instructional models for talented students. *Gifted Child Quarterly, 30,* 164–169.

VanTassel-Baska, J., Bracken, B., Brown, E., & Feng, A. (2005). *Project Athena year three student data report.* Williamsburg, VA: The College of William and Mary, Center for Gifted Education.

Wright, P. S., Horn, S. P., & Sanders, W. L. (1997). Teacher and classroom context effects on student achievement: Implications for teacher evaluation. *Journal of Personnel Evaluation in Education, 11*(1), 57–67.

CHAPTER 36

THE USE OF QUALITATIVE METHODOLOGY TOOLS IN GIFTED EDUCATION RESEARCH

by

LAURENCE J. COLEMAN

Qualitative research is many things to many people. Its essence is twofold: a commitment to some version of the naturalistic, interpretive approach to its subject matter and ongoing critique of the politics and methods of postpositivism.
—Norman K. Denzin and Yvonna Lincoln (2000)

Research, as this section notes, is the foundation for the claims we make for the benefits of education of gifted and talented children. Without a solid research base, gifted child education will continue to have problems arguing for programs in the general anti-intellectual environment of American society. Many of the problems we have sustaining resources and programs are linked to our limited research base. Joyce VanTassel-Baska knows this and she has been an advocate for research and the value it adds to our field. She has made significant contributions on topics such as identification, policy, teacher standards, family, evaluation, and so forth. As director of the Center for Gifted Education at The College of William and Mary, Dr. VanTassel-Baska's studies about curriculum are her most significant scholarly contributions. These studies are a rich vein for curriculum development (Little, Feng, VanTassel-Baska, Rogers, & Avery, 2007) and program development for future research. Her group has produced a body of validated curriculum units, a rarity in our field, demonstrating that gifted students learn best by providing teachers with field-tested curriculum (Feng, VanTassel-Baska, Quek, O'Neill, & Bai, 2005; VanTassel-Baska et al., 2008). The strength of Joyce's research is that she has pushed the field away from a heavy psychological orientation on research about gifted children toward an educational orientation. Along with the customary quantitative research and evaluation research, VanTassel-Baska has used unstructured methods, a hallmark of qualitative inquiry, and has supported qualitative research in writings on diversity (VanTassel-Baska & Stambaugh, 2008) and on alternative forms of identification education (VanTassel-Baska, 2007; VanTassel-Baska, Feng, & Evans, 2007).

In this paper, the place of qualitative research in gifted education and its future role in gifted research is described. I argue that qualitative research is a misunderstood and underused form of scholarship that offers important insights into the development of giftedness. I highlight attributes of the genre and provide illustrations of how qualitative research takes place. I end with examples of completed research topics and some commentary on future research.

Although qualitative inquiry has useful tools for research, qualitative research is neither an isolated tool, nor a collection of tools or procedures; rather, it is a broader, paradigmatic way of looking at the world that employs methods in systematic ways for the purpose of understanding phenomenon and uncovering the meanings of persons in cultures. Unlike quantitative research, its conventional cousin, it makes no pretense at generalization, prediction, or objectivity; instead, it uncovers the meanings and behaviors of persons in context from their perspective. Using unstructured interviews, narrative data, observations, and field notes by themselves or in combination is not doing qualitative research. When used for the purposes consistent with the goals of quantitative research, they are still quantitative procedures. The two paradigms for research see the world much differently and are logically at cross purposes. Using them together in a research project appropriately is very difficult because they are not naturally complementary. To use both appropriately, neither should have primacy. The logic and reasoning powers of the researcher brings them together in a well-written paper. An excellent example is Borland, Schnur, and Wright (2000).

In the time that Joyce VanTassel-Baska has been in the field, qualitative research has moved from being ignored and unaccepted to becoming a regular part of scholarly activity (Coleman, Guo, & Dabbs, 2007). Qualitative research has qualities distinguishing it from conventional educational research. These attributes convey much about the genre and underscore the particular strengths of it. Twelve are briefly presented.

1. *Participant selection.* Qualitative researchers do not use the term *subject* to describe the people they study. The goal is to select informants who possess knowledge of the phenomenon being investigated. Participant sampling refers to persons as well as settings or context because meaning comes out of context. The preferred terms are *purposive sample* or *theoretically relevant sample.* Random sampling is not a goal. Convenience should not trump the scholarly reason for selecting participants. Qualitative researchers should

provide enough information so the reader can understand the composition of the sample, their context, and their relevance to the research question.

2. *Insider perspective.* The goal of qualitative inquiry is to capture the perspective of people in particular contexts. Describing a situation and its participants are worthy but insufficient outcomes for qualitative research. Insiders see meaning in actions and situations in a manner that differs from outsiders. For example, in a classroom children can be heard referring to the class as "boring," yet looking inside reveals that the term refers to the "already known" content, nor the general subject matter of the class (Peine, 2003).

3. *Data collection.* Systematic observation of the phenomena is at the center of every scientific inquiry. Observing, interviewing, and collecting artifacts are the broad categories of procedures for gathering data. The observations are written narratives or fieldnotes of the situation. The interviews are unstructured and open-ended. The artifacts are documents in the form of papers, products, announcements, objects, and so forth present in the situation. The more variety of data sources used, the stronger the research.

4. *Disclosure.* The primary research instrument is the researcher. Everything (data collection, analysis, interpretation) is filtered through the mind of the inquirer. Therefore, the investigator is obliged to "unpack" her subjectivity so that readers can discern whether the findings are actually in the situation and not invented by the investigator. Subjectivity cannot be removed, but it can be known.

5. *Data analysis.* The process is inductive, not deductive, and recursive. The goal is to discover what is happening beneath the surface of a particular situation. Repeated reading of data sources bounded by the research question reveals meaning in that context. These meanings are patterns induced from the data, which are called codes, categories, or themes. Interpretations are drawn from the meaning and processes found in the context.

6. *Interpretation.* The findings of any study are interpretations of what is happening in that context. The interpretive process moves from description toward the uncovering of meanings of participants. The process is validated by doing the earlier elements in this list and the process should be transparent.

7. *Voice.* Bringing forth the voice of participants is a goal of qualitative research. The actual meanings are created by the actors interacting in the situation. Unearthing the tacit meanings of persons in context and making them visible accomplishes this goal.

8. *Rich description.* Rich description is when the reader is given enough detail to enter the world of the participants and the participants would recognize the place described by the investigator. This requires that the researcher fills the story with subtle comprehendible variations of participants' meaning,

9. *Triangulation.* Much like a global positioning system (GPS) in one's car, the qualitative researcher uses data from multiple sources (e.g., people, newspapers, informal surveys) and multiple methods (e.g., interviews, videos,

observations, artifacts) to locate the meaning in the situation. The stronger the links to the context, the more the investigator validates her work.

10. *Alternate explanations.* Alternate explanations for what is uncovered must be explored. Looking for the discrepant case or instances that do not match the findings to reexamine findings is mandatory. Studies presenting no alternative explanations are not as valuable as those that do.

11. *Credibility and trustworthiness.* Reliability and validity are analogous terms in quantitative research. This is accomplished by how the story of the study is told. Credibility is established through rich description, length of time in the context observing, the clarity of voices of the participants, discrepant cases discussed, and disclosure. Trustworthiness is engendered by offering a description of how the interpretation was made. Obtaining feedback from participants (member checking), asking others to examine the study, and constructing an audit trail builds the trust of readers.

12. *Theory. Grounded theory* is the name for theory induced directly from the data because it is derived from the soil of the situation. A sound theory should make sense to the participant, use understandable language, and provide data that the participants could use to change the situation should they wish to do it.

Although qualitative research shares these attributes, considerable variation across studies occurs. Unlike quantitative research where many terms have such high consensual meaning, such as analysis of variance, validity coefficient, and so forth, that they require little further explanation, in qualitative research this is not the case. Terms, such as interview and themes, cannot be treated as code words because the processes used by researchers are too variable to forego explanation.

Interviews, field notes, and artifact collection can take place in vastly different ways. Therefore, the researcher's responsibility is to explain what she did in terms that are understandable to the reader. The situation is made more complex by the fact that there are schools of research with their own traditions within the qualitative research paradigm that use the terms differently. To illustrate this point, consider four kinds of qualitative research: phenomenology, ethnography, evaluation, and action research. Each form uses interviews, but the questions they tend to ask differ. For example, a phenomenologist might ask, "What stands out in your mind about the experience?"; the ethnographer might lead, "Take me through a typical school day"; an evaluator might ask, "Which objective of the program was met and how did this happen?"; and the action researcher might ask, "Given what you know about the situation now, how might you reconceptualize your problem?" These examples illustrate that the investigator must provide complete explanation in order for the reader to comprehend the research. Sound qualitative research follows these precepts. Studies should be organized with these precepts in mind.

HOW TO DO A STUDY

With conventional knowledge to conduct a study, one starts with the research question. I would suggest that is not the place to start. The starting point is: What does the investigator want to learn and for what purpose? If one wants to be able to control and predict behavior, then quantitative study is appropriate. If one wants to understand how people experience a program or curriculum on their own terms, they should be asked. Qualitative research will not tell you how to make something work; it will give you information on how a process works from the perspective of the participants.

Because using qualitative research is our topic, I will describe the process of conducting two studies, paying attention to the attributes of the qualitative research. Because I know best my own research, I will immodestly use them for qualitative methods discussion purposes but I make no claim that my process is the only or the best way to study the topic. My process is an example, as imperfect as it is, of how qualitative scholarship is enacted.

GETTING STARTED

Qualitative research often starts off with a general informed notion of a question or situation. A process of refining and focusing happens as the study develops and more about the context and participants are known. The result is a planned study becomes an enacted study. The tradition of qualitative research is to be transparent about the process.

The Alex Study

As a qualitative researcher, I wanted to learn how teachers of the gifted thought while teaching without the filter of what experts say they should think. Finding no such previous studies in gifted education, the general education literature provided background. I needed to find teachers willing to let me enter their world and who would be available for discussion and reflection. Once I started the process, I had to establish some criteria for picking teachers and a means for gathering data that made sense to the teachers and fit their context. My preference was to study experienced, highly competent teachers, as judged by colleagues, who taught in different educational settings. As I assembled a pool of teachers' names, I approached several to explain my interest and our conversations led me to rethink the study. Because teacher thought is unexpressed and unseen, we needed time to talk in order to develop a shared vocabulary based on my observations and their recollections. It became clear that trying to study several teachers at once in different settings was logistically a nightmare.

The study planned. I planned that I would study one teacher at a time in a class of some type. I would observe classes and parts of classes during the day for a minimum of 2 weeks. We would meet as soon as possible afterward to discuss what I saw and what the teacher recalled about his thoughts. The teacher would share his plans for the day and for the 2 weeks. I would collect all artifacts, such as handouts and so forth. At the end of the process, we would have a summative interview. Once the preliminary analysis was done, I would bring it back to the teacher to be certain it represented his thoughts.

The study enacted. The teacher interviewed was an award-winning teacher who taught in a special summer program for gifted elementary and middle school children. He taught philosophy in four classes of 90 minutes in the day. Because his classes were back-to-back, we could find no time to talk. The solution was to give him a tape recorder in which he was to describe his thoughts about the class I observed during his break or as soon as possible. We met after school for about 40 minutes to review his class and to discuss what he was thinking. He gave me copies of his lesson plans, notes he made during class, and any collectibles. I kept field notes of his classes and a diary of my own thoughts. Our discussions and his own recordings were taped and transcribed. At the end of each week, we had a summative interview.

The findings. The analysis took place over many months of pouring repeatedly through the data sources looking for patterns about my research question. Three major themes emerged that became published papers. Only one was anticipated—that was a paper of the teacher's professional practical knowledge. The second paper focused on the teacher's thoughts on carrying on an active discussion with a class, which was captured in a 'cognitive map' of thoughts and teaching procedures. The third paper focused on the emotional experiences of teaching and more specifically, the teacher's tacit goal to create a "flow" experience for himself. I shared my findings with the teacher and he confirmed my descriptions.

The Greenhouse Institute Study

The question of how talent develops in settings that encourage and promote that talent was my general concern. I thought I would start small with a setting like a chess club to see what I could learn about the talent development process. Shortly, after musing with a friend about doing studies like this, my friend changed jobs and invited me to study a special environment of a high school for gifted and talented children. I narrowed my focus to studying academically talented children in a public residential high school. The study grew into an ethnography that involved leaving my home and living in another state at the school for one year. The first difficulty was to rearrange my life so that I could do the study. This required long conversations with my family and colleagues to work out the details.

The study planned. As a researcher, I planned that I would travel to the school before students arrived and move into the dorm. The year would be divided in two spheres: The first semester would be "hanging out" in order to learn about the school, the students, teachers, administration, the curriculum, and becoming part of the place as I would live at the school for 3 weeks out of the month; the second semester I would interview my primary informants, continue to hang out, and work to confirm my tentative thoughts. I kept a journal that I wrote in daily. I lived at the school for 10 days out of each month and left following graduation.

I planned to keep daily field notes, a running journal of my thoughts and impressions, and collect papers and announcements. I planned to have informal interviews, but not scripted scheduled interviews in the fall with repeated interviews of 30 students in the spring.

The study enacted. Keeping up-to-date on my field notes and my journal consumed so much time that first month, I became more focused in observing situations for which I had insufficient information. I developed a strategy of appearing at key points during the day to hang out in the dining hall, in the student lounge in the early afternoon, in a local coffee shop, in the dorm on the floor during study hours, and at extracurricular meetings. I reduced the number of prime informants to eight once I realized how difficult it was for students to find open spots to talk with me and the amount of time it took to conduct an interview. I added focus group interviews to learn more about senior girls, Black students, best friends, and single interviews with students when they asked to talk with me.

Findings. I discovered two worlds nested within a larger institutional community, that is, academic life and residential life. The interaction between students and school produced a high-energy, fast-paced environment that prompted me to call it "life in the fast lane." I discovered a unique social system that seems to be able to foster excellence and equity and proposed a grounded theory of it.

ANALYSIS AND FINDINGS

Qualitative research produces more data than one can ever use in telling the story in the data. I always find so many details and themes that are fascinating and worthy of deeper study. To extract oneself from the data in order to produce a story, that is on paper, of the study, one must prioritize findings and discard data. Letting go of your hard work to tell the story is the hardest part of doing analysis. Being disciplined is a struggle.

Looking for instances in your data that do not support your analysis is crucial. The resolution of discrepant instances and conflicts in the data are the paths toward extracting the meaning of the data. The researcher must be mindful that it is the meanings of the participants that are most important.

In every study I have done, with the exception of evaluation research, I have ended up in a place I had not anticipated because the data took me there. In the Alex study, I discovered the emotional life of teaching and that optimal experience was his daily teaching goal, while conducting an active discussion requires planning, alertness, and risk taking. In the Greenhouse Institute study, I found a social system that I was compelled to describe. I came to appreciate the synergistic effect that matching bright motivated children with teachers who love their content produces a wonderful learning experience. Replication of this condition is the heart of gifted education.

EXAMPLES OF QUALITATIVE RESEARCH

Many aspects of our field have been studied (Coleman et al., 2007). A greater variety of topics, questions, and phenomenon have and could be studied using qualitative research. The flexibility of qualitative research to answer a wide variety of questions in different topic areas is illustrated below.

Topics	*Example*
Motivation	Success stories of girls
Process	Crystallizing experiences of children in music setting
	Spatial temporal intelligence of inventors
	Compensation strategies of gifted learning-disabled college students
	Studying and homework in a challenging high school
Emotions	Depression in adolescent males
	Struggles of a highly verbal nonreader
	Intensities of three boys, two girls
	Cross-generational life stories of women
	Emotions experienced while teaching
Life Stories	Women of four ethnicities (Asian, African American, Latina, and European American)
	Jimi Hendrix
	College students who define themselves as intellectuals
Evaluation	Families views of ending enrichment programs
	Transition from TAG to general education of four African American males
	Mentoring by three university students of 6 fourth graders
	Social system formation in high school
	Family home/school factors and success of second and third graders at risk
	Advocacy in action (multiple case studies)
	Experiential learning of six college females
Teachers	Career path of future elementary teachers
	Tacit invisible knowledge of a teacher
Curriculum	Open-ended language arts/humanities in third and fourth graders
	Collaboration in a challenging math class of 11-year-olds
	Research processes used by junior high students

Reading these examples reinforces several impressions about qualitative research. First, studies are in-depth descriptions of participants (individuals, small groups, or programs). Less is more in the sense that depth is preferred over survey responses. Second, the context or situation forms a boundary within which the study takes place. Case study is how studies are often conceived. Third, description is the starting point of analysis, but interpretation of the data is the real work for the researcher. The same data set might lead to a different interpretation by other investigators. Fourth, the studies are of particular situations, yet the tendency to generalize occurs in the reader. Fifth, the heart of qualitative research is face-to-face interaction through interviews and observations of the researcher and the participants. Sixth, qualitative research takes one inside the situation from the perspective of the participants. Seventh, thoughtful researchers can use their creativity to conceptualize studies on most phenomena. Researchers who are attracted by these points will find qualitative research to be rewarding.

FINAL WORDS

Qualitative research has been underused in our field. All development happens in context, so qualitative research is a natural and powerful way to understand the growth of talented and gifted children in the various settings of life, such as family, peer group, club, church, classroom, program, and so forth. Qualitative inquiry enables the researcher to get an insider perspective on phenomena that is relatively impossible with quantitative research. For example, if we are to understand how curriculum is enacted by teachers or how children make sense of the curriculum, we need to ask them directly.

I am pleased to contribute to this text honoring the work of Joyce VanTassel-Baska. Her productivity has been prodigious, as it reflects her passion for improving the lives of gifted and talented children. Her commitment to examine issues from multiple perspectives has helped us all. I have benefited from her support of my work, her acknowledgment of the role of qualitative research in improving our understanding of the gifted and talented education, and numerous conversations. Joyce may be able to step away from her role as an advocate for gifted children, but I suspect her active way of being in the world will impel her to be a thoughtful contributor in every future endeavor.

REFERENCES

Borland, J., Schnur, R., & Wright, L. (2000). Economically disadvantaged students in a school for the academically gifted: A postpositivist inquiry into individual and family adjustment. *Gifted Child Quarterly, 44,* 13–32.

Coleman, L. J., Guo, A., & Dabbs, C. (2007). The state of qualitative research in gifted education as published in American journals: An analysis and critique. *Gifted Child Quarterly, 51,* 51–63.

Feng, A., VanTassel-Baska, J., Quek, C., O'Neill, B., & Bai, W. (2005). A longitudinal assessment of gifted students' learning using the Integrated Curriculum Model: Impacts and perceptions of the William and Mary language arts and science curriculum. *Roeper Review, 27,* 78–83.

Little, C. A., Feng, A. X., VanTassel-Baska, J., Rogers, K., & Avery, L. (2007). A study of curriculum effectiveness in social studies. *Gifted Child Quarterly, 51,* 272–284.

McDuffie, K. A., & Scruggs, T. E. (2008). The contributions of qualitative research to discussions of evidence-based practice in special education. *Intervention in School and Clinic, 44*(2), 91–97.

Peine, M. (2003). Doing grounded theory research with gifted student. *Journal for the Education of the Gifted, 26,* 184–200.

Van Tassel-Baska, J. (Ed.). (2007). *Serving gifted learners beyond the traditional classroom: A guide to alternative programs and services.* Waco, TX: Prufrock Press.

VanTassel-Baska, J., Feng, A., Brown, E., Bracken, B., Stambaugh, T., French, H., et al. (2008). A study of differentiated instructional change over three years. *Gifted Child Quarterly, 52,* 297–312.

VanTassel-Baska, J., Feng, A., & Evans, B. L. (2007). Patterns of identification and performance among gifted students identified through performance tasks: A three-year analysis. *Gifted Child Quarterly, 51,* 218–231.

VanTassel-Baska, J., & Stambaugh, T. (2008). *Overlooked gems: A national perspective on low-income promising learners.* Washington, DC: National Association for Gifted Children.

CHAPTER 37

EVALUATION RESEARCH IN GIFTED EDUCATION

by

ANNIE
XUEMEI FENG

While educators of the gifted can help improve general education in many ways, the most powerful approach would be to build quality gifted programs in every district in this country to serve as visible standards of excellence in schooling.

—Joyce VanTassel-Baska

I t is an honor for me to contribute a chapter to this festschrift, because a major purpose of this volume is to celebrate Joyce VanTassel-Baska's accomplishments, contribution to, and influence on the field of gifted education. The wide coverage of topical areas in this volume is itself a testimony to the broad impact she has had in the gifted education community.

STARTING OUT

Just after graduating with my doctorate in June 2001, I was hired as a postdoctoral fellow, serving as the Coordinator of Research and Evaluation at the Center for Gifted Education at The College of William and Mary under the leadership of Joyce VanTassel-Baska. I soon was engaged in an evaluation project of a state gifted training grant's impact on local gifted programs of a northwestern state. Our Center-based evaluation team implemented the mutually agreed-upon evaluation design of the state gifted program, and collected data from 12 sampled school districts, geographically diffused in four regions of the state. I had the opportunity to team with Joyce and another colleague in one of the sampled regions. We observed classroom teaching, interviewed key program personnel, and conducted focus group interviews with different stakeholder groups. It was in this initial intensive working relationship that I started to get to know Joyce. Her deep knowledge and insights about the gifted community, her passion for the field, her scholarly spirit in conducting evaluation research, and her charisma all came alive to me. I started to understand why people at the Center, graduate students and staff alike, admired her so much.

In one of the school districts we visited, we encountered a rather cold reception from the associate superintendent. The district did not have a gifted program coordinator and about five percent of this associate superintendent's job responsibility was allocated to supervising the district's gifted programs. Although we had scheduled this meeting with the associate superintendent in advance, he was quite impatient with us at the beginning of his interview. Flurries of snow danced outside this early December morning, yet the chill inside the office was even more palpable. As if she was not aware of the atmosphere of the conversation, Joyce continued the interview, communicating the purpose of our evaluation, and asking several semistructured interview questions. Somehow, the conversation was ignited as Joyce began to help the dismal associate superintendent to solve the problems he was facing: his lack of personnel for the district and his competing priorities for the paucity of resources. The conversation began to bring forward the larger context in which the district programs operated. Aside from collecting the data we needed, Joyce provided guidance to this gloomy superintendent on a set of strategies he might use to leverage available resources for the gifted program service and delivery as well as other priorities for programs in the district. By the end of the meeting, not only was the ice broken, a constructive dialogue followed. The associate superintendent even offered to drive us around his district during our site visits. I believe the associate superintendent was amazed by Joyce's deep knowledge of the gifted program landscape and her down-to-the-earth spirit in helping him and his district to strategize his use of limited resources. I also was amazed by her care for the gifted community, her expertise in quickly grasping the major issues, and her charisma in helping local practitioners solve problems.

Joyce's influence on my scholarship, attitude, and practice in gifted program evaluation has been tremendous. I have been very fortunate to work with her and witness her impact on the field in many aspects. I remember that at the 2002 Belin-Blank conference, I had an opportunity to chat with Julian Stanley about my work, and when he discovered that I worked for Joyce, he said, "Isn't it a fortune that you work with Joyce?" I replied, "Yes, Dr. Stanley, that's very true."

Many fond memories about Joyce came back when thinking about her influence on evaluation research and on my evaluation practice, but let me now write about evaluation research per se and share with you how Joyce's scholarly work has influenced gifted program evaluation thinking and practice.

WHAT IS EVALUATION RESEARCH?

The terms *evaluation*, *evaluation research*, and *program evaluation* have been used interchangeably in various textbooks, professional journals, and evaluation theories. Program evaluation is defined as the "use of social research methods to systematically investigate the effectiveness of social intervention programs in ways that are adapted to their political and organizational environments and are designed to inform social action to improve social conditions" (Rossi, Lipsey, & Freeman, 2004, p. 16). Trochim (2005) defined evaluation as "the systematic acquisition and assessment of information to provide useful feedback about some object" (para. 2). He further argued that

> Evaluation is a methodological area that is closely related to, but distinguishable from more traditional social research. Evaluation utilizes many of the same methodologies used in traditional social research, but because evaluation takes place within a political and organizational context, it requires group skills, management ability, political dexterity, sensitivity to multiple stakeholders and other skills that social research in general does not rely on as much. (para. 1)

The American Evaluation Association (n.d.) noted that

> evaluation involves assessing the strengths and weaknesses of programs, policies, personnel, products, and organizations to improve their effectiveness. Evaluation is the systematic collection and analysis of data needed to make decisions, a process in which most well-run programs engage from the outset. (para. 1)

THE FIVE COMPONENTS OF EVALUATION THEORIES

The above definitions of evaluation research appear to reflect the common methodological thread as well as diverse emphases of program evaluation. Shadish, Cook, and Leviton (1991) reviewed the evolutionary history of evaluation research theories and practices and summarized program evaluation into five componential theories and relevant questions each component mainly addressed:

1. *Social programming*: What are the important problems this program could address? Can the program be improved? Is it worth doing so? If not, what is worth doing?
2. *Knowledge use*: How can I make sure my results get used quickly to help this program? Do I want to do so? If not, can my evaluation be useful in other ways?
3. *Valuing*: Is this a good program? By which notion of "good"? What justifies the conclusion?

4. *Knowledge construction*: How do I know all this? What counts as a confident answer? What causes that confidence?

5. *Evaluation practice*: Given my limited skills, time, and resources, and given the seemingly unlimited possibilities, how can I narrow my options to a feasible evaluation? What is my role—educator, methodological expert, judge of program—worth? What questions should I ask, and what methods should I use? (p. 35)

These five components of evaluation theories synthesized well the complexity of evaluation research in a better understood and organized manner. In the current landscape of gifted program evaluation, the two thorny dimensions appear to be in the knowledge use and knowledge construction areas.

KNOWLEDGE CONSTRUCTION AND GIFTED PROGRAM EVALUATION METHODOLOGY

It is not new to the evaluation field that evaluation research often is categorized and studied in the methodological arena. This is understandable because evaluation, heavily borrowed from social research methods for its practice, and as an evolved profession comprising many social research methodologists like Donald Campbell and Lee Cronbach, has been dominated for a long time by the argument over the best method for conducting sound evaluation practice. The methodological debate has evolved from the dichotomy between quantitative and qualitative methods to a more convergent mixed-method and multimethod approach over the last few decades (Green, 2006).

Evaluation research in the gifted education community was not immune to such a debate. Evaluation of gifted programs often was equivalent to the assessment of student performances on an array of test batteries by utilizing a number of methodological designs to gauge gifted program effectiveness or impact (Carter, 1991; Hunsaker & Callahan, 1993). The current evaluation method also has been tremendously affected by the No Child Left Behind Act (NCLB; 2001), whereas the Department of Education was charged with identifying the evidence-based educational interventions, utilizing the gold standard of randomized control experimental design, a priority that is tied into the funding eligibility of a proposed study. Under the requirement of NCLB, the evaluation of gifted program effectiveness also has been pushed toward identifying evidence that gifted students' achievement (i.e., performance on high-stake standardized tests) can be attributable to gifted program membership.

The use of experimental and quasi-experimental designs to discern gifted program outcomes and impact appeared to be an effort in vain, not because these methods themselves are not well established, but due to the reality that the choice of appropriate methods was driven by the real world of gifted education practice and the evaluation questions of interest to clients. Moreover, the state testing model for judging a gifted program was a mismatch between the focus of the test and the intent of most gifted programs, which emphasize higher level thinking and advanced content, well beyond the test content.

Gifted program evaluation particularly has to adopt flexible approaches and/or models in order to achieve effective evaluation. VanTassel-Baska (2004a) articulated the William and Mary Eclectic Model of Gifted Program Evaluation (WMEM) that has spearheaded the field of gifted program evaluation by exercising flexible yet responsible practices to improve gifted program services, providing rich evidence for local leadership when decisions are to be made. A framework of six major evaluation approaches (CIPP, responsive evaluation, case study method, connoisseurship, utilization-based methods, and accreditation approach) have been captured in this eclectic model to respond to the needs of local gifted programs. By utilizing WMEM, the choices of an evaluation method are driven by invested questions and immediate issues to be resolved by a local program, not the other way around as the use of state tests imposes.

It is important to develop a comprehensive evaluation plan in order to assess program effectiveness. A logic model documenting the program input, output, process, and short- and long-term outcomes can be a viable way to achieve such a goal. A more detailed description of using logic models in gifted program evaluation for methodological enhancement and evaluative comprehensiveness will be discussed in a later section of the chapter.

UTILIZATION-BASED EVALUATION

Evaluators hope that their work is useful in solving a social problem, improving a program, and helping decision makers, policy makers, program managers, and other stakeholder groups. However, evaluations do not always have the influence on policy, practice, and decision making as evaluators assumed or expected. In a review of evaluation use literature, Weiss, Murphy-Graham, Petrosino, & Gandhi (2008) found that many investigations in many countries have shown only limited and modest influence on policy and practice (Baklien, 1983; Becker, 1984; Breslau, 1998; Bulmer, 1986; Furubo, 1994; Lampinen, 1992) with only a few notable exceptions (e.g., Gueron & Pauly, 1991; Henig, 2007; Schweinhart, Barnes, & Weikart, 1993). Most studies seem to be used in selective bits, reinterpreted to fit existing preferences or ignored altogether (Lemieux-Charles & Champagne, 2004; Rosenstock & Lee, 2002).

The utilization of gifted program evaluation in general suffers from a lack of attention as well (VanTassel-Baska, 2004b). In a survey of all states with legislation regarding the provision of services to gifted and talented students (Council of State Directors of Programs for the Gifted, 1998), only eight states had conducted a statewide evaluation of gifted programs in the previous 7 years. It was unclear what the percentage of local districts was within states who had taken initiatives to utilize evaluation as a tool for program improvement. Furthermore, for those districts that have conducted evaluations, it is rare that evaluation results are fully used as recommended. In a follow-up analysis of the use status of seven state or local gifted program evaluations after 6 months of the completion of the evaluation, VanTassel-Baska (2004b) found several prevalent themes about the role of these evaluations: (1) the evaluation confirmed or disconfirmed preexisting perceptions about the program; (2) the evaluation positively impacted the status and importance of the program in local districts; (3) the evaluation helped the program personnel and teachers to reflect upon best practices with gifted students; and (4) a clearer direction for gifted program improvement was developed. She further observed that although there were these positive impacts on program staff and district personnel in heightened awareness of the importance of gifted programs, expectations for better practices in program delivery, and elevated awareness of the legitimacy of the enterprise of gifted education, the long-term utilization of the recommendations for improving the program had yet to occur. The lack of resources and leadership expertise at local districts, coupled with the sophistication of the political process propelling the NCLB priorities, are impeding the immediate actions to move gifted program agendas forward.

THREE EVALUATION STRATEGIES TO ENHANCE METHODOLOGICAL CHOICES AND EVALUATION USE

No evaluator is in doubt that the ultimate goal of evaluation is to enact program change. Evaluation use is actually central to justifying the evaluation field itself. In the next section of this chapter, I will discuss several evaluation strategies that can be helpful in enacting program change by strengthening evaluation method choices as well as increasing the likelihood of evaluation use. The three strategies include: the logic model, stakeholder engagement and analysis, and evaluation capacity building.

Logic Model

As described before in this chapter, the evaluation of gifted program is often tied to program outcomes and impact. More often than not, outcomes are measured and expected to be measured by using a rigorous design (experimental or quasi-experimental) and assessing students' performance on a number of high-stakes standardized achievement tests. This approach to evaluation program outcomes and impact is flawed indeed. The gifted program operates in a much more complex system involving curriculum delivery, instructional differentiation, service delivery model, staff training, identification, parental involvement, and demographic composition, as well as an array of different levels of implementation even within the same school district. A program logic model can serve as a tool in laying out a comprehensive evaluation plan that derives a logic link between the input, activities, output, and program outcomes, taking into considerations contexts, assumptions, and stage of program development. As an external evaluator, it is crucial to work with stakeholders and identify the content for each specific step of program development and relevant indicators for measurement.

Moreover, the program outcomes are not only reflected by student performance on various tests but also in the social and behavioral aspects of the intended program outcomes. Coleman (1995) called for the assessment of both "cognitive abilities" and "insider qualities," as students who participated in the program also can increase their social and emotional skills. Coleman and Cross (1993) found program change was connected to students' self-ratings of program satisfaction. Figure 37.1 shows an example of the multidimensionality of program outcomes which can occur at different stages of program development.

By working with stakeholders on a mutually agreed-upon logic model of gifted program development, a comprehensive evaluation plan can be developed, and program outcome indicators identified. By considering the near- and-long term outcomes of a gifted program, tangible program effectiveness can be discerned through the examination of near-term affective impact of the program on students, teachers, and other stakeholder groups with vested interest in the program. A stage-dependent logic model also can alleviate the problem of using a rigid evaluation design method, and flexible approaches responsive to the identified areas for investigation can be exercised.

Stakeholder Engagement and Analysis

"Whether evaluations are used depends largely on forces in the social and political contexts in which the evaluations are undertaken. Consequently, to conduct successful evaluation, evaluators need to continually assess the social ecology of the arena in which they work." (Rossi, Lipsey, & Freeman, 2004, p. 373). The impetus and support for an evaluation might come from the decision makers and the leadership of a district. However, the evaluators' work is conducted in real-world settings of multiple and often conflicting interests of various individuals, groups, and departments of an organization. In order to conduct an evaluation successfully, getting stakeholders engaged has become a crucial step in the whole evaluation process.

In a gifted program evaluation, gifted students, teachers of the gifted, building and program administrators, and parents comprise the typical and salient stakeholder groups. Political constituencies, however, such as board members; the district superintendent; and evaluation, assessment, and accountability officers, also are crucial players in the evaluation process. In the initial negotiation process of an evaluation proposal, it is very helpful to conduct a stakeholder analysis, understanding the dynamics of stakeholder constituencies, the priority landscape of the local agency, and the relevant resources available to move a program change agenda forward.

The Power versus Interest Grids developed by Eden and Ackermann (1998, as cited in Bryson, 2004; see Figure 37.2) that often have been used in the strategic management literature can be a useful tool in identifying stakeholders' interest in an organization or issue at hand, and the stakeholder's power to affect the

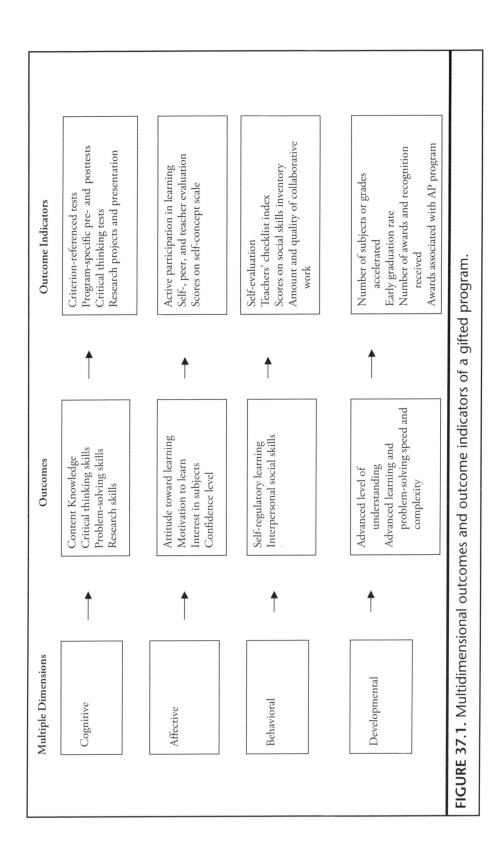

FIGURE 37.1. Multidimensional outcomes and outcome indicators of a gifted program.

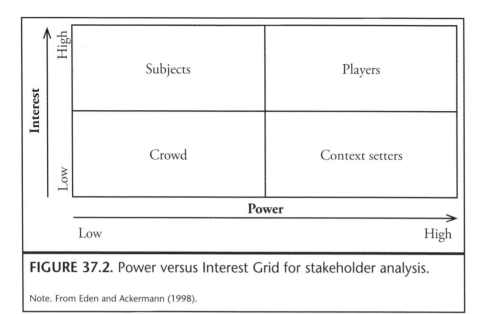

FIGURE 37.2. Power versus Interest Grid for stakeholder analysis.

Note. From Eden and Ackermann (1998).

organization's or program's future. In the grid, stakeholders can be categorized into four types: players who have both an interest and significant power; subjects who have an interest but little power; context setters who have power but little direct interest; and the crowd which consists of stakeholders with little interest or power (Bryson, 2004, p. 31). Power versus interest grids help evaluators determine which players' interests and power base must be taken into account in order to address the problem. They also help highlight coalitions to be encouraged or discouraged, what behavior should be fostered, and whose "buy in" should be sought or who should be "co-opted" (Bryson, 2004). The information gathered through this grid analysis will help the evaluator to develop strategies to convince stakeholders to change their views and enact change toward expected direction.

Evaluators have long been lamenting the underutilization of evaluation results. However, the problem that caused the underuse of results to a large extent might be attributable to the initial ambiguity about the target audiences for change, and the central leverage that can enable change, given the availability of resources. By a power versus interest reality check of the stakeholders, evaluators will understand more clearly the role of various stakeholder groups in the evaluation process; and identify which group or groups the evaluator will inform, consult, involve, collaborate with, or empower in the cycle of evaluation planning and implementing process. A clear agenda of the various types of involvement of stakeholder groups will ultimately help to move the evaluation use agenda forward more smoothly.

Evaluation Capacity Building

A third strategy that can help enhance evaluation quality and use is to empower stakeholders through evaluation capacity building process. Shadish et al. (1991) categorized evaluation use into three kinds: the instrumental use where direct decisions about program change are made based on the evaluation results; the "conceptual use" (Leviton & Hughes, 1981) where results were not used instrumentally to make changes, but still affected how people thought about an issue; and persuasion use. Persuasive use is another form of getting evaluation results used to persuade people of a position already taken, such as what lobbyists, advocacy groups, and think tanks do by using authoritative evaluation results for achieving a goal.

Although the instrumental use of evaluation results often is rare after the immediate evaluation results are shared and disseminated, the conceptual use of the evaluation results often are tangible. Evaluators learn various techniques to facilitate evaluation use, including stakeholder involvement at an earlier stage and frequent contact with users, to identify priority areas that can be put into practice in a short-term evaluation capacity-building process.

Evaluation Capacity Building (ECB) is defined as "the intentional work to continuously create and sustain overall organizational processes that make quality evaluation and its uses routine" (Stockdill, Baizerman, & Compton, 2002, p. 14). ECB helps build the learning component of evaluation. Preskill and Boyle (2007) identified 36 learning objectives that could facilitate efforts to build organization members' ability to think evaluatively and to engage in evaluation practice. These ECB objectives may help participants in understanding key evaluation terms and concepts, the strengths and weaknesses of different data collection methods, and the importance of using culturally appropriate and responsive evaluation approaches. The ECB process also can help participants to enhance their abilities to develop program logic models, determine evaluation questions, construct data collection instruments, and develop sound evaluation budgets. The ECB, if well implemented, can influence a change in attitudes, perceptions, values, and beliefs about evaluation value to the organization (Preskill, 2008, p. 131).

Three ECB strategies, discussion, practice by doing, and teaching others were found to be the more effective approaches that lead to greater levels of retention among participants (Preskill, 2008; Preskill & Russ-Eft, 2005). Engaging stakeholders in a collaborative learning process can tremendously help their active participation in an ongoing evaluation project, develop the "buy-in" attitude, and nurture stakeholders to identify themselves as the agent of change.

CONCLUDING REMARKS

Evaluation research is a fascinating field to study, reflect on, and practice. I am in debt to the field experiences I have accumulated from my work at the Center for Gifted Education, my apprenticeship under Joyce's mentorship, and the opportunities and encouragement Joyce has often given me. I bear witness to a great scholar wearing the shoes of a practitioner, who cared for the gifted education community immensely, and who exercised great sensitivity and responsibility to a vulnerable field that often sustains attacks and negligence due to judgments being made based on assumptions rather than empirical evidence. I believe Joyce's legacy and influence in many areas of this field have yet to be fully realized. Certainly, her contribution to evaluation research will be remembered and used as a model for others.

REFERENCES

American Evaluation Association. (n.d.). *About us.* Retrieved December 9, 2008, from http://www.eval.org/aboutus/organization/aboutus.asp

Baklien, B. (1983). The use of social science in a Norwegian ministry, as a tool of policy or a mode of thinking? *Acta Sociologica, 26,* 33–47.

Becker, H. (1984). The case of Germany: Experiences from the education council. In T. Husen & M. Kogan (Eds.), *Educational research and policy: How do they relate?* (pp. 103–119). Oxford, UK: Pergamon.

Breslau, D. (1998). *In search of the unequivocal: The political economy of measurement in U.S. labor market policy.* Westport, CT: Praeger.

Bryson, J. M. (2004). *Strategic planning for public and nonprofit organizations: A guide to strengthening and sustaining organizational achievement* (3rd ed.). San Francisco: Jossey-Bass.

Bulmer, M. (1986). *Social science and social policy.* London: Allen and Unwin.

Carter, K. R. (1991). Evaluation of gifted programs. In N. K. Buchanan & J. F. Feldhusen (Eds.), *Conducting research and evaluation in gifted education: A handbook of methods and applications* (pp. 245–276). New York: Teacher College Press.

Coleman, L. J. (1995). The power of specialized educational environments in the development of giftedness: The need for research on social context. *Gifted Child Quarterly, 39,* 171–176.

Coleman, L. J., & Cross, T. L. (1993). Relationships between programming practices and outcomes in a summer residential school for gifted adolescents. *Journal for the Education of the Gifted, 16,* 420–441.

Council of State Directors of Programs for the Gifted. (1998). The 1998 state of the states gifted and talented education report. Denver, CO: Author.

Furubo, J. E. (1994). Learning from evaluation: The Swedish experience. In F. L. Leeuw, R. C. Rist, & R. E. Sonnichsen (Eds.), *Can governments learn? Comparative perspectives on evaluation and organizational learning* (pp. 45–65). New Brunswick, NJ: Transaction.

Green, J. C. (2006). Toward a methodology of mixed methods social inquiry. *Research in the Schools, 13*(1), 93–99.

Gueron, J. M., & Pauly, E. (1991). *From welfare to work.* New York: Russell Sage.

Henig, J. R. (2007, May). *The evolving relationship between researchers and public policy.* Paper presented at American Enterprise Institute Conference, Washington, DC.

Hunsaker, S. L., & Callahan, C. M. (1993). Evaluation of gifted programs: Current practices. *Journal for the Education of the Gifted, 16,* 190–200.

Lampinen, O. (1992). *The utilization of social science research in public policy.* Helsinki, Finland: VAPK.

Lemieux-Charles, L., & Champagne, F. (Eds.). (2004). *Using knowledge and evidence in health care: Multidisciplinary perspectives.* Toronto, Ontario, Canada: University of Toronto Press.

Leviton, L. C., & Hughes, E. F. X. (1981). Research on the utilization of evaluations: A review and synthesis. *Evaluation Reviews, 5,* 525–548.

No Child Left Behind Act, 20 U.S.C. §6301 (2001).

Preskill, H. (2008). Evaluation's second act: A spotlight on learning. *American Journal of Evaluation, 29,* 127–138.

Preskill, H., & Boyle, S. (2007, November). *Evaluation capacity building unplugged.* Think tank session presented at the American Evaluation Association annual conference, Baltimore.

Preskill, H., & Russ-Eft, D. (2005). *Building evaluation capacity: 72 activities for teaching and training.* Thousand Oaks, CA: Sage.

Rosenstock, L., & Lee, L. J. (2002). Attacks on science: The risks to evidence-based policy. *American Journal of Public Health, 92*(1), 14–18.

Rossi, P. H., Lipsey, M. W., & Freeman, H. E. (2004). *Evaluation: A systematic approach* (7th ed.). Thousand Oaks, CA: Sage.

Schweinhart, L. J., Barnes, H. V., & Weikart, D. P. (1993). *Significant benefits: The High/Scope Perry Preschool study through age 27.* Ypsilanti, MI: High/Scope Press.

Shadish, W. R., Cook, T. D., & Leviton, L. C. (1991). Good theory for social program evaluation. In W. R. Shadish, T. D. Cook, & L. C. Leviton (Eds.), *Foundations of program evaluation* (pp. 36–68). Newbury Park, CA: Sage.

Stockdill, S. H., Baizerman, M., & Compton, D. W. (2002). Toward a definition of the ECB process: A conversation with the ECB literature. In D. W. Compton, M. Baizerman, & S. H. Stockdill (Eds.), *The art, craft, and science of evaluation capacity building: New directions for evaluation* (Vol. 93, pp. 7–25). San Francisco: Jossey-Bass.

Trochim, M. K. W. (2005). *Research methods knowledge base.* Retrieved from http://www.socialresearchmethods.net/kb/intreval.htm

VanTassel-Baska, J. (2004a). Introduction to the William and Mary Eclectic Model of Gifted Program Evaluation. In J. VanTassel-Baska & A. X. Feng (Eds.), *Designing and utilizing evaluation for gifted program improvement* (pp. 1–22). Waco, TX: Prufrock Press.

VanTassel-Baska, J. (2004b). Metafindings on the utilization of evaluations. In J. VanTassel-Baska & A. X. Feng (Eds.), *Designing and utilizing evaluation for gifted program improvement* (pp. 155–176). Waco, TX: Prufrock Press.

Weiss, C. H., Murphy-Graham, E., Petrosino, A., & Gandhi, A. G. (2008). The fairy godmother—and her warts: Making the dream of evidence-based policy come true. *American Journal of Evaluation, 29,* 29–47.

CHAPTER 38

BIOGRAPHY, EMINENCE, AND TALENT DEVELOPMENT:

The Lure of Lives

by

ANN ROBINSON

We read biography to see how others live and to improve how we might live . . .

—As paraphrased by a number of biographers

A great reader of biographies, Catherine Morris Cox (later Miles; 1926) noted in the second chapter of the second volume of the Terman studies, "Because history deals with unusual personages, it offers especially reliable matter for the study of exceptional ability, or genius" (p. 23). The history of an individual is captured in life stories, life depiction, and biography; the lure of lives has attracted both researchers and practitioners in the field of gifted education.

In what ways has the field of gifted education used biography? This chapter explores two different, but complementary, strands of work that use life writing to investigate and to develop talents. First, biography has been used as the material and the method of investigating eminence and giftedness. From influential figures such as Sir Francis Galton, Sigmund Freud, and Howard Gruber, as well as Catherine Cox Miles, life writing has contributed to our psychological research canon. Second, biography has been used as an instructional resource for talented learners in the schools. Beginning with the work of Leta Hollingworth in the 1920s and continuing to the present day, biographies appear in popular program and curriculum models in the field.

The purpose of this chapter is to review briefly the work of selected figures in gifted education who fell victim to the lure of life depiction—either as a research tool or as a curricular intervention. Next, major themes with respect to the use of biography in gifted education will be explored. And, finally, unresolved questions about biography as a researcher's tool or as the teacher's instructional approach are posed. The field can learn much about the development of talent in young people by looking to the fully deployed achievements of eminent adults.

BIOGRAPHY AND BIOGRAPHICAL RESEARCH— A BRIEF LOOK BACK

Biography has a considerable history in the study of talent development. Certainly, biography in the Western tradition is traceable to the summaries of eminent Greeks and Romans in Plutarch's *Lives* and even earlier, but gifted education and its use of biography are predominantly 19th century phenomena. Simonton (1984, 1998a) situated the first quantitative biographical investigation of attainment in Quetelet's study of English and French playwrights, an examination of the relationship between age and achievement in a specific domain. In 19th-century England, biographical and archival data were examined to document the accomplishments of eminent persons (Ellis, 1926; Galton, 1874). The Victorian heyday gave rise to the modern roots of gifted education when Galton undertook his analysis of intergenerational pedigrees through the use of biographical analysis of members of prominent families. In the 20th century, biographies were used to investigate the development of talent as part of the Terman studies and conceptualized as a retrospective companion piece to the longitudinal study of bright children in California. Other late 20th- and early 21st-century biographically based research studies have advanced our understanding of talent development through the study of historical figures, their family constellations, and their milieu (Gardner, 1993; Goertzel, Goertzel, & Goertzel, 1978; Gruber & Barrett, 1980; Raskin, 1936; Robinson, 2003; Simonton, 1984; VanTassel-Baska, 1996; Walberg, Rasher, & Parkerson, 1980).

CONTRASTING APPROACHES TO BIOGRAPHICAL RESEARCH IN GIFTED EDUCATION

Both in the past and now, the use of biographical research methods in gifted education represents the confluence of two different theoretical and methodological perspectives: qualitative and quantitative. Specifically, the two major biographical approaches in gifted education are historiometry and case study. The methods differ dramatically, but researchers employing the two approaches frequently investigate similar questions of creativity, eminence, and talent development in specific content domains.

First, the tradition of historiometry is highly quantitative and requires multiple biographies or biographical materials usually about many *different* individuals practicing in a specific domain such as music, science, or political leadership. Simonton (1998a) defined historiometry as a correlational methodology that applies quantitative analyses to archival data concerning historical individuals and events in order to test hypotheses. He emphasizes the scientific and empirical perspective of this quantitative method applied to historical data and historical questions. Historiometry provides a grand sweep through numerous lives and/or events to find patterns.

In contrast to the quantitative approach, the second tradition, case study, is the close exploration of the particular. According to Stake (1995), "case study is the study of the particularity and complexity of a single case, coming to understand its activity . . ." (p. xi). Stake viewed the biographer as one of the roles available to the modern social sciences case study researcher. The biographical case study tradition is characterized by the humanities disciplines; the work of great 18th- and 19th-century English biographers such as Samuel Johnson, James Boswell, and Thomas Carlyle and 20th-century biographical theorists such as Virginia Woolf (1927, 1939) and Harold Nicholson (1927) laid the groundwork for the modern biographical method. In addition to the influence of literary thinkers, biographical case study also was annexed by the psychoanalytic school of Sigmund Freud. According to historian of biography Nigel Hamilton (2007), Freud sought to "colonize biography" by wresting the form from the hands of historians, journalists, and novelists and turning it to the service of psychology. Ultimately, Freud was not successful in running off historians or writers, but he did encourage other psychologists to use biographical materials and methods in clinical case study.

Research from both the quantitative and qualitative traditions is represented in the major themes that characterize biographical research in gifted education. It is possible to find biographical studies with the "grand sweep" of history and with the close attention to the particular case informing our understanding of creativity, eminence, and talent development.

Major Themes in Biographical Research in Gifted Education

Although there are numerous themes in biographical research, three are especially relevant to the body of work in gifted education. First, biographically based investigations often focus on adult creativity and eminence in specific talent domains. Biography is especially well suited to studies that are domain-specific. Full-scale biographical work generally is focused on the life of an individual scientist, artist, writer, musician, or mathematician and the contributions of that person to a field of expertise. Second, a smaller subset of studies search for childhood markers or patterns of talent development that presage the adult attainments; these studies emphasize a search for evidence of childhood precocity or for the family environment that fostered the development of talents. Finally, biography frequently is instructive; it includes a didactic undercurrent whether its application be in research or in classroom instruction.

Adult Eminence in Specific Domains

Twentieth century examples of biographical inquiry of eminent adults include the works of Howard Gardner, Howard Gruber, and Dean Keith Simonton. Moving from the broadest sweep in terms of numbers of biographical "subjects" to the most particular, this summary treats the historiometric work of Simonton (1998a) first, moves on to the collections of case studies of creative adults by Gardner (1993) and Wallace and Gruber (1989), and concludes with Gruber's massive examination of a particular phase of work from a single eminent individual, Charles Darwin (Gruber & Barrett, 1980).

Simonton (1981, 1984, 1998, 1999) has argued for the use of historical, biographical, and archival data to investigate eminence and adult creativity. He has undertaken a number of historiometric investigations in numerous domains of achievement and creativity. For example, he has investigated leadership in both multiple subject (1988) and single-subject designs (1998b), in music composition (1991), and literary creativity (1989). Although historiometry can focus on single individuals through analysis of one eminent person's creative products or actions, the more frequent application uses many biographical cases. In fact, from Simonton's perspective, one of the reasons for using this method is to increase the access we have to "significant samples," in other words, samples of individuals who are not drawn at random to represent everyman or everywoman, but who represent extreme cases in adult accomplishment (Simonton, 1999).

In contrast to the quantitative, historiometric method of studying domain-specific creativity, Gardner (1993) took an historical and psychological approach to examine biographies across several content domains. He drew lessons from the lives of Freud, Einstein, Picasso, Stravinsky, T. S. Eliot, Martha Graham, and Mahatma Gandhi to understand how individuals creatively shifted the focus of the field in which they worked. Gardner acknowledged that he was inspired by Csikszentmihalyi's framework for investigating creativity that combines an examination of an individual who excelled in a specific *domain* or symbol system (or as Gardner defined it—a type of intelligence) coupled with the investigation of a knowledgeable group of people in that domain characterized as the *field* (Csikszentmihalyi, 1988). Early in *Creating Minds*, Gardner (1993) stated that he sought

> to enter into the worlds that each of the seven figures occupied during the period under investigation—roughly speaking, the half century of 1885 to 1935. In so doing, I hope to illuminate the nature of their own particular, often peculiar, intellectual capacities, personality con-

figurations, social arrangements, and creative agendas, struggles, and accomplishments. (p. 6)

He further stated that he approached this biographical work as a social scientist and therefore looked for patterns that allowed him to understand "the Creative Enterprise writ large." So, although Gardner examined seven cases in comparison to the hundreds that might be the subjects of historiometry, he intended to generalize across domains once he peered into them through the life trajectories of eminent adults.

In contrast, Howard Gruber focused his biographical case study on a single individual working in a specific domain—science. His most in-depth study was the analysis of the work of Charles Darwin on the theory of evolution (Gruber & Barrett, 1980). Working with a scientist that he met in the reading room of the Cambridge Library where the major Darwin archive is located, Gruber focused on tracing the development of Darwin's thinking over the course of 2 key years in the formulation of his theory of natural selection. Thus, Gruber's focus was not only domain specific, but within the domain of science, he traced the more particular creative development of a web of Darwin's ideas.

Childhood Markers as the Focus of Biographical Research

From the historiometric methods of Galton (and his enthusiastic intellectual descendent, James McKeen Cattell), Lewis Terman guided Catherine Cox Miles (1926) to conduct a retrospective study of 301 individuals who had attained eminence between 1450 and 1850. Her massive biographical work was the second volume of Terman's research, *The Genetic Studies of Genius*. Although she began by reading multiple biographies of her 301 adult subjects, Catherine Cox Miles intended to search the materials for key developmental markers that would permit her to estimate the childhood IQ's of the eminent adults who were the subjects of these biographies. In the preface to the second volume, she explained that Terman believed that such a biographical study of eminent adults would complement the prospective, longitudinal studies of the 1,400 children in the Terman sample.

The Cox sample was drawn from the list of 1,000 individuals included in James McKeen Cattell's statistical study of eminent men (some of whom were women). Cattell (1903) had selected the individuals based on the numbers of inches of text devoted to them in at least three biographical dictionaries. Cox removed adults who achieved eminence through inherited royalty. Her original list contained 312 individuals, but she dropped 11 of these cases when no evidence of childhood accomplishments or milestones could be found in the biographical sources. She stated,

. . . the method of approach to the study of the native ability of eminent men, employed in the present investigation, i.e., the application of mental-test standards to behavior and performance in childhood as reported in history and biography, furnishes, where reliable and sufficiently complete data are available, a means of determining the "brightness" of the youths who afterwards achieved eminence. (Cox, 1926, p. 29)

For each of the individuals studied, Cox constructed a separate bibliography; typewritten copies of each of her sets of notes can be found in the Terman Archives at Stanford University. The bibliographies indicate that multiple biographies and biographical compendia were consulted. In fact, Cox and her army of assistants (who included Florence Goodenough and Lulu Stedman at some point in the project) examined 1,500 biographical sources. They looked for evidence of childhood milestones either in the dated incidents of childhood achievements, behaviors, or (if they were very fortunate), in the childhood writing samples of the eminent. To these chronologies, they applied standard psychological indices carried out by more than one rater to secure estimates of childhood I.Q. Cox arrived at three main conclusions from her examination of the biographies and biographical materials. First, she noted that eminent adults had the advantage of family background and of the opportunity for an excellent education, often through individual tutoring or mentoring. Second, she noted that the highly eminent adults in her sample would have been discovered by intelligence tests when they were young children. And, third, she concluded that childhood intelligence alone did not account for eminence, but rather persistence, effort, confidence in one's abilities, and "force" of character.

Other biographical studies have been undertaken, but with more qualitative approaches. The Goertzels (1962) examined the childhoods of more than 300 eminent persons to find patterns in the home lives that fostered such talents in children. Other researchers focused on the early descriptions of children's behavior, accomplishments, and the childhood experiences that produced extraordinary achievements. For example, McGreevey (1995) examined the lives of the three Brontë sisters and their brother in remote Yorkshire. Using primary sources as well as biographies, she developed a picture of childhood creativity, collaboration, and isolation that presaged the development of adult writers. Using documents and contemporaneous 18th-century biographies, Robinson (2003) examined the development of a Prussian child prodigy who attained eminence in Europe for his abilities with multiple languages and translations. The goal of that study was to map the life experiences related in the biographical materials to Feldman's co-incidence theory in order to determine if the case added to the literature on child prodigies.

The themes of biographical studies focused on adults in a particular domain and those focused on the childhoods of individuals who later attained eminence do not disentangle easily. Several biographically based studies involve both themes, adult creativity in a domain, and childhood markers that are related to it, in equal measure. For example, VanTassel-Baska (1995, 1996) examined the lifespan development of Charlotte Brontë and Virginia Woolf as writers. She concentrated on the domain of writing, examined both primary and secondary sources, and drew comparisons across the two novelists "to explore the inner and outer forces that energized the lives of Charlotte Brontë and Virginia Woolf and accounted for their creative productivity" (VanTassel-Baska, 1996, p. 295).

Gardner's (1993) historical case studies also exemplified these two themes. ↓ focused on the emergence of the life's work of his seven creative, eminent individ als in the separate chapters detailing their work and its influence on their respective fields, but he also drew the inferences and conclusions of a psychologist about the youthful antecedents of eminence.

And, finally, Walberg even went so far as to draw practical lessons about the upbringing and education of children from the lives of the eminent as reflected in his investigations of their biographies (Walberg et al., 1980; Walberg & Wynne, 1993). For example, he advised educators that five childhood activities are frequently associated with adult eminence: diligent work habits, the acquisition of a large fund of personal knowledge that can be applied to a broad array of problems, the opportunity for support *and* constructive criticism from others, a commitment to arduous goals, and managing their activities so they succeed at those goals.

BIOGRAPHY AS LIFE LESSONS

Keeping Walberg's suggestions in mind, it is a short distance from the research in gifted education using biography as a methodology to the use of biography as a teaching tool. As early as 1923, Leta Hollingworth used biography "to enrich the curriculum of the elementary school, for young, intellectually gifted children" (Hollingworth, 1924, p. 277). Funded by the Carnegie Corporation, Hollingworth worked with two classes of high-ability students in New York City to investigate how young learners pursued their studies and how they benefited from the study of biography (Hollingworth, 1924).

Hollingworth's students, who were 8–10 years old, organized much of their own instruction. After an introduction to the meaning of biography in the fall of the year, children began spring discussions of their self-selected biographies every Tuesday morning for 40 minutes. Two biographies were considered each week and managed by a committee of children elected by the class. Children selected their own biographies; however, Hollingworth noted that children did not tend to choose outside the fields of "warfare, government and mechanical invention" when left without guidance. Therefore, she provided a list of possible individuals for investigation and spent time and money to acquire a classroom library. Instruction was organized like a seminar with children reading or reporting orally on their biographical figure and leading a discussion. Student questions were so numerous that the class instituted a box for questions not addressed during the time allotted for the seminar. After working with students for a year, Hollingworth decided that one hour per week for a year should be devoted to the study of biography with high-ability learners.

Although Leta Hollingworth led the way, biography as a curricular strategy appears in more recent models in gifted education. For example, the Autonomous Learner Model developed by Betts (1986) incorporated extended use of biography in the second dimension of the model, Understanding Giftedness. Betts described three specific instructional activities based on biography: the Biographical Sketch, the Eminent People News Conference, and the Eminent People Open House or the Night of the Notables. These build upon one another as students research individuals to produce a biographical sketch, develop questions for role-playing in class news conference, and "become the person" through an evening, interactive performance in the community.

Biography appears in other instructional approaches as well. Frasier and her colleagues (1981) and Hébert and his colleagues (1995; Hébert, Long, & Speirs Neumeister, 2001) have recommended biography as the raw material for bibliotherapy for gifted students. Reading about the challenges, problems, and resolutions experienced by others provides an affective support for gifted students. Finally, both Sternberg and Grigorenko (2002) and Reis and colleagues (2007) have incorporated biography into the Teaching for Successful Intelligence Model and the Schoolwide Enrichment Model for Reading, respectively; VanTassel-Baska has drilled down to the materials level with a specific unit on autobiography developed within the framework of the Integrated Curriculum Model (VanTassel-Baska, 1986).

Our work at the Center for Gifted Education in Arkansas has focused on biography as a means to extend curriculum units, to provide experience with primary source materials, and to encourage students' thinking about talent development (Robinson & Schatz, 2002). To that end, we developed teacher guides that we termed "Blueprints for Biography." A Blueprint is keyed to a specific biography, but includes common lesson formats. For example, the discussion questions for a biography are divided into three sections (Robinson, 2006). The first set of questions, Before the Book, focuses children's attention on the biography to be read and asks students to make predictions. The second set of questions, By the Book, includes reading comprehension, vocabulary study, and textual and graphic analysis. The third set of questions, Beyond the Book, emphasizes talent development. In addition to the question sets, Blueprints include four types of extension activities called P-Quads: Prompts for writing, Primary source analysis, Portrait study, and Point-of-view analysis (Robinson & Cotabish, 2005). Teachers can use Blueprints with small or large groups or they can form the nucleus of an independent study or learning center. The goal of the Blueprints initiative was to locate exemplary biographies for gifted students and to provide their teachers with instructional support.

The aim of biography often has been instruction. To paraphrase any number of biographers, "We read biography to see how others live and to improve how we might live. . . ." At the hands of model builders and curriculum developers, the life lessons that gifted children and adolescents can gain from reading the biographies of eminent adults found their way into instructional practice in the field of gifted education.

QUESTIONS FOR THE FUTURE

Despite its long history in gifted education and its appearance in both research and practice, there are unresolved issues with respect to the use of biography in the field.

In terms of the use of biography as a research method, there are many, many unresolved issues in the biographical approach. Two are especially useful for gifted education scholars to consider in the immediate future. The more sophisticated the field becomes in its understanding of biography as a research method, the more we will understand the complexities and limitations of this kind of research and the more we will appreciate its richness. First, biography *is* interpretation from the particular, so biographical methods are inherently susceptible to bias. Life depiction is a view of one individual through the lens of another. One scholar of life writing refers to the evidence as passing "through the alembic of the biographer" (Saintsbury, 1892/1923, p. 103). An alembic is a glass laboratory device for distilling substances to draw off essences; in so doing, the alembic changes the material. There are not one, but two "subjects" in any biography—the eminent figure and the writer who depicts that life. Researchers in gifted education who use biographies as part of their raw material as did Galton, Cox, Gardner, Simonton, and Walberg ignore this relationship at their peril. Yes, concrete events did occur and through the methods of the historian, these events and details can often be substantiated, but different biographers of the same individual or a group of individuals will choose and arrange their primary materials in different ways. Thus, researchers who depend on biographies either to explore adult creativity and eminence or to search for childhood markers and experiences that might explain them will engage in more rigorous work if they use multiple biographies and, where possible, drill down to some primary sources themselves.

Second, we need to explore the similarities and differences between biography proper and historical case study. Are they the same? Are they different? Within the literature on the theory of biography, the debate over biography as a craft or as an art has extended for decades. Historians and novelists hold differing beliefs about biography, and they practice it differently. From the time of Freud, psychology was viewed as a latecomer to biography. Only now is our applied field pulling up to the engine of biographical inquiry. Gifted education should join the debates that engage the historians, novelists, psychologists, and journalists. As educators, we borrowed biography from them. As a field, we now need to examine the possible permutations and uses of biography more closely. Although informative biographies that touch on the development of talents and explore the complexities of creativity exist in the biographical canon, we do not have a deep well of lengthy examples from scholars in gifted education. To enlarge our scope, we need a better understanding of the ways we can use biographers' methods to produce more rigorous biographical case studies from perspectives that interest the field. We can borrow some qualitative principles and tools from researchers and apply them to biographical case study research in gifted education, but we need more explicit guidance for conducting and reporting such work (Smith, 1994). Biographers with either a literary or an historical bent have confronted many of theoretical and methodological issues for centuries. As Robert Stake (1995) cautioned, we would be well advised to consult them.

With respect to biography in the curriculum, there also are unresolved issues. We use biography in specific curriculum units or strategies, but we do not have a sense of what children and adolescents, let alone gifted students, should learn about biography and when they should learn it. In other words, we have no scope and sequence for learning about this important form of writing. A host of unresolved questions can be derived from such an overarching issue. For example, when should biography be introduced in the curriculum? How much time should be devoted to it? When should we teach the important differences and similarities between biography and autobiography? What are key biographies that should be part of the reading canon in elementary school? In middle school? In high school? When should students investigate the relationship of the biographer to his or her subject? When do we link key skills in historiography or primary source investigations to the understanding of biography? When do students learn about the biographical fallacy? The problems of presentism? To what degree and when are students exposed to the theories of biography? The history of biography? The various forms of life depiction? The purposes of biography? It is our intent through our work with Blueprints for Biography to investigate some of these scope and sequence questions about biography in the curriculum.

In this regard, the work of Joyce VanTassel-Baska, who has undertaken extensive curriculum development, implementation, and evaluation, including strategies for developing scope and sequence, could be emulated by educators interested in laying out a reasonable K–12 scope and sequence document for the content and skills of biography.

Life writing, life depiction, biography—these are important as a means of investigating eminence, creativity, and giftedness and as a means of teaching our gifted students about talent development. At this point in the use of and familiarity with biography in the field, Leon Edel (1988) is refreshingly plain spoken:

> The secret of biography resides in finding the link between talent and achievement. A biography seems irrelevant if it doesn't discover the overlap between what the individual did and the life that made that possible. Without discovering that, you have shapeless happenings and gossip. (p. 39)

References

Betts, G. T. (1986). The Autonomous Learner Model for the gifted and talented. In J. S. Renzulli (Ed.), *Systems and models for developing programs for the gifted and talented* (pp. 27–55). Mansfield Center, CT: Creative Learning Press.

Cattell, J. M. (1903). A statistical study of eminent men. *Popular Science Monthly, 62,* 359–377.

Cox, C. M. (1926). *The early mental traits of three hundred geniuses. Genetic studies of genius, Volume II.* Palo Alto, CA: Stanford University Press.

Csikszentmihalyi, M. (1988). Society, culture, and person: A systems view of creativity. In R. J. Sternberg (Ed.), *The nature of creativity* (pp. 329–339). New York: Cambridge University Press.

Edel, L. (1987). *Writing lives: Principia biographia.* New York: Norton.

Edel, L. (1988). Interview. In G. Plimpton (Ed.), *Writers at work: The Paris Review interviews, eighth series* (pp. 25–72). New York: Penguin.

Ellis, H. (1926). *A study of British genius.* Boston: Houghton Mifflin.

Frasier, M. M., & McCannon, C. (1981). Using bibliotherapy with gifted children. *Gifted Child Quarterly, 25,* 81–84.

Galton, F. (1874). *English men of science: Their nature and nurture.* London: Macmillan.

Gardner, H. (1993). *Creating minds: An anatomy of creativity seen through the lives of Freud, Einstein, Picasso, Stravinsky, Eliot, Graham, and Gandhi.* New York: Basic Books.

Goertzel, T., & Goertzel, M.G. (1962). *Cradles of eminence.* Boston: Little Brown.

Goertzel, M. G., Goertzel, V., & Goertzel, T. G. (1978). *300 eminent personalities: A psychosocial analysis of the famous.* San Francisco: Jossey-Bass.

Gruber, H. E., & Barrett, P. H. (1980). *Darwin on man: A psychological study of scientific creativity.* Chicago: University of Chicago Press.

Hamilton, N. (2007). *Biography: A brief history.* Cambridge, MA: Harvard University Press.

Hébert, T. P. (1995). Using biography to counsel gifted young men. *Journal of Secondary Gifted Education, 6,* 208–219.

Hébert, T. P., Long, L.A., & Speirs Neumeister, K. (2001). Using biography to counsel gifted young women. *Journal of Secondary Gifted Education, 12,* 62–79.

Hollingworth, L. S. (1924). Introduction to biography for young children who test above 150 IQ. *Teachers College Record, 26,* 277–287.

McGreevy, A. L. (1995). The parsonage children: An analysis of the creative early years of the Brontës at Haworth. *Gifted Child Quarterly, 39,* 146–153.

Nicholson, H. (1927). *The development of English biography.* London: Hogarth Press.

Raskin, E. A. (1936). Comparison of scientific and literary ability: A biographical study of eminent scientists and men of letters. *Journal of Abnormal and Social Psychology, 31,* 20–35.

Reis, S. M., McCoach, D. B., Coyne, M., Schreiber, F. J., Eckert, R. D., & Gubbins, E. J. (2007). Using planned enrichment strategies with direct instruction to improve reading fluency, comprehension, and attitude toward reading: An evidence-based study. *The Elementary School Journal, 108*(1), 3–23.

Robinson, A. (2003, April). *Biographical research on talent development: Learning from the life of a child prodigy.* Paper presented at the annual meeting of the American Educational Research Association, Chicago.

Robinson, A. (2006, Fall). Blueprints for biography: Differentiating the curriculum for talented readers. *Teaching for High Potential,* 7–8.

Robinson, A., & Cotabish, A. (2005). Biography and young gifted learners: Connecting to commercially available curriculum. *Understanding Our Gifted, 17*(2), 3–6.

Robinson, A., & Schatz, A. (2002). Biography for talented learners: Enriching the curriculum across the disciplines. *Gifted Education Communicator, 33*(3), 12–15, 38–39.

Saintsbury, G. (1923). Some great biographies. In *The collected essays and papers of George Saintsbury* (pp. 409–412, 432–433). Boston: E. P. Dutton. (Reprinted from *Macmillan's Magazine,* pp. 97–107, 1892)

Simonton, D. K. (1981). The library laboratory: Archival data in personality and social psychology. In L. Wheeler (Ed.), *Review of personality and social psychology, vol. 2,* (pp. 217–243). Beverly Hills, CA: Sage.

Simonton, D. K. (1984). *Genius, creativity, and leadership: Historiometric inquiries.* Cambridge, MA: Harvard University Press.

Simonton, D. K. (1988). Presidential style: Personality, biography, and performance. *Journal of Personality and Social Psychology, 55,* 928–936.

Simonton, D. K. (1989). Shakespeare's sonnets: A case of and for single-case historiometry. *Journal of Personality, 57,* 695–721.

Simonton, D. K. (1991). Emergence and realization of genius: The lives and works of 120 classical composers. *Journal of Personality and Social Psychology, 61,* 829–840.

Simonton, D. K. (1998a). Historiometric methods in social psychology. *European Review of Social Psychology, 9,* 267–293.

Simonton, D. K. (1998b). Mad King George: The impact of personal and political stress on mental and physical health. *Journal of Personality, 66,* 443–466.

Simonton, D. K. (1999). Significant samples: The psychological study of eminent individuals. *Psychological Methods, 4,* 425–451.

Smith, L. M. (1994). Biographical method. In N. K. Denzin & Y. S. Lincoln (Eds.), *Handbook of qualitative research* (pp. 286–305). Thousand Oaks, CA: Sage.

Stake, R. E. (1995). *The art of case study research: Perspectives on practice.* Thousand Oaks, CA: Sage.

Sternberg, R. J., & Grigorenko, E. L. (2002). The theory of successful intelligence as a basis for gifted education. *Gifted Child Quarterly, 46,* 265–277.

Van Tassel-Baska, J. (1986). Acceleration. In J. Maker (Ed.), *Critical issues in gifted education* (pp. 179–186). Rockville, MD: Aspen.

Van Tassel-Baska, J. (1995). Study of life themes in Charlotte Brontë and Virginia Woolf. *Roeper Review, 18,* 14–19.

Van Tassel-Baska, J. (1996). The talent development process in women writers: A study of Charlotte Brontë and Virginia Woolf. In K. Arnold, K. D. Noble, & R. F. Subotnik (Eds.), *Remarkable women: Perspectives on female talent development* (pp. 295–316). Cresskill, NJ: Hampton Press.

Walberg, H. J., Rasher, S. P., & Parkerson, J. (1980). Childhood and eminence. *Journal of Creative Behavior, 13,* 225–231.

Walberg, H., & Wynne, E. A. (1993). Education for eminence. *Gifted Child Today, 16*(6), 28–32.

Wallace, D. B., & Gruber, H.E. (Eds.). (1989). *Creative people at work: Twelve cognitive case studies.* New York: Oxford University Press.

Woolf, V. (1927). *The new biography.* New York: Herald Tribune Books.

Woolf, V. (1939, April). The art of biography. *Atlantic Monthly,* 506–510.

CHAPTER 39

EMINENT REMAINS:

The Life, Studies, and Archives of Sir Francis Galton

by

ARIEL
BASKA

Everything we possess at our birth is a heritage from our ancestors.
—Sir Francis Galton

On a cold day in March, Joyce Van Tassel-Baska (or as I know her, Mom) and I went on an adventure in London. We've been used to adventuring around our favorite city for the past 15 years, but in March of 2008, we did something we simply had never done. We took the number 8 bus to switch to the number 52 bus, walking through winding university streets and commercial roads to arrive at the University College of London's (UCL) Archive buildings. Where, at the recommendation of our long-time friend, Ann Robinson, we spent days of our spring vacation delving into the personal papers and private notes of Sir Francis Galton.

The UCL Special Collections Building, situated next to a petrol station in Camden, is hardly prepossessing. As we buzzed in to enter this fine example of brutalist architecture, my thoughts turned to why our good friend Ann would set us on such a strange quest. As I pondered whether a cousin of Darwin was really worth all this, or if this was some bizarre hazing ritual for anglophiles involved in gifted education, a voice called us up to the third floor of this dingy building with an overworking radiator (most uncharacteristic of England) and rickety elevator (somewhat more characteristic of all academic buildings everywhere). Another voice rasped from another intercom, as we peered into a locked door to a tiny library. Another loud buzz and we were inside the tiny library, reading through the typewritten list of their enormous collections (clearly beyond the librarian's desk lies a room as large as Mary Poppins' carpet bag), filling in cards to request boxes, completely ignorant as to what they might contain. Another glance around the room, and I saw the two rectangular tables, three steel shelves, eight chairs, and one research desk with one research assistant who held the keys to the kingdom, a kingdom of people who have lived and died and found their rest on the shelves of this small building. Scientists, writers, educators, artists, and politicians—all these lives gently wrapped up in delicate tissue paper.

Although we had never before ventured out to the University College of London's Special Collections, I have memories dating to age 11 of my mother poring over original manuscripts. Our love affair with London first began when mom spent a sabbatical in Cambridge, researching the creative genius of the Woolf and Brontë families. At that age, I was hooked on England for a lot of reasons. There was the Latin my mother taught me in the afternoons over hot Knorr's soup, followed by weekend trips to see classical sculpture in the British Museum and amazing theatricals in London's West End. There also were the frequent visits to bookstores, both new and antique, and of course BBC 4, my favorite of the four television stations, which broadcast silly melodramas from the 1930s every day at 4 p.m., and documentaries about Hitler or penguins at every other hour. When my mother first introduced me to England, I confess I could not quite have grasped the wonder my mother felt holding original works, scrawled in the author's own hand. Still, I tried my best, clutching my tattered paperback copy of *Jane Eyre* as she leafed gingerly through the original in the back rooms of the Haworth Parsonage Museum. Then, as now, my mother has appreciated the significance of the biography of eminent lives.

As we began to muddle our way through the myriad boxes we requested, a small shape of the life of Sir Francis Galton began to emerge from the little green catalogue that seemed to map out the contents of the archives and his life.

Precocity and Giftedness

Born the youngest of seven children to a good English Quaker family in 1822, his family stock presaged much of his career. His parents both came from eminent families, notable respectably for the banking trade and scientific research. His grandfather, Erasmus Darwin, was a physician, responsible for writing many works and proposing a theory of evolution, which his other grandson, Charles Darwin, devoted his life to proving. As a child, both Galton and his sister Adele exhibited precocious behaviors. Adele took her younger brother under her wing from birth, teaching him letters and using the reading method to help him understand language. She taught herself Greek and Latin so that she could teach him and informally trained him in the study of insects at home. The day before his fifth birthday, Francis wrote a letter to his sister:

> My dear Adele,
> I am four years old and I can read any English book. I can say all the Latin Substantives and Adjectives and active verbs besides 52 lines of Latin poetry. I can cast up any sum in addition and can multiply by 2, 3, 4, 5, 6, 7, 8, 9, 10, 11. I can also say the pence table, I read French a little and I know the clock.
>
> Francis Galton
Febuary [sic] 15, 1827

By age 6, Francis and Adele had mastered Homer's *Iliad* and *Odyssey*, even beginning their own compositions in ancient Greek and Latin, a task still considered challenging for many graduate students of the classics. Although many refer to Galton as being a prime example of a late bloomer from a prodigious family (his most lasting work was not completed until his 80s), Lewis Terman published a study on Galton's precocity in 1917, projecting his childhood IQ around the 200 range. Even without quantifying the behaviors, his intelligence and intellectual curiosity are clearly evident from an early age.

EDUCATION

In Galton's early life, he attended the local schools around the area of Birmingham. In 1836, he entered the local King Edward's School, where he learned much about the classics and religion, but his parents withdrew him because of failed expectations and encouraged him in the pursuit of a medical career instead. To this end, he studied at Birmingham General Hospital from the age of 16. Galton wrote in his memoirs that he relished his time on ward duty, even while he spent time tending to men who had been injured in fights. He cavalierly noted in *Memories*, "it was my part to shave the head, using the blood as lather, which makes a far better preparation for shaving than soap" (Galton, 1908, p. 42). After his year apprenticing with local doctors at Birmingham General, he attended medical school at King's College for a year, where he again showed a predilection for morbid topics in his studies. He commented rather ghoulishly to his father, "dissecting increases the appetite wonderfully." Already in his adolescence, he had developed a somewhat macabre and distanced attitude toward patients and the medical profession in general that would follow him in his later career.

He then went to Cambridge and entered Trinity College in 1840, studying mathematics and medicine, but did not take well to the rigors of academic life. After a difficult start, he took a year off to recover from mental overexertion. He writes in his memoirs of this period: "It was as if I had asked a steam engine to perform more work than it was constructed for, by tampering with its safety valve, had strained the mechanism. Happily, a human body may repair itself" (Galton, 1908, p. 97). When his father died in 1844, he realized he could live well without an income and made the decision to discontinue his dalliance with medicine. He graduated from Cambridge without distinction and unsure of his future. For a few years, he indulged in sports and lived a life of leisure while recovering his health, but became bored and decided to engage in extensive travel, which he found more to his liking.

GALTON'S TRAVELS

Galton had an insatiable appetite for world travel, a taste first developed on an extensive trip through Europe. Yet, his passion for travel was only beginning. He went to Egypt and explored the Nile River all the way to its origin in Khartoum, sketching images of interest along the way and corresponding with his friends about the wonders of the country. He continued on in the continent of Africa, developing both personal and professional interest in the place. He explored the inland areas of South Africa, current-day Namibia, for a period of 2 years, leading an expedition of 28 men. He mapped the region geologically and astronomically, made contact with the people of the region, and brought back flora and other artifacts of the area. He later compiled his collections and sketches to write two travel books, one an account of his journey (Galton, 1853), and one for the lay person who would be interested in traveling, an early Frommer's Guide to the art of successful travel (Galton, 1855). For his groundbreaking work in Africa, he received the Royal Geographical Society gold medal and three years later, in 1856, was made a Fellow of the Royal Society.

SCIENTIFIC CAREER

The momentous discoveries of his cousin Charles Darwin and the publication of *Origin of the Species* in 1859 led Galton to discover himself as a scientist. After reading the work, Galton wrote in a letter: "I devoured its contents and assimilated them as fast as they were devoured—a fact to which I am inclined to ascribe to a natural bent of mind that both its illustrious author and myself have inherited from our common grandfather Erasmus Darwin." From the moment he read it, he began applying the concepts of heredity to human capacity.

After much correspondence with Darwin and study of his work, Galton became convinced that the development of eminence as a human trait was due almost entirely to heredity. Regardless of academic field or talent, Galton believed that eminence was a heritable characteristic, a belief very much at odds with the more popular sentiment of the time that claimed that all individuals possessed equal ability. Even Darwin believed that all he had learned of value was self-taught, and that people should credit no one but themselves for their achievements.

However, Darwin had to recant these opinions after reading *Hereditary Genius,* Galton's (1869) first professionally important work. Darwin's letter from 1869 reads: "You have made a convert of an opponent in one sense for I have always maintained that, excepting fools, men did not differ much in intellect, only in zeal and hard work."

To Galton, genius was innate talent and skill, sometimes shaped by circumstance, but always passed down from former generations. He set out to study this idea extensively through his lifetime in various ways. In the process, he invented statistical methods, developed a survey method for collecting data, and calibrated differences in human response to various items through use of a scale. His first studies of eminence focused on great men of science, many of whom he knew personally, collecting data on their families and their personal characteristics, their predilections and habits of mind. In *English Men of Science* (1874), he wrote of Darwin that he was very bad at modern languages and learning by rote but that he had a good memory for concepts and excellent metacognitive skills.

Just as in preparation for his later work, *Hereditary Genius*, Galton studied genealogies and obituaries for clues to support his emergent ideas. Both *English Men of Science* (1874) and *Hereditary Genius* (1869) celebrated his thesis that genius ran in families, mining the data from those he knew personally, such as family members and Royal Society colleagues, and those whose work he admired, such as Plato, Newton, Michelangelo, and the Brontë sisters. He once remarked at a talk on his work in Paris:

> It must be recollected that we have to work not only for ourselves but for future generations of scientific men and that we are doing really good science if we can succeed in the establishing of family records that will afford information to others of a kind inaccessible to ourselves. (Galton, 1883)

Galton's work propagated the idea of nature versus nurture and he spent much of his life trying to help others understand the strong influence of natural traits. He initiated the first studies of twins, attempting to show indisputable aspects of heritability in the same family. He also became interested in census-taking among school children to predict and diagnose problems in physical health such as vision or mental capacity that would affect learning. Although he never created an IQ test, his ideas were very influential on Binet, who first developed such an instrument.

A natural outgrowth of these interests was Galton's more infamous association with eugenics. Galton believed that Darwin's idea of "survival of the fittest" should be applied to human society, where he believed that desirable traits should be passed down to future generations to benefit the world as a whole. He wrote:

> The living world does not consist of a repetition of similar elements, but of an endless variety of them that have grown, body and soul, through selective influences into close adaptation to their contemporaries, and to

the physical circumstances of the localities they inhabit. The moral and intellectual wealth of a nation largely consists in the multifarious variety of the gifts of the men who compose it, and it would be the very reverse of improvement to make all its members assimilate to a common type. (Galton, 1883, p. 2)

Galton's philosophical focus in eugenics always tended toward the encouragement of talent, and the natural development of such gifts passed on for prosperity. In the introductory chapter to *Hereditary Genius*, he analyzed eugenics from an historical perspective, discussing the tragedy of the monastic movement that appealed to the great intellectuals of the medieval era. According to Galton, the great men of the Middle Ages devoted themselves to Christian celibacy, thus depriving the world of stronger, intellectually powerful, and morally superior men. His protégé Karl Pearson (1914–1930) later distilled Galton's idea of eugenics into a metaphor,

The garden of humanity is very full of weeds. Nurture will never transform them into flowers; the eugenist calls upon the rulers of mankind to see that there shall be space in the garden, freed of weeds, for individuals and races of finer growth to develop with the full bloom possible to their species. (p. 220)

This more reductive view of Galton's theory of eugenics would be used later to argue for supremacist ideology, but Galton himself was far more focused on the possible accomplishments of the genetically gifted individual, rather than the concept of a "master race."

OTHER ACCOMPLISHMENTS

Although Galton's eminence was guaranteed with his contributions to the psychology of individual differences, he made contributions at world-class levels to other fields as well. He was the first to use pictures to analyze weather patterns, tracking trends in maps of Europe—techniques still used today by meteorologists. He also discovered the unique properties of fingerprints. He wrote two books on the subject that proposed fingerprints as an ideal way to track criminals, a suggestion implemented and institutionalized by Scotland Yard 5 years after his groundbreaking work on the subject.

He developed the science of biometrics, the application of statistical techniques to the understanding of living forms. He founded inferential statistics by working through the concept of correlation and regression, which put him on the forefront of a completely new scientific and mathematical process. In 1889, Galton published *Natural Inheritance*, a summary of his work on correlation and regression and the techniques he had worked out. His graduate student, protégé, and biographer Karl Pearson noted how impressed he was with Galton's work in this area:

> It was Galton who first freed me from the prejudice that sound mathematics could only be applied to natural phenomena under the category of causation. Here for the first time there was a possibility . . . of reaching knowledge as valid as physical knowledge was thought to be, in the field of living forms and above all in the field of human conduct. (E. S. Pearson, 1938, p. 19)

LAST YEARS

Galton received many awards throughout his long life of 89 years. He even received a knighthood from the queen in the year of his death. He grew increasingly infirm, first unable to hear and then to walk. In spite of his physical condition, he still loved the outdoors and valued a close connection to the natural world. He died of acute bronchitis in 1911, leaving the bulk of his estate to an endowed chair in eugenics at the University of London where he began his anthropogenic laboratory so many years before in 1884. Karl Pearson was its first occupant. His last words were said to be: "One must learn to suffer and not complain" (Brookes, 2004).

GALTON, THE MAN

Many biographers have tried to analyze Galton and the characteristics that drove him to accomplish so much in his lifetime. The mark of an omnibus gifted personality is the extent to which it has impacted on multiple fields. Galton did just that as an explorer, meteorologist, biometrist, and scientist, yet today he is still best known as a researcher of heritability and the father of the eugenics movement.

Galton had great intellectual drive and energy, particularly for a man who could so easily have lived a life of gentlemanly leisure. He accomplished a lot in the public eye, but also steered the organizations he cared about through several periods of his life. He served as president, secretary, and other offices for most of the organizations with which he was affiliated, including the British Association, The Royal Society, and the Anthropological Association. He began new projects and research studies as they came to interest him. By all biographical accounts, Galton also was highly social and an affable personality (Gillham, 2001). He managed an active social life, with the help of his wife who had strong connections and helped him entertain at home on Rutledge Street in Kensington, London, or on picnics in various favorite spots throughout England.

Galton spent much of his life trying to live up to his own illustrious heritage. The sizeable shadows cast by his grandfather and cousin intimidated him, and in many ways spurred him to look for new areas of science to define. He once observed: "the world is beginning to awaken to the fact that the life of the individual is in some real sense a prolongation of those of his ancestry. The life histories of our relatives are prophetic of our own futures . . ." Not only was this comment indicative of his work to date, but it presages our own contemporary understanding of population genetics and its application to health care.

His biographer, Bulmer (2003), described him as a man whose creativity exceeded his intellect. His capacity for ideas extended beyond his capacity to carry them out to the deepest level necessary for logical conclusions to be drawn from all aspects of the work. Consequently, the world has forgotten nearly all of the spheres to which he contributed because others have made a deeper mark on the intellectual canvas and because modern history has given eugenics a bad name. Yet, no man has exceeded Galton in the sheer scope of his imagination to understand individual differences and apply them to his work.

One puzzling issue that remains is his relationship with women in his personal life. He never directly acknowledges his debt to the women in his life. The documentary evidence left behind clearly shows that his sister took responsibility for most of his early education, and shaped his understanding of many of his lifelong interests. His journals and correspondences reveal that his mother was his close confidant well into his 20s. His wife also hardly merits mention in his memoirs, although she supported his intellectual efforts and helped him to succeed in the social climate of Victorian England. Galton even goes so far as to accuse his wife of having "little or no imagination" (Forrest, 1974). However, given his evaluations of the contributions of mothers in his works on great men in the arts and sciences, it is inexplicable as to why he gives all the women in his own life such short shrift. Of his mother, he noted only that she had good perspective in drawing, even though she held the family together for 30 years after her husband's death. His sister also suffers from limited commentary and receives no credit for her intellectual contributions to his development. He noted in the *Memoirs*: "I owe enormously to her pious, serene, and resolute disposition." (Galton, 1908, p. 11).

Galton was a private person when it came to personal feelings (Brookes, 2004). His memoirs reveal little of the man, only of what he did at different stages of life. Because he never had a child, he once admitted in a candid moment that he lacked the same motivation for succeeding that other men possess because of family obligations and duties. He probably perceived the lack of an heir as a personal failure, given his focus on heritable characteristics. At his funeral and quoted in published obituaries, the Reverend Blake of Trinity College addressed the worthiness of Galton the man:

> He was a man of singular sweetness of temper, courteous, considerate, prompt to sympathize in little things as well as great. He was a stimulating conversationalist . . . charming travel companion who could solve problems well . . . had a keen intellect, vigilant for something new, beautiful, or wonderful.

Galton, the Father of Gifted Education

Although the field of gifted education as it has evolved in the United States tends to credit Lewis Terman and Leta Hollingworth with the progenitor label, it is difficult to ascribe that ancestral laurel to anyone but Francis Galton. He conceptualized the theories that guide our thinking today—the role of families, the boundaries of heredity, the role of individual differences in performance in all fields, and the special nature of eminence. He also created the methodologies and tools by which we conduct research in gifted education, from biographical techniques to inventing our statistical methods, still used today. He also crafted the research agenda we still follow—twin studies, biographical inquiry into the lives and family background of contemporary eminent people, and large-scale longitudinal studies that allow us to understand the development of talent over time on key dimensions. Although revisionists among us may be quick to dismiss his ideas as racist, sexist, and inaccurate in light of contemporary understanding, it seems fair to judge Galton as a product of his time and his culture and to give him a leading place in the pantheon of individuals who have contributed greatly both to understanding genius and the mark it makes on societies and choosing to exhibit it by the exemplum of his own life.

Galton's Archive

As my mother and I sifted through personal correspondences, original proofs, notes, photographs, and sketches, we found ourselves constantly proclaiming our joy at unwrapping the secrets of past lives. I may not have understood this passion of my mother's when we first traveled to the Haworth Parsonage, but sadly I can not find a more erudite term that fully captures our reaction quite like the phrase "geeking out." Like the characters in *Possession*, the wonderful novel by A. S. Byatt, we allowed the research and the life behind it to dictate our lives for those few days in March, reveling over a found letter here and an unexpected photograph there. There is a luxury to examining 75 boxes of material as if no one else has seen it or cares about what it may all mean. There also is the overwhelming realization that we viewed only a third of the archived boxes of material in that library, as Galton has letters and papers scattered in other archives worldwide.

The joy of archival research, however, cannot be overstated. Although the access to the archive is formal and stringent in respect to your credentials, your purpose, and the times the library is open, the opportunity to request and handle anything you want, to take digital pictures of the contents, and to type in your notes on your own laptop was quite freeing. We decided to focus on biographical material, Galton's works in the original, including his memoir, and selected letters written by and to him. The catalogue allowed us to decide what was most important and how to attack the sheer volume of material. Reviewing our notes each night back at the hotel led us to consider what we understood and what needed greater clarification. It also allowed us to realize how exciting certain finds—the original copies of *English Men of Science* and *Hereditary Genius,* still tied up with twine, the letters from Darwin, and Galton's original sketches from Egypt— were particularly meaningful as we had just returned from our own trip of a lifetime to the sandy land of the pyramids. No other kind of research sparks quite the same fire or bears such personal relevance as the biographical study of one man's possessions.

My mother's life, work, and personal interests also parallel Galton's in their own way. Just as Galton dove into the archives of great men (and a few women) of science, arts, and the humanities, my mother has enjoyed the study of creativity in eminent families—those of Charlotte Brontë, Virginia Woolf, and Sir Francis Galton. My mother, like Galton, also has tried to develop her own creativity, independent of formal study. Like Galton, she has kept very personal and creative ruminations on her travels, from poetry to journals, to simple sketches, and even shares a similar passion for photography. Beyond the personal though, both my mother and Galton devoted their life's work to ideas, whether or not their enthusiasm surpassed their ability to execute those ideas at an expert level. My mother's interests in gifted education have been broad in scope, working in most facets of the field with a variety of different colleagues and school systems. Like Galton, she started as an amateur who attacked with relish new areas that needed to be developed—curriculum, low-income promising learners, teacher standards. She has left a great body of work—both that which she has done, and that which future generations need to do. Although her personal archives may never be collected and stored in a dingy building in Camden, the sum of her life and her work will continue to inspire others in the field of gifted education to carry on the great tasks she has begun.

References

Brookes, M. (2004). *Extreme measures: The dark visions and bright ideas of Francis Galton.* New York: Bloomsbury.

Bulmer, M. G. (2003). *Francis Galton: Pioneer of heredity and biometry.* Baltimore: Johns Hopkins University. Press.

Darwin, C. (1859). *On the origin of species by means of natural selection, or the preservation of favoured races in the struggle for life.* London: John Murray

Forrest, D. W. (1974) *The life and work of a Victorian genius.* London: Paul Elek.

Galton, F. (1853). *Narrative of an explorer in tropical South Africa,* London: John Murray.

Galton, F. (1855). *The art of travel.* London: John Murray.

Galton, F. (1869) *Hereditary genius.* New York: Macmillan.

Galton, F. (1874). *English men of science.* New York: Macmillan.

Galton, F. (1883). *Inquiries into human faculty.* New York: Macmillan.

Galton, F. (1889). *Natural inheritance.* New York: Macmillan.

Galton, F. (1908) *Memories of my life.* London: Methuen.

Gillham, N. W. (2001). *A life of Sir Francis Galton: From African exploration to the birth of eugenics.* Oxford, UK: Oxford University Press.

Pearson, K. (1914–1930). *The life, letters and labours of Francis Galton* (3 Vols.) London: Cambridge University Press.

Pearson, E. S. (1938). *Karl Pearson: An appreciation of some aspects of his life and work.* Cambridge, UK: Cambridge University Press.

Terman, T. (1917). The intelligence quotient of Francis Galton in childhood. *American Journal of Psychology, 28,* 209–215.

CHAPTER 40

THE PUBLIC POLICY LANDSCAPE FOR GIFTED EDUCATION

by

JAMES GALLAGHER

Developing and implementing national, state, and local policies that govern the administration of gifted programs and services is the glue that holds gifted education together.

—Joyce VanTassel-Baska

INTRODUCTION

There has been increasing interest in the role that public policy plays in the program directions for educating gifted students. There is a growing realization that policy standards, once established, can determine who the gifted student is, who should teach him or her, what the special education services should be, and in what context (e.g., regular classroom) these special education services will be delivered.

Policies are not only the orders that direct our own behaviors in education, but those of others as well. We know that policies can be shaped by our own efforts if we understand the policy-making process well enough. Public policy is, in fact, the vehicle through which the American public expresses its goals and priorities. One common definition of public policy has been: Policies are the rules and standards by which we allocate scarce resources to almost unlimited social needs (Gallagher, 2002). Such a statement clearly indicates that not

Table 40.1

EXAMPLES OF ENGINES OF CHANGE

	Children With Disabilities	**Gifted Students**
Legislation	Individuals with Disabilities Education Act (IDEA; 1990) (More than 2 billion dollars)	Jacob K. Javits Gifted and Talented Students Education Act of 1988 (Less than 10 million dollars)
Court Actions	*PARC vs. Commonwealth of Pennsylvania* (1972) (affirms the rights of children with disabilities to a free and appropriate public education)	Office of Civil Rights concerns over discrimination of minority students in programs for gifted
Administrative Actions	Various rules around mandated Individualized Education Programs (IEPs) for each student	Local decisions on rules for grouping of gifted students
Professional and Private Initiatives	Establishment of parent groups to help lobby for parental rights and education of their children	Producing differentiated curricula for the gifted

all desirable social goals will be met and that it is critical to have a spending priority if your goals are to be attended to.

If we are interested in changing public policy, we need to pay attention to the mechanisms for change. Public policies are established mainly through the four engines of change noted earlier by Gallagher (2006): legislation, court actions, administrative rules, and professional initiatives. It seems clear that the American public has not yet reached a consensus on how we should respond to gifted students. This ambivalence of the American public to gifted students can best be shown by contrasting policies related to gifted students with children with disabilities who have clearly received societal approval on these four engines of change.

Legislation

Table 40.1 shows that the legislation for children with disabilities has yielded billions of federal dollars, and every state receives a portion of these resources to educate children with disabilities. In contrast, gifted students have only a small federal demonstration program (Jacob J. Javits) that yields less than 10 million dollars annually.

Courts

Similarly, the court actions taken on behalf of children with disabilities have brought forth a decision that affects every child with disabilities in the nation, guaranteeing a free and appropriate public education (FAPE). For the education of the gifted, in contrast, the Office of Civil Rights actions have focused on the right of minority students to participate in programs for gifted students.

Administrative Rules

Table 40.1 also shows the power of administrative rule making. Neither legislation nor court decisions can be specific enough to cover all of the implications of their actions. Therefore, additional sets of rules must be written that often direct and shape the actions taken to implement the laws or decisions. In the case of children with disabilities, a long set of rules have been necessary to follow onto the implementation of an Individualized Education Plan (IEP). Those regulations impact on family participation and teacher flexibility to cope with the needs of the child. The federal administrative rules that place emphasis on low-income and minority gifted have shaped the awarding of grants and the general direction of the field.

Professional and Private Initiatives

Finally, professional and private initiatives have played a major role in shaping policy for both children with disabilities and children with special gifts. The parent group movement became a powerful factor in getting resources for children with disabilities, while the professional initiatives focused on curriculum development and acceleration were two policy areas where actions have been taken on behalf of the gifted, at least at state and local levels.

EDUCATION POLICY PRIORITIES

For several decades there has been a struggle for scarce resources between two major values in American society, equity and excellence. At the present writing, equity appears to have the better of the conflict with billions of dollars being spent for Head Start (Styfco & Zigler, 2003) and on the No Child Left Behind Act (NCLB; 2001). In both of these legislative initiatives, the concept of vertical equity or the "unequal treatment of unequals in order to make them more equal" has been employed (Gallagher, 2002). The emphasis on equity rings true in American society whereas excellence has an elitist flavor that hinders policy making in that direction. For example, almost 40 years ago the Marland Report (Marland, 1972) presented the unmet needs of gifted students in the United States:

- ► Existing services to the gifted do not, in general, reach a large number of students and significant subpopulations are strikingly underserved.
- ► Special programming for the gifted is a low priority at all levels of government. The federal role in services to the gifted is all but nonexistent.
- ► Enormous individual and societal losses occur because the talents of the gifted are undiscovered and undeveloped.

It is not stretching reality too far to say that the same statements could be made today, a sober commentary on our lack of ability to mobilize public effort. However, three areas of policy interest are deserving of special note.

Minority Gifted

One of the most serious and continuing policy issues involves the inclusion or exclusion of children of diverse race and ethnic background in programs for gifted students. There is no disagreement about the major disproportion of these groups in special education programs for gifted students. Ford and Whiting (2008) present figures that suggest that African American students and Hispanic students appear in such programs at only about 50% of their proportions in the general population.

However, there is a great disparity among professionals about the reasons for these disproportions. For a few, these data suggest that such differences represent inherent differences between the races and use the student IQ results as supporting such an explanation (Hernstein & Murray, 1994).

To others, the fault lies in the biased instruments (IQ tests) being used for identification and a lack of understanding of the role that culture plays in the development of young children. For example, African American children place more emphasis on oral rather than verbal communication, are more influenced by social factors, and possess a high energy level that may be misinterpreted as hyperactivity or aggression (Ford & Whiting, 2008).

To yet others, such differences reflect the rejection of the dominant White culture by African American students who condemn achieving Black students as "Whitey" or "Oreos," thus discouraging them from pursuing academic excellence as it has been traditionally defined (Ogbu, 2004). The notion that special programs for gifted students have been, in fact, "back door segregation" efforts, has alerted the Office of Civil Rights to hold a series of investigations of individual school systems to determine how their selection process for membership in special programs might have been biased against minority students. If the procedures were judged to be unbiased, then the school systems were not held responsible for the disproportions that occurred.

There is an additional unusual finding that needs to be factored into the discussion. Asian students appear to be overrepresented in programs for the gifted. Because there is little reason to believe their families have been received more positively than other minority groups, the question becomes "What is different?" Some believe that it is the commitment to learning and academic discipline in many Asian families that accounts for such figures (Kitano & DiJiosia, 2002).

Gallagher (2008) has proposed a different and more serious consequence. If developing intelligence is a continuing mixture of the sequential interaction of heredity and environment, then a lack of early stimulation or practice on intellectual tasks can cast long shadows into the future. It may result in real differences in intellectual performance at school age and beyond, even if there were no differences in native ability in the first place. The solution then lies, not in finding new nonverbal ability tests, but in stressing early developmental stimulation and family counseling on the importance of the early years and in supporting policies that stress early childhood education.

Differentiated Curriculum

One of the most useful of the infrastructure components described by Gallagher (2008) is curriculum development. If the gifted student is clearly superior in thinking abilities and able to learn more knowledge more quickly than the average student, then it seems logical that he or she should receive an adaptive curriculum. But, what should it be and who should produce it?

Renzulli (1988) has produced a Schoolwide Enrichment Model that enables bright students to start from the experiences presented to all students and then have advanced students move through advanced thinking processes to problem solving through, to independent investigation and data collection. Feldhusen also has produced a three-stage model that stresses the use of advanced thinking processes to develop independent study techniques and problem solving (Feldhusen & Kolloff, 1986). Both Renzulli and Feldhusen stressed the development of thinking processes rather than content modification.

VanTassel-Baska (VanTassel-Baska & Stambaugh, 2008) also used a problem-based approach, but, in addition, produced major content modifications for gifted students in the areas of science, language arts, mathematics, and social science (VanTassel-Baska, 2003). These curriculum modifications have been widely distributed, thanks to an aggressive implementation policy by VanTassel-Baska's Center for Gifted Education at The College of William and Mary. In addition, VanTassel-Baska has been a leader in attempts to create sophisticated assessment models so that the utility of the curricula that has been developed was appropriately assessed in classroom settings (VanTassel-Baska & Stambaugh, 2008). Her Center for Gifted Education has been an important influence in the system of differentiated education for gifted students for two decades.

Acceleration

One of the policy decisions that has taken place largely at the local level has been that of pupil acceleration. The reason for such a policy is twofold: first to place the student in a group that more nearly reflects the student's advanced development and second to reduce the total amount of time that the student may stay in the educational system. Many gifted students may spend as much as a quarter of a century in school ending with a medical or law degree or a doctorate in the sciences. When that length of time can be shaved off, it will be important to the student and to the society.

The policy of acceleration is one fine example of how *facts* tend to lose out to *cultural values*, at least in the short run. There is a widespread feeling, among teachers and parents, that student acceleration can lead to social relationship problems and the skipping over of key knowledge. There has been considerable data collected on what happens to students who have been accelerated and the overall portrait is clear and positive (Colangelo, Assouline, & Gross, 2004).

The fears of social disruption in the life of student accelerants has been much overplayed. Those who have been accelerated have done well academically and in creative productivity and feel good about the accelerative moves in retrospect, especially as it enabled them to get a jump-start on their career (Wai, Lubinski, & Benbow, 2005).

FUTURE POLICY NEEDS

For the past few decades, those interested in education for gifted students have been forced to separate themselves from general education in order to demonstrate what should be done for these especially gifted students. Now that these demonstrations have occurred in curriculum development and leadership, it may be necessary to join together with other educational reform movements to build on initiatives for the gifted.

Preschool Initiatives

The prekindergarten movement has flourished despite tight state and local budgets because of the public recognition of the overwhelming importance of this developmental period (Hodgkinson, 2001; Ramey & Ramey, 1998). This emphasis on the preschool age range also gives us the ability to discover early talent and prodigies and nourish them before formal schooling even begins. This is particularly true in cultural settings not attuned to intellectual development, where talent can be suppressed before it can properly flower.

Long-Range Planning

The federal government can give states starter funds for long-range planning at the state level. Such multidisciplinary long-range planning reporting to the governor or state legislature can include how to utilize the educational infrastructure to meet societal goals, one of which is the freeing of intellectual talent through differentiated curriculum development and planned acceleration.

Leadership Training

Advanced education at the doctoral level too often has focused on children in academic trouble to the exclusion of top performers. The support of postdoctoral fellowships or dedicated research funds can be used to place a spotlight on the development of excellence through careful seeding of new researchers.

Future Curricula

The professional marriage of content experts and experts in thinking processes could yield additional curricula in the arts and sciences to challenge the best minds at the middle and secondary level.

It should be noted that none of the above policy suggestions mean substantial expenditure of funds when one considers the overall costs of educational systems. For a small amount, we can make major changes as a nation in the way we nurture talent.

THE WAY FORWARD

However, even these modest ventures described here will not likely be made if we ignore the problems we have had in the past in dealing with excellence and the political model of democratic government, which has special pitfalls. There have been periodic attempts to rouse the nation on the importance of providing educational assistance to outstanding students.

The report *A Nation at Risk* (National Commission on Excellence in Education, 1983) detailed the risk we run as a nation by ignoring the needs of gifted students. Ten years later, the U.S. Department of Education (1993) brought forth *National Excellence,* which decried the lack of attention that bright students received in our educational system. Although such reports stirred much discussion, they did not seem to result in major legislative or even professional initiatives.

THE TROUBLE WITH DEMOCRACY

The obvious values of a democratic government are so apparent that we sometimes forget that there are substantial downsides as well for particular goals. As Winston Churchill once remarked, "No one pretends that democracy is perfect or all wise. Indeed, it has been said that democracy is the worst form of government, except for all those other forms that have been tried from time to time" (Petrie, 2006).

The problem of education, and education of the gifted in particular, is that it is a long-term issue such as is global warming and creating a transportation infrastructure, not an immediate crisis such as a hurricane or train wreck, which does stir decision makers to act.

What is clearly needed is the development of an educational infrastructure (Gallagher, 2008) that can support the development of research, leadership training, curriculum development, technical assistance, and the like over an extended period of time. Such long-term planning requires setting aside a portion of our scarce yearly resources and that requires foresight and political courage of the type we have not seen in a long while.

Unfortunately, the major impetus for support of the education of gifted students appears to be fear. When we feared the Russians in the Cold War, we provided major support for curriculum development in mathematics (e.g., School Mathematics Study Group [SMSG]) and Sciences (e.g., Biological Sciences Curriculum Study [BSCS], Physical Science Study Committee [PSSC]) so that our bright students could become competent scientists and protect us against the threat of Russian science.

Now we seem to face a similar situation with the rapid emergence of China, India, and Japan, among others, to challenge our economic security. We have responded with a report, *Rising Above the Gathering Storm* (Committee on Science, Engineering, and Public Policy, 2005), that has been put into legislation under the America Competes Act of 2006, which proposes to support research in the sciences and educational improvements to meet this new threat. It is not clear how many resources will be put on the table, but it is clear that gifted students can profit from this new initiative just as they did from the curriculum blizzard of the 1960s and 1970s.

We understand that policy statements are a type of social hypotheses, hoping that when we enact policy we will see some beneficial results. There are no guarantees for such actions, but we do know that if we do not act, the results will surely not be in our favor.

REFERENCES

Colangelo, N., Assouline, S. G., & Gross, M. U. M. (2004). *A nation deceived: How schools hold back America's brightest students* (Vol. 1). Iowa City: The University of Iowa, The Connie Belin & Jacqueline N. Blank International Center for Gifted Education and Talent Development.

Committee on Science, Engineering, and Public Policy. (2005). *Rising above the gathering storm: Energizing and employing America for a brighter economic future.* Washington, DC: National Academies Press.

Feldhusen, J. F., & Kolloff, P. B. (1986). Seminar: An instructional approach for gifted students. *Gifted Child Today, 9*(5), 2–7.

Ford, D., & Whiting, G. (2008). Recruiting and retaining underrepresented gifted students. In S. Pfeiffer (Ed.), *Handbook of giftedness in children* (pp. 293–308). New York: Springer.

Gallagher, J. (2002). *Society's role in education gifted students: The role of public policy.* Storrs: University of Connecticut, The National Research Center on Gifted and Talented.

Gallagher, J. (2006). *Driving change in special education.* Baltimore: Paul H. Brookes.

Gallagher, J. (2008). According to Jim: Necessary components of national infrastructure to support the development of brilliant minds. *Roeper Review, 30,* 5.

Hernstein, R. J., & Murray, C. (1994). *The bell curve.* New York: The Free Press.

Hodgkinson, H. (2001). Educational demographics: What teachers should know. *Educational Leadership, 58*(4), 6–11.

Individuals With Disabilities Education Act, 20 U.S.C. §1401 et seq. (1990).

Kitano, M. K., & DiJiosia, M. (2002). Are Asian and Pacific Americans overrepresented in programs for the gifted? *Roeper Review, 24,* 76–81.

Marland, S. P., Jr. (1972). *Education of the gifted and talented: Report to the Congress of the United States by the U.S. Commissioner of Education and background papers submitted to the U.S. Office of Education,* 2 vols. Washington, DC: U.S. Government Printing Office. (Government Documents, Y4.L 11/2: G36)

National Commission on Excellence in Education. (1983). *A nation at risk: The imperative for educational reform.* Washington, DC: U.S. Government Printing Office.

No Child Left Behind Act, 20 U.S.C. §6301 (2001).

Ogbu, J. U. (2004). Collective identity and the burden of "acting White" in Black history, community, and education. *Urban Review, 36*(1), 1–35.

PARC v. Pennsylvania, 334 F.Supp. 1257 (E.D. PA 1972)

Petrie, J. (2006). *Collection of Winston Churchill quotes.* Retrieved November 12, 2008, from http://jpetrie.myweb.uga.edu/bulldog.html

Ramey C. T., & Ramey, S. L. (1998). Early intervention and early experience. *American Psychologist, 53,* 109–120.

Renzulli, J. S. (1988). The search for excellence—A modest proposal for schoolwide change. *Roeper Review, 10,* 200–204.

Styfco, S. J., & Zigler, E. (2003). The federal commitment to preschool education: Lessons from and for Head Start. In A. Reynolds, M. Wang, & H. Walberg (Eds.), *Early childhood programs for a new century* (pp. 3–34). Chicago: Child Welfare League of America.

Title V, Part D. [Jacob K. Javits Gifted and Talented Students Education Act of 1988], Elementary and Secondary Education Act of 1988 (2002), 20 U.S.C. sec. 7253 et seq.

U.S. Department of Education, Office of Educational Research and Improvement. (1993). *National excellence: A case for developing America's talent.* Washington, DC: U.S. Government Printing Office.

VanTassel-Baska, J. (2003). Selecting instructional strategies for gifted learners. *Focus on Exceptional Children, 36*(3), 1–12.

VanTassel-Baska, J., & Stambaugh, T. (2008). Curriculum and instructional considerations in programs for the gifted. In S. Pfeiffer (Ed.), *Handbook of giftedness in children* (pp. 347–366). New York: Springer.

Wai, J., Lubinski, D., & Benbow, C. P. (2005). Creativity and occupational accomplishments among intellectually precocious youths: An age 13 to age 33 longitudinal study. *Journal of Educational Psychology, 97,* 484–492.

CHAPTER 41

NATIONAL PRIORITIES AND EDUCATING THE GIFTED:

Substantive Foundations for Policy

by

DAVID
W. LESLIE

A bill for the more general diffusion of learning . . .
—Thomas Jefferson to John Adams (1813)

Gifted education, at its heart, recognizes the unique and special educational needs of students whose abilities are exceptional—and, by definition, different from those of most students. To the extent that they do differ in ability, and given the recognition that special needs students merit special education, educators understand the need for differential treatment of the gifted. This much is not controversial.

But, differential treatment implies a responsibility to (a) reliably and validly identify underlying abilities that merit differential treatment, and (b) design valid ways to "treat" those differences (c) without overburdening taxpayers or denying support to others commensurate with their own educational needs.

The politics of competing claims in regard to (a), (b), and (c) move me to search for a policy framework that can provide a structure within which to pursue those claims in a fair way. I will propose a loose adaptation of elementary substantive and procedural due process and equal protection concepts as a starting point for elaborating that structure.

This volume is dedicated to the career and work of Joyce VanTassel-Baska, founding director of the Center for Gifted

Education at The College of William and Mary. The principal focus of her research has been on "what works" in curriculum—namely, how should gifted students be "treated?" The knowledge base generated by the Center's programmatic efforts for more than 20 years have provided a set of principles that stand the tests of empirical validation. Without knowing "what works," educators cannot satisfy the most fundamental questions in policy. In this sense, Professor VanTassel-Baska has served her profession in the most exemplary way—by advancing the foundations for policy with essential knowledge.

THE PROBLEM(S)

Two fundamental problems beset the development and implementation of gifted education policy. These are (a) the age-old tension between merit and equality that has driven pendulum swings in public policy across wide areas of concern to Americans[1], and (b) the problem of a fair way to allocate resources in the differential treatment of groups and individuals.[2] The first problem might be analyzed with a framework provided by the concept of substantive due process. The second might be analyzed with a procedural due process framework.

Thomas Jefferson probably was the earliest and most eloquent advocate for gifted education. His famous design for Virginia's education system attempted to assure equal access to elementary education for all, but he conditioned access to further (secondary and higher) education on merit:

> A bill for the more general diffusion of learning . . . proposed to divide every county into wards of five or six miles square; . . . to establish in each ward a free school for reading, writing and common arithmetic; to provide for the annual selection of the best subjects from these schools, who might receive at the public expense a higher degree of education at a district school; and from these district schools to select a certain number of the most promising subjects, to be completed at an University where all the useful sciences should be taught. Worth and genius would thus have been sought out from every condition of life, and completely prepared by education for defeating the competition of wealth and birth for public trusts. (Jefferson, 1813, para. 8)

He felt that merit was the best way to assure wise civic leadership. In his plan, scarce public resources would have to be distributed in a way that assured merit was the basis of access to opportunity once provision for broad elementary education was assured. The return on investment in education would be general public literacy, assuring informed voting, and wise public leadership based on knowledge and understanding.

Jefferson's basic idea, of course, has been radically expanded in America through the centuries, but not without clashes. Only in comparatively recent times have opportunities for even basic education been extended to minorities, women, and individuals with special needs. In fact, "merit" was long understood to be code for wealthy White males. But, merit has a more complex history in the evolving value system of American culture. Threats to security, especially in the 1940s and 1950s, focused attention on talent identification and development (Flattau et al., 2006), just as the nation was awakening to a new imperative in race relations (Boyd, 2004).

Coming as close together as they did, the Supreme Court's *Brown v. Board of Education of Topeka* (1954) decision and passage of the National Defense Education Act (1958) juxtaposed the conflicting values of merit and equality as moving forces in public policy. In the contest between the two, the push for equality was (as measured by legislation and litigation) plainly the more urgent on the nation's agenda. The Elementary and Secondary Education Act of 1965, not to mention litigation spawned by *Brown*, committed the federal government to support for the nation's poorest students to an extent that it has not supported the nation's most gifted in the early grades.

More recent public policy has brought special support for students with disabilities (e.g., Education for all Handicapped Children Act of 1975), women (Title IX of the Higher Education Amendments of 1972), and the institutionalization of Title I of the Elementary and Secondary Education Act of 1965 to support those from economically disadvantaged homes and communities. Meanwhile, intermittent funding of gifted programs (e.g., Javits acts) has left them with too little depth and continuity to have commensurate impact. But, even as the federal government (and most states) were opting to realize the aspirations of Jefferson's elementary and secondary education systems to assure a fully literate citizenry, merit won an extraordinary measure of support in the form of funding for an exponentially expanded system of postsecondary education. What may have been denied to gifted students in the early years was provided to them in lavish form at the college level. The American system of higher education broadened access and deepened its impact on the best and brightest between 1950 and about 1990 in ways that had no historic or international parallels (Trow, 1999). It often was called "the envy of the world," and produced extraordinarily talented generations of Ph.D.s whose research won a hugely disproportionate share of Nobel (and other) Prizes (Commission on the Future of Higher Education, 2006).

In one sense then, perhaps the nation has—in however disjointed form—realized the outlines of Jefferson's prescription. It has respected and achieved an exceptionally broad distribution of basic educational opportunity through a variety of policy measures—legislation, funding, and the courts. At the same time, it has created a system through which access to the highest levels of intellectual and artistic opportunity are widely available to individuals of talent.

But, the system is cobbled together and is betrayed by many inefficiencies. Not least among these inefficiencies is simultaneous overfunding and underfunding. And, of equal concern is the extent to which the gifted, especially those in historically disadvantaged racial, gender, or economic groups, are randomly "treated" in programs that neither address their needs nor select them with care.

How, then, to begin assessing these policy problems? What framework(s) might provide the leverage to better understand and address the shortcomings of gifted education in 21st-century America?

I will propose to frame the problems in terms of substantive and procedural due process and equal protection, not to engage in a scholarly or philosophical exegesis of due process jurisprudence, but to begin the construction of a pragmatic way to justify, design, and support programs for the gifted.

DUE PROCESS AND EQUAL PROTECTION: THE CONCEPTS AND THEIR APPLICATION

The Fifth Amendment to the federal constitution reads (in part) as follows: ["no person shall be . . .] deprived of life, liberty, or property, without due process of law" (USCS Constitution, Amend. 5). The post-Civil War 14th Amendment extended the right to due process to actions taken by states, and added a clause, "nor deny to any person within its jurisdiction the equal protection of the laws" (USCS Constitution, Amend. 14). The equal protection clause underlay the *Brown v. Board of Education* (1954) conclusion that (de jure) separate education for Blacks and Whites was "inherently unequal." Revolutionary at its time, *Brown* was the kick-start to the vast effort to assure equal opportunity at the elementary and secondary levels. It led to the legal stratification of any kind of classification in a hierarchy: suspect classifications.[3] Race or (more slowly and conditionally) gender or classifications that implicated some fundamental right like religious speech had to be rationalized by proving that the state had no other alternative.[4] Giftedness is not a suspect classification, either constitutionally or otherwise, so differential treatment of gifted children and the lack of opportunity for them are more easily rationalized by states that are short of resources, personnel, and know-how.

The due process clause contemplates both substance and process in assessing state actions. Its history is too extensive to elaborate, but in the simplest possible terms, the "process" that is due an individual who may be affected by a state action must be commensurate with the possible harm. So, if the state were to contemplate depriving an individual of "life," the most Draconian protections would be due. More difficult to parse are the array of other "liberties" that may or may not be "fundamental."[5] Yet, if the state were to fine someone $25 for speeding, it would have a very low burden of proof indeed. ("Any evidence" at all might be enough in the latter case; "proof beyond the shadow of a doubt" would be required in the death penalty case.)

APPLYING DUE PROCESS AND EQUAL PROTECTION FRAMEWORKS TO GIFTED EDUCATION POLICY

The goal of this section is to set up a practical framework to evaluate existing policy and to modify it in ways that provide for educating the gifted commensurately with the prospective return on investment in them—both socially and individually.

Equal Protection for the Gifted?

The gifted do not constitute a suspect class under existing equal protection law. Nor do the gifted enjoy the level of compensatory protections available for some groups under statutory law. In other words, the presumptions underlying equal protection tend to run against the interests of the gifted. Historically, those who have benefited from educational advantages have been protected through the allocation of resources, the distribution of all kinds of privileges, and presumptions of entitlement. Because educational advantages have accrued disproportionately to wealthy White males through the course of U.S. history, race, gender, and economic condition became protected in the reallocation of opportunity to "others."[6] The post-*Brown* era has largely represented an effort to remedy both de jure and de facto discrimination.

I contend that the consequent redistribution of resources and opportunities has had enormous good effects in the direction of civic literacy, per Jefferson's design. But, it has narrowed the rationale for that redistribution in ways that attenuate the nation's ability to identify talent and encourage its development.

Returning to the National Defense Education Act (NDEA) of 1958, we may recall that it emerged from a national priority to identify talent in science and technology and to invest in that talent in the national interest. Likewise, looking back to Jefferson's ideas, "merit" clearly was the criterion he had in mind in thinking about how to assure wise leadership for the nation. And, in *A Nation at Risk* (National Commission on Excellence in Education, 1983), the authors urged the nation to refocus education on "excellence," answering John Gardner's (1961) provocative "can we be equal and excellent, too?" question in the affirmative. Myriad other reports have concentrated on the nation's need to compete in the increasingly international economy by fostering talent.

How does the idea of equal protection help us to rationalize the distribution of resources when merit and equality collide as imperatives?

Equal protection jurisprudence focuses on the rights of individuals and, where past discrimination has implicated classes of people, on the rights of those classes. It has been less actively employed in thinking through the nature of collective rights, though. Enumerated rights in the Bill of Rights cover an array of historically important liberties and are traceable at least to the Magna Carta of 1215—often taken as the landmark event limiting the power of the king (who was the state; National Archives and Records Administration, n.d.). Individual rights and liberties therefore have been at the core of equal protection jurisprudence as the U.S. Constitution has matured through case-by-case litigation.

Are collective rights—those fundamental expectations underlying the social order—of concern in equal protection analysis? What is so fundamental to society that it should enjoy protection? Obviously, recent history shows that national security, international awareness, and economic competitiveness—as well as civic engagement—are all keys to the nation's viability. (Its viability has rarely been questioned, but on both security and economic fronts, events of the early 2000s have challenged the nation's complacency.)

The challenges facing the nation lead directly to the fundamental question: What is the best way to invest (and in whom) to overcome the challenges and strengthen the nation's future? Just as the NDEA was the answer in 1958, so might reconsidering investments in education be a substantial part of the answer 50 years later.

Equal protection analysis, curiously enough, might lead to a somewhat different answer than we reached in the post-*Brown*, post-Jim Crow era. If the nation faces existential threats, as is often alleged[7], then perhaps a compelling argument can be developed about how to invest in education that advances the gifted and talented—at least in fields that address the existential threat. Although the current neglected state of gifted education can be justified by almost any legitimate state interest—against the more compelling argument that compensation for past discrimination requires certain kinds of investment—the "existential threat" interest of the state may justify a search for and attention to the most gifted and talented and to the kind and depth of education they are given. Much as has been the case during periods of existential threat in the past—namely wartime—compelling need can legitimately compel the investment in "defense."

Put succinctly, this argument suggests that the nation needs to recognize and affirmatively assure that the talents it needs are nurtured effectively in the larger interest of overcoming serious threats. This is an active/positive defense of education for the gifted that rationalizes their (valid) selection and (purposeful) education. In the current environment, gifted educators and the parents of gifted children are usually burdened with answering "why?" because the gifted are so often able to find their own way.[8] By classifying the gifted (or at least their talents) as essential to the national interest, it becomes morally, politically, and legally *necessary* to single them out for support.

Because this argument can be misinterpreted as a not-so-subtle approach to eviscerating other compensatory programs, I should be clear that the distribution of talent across ethnic, gender, and nationality lines should separate the two issues. Identifying talent, though, is so important to the whole classification problem that the methods used have to be carefully validated and prudently applied. They must especially not show bias.

In the case of a fundamental national interest, though, classification methods may legitimately overselect because it in the national interest to err on the side of overinclusion, but presumptively to eliminate every possible error that might lead to underinclusion. Missing a talented person might mean missing some important advance in science, technology, or other field that contributes to national security. (On the other hand, including someone who is not as highly talented as expected might nevertheless provide an opportunity for that person to make an unanticipated contribution.)

So, much hinges on the logic and technology of selection. To explore the way such policy might look, I will rely on a parallel use of the concept of due process.

SUBSTANTIVE AND PROCEDURAL DUE PROCESS: HOW TO SORT OUT THE GIFTED FROM THE OTHERS?

Although equal protection may justify (or forbid) the classification of people, the idea of due process underlies the fair treatment of individuals. The 14th Amendment says, in part, " . . . nor shall any State deprive any person of life, liberty, or property without due process of law." The courts have wrangled over the meaning of each phrase of this clause, but often retreat to the concept of simple fairness in cases where little is at stake. On the other hand, when much is at stake, the state bears an increasing burden to prove its case.[9]

There are (in very simple terms) two different kinds of due process: substantive and procedural. Although it is far more complex and although the law continues to evolve, we can boil these two components of due process down to practical (if simplistic) terms.

Substantive due process requires that the evidence a state uses in its decisions bear a commensurately more direct relationship to outcomes with higher stakes, especially stakes that may affect individuals' most fundamental life, liberty, or property interests.[10] (Death penalty cases, for an extreme example, can't be sustained if the evidence is only circumstantial.)

Procedural due process requires that opportunities to rebut the state's case or decision be provided in degrees of elaboration that also are commensurate with the effects on individuals' life, liberty, or property interests. (Death penalty cases often are tied in procedural knots for years and even decades because "every" avenue for rebuttal must remain open.)

Once the principal policy decision has been made to support a selective gifted education program in the national interest, the ensuing questions will be about who is selected, how they are selected, and how they will be educated. Because the state is both classifying people and treating some differently than others, presumably it will have fairly wide latitude "in the national interest" if our formulation above holds up.

But, having justified its ends, it will still have to justify its means.

Substantively, this boils down to using valid selection methods and implementing proven curricula. It is at this critical juncture that research of the kind the Center for Gifted Education has promoted comes to the service of the state.

First, who is gifted, but equally important, how does the state know? With a national interest rationale, the state will have relatively broad discretion in answering these questions. But, it will be in a better position to the extent that it has substantive answers. Instead of working from a perspective that focuses on the individual learner, a substantive case might better be built from the other end of the logical continuum. Specifically, what are the national interests and needs that require the state's attention? This is a decision, not for schools or districts or parents and communities, but for legislatures. Only at that level can the state authoritatively say what its goals are and why. From that point, the rest follows more or less logically. Defense requires X, competitiveness requires Y, national solidarity requires Z.

X, Y, and Z would (obviously) require talented people, so one might "map backward" (Elmore, 1979/1980) from experts in X, Y, and Z. The requisite talents and abilities, as well as what kinds of educational foundation may be required, can be assessed and defined. And, selection and curriculum methods can be inferred and tested. Working (backward as well as forward) through the substance of each step builds the legitimacy of the state's policy framework for educating gifted people to the extent that each step brings experience and evidence to bear and to the extent that direct relationships are established.

The risks both politically and legally multiply when this chain of logic leads to either over- or underselection of individuals, or to over- or undereducating them. (The greater risk in both cases is probably on the "under-" end, but both will be explored briefly.)

Getting the substance wrong, whether well-intentioned or simply careless, means the state is vulnerable to a substantive due process attack, which can be boiled down to a simple accusation: "You don't know what you are doing. . . ." For its part, the state has to answer that it clearly and justifiably does know what it is doing and why. (It also has to justify what it is doing as a legitimate—or, in this case, compelling—function.)

It can err by overselecting individuals, but doing so can be costly to the taxpayers (i.e., too many unqualified engineers can lead to poorly executed projects.) It can err by underselecting individuals, but doing so may limit the effectiveness of the program in meeting state goals (i.e., too few engineers, when there are more who can do the work, might slow or hamper work on critical projects).

The state can err by overeducating them. Ph.D.'s may not be required to assure that certain projects are completed efficiently and work as intended. The state can err by undereducating them. Examples are probably not needed here, but imagine undergoing heart surgery at the hands of physicians' assistants.

Overselection and overeducating would appear to do little damage to any individual. Obviously, though, too far "over-" in either case means the program will chew into resources needed for other state priorities. That is a political problem and one that requires political judgment. On the other hand, underselection and undereducating pose dangers. Underselection, if history means anything, is often correlated with discrimination against otherwise protected groups: women, minorities, and the poor. And undereducating leads to multiplying inefficiencies—such as bridges or dams that fail and correctives to those failures that also fail because people are in over their heads in trying to solve problems for which they have inadequate training. This is where the national need argument comes to the point.

Because the contours of error implicate public policy—particularly on the question of how much to spend, on whom to spend it, and on what kind of education to spend it—gifted education, however well rationalized in the national interest, has to be substantively justified and the terms on which it is provided politically supported. The more substantive justification is provided, the easier it will be to rally political support.

Gifted education has never been a particularly easy sell in political circles, but my position in this paper is that there are some clear avenues providing compelling foundational rationales. The field can, as the Center's work shows, satisfy the sort of substantive due process concerns that might otherwise derail legislative support.

The argument needs to be less about abstract "opportunities" for the gifted and talented, and more about how to meet legitimate national needs in valid and effective ways. I have presented the substantive due process concept as a way to suggest the field organize its research and mount its case.

Procedural due process also provides a framework that supports the selectivity and differential treatment that may be needed, but that are politically unpopular.

In general, gifted education may provide special benefits for some, but only some, individuals. Therefore, most will be denied these opportunities and may seek to rebut individual decisions. Decisions that are based on the kind of substantive, evidence-based research rationalizing selection processes and criteria are more readily defensible. But, in the arena of talent identification, it generally is accepted that casting broad nets is important. So, an argument can be made that the state's goals are so fundamentally important that overselection is better than underselection.

With that general approach, the state may be better positioned to rebut individuals' contention that they were unjustly denied opportunity. The state can show (if it has done its homework) how its evidence demonstrates it is overselecting, and therefore "bending over backward" to offer opportunities.

To the extent that the state employs multiple criteria and multiple methods in its selection of individuals, and to the extent that it uses "panels" of data rather than individual data points or cut-offs, to that extent, it may be in a better position to show that it is overselecting. But, substantively, overselection is most readily justified when it is shown to be an essential strategy in meeting national needs through talent development.

CONCLUSION

Equal protection and due process ideas may be helpful to the advancement of gifted education policy. The state of the public's commitment has varied over the decades, but strong rationales and methods for strengthening the commitment and the means to implement that commitment may be available in the kind of informal "framing" attempted in this chapter.

The bottom line lies in how substantively gifted educators are able to tie their work, both in talent identification and curriculum development, to the attainment of broader goals.

The Center for Gifted Education, under Joyce VanTassel-Baska's leadership, has done as much as any other group to advance the substance of gifted education's "connect" to these broader goals. This festschrift celebrates those achievements;

and this brief essay helps to emphasize why the "connect" is important and why research is so fundamental to the validation of that "connect."

REFERENCES

Amendment 5, Constitution of the United States of America. U.S.C.S. Const. Amend. 5 (1791). Retrieved from http://www.consource.org

Amendment 14, Constitution of the United States of America. U.S.C.S. Const. Amend. 14 (1868). Retrieved from http://www.consource.org

Boyd, H. (2004). Speaking volumes about *Brown*: Scholarly works review the record of the landmark mid-20th century ruling. *Black Issues Book Review, 6*(3), 20–21.

Brown v. Board of Education of Topeka. 347 U.S. 483 (1954).

Caputo, R. K. (2002). Discrimination and human capital: A challenge to economic theory & social justice. *Journal of Sociology & Social Welfare, 29,* 105–124.

Commission on the Future of Higher Education. (2006). *A test of leadership: Charting the future of U.S. higher education.* Washington, DC: U. S. Department of Education. Retrieved from http://www.ed.gov/about/bdscomm/list/hiedfuture/reports/final-report.pdf

Education for all Handicapped Children Act of 1975, P.L. 94-142, 105th Cong. (1975).

Elementary and Secondary Education Act of 1965, P.L. 89-10, 89th Cong. (1965).

Elmore, R. F. (1979/1980). Backward mapping: Implementation research and policy decisions. *Political Science Quarterly, 94,* 601–616.

Flattau, P. E., Bracken, J., van Atta, R., Bandeh-Ahmadi, A., de la Cruz, R., & Sullivan, K. (2006). *The National Defense Education Act of 1958: Selected outcomes* (IDA Document D-3306). Washington, DC: Science and Technology Policy Institute.

Friedman, L. (2006). Ordinary and enhanced rational basis review in the Massachusetts Supreme Judicial Court: A preliminary investigation. *Albany Law Review, 69,* 415–448.

Gardner, J. (1961). *Excellence: Can we be equal and excellent, too?* New York: Norton.

Herman, D. A. (2007). Juvenile curfews and the breakdown of the tiered approach to equal protection. *New York University Law Review, 82,* 1857–1894.

Higher Education Amendments of 1972, 20 U.S.C. §1681 *et seq.* (1972).

Individuals with Disabilities Education Act of 1990, P.L. 101-476, 101st Cong. (1990).

Jefferson, T. (1813). *Thomas Jefferson on politics & government.* Retrieved from http://etext.virginia.edu/jefferson/quotations/jeff1370.htm

Kuckes, N. (2006). Civil due process, criminal due process. *Yale Law & Policy Review, 25,* 1–62.

Manara, N. (2008). A process long overdue: Finding a fundamental right to bear arms. *The Georgetown Journal of Law & Public Policy, 6,* 729–752.

National Archives and Records Administration. (n.d.). *Magna Carta and its American legacy.* Retrieved October 16, 2008, from http://www.archives.gov/exhibits/featured_documents/magna_carta/legacy.html

National Association for Gifted Children. (n.d.). *Why should gifted education be supported?* Retrieved from http://old.nagc.org/NSBA/Whysupportgifted.PDF

National Commission on Excellence in Education. (1983). *A nation at risk: The imperative for educational reform.* Washington, DC: U.S. Government Printing Office. Retrieved from http://www.ed.gov/pubs/NatAtRisk/index.html

National Defense Education Act of 1958. P.L. 85-864, 85th Cong. (1958).

Trow, M. (1999). From mass higher education to universal access: The American advantage. *Minerva: A Review of Science, Learning & Policy, 37,* 303–328.

Viteritti, J. P. (2007). The inadequacy of adequacy guarantees: A historical commentary on state constitutional provisions that are the basis for school finance litigation. *University of Maryland Law Journal of Race, Religion, Gender and Class, 7,* 58–92.

END NOTES

1. John Gardner's (1961) classic, *Excellence: Can We Be Equal and Excellent, Too?,* framed the tension and its implications this way: "If we scorn . . . excellent plumbers and tolerate . . . slovenly philosophers, neither our pipes nor our theories will hold water."

2. See extensive analyses (Viteritti, 2007) of litigation that pits equity in the distribution of funds for education against adequate substantive provisions for education implied in state constitutions.

3. ". . . government action that affects a fundamental interest or creates a suspect classification will receive the strictest scrutiny from the courts" (Friedman, 2006, p. 417).

4. "Some of today's hardest constitutional cases involve challenges to laws that share two common characteristics. First, the laws burden a class of citizens that is not quite 'suspect' (e.g., defined by race), but still possesses some attributes of a suspect class (e.g., defined by inherent characteristics, poorly represented in the political process, or historically disfavored by legislation). Second, the laws affect freedoms that, although not categorical (i.e., enumerated constitutional rights), are still very important. These 'hybrid' cases integrate issues from both the suspect classification and fundamental interest strands of equal protection jurisprudence. They involve legislation that may not violate substantive constitutional provisions, but nevertheless imposes a substantial burden on a particularly vulnerable group" (Herman, 2007, p. 1859). Herman notes struggles over whether gender is or is not "suspect," noting an intermediate standard has generally been used in this situation.

5. ". . . the key determination in any substantive due process case is whether or not the right at issue is 'fundamental.' This determination informs the level of scrutiny applied to the challenged legislation, with legislation [or a state's act implementing it] that infringes on fundamental rights typically demanding a more intensified form of means-end scrutiny" (Manara, 2008, p. 745).

6. See Caputo's (2002) analysis showing these effects and contending that affirmative action remains justified as a result.

7. There simply are too many grave issues on the nation's agenda to enumerate, but financial and military security, nuclear proliferation, energy, climate change, poverty, inequality, technology and its impact, health, demographic change, education, and more can be found among agendas identified by such independent "think tanks" as Brookings, American Enterprise Institute, Rand, and the like.

8. The National Association for Gifted Children (NAGC) poses these common questions and allegations: "Why should gifted education be supported? This question is often asked in a confrontational manner by those who believe that gifted individuals do not need special educational provisions. Some sincerely feel that truly gifted children will remain gifted and fulfill their educational needs on their own. Others feel that if teachers are doing their job, the gifted should be able to get by without the special attention that other atypical learners need." (NAGC, n.d., para 1.)

9. "The three-part Mathews test provides that for any cognizable deprivation of liberty or property, the procedures constitutionally due are determined by considering: First, the private interest that will be affected by the official action; second, the risk of an erroneous deprivation of such interest through the procedures used, and the probable value, if any, of additional or substitute procedural safeguards; and finally, the Government's interest, including the function involved and the fiscal and administrative burdens that the additional or substitute procedural requirement would entail" (Kuckes, 2006, citing Mathews v. Eldridge, 424 U.S. at 333).

10. See Daniels v. Williams, 474 U.S. 327 (1986), for example. ". . . substantive due process," . . . bars certain arbitrary government actions . . . regardless of the fairness of the procedures used to implement them . . . [and] procedural due process [which means] the State may not execute, imprison, or fine a defendant without giving him a fair trial, nor may it take property without providing appropriate procedural safeguards" (p. 337).

CHAPTER 42

POLICY IN ACTION:

A Memoir of the Illinois Years at the Helm of the State Gifted Education Program

by

LINDA
D. AVERY

The real role of educational leaders is to effect positive change in environments and other people as well as in oneself.

—Joyce VanTassel-Baska

THE STAGE IS SET

As I look back on my professional career, I find I can identify in hindsight a perspective that was unavailable to me as I lived the actual experience. My work with Dr. Joyce VanTassel-Baska during her tenure as the state gifted education coordinator in Illinois in the late 1970s was such a period in my life. At the time, it seemed a blur, but in calm recollection, it achieves a definition, order, and clarity that was unknowable then. Part of that haze was attributable to Joyce's modus operandi as a whirlwind, a highly charged and targeted force, eliminating most obstacles in unwavering pursuit of a vision of excellence. Another part of that haze was my own naiveté and lack of experience.

Perhaps I was too close to the events to see the forest for the trees. I lacked the distance necessary to recognize the extent of the impact that was reverberating through the state program as a result of her stewardship in that post. I do remember quite viscerally what the experience felt like.

Imagine a dream in which you find yourself tooling along a country road on your way to a family picnic in a Ford station wagon being driven by your grandmother. This image dissolves and suddenly you are strapped into a racecar at the Indianapolis 500 with Mario Andretti at the wheel. Adapt or die, as Darwin would have said.

I watched with sheer admiration how Joyce, even as a young professional, honed and dedicated her talents to the advancement of the field of gifted education and to the development of the next generation of leaders in it. For this small window in time (1976–1979), I can be Boswell, both accomplice and witness to the events that transpired. It seems fitting that on the occasion of her retirement that I take a moment to ponder and record her contributions during this period in her long and distinguished career. Because our histories are intertwined, I also will share a bit of my own vocational journey.

While a graduate student at Michigan State University, I obtained a contract for summer employment at the Michigan Department of Education, a fortuitous circumstance that led to being hired as a full-time employee the following winter (1971), and ultimately I was promoted to the level of educational consultant (1976). During that time, the state legislature approved the first statewide funding for gifted education. It was a small appropriation, about $600,000, and the money was awarded on a competitive grant basis to a few local districts each year.

Only a handful of states at this time even had state coordinators for gifted education, and fewer still had state funding to support programs. This was the period just before a small appropriation was made at the federal level to encourage the creation of full-time state gifted education coordinator positions. This federal program was quite ingenious. States were awarded money to recruit and hire these positions, but the money was time-limited, the expectation being that states would see the value of these jobs and support them with their own revenues after the grant period lapsed. This is exactly what happened. By doing this, the leadership at the federal level created a mechanism to promote, organize, and consolidate effective advocacy efforts, first at the state and then through the state, at the grass-roots level. Although there was a 7-year hiatus in federal funding from 1981 until 1988, state and local support continued to germinate and grow. This support ultimately culminated in the creation of the Javits funding, and Javits money has been the primary catalyst for research and innovation in the field since its inception.

In Michigan, the in-house person who developed the guidelines and carried responsibility for the distribution of the money, Dr. Robert Trezise, was at the time the state consultant in social studies curriculum. Bob did double duty in administering the new state funding for gifted services. Although I was one of the staff primarily responsible for innovation in education (ESEA Title IV–C), I teamed with Bob to launch and monitor the newly created state gifted program. He also was the primary mentor for Michael Grost, a mathematics prodigy who attended Michigan State University as a young accelerant during the years that Dr. Elizabeth Drew worked in gifted education there, as has been chronicled in the book *Genius in Residence,* written by Michael's mother Audrey.

To beef up my own knowledge base in the field, I attended a gifted conference in Toledo, OH, hosted by Joyce VanTassel. (She was neither a doctor, nor a Baska at that time.) Shortly thereafter, Joyce left the Toledo district coordinator position to become the state coordinator for gifted education in Illinois. The Illinois program was the second oldest state-funded program in the country and had already been in existence for 14 years. When an opening occurred for an assistant to Joyce, I leapt at the opportunity and was lucky enough to be selected. I packed up my belongings and my cat and moved to another state capitol in search of adventure and challenge.

Although I was not new to state government work (a key factor in Ms. VanTassel's decision to hire me for the job), I had not seriously thought about government work at the macro level. I knew how to develop application forms and approval procedures, organize conferences, collect and analyze evaluation data, conduct needs assessments and use results to develop planning documents, and other tasks of this nature. I was clearly a technician, albeit a good and highly productive technician, but I was content to be the banderillero, not the matador.

THE CURTAIN IS DRAWN

It was not until I attended an in-house seminar given by the assistant superintendent for public instruction that I began to consciously examine and understand the role of state government across all of its programs and services. That role, as Dr. Ashline so succinctly described it, was threefold: (1) the distribution of money, (2) the translation of law into rules and regulations to carry out legislative intent, and (3) the monitoring and auditing of these funds and respective programs to ensure accountability. Not captured in this analysis was the role of leadership in the process. What I had a ringside seat to observe first-hand in those extraordinary years was the remarkable artistry that Joyce VanTassel possessed to propel a program forward by creating synergy in the implementation of these elements.

Richard Ronvik, the director of the Chicago Public School's gifted program, once said that no coordinator in the prior history of the Illinois state program had done as much as Ms. VanTassel did in her first few months on the job. Joyce redefined and ignited the role of the state gifted education coordinator. As Joyce's own expertise and awareness grew, her vision of what could be accomplished flourished. She didn't have a fixed blueprint, but rather a fluid and evolving sense of how to integrate all the disparate program functions and components into an ontogenic whole.

Now, in the rearview mirror, I can see clearly the ripples that were made across the 630 school districts educating gifted students and the 9 technical support centers providing regional assistance with program and professional development. Just as ripples can turn into waves, these calculated, as well as intuitive, decisions and actions laid a foundation that grounded and supported the burgeoning service delivery system for decades to come.

RISING ACTION

Under Ms. VanTassel's leadership, a decisive impact was made in the amount of state funding for gifted education. The funding formula for the Illinois program entitled districts with programs meeting state guidelines to claim $60.00 per student for up to 5% of the total student population. Under Joyce's advocacy, this formula was changed to $100 per student, an increase of 67%, and the corresponding appropriation was augmented to support this change. This move assured district-level personnel that resources were available to support program growth and development. The actual dollars were quite small in comparison to the vast investments that were plowed into special and compensatory education programs, but the moral victory of getting the first increase in state funding in many years was profound in encouraging local program development efforts.

A second substantive change was in the utilization of the nine regional service centers that were state funded. For years, these centers saw their primary responsibility as pleasing their constituent districts by helping with the identification processes and by providing staff development that was fun for teachers. Ms. VanTassel set a higher level of expectation for their performance. She brought them into the processes for approving district applications and monitoring district implementation, processes that had been little more than rubber stamps in the past. In this way, these regional staff members were more empowered and better versed in the goal of *program* development, which was to take a program at its current level of evolution and move it to a higher level by promoting both acceleration and articulation across the K–12 span (VanTassel-Baska, 1986). Regional staff now had to get districts beyond the absorbing emphasis on the identification and selection of students and to address other key variables such as grouping strategies, curriculum design, and program planning and evaluation. Most regional staff welcomed and thrived on these new expectations; the few who failed to embrace these changes were replaced in subsequent funding cycles.

District gifted programs were a motley mix at this time (Avery & Bartolini, 1979). Of course, a few districts, most notably Chicago and its affluent suburbs, were very sophisticated and had well-conceptualized and developed services, already addressing issues of program depth and linkage across grade levels. Many districts had modest to competent programs, especially at the upper elementary level, utilizing a variety of organizational models (e.g., self-contained classrooms, pull-out) across the state. Most districts did not start programs until grade 3, did little at the middle and high school levels, ignored the research on early admission and grade skipping, and lacked curricula that were content-driven. Of course, some programs were quite primitive. The worst example was the district (small, rural) that used its money to buy library books targeted to advanced learners; that was the extent of the whole program.

There were a plethora of needs across district programs including the lack of K–12 articulation, insufficient acceleration options, scatter-shot staff development, ineffective parent involvement, virtually nonexistent program planning and evaluation. Only a handful of urban districts had Advanced Placement (AP) options available at the secondary level; there were only one or two International Baccalaureate (IB) programs getting started in the whole state. No requirements were in place for certification of teachers of the gifted so interested staff moved from the regular classroom to gifted classroom or coordinator positions with little specialized training and preparation. The field was still finding its bearings.

Several strategies were undertaken at the state level to elevate expectations and requirements for local program operations, but two will be mentioned here: the carrot and the stick. The carrot was the more inventive and interesting. In collaboration with local district and regional gifted education staff, the state identified a set of parameters against which local services could be measured to determine if the district reached the status of having an "exemplary gifted program." Districts could self-nominate for this recognition, or could be nominated by regional staff. The nomination process involved the completion of a questionnaire that was reviewed in-house and followed up with an on-site visit. The pay off for districts willing to seek this designation was recognition at the statewide conference and their inclusion in a widely disseminated public relations brochure describing their program.

The value of this initiative was in communicating a set of standards that local programs could aspire to address. In effect, Illinois was defining for the first time the components of and expectations for high-quality gifted programs. Earlier work had focused exclusively on minimum expectations, but this effort transcended the emphasis on mere compliance. This was in some ways a precursor to the initiative launched by NAGC many years later to articulate standards for sound program design, development, and implementation. The Illinois initiative also turned out to be a very effective staff development tool for use with gifted program coordinators by giving them a more rigorous template against which they could assess their program's level of development.

The "stick" addressed the programs at the bottom of the barrel. For the first time ever, program applications that described insufficient service options or that used spurious identification procedures were put on probationary status. The funding was not withheld during the first year, but these districts were required to make program adjustments if they wanted to secure future funding. A process was set up to involve local district personnel in the review of program applications. The rule was that one could not review schools from the same region in which one's own district was located. This provided some level of objectivity in the decision-making and reduced the potential for premature leakage of the approval decisions that were made. Before a district was put on probation, the state staff reviewed the recommendation of the review team, scrutinized the application itself, and made the final judgment call.

Again, this approach had far-reaching consequences. Prior to the institution of this process, local coordinators had only seen their own district applications and had little sense of how their programs matched up against other programs across the state. Through this collaborative examination of applications, they began to see the common problems in program development that were unveiled. Although the written applications could be distorted to inflate the actual nature of the program, in most cases, the applications were honest and reasonable representations of actual services. At the conclusion of these massive, 2-day review sessions for all the district applications, a debriefing of the small groups was held to analyze what had been learned from the process itself and to extract broad-based observations of program needs. These groups also were polled to make recommendations to strengthen future application requirements.

Hand-in-hand with the involvement of the field in the application review process, the regulatory framework itself also was revised. Because rules and regulations carry the force of law, any changes at this level must go through layers of review and approval. By including local district staff in the application review, they began to see the connection between the regulation requirements and the programs that were developed to meet them. There always is resistance when state government tries to shore up and tighten regulatory expectations, but by educating the field as to critical linkage between the regulations and the results that accrue, Ms. VanTassel was able to mobilize advocacy for the proposed changes.

An example of a revision in the program regulations was the tightening of the definition of giftedness. Illinois used the same definition that was used in the Marland (1972) report, which highlighted six categories (general intellectual ability, specific academic aptitude, creative thinking, leadership, visual and performing arts, and psychomotor). Some districts saw this as a menu of options, and targeted the district's funds to support athletic programs or summer institutes for students with leadership abilities. The changes made in the program requirements called for a more hierarchical approach. Districts were expected to develop programs in the first two categories (intellectual ability and academic aptitude) before they could move on to the other categories. Eventually the category of psychomotor was eliminated entirely.

Both of these strategies, the carrot and the stick, relied on two-way channels of communication: top-down and bottom-up. The state personnel, the regional staff, and local program coordinators and their constituencies, were constantly engaged in dialogue and decision making. The carrot gave the field a healthy vision to aspire to; the stick weeded out the programs that refused to grow.

One of the most powerful impacts of Ms. VanTassel's tenure in Springfield was her introduction of the Study of Mathematically Precocious Youth (SMPY) project and her establishment of a statewide mechanism for its implementation (VanTassel-Baska, 1983). Many states since that time have chosen to replicate her work. Joyce recognized early on that Julian Stanley and his colleagues at Johns Hopkins University had figured out how to break through the ceiling of gifted student identification and also to design interventions that would respond to the needs of a previously invisible population uncovered by this methodology. Perhaps this innovation, more than any other, has transformed how public schools have come to appreciate the ranges of intellectual giftedness embedded in the top 5% of bright students. The follow-up interventions are mostly carried out on university campuses that sponsor compressed content and/or enrichment programs to qualified adolescents and that often offer a mechanism to award college credit for successful completion. Local schools have become quite sophisticated in linking parents and kids with these services in order to complement what can be done in the local system. Joyce was the first to validate the breakthrough achieved by Dr. Stanley and show how his ideas could be translated into a statewide initiative, and Illinois was the landscape. To demonstrate his gratitude, Julian became a lifelong mentor and advocate of Joyce's contributions to the field.

Under VanTassel's leadership, the overall program for gifted education in Illinois took significant steps forward. She was able to accomplish this by recognizing and organizing dedicated and creative individuals at the regional and local levels, working with and through them to shape and execute an agenda for positive change, and by always extending the frontiers of possibility and pushing the boundaries of the tasks at hand. She was at the epicenter of some remarkably talented people whose objectives coalesced to bring programs and services to new heights. She understood the opportunity at hand and put boundless energy and enthusiasm into seizing a small moment in time in order to unleash a big difference across the state.

THE TURNING POINT

Joyce's departure from the Illinois State Board of Education was spurred by several factors. One of these factors was the structural change undertaken by the Department of Special Education Services, the division in which the gifted program was housed. This department originally had been organized by categorical programs and during Joyce's tenure, shifted to a systemic model based on program functions. Instead of focusing on program areas such as learning disabled, hard-of-hearing, developmentally disabled, and the like, the new structure created units around program functions, such as application and approval procedures, program development and staff training, and program monitoring. This strategy streamlined procedures for special education program compliance at both the state and district levels and maximized staff output by cross-pollination of manpower. It was a smart move for special education, but a potentially disastrous move for gifted.

The reason was that the gifted education, unlike special education, was not a mandated program, nor did it have the magnitude of funding to maintain its identify in this consolidated schematic. The program was still fragile and needed discrete advocacy to sustain and nurture the gains that had been made. When Joyce left the state agency, she was able to participate in an effort to relocate the program from the special education division and into one that allowed it to keep its discrete identity. What was lost in this move was the chance to leverage other employees to carry out functional tasks in gifted education when Joyce had been promoted to a division manager position. However, what was gained was greater autonomy in establishing the priorities and initiatives for the field as well as the opportunity to maintain the bully pulpit and to sound the clarion call. Educators of the gifted often felt like voices in the wilderness; at least with this change, their megaphone was not taken away.

Another salient factor in Joyce's decision to leave Springfield was personal. She had met Leland Baska, a bright, handsome school psychologist from Chicago, and she wanted to pursue the relationship in closer proximity to him. Her success with this venture is well documented. She also found the time to complete her doctorate in educational administration.

Just as people have periods in their lives marked by growth and stasis, contentment and discord, excitement and boredom, programs, too, can go through cycles of popularity and invisibility, attention and disregard, up-ticks and downturns. In recent years, state funding for gifted education in Illinois was discontinued. A state with a venerable history of being an early advocate for services to high-ability students no longer saw the need to sustain a discrete line item in the state budget to support this population of learners. This didn't mean that programs were completely dismantled at the local level. It did mean that values had shifted. An old adage proclaims, "If you want to know what the priorities are, look to see where the money is spent."

In spite of some setbacks, many strides have been made in the field of gifted education from the late 1970s until now. Across her career, Joyce has contributed to many of them, and her tenure during her time at The College of William and Mary has given her a national and international platform for shaping and sharing her ideas and insights. Her work on curriculum development has been seminal in stressing the integration of advanced content tied to standards with higher level thinking and reasoning skills. The Center's curriculum units are both a tool for classroom teachers as well as a model for local districts on how to create and assess powerful learning experiences for gifted children. Joyce has been a vibrant voice in linking professional development to research-based best practice and in calling attention to the need for data collection and analysis in decision making at the classroom and program levels. During her presidency of the National Association for Gifted Children (NAGC), Joyce fused the interests of that organization with the Council for Exceptional Children, The Association for the Gifted (CEC-TAG) to craft a set of teacher competencies for the field that are endorsed by both organizations and are a basis for teacher certification programs.

These achievements grew from the needs that Dr. VanTassel-Baska and her colleagues identified and the solutions that they designed. I like to think that Joyce's years in state government were the catalyst for seeing the possibilities beyond leadership at the local district level; these were the years that initiated her into the world of upper level administration, high-stakes decision making, and complex politics and prepared her for tackling big problems and systemic challenges. If this were the case, then I was blessed indeed to share the cockpit on this magnificent ride.

CLIMAX

Alfred, Lord Tennyson wrote in the poem "Locksley Hall" that "knowledge comes, but wisdom lingers." Looking back on these early years in my career under the tutelage of Dr. VanTassel-Baska, I think it was a period in which I formulated some essential insights about policy development and leadership abilities. These are the key observations I made:

1. Good policies like good programs are always evolving. The factors that impinge on both of these domains are never static, and as our experience deepens and the contextual variables change over time, both the conceptual design features and the implementation elements must adapt and grow. There is no "perfect" policy or program; what constitutes high quality at one point in time, often becomes the threshold for the next tier of progress.

2. Good policy frameworks are stretched like a tight-rope between prescription and proscription but have enough slack to allow for the strong winds of individuation. They articulate what one must do and what one cannot do, but they also accommodate some flexibility across and between these poles to permit a variety of field-based responses. The political process itself tends to be remarkably effective in shaping these parameters, but without aggressive advocacy balanced across a range of interests, it is possible for policies to stifle as well as to enrich and encourage.

3. The consequences of decisions, particularly those that have impact across large sectors of the society, can never be fully forecasted. No one dreamed that the replication of the SMPY project would become a staple of gifted education services across the entire country; no one foretold that the emphasis on underidentification of selected minorities would still be driving large allocations of time and resources at the district level. One proceeds on the basis of one's best judgment at the time, knowing that there can be negative as well as positive outcomes.

4. This uncertainty or ambiguity in predicting outcomes can arouse tension in the psyche. In order to lead, the individual must recognize and overcome this inertia. Many people do not pursue positions of authority because of this tension. A good leader also is a mentor to his or her followers and helps them to understand and counteract this psychological dissonance so that new voices and talents can step into the spotlight.

5. There is no more powerful leadership tool in a democracy than leading by example. An administrator who puts his or her heart and soul into an endeavor, who listens patiently and wisely to the input of both trusted advisors and professed antagonists, who communicates and explains the rationale for the course of action, and who acts decisively in accordance with strong values toward a vision of the common good will engender support and mobilize resources beyond one's wildest imagination. I do not mean to imply that one should become a fanatic in one's chosen field,

but a person does pay a price for taking on the mantle of top responsibility in addition to getting a pay off.

DENOUEMENT

I left the Illinois State Board of Education about one year after Joyce's departure to accept an administrative position with the Illinois Department of Children and Family Services, one of only two cabinet-level child welfare agencies in the United States. I stayed with this agency for the next 12 years in a variety of management roles. In my late 40s, I decided to pursue a doctorate and left full-time employment to become a graduate student. I enrolled at The College of William and Mary and moved to Virginia to once again work with Joyce. A line by T.S. Eliot in "The Four Quartets" comes to mind: "And the end of all our exploring will be to arrive where we started and know the place for the first time." Although I have come to see life as a spiral, rather than a circle, there were many similarities between my early years in Springfield and my later years in Williamsburg. Probably at no other junctures in my life did I feel so invited to grow as a practicing professional. At no other times did I achieve the level of sustained productivity that was necessary to meet performance expectations. I learned a lot about my limits and my limitations through both of these experiences.

I continue to marvel at Joyce's capacity to inspire and elevate. In our work together, she gave me a cherished gift, the gift of realizing that my reach may exceed my grasp. I can only hope that in the years I served in supervisory or collegial roles, I was able to pass on to others, at least in some small measure, the treasure she bestowed on me.

REFERENCES

Avery, L. D., & Bartolini, L. (1979). Survey of provisions for gifted children in Illinois: A summary paper. *Journal for the Education of the Gifted, 2*, 132–140.

Marland, S. P., Jr. (1972). *Education of the gifted and talented: Report to the Congress of the United States by the U.S. Commissioner of Education and background papers submitted to the U.S. Office of Education,* 2 vols. Washington, DC: U.S. Government Printing Office. (Government Documents, Y4.L 11/2: G36)

VanTassel-Baska, J. (1983). State-wide replication in Illinois of the Johns Hopkins Study Of Mathematically Precocious Youth. In C. P. Benbow & J. C. Stanley (Eds.), *Academic precocity: Aspects of its development* (pp. 179–191). Baltimore: The Johns Hopkins University Press.

VanTassel-Baska, J. (1986). Lessons from the history of teacher inservice in Illinois: Effective staff development in the education of the gifted. *Gifted Child Quarterly, 30*, 124–126.

CHAPTER 43

LEADERSHIP AND GIFTEDNESS

by

ROBERT
J. STERNBERG

Giftedness in leadership is, in large part, a function of creativity, analytical intelligence, practical intelligence, and wisdom. Gifted leaders are not necessarily good at everything. Rather, they know their own strengths and weaknesses. They make the most of the strengths and find ways to deal with the weaknesses.

—Robert J. Sternberg

Which of the following is impossible? (1) bicycling to the edge of the universe; (2) counting the precise number of bacteria in the human body at a given moment in time; (3) writing a chapter on leadership and giftedness without saluting Joyce VanTassel-Baska; (4) all of the above; (5) none of the above.

The correct answer to this challenging problem is (4). They are all impossible. So, I will not try to bicycle to the edge of the universe nor will I start counting bacteria. And, I will certainly not fail to open this chapter without saluting one of the handful of greatest leaders in the field of gifted education for the latter half of the 20th century into the early part of the 21st century: Joyce VanTassel-Baska. Joyce is the Jody and Layton Smith Professor in Education, School of Education, and Executive Director, Center for Gifted Education at William and Mary. She has worked in the field of educational leadership and has started a master's and doctoral program emphasizing gifted education in the educational-leadership program. She has won countless awards and received more recognitions than I could fit within the allowable page limit for this article. And, most importantly, she is a wonderful person of whom we all can be proud. She is the prototype of the leader of whom I speak in this chapter.

Where does leadership fit with giftedness? In the United States, we often think of giftedness in terms of IQ and school achievement, and possibly a few other qualities (Kaufman & Sternberg, 2007), although some other cultures have a broader view (Sternberg, 2007a). But, what was Mother Teresa's IQ? Or Abraham Lincoln's? Some scholars who are focused on IQ may ponder questions such as these. The questions are red herrings, because the IQs of these individuals are not what made them gifted leaders. Adults usually are identified as such by the leadership roles they take in their fields. Many of us do not know, and do not care about, how quickly they learned about their fields. Their poor childhood academic performance (Albert Einstein) or their outstanding childhood feats (John Stuart Mill) later become mere curiosities. Joyce VanTassel-Baska did not attain her eminence in the field of gifted education by memorizing a textbook on gifted education, nor by solving puzzle-like IQ test problems that predict how rapidly or thoroughly one will be able to learn the contents of that book. Do any of you reading this chapter know her childhood test scores or school grades? I certainly don't. Instead, eminent leaders like Joyce achieve their position by leading the field with their ideas.

In this chapter, I argue that giftedness in leadership is, in large part, a function of *creativity* in generating ideas, *analytical intelligence* in evaluating the quality of these ideas, *practical intelligence* in implementing the ideas and convincing others to value and follow the ideas, and *wisdom* to ensure that the decisions and their implementation represent positive values directed for the common good, over the long and short terms, of all stakeholders. The model is referred to as WICS— *w*isdom, *i*ntelligence, *c*reativity, *s*ynthesized—although the order of elements in the acronym is intended only to make it pronounceable (Sternberg, 2003b, 2003c).

EMPIRICAL LITERATURE

Creativity, intelligence, and wisdom are not innate, unmodifiable characteristics. Although these attributes may be partially heritable, heritability is distinct from modifiability (Sternberg & Grigorenko, 1999). Leaders can develop their creativity, intelligence, and wisdom. One is not "born" a gifted leader. Rather, giftedness in wisdom, intelligence, and creativity—the ingredients of gifted leadership—is a form of developing competency and expertise (Sternberg, 2003a) that one can decide to utilize or not in actual leadership decisions. The environment strongly influences the extent to which we are able to utilize and develop whatever genetic potentials we have (Sternberg & Grigorenko, 2002). Joyce VanTassel-Baska's considerable skills interacted with her environments at Northwestern University and The College of William and Mary to allow her to lead brilliantly.

Leadership comprises both skills and attitudes that almost anyone can develop. This view of leadership contrasts with many traditional views. Traditional models of leadership often stress identification of "fixed" traits or behaviors that make leaders gifted; other models instead emphasize the interaction between internal attributes and situations (Antonakis, Cianciolo, & Sternberg, 2004).

For example, one can compare my view with that of transactional and transformational leadership (Bass, Avolio, & Atwater, 1996). Transactional leaders emphasize the contractual relationship between leader and follower. For example, an employee might agree to engage in certain activities in exchange for certain rewards from the leadership of organization by which he is employed (Sashkin, 2004). Transformational leaders emphasize higher needs and a relationship in which followers may become leaders and leaders into moral agents (Burns, 1978; Sashkin, 2004). Transactional leaders are more likely to pursue options that preserve current paradigms. Transformational leaders, on the other hand, are more likely to pursue any options that reject current paradigms. They are crowd-defiers. In terms of Kuhn's (1970) theory of scientific revolutions, which applies to ideas outside the sciences as well, these are the leaders who revolutionize ways of thinking. In other words, transformational leaders exhibit a more creative leadership style, on average, than do transactional leaders.

WHAT ARE THE MAJOR THEMES FOR THE FIELD OF GIFTED EDUCATION?

The major themes for gifted education are the importance of creativity, academic and practical intelligence, and wisdom for leadership. The article considers these three elements, in that order, because it represents the order in which the elements often are initially used. As leadership decisions evolve, the elements become interactive and so order becomes less relevant.

Creativity

Creativity refers to the skills and attitudes needed for generating ideas and products that are (a) relatively novel, (b) high in quality, and (c) appropriate to the task at hand (Sternberg & Lubart, 1995). Creativity is important for leadership because it is the component whereby one generates the ideas that others will follow. A good leader, on this view, is one who embodies a creative vision, as Joyce VanTassel-Baska has, first in her work at Northwestern, and then in her work at William and Mary.

Creative leadership as a confluence of skills and attitudes. A confluence model of creativity (Sternberg & Lubart, 1995) suggests that creative people show a variety of characteristics. These characteristics represent not innate abilities, but rather, largely, decisions. In other words, to a large extent, people decide to be creative. People who decide to be creative exhibit a creative attitude toward leadership.

What are the elements of a creative attitude toward leadership?

1. *Problem redefinition.* Creative leaders do not define a problem the way every-one else does, simply because everyone else defines the problem that way. They decide on the exact nature of the problem using their own judgment. Most importantly, they are willing to defy the crowd in defining a problem differently from the way others do (Sternberg & Lubart, 1995). Gifted leaders are more willing to redefine problems and better able to do so.

2. *Problem analysis.* Creative leaders are willing to analyze whether their solution to the problem is the best one possible. Gifted leaders are more willing to analyze their own decisions, and better see their strengths and weaknesses.

3. *Selling a solution.* Creative leaders realize that creative ideas do not sell themselves; rather, creators have to decide to sell their ideas, and then decide to put in the effort to do so. Gifted leaders are better salespeople. They persuade others of the value of their ideas and to follow those ideas. They thus need to be able to articulate the value of their idea in a clear and persuasive way.

4. *Recognizing how knowledge can both help and hinder creative thinking.* Creative leaders realize that knowledge can hinder as well as facilitate creative thinking. Sometimes leaders become entrenched and susceptible to tunnel vision, letting their expertise hinder rather than facilitate their exercise of leadership. Gifted leaders are more likely to recognize their own suscepti-bility to entrenchment and take steps to battle against it, such as seeking able advisors, new ideas from novices, and so forth.

5. *Willingness to take sensible risks.* Creative leaders recognize that they must decide to take sensible risks, which can lead them to success but also can lead them, from time to time, to failure. Gifted leaders are more willing to take large risks and to fail as often as they need in order to accomplish their long-term goals.

6. *Willingness to surmount obstacles.* Creative leaders are willing to surmount the obstacles that confront anyone who decides to defy the crowd. Such obstacles result when those who accept paradigms confront those who do not (Kuhn, 1970; Sternberg & Lubart, 1995). All leaders encounter obstacles. Curiously, gifted leaders are particularly susceptible to obstacles, because they often want to move followers more quickly and further than the followers might be ready for. So, the gifted leader needs great resilience in order to accomplish his or her goals.

7. *Belief in one's ability to accomplish the task at hand.* Creative leaders believe in their ability to get the job done. This belief is sometimes referred to as self-efficacy (Bandura, 1996). Gifted leaders believe in themselves and their ideas—not necessarily in the value of every single idea, but in the value of their overall strategy for leadership.

8. *Willingness to tolerate ambiguity.* Creative leaders recognize that there may be long periods of uncertainty during which they cannot be certain they are doing the right thing or that what they are doing will have the outcome

they hope for. The more gifted the leaders, the greater the ambiguity, because these leaders try to make large changes that can create shock waves for followers but also for themselves.

9. *Willingness to find extrinsic rewards for the things one is intrinsically motivated to do.* Creative leaders almost always are intrinsically motivated for the work they do (Amabile, 1983). Creative leaders find environments in which they receive extrinsic rewards for the things they like to do anyway. Gifted leaders almost always love what they do.

10. *Continuing to grow intellectually rather than to stagnate.* Creative leaders do not get stuck in their patterns of leadership. Their leadership evolves as they accumulate experience and expertise. They learn from experience rather than simply letting its lessons pass them by. Gifted leaders do not flame out as time passes them by. Rather, they adapt to changing circumstances.

Types of creative leadership. The creative ideas leaders propose can be of different types (Sternberg, Kaufman, & Pretz, 2003). Consider each type of leadership in turn:

1. *Conceptual replication.* This type of leadership is an attempt to show that a field or organization is in the right place at the right time.

2. *Redefinition.* This type of leadership is an attempt to show that a field or organization is in the right place, but not for the reason(s) that others, including previous leaders, think it is.

3. *Forward incrementation.* This type of leadership is an attempt to lead a field or an organization forward in the direction it already is going.

4. *Advance forward incrementation.* This type of leadership is an attempt to move an organization forward in the direction it is already going, but by moving beyond where others are ready for it to go.

5. *Redirection.* This type of leadership is an attempt to redirect an organization, field, or product line from where it is headed toward a different direction.

6. *Reconstruction/redirection.* This type of creative leadership is an attempt to move a field or an organization or a product line back to where it once was (a reconstruction of the past) so that it may move onward from that point, but in a direction different from the one it took from that point onward.

7. *Reinitiation.* This type of leadership is an attempt to move a field, organization, or product line to a different, as yet unreached starting point and then to move from that point.

8. *Synthesis.* In this type of creative leadership, the creator integrates two or more ideas that previously were seen as unrelated or even as opposed.

Various forms of creative contributions engender different kinds of leadership. Some leaders transform the nature of an organization, whereas others do not. At a given time, in a given place, transformation may or may not be called for. So, transformation is not necessarily needed in every leadership situation. But, the leaders who tend to be remembered over the course of history are probably, in most cases, those who transform organizations or, more generally, ways of thinking.

One might ask whether gifted leaders are more likely to show one or another form of creativity. For example, are gifted leaders more likely to be reinitiators than to be replicators? Probably, on average, gifted leaders are more likely to adopt leadership styles that involve challenging existing paradigms. But, two important points must be kept in mind. First, the various types of creativity refer to kinds of novelty, not quality. Creativity, however, involves quality as well as novelty. One can have a very novel idea that nevertheless is not good. Second, even the more mundane forms of creativity can lead someone to be labeled as gifted. If a leader were able to replicate within a society some of the creativity of the Renaissance in art, literature, and science, he or she might be considered to be quite gifted. So, the type of creativity does not necessarily speak to whether a leader is gifted. Even more modest types of creativity can result in gifted performance.

Our research on creativity (Sternberg & Lubart, 1995) has yielded several conclusions. First, creativity often involves defying the crowd, or as we have put it, buying low and selling high in the world of ideas. Creative leaders are good investors: They do what needs to be done, rather than just what other people or polls tell them to do. Second, creativity is relatively domain specific. Third, creativity is weakly related to traditional intelligence, but certainly is not the same thing as academic intelligence. In general, it appears that there is a threshold of IQ for creativity, but it is probably about 120 or even lower (see review in Sternberg & O'Hara, 2000). So, let's next consider the role of intelligence in leadership.

Intelligence

Intelligence would seem to be important to leadership, but how important? Indeed, if the conventional intelligence of a leader is too much higher than that of the people he or she leads, the leader may not connect with those people and become ineffective. Intelligence, as conceived of here, is not just intelligence in its conventional narrow sense—some kind of general factor (g; Jensen, 1998, 2002; Sternberg & Grigorenko, 2002) or as IQ (Kaufman, 2000), but rather, in terms of the theory of successful intelligence (Sternberg, 2005b). Successful intelligence is defined as the skills and attitudes needed to succeed in life, given one's own conception of success, within one's sociocultural environment. Successfully intelligent people balance adaptation to, shaping of, and selection of environments by capitalizing on strengths and compensating for or correcting weaknesses. Many a leader who had a spectacular fall did so because he or she was unable to control or counteract the effects of his or her weaknesses. Two particular aspects of the theory of successful intelligence are especially relevant. These are academic and practical intelligence.

Academic intelligence. Academic intelligence refers to the memory and analytical skills and attitudes that in combination largely constitute the conventional notion of intelligence—the skills and attitudes needed to recall and recognize but also to analyze, evaluate, and judge information. There is a long history of research on the relation between these skills and attitudes and leadership, going back at least to Stogdill (1948), and the results are ambiguous. Although there seems to be a modest correlation between intelligence and leadership effectiveness (Stogdill, 1948), the correlation is moderated by factors such as the stress experienced by the leader (Fiedler, 2002), which apparently even can change the direction of the correlation. Intelligence matters to leadership under conditions of low stress, but actually can impede performance under high stress. Experience is more helpful to leaders under conditions of high stress, when they do not have the luxury of applying analytical techniques to the solution of problems and need to draw from experience to solve problems that confront them.

The literature on giftedness is in large part a literature on academic intelligence (see, e.g., essays in Sternberg & Davidson, 2005). Certainly, academic intelligence is important to giftedness and to gifted leadership. But, there are many people who have been gifted intellectually who have not become gifted leaders. They lacked the other qualities of WICS.

The academic skills and attitudes matter for leadership, because leaders need to be able to retrieve information that is relevant to leadership decisions (memory) and to analyze and evaluate different courses of action, whether proposed by themselves or by others (analysis). But, a good analyst is not necessarily a good leader.

The long-time primary emphasis on *academic* intelligence (IQ) in the literature relating intelligence to leadership perhaps has been unfortunate. Indeed, recent theorists have been emphasizing other aspects of intelligence, such as emotional intelligence (e.g., Caruso, Mayer, & Salovey, 2002; Goleman, 1998a, 1998b) or multiple intelligences (Gardner, 1995), in their theories. Here the emphasis is on practical intelligence (Sternberg & Hedlund, 2002), which has a somewhat different focus from emotional intelligence. Practical intelligence is a part of successful intelligence. Practical intelligence is a core component of leadership, and thus will receive special attention here.

Practical intelligence. Practical intelligence is the set of skills and attitudes to solve everyday problems by utilizing knowledge gained from experience in order purposefully to adapt to, shape, and select environments. It thus involves changing oneself to suit the environment (adaptation), changing the environment to suit oneself (shaping), or finding a new environment within which to work (selection). One uses these skills to (a) manage oneself, (b) manage others, and (c) manage tasks.

Giftedness in "transactional leadership" (Bass et al., 1996) derives, in large part, although not exclusively, from the adaptive function of practical intelligence. Transactional leaders are largely adapters: They work toward the mutual fulfillment with their followers of essentially contractual obligations. The leaders typically provide contingent rewards, specifying role and task requirements and rewarding desired performance. Or, the leaders may manage by exception, in which case they monitor meeting of standards and intervene when these standards are not met.

Sternberg and his colleagues (e.g., Sternberg & Hedlund, 2002) have taken a knowledge-based approach to understanding practical intelligence. Individuals draw on a broad base of knowledge in solving practical problems, some of which is acquired through formal training and some of which is derived from personal experience. Much of the knowledge associated with successful problem solving can be characterized as tacit. It is knowledge that may not be openly expressed or stated; thus, individuals must acquire such knowledge through their own experiences. Furthermore, although people's actions may reflect their knowledge, they may find it difficult to articulate what they know. For their own leadership, what matters is not so much what tacit knowledge they can articulate, but rather, how much of this knowledge they can apply. However, to serve as effective mentors, it helps greatly if they can articulate as well as act on this knowledge.

The main findings from tacit-knowledge research are that (a) tacit knowledge tends to increase with experience; (b) it correlates minimally and sometimes not at all with scores on tests of academic intelligence; (c) it does not correlate with personality; (d) it predicts job performance significantly; and (e) it provides significant incremental prediction over conventional academic-intelligence measures.

Wisdom

A leader can have all of the above skills and attitudes and still lack an additional quality that, arguably, is the most important quality a leader can have, but perhaps, also the rarest. This additional quality is wisdom. Wisdom is viewed here in terms of a proposed balance theory of wisdom (Sternberg, 1998), according to which an individual is wise to the extent he or she uses successful intelligence, creativity, and knowledge as moderated by values to (a) seek to reach a common good, (b) by balancing intrapersonal (one's own), interpersonal (others'), and extrapersonal (organizational/institutional/spiritual) interests, (c) over the short and long terms, to (d) adapt to, shape, and select environments. Wisdom is in large part a decision to use one's intelligence, creativity, and knowledge for a common good.

Wise leaders do not look out just for their own interests, nor do they ignore these interests. Rather, they skillfully balance interests of varying kinds, including their own, those of their followers, and those of the organization for which they are responsible. They also recognize that they need to align the interests of their group or organization with those of other groups or organizations because no group operates within a vacuum. Wise leaders realize that what may appear to be a prudent course of action over the short term does not necessarily appear so over the long term. Giftedness in wisdom is a matter of balance—skillful balance of the various interests and of the short and long terms in making decisions.

Unsuccessful leaders often show certain stereotyped fallacies in their thinking. Consider six such flaws (Sternberg, 2002, 2005a). The first, the *unrealistic-optimism fallacy*, occurs when they think they are so smart and effective that they can do whatever they want. The second, *egocentrism fallacy*, occurs when successful leaders start to think that they are the only ones that matter, not the people who rely on them for leadership. The third, *omniscience fallacy*, occurs when leaders think that they know everything, and lose sight of the limitations of their own knowledge. People who commit this fallacy do not learn from mistakes, and often ignore the advice of others. They and their team become susceptible to groupthink (Janis, 1972). The fourth, *omnipotence fallacy*, occurs when leaders think they are all-powerful and can do whatever they want. The fifth, *invulnerability fallacy*, occurs when leaders think they can get away with anything, because they are too clever to be caught; and even if they are caught, they figure that they can get away with what they have done because of who they imagine themselves to be. The sixth, *ethical disengagement fallacy*, occurs when a leader starts to believe that ethical behavior is relevant to others but not to him- or herself.

Leaders can be intelligent in various ways and creative in various ways; it does not guarantee they are wise. Indeed, probably relatively few leaders at any level are particularly wise. Yet, the few leaders who are wise to the point of being gifted—perhaps Nelson Mandela, Martin Luther King, Jr., Mahatma Gandhi, Winston Churchill, Mother Teresa—leave an indelible mark on the people they lead and, potentially, on history. It is important to note that wise leaders are probably usually charismatic, but charismatic leaders are not necessarily wise, as Hitler, Stalin, and many other charismatic leaders have demonstrated over the course of time.

Much of the empirical data on wisdom has been collected by Paul Baltes and his colleagues. Over time, they collected a wide range of data showing the relevance of wisdom for gifted performance. For example, Staudinger, Lopez, and Baltes (1997) found that measures of intelligence and personality, as well as their interface, overlap with but are nonidentical to measures of wisdom in terms of constructs measured. Baltes, Staudinger, Maercker, and Smith (1995) found that older individuals in leadership positions who were nominated for their wisdom performed as well as did clinical psychologists on wisdom-related tasks. They also showed that up to the age of 80, older adults performed as well on such tasks as did younger adults. In a further set of studies, Staudinger and Baltes (1996) found that performance settings that were ecologically relevant to the lives of their participants and that provided for actual or "virtual" interaction of minds increased wisdom-related performance substantially. These results suggest that part of wise leadership is achieving a meeting of minds, rather than merely imposing the view of the leader's mind on the minds of the followers.

SYNTHESIS

One of the most gifted leaders of the 20th century was Nelson Mandela. He transformed South Africa from a repressive Apartheid state into a model of modern democracy. It did not become a country without problems. But, if one looks at the alternative model provided by Robert Mugabe in Zimbabwe, economically, politically, and morally a failed state, one can see how badly things could have gone.

What made Nelson Mandela so successful? He had the creativity to envision a transformation of South Africa from a state that deprived the large majority of its citizens of human rights to one that would embrace human rights for all, including the former oppressors. He had the analytical intelligence to evaluate his plan and to fine-tune it as it was implemented. He had the practical intelligence to implement the plan with great success and to persuade a very broad range of constituencies that his plan was a good one. Such persuasion was no mean feat, especially in largely preventing a massive exodus of White people and in convincing Black people that reconciliation rather than retribution was the key to success in the new democratic state. And, he had the wisdom to let go of the massive abuse of human rights to which he himself had been subjected in prison, and to propose a plan that was for the common good of all stakeholders.

Gifted leadership requires each of the elements of WICS. Without creativity, one cannot truly be a gifted leader. Leaders constantly confront novel tasks and situations. If they lack the creativity to deal with them effectively, they fail. Mugabe, in place of creating a new vision, essentially copied the model of divisive dictators such as Stalin, pitting one group against the other, and has presided over a state in radical decline on all measures of well-being. Without the application of a high level of intelligence, one cannot be a gifted leader. Any leader may have creative ideas, but ones that are either flawed from the outset or that fail in implementation. The leader needs the intelligence to distinguish good from bad ideas, and to ensure that followers follow rather than ignore or rebel against the leader. And, without wisdom, a leader may choose a path that benefits his or her cronies, as in the case of Mugabe or Saddam Hussein, but few others. Gifted leadership requires WICS.

WHAT ARE THE NEW TRENDS OR DIRECTIONS?

It is possible to translate these ideas into operational measures. In our Rainbow Project, designed to assess the analytical, creative, and practical aspects of intelligence, we designed assessments that went beyond traditional measures for helping in decisions about admitting high school students to college (Sternberg & The Rainbow Project Collaborators, 2006). Our analytical measures were conventional—learning meanings of words from context, number series, and figural matrices. To assess creative thinking, we had tests such as of writing creative stories and captioning cartoons. To assess practical thinking, we had paper-and-pencil and movie-based tests presenting practical problems that students had to solve. We found we could double prediction of first-year college grades over SAT alone and could greatly reduce ethnic-group differences among those who had taken the test. In other words, we increased both academic excellence *and* diversity through the use of broader tests.

In a follow-up, the Kaleidoscope Project, conducted at Tufts University, all of the more than 15,000 applicants to Tufts were invited to answer questions that were analytical, creative, practical, or wisdom-based (Sternberg, 2007b, 2007c). We found that asking such questions gave a totally different slant to admissions. It enabled us to identify leadership skills that we would not otherwise have been able to identify. We did not find ethnic-group differences penalizing underrepresented minorities. Students who did well on Kaleidoscope did just as well in their first year at Tufts as did students whose admissions were more closely connected to other assessments.

These same ideas can be applied to testing of achievement as well as of abilities. We found we could expand assessments of knowledge and thinking on Advanced Placement Psychology and Statistics tests by measuring creative and practical thinking in these subject-matter areas. When these new assessments were added, ethnic-group differences decreased (Stemler, Grigorenko, Jarvin, & Sternberg, 2006).

It also is possible to teach for wisdom, intelligence, and creativity synthesized (Sternberg, Jarvin, & Grigorenko, 2009). When one teaches more broadly, one develops the kinds of leadership skills students will need to be not just gifted students, but also, gifted adults.

What Are the Unresolved Issues and Questions?

There probably is no model of leadership that will totally capture all of the many facets—both internal and external to the individual—that make for a gifted leader. The WICS model may come closer than some models, however, in capturing dimensions that are important. It is based upon the notion that a gifted leader decides to synthesize wisdom, intelligence, and creativity. We do not yet know just how leaders do such a synthesis, or learn how to do it.

A gifted leader needs exceptional creative skills and attitudes to come up with ideas; academic skills and attitudes to decide whether they are good ideas; practical skills and attitudes to make the ideas work and convince others of the value of the ideas; and wisdom-based skills and attitudes to ensure that the ideas are in the service of the common good rather than just the good of the leader or some clique of family members or followers. A leader lacking in creativity will be unable to deal with novel and difficult situations, such as a new and unexpected source of hostility. A leader lacking in academic intelligence will not be able to decide whether his or her ideas are viable, and a leader lacking in practical intelligence will be unable to implement his or her ideas effectively. An unwise leader may succeed in implementing ideas, but may end up implementing ideas that are contrary to the best interests of the people he or she leads.

The WICS model is related to many other models. It incorporates elements of transformational as well as transactional leadership (Bass et al., 1996), emotionally intelligent leadership (Goleman, 1998b), visionary leadership (Sashkin, 2004), and charismatic leadership (Conger & Kanugo, 1998). Eventually a model of leadership will appear that integrates all the strengths of these various models. In the meantime, the WICS model seems like a start.

We may look at WICS as a model just for adults, but that is not what it is at all. The WICS model suggests we need to broaden the way we conceive of giftedness in childhood. Giftedness is not just a matter of ability-test scores or of grades.

The state of the world makes clear that what the nations of the world need most are *gifted leaders,* not just individuals who get good grades, good test scores, or who have the skills that will get them into elite colleges, which in turn will prepare them to make a lot of money. The United States is so individualistic that it is working against its own self-interests. We risk developing successive generations of self-interested gifted individuals who view their gifts primarily as a means to serve their own needs and desires. The country needs leaders, and WICS provides a model for developing leadership in its young.

The best way to develop WICS in our young people is through role models. The field of gifted education has had such a role model in Joyce VanTassel-Baska. She has been creative, intelligent, and wise in her work and in her life. She has developed the kind of wisdom coupled with humility that one only sees in the greats of a field. It has been a pleasure to know her, to be her colleague and, I hope, to be her friend. Her leadership will continue to influence the field of gifted education long after she retires and, I suspect, after I do as well! The field can be grateful for such a superb role model for what leadership is about.

REFERENCES

Amabile, T. M. (1983). *The social psychology of creativity.* New York: Springer-Verlag.

Antonakis, J., Cianciolo, A., & Sternberg, R. J. (Eds.). (2004). *Handbook of leadership.* Thousand Oaks, CA: Sage.

Baltes, P. B., Staudinger, U. M., Maercker, A., & Smith, J. (1995). People nominated as wise: A comparative study of wisdom-related knowledge. *Psychology and Aging, 10,* 155–166.

Bandura, A. (1996). *Self-efficacy: The exercise of control.* New York: Freeman.

Bass, B. M., Avolio, B. J., & Atwater, L. (1996). The transformational and transactional leadership of men and women. *International Review of Applied Psychology, 45,* 5-34.

Burns, J. M. (1978). *Leadership.* New York : Harper & Row.

Caruso, D. R., Mayer, J. D., & Salovey, P. (2002). Emotional intelligence and emotional leadership. In R. E. Riggio, S. E. Murphy, & F. J. Pirozzolo, *Multiple intelligences and leadership* (pp. 55–74). Mahwah, NJ: Lawrence Erlbaum.

Conger, J. A., & Kanugo, R. N. (1998). *Charismatic leadership in organizations.* Thousand Oaks, CA: Sage.

Fiedler, F. E. (2002). The curious role of cognitive resources in leadership. In R. E. Riggio, S. E. Murphy, & F. J. Pirozzolo, *Multiple intelligences and leadership* (pp. 91–104). Mahwah, NJ: Lawrence Erlbaum.

Gardner, H. (1995). *Leading minds.* New York: Basic Books.

Goleman, D. (1998a). *Working with emotional intelligence.* New York: Bantam.

Goleman, D. (1998b, *November–December*). What makes a good leader? *Harvard Business Review, 76,* 93–102.

Janis, I. L. (1972). *Victims of groupthink.* Boston: Houghton Mifflin.

Jensen, A. R. (1998). *The g factor.* Westport, CT: Greenwood/Praeger.

Jensen, A. R. (2002). Psychometric *g*: Definition and substantiation. In R. J. Sternberg & E. L. Grigorenko (Eds.), *The general factor of intelligence: How general is it?* (pp. 39–53). Mahwah, NJ: Lawrence Erlbaum.

Kaufman, A. S. (2000). Tests of intelligence. In R. J. Sternberg (Ed.), *Handbook of intelligence* (pp. 445–476). New York: Cambridge University Press.

Kaufman, S. B., & Sternberg, R. J. (2007). Giftedness in the Euro-American culture. In S. N. Phillipson & M. McCann (Eds.), *Conceptions of giftedness: Socio-cultural perspectives*. Mahwah, NJ: Lawrence Erlbaum.

Kuhn, T. S. (1970). *The structure of scientific revolutions* (2nd ed.). Chicago: University of Chicago Press.

Sashkin, M. (2004). Transformational leadership approaches: A review and synthesis. In J. Antonakis, A. Cianciolo, & R. J. Sternberg (Eds.), *The nature of leadership* (pp. 171–196). Thousand Oaks, CA: Sage.

Staudinger, U. M., & Baltes, P. M. (1996). Interactive minds: A facilitative setting for wisdom-related performance? *Journal of Personality and Social Psychology, 71,* 746–762.

Staudinger, U. M., Lopez, D. F., & Baltes, P. B. (1997). The psychometric location of wisdom-related performance: Intelligence, personality, and more? *Personality & Social Psychology Bulletin, 23,* 120–1214.

Stemler, S. E., Grigorenko, E. L., Jarvin, L., & Sternberg, R. J. (2006). Using the theory of successful intelligence as a basis for augmenting AP exams in psychology and statistics. *Contemporary Educational Psychology, 31,* 344–376.

Sternberg, R. J. (1998). A balance theory of wisdom. *Review of General Psychology, 2,* 347–365.

Sternberg, R. J. (2002). Successful intelligence: A new approach to leadership. In R. E. Riggio, S. E. Murphy, & F. J. Pirozzolo (Eds.), *Multiple intelligences and leadership* (pp. 9–28). Mahwah, NJ: Lawrence Erlbaum.

Sternberg, R. J. (2003a). What is an expert student? *Educational Researcher, 32*(8), 5–9.

Sternberg, R. J. (2003b). WICS: A model of leadership in organizations. *Academy of Management Learning and Education, 2,* 386–401.

Sternberg, R. J. (2003c). *Wisdom, intelligence, and creativity, synthesized.* New York: Cambridge University Press.

Sternberg, R. J. (2005a). Foolishness. In R. J. Sternberg & J. Jordan (Eds.), *Handbook of wisdom: Psychological perspectives* (pp. 331–352). New York: Cambridge University Press.

Sternberg, R. J. (2005b). The theory of successful intelligence. *Interamerican Journal of Psychology, 39,* 189–202.

Sternberg, R. J. (2007a). Cultural concepts of giftedness. *Roeper Review, 29,* 160–166.

Sternberg, R. J. (2007b). Finding students who are wise, practical, and creative. *The Chronicle of Higher Education, 53*(44), B11.

Sternberg, R. J. (2007c). New ways of identifying gifted children: Rainbow & Aurora batteries. *Gifted Education Communicator, 38*(1), 32–36.

Sternberg, R. J., & Davidson, J. E. (Eds.). (2005). *Conceptions of giftedness* (2nd ed.). New York: Cambridge University Press.

Sternberg, R. J., & Grigorenko, E. L. (1999). Myths in psychology and education regarding the gene environment debate. *Teachers College Record, 100,* 536–553.

Sternberg, R. J., & Grigorenko, E. L. (Eds.). (2002). *The general factor of intelligence: How general is it?* Mahwah, NJ: Lawrence Erlbaum.

Sternberg, R. J., & Hedlund, J. (2002). Practical intelligence, *g*, and work psychology. *Human Performance, 15,* 143–160.

Sternberg, R. J., Jarvin, L., & Grigorenko, E. L. (2009). *Teaching for intelligence, creativity, and wisdom.* Thousand Oaks, CA: Corwin Press.

Sternberg, R. J., Kaufman, J. C., & Pretz, J. E. (2003). A propulsion model of creative leadership. *Leadership Quarterly, 14,* 453–473.

Sternberg, R. J., & Lubart, T. I. (1995). *Defying the crowd: Cultivating creativity in a culture of conformity.* New York: Free Press.

Sternberg, R. J., & O'Hara, L. A. (2000). Intelligence and creativity. In R. J. Sternberg (Ed.), *Handbook of intelligence* (pp. 609–628). New York: Cambridge University Press.

Sternberg, R. J., & The Rainbow Project Collaborators. (2006). The Rainbow Project: Enhancing the SAT through assessments of analytical, practical and creative skills. *Intelligence, 34,* 321–350.

Stogdill, R. M. (1948). Personal factors associated with leadership: A survey of the literature. *Journal of Psychology, 25,* 35–71.

CHAPTER 44

LEADERSHIP AND SUSTAINABILITY FOR EDUCATION:

Different Perspectives to Inform Gifted Education

by

KEN SEELEY

The domain of leaders is the future. The leader's unique legacy is the creation of valued institutions that survive over time. The most significant contribution leaders make is not simply to today's bottom line; it is to the long term development of people and institutions so they can adapt, change, prosper and grow.
—J. M. Kouzes and B. Z. Posner (2002, p. xxviii)

INTRODUCTION

The above quote sets the stage for our look at leadership and how it plays out in education and ultimately to the field of gifted education. The relationship of leadership to both institutions and people is inherent in the information covered here, because it is what creates the future.

Leadership has many definitions and frameworks and this chapter will start broad and then focus on the implications for gifted education leadership. Northouse (2004) defined leadership broadly, stating that leadership is a process whereby an individual influences a group of individuals to achieve a common goal (p. 3). According to Northouse, leadership produces change and movement by establishing direction, aligning people, and motivating and inspiring others.

Early conceptions of leadership focused on the "trait" approach proposed in recent times by Stodgill (1974), who identified 10 traits of leaders that are largely personality characteristics:

1. drive for responsibility and task completion,
2. vigor and persistence in pursuit of goals,
3. venturesomeness and originality in problem solving,
4. drive to exercise initiative in social situations,
5. self confidence and sense of personal identity,
6. willingness to accept consequences of decision and action,
7. readiness to absorb interpersonal stress,
8. willingness to tolerate frustration and delay,
9. ability to influence other persons' behavior, and
10. capacity to structure social interaction systems to the purpose at hand.

The trait theory is presented here because so many people describe leadership in these ways. Most current leadership authors do not like trait theory because it implies inherent personality conditions that are not teachable in developing leaders. Indeed, for education, the more appropriate theory of leadership is the "skills theory" that implies leadership can be learned and developed. The early proponent of the skills approach to leadership was Robert Katz, who wrote for the *Harvard Business Review* in 1955 that he viewed leadership as a set of "developable" skills (Katz, as cited in Northouse, 2004, p. 35). However, the interaction of traits and skills defines leadership at the personal and individual level. It is useful to apply these broad concepts as we look at the educational leadership literature.

COLLABORATIVE LEADERSHIP FOR EDUCATION

Leadership that both creates and influences institutions, like schools and education, needs to be collaborative in nature. Schools are grounded in community that necessarily brings diversity and complexity for leaders who seek to change and improve education. Chrislip and Larsen (1994) made important observations that are as relevant today as when they were when written 15 years ago:

Achieving meaningful reform in education has been a frustrating and often fruitless endeavor. On no other issue is there more public desire for change and less institutional or political will to create it. Each new wave of the reform movement emphasizes the need for deeper and more fundamental changes in the way we conceive of education and the way it is delivered. And with each new wave of reform, real sustainable change seems more elusive. (p. 7)

The authors' remedy for lack of progress in educational reform is for leaders to collaborate on implementation to create the change. They believe that the failure has not been a shortage of good ideas, but rather poor implementation of those ideas into practice. Most educators agree that all students can learn, that excellence and high standards need to guide us, and that we also need to improve graduation rates and close achievement gaps. How we get there will require a collaboration of teachers, principals, parents, students, higher education, and community members. Similarly, Jim Collins (2001), in his best-selling book *Good to Great*, described the collaborative leadership process in simple terms: "The good-to-great leaders began the transformation by first getting the right people on the bus (and the wrong people off the bus) and then figured out where to drive it" (p. 63). Collins made the compelling case that the biggest reason we do not go from good to great is that people are satisfied with "good enough." So, "good" is the enemy of "great." The settling for "good enough" in education has been the major barrier to developing adequate opportunities for gifted students as well as sufficient support for low achieving students. Too often we hear from educators, "We're doing the best we can." As leaders for change and reform we cannot accept these excuses. To move from good to great and to improve implementation of great ideas, we need collaborative leadership. "Underlying this premise is an implicit trust that diverse people engaged in constructive ways and provided with the necessary information to make good decisions can be relied upon to create appropriate answers to the most pressing problems" (Chrislip & Larsen, 1994, p. 14).

LEADERSHIP FOR SYSTEMS CHANGE AND SUSTAINABILITY

Implicit in the opening theme of this chapter is that leadership must ". . . create valued institutions that survive over time." This raises the bar as a conception of leadership from merely influencing groups to putting in place meaningful and lasting institutional change. The recent work of Michael Fullan (2005) in his book, *Leadership and Sustainability*, reinforces this idea that leadership necessarily includes sustainability and institutionalization that Fullan described as "systems change." Fullan acknowledged the work of Andy Hargreaves as influential on his ideas about sustainability. Hargreaves stated that " . . . sustainability does not simply mean whether something will last. It addresses how particular initiatives can be developed without compromising the development of others in the surrounding environment now and in the future" (Hargreaves & Fink, 2000, p. 30). Fullan defined sustainability generally: "Sustainability is the capacity of a system to engage in the complexities of continuous improvement consistent with deep values of human purpose" (p. ix).

Leadership for sustainability is a theme that should surely resonate with the field of gifted education. Gifted programs in schools, often viewed as a "fad," always have labored under almost no resources that could come and go from year to year. As a field of academic study, gifted education has been suspect among many mainstream leaders in the fields of education and psychology. Leaders in the field of gifted education, like Joyce VanTassel-Baska (2002; VanTassel-Baska

& Olszewski, 1989), exemplify the notion of leadership espoused by Fullan, as she has pushed for continuous improvement, building capacity in the system through training, research and institutional development of programs for gifted children built on solid educational foundations in mainstream curriculum adapted for gifted learners, and instruction with acceleration. In one of VanTassel-Baska's (1985) early publications, she made a strong case for sustainability for the field, based on building from the existing curriculum content areas rather than what she called "creative dabbling":

> To satisfy gifted students' need for depth, exposure to these traditional areas of learning is essential, not only to develop and refine proficiency skills in verbal and quantitative areas, but to allow for expanded growth into related disciplines and interdisciplinary studies. . . . A curriculum that does not have a strong content base or focus has little richness. (p. 50)

LEADERSHIP AS A TALENT AREA

One of the early definitions of giftedness that includes leadership abilities is found in the work of DeHahn and Havighurst (1957), which laid the groundwork for the multiple definitions adopted by The U.S. Department of Health, Education, and Welfare's Office of Gifted and Talented in 1972. Social leadership was included among the six domains of giftedness and defined as:

> . . . specifically the ability to help a group reach its goals and to improve human relationships within a group. Such skills are necessary for those who will eventually assume leadership positions in business and industry, labor unions, professional organizations, community groups, government and international agencies. (DeHahn & Havighurst, 1957, as cited in Tannenbaum, 1983, p. 10)

The DeHahn and Havighurst definition above may seem somewhat elusive when trying to find a definitive set of identifying characteristics that could lead to a program for young learners with leadership skills to be developed. Tannenbaum (1983) reported a positive relationship between leadership skills and general intelligence based on the work of Terman and Hollingworth (p. 71). Karnes and Bean (1996) stated that, "leadership is often a range of experiences in the life of a person, which suggests the changing nature of the elusive concept" (p. 2). Karnes and Bean (1996) also suggested that more recent research continues to support the leadership-high intellectual ability relationship: "Many parallels exist between the characteristics used to define an effective leader and the characteristics used to describe a gifted individual" (p. 3). However, there seems to be no support for adding creativity to the correlates for leadership as there has been no strong relationship found (Frasier & Passow, 1994). Rogers (2002) suggested that identification of the leadership domain is limited to subjective peer nominations or teacher nominations. She stated that, "Thus far, researchers have not discovered a valid and reliable written test for identifying giftedness in leadership" (p. 25).

Meanwhile, Sternberg (2005) suggested that leadership is demonstrated by evidence of advanced level on performance assessments. "Leadership involves both skills and attitudes. The skills are developing competencies and expertise based on how well one can execute certain functions of leadership" (p. *37*). This is consistent with other related research on the leadership domain of giftedness (Addison, 1985; Davis & Rimm, 1994; Frasier & Passow, 1994; Renzulli, 1983).

Stodgill (1974) examined 124 personality factors associated with leadership. He concluded that, "Leadership is found to be an active process and not merely the result of a combination of traits" (as cited in Sisk, 1985, p. 48). Sisk (1985) stated that, "The ability to evaluate one's self, situations, and the interrelation of situations and people is essential for students gifted in leadership" (p. 50), and listed the necessary abilities, or skills, for leadership:

1. Carries responsibility well and can be counted on to do what has been promised.
2. Is self-confident with both age-mates and adults; seems comfortable when showing personal work to the class.
3. Is well liked.
4. Is cooperative, avoids bickering, and is generally easy to get along with.
5. Can express him- or herself clearly.
6. Adapts to new situations; is flexible in thought and action and is not disturbed when the normal routine is changed.
7. Enjoys being around other people.
8. Tends to dominate; usually directs activities.
9. Participates in most school social activities; can be counted on to be there. (p. 49)

McCarney and Anderson (1998) created The Gifted Evaluation Scale (GES). The leadership domain on the scale is consistent with the Marland (1972) definition of giftedness. The subscale lists 10 observable leadership traits:

1. Takes a leadership role.
2. Enjoys working towards goals.
3. Demonstrated character and integrity.
4. Takes an active role in elected offices.
5. Facilitates group activities.
6. Presents ideas, clarifies information, and influences others.
7. Facilitates positive interpersonal relations within a group.
8. Organizes and leads groups.
9. Is chosen or elected to a leadership position by peers.
10. Naturally assumes leadership roles.

Lester (2008) synthesized gifted leadership abilities found across the research literature into 10 observable skills. Lester believes that these skills are more useful to teachers because they can be observed for the purposes of identification:

► Volunteers for tasks.
► Takes charge of group games or activities.
► Excels at making decisions or solving problems.
► Embraces new challenges or initiatives.
► Is well liked by peers.
► Influences the behavior, beliefs, or actions of peers.
► Excels in academic achievement or intellectual pursuits.
► Shows an interest in the welfare of others.
► Exhibits a natural competitive spirit.
► Displays an energetic drive or high levels of ambition. (p. 1)

Another list of attributes of leadership among gifted learners was suggested by Karnes and Bean (1990):

► The desire to be challenged.
► The ability to solve problems creatively.
► The ability to reason critically.
► The ability to see new relationships.
► Facility of verbal expression.
► Flexibility in thought and action.
► The ability to tolerate ambiguity.
► The ability to motivate others. (p. 2)

Generally, we find lists of attributes that include a range of what Frazier and Passow (1994) referred to as

. . . traits, aptitudes, and behaviors as the gifted child's: (a) facility in manipulating abstract symbol systems, (b) early language interest and development, (c) unusually well developed memory, (d) ability to generate original ideas, (e) precocious language and thought, (f) superior humor, (g) high moral thinking, (h) independence in thinking, (i) emotional intensity, (j) high levels of energy, (k) early reading and advanced comprehension, (l) logical thinking abilities, (m) high levels of motivation, (n) insights, and (o) advanced interests. (p. xvi)

THE CONCEPTUAL CONUNDRUM FOR GIFTED LEADERSHIP CONTENT AREA

The examples above of lists and conceptions of leadership among gifted learners suggest that we can and should identify such abilities or potential abilities in students and then set up a program to serve their needs. As a practical matter, it is unclear whether we should set up separate gifted leadership programs. The literature reports many such efforts (Addison, 1985; Davis & Rimm, 1994; Karnes & Bean, 1990, 1996; Karnes & Chauvin, 2000; Karnes & Stephens, 1999). There have been further efforts at measuring leadership ability with scales, inventories, and checklists, but many of these efforts have lacked validity and reliability (Plucker & Callahan, 2008).

In reflecting on the literature in this area and the conundrum of program development following identification of ability areas, it seems to me that rather than setting up gifted leadership programs, we should embed leadership in all gifted programs. This recognizes the connection between leadership and intellectual abilities upon which the whole content area is based. Further, it combines the skill and trait theories of leadership, assuming that educators can build on traits and teach leadership skills explicitly. Gifted education programs should be educating the future leaders in academic, intellectual, and arts areas so it follows that educators also should provide direct instruction about leadership to all gifted learners because of this implied potential. This makes the assumption that, because of the connections between intellectual ability and leadership, most gifted learners have the potential to be leaders and therefore we should develop their skills to the fullest extent possible.

THE LONG LEVER OF LEADERSHIP: THE TIES THAT BIND

Archimedes' famous saying was, "Give me a lever long enough and I can change the world." Developing this metaphor, Fullan (2005) described an essential ingredient for educational leadership and sustainability as "the long lever of leadership." This concept is proposed here as a new conceptual model for including leadership skill development in all gifted programs. Reflecting on Archimedes, Fullan stated:

> For sustainability that lever is leadership—a certain kind of new leadership . . . leadership that operates very differently than is the case at present, that is valued differently by societies seeking greater sustainability, and that helps produce other similar leaders to create a critical mass. This critical mass is the long lever of leadership. If a system is to be mobilized in the direction of sustainability, leadership at all levels must be the primary engine . . . We need a system laced with leaders who are trained to think in bigger terms and to act in ways that affect larger parts of the system as a whole: the new theoreticians. (p. 27)

I propose this bold idea that the long lever of leadership should extend to all gifted learners. This will promote sustainability, which is a foundation of our definition of leadership at the outset of this chapter. It is about creating institutions that survive over time. Further, it promotes the concept that gifted learners should be "trained to think in bigger terms" on a life course and that these young people will be "the new theoreticians." Fullan's ideas that are grounded in mainstream educational leadership also can be a foundation for gifted education leadership skill training at the learner level all the way to the need for new leaders in the field. These notions of sustainability should be given serious consideration by the future leaders in gifted education. Sustaining attention to gifted learners from the mainstream educational community always has been an elusive process with mixed results. By including leadership skill development as an integral part of any comprehensive program for gifted learners, it develops potential in those with above-average abilities and moves leadership from being an add-on program to becoming an integral part of the curriculum.

THE PAST, THE FUTURE, AND A TRIBUTE

The definition of leadership chosen for this chapter was taken from many possibilities with great care to find a fit for gifted education and as a tribute to Dr. Joyce VanTassel-Baska, to whom this book and this chapter are dedicated. Joyce personifies great leadership and fits the definition posited by Kouzes and Posner perfectly. Having known Joyce through the Keystone Consortium and personally as a friend and colleague for 30 years, I speak with good knowledge about her leadership and contributions that created institutions that survive; the long-term development of people and institutions; and creating leaders for the future. Joyce's career defines leadership for all of us.

This book is created for Joyce VanTassel-Baska as a tribute to an outstanding, productive career on the occasion of her retirement from The College of William and Mary. Joyce always has stood for a commitment to excellence and to the highest standards for herself and the field of gifted education. From a leadership perspective, Joyce has trained new generations of leaders from her role as professor and researcher and also from her national and international presentations that touched the lives of so many who seek new, substantive ways, to create and maintain educational programs for gifted learners.

AFTERWORD

I close on a personal note as one who teaches leadership to educators and I reflect on my own career contemplating what may lie ahead. My hope for Joyce VanTassel-Baska is the same that it is for myself. I hope we find in the latter portion of our lives new ways to lead, to contribute, to mentor, and to leave a legacy for future leaders in education. I want to wish Joyce the best on her next journey, which will surely be a new beginning.

REFERENCES

Addison, L. (1985). *Leadership skills among the gifted and talented.* Reston, VA: ERIC Clearinghouse on Handicapped and Gifted Children. (ERIC Document Reproduction Service No. ED262511).

Chrislip, D., & Larson, C. (1994). *Collaborative leadership: How citizens and civic leaders can make a difference.* San Francisco: Jossey-Bass.

Collins, J. (2001). *Good to great.* New York: Harper Collins.

Davis, G. A., & Rimm, S. (1994). *Education of the gifted and talented.* Englewood Cliffs, NJ: Prentice Hall.

Frasier, M. M., & Passow, A. H. (1994). *Toward a new paradigm for identifying talent potential* (Research Monograph No. 94112). Storrs: University of Connecticut, The National Research Center on the Gifted and Talented.

Fullan, M. (2005). *Leadership and sustainability.* Thousand Oaks, CA: Corwin Press.

Hargreaves, A., & Fink, D. (2000). The three dimensions of reform. *Educational leadership, 57*(7), 30–34.

Karnes, F. A., & Bean, S. (1990). *Developing leadership in gifted youth.* Reston, VA: ERIC Clearinghouse on Handicapped and Gifted Children. (ERIC Document Reproduction Service No. E485)

Karnes, F. A., & Bean, S. (1996). Leadership and the gifted. *Focus on Exceptional Children, 29*(1), 1–12.

Karnes, F. A., & Chauvin, J. C. (2000). *Leadership Skills Inventory.* Scottsdale, AZ: Gifted Psychology Press.

Karnes, F. A., & Stephens, K. (1999). Lead the way to leadership education. *Education Digest, 64*(8), 62–66.

Kouzes, J., & Posner, P. (2002). *The leadership challenge* (3rd ed.). San Francisco: Jossey-Bass.

Lester, J. (2008). *Leadership development: Identifying, initiating, and implementing leadership development for all students.* Manuscript in preparation.

Marland, S. P., Jr. (1972). *Education of the gifted and talented: Report to the Congress of the United States by the U.S. Commissioner of Education and background papers submitted to the U.S. Office of Education,* 2 vols. Washington, DC: U.S. Government Printing Office. (Government Documents, Y4.L 11/2: G36)

McCarney, S. B., & Anderson, P. D. (1998). *The Gifted Evaluation Scale* (2nd ed.). Columbia, MO: Hawthorne Educational Services.

Northouse, P. (2004). *Leadership theory and practice.* Thousand Oaks, CA: Sage.

Plucker, J. A., & Callahan, C. M. (2008). *Critical issues and practices in gifted education: What the research says.* Waco, TX: Prufrock Press.

Renzulli, J. S. (1983). Rating the behavioral characteristics of superior students. *Gifted Child Today, 29,* 30–35.

Rogers, K. B. (2002). *Re-forming gifted education: Matching the program to the child.* Scottsdale, AZ: Great Potential Press.

Sisk, D. A. (1985, September). Leadership development: Its importance in programs for gifted youth. *NASSP Bulletin, 69*(482), 48–54.

Sternberg, R. J. (2005). WICS: A model of giftedness in leadership. *Roeper Review, 28,* 37–44.

Stodgill, R. M. (1974). *Handbook of leadership: A survey of theory and research.* New York: Free Press.

Tannenbaum, A. J. (1983). *Gifted children: Psychological and educational perspectives.* New York: Macmillan.

VanTassel-Baska, J. (1985). Key administrative concepts in gifted program development. In J. Feldhusen (Ed.), *Toward excellence in gifted education* (pp. 85–104). Denver, CO: Love.

VanTassel-Baska, J., & Olszewski, P. (Eds.). (1989). *Patterns of influence on gifted learners: The home, the self, and the school.* New York: Teachers' College Press.

VanTassel-Baska, J. (2002). What matters in curriculum for gifted learners: Reflections on theory, research, and practice. In G. A. Davis & N. Colangelo (Eds.), *Handbook on gifted education* (3rd ed., pp. 174–183). Boston: Allyn & Bacon.

CHAPTER 45

LEADERSHIP:

An Integrated Approach

by

ELISSA
F. BROWN

Leadership in gifted education rests on simultaneously recogniz-
ing the twin realities of improving educational opportunities for
our best learners even as we work side by side with general and
special educators to improve the education of all learners.
—Joyce VanTassel-Baska

INTRODUCTION

It is a complex, yet exciting, time to be an educational
leader in the field of gifted education. The demands of
advocating for gifted learners within an educational context that focuses learning toward a reductionist level, due
in large part to the No Child Left Behind Act (2001), coupled
with multiple demands for limited resources leaves many leaders in the field wondering how much longer they can persevere against seemingly insurmountable odds. The challenges
implicate not only individual leaders but the collective efforts
of teachers of the gifted and ultimately gifted students.

In her presidential address to the members of the National
Association of Gifted Children (NAGC), Dr. Joyce VanTassel-
Baska (2007) presented a 10-step program for administrators
and teachers as a call to action in order to improve learning
outcomes for our best learners. Her charge was a "systemic
approach to meeting the needs of gifted learners," (p. 5). Dr.

VanTassel-Baska laid out an ambitious plan of action, which is indicative of her leadership in the field of gifted education. Examples of Joyce's leadership include positions she has held, such as her recent NAGC presidency, her scholarship, having been the recipient of Javits grants since the program's inception in 1988, her mentorship of graduate students spanning more than 20 years, and her many products, whether they are peer-reviewed publications or a plethora of curriculum units. In honoring her with this chapter, I will employ the Integrated Curriculum Model (ICM; VanTassel-Baska, 1992, 1994, 1998; VanTassel-Baska & Little, 2003) as a conceptual framework for leadership in the field of gifted education.

The Integrated Curriculum Model (VanTassel-Baska, 1986) was derived from consideration of key characteristics of gifted learners and corresponding curriculum dimensions that respond to those characteristics. It is comprised of three interrelated dimensions: advanced content, process/product, and issues/themes. This model has been used as a framework for developing curriculum at the Center for Gifted Education at The College of William and Mary for more than 20 years and is employed for curriculum design in all of the William and Mary units of study. With funding from the Jacob K. Javits Program, VanTassel-Baska and her project staff have developed curriculum units in language arts, science, and social studies. Research has been conducted to support the efficacy of these curriculum units with both gifted and nongifted populations within a variety of educational settings. Additionally, teacher training on the ICM model has allowed for improved fidelity of curriculum implementation. The curriculum units are used throughout the United States as well as in more than two dozen countries.

THE ICM AS A FRAMEWORK FOR LEADERSHIP

Adapting the ICM framework to leadership in gifted education allows us to consider the interlocking dimensions as a way to conceptualize how leaders in gifted education employ advanced content, processes, and understandings in order to respond to the diverse needs of gifted learners. Schools, school systems, and states need leaders who know the content of gifted education, who understand through their leadership skills when to push systems toward change balanced with when to honor the systems in place. Lastly, leaders in gifted education must value high-end learning and belief in assumptions about improving teacher quality and student outcomes. They must be leaders who can pursue a single-minded pursuit in the belief that gifted learners must have their individual needs met in order to realize their potential. Figure 45.1 overlays the construct of leadership onto the ICM framework.

Advanced Content

Leaders in gifted education must deeply understand their content; the content of gifted education. They should have grounding in the empirical literature in gifted education such as the longitudinal research on acceleration (Colangelo,

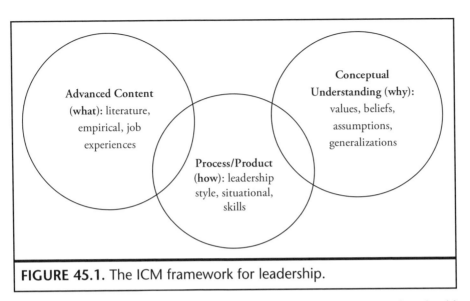

FIGURE 45.1. The ICM framework for leadership.

Assouline, & Gross, 2004) or deep expertise from educational practice. They should know, from a content perspective, how to respond to questions about ways to be responsive and nurture potential from promising students from economically disadvantaged backgrounds (VanTassel-Baska & Stambaugh, 2007). Leaders in gifted education, for example, should be able to respond to other administrators and policy makers about the benefits and limitations of grouping practices (Kulik & Kulik, 1992; Rogers, 1998, 2002), research on the efficacy of curriculum models typically employed in gifted programs (VanTassel-Baska & Brown, 2007), and the importance of teacher preparation (Hansen & Feldhusen, 1994) when working with gifted learners. The quality of teaching influences student learning. If program services and curriculum are to be delivered effectively, teachers with specific knowledge and skills in gifted education must be employed (Leppien & Westberg, 2006). Advanced content knowledge can be job embedded as well as gleaned from the robust literature and empirical evidence base of the field. Advanced content in understanding the field of gifted education can equip an individual to understand multiple perspectives, such as the resistance toward acceleration, yet respond with the research and variety of accelerative options so that a gifted learner can receive appropriate services based on his or her strength domains. Being a content expert provides the underpinnings of credibility for a leader.

Process/Product

The skills, processes, and styles are the conduits for leaders to translate their content knowledge about gifted education and apply it across classrooms, schools, districts, and states. Leaders in gifted education need to know how to secure resources, improve programming, support teacher preparation in gifted, and advocate for students within a context of impeding influences. Leaders in gifted education, possibly more than other fields, must be resilient because they are advocating for a group of students who display exceptional cognitive ability while challenging the sensitivities of critics who contend that appropriately differentiated academic experiences for highly able children are somehow unfair to other children (Spielhagen & Brown, 2008). They must know when to push for change and from whom they can garner support.

Leadership skills in gifted education are similar to the characteristics cited in the leadership literature such as being a problem solver and visionary, and the ability to build capacity. Yet, even employing these sets of skills does not predict success in gifted education because of the nature of the target population and the contextual environment of education. With competing demands of limited resources and educational reforms targeted at below proficiency standards, it is difficult for a leader in gifted education, even one that may be politically astute, to garner support (Gallagher, 2002). Change is not unidirectional. When change is introduced, the context is affected by the change, and change is affected by the context. Therefore, even going for subtle changes in gifted education is being proactive. For example, rather than change an entire identification process in a school system, one could begin by changing the ability measures or practices employed within that process. Or, one could consider a goal such as changing the program or services to match the identification system and then determine which stakeholders need to be involved in the change process. There are many incremental changes that a leader can exercise within any context for gifted education that ultimately leads to program.

Conceptual Understanding

Conceptual understanding for leaders in gifted education includes holding certain assumptions based on values and beliefs about gifted learners, as well understanding contextual generalizations about the system within which one works, and the ability to hold both in tandem. Leaders in gifted education need to understand their assumptions and recognize that those assumptions may be very different than the people they work with or the context they work within. Some of the contextual generalizations and key assumptions for leaders in gifted education include the following listed below.

Contextual Generalizations:
- ▸ The current context of the general educational system, including state-mandated courses of study and their matching state assessments, are insufficient to meet the intellectual needs of gifted learners.
- ▸ Tensions between excellence and equity continue to affect key dimensions of programming such as identification, service delivery, and advocacy for gifted learners. Learning how to negotiate those tensions, and find levers of change that benefit gifted learners is a critical component for leaders in gifted education at all levels of the educational enterprise.
- ▸ Limited resources coupled with increasing demands for qualified personnel, realities of inequality among schools, and competing priorities will

continue to affect the degree to which systemic reform can be implemented and sustained in gifted education (Brown, 2007).

Key Assumptions About Gifted Learners:
- ▸ High intelligence, either general or domain-specific (e.g., mathematics), is a central ingredient for giftedness.
- ▸ In order for gifted learners to be challenged sufficiently to match their potential level of achievement, they require modifications in curriculum, instruction, and assessment, as well as flexibility with regard to grouping options.
- ▸ The talent development process for gifted learners involves a developmental trajectory that is different from the normal population.
- ▸ Giftedness exists in all cultural groups, across all economic strata, and in all areas of human endeavor.

Understanding contextual generalizations and holding certain assumptions about gifted learners helps leaders operationalize a delivery system to facilitate gifted student learning and growth.

REVIEW OF THE LITERATURE ON LEADERSHIP

Most leadership theories guiding educational leaders focus on leadership skills, style, and processes of leadership (Blanchard & Hersey, 1996; Burns, 1978; Spillane & Sherer, 2004). Terms such as *transformational leadership*, *situational leadership*, and *distributed leadership* serve as reference points for these theories and deepen our understanding of the "how" of leadership represented by the process/product dimension of the ICM model for leadership.

Burns (1978) introduced transformational leadership and is considered the founder of modern leadership theory. His definitional structure of leadership included ideas about the manner in which leaders see and act in order for their followers to act based on certain goals representing values and motivations of both the leader and follower. Transactional leadership, according to Burns, focuses on trading one thing for another, whereas transformational leadership, which is more commonly referred to in educational circles, is focused on change. Transformational leaders assume that the results will be beyond expectations and that leaders form a "relationship of mutual stimulation and elevation that converts followers into leaders and may convert leaders into moral agents (Burns, 1978, p. 4) Influence is characterized by modeling behavior through exemplary character. There is an assumption that leaders in gifted education are looked upon to bring about the transformation of a program.

Blanchard and Hersey' s (1996) theory of leadership called for a leader to constantly assess the situation and adapt his or her style accordingly. Known as situational leadership, their model has the leader changing behavior based on the perceived followers' maturity. They posit four styles that match high and low willingness and ability to perform a task, resulting in the following leadership styles; telling, participating, selling, or delegating. The effective leader is skilled in all four styles and discerns which styles are appropriate, depending upon the followers' abilities and the tasks required. These leaders recognize situations, assess individual differences, and create learning opportunities in a supportive climate, depending upon the situation.

Spillane and Sherer (2004) called for distributed leadership characterized by a large degree of interaction among leaders and followers such that depending upon the task, roles may change as the situation warrants. Leaders can function as collaborators, collectors, or coordinators. Distributed leadership builds commitment to the organization's mission and goals, and empowers others to achieve the objectives.

Leaders must be inspirational in order to motivate teachers and other school personnel to be engaged in meaningful work to enhance the learning of gifted students. Priority should be placed on honoring student work that represents rigor and rewarding teachers who can demonstrate consistently high levels of differentiated teaching behaviors. Rewarding the talent development of teachers and students shows that value is placed on it within a school or district context. Research from educational reform projects suggests that teachers need a climate of collegiality and support for innovation to effect meaningful change in classroom practice (Wolf, Borko, McIver, & Elliott, 1999).

Leaders in gifted education must accept the multiple realties of working in an organization and the degree to which one must use advanced content, conceptual understanding, and leadership processes such as distributed leadership or transformation leadership in order to be effective in implementing learning reforms. Leaders in the field of gifted education can use these theories of leadership, as well as many others, as the foundation for interacting with others in order to achieve common outcomes.

Major Themes for the Field of Gifted Education

Major themes affecting leaders in gifted education focus on giftedness as a lifelong endeavor, the teacher/facilitator, documenting program effectiveness, and understanding the environmental educational context. A sample of themes is as follows:

▶ *Giftedness as a talent development process.* Viewing gifted development as a lifelong process is one of Dr. VanTassel-Baska's most remarkable accomplishments related to leadership in gifted education. The Center for Gifted Education's mission is: "a learning community that values and fosters the talent development process of individuals over the lifespan." To that end, programs and services have been created and implemented that operationalize the mission. The Saturday/Summer Enrichment Program (SEP) has been serving tens of thousands of students pre-K–10 for more than 20 years. Graduate students of all ages have worked at the Center, fostering their own linkages of research to practice. The William and Mary curriculum units have changed students and teachers in responding to high-end learning. The research studies conducted through the Center have shaped state policies, local programs, and individuals by informing practice with data. Viewing giftedness as a lifelong talent development process with fluidity and then providing targeted programs at various entry points along the way is a model that the Center for Gifted Education has exemplified throughout its 20 years of existence.

▶ *Personnel preparation.* Leaders in gifted education must be able to influence teachers' pedagogical practices and facilitate teachers' talent development process. The use of content-relevant pedagogy delivered in a context of application and reflection has been found crucial to the transfer of professional development to practice (Guskey, 2000). Recently, national teacher standards in gifted education were cocreated and adopted by NAGC and the Council for Exceptional Children (CEC). These standards provide the framework for undergraduate and graduate programs in gifted education and the requisite knowledge and skills that teachers must acquire and demonstrate competence in. Employing teachers and administrators who have specific training and content knowledge in gifted education builds the capacity of teachers to deliver differentiated instructional practices and curriculum efficacy with gifted learners.

▶ *Documenting program effectiveness.* Although there has been an increasing number of studies in gifted education on program effectiveness, it is still an area that needs attention. Until the field can document that programs are not only value-added but integral to the intellectual and emotional development of gifted learners through documentation of effectiveness, they will continue to be in jeopardy in an era of limited resources.

▶ *Utilization of research for informed decision making.* The importance of guiding educational decisions from the empirical research base to practice is paramount and yet, to date, is a loosely coupled system. Practitioners are not typical consumers of research, and scholars often do not translate the implications of their findings for practice. The Robinson, Shore, and Enersen (2007) evidence-based best practice book in gifted education and NAGC's publication *Teaching for High Potential,* are two examples of how leaders can utilize research to guide decision-making.

▶ *Focusing attention and resources on high-end learning within a context of "just good enough."* There is no incentive for schools or school systems to attend to the growth of students once they attain proficiency, or to spur students who are already proficient to higher levels of attainment. Leaders in gifted education will continue to struggle with this dilemma of raising expectations within a context of minimum standards (Tomlinson, 2002).

> ▸ *Strengthening the infrastructure at state and local levels in the absence of federal legislation.* Without a federal mandate, state policies tend to be less comprehensive and are ceded to the local agency for interpretation. The strength of gifted programs rests with the policies, personnel, and programming at state and local levels (Clinkenbeard, Kolloff, & Lord, 2007). The degree to which state policy makers can enact legislation coupled with commensurate funding levels and local school systems can bring coherence among program components, such as identification and services, will determine the sustainability and institutionalization of gifted education. Leadership at state and local levels is paramount to strengthening the infrastructure.

NEW TRENDS

New trends will require leaders in gifted education to apply their leadership skills more broadly and become increasingly situational leaders. Although some trends will continue to plague the field, such as working in a field of limited resources, others such as virtual learning will require leaders to strategically think about the learning environment as being "flat" and thus the classroom no longer a boundary for learning.

> ▸ *Virtual learning.* Friedman's (2007) book, *The World Is Flat*, documents how globalization and the convergence of political events and innovations have "flattened the world" (p. 5). His work has implications for education and educational delivery systems. Several school districts and some states are launching new innovation in technology that allow students to access learning virtually. Enrollments in virtual schools have continued to grow nationwide, with some online schools seeing their numbers double from year to year. This growth is fueled in large part by greater demand for quality courses not available at traditional high schools, such as Advanced Placement courses, science and math classes, and foreign language courses. Virtual learning will continue to expand and create a paradigm shift for leaders in gifted education with regard to instruction, service providers, programming, and policies.

> ▸ *Data-based decision making.* In an age of accountability, leaders should attend to making decisions based on requisite data. Today, the majority of state budgets are targeted toward education expenditures, and school district leaders are held more accountable for student outcomes. Legislators want to know that their earmarked funds produce results. Consequently, gifted education should continue to monitor and assess program effectiveness.

> ▸ *Diversity of learners.* According to Hodgkinson (2003), shifting demographics and migration patterns will have large implications for teaching and learning. He noted that the United States' most diverse group is our

youngest children, under the age of 5, and they will make the nation more diverse as they age. Almost 9 million children between the ages of 5–17 speak a language other than English in their home.

▶ *Teacher attrition and preparation.* The field of education is plagued with the realization that the majority of teachers and administrators will soon retire, and there is a paucity of educators to fill their positions. Already there is a plethora of alternative teacher preparation programs (e.g., Teach for America), and this trend will continue. This trend has implications for teacher quality as well as specialized training needed, for example, to work competently with gifted students.

Unresolved Issues/Questions

From my varied leadership experiences as a district coordinator for gifted, school principal, director of the Center for Gifted Education at The College of William and Mary, and state director of gifted education, it concerns me that some of the field's unresolved issues continue to preclude gifted education from leveraging its assets, such as the robust research base on curriculum efficacy with gifted learners conducted by Joyce VanTassel-Baska and her colleagues over the years, pitted against a reductionist movement toward curriculum and pedagogical practices. Many in the field continue to wrestle with issues that hinder advances in gifted education. Until we can focus our energies, resources, and personnel on creating coherence among program components and partnering with agencies and organizations to collaborate and maximize our efforts, these unresolved issues will limit the advances that we make. There are many unresolved issues for leaders in gifted education, but the three most critical are as follows:

▶ *Identification still plagues the field.* It requires people resources, fiscal commitment, and valuable time away from servicing students. Even though Joyce's work for more than 30 years has focused, almost exclusively, on the efficacy of high-end curriculum on learning outcomes, many school districts are still wrestling with which tests should be employed to identify gifted students. Identification matters, but not much. Until we can move away from *who* is gifted to what robust experiences we can provide to students to nurture and develop over time their propensities, this will continue to be an unresolved issue.

▶ *Being a leader in gifted education is like being a salmon swimming upstream, against the tide.* Being a leader in the field of gifted education is not for the timid or for someone who acquiesces in order for everyone to get along. It does not mean that one has to be aggressive to get things to change, but it does mean that one must always see an opening or another way to approach the process. It's about being flexible but with a single-minded pursuit. It's about building others' capacity but persuading them to support gifted education. It's about joining forces with other stakeholders without losing one's identity. It's about listening to policy makers describe how students need to be able to compete in a global market, and yet, watching valuable resources being targeted at remediation and intervention to help students become barely proficient on state assessment measures.

► *The misconception that being an advocate for a specialized group of learners automatically assumes that you are not an advocate for other learners.* There is a misconception that advocacy is an either/or proposition that presents itself as an *us or them mentality.* If we accept the premise that giftedness is a lifelong process, that it occurs in all cultural groups, in all economic strata, and in all areas of human endeavor, then we must be willing to support high expectations, customization of learning, and garnering potential from each individual. And yet, there are many professionals who seem to believe that if you are an advocate for gifted learners, then you cannot be an advocate for other learners; or if you support acceleration, then you must not support enrichment. Educating gifted learners is not a competition. It is an ethical, educational imperative.

Leaders in gifted education must continue to address these unresolved issues even as they pursue targeted goals.

CONCLUSION

Joyce VanTassel-Baska's leadership in gifted education manifests itself in her scholarship, mentorship, and teaching of graduate students, and most importantly in her translation of 20 years of curriculum development and research for gifted learners into curriculum units that have influenced more than 600,000 students in the United States and 28 other countries (VanTassel-Baska & Stambaugh, 2008). This chapter is to honor her by viewing leadership through employing the dimensions of the Integrated Curriculum Model. It provides a practical framework for leaders in gifted education because all three dimensions—advanced content, process-product, and real-world concepts and issues—must be held in tandem as leaders continue to advocate, promote excellence, improve programs, and lead the talent development process of gifted learners.

REFERENCES

Brown, E. (2007, April). *Case studies of school reform and innovation: Project Athena findings.* Paper presented at the annual American Education Research Association conference, Chicago.

Blanchard, K. H., & Hersey, F. (1996, January). Great ideas revisited. *Training and Development, 50*(1), 42–47.

Burns, J. M. (1978). *Leadership.* New York: Harper & Row.

Clinkenbeard, P. R., Kolloff, P. B., & Lord, E. W. (2007). *A guide to state policies in gifted education.* Washington, DC: National Association for Gifted Children.

Colangelo, N., Assouline, S. G., & Gross, M. U. M. (2004). *A nation deceived: How schools hold back America's brightest students* (Vol. 1). Iowa City: The University of Iowa, The Connie Belin & Jacqueline N. Blank International Center for Gifted Education and Talent Development.

Friedman, T. (2007). *The world is flat.* New York: Farrar, Straus, and Giroux.

Gallagher, J. J. (2002). *Society's role in educating gifted students: The role of public policy.* Storrs: University of Connecticut, The National Research Center on the Gifted and Talented.

Guskey, T. R. (2000). *Evaluating professional development.* Thousand Oaks, CA: Corwin Press.

Hansen, J. B., & Feldhusen, J. F. (1994). Comparison of trained and untrained teachers of gifted students. *Gifted Child Quarterly, 38,* 115–121.

Hodgkinson, H. L. (2003). *Leaving too many children behind: A demographer's view on the neglect of America's youngest children.* Washington, DC: The Institute for Educational Leadership.

Kulik, J. A., & Kulik, C. L. (1992). Meta-analysis findings on grouping programs. *Gifted Child Quarterly, 36,* 73–77.

Leppien, J. J., & Westberg, K. L. (2006). Roles, responsibilities, and professional qualifications of key personnel for gifted education services. In J. H. Purcell & R. D. Eckert (Eds.), *Designing services and programs for high-ability learners* (pp. 161–182). Thousand Oaks, CA: Corwin Press.

No Child Left Behind Act, 20 U.S.C. §6301 (2001).

Robinson, A., Shore, B. M., & Enersen, D. L. (2007). *Best practices in gifted education: An evidence-based guide.* Waco, TX: Prufrock Press.

Rogers, K. B. (1998). Using current research to make "good" decisions about grouping. *NASSP Bulletin, 82,* 38–46.

Rogers, K. (2002). *Re-forming gifted education: Matching the program to the child.* Scottsdale, AZ: Great Potential Press.

Spielhagen, F. R., & Brown, E. F. (2008). Excellence vs. equity: Political forces in the education of gifted students. In B. S. Cooper, L. Fusarelli, & J. Cibulka (Eds.), *Politics of K–12 education: A handbook of theory, applications, and reform* (pp. 820–851). Mahwah, NJ: Lawrence Erlbaum.

Spillane, J. P., & Sherer, J. Z. (2004). *A distributed perspective on school leadership: Leadership practices as stretched over people and place.* Evanston, IL: Northwestern University.

Tomlinson, C. A. (2002, November 6). Proficiency is not enough. *Education Week, 22,* 36, 38.

VanTassel-Baska, J. (1986). Effective curriculum and instructional models for talented students. *Gifted Child Quarterly, 30,* 164–169.

VanTassel-Baska, J. (1992). *Effective curriculum planning for gifted learners.* Denver: Love.

VanTassel-Baska, J. (1994). *Comprehensive curriculum for gifted learners* (2nd ed.). Boston: Allyn & Bacon.

VanTassel-Baska, J. (1998). *Excellence in educating gifted and talented learners* (3rd ed.). Denver: Love.

VanTassel-Baska, J. (2007). Leadership for the future in gifted education: Presidential address, NAGC 2006. *Gifted Child Quarterly, 51,* 5–10.

VanTassel-Baska, J., & Brown, E. (2007). Toward best practice: An analysis of the efficacy of curriculum models in gifted education. *Gifted Child Quarterly, 51,* 342–358.

VanTassel-Baska, J., & Little, C. A. (2003). *Content-based curriculum for high-ability learners.* Waco, TX: Prufrock Press.

VanTassel-Baska, J., & Stambaugh, T. (2007). *Overlooked gems: A national perspective on low-income promising learners.* Washington, DC: National Association for Gifted Children.

VanTassel-Baska, J., & Stambaugh, T. (Eds.). (2008). *What works: 20 years of curriculum development and research for advanced learners.* Waco, TX: Prufrock Press.

Wolf, S., Borko, H., McIver, M., & Elliot, R. (1999). *"No excuses": School reform efforts in exemplary schools of Kentucky.* Washington, DC: Office of Educational Research and Improvement.

REFLECTIONS

by

Joyce
VanTassel-
Baska

Learning is not attained by chance. It must be sought for with ardor and attended to with diligence.

—Abigail Adams

This volume is meant to highlight contributions I have made to the field of gifted education as judged by my peers and former students. Yet, the contents may prove to be unsatisfactory in explaining the modest sum of my accomplishments in relation to real breakthroughs made by luminaries in the field whose shadow I merely inhabit. However, the work may seem more important perhaps if judged in light of where I started and where I am now after 44 years of work in education, the scope and diversity of effort, and the multiple contexts in which I have worked. Most importantly, I have focused my efforts on "small ponds" in education in which few educators have had the privilege to work—the small pond of Latin and the small pond of gifted education, both causes I have championed throughout my career. I offer the following overview of my life and work, highlighting the major events that have shaped my thinking and my doing. Some of these are highlighted also by authors in this volume while others are clearly influences only I could know from the vantage point of lived experience.

Major themes that emerge from this portrait include the role of intrapersonal characteristics like self-reliance and motivation, perseverance and commitment—all nonintellectual traits that I have been able to use to my advantage. At all stages of life, these qualities have been at the forefront of the modest successes I have achieved. Although the nice term to use for my proactive nature might be "courage to act," I prefer the Yiddish word *chutzpah*, a quality of assertiveness that has pervaded my thinking and doing gifted education in all of the venues in which I have worked. Perhaps the pinnacle of its application came with my movement from K–12 work to higher education through the replication of Julian Stanley's talent search model at Northwestern University. Leaping microworlds, I encountered a different view of gifted education from what I was used to—a view of high socioeconomic level families confirming the level of ability of their offspring and searching for ways to give them even more advantages. I also encountered the world of a first-class university where research ruled supreme and application work with schools was judged to be a second-rate enterprise. The move to William and Mary also represented a leap of faith, encountering a culture completely different from the Midwest and a different academic culture as well, one that valued social-political connections above all else and accommodated the uneasy alliance of the Eastern intellectual with the Southern politician.

Also of import were the people in my life who encouraged, inspired, or nurtured me in the right direction at the right time. Some were family like my grandmother, others were teachers, and still others mentors who came into my life and made it richer and more meaningful by their presence. My grandmother was my lifeline. It is often said we only need one person to love us unconditionally as a child. For me, that person was my grandmother who conversed with me as if I were an adult, confided in me, and comforted me when I was upset. She encouraged my academic interests and taught me to make pies. She was high strung and suffered from a nervous condition through most of her life. Yet, her emotionality was a welcome balm to the indifference I felt from others in my environment. We were connected intuitively, she knew my moods and problems, many times without speaking. She gave me the sense of self so necessary to growing up and being confident in the world.

Teachers like Mr. Lawniczak in junior high language arts provided an excitement about learning I had never discovered before nor would experience again before college and my beloved professors, Dr. Wheelock in classics and Dr. Schoelton in English. Both of them exuded passion for their subject and great humility in the face of all that needed to be known and learned. Dr. Wheelock often commented on his laboring in the classical vineyards as a "field hand" of no importance, yet his introductory college text on Latin is still in print and in its ninth edition. He was a scholar of the first rank, a graduate of Harvard, and the most enthusiastic teacher I ever encountered for all things Roman and Greek. Dr. Schoelton was given the nickname "shaky Schoelton" because he could not stop his hands from moving, a vestige of his time as a soldier in World War II. He was luminous and transfixed in his discussion of John Donne and the other metaphysical poets, weaving their secular appetites with their spiritual ecstasies like no other professor of English literature. He made poetry the study of all that was meaningful in life, a tableland where cognition and emotion met. I was entranced and hooked thereafter on English poets of any age. These teachers opened up the world of learning for me, and I gratefully walked through it.

I have been most fortunate across my professional life to have had attention and real support from luminaries in education—giants who made time for me and provided opportunities, even though I was no one's graduate student. Jacob Getzels took me to lunch at the faculty club at The University of Chicago and pointed out the spot where the Manhattan Project began after meeting him in his office to discuss a potential grant, an experience that prompted me to write a reflective poem. Julian Stanley graciously invited me into his world of the talent search and opened doors to allow me to establish the model at Northwestern University. Jim Gallagher asked me to teach a class for him at the University of North Carolina–Chapel Hill the summer after Ariel was born, encouraging my pursuit of a career in higher education as he had before at different junctures of my earlier work in the field. His firm grasp of issues, his Irish wit and humor, and his vision for what gifted education needs have been major inspirations in all professional settings in which I have worked. A. Harry Passow became my informal mentor, most especially in how to behave like a "mensch" and pursue charity and excellence in tandem, as he did so well in his life. John Feldhusen became my friend and colleague over many years, sharing his thoughts and insights with me. He was a gentle and powerful model for how to be both a teacher and a scholar in higher education at the highest level of excellence. For me, there has never been a line of distinction drawn between the personal and the professional. Thus, my closest friends are people I have met professionally, and my notions of friendship are strongly interwoven with the professional mission of gifted education.

Although many of my educational experiences were generally unsatisfactory and banal before college, the university has opened up a wealth of opportunity for me ever since, providing intellectual stimulation in ways I never had experienced. Nevertheless, public schooling for me has been a consistent thread of support for the continued accrual of educational advantage, even when it was substandard. At all ages, school was something I looked forward to because it was by far the most interesting part of my life. For students who come out of working-class roots, school is the one place they have to go that affords credentials, organization, structure, and control. There was always the illusion of movement forward with a diploma or degree. For me, it was a lifeline to social mobility.

Aspiration level that exceeds prediction for success is another theme that has been relevant to my life and work. Some might label it "overweening ambition," but I always moved out of my comfort zone to achieve what I thought was important work at a level beyond my competence at the time. This has been true for everything from coaching basketball to writing books to doing research to taking on megaprojects. If I had waited to become fully competent or thought that I had to, I would not have done most of what now comprises my professional vita.

Collaboration as a way of working also has been important to my career, but especially at university level. What I have learned is that no one individual can accomplish much at the institutional levels of society alone. A cadre of caring colleagues must combine their efforts to make good things happen. I have been most fortunate in finding the right people at the right time for the tasks that needed doing. My wonderful colleagues from the Keystone Consortium—Ken Seeley, Linda Silverman, Camilla Benbow, and John Feldhusen—all were wonderful collaborators for 18 years in writing books and leading workshops. At Northwestern, I encountered wonderful postdoctoral students in the form of Paula Olszewski-Kubilius, Marilyn Kulieke, and Marsha Landau. We shared ideas, conducted research, wrote articles together, and accomplished much in that environment. Benjamin Bloom also took an interest in my work as did Michael Piechowski who provided extensive critiques of my early academic writing always with his characteristic kindness. At William and Mary, I have encountered waves of collaborators over the years. In the first decade, Linda Boyce, Dana Johnson, and Beverly Sher were crucial to the development of the language arts and science high-quality curriculum our Center came to be known for. In the second decade, my friend and colleague Bruce Bracken applied important expertise in assessment and research to our curriculum efforts, elevating the work I was trying to do to more rigorous levels. Collaboration is just as necessary for affective support as for cognitive and academic skills in accomplishing hard challenges. I believe I understand the wisdom of that idea even more now than I did at earlier stages of my career.

Finally, the theme of change is relevant to the following chronicle. Lucretius said in his *De Rerum Natura* that all things change—the state in which we know them melts away, and they no longer resemble what they once were. As I reflect on my professional career, I am struck by how much my life has changed. I was a solitary only child, cut off from life's advantages by virtue of family circumstance. I lacked any awareness of the world of possibilities for the first two decades of my life and did not move out of my hometown of Toledo, OH, until I was 30. Yet, I have become a world traveler, conversant in the ways of multiple cultures and countries, if not languages. I have worked in three states at all levels of education. I have lived a comfortable upper middle class life for the past 25 years. I have developed my own model for family life, different from my ancestors, two earlier generations of divorced women raising daughters alone without financial support. I raised my daughter to have material and educational advantages afforded her without question of expense.

My mind also has changed and expanded in respect to ideas, deepened in the understanding of topics and issues I have studied well and over time. New ideas have come to be a part of my mental repertoire of ongoing lifelong learning in more structured and connected ways. Where I was once very limited as a writer, I have learned a system that works for me, gaining the fluency and elaboration necessary to be "in the game" of academic discourse. Where once I spoke without notes or careful preparation, I now prepare talks more carefully, often writing them out entirely. I have now become a practicing academic, where once I was merely an impostor, romanticizing the role and mimicking the lives of others. My early lack of discipline and "in the moment thinking" has given way to more planful approaches to work and life.

Yet, my basic values remain. I continue to believe that education is the most important gift one can ever give or receive. I believe that growing up in poverty is among the most limiting experiences to human potential imaginable. I believe that people can outperform early predictions about their ability, given opportunity and hard work. I believe that, in the end, the willingness to work hard on the right issues counts the most for making a difference in the world.

Finally, I believe that I have been one of the lucky ones. The chances that I would have had the career I do or enjoy the lifestyle to which I have become accustomed had a probability of less than one tenth of 1%. Individuals with my personal background demographic factors—coming from poverty, single parent status, first generation college-bound—are far more likely to experience educational disadvantages than culminate their education with a terminal degree. Girls who grow up without fathers are less likely to overcome the psychological stressors associated with that condition to become contributors to society rather than spending their lives seeking approval and depending on men. An individual who attends a fourth-tier educational institution rarely winds up working in two of the top universities in the country. Women are still underrepresented at the upper levels of the tenure process in universities, constituting only 10% of full professors across all fields. Even now, women in endowed chair positions like mine for the past 22 years constitute fewer than 1% of women in higher education.

It is therefore rather miraculous that anything of lasting worth has been accomplished through my agency, but I am most grateful to know that two university centers that I started continue to thrive, that graduate students I have mentored are placed throughout the world doing good work in education, and that publications that I have authored continue to inform the enterprise of gifted education. No one individual has a right to expect this much in return for only reasonably good ideas, though ideas born of good intentions, and acted upon with zeal.

LIFE AND CAREER HIGHLIGHTS OF JOYCE VANTASSEL-BASKA

Born into poverty without a father I ever saw and raised in a household of four generations by my grandmother while my mother worked. My mother never received child support and was forced to support the family by going to work at the telephone company right out of high school. I was raised at 1065 Palmwood in Toledo, OH, a mostly Black neighborhood when I was growing up.

I was a solitary child, having no brothers and sisters and being told not to play with the neighborhood children because they were "not like us." I loved books and reading, playing outside, and riding first my tricycle, then my bicycle around the neighborhood. We had few books on the family shelves but early on I became a frequenter of the public library. I never had lessons as a child in anything but dancing, but they were stopped when we couldn't afford a costume for the recital. My family liked to play cards, make social calls on distant cousins, and visit with neighbors. Conversations were limited to daily topics like food, the weather, and what each family member had done that day. My early claim to verbal precocity was my recitation of "The Night Before Christmas" before the church congregation at age 4.

Attended Roosevelt Elementary School, a block away from my home, for kindergarten and first grade. My best friend at Roosevelt was a Black girl whose father was a physician. My mother thought that relationship was fine for me—class mattered more than race. I have only glimpses left of life at this school. My kindergarten teacher Miss Budd chastised me for liking to watch fish too long and banished me to the hall one afternoon to stare at them rather than doing the "coloring within lines" of animals, which was our daily fare. My first-grade teacher also was my mother's teacher, Miss Purtle. She felt I should be accelerated to third grade after first because of my advanced reading capacity. However, I was moving the next year from a mostly all-Black school to one that was all-White, even though it was located in a working class neighborhood. Thus, the administration overrode her suggestion.

Attended Whittier Elementary School, a half block away from the modest bungalow home we moved to in 1951. At Whittier, my second-grade teacher Miss R. thought I was bright and took me home to meet her niece and tried to interest me in piano. However, when she saw my scores on the California Test of Mental Maturity (CTMM), taken in second grade, she reconsidered and paid less attention to me thereafter. I had scored a 112. To this day, I remember contorting my body to answer the directionality questions based on looking at pictures and having to visualize spatial rotations. Needless to say, it was not my best test performance. I was to prove her IQ-based assessment wrong years later when ironically I became her assistant principal for a few months. The rest of my elementary years in school were unremarkable from both the vantage point of teaching and learning. However, in junior high, I encountered Mr. Lawniczak's English classes where I flourished. He was an ugly man physically but an intellectual force I had never encountered before. He had us write poetry, sing classical songs while he played piano, and discuss great literature. I fell madly in love with him. He reciprocated by taking a special interest in me and encouraging me to write more and gave me suggestions for reading. The English supervisor for Toledo Public Schools thought he was a terrible teacher, as he used methods unconventional and talked and thought at lofty levels, well over the head of some of my classmates. Later he went on to get his doctorate in English at the University of Toledo under the tutelage of Dr. Martin Schoelton who would also inspire me in English classes there.

Life beyond school. The move to the new house and neighborhood brought new challenges at every level. I slept on a cot in the dining room when we moved to 4051 Walker Avenue because the house only had two bedrooms. When my great-grandfather died in 1955 at age 95, I moved into his bedroom. My mother and grandmother shared a bedroom. We had meat once or twice a week for dinner, usually roasts, hamburgers, or hot dogs. Pancakes were a regular staple for supper as were macaroni and cheese. We did not have a car as no one in the family knew how to drive so we took public transportation everywhere. We obtained a television in 1955, and I became an early and avid watcher of shows like *Ed Sullivan*, which featured new talent in the culture, including Elvis Presley and The Beatles. I started a collection of movie stars that I kept in the basement next to the coal bin and tended to when I wanted, dreaming of a life beyond my current one.

Growing up from age 7 through high school in a working-class White neighborhood also was a different kind of social experience. I was encouraged to make friends in this setting, and I tried mightily. The two girls on my block were both tomboys and much more adept than I at all things physical. They taught me to jump off garage roofs into large mounds of dirt being readied for construction, bicycle polo, and tree climbing. Summers were spent playing tetherball in the local park, tennis, and softball. I did well enough to be accepted by them and even became their friend.

My career aspirations were shaped by my grandmother, who had been a first-grade teacher in a rural school system in Wauseon, OH, for 2 years. She had attended a 6-week training program at Oxford University in Ohio to qualify. She told me I should be a teacher and that I should take Latin, both pieces of advice I took to heart. A part of me did aspire to dancing, however, and I dreamed of being able to make a living at it by dancing on tabletops at Rudy's Hot Dog, a local Toledo establishment. Obviously, this dream was neither encouraged nor fulfilled.

Self-reliance. At age 13, I became an early version of a "latchkey kid," living at home and caring for myself after my beloved grandmother was committed to Toledo State Hospital for depression while my mother worked nights. I learned to get myself off to school, do my homework when I returned, and usually fix my own dinner.

I learned to drive in three lessons at age 16, got a used 1956 Plymouth with push button controls, and began to take driving trips and vacations with my mother. I had five accidents my first year but ultimately settled down as a driver. My high school friend, who also was valedictorian of my high school class, said years later that it was my independence and self-reliance during these years that allowed me to move beyond my peers professionally in later life.

Attended Woodward High School. Although I hung out with the gifted group in high school, most of my friends did better academically than I did. I finished 12th in a class of 483. When we received our SAT scores, my verbal score was the highest in the school at 620. Math was more modest at 560. However, my peer group's and my IQ scores were only three points apart on the Otis Lennon taken during the junior year, each of us scoring in the range of 130–133. I clearly identified with and liked this group of girls who were studious and serious, all coming from modest means and wanting to succeed in school. Yet, my own interests tended to be more on boys at this stage of life.

All in all, I had poor teachers in my high school, which sent fewer than one third of its graduates to college. It was located in a low socioeconomic level neighborhood of the city and was considered one of the poor schools in Toledo. Although honors classes were available in some subjects, no Advanced Placement

(AP) courses, which had just started in 1958, were available at the school. I was no prize student either. Erratic in my performance, interested only in the subjects I was a natural in, and gravitating only to the few teachers I liked and who liked me, I was ill-prepared for serious academic challenge and study.

My biggest academic distinction during high school was placing every year in the State of Ohio English Examinations, taken by selected students in all schools statewide. Other notable feats during high school were playing the lead in the senior class play, entitled *Breath of Spring*. I belonged to a lot of clubs and enjoyed the social contact they provided. I also avidly loved sports, especially basketball, and fell out of the stands once cheering for our star guard Butch Komives who took the school to the state title.

Ultimately I was able to get a need-based scholarship to the University of Toledo for 4 years, after having an interview with the female dean of students who pointedly asked me if I intended to quit, get married, and have children rather than finish my degree. I evidently satisfied her with my response as I got the support. I also received a PTA scholarship for 2 years, with the promise to teach in Toledo Public Schools for at least that period of time as a payback. To supplement my scholarship aid, I worked for 4 summers as a long-distance operator at The Ohio Bell Telephone Company, a job my mother got for me as she had worked for the company since she was 18. I started the summer after graduation. Between the money I was able to save from the job and the scholarships, I was able to attend and pay for college, the first member of my family to do so.

Attended the University of Toledo as an honors student in English. I enjoyed my Latin classes with Dr. Fredrick Wheelock, an amazing enthusiast for the language and all things ancient. I also enjoyed my English classes with Dr. Martin Schoelton, whose discussion of 17th-century metaphysical poetry caused frisson on the back of my neck, the first of many visceral reactions to poetry that I have had over the years. I found my education classes boring and irrelevant to my interests. I almost failed prestudent teaching, as I misspelled the word "holistic" on the board of an English class. I loved student teaching, however, and had a great cooperating teacher in Medora Cox who nurtured me well and realized my affinity for working with bright students. My cooperating teacher in Latin, Wesley Jones, was a once-in-a-lifetime Latin teacher—very good with students and very academically demanding. I learned much under his tutelage. He also was an African American in an all-White high school. I ultimately graduated from the university *cum laude,* one semester late due to starting my teaching career early.

Eloped with Tom VanTassel to Monroe, MI, in May of our sophomore year of college at age 19. We had met one year prior at the freshman mixer at the university. He was like me in many ways—an honors student from one of the other poor high schools in the city and from a working class family albeit much larger than mine. Through our marriage, I became part of a large and wonderful family, who continue to be a part of my life even today.

Taught English and Latin at Bowsher High School, the most academically challenging high school in the city. Hired without a degree to take over my cooperating teacher's schedule, I taught five classes and supervised a study hall for $4,300 per year. I was so caught up in teaching that I was amazed that I was paid at all for the experience.

Working with gifted learners and developmentally delayed learners made me appreciate group differences in learning and caused me to realize my affinity for working with the gifted in honors and AP classes. My most powerful teaching experience was with an English honors class that I had for 3 years who demonstrated to me the capacity of gifted learners for handling more challenging work, the progress they can make, especially in sophistication of their arguments and writing, and their strong positive affective traits. Years later, one of them credited me with inspiring her to become a teacher, a girl who was so quiet and shy at the time that I never would have suspected. The best student in the class was a lively girl with verbal quips to spare whose father was the school custodian.

Coaching girls' basketball, track, and tennis made me more aware of individual differences and the power of motivation in learning. Most of the basketball team were not strong in academics but were adept at sports although unschooled. I found that I could motivate the girls well to play but needed the expertise of one of the fathers to provide the technical aspect. We made it to second place in the city with this combination. One of the starting five still contacts me to this day.

I invited a young man I taught in the summer Upward Bound Program at Bowling Green State University to attend Bowsher. He was the first Black student to attend the school and had wonderful potential for being able to take our advanced English courses, including AP, and benefit from them. He attended an all-Black high school in the city prior to this move. John Scott did well, going on to college and an ultimate career as an English professor.

I made many friends on the high school faculty. We traveled together annually to Stratford, Ontario, Canada for Shakespeare plays; played volleyball together on a city-wide winning team; and socialized in other venues as well.

I was a major leader in the teacher strike of 1970, encouraging faculty to stay home and working a picket line at the school. I went on the radio to explain the union position, interviewed near the lettuce in a local supermarket and accused my assistant principal of lying to us about the issues. We lost the strike and returned after 8 days but gained more respect. I became an officer in the state American Federation of Teachers union and was soon targeted for becoming an administrator, as were other standouts from the striking teachers. I learned from this experience to trust my ability to think through issues rather than accepting authority and its point of view. Although the rebel instinct had always been a part of my nature, this event shaped my understanding of the power of thinking and acting on that understanding rather than cowering. I became emboldened to project my ideas on others rather than the other way around. I also became even more proud of my profession, a group of teachers willing to risk being fired for what they believed in to garner respect, better working conditions and salary, and opportunities for students.

Received masters' degrees in English and education by attending classes part time in the evening. I was offered a fellowship to get a doctorate in English and one in education as well. I turned both down in favor of maintaining economic independence. Based on family background, I understood all too well the dangers of becoming economically dependent on males. I began law school at night at The University of Toledo and neither did well nor enjoyed it so I quit after one semester. On reflection, I realized that law is about a particular way of thinking, not just oratory. I also realized the preparation of lawyers is an adversarial model, where the student must be prepared to argue even the smallest point to win a case. As one of five female law students in a class of 150 new students, I encountered gender discrimination for the first time that I was aware of in my professional life. I chafed at the style of teaching and the relentlessness of the badgering of students, especially the females. Also during these years I taught a night school class in writing at the University of Toledo and supervised student teachers. I learned from these experiences that I needed to find a niche, rather than continuing to explore possible avenues that turned out to be blind alleys.

Began my administrative intern year in Toledo Public Schools, serving as assistant principal in an elementary school, then a high school, then serving as an assistant in the Office of Staff Development. Walter Bonkowski, the head of staff development and former principal, became my friend and mentor.

I worked at McKinley Elementary School, a K–8 building, as an assistant principal for 3 months. My worst nightmares emerged in this setting. My own second-grade teacher was a teacher in the building and came to me to settle little problems she had in her classroom, like a student who had lost small change. A second nightmare was a bad automobile accident outside my office window that involved one of our students during my first few weeks. I handled the communications with parents and with on-the-scene emergency workers. I learned from this experience my fear and revulsion of taking a line position in administration as the unpredictability and trivial nature of how time may be spent is not to my liking. My greatest lesson was how to build a middle school master schedule. I also enjoyed my relationship with Roger Moser, the principal, finding him a steady and stable head of the school.

My second intern placement was at Start High School, one of the newest of the 10 high schools in the city. Here I served as the assistant principal for guidance and scheduling. Again, I enjoyed building the master schedule for the high school. In this setting, I also learned about the underachieving gifted as I was allowed to examine the records of students in the sophomore class who had a 130 IQ but were not performing well in school, who were truant, or often on the doorstep of my office. I learned that of the group functioning at that range of giftedness, 63% were making C's or lower and experiencing other problems. The Marland Report had just come out, citing 55% as the national figure of gifted underachievers. I could clearly see that underachievement was a huge problem among the gifted in this urban school district, even at one of its higher SES level schools.

My third placement was the most to my liking. It was in central office, working as an assistant to the director of staff development, a new office in Toledo Public Schools. Here I was given free reign to be creative with developing materials, reading relevant books, writing letters, and hosting various school events for the system. I learned from Walter the do's and don'ts of administration—grandmother and grandfather rules. I remember the ones that have served me the best over time—"once stabbed in the back, always expect to be from that person"; "work hard but play hard too"; and "because people want to do a good job, they are usually trying even if they are not succeeding up to external expectations." Walter's wise counsel kept me out of trouble in many situations, and he often remarked that I had little insight when it came to dealing with other people even though I had a huge capacity for work and getting a job done, a statement that could as easily be uttered about me even today.

Found my niche in gifted education as the first coordinator of gifted programs in Toledo Public Schools. I was most fortunate that this new position opened just as I finished my internship. My mentor Walter suggested it was a natural for me, and I took it instead of the assistant principalship also offered at the same time. I identified 1,300 students for services in my first year and set up pilot programs in selected elementary, middle, and high schools. I instituted and taught a film seminar in one inner city high school and offered Junior Great Books in an elementary school two mornings a week. From these direct teaching experiences, I learned what gifted students can do when they have targeted opportunities, not confounded by age or socioeconomic background. I immersed myself in the field of gifted education, reading Milton Gold's classic book, entitled *Education of the Intellectually Gifted*. My first federal grant was written and received (Title III) during my second year on the job. I conducted numerous workshops throughout Ohio during these years and served on the state team that wrote the Ohio plan in Aspen, CO. I organized a CEC-TAG regional conference in Toledo in 1976, attended by more than 300 people in the Midwest region. I started The Toledo Area Association for the Gifted, an educator and parent group, devoted to the needs of gifted children. Clearly, I was hooked on gifted education and had a vision of what could happen in an urban district like Toledo. I had great support from other administrators, helpful parents, and docile students. The 1970s were a time when looking at gifted education was viewed as a reasonable thing to be doing in school districts, even though state funding lagged behind. Everyone was excited about the possibility of what could be done so it was easy to motivate even jaded administrators that good opportunities could flow to poor kids who were smart.

Project Phoenix, the Title III project we received, was an interdisciplinary program of study for high school students in our most segregated inner-city schools. The program model also had a full-time counselor assigned to the freshmen and sophomores, targeted for the program. Right away, I was immersed in curriculum development, professional development, and working with children and families from poverty. When I held parent meetings, there was strong turnout, with wonderful questions. I also learned early on the difficulty of increasing critical thinking abilities from a short-term intervention, the problem with finding a test that was consonant to the curriculum being used, and the issues associated with running a large-scale project. This foundation in project work was replicated many times later in my career, and the Toledo experience taught me much about the complexity of the process.

I began teaching classes in gifted education at Bowling Green State University before I had even taken one. The field was just evolving, and I was excited about its potential and all the work that needed to be done, including the serious preparation of professionals.

Moved to Springfield, IL, to become State Director of Gifted Education. My 3 years in the Illinois Department of Education taught me much about the educational process writ large at the state level, state politics in education, and the uneasy relationship between state departments and state legislatures. It also gave me important insights into gifted education and how it worked in the second oldest state-funded gifted program in the country, with more than 630 district programs operating. I learned, for example, that professional development alone was not a sufficient mechanism to spur lasting program development for gifted learners in school districts. Even though Illinois had 9 area service centers and a cadre of 18 professionals who delivered workshops to a legion of schools on gifted education topics, there was little evidence of impact at the programmatic level. I also learned that Chicago Public Schools ran one of the truly great gifted programs in the country under the leadership of Richard Ronvik, offering a pyramid of services from city-wide to regional centers to school-based opportunities. Illinois also was a context where I could make an impact statewide in a variety of ways. My contributions in the state that were the most lasting were setting up the Illinois Talent Search, a replication of the Johns Hopkins model, and identifying 22 school districts as exemplary in programming through a collaborative team approach that included paper reviews and site visits.

Became a founding member of The Keystone Consortium. This "think tank" group began after meeting at a leadership conference in 1978 in Terre Haute, IN, and a later conference that same year in Albuquerque, NM. John Feldhusen grabbed my head at dinner and proclaimed it to be extraordinary at organization in this field and suggested the need to have opportunities for regular collaboration.

The group conducted workshops nationally and published books in the field. Original members were John Feldhusen and Grayson Wheatley (Purdue), Ken Seeley (University of Denver), Bill Foster (Rutgers), my husband Lee, and I. Other players became Linda Silverman and Camilla Benbow. We met annually in the mountains of Colorado and plotted out what matters in gifted education, argued about approaches, and enjoyed each other's company. We also wrote influential books together. John took the leadership on the first edition of the *Toward Excellence in Gifted Education* book, later a three-edition book. Linda's counseling book was a product of the group as was my *Comprehensive Curriculum for Gifted Learners* book, both first and second editions.

Working in this group provided me the support I needed to begin publishing seriously in the field and feeling that I could handle a university-level position in gifted education. John had me teach summer classes at Purdue in curriculum to further bolster that perception. Initially, I was the only female member of the group, the only one without a doctorate, and the only one without a university job. The Keystone group also socialized me to the type of lifestyle I would come to lead as an academic—time spent thinking, talking with colleagues, and producing. It was a good model to have before hitting the halls of Northwestern University.

Served as president of CEC-TAG. My presidential address in Philadelphia, published in *Journal for the Education of the Gifted*, dealt with the need to develop programs and services for gifted learners in a systematic way across the country, heavily influenced by my roles as local and state director of gifted programs.

Married Lee Baska and gave birth to Ariel. My personal life was greatly enriched by meeting Lee through the Chicago gifted program where he was a school psychologist and joining our lives together. When Ariel was born, we moved to 2607 Noyes in Evanston, IL, where I started work at Northwestern University. I divided my time in Evanston between my new position at Northwestern, and watching my daughter grow, from her first steps to her frantic attempts to dance to "The Nutcracker."

For 3 years prior, I directed the Area Service Center in Matteson, IL, and worked with a wonderful crew of educators—Judy Lipschutz, Anne Shuler, Alan Dornseif, and Jake Schneider, the superintendent. This opportunity allowed me to move up to the Chicago area to be with Lee as we began our relationship and to finish my doctoral degree, being near universities where I could access coursework. We lived first at an apartment in Tinley Park and then at an old farmhouse in Crete, IL.

Graduated from The University of Toledo with a doctorate in education. I pieced together my doctoral program after leaving Toledo with courses from Chicago State. I also took and taught courses at Purdue where John Feldhusen helped me socialize to university-level teaching and served on my dissertation committee as a fourth examiner. My major was educational administration and my minor was curriculum and instruction. I fulfilled my residency requirements while working as a full-time administrator by taking 9 semester hours of coursework each semester for the academic year of 1975–1976 at The University of Toledo before moving to Illinois. I drove back to Toledo to take my comprehensive exams and do orals. My dissertation was on the teaching of Latin to verbally precocious seventh graders, a topic that allowed me to test out the fast-paced classroom model in foreign language instruction for talent search students in Illinois.

Established the Midwest Talent Search and Center for Talent Development at Northwestern University. The decision to create and take the talent search model to Northwestern University was arrived at after much debate and discussion. The project also was pitched to Purdue and The University of Chicago. It was with Julian Stanley's help that the project was so well-received at Northwestern, as the dean of the School of Education, David Wiley, had been Julian's graduate student at the University of Wisconsin many years before. At Northwestern I had access to Benjamin Bloom and Michael Piechowski, both of whom were making important contributions to the field of talent development. I also had access to talented graduates like Paula Olszewski-Kubilius, Marcia Landau, and Marilyn Kulieke who began working with me in the evolving Center. We identified 25,000 students annually throughout the Midwest region and offered the first 3-week residential program in 1983. We also organized an annual awards ceremony, a Saturday commuter program for gifted children in the Chicago area, and various teacher workshops. A research plan was devised so that we could publish on our findings about these students. In 1984, the Center for Talent Development was officially launched. These 5 years at Northwestern became my apprenticeship at a university in a nontenure track position to learn how to function as an academic. The context was invaluable for helping me understand the level to which I needed to aspire to be successful in higher education.

Received the Early Leader Award from NAGC. This award was important to me as a sign that my work was nationally recognized in the field and found to be indicative of high-quality leadership, even if it was primarily in the eight state region of the Midwest.

Moved to Williamsburg, VA, to take an endowed chair in gifted education. This was perhaps the biggest move of my career. I was taking on a tenure-track position at the second oldest college in the country and leaving behind the Midwest, the land where my values were shaped and my ancestors' bones reside. I received tenure as an associate professor one year after my arrival and went on to become a full professor in 3 more years in 1991. Jack Nagle, the dean in the School of Education, became my mentor and friend during these years. He was an excellent tutor in the ways of the College, the town, the South, and the East—all cultures that I needed to learn well enough to thrive here. To this day, I owe him a debt of gratitude for his wise counsel and support. I developed a master's program in 1989 and in 1992, I started a doctoral-level program for budding administrators and university researchers who wished to work in the field of gifted education.

Established a second center in gifted education. I began the process of Center development very differently at The College of William and Mary than at Northwestern where I brought in a replicable project. I invited a core group of interested faculty to join me in the initiatory stages of the venture, followed by a team of school district personnel from the area. A plan was crafted that included the development of a master's program, a precollegiate learner program, and several outreach activities for teachers and parents. These were mounted quickly, and I turned to grant activities to sustain the enterprise. Over 22 years, I brought in more than $12 million to the Center for a variety of activities, ranging from 6-year grants from the state of Virginia to run the Governor's School of Math, Science, and Technology, to seven different State Council in Higher Education grants to offer professional development to teachers in math and science to 20 years of funding for research and development of effective curriculum from the United States Department of Education.

The Center changed as new graduate students came and went, staff changed, and new opportunities emerged. We began in 1994 to do serious program development and evaluation work with selected school districts, work that informed every other facet of our efforts as well. Evaluation contracts became a staple of Center activity over the following years.

The first edition of *Comprehensive Curriculum for Gifted Learners* was published by Allyn & Bacon in 1988, shortly after my arrival in Williamsburg. *Patterns of Influence: The Home, the Self, and the School* was published the same year by Teachers' College Press.

Led world-wide consulting in gifted education. Professional opportunities were provided through The World Council on Gifted conferences held in Hamburg, Barcelona, Istanbul, Adelaide, Sydney, and Toronto. Long-term consulting began in Australia in 1989 and continued through teaching almost annually for Miraca Gross at the University of New South Wales. I began consulting in Singapore in 1992 and continued the relationship even now, having trained teachers there, led the development of curriculum in their secondary schools, and led the evaluation team to evaluate their program in 2001. Other opportunities to consult emerged in England, the Netherlands, Jordan, the United Arab Emirates, Saudi Arabia, Korea, New Zealand, and Germany.

I had the pleasure of leading three delegations in gifted education, comprised of 85 individuals across the United States, to China, Russia, and Egypt through the People to People Ambassador Program. This experience provided access to gifted schools in these countries as well as educators who had similar goals as mine to internationalize gifted education.

The international opportunities for consulting work have been among the richest I have enjoyed as they have taught me the value of travel itself as a profound learning experience, the wonder of other cultures so different from my own, and the powerful human connections that bind me to other peoples of the world through our common interest in giftedness. I made lifelong friendships in both Singapore and Australia.

Received the Lifetime Achievement Award from the Virginia Association for the Education of the Gifted. I acknowledged my students as the centerpiece of my work at William and Mary.

Received the Hall of Fame Award from Woodward High School. I delivered a speech that suggested we need to focus more on developing talent in a broader range of students and paying attention to nurturing students from poverty backgrounds. To date, I am the only doctoral graduate of my class of 483 students. There was one pharmacist and two attorneys, all male.

Appointed Visiting Scholar to Cambridge University in England. I conducted archival research on the talent development process in Charlotte Brontë and Virginia Woolf. On the side, I taught Ariel Latin, using the *Ecce Romani* Latin series, from which my daughter now teaches.

This year was a pivotal one in my career and life, as I had the unique opportunity to live in another country for 3 months, the country of my heritage, with access to the great and historic university libraries, archives, and resources at Cambridge. Not only that, but London was an hour's train ride away. We spent many days in London, exploring the British Museum among others and attending plays. We visited Haworth, and Ariel sat beside me reading *Jane Eyre* for the first time as I explored the Brontë archive at the Parsonage. We attended a seminar on Virginia

Woolf at Newnham College in the same room where she delivered her *Room of One's Own* lecture. We attended special lectures at the Scott Polar Institute on the exploits of Sir Ranulph Fiennes and other explorers to Antarctica. My favorite lecture, because of its esoteric nature, was given at Sidney Sussex College on the whereabouts of Oliver Cromwell's head in the walls of the college and the probable location of his body, conducted by the dean of the Cambridge Medical College.

I read all day the primary and secondary sources on both Charlotte Brontë and Virginia Woolf. I found the task overwhelming and humbling. I realized I may have little insight to contribute to the existing scholarship, even by taking the perspective of talent development. I became aware of my limitations as a scholar and realized that my lack of affinity for the daily grind of academic texts over the years had left me without the habits of mind to make real progress in this kind of work. I could only hope to write to a new angle regarding the lives of these great women writers. I also realized my lack of methodological skills in making new sense of old material. Yet, I persisted and found some joy in the archival approach to research. The result was an article published in *Roeper Review* in 1995 and a chapter in *Remarkable Women* in 1996. Although these two pieces are strong in respect to my writing and the content explored, they pointed out to me the reality of doing scholarship on a timetable; I realized it takes years to become immersed in a subject of interest. The whole experience caused me to reevaluate my strengths and limitations.

Received the SCHEV Faculty Award. To date, I am the only School of Education professor to receive this award. The ceremony was held in the Virginia Museum of Fine Arts in Richmond, and I received the award from Gerald Baliles, then governor of Virginia. It was a $5,000 cash prize and a lovely glass sculpture. Larry Sabato, the media-savvy political science professor from the University of Virginia, also received the award at the same time. Governor Baliles and I chatted about the importance of our respective grandmothers in shaping our desire to go into education.

Received the faculty award from Phi Beta Kappa, the Alpha Chapter at William and Mary. I gave a short speech, highlighting the importance of making the world more beautiful, a nod to Miss Rumphius and all others like her.

Offered the executive directorship at The Center for Talented Youth at Johns Hopkins University. I was offered the position but declined based on my daughter's strong objection to moving and leaving her friends and schooling in Williamsburg. I also had doubts about leaving the Center and the graduate students in the midst of their program.

Received the Distinguished Scholar Award from NAGC. This award represented an arrival into the club of people who have contributed greatly to the scholarship in the field of gifted education. I am humbled to be counted among them.

Served as editor of *Gifted and Talented International*, a research journal of The World Council on the Gifted and Talented for 7 years. Editing this international journal connected me even more to the international community of scholars in the field and provided several of my most talented graduate students the opportunity to be assistant editors as part of their graduate experience.

Developed Project STAR. I worked collaboratively with the state of South Carolina to develop performance-based assessments to identify more low-income and minority students in that state. The Center for Gifted Education staff and graduate students tackled the test development and validation work. We then did the follow-up studies to assess what difference it made in increasing access and making a difference in lives.

This work was tremendously gratifying in its purpose, execution, and collaborative spirit. It resulted in several publications in the field, including five refereed journal articles. It also was the basis for the last book in the *Critical Issues in Equity and Excellence in Gifted Education* series that profiled patterns of low-income and minority learners. I received the Richard Riley Award from South Carolina, their highest honor, for my leadership in this work.

Received a Fulbright Teaching Award to New Zealand. Ariel accompanied me on the lecture tour, which took me to Massey University in North Palmerston for my SCION keynote lecture on problem-based learning (PBL) science teaching for the gifted, and on to Christchurch to Wellington and to Hamilton for lectures in schools and other universities. We enjoyed the country and the people we met, especially in Wellington, the capital of the country whose natural location is beautiful and whose urban culture we found fascinating. We inhabited an historic house down the street and around the corner from where the English short story writer Katherine Mansfield lived. We explored the mall area and the great new Maori museum that had just opened. We also did mundane tasks like washing clothes and hanging them out to dry in the backyard amid New Zealand's flora.

Offered two deanships, one from the School of Education at my alma mater, the University of Toledo, and one from Purdue University, but decided to stay in gifted education at William and Mary until I retired. Again, family considerations intervened, with Ariel wanting to stay at William and Mary and graduate and Lee preferring to stay in familiar surroundings.

Received two large Javits grants from the U.S. Department of Education to research and develop curriculum and assessment tools to use in Title I settings. Project Athena and Project Clarion brought $6 million to the College over the 5 years of their operation. These projects began a strong collaboration with Bruce Bracken, who is a top assessment expert in the country. We conducted longitudinal studies of curriculum effectiveness with all learners. After being in the Stetson House on campus for 10 years, we moved to a new house for Project Athena (The Young House). Upon receipt of the Project Clarion grant, we moved to a wonderful house on the edge of campus at 427 Scotland Street, which housed all of our projects and the mainstream work of the Center in 2003.

Received the Alumni Achievement Award from the College of Education at the University of Toledo. I delivered a speech that praised my arts and science professors, thanked my family, and suggested my gratitude to the institution that did so much for my educational development.

Published important texts in the field. *Content-Based Curriculum for High-Ability Learners* was published by Prufrock Press, chronicling the curriculum development models and strategies used in the William and Mary curriculum materials. My coeditor on the book is Catherine Little, graduate of the William and Mary doctoral program in 2000 and curriculum coordinator at the Center for 6 years. Also published this year by Love Publishers is *Curriculum Planning and Instructional Design for Gifted Learners.*

Utilizing Evaluation for Gifted Program Improvement was published, chronicling a decade of evaluation research conducted through The Center for Gifted Education. My coeditor on this book is Annie Feng, the Center's research and evaluation director. Individual studies were published in seven separate peer-reviewed journal articles.

The third edition of *Comprehensive Curriculum for Gifted Learners* was published by Pearson. My coauthor is Tamra Stambaugh, William and Mary gifted program graduate of 2007, who read the first edition of the book as her first exposure to gifted education. Coincidentally, the book was my first to write in the field.

Served as president-elect, president, and past president of the National Association of Gifted Children. I attacked the role of president of the organization with a sense of purpose and vision for the field. I believed our number one problem was a lack of infrastructure to keep the field viable at district, state, and university levels. Thus, the thrust of my energy went to these areas through work on establishing a set of teacher education standards to lure new institutions to gifted education and keep existing ones in the fold, work on state regulations that are weak and outmoded, based on our contemporary research base, and work on specific issues that appear intractable like promising children in poverty, identification, and service delivery models that work. Several notable achievements occurred during this time.

The teacher education standards in gifted education were approved by NCATE. A dissemination plan was developed and guides for higher education and K–12 were published in 2008.

As president, I wrote a grant to the Jack Kent Cooke Foundation for NAGC to cohost with our Center a national conference on promising students from poverty. We held the conference at the William and Mary offices in Washington, where it was attended by almost 90 leaders from local, state, and national levels. Our resulting publication entitled *Overlooked Gems* was widely disseminated to the field.

A CD-ROM was published for use by advocacy and policy groups at state level to provide research-based rules and regulations for the state administration of gifted programs, using sample language from current state policies.

The *Critical Issues in Equity and Excellence in Gifted Education* series of four volumes was launched, with a book published each year from 2006–2009, with all proceeds going to benefit the organization.

Received the CEC-TAG Achievement Award for collaborative leadership on the teacher education standards. This award, given to me at the CEC-TAG convention in Louisville, KY, was very meaningful because it acknowledged the unique confluence of events that allowed us to get traction on passing the teacher education standards for the field through the two national organizations and NCATE with a major emphasis on diversity.

Received the Mensa International Award for Research for the fourth time. This award recognized empirical research I have conducted in the field over the last year as earlier awards did likewise in 1999, 2001, and 2007.

Appointed Professor Emerita at The College of William and Mary. In August, I retire from The College of William and Mary with ongoing research and writing projects stretching before me.

> *Time is like a series of liquid transparencies.*
> *You don't look back*
> *Along time,*
> *But through it like water.*
>
> —Margaret Atwood

CONCLUDING THOUGHTS

I have come a long way from the little girl in Toledo, OH, who lived a sheltered and narrow life, surrounded by the realities of daily life necessities. I have grown into a woman of independence, resolve, and commitment to a lifetime devoted to the mission of gifted students, their families, and the institutions responsible for educating them. I have benefited from taking on this mission in significant ways, both personally and professionally. Through it, I have come to understand my own giftedness, accepting my uneven talents and building on my strengths. I have come to identify abilities in others, confident that I can bring out the best they have to offer at a given stage of development as others did for me. I also have become a lifelong advocate for intervention for the gifted in respect to programs, services, and curriculum. My core belief in the field is related to the importance of providing such interventions across the span of the schooling years in areas of greatest need. Despite the grass roots efforts of the 1970s when I entered the field, gifted education has not advanced much in program development at local or state levels. We have continuously suffered from lack of support for funding and other resources to keep pace with needs to advance the field in appropriate ways and in recent years also have suffered from the biases of those who see services to the gifted as elitist.

In spite of this, promising work still continues on several fronts:

1. *The ability to embrace low-income and minority learners as an important part of our mission as advocates of the gifted.* We can see the evidence of this expanded mission in the requirements of the Javits program to serve low-income students as a target group. By using the Javits funding across two decades to address this target population, we have learned much about both identification and programs and services needed. Identification procedures in many states now include assessments that are more favorable

for finding underrepresented groups. Outstanding model programs are in place across the country from which we can learn much about the tailored efforts needed to serve these students well. Many foundations support this area of programming as well. The Jack Kent Cooke Foundation has shown great leadership in this area, improving the lives of promising learners from poverty through direct and individualized intervention over multiple years.

2. *The ability to mobilize support for gifted students and prepare teachers and leaders in the field.* The leadership of The National Research Center on the Gifted and Talented has been pivotal to conducting research and disseminating the work of the field on critical issues that impact the lives of gifted learners. The University of Connecticut as a part of that consortium of universities has been stellar in producing leaders in this field over the past three decades and preparing teachers through the work of Confratute, their summer training mechanism for professional development. No other institution has been as successful in attracting educators to gifted education and converting them to become advocates. Joe Renzulli, as the leader of these efforts, has left a legacy untouched by others in its scope and ultimate impact on the future of this field.

3. *The progress of targeted programs to deepen program development efforts through systematizing interventions and collecting data on student impact.* We have a few stellar programs throughout the United States where systematic and ongoing efforts have created and sustained program opportunities for our best learners. Many of these have been in the context of full-time schools such as our 12 residential high schools while others have been district efforts using center-based programs to accomplish this integrated and comprehensive outcome for gifted learners such as in Virginia Beach and Fairfax County, VA. The hallmark of these programs has been the articulation of services in K–12 or 9–12, in all areas of the curriculum, ensuring ongoing challenge across the schooling years. Although these programs are not "popular" in this climate of antipathy toward the gifted, they do bode well for the continued interest and seriousness with which some educators and policy makers approach serving our best learners.

4. *The use of research-based curriculum.* In spite of troubled times for education budgets everywhere, I'm gratified to know that research-based curriculum like the units produced by our Center at William and Mary are being used nation-wide and abroad to model exemplary curriculum in the subject areas. The evidence base supporting their use with gifted learners and even with more typical learners has been solid in respect to academic gains in core subject areas and in critical thinking. Due to Javits Program funding, we have seen curriculum for the gifted developed, tested in classrooms nationwide, revised, and assessed for its effectiveness. Much work remains to be done in the dissemination of materials. Educators need to understand that carefully designed differentiated units of study are always preferable to basal materials and unconnected activities.

5. *Progress in the use of acceleration.* Due in no small part to the ongoing legacy of Julian Stanley, acceleration has gained a new foothold in our work in gifted education. The talent search model has impacted the ways we identify and serve the gifted nationally. Perhaps the most important aspects of this renaissance owe their origin to the fine work of the Belin-Blank Center in crafting and disseminating *A Nation Deceived*, a report that dispels the myths about the value of acceleration as a tool to be used in the lives of most gifted learners. The report also has influenced state and local policy to include accelerative opportunities as a research-based option for programs. This growth in the use of one of our most powerful strategies we have to serve the gifted is a true blessing to the field and the individual lives of gifted students everywhere.

6. *The growth of alternative programs and services outside of schools.* As I reported in another volume, *Serving Gifted Learners Beyond the Traditional Classroom,* the majority of well-designed and articulated programs and services for the gifted are occurring in contexts other than public and private schools. The talent search universities, notably Johns Hopkins, Duke, and Northwestern, provide fast-paced and accelerative programs in summer, academic year, and online environments. These opportunities have proliferated over the past 20 years to become the models for what gifted learners need. My only wish would be that the rigor and quality of these options might be replicated in traditional school settings. Other opportunities external to school, including mentorships and internships, personalized options provided by adult professionals, and an array of online coursework, have all shown positive impact on gifted lives. Service-learning opportunities also offer real-world learning that impacts both cognitive and affective growth.

These very real trends will affect the next decade of work in this field, encouraging more advocates to join the cause to address the needs of this special population of learners. Some might say that the gifted have all the advantages and do not deserve public resources. Others, like myself, have always believed that all students have a right to an appropriate education, regardless of the nature and quality of mind they bring to the enterprise of learning. If we want to level the playing field and preserve equity in education, we will need to do more for the gifted, not less. It has been my pleasure to work relentlessly toward that end, advocating for children from backgrounds similar to mine. My greatest hope, after 44 years of work, is that others will take up the cause of children from different cultural groups, children from poverty, and children with uneven abilities, so that all will have access to the social and intellectual capital necessary to develop into the eminent leaders of tomorrow.

Adults can change their circumstances; children cannot. Children are powerless, and in difficult situations they are the victims of every sorrow and

mischance and rage around them, for children feel all of these things but without any of the ability that adults have to change them. Whatever can take a child beyond such circumstances, therefore, is an alleviation and a blessing.
—Mary Oliver

AFTERWORD

I t would be remiss to close the volume on this scholar's illustrious career without addressing the word origin of this culminating publication. Meaning "a celebration of academic work" in German, this festschrift is the capstone publication celebrating Dr. Van Tassel-Baska's distinguished scholastic career at The College of William and Mary. Her career, in which she began as an enthusiastic English and Latin teacher and developed into one of the great leaders in the field of gifted education, is a shining hallmark gold standard of a master teacher and impassioned leader in educational reform and progress around the world. This volume brings together her colleagues, graduate students, and friends; cohesively binding the strands of research and development in gifted education; examining the past and the present; and looking to the future for leading change in gifted education.

It is rare that one person is capable of contributing so much to a field, spanning an array of topics and illustrating expertise and worthwhile contributions in each. However, as evidenced by this volume, Joyce has successfully done so, and with great impact. Although many attribute the work of Dr. Joyce Van Tassel-Baska primarily to curriculum, this compendium evidences her far-reaching and broad contributions to the field of gifted education in a myriad of areas including alternative identification measures, contributing factors and inhibitors to talent development, policy initiatives, leadership, professional development, special populations, and of course, differentiated curriculum. Her contributions in each of these areas will continue to guide the field for years to come and have already made significant contributions and policy changes that enhance gifted services for more than 600,000 students in school districts across the United States and 28 additional countries.

Thank you, Joyce, for all that you have done and all that you will do ahead. Thank you for your kind and meaningful invitations to work and learn with you. The educational changes that ripple as a result of your work will go on and on from your teaching, your mentoring, your writing, your curriculum, your research, your service, and your leadership in gifted education.

With love,

Bronwyn MacFarlane   Tamra Stambaugh
Editor   Editor

THE PUBLICATIONS OF JOYCE VANTASSEL-BASKA

D
r. VanTassel-Baska has authored or edited 26 books and 450 other publications since 1977. She also has held major editorial positions with journals in the field. Although she formally entered higher education in 1982, she has been publishing in the field for 32 years.

BOOKS AND EDITED VOLUMES

Authored, coauthored, or edited 26 books and monographs, including two third and two second editions since 1981.

VanTassel-Baska, J. (Ed.). (in press). *Patterns and profiles of low-income gifted learners.* Waco, TX: Prufrock Press.

VanTassel-Baska, J., & Little, C. (Eds.). (in press). *Content-based curriculum for high-ability learners* (2nd ed.). Waco, TX: Prufrock Press.

VanTassel-Baska, J., Cross, T. L., & Olenchak, F. R. (Eds.). (2009). *Social-emotional curriculum with gifted and talented learners.* Waco, TX: Prufrock Press.

Johnsen, S. K., VanTassel-Baska, J. L., & Robinson, A. (2008). *Using the national gifted education standards for university teacher preparation programs.* Thousand Oaks, CA: Corwin Press.

Kitano, M., Montgomery, D., VanTassel-Baska, J. L., & Johnsen, S. K. (2008). *Using the national gifted education standards for preK–12 professional development.* Thousand Oaks, CA: Corwin Press.

VanTassel-Baska, J. (Ed.). (2007). *Alternative assessment with gifted and talented students.* Waco, TX: Prufrock Press.

VanTassel-Baska, J. (Ed.). (2006). *Serving gifted learners beyond the traditional classroom: A guide to alternative programs and services.* Waco, TX: Prufrock Press.

VanTassel-Baska, J., & Stambaugh, T. (2006). *Comprehensive curriculum for gifted learners* (3rd ed.). Needham Heights, MA: Allyn & Bacon.

VanTassel-Baska, J. & Stambaugh, T. (Eds.). (2006). *Overlooked gems: A national perspective on low-income promising learners.* Washington, DC: National Association for Gifted Children.

VanTassel-Baska, J., & Feng, A. (Eds.). (2004). *Designing and utilizing evaluation for gifted program improvement.* Waco, TX: Prufrock Press.

VanTassel-Baska, J. (2004). *Acceleration strategies for teaching gifted learners.* Waco, TX: Prufrock Press.

VanTassel-Baska, J. (Ed.). (2004). *Curriculum for gifted and talented students.* Thousand Oaks, CO: Corwin Press.

VanTassel-Baska, J., & Little, C. (Eds.). (2003) *Content-based curriculum for high-ability learners.* Waco, TX: Prufrock Press.

VanTassel-Baska, J. (2003). *Curriculum planning and instructional design for gifted learners.* Denver, CO: Love.

VanTassel-Baska, J. (2003). *Content-based curriculum for low income and minority gifted learners* (Research Monograph No. 03180). Storrs: University of Connecticut, The National Research Center on the Gifted and Talented.

VanTassel-Baska, J. (1998). *Excellence in educating gifted and talented learners* (3rd ed.). Denver, CO: Love.

VanTassel-Baska, J., Johnson, D. T., & Boyce, L. N. (Eds.). (1996). *Developing verbal talent: Ideas and strategies for teachers of elementary and middle school students.* Boston: Allyn & Bacon.

VanTassel-Baska, J. (1994). *Comprehensive curriculum for gifted learners* (2nd ed.). Boston: Allyn & Bacon.

VanTassel-Baska, J. (1992). *Planning effective curriculum for gifted learners.* Denver, CO: Love.

VanTassel-Baska, J., Patton, J., & Prillaman, D. (1991). *Gifted youth at risk: A report of a national study.* Reston, VA: Council for Exceptional Children.

VanTassel-Baska, J. (Ed.). (1990). *A practical guide to counseling the gifted in a school setting* (2nd ed.). Reston, VA: Council for Exceptional Children.

Feldhusen, J., VanTassel-Baska, J., & Seeley, K. (1989). *Excellence in educating the gifted.* Denver, CO: Love.

VanTassel-Baska, J., & Olszewski-Kubilius, P. (Eds.). (1989). *Patterns of influence on gifted learners: The home, the self, and the school.* New York: Teachers College Press.

VanTassel-Baska, J., Feldhusen, J., Seeley, K., Wheatley, G., Silverman, L., & Foster, W. (1988). *Comprehensive curriculum for gifted learners.* Boston: Allyn & Bacon.

VanTassel-Baska, J. (Ed.). (1983). *A practical guide to counseling the gifted in a school setting.* Reston, VA: Council for Exceptional Children.

VanTassel-Baska, J. (1981). *An administrator's guide to the education of gifted and talented children.* Washington, DC: National Association of State Boards of Education.

REFEREED PUBLICATIONS IN PERIODICALS

Authored or coauthored 112 refereed publications in periodicals since 1979.

Ambrose, D., VanTassel-Baska, J., Coleman, L., & Cross, T. (in press). Gifted education as a porous fragmented discipline. *Gifted Child Quarterly.*

VanTassel-Baska, J., Bracken, B., Feng, A., & Brown, E. (in press). A longitudinal study of reading comprehension and reasoning ability of students in elementary Title I schools. *Journal for the Education of the Gifted.*

VanTassel-Baska, J. (in press). Working with urban students of poverty: Overlooked gems. *Journal of Urban Education.*

VanTassel-Baska, J., Brown, E. & Tieso, C. (2009). *A study of successful scale-up Title I schools using a gifted language arts curriculum.* Manuscript in preparation.

Tieso, C., Brown, E., & VanTassel-Baska, J. (2009). *The validation of ASPIRE, a scale to assess school readiness for innovation.* Manuscript in preparation.

Kim, K., VanTassel-Baska, J., Bracken, B., Feng, A. & Bland, L. (2008). *A study of science learning for primary students in Title I schools: Project Clarion.* Manuscript submitted for publication.

Bland, L., VanTassel-Baska, J., Bracken, B., Stambaugh, T., Feng, A., & Kim, K. (2008). *The use of performance-based assessment to document science learning in young Title I students.* Manuscript submitted for publication.

VanTassel-Baska, J. (2008). *Gifted children curriculum and programs: How to meet intellectual and personal needs.* Manuscript submitted for publication.

Chandler, K., & VanTassel-Baska, J. (2008). Working with twice-exceptional learners. Manuscript submitted for publication.

VanTassel-Baska, J., Feng, A., Chandler, K., Quek, C., & Swanson, J. (2008). *The benefits of performance-based gifted identification approaches on middle school students' academic and affective profiles.* Manuscript submitted for publication.

VanTassel-Baska, J. (2008). Curriculum development for gifted learners in science at the primary level. *Revista Espanola de Pedagogia, 66,* 283–296.

VanTassel-Baska, J., Feng, A., MacFarlane, B., Heng, M. A., Teo, C. T., Wong, M. L., et al. (2008). A cross-cultural study of teachers' instructional practices in Singapore and the United States. *Journal for the Education of the Gifted, 31,* 338–363.

VanTassel-Baska, J., Feng, A., Brown, E., Bracken, B., Stambaugh, T., French, H., et al. (2008). A study of differentiated instructional change over three years. *Gifted Child Quarterly, 52,* 297–312.

VanTassel-Baska, J., Feng, A., & de Brux, E. (2007). A study of identification and achievement profiles of performance task-identified gifted students over 6 years. *Journal for the Education of the Gifted, 31,* 7–34.

VanTassel-Baska, J., Feng, A., & Evans, B. (2007). Patterns of identification and performance among gifted students identified through performance tasks: A three-year analysis. *Gifted Child Quarterly, 51,* 218–231.

Little, C. A., Feng, A., VanTassel-Baska, J., Rogers, K., & Avery, L. (2007) A study of curriculum effectiveness in social studies. *Gifted Child Quarterly, 51,* 272–284.

VanTassel-Baska, J., & Brown, E. (2007). Toward best practice: An analysis of the efficacy of curriculum models in gifted education. *Gifted Child Quarterly, 51,* 342–358.

VanTassel-Baska, J., Quek, C., & Feng, A. (2007). Developing structured observation scales for instructional improvements in classrooms accommodating gifted learners. *Roeper Review, 29,* 84–92.

VanTassel-Baska, J., & Johnsen, S. K. (2007). Teacher education standards for the field of gifted education: A vision of coherence for personnel preparation in the 21st century. *Gifted Child Quarterly, 51,* 182–205.

VanTassel-Baska, J. (2007). Leadership for the future in gifted education: Presidential address, NAGC 2006. *Gifted Child Quarterly, 51,* 5–10.

VanTassel-Baska, J., MacFarlane, B., & Feng, A. (2006). A cross-cultural study of exemplary teaching: What do Singapore and the United States secondary gifted class teachers say? *Gifted and Talented International, 21*(2), 38–47.

VanTassel-Baska, J. (2006). NAGC symposium: A report card on the state of research in the field of gifted education. *Gifted Child Quarterly, 50,* 339–341.

Brown, E., Avery, L., VanTassel-Baska, J., Worley, B., & Stambaugh, T. (2006). A five-state analysis of gifted education policies. *Roeper Review, 29,* 11–23.

VanTassel-Baska, J., & Stambaugh, T. (2006). Project Athena: A pathway to advanced literacy development for children of poverty. *Gifted Child Today, 29*(2), 58–63.

VanTassel-Baska, J. (2006). A content analysis of evaluation findings across 20 gifted programs: A clarion call for enhanced gifted program development. *Gifted Child Quarterly, 50,* 199–215.

VanTassel-Baska, J., & Stambaugh, T. (2005). Challenges and possibilities for serving gifted learners in the regular classroom. *Theory into Practice, 44,* 211–217.

Feng, A., VanTassel-Baska, J., Quek, C., O'Neill, B., & Bai, W. (2005). A longitudinal assessment of gifted students' learning using the Integrated Curriculum Model: Impacts and perceptions of the William and Mary language arts and science curriculum. *Roeper Review, 27,* 78–83.

VanTassel-Baska, J. (2005). Gifted programs and services: What are the nonnegotiables? *Theory Into Practice, 44,* 90–97.

VanTassel-Baska, J., Feng, A., Quek, C., & Struck, J. (2004). A study of educators' and students' perceptions of academic success for underrepresented populations identified for gifted programs. *Psychology Science, 46,* 363–378.

VanTassel-Baska, J. (2004). Building a research agenda: The William and Mary Model. *Quest, 15*(2), 1–6.

VanTassel-Baska, J., & Baska, A. (2004). Working with gifted students with special needs: A curriculum and program challenge. *Gifted Education Communicator, 35*(2), 4–27.

VanTassel-Baska, J. (2004). The case for a systems approach to curriculum differentiation. *Tempo, 24*(1), 5–24.

VanTassel-Baska, J. (2004). Expert's forum: Program delivery models for the gifted. *Duke Gifted Letter, 5*(1), 8–9.

VanTassel-Baska, J., Feng, A., Quek, C., & Struck, J. (2004). A study of educators' and students' perceptions of academic success for underrepresented populations identified for gifted programs. *Psychology Science, 46,* 363–378.

VanTassel-Baska, J. (2004). Quo vadis? Laboring in the classical vineyards: An optimal challenge for gifted secondary students. *Journal of Secondary Gifted Education, 15,* 56–60.

VanTassel-Baska, J. (2003, September). Differentiating curriculum experiences for the gifted and talented: A parent's guide to best practice in school and at home. *Parenting for High Potential,* 18–21, 29.

VanTassel-Baska, J. (2003). *Differentiating the language arts for high ability learners, K–8.* Arlington, VA: ERIC Clearinghouse on Disabilities and Gifted Education. (ERIC Document Reproductive Service No. ED474306)

VanTassel-Baska, J., & Feng, A. (2002). *Evaluation of the Idaho state gifted program: Lessons on the impact of training.* Washington, DC: National Association for Gifted Children.

VanTassel-Baska, J., Zuo, L., Avery, L., & Little, C. (2002). A curriculum study of gifted-student learning in the language arts. *Gifted Child Quarterly, 46,* 30–43.

VanTassel-Baska, J. (2002). Considerations in evaluating gifted programs. *The Communicator, 33*(2), 20–24.

VanTassel-Baska, J. (2002). Assessment of gifted students' learning in the language arts. *Journal for Secondary Gifted Education, 13,* 67–72.

VanTassel-Baska, J., Johnson, D., & Avery, L. D. (2002). Using performance tasks in the identification of economically disadvantaged and minority gifted learners: Findings from Project STAR. *Gifted Child Quarterly, 46,* 110–123.

Avery, L., & VanTassel-Baska, J. (2001). Investigating the impact of gifted education evaluation at state and local levels: Problems with traction. *Journal for the Education of the Gifted, 25,* 153–176.

VanTassel-Baska, J. (2001). The role of Advanced Placement in talent development. *Journal of Secondary Gifted Education, 12,* 126–132.

VanTassel-Baska, J. (2001). Creativity as an elusive factor in giftedness. *New Zealand Journal of Gifted Education, 13*(1), 33–37.

VanTassel-Baska, J. (2001). The talent development process: What we know and what we don't know. *Gifted Education International, 16*(1), 20–28.

VanTassel-Baska, J. (2000). The on-going dilemma of identification practices in gifted education. *The Communicator, 31*(2), 39–41.

VanTassel-Baska, J. (2000). Standards of learning and goodness of fit. *Tempo, 20*(3), 8–10.

VanTassel-Baska, J., Avery, L. D., Little, C. A., & Hughes, C. E. (2000). An evaluation of the implementation of curriculum innovation: The impact of the William and Mary units on schools. *Journal for the Education of the Gifted, 23,* 244–270.

VanTassel-Baska, J. (2000). Curriculum policy development for secondary gifted programs: A prescription for reform coherence. *NASSP Bulletin, 84*(615), 14–29.

VanTassel-Baska, J. (1999). Challenging language arts curriculum for high-ability learners. *Alberta Journal on Gifted Education, 12*(2), 4–14.

VanTassel-Baska, J., Leonhard, P., Glenn, C. B., Poland, D., Brown, E., & Johnson, D. (1999). Curriculum review as a catalyst for gifted education reform at the secondary level. *Journal of Secondary Gifted Education, 4,* 173–183.

VanTassel-Baska, J. (1998). *Honoring intellectual diversity.* Reston, VA: National Council of Teachers of Mathematics.

VanTassel-Baska, J. (1998). A critique of the talent searches: Issues, problems, and possibilities. *Journal of Secondary Gifted Education, 9,* 139–144.

VanTassel-Baska, J. (1998). *Planning science programs for high ability learners.* Reston, VA: Council for Exceptional Children.

VanTassel-Baska, J., Bass, G., Ries, R., Poland, D., & Avery, L. (1998). A national pilot study of science curriculum effectiveness with high ability students. *Gifted Child Quarterly, 42,* 200–211.

VanTassel-Baska, J. (1998). The development of academic talent: A mandate for educational best practice. *Phi Delta Kappan, 79,* 760–763.

Avery, L. D., VanTassel-Baska, J., & O'Neill, B. (1997). Making evaluation work: One school district's experience. *Gifted Child Quarterly, 41,* 28–37

VanTassel-Baska, J. (1997). Excellence as a standard for all education. *Roeper Review, 20,* 9–12.

VanTassel-Baska, J. (1997). Counseling talented teachers. *Counseling and Human Development, 29*(9), 1–12.

Boyce, L. N., VanTassel-Baska, J., Burruss, J., Sher, B. T., & Johnson, D. T. (1997). A problem-based curriculum: Parallel learning opportunities for students and teachers. *Journal for the Education of the Gifted, 20,* 363–379.

VanTassel-Baska, J. (1997). Responses to "varieties of intellectual talent." *Journal of Creative Behavior, 31*(2), 125–130.

VanTassel-Baska, J., & Avery, L. D. (1997). *Perspectives on evaluation: Local considerations.* Washington, DC: National Association of Gifted Children.

VanTassel-Baska, J., Johnson, D. T., Hughes, C. E., & Boyce, L. N. (1996). A study of language arts curriculum effectiveness with gifted learners. *Journal for the Education of the Gifted, 19,* 461–480.

VanTassel-Baska, J., Bailey, J., & Hall, K. H. (1996). Case studies of promising middle schools. *Research in Middle Level Education Quarterly, 19,* 89–116.

VanTassel-Baska, J. (1995). The development of talent through curriculum. *Roeper Review, 18,* 98–102.

VanTassel-Baska, J. (1995). A study of life themes in Charlotte Brontë and Virginia Woolf. *Roeper Review, 18,* 14–19.

Johnson, D., Boyce, L. N., & VanTassel-Baska, J. (1995). Science curriculum review: Evaluating materials for high-ability learners. *Gifted Child Quarterly, 39,* 36–43.

VanTassel-Baska, J., Olszewski-Kubilius, P., & Kulieke, M. (1994). A study of self-concept and social support in advantaged and disadvantaged seventh and eighth grade gifted students. *Roeper Review, 16,* 186–191.

VanTassel-Baska, J. (1994). Development and assessment of integrated curriculum: A worthy challenge. *Quest, 5*(2), 1–6.

VanTassel-Baska, J. (1993). The development of academic talent. *The Communicator, 23*(4), 14–21.

VanTassel-Baska, J., Gallagher, S., Bailey, J., & Sher, B. (1993). Scientific experimentation. *Gifted Child Today, 16*(5), 42–46.

VanTassel-Baska, J. (1993). Linking curriculum development for the gifted to school reform and restructuring. *Gifted Child Today, 16*(4), 34–37.

Bessemer, K., VanTassel-Baska, J., & Bailey, J. M. (1992). Saturday and summer programs for gifted learners at The College of William and Mary. *Gifted Child Today, 15*(4), 3–8.

VanTassel-Baska, J. (1992). Developing learner outcomes for gifted students. Reston, VA: ERIC Clearinghouse on Disabilities and Gifted Education.

VanTassel-Baska, J., Landrum, M., & Peterson, K. (1992). Cooperative learning and the gifted. *Journal of Behavioral Education, 2,* 314–323.

VanTassel-Baska, J. (1992). Educational decision making on acceleration and grouping. *Gifted Child Quarterly, 36,* 68–72. (*Note.* Paper received American Mensa Research Award.)

VanTassel-Baska, J. (1991). Gifted education in the balance: Building relationships with general education. *Gifted Child Quarterly, 35,* 20–25.

VanTassel-Baska, J. (1991). Serving the disabled gifted through educational collaboration. *Journal for the Education of the Gifted, 14,* 246–266.

Patton, J., Prillaman, D., & VanTassel-Baska, J. (1990). The nature and extent of programs for the disadvantaged gifted in the United States and territories. *Gifted Child Quarterly, 34,* 94–96.

VanTassel-Baska, J., & McEachron-Hirsch, G. (1990). Global education for the gifted: A curriculum focus for the 21st century. *Gifted International, 6*(1), 35–45.

VanTassel-Baska, J. (1989). The role of the family in the success of disadvantaged gifted learners. *Journal for the Education of the Gifted, 13,* 22–36.

VanTassel-Baska, J. (1989). Appropriate curriculum for gifted learners. *Educational Leadership, 46*(6), 13–15.

VanTassel-Baska, J., Willis, G., & Meyers, D. (1989). Evaluation of a full-time self-contained class for gifted students. *Gifted Child Quarterly, 33,* 7–10

VanTassel-Baska, J., Patton, J., & Prillaman, D. (1989). Disadvantaged gifted learners at-risk for educational attention. *Focus on Exceptional Children, 22*(3), 1–15.

VanTassel-Baska, J., & McEachron-Hirsch, G. (1989). International education for the gifted at William and Mary College. *Gifted Child Today, 12*(3), 2–5, 37–39

VanTassel-Baska, J. (1988). The preparation of manuscripts: Some reflections. *Gifted Child Quarterly, 32,* 366.

VanTassel-Baska, J., & Willis, G. (1988). A three year study of the effects of low income on SAT scores among the academically able. *Gifted Child Quarterly, 31,* 169–173.

VanTassel-Baska, J. (1988). The ineffectiveness of the pull-out model in gifted education: A minority perspective. *Journal for the Education of the Gifted, 10,* 255–264.

VanTassel-Baska, J., & Campbell, M. (1988). Developing a comprehensive approach to scope and sequence: Implementation considerations. *Gifted Child Today, 11*(6), 8–12.

VanTassel-Baska, J. (1988). Developing a comprehensive approach to scope and sequence: Curriculum alignment. *Gifted Child Today, 11*(5), 42–45.

VanTassel-Baska, J. (1988). Developing a comprehensive approach to scope and sequence: Curriculum frameworks in the content areas. *Gifted Child Today, 11*(4), 58–61.

VanTassel-Baska, J. (1988). Developing a comprehensive approach to scope and sequence: Curriculum needs assessment. *Gifted Child Today, 11*(3), 29–34.

VanTassel-Baska, J., & Campbell, M. (1988). Developing scope and sequence for the gifted learner: A comprehensive approach. *Gifted Child Today, 11*(2), 2–7.

VanTassel-Baska, J., & Kulieke, M. J. (1987). The role of the community-based scientific resources in developing scientific talent: A case study. *Gifted Child Quarterly, 30,* 111–115.

VanTassel-Baska, J. (1987). A case for the teaching of Latin to the verbally talented. *Roeper Review, 9,* 159–161.

VanTassel-Baska, J. (1986). Effective curriculum and instructional models for talented students. *Gifted Child Quarterly, 30,* 164–169.

VanTassel-Baska, J. (1986). Lessons from the history of teacher inservice in Illinois: Effective staff development in the education of gifted students. *Gifted Child Quarterly, 30,* 124–126.

VanTassel-Baska, J. (1986). The use of aptitude tests for identifying the gifted: The talent search concept. *Roeper Review, 8,* 185–189.

VanTassel-Baska, J. (1985, Winter). The case for acceleration. *Private School Quarterly*, 14–26.

VanTassel-Baska, J. (1985). The talent search model: Implications for secondary school reform. *National Association of Secondary School Principals Journal, 69*(482), 39–47.

VanTassel-Baska, J., & Prentice, M. (1985). The Midwest Talent Search: Catalyst for local and statewide program development on behalf of the talented. *Roeper Review, 7,* 167–170.

VanTassel-Baska, J., Olszewski, P., & Landau, M. (1985). Toward developing an appropriate math/science curriculum for gifted learners. *Journal for the Education of the Gifted, 8,* 257–272.

VanTassel-Baska, J. (1984). The talent search as an identification model. *Gifted Child Quarterly, 28,* 172–176.

VanTassel-Baska, J., Landau, M., & Olszewski, P. (1984). The benefits of summer programming for gifted adolescents. *Journal for the Education of the Gifted, 8,* 73–82.

VanTassel-Baska, J. (1983). Profiles of precocity: The 1982 Midwest Talent Search finalists. *Gifted Child Quarterly, 27,* 139–144.

VanTassel-Baska, J. (1983). The teacher as counselor of the gifted. *Teaching Exceptional Children, 15,* 144–150.

VanTassel-Baska, J., Schuler, A., & Lipschutz, J. (1982). An experimental program for gifted four year olds. *Journal for the Education of the Gifted, 5,* 44–55.

VanTassel-Baska, J. (1982). Results of a Latin-based experimental study of the verbally precocious. *Roeper Review, 4,* 35–37.

VanTassel-Baska, J. (1981, June). A comprehensive model of career education for gifted and talented. *Journal of Career Education,* 325–331.

VanTassel-Baska, J. (1980). Gifted education in the '80s: Pitfalls and possibilities. *Journal for the Education of the Gifted, 3,* 1–4.

VanTassel-Baska, J. (1979). A needs assessment model for gifted education. *Journal for the Education of the Gifted, 2,* 141–148.

VanTassel-Baska, J. (1977). The role of the library in gifted child education. *Illinois Libraries, 59,* 498–500.

Refereed Conference Proceedings

Authored 26 articles for conference proceedings and edited 4 conference proceedings since 1982.

VanTassel-Baska, J. (2008). What works in curriculum for gifted learners: The evidence base. In *Conference Proceedings from the 10th Asia Pacific Conference On Giftedness*, Singapore.

VanTassel-Baska, J. (2008). The non-negotiables of gifted education. In *Talent Development: Conference Proceedings*, Einhoven, The Netherlands.

VanTassel-Baska, J. (2006). Models for teaching content-based curriculum for gifted learners: Research findings on curriculum effectiveness studies. In *Beyond Standards: Conference Proceedings*, Evangelische Academie, Bad Boll, Germany.

VanTassel-Baska, J., Burrus, J., Avery, L., Little, C., & Poland, D. (2001). Curriculum effectiveness studies in social and language arts for gifted learners. In N. Colangelo

& S. G. Assouline (Eds.), *Talent development IV: Proceedings from the 1998 Wallace Symposium on Research in Gifted Education* (pp. 463–466). Scottsdale, AZ: Great Potential Press.

Avery, L. D., & VanTassel-Baska, J. (1999, April). *The impact of gifted education: Evaluation at state and local levels: Translating results into action.* Paper presented at the American Education Research Association (AERA) Conference, Montreal, Canada.

VanTassel-Baska, J. (1999). The talent search model as a systemic initiative for talent development. In S. G. Assouline & N. Colangelo (Eds.), *Talent development III: Proceedings from the 1995 Wallace Symposium on Research in Gifted Education* (pp. 135–138). Scottsdale, AZ: Gifted Psychology Press.

VanTassel-Baska, J. (1999). The talent development process in women writers. In S. G. Assouline & N. Colangelo (Eds.), *Talent development III: Proceedings from the 1995 Wallace Symposium on Research in Gifted Education* (pp. 417–420). Scottsdale, AZ: Gifted Psychology Press.

VanTassel-Baska, J. (1999). The talent searches: Counseling and mentoring activities. In S. G. Assouline & N. Colangelo (Eds.), *Talent development III: Proceedings from the 1995 Wallace Symposium on Research in Gifted Education* (pp. 153–158). Scottsdale, AZ: Gifted Psychology Press.

VanTassel-Baska, J. (1998). Can appropriate curriculum become a reality in schools? In J. LeRoux (Ed.), *Connecting the gifted community worldwide: Selected proceedings from the World Conference on the Gifted* (pp. 71–80). Ottawa, Canada: University of Ottawa.

VanTassel-Baska, J. (1998, August). *What makes giftedness work in schools?* Paper presented at the American Psychological Association Symposium, San Francisco, CA.

VanTassel-Baska, J. (1998, August). *Promoting excellence within a world community.* Paper presented at the Third Ibero-American Conference on Gifted Education, Brasilia, Brazil.

VanTassel-Baska, J. (1995). Key features of successful science and mathematics educational reform initiatives. In *Proceedings from making it happen: First in the world in science and mathematics education* (pp. 45–48). Washington, DC: Executive Office of the President.

VanTassel-Baska, J. (1994). National science and language arts curriculum projects. In S. G. Assouline and N. Colangelo (Eds.), *Talent Development: Proceedings from the Wallace Symposium on Research in Gifted Education* (pp. 19–38). Ames, IA: University of Iowa.

VanTassel-Baska, J. (1994). Needed research about the gifted and talented. In S. G. Assouline and N. Colangelo (Eds.), *Talent Development: Proceedings from the Wallace Symposium on Research in Gifted Education* (pp. 123–150). Ames, IA: University of Iowa.

VanTassel-Baska, J. (1994). Findings from the National Curriculum Projects in science and language arts. In S. G. Assouline & N. Colangelo (Eds.), *Talent Development: Proceedings from the Wallace Symposium on Research in Gifted Education* (pp. 1–28). Ames: University of Iowa.

VanTassel-Baska, J. (1993). Curriculum interventions for the disadvantaged gifted. In F. Mönks (Ed.), *Proceedings from the Ninth World Conference on the Gifted* (pp. 81–89). The Hague, Netherlands: World Council on the Gifted.

VanTassel-Baska, J. (1993). Gifted education and middle school education at the crossroads. In *Proceedings from North Carolina Conference on Middle Schools and the Gifted.* Raleigh, NC: ASCD.

Ventis, D., & VanTassel-Baska, J. (Eds.). (1990). *Proceedings and occasional papers from a symposium on the developmental potential of the gifted.* Williamsburg, VA: The College of William and Mary, Center for Gifted Education.

VanTassel-Baska, J. (1989). General education trends and implications for gifted education. In L. Ganschow (Ed.), *Proceedings: Cooperative planning for excellence in schools: Implications for gifted/talented education* (pp. 1–14). Oxford, OH: Miami University.

VanTassel-Baska, J. (Ed.). (1986). *Proceedings from the Tenth Annual Phi Delta/Kappa Research Symposium: The world of the mind: Insights into human potential.* Evanston, IL: Northwestern University.

VanTassel-Baska, J. (Ed.). (1986). *Proceedings from the Ninth Annual Phi Delta Kappa Research Symposium: The nature of science and mathematics education in a global society.* Evanston, IL: Northwestern University.

VanTassel-Baska, J. (Ed.). (1986). *The Richardson study: A catalyst for policy change in gifted education: Proceedings from the Midwest policy conference on gifted education.* Evanston, IL: Northwestern University.

VanTassel-Baska, J. (1985). Between Scylla and Charybdis: The dilemma of providing counseling services to the gifted. In *Promising practices: Its role in gifted education: Proceedings of the second annual distinguished lecture series on gifted education* (pp. 43–53). San Diego, CA: San Diego United School District.

VanTassel-Baska, J. (1984). Programs for pre-high school students. In *Proceedings from the Argonne National Laboratory Conference on the role of national laboratories in precollegiate science education* (pp. 71–74). Argonne, IL: Argonne National Laboratory.

VanTassel-Baska, J. (1983). Talented youth in a changing society: Exploring backgrounds, influences, and implications for education. In M. Hastings (Ed.), *Education and the changing fabric of American society, a monograph of the proceedings from the Ninth Annual Research Symposium* (pp. 33–36). Evanston, IL: Northwestern University.

VanTassel-Baska, J. (1982). The Midwest Talent Search project. In R. Brodsky (Ed.), *The three faces of gifted: Monograph from the fourth annual conference* (pp. 54–60). Bloomfield Hills, MI: Roeper Review and Academy for the Gifted.

CHAPTERS IN BOOKS

Authored 87 book chapters since 1980.

VanTassel-Baska, J. (in press). Elementary social studies curriculum. In B. Kerr's (Ed.), *The encyclopedia for giftedness and creativity.* Thousand Oaks, CA: Sage.

VanTassel-Baska, J. (in press). Elementary writing curriculum. In B. Kerr's (Ed.), *The encyclopedia for giftedness and creativity.* Thousand Oaks, CA: Sage.

VanTassel-Baska, J. (in press). Verbal ability. In B. Kerr's (Ed.), *The encyclopedia for giftedness and creativity.* Thousand Oaks, CA: Sage.

VanTassel-Baska, J., & Wood, S. (in press). The Integrated Curriculum Model. In J. Renzulli (Ed.), *Systems and models in gifted education.* Mansfield Center, CT: Creative Learning Press.

VanTassel-Baska, J. (in press). Designing creative and innovative curriculum for gifted learners. In L. Shavinina (Ed.), *The handbook on giftedness.* London: Springer.

VanTassel-Baska, J. (in press). Recent advances in gifted education policy. In L. Shavinina (Ed.), *The handbook on giftedness.* London: Springer.

VanTassel-Baska, J. (in press). Introduction. In J. VanTassel-Baska (Ed.), *Patterns and profiles of low-income gifted learners.* Waco: TX: Prufrock Press.

VanTassel-Baska, J. (in press). Curriculum interventions for low-income learners. In J. VanTassel-Baska (Ed.), *Patterns and profiles of low-income gifted learners.* Waco: TX: Prufrock Press.

VanTassel-Baska, J. (in press) A model for serving low-income learners. In J. VanTassel-Baska (Ed.), *Patterns and profiles of low-income gifted learners.* Waco: TX: Prufrock Press.

VanTassel-Baska, J. (2009). Affective curriculum and instruction for gifted learners. In J. VanTassel-Baska, T. L. Cross, & F. R. Olenchak (Eds.), *Social and emotional curriculum with gifted and talented students* (pp. 113–132). Waco, TX: Prufrock Press.

VanTassel-Baska, J. (2009). Introduction. In J. VanTassel-Baska, T. L. Cross, & F. R. Olenchak (Eds.), *Social and emotional curriculum with gifted and talented students* (pp. 1–10). Waco, TX: Prufrock.

VanTassel-Baska, J. (2009). Reflections. In T. Stambaugh & B. MacFarlane (Eds.), *Leadership for change in gifted education: The festschrift of Joyce VanTassel-Baska* (pp. 549–570). Waco, TX: Prufrock Press.

VanTassel-Baska, J., & Brown, E. (2009). An analysis of gifted education curriculum models. In F. A. Karnes & Suzanne M. Bean (Eds.), *Methods and materials for teaching the gifted* (3rd ed., pp. 75–106). Waco, TX: Prufrock Press.

VanTassel-Baska, J., Evans, B., & Baska, A. (2009). The role of the arts in the socioemotional development of the gifted. In J. VanTassel-Baska, T. L. Cross, & F. R. Olenchak (Eds.), *Social and emotional curriculum with gifted and talented students* (pp. 227–257). Waco, TX: Prufrock Press.

Cross, T. L., VanTassel-Baska, & Olenchak, F. R. (2009). Creating gifted lives: Concluding thoughts. In J. VanTassel-Baska, T. L. Cross, & F. R. Olenchak (Eds.), *Social and emotional curriculum with gifted and talented students* (pp. 361–372). Waco, TX: Prufrock Press.

VanTassel-Baska, J. (2008). The role of cultural diversity in gifted education. In T. Balchin, B. Hymer, & D. Matthews (Eds.), *Encyclopedia of gifted education* (pp. 273–280). London: Routledge.

VanTassel-Baska, J., & Stambaugh, T. (2008). Curriculum and instructional considerations in programs for the gifted. In S. Pfeiffer (Ed.), *Handbook of giftedness in children: Psychoeducational theory, research, and best practices* (pp. 347–366). New York: Springer.

VanTassel-Baska, J. (2008). An overview of alternative assessment measures for gifted learners and the issues that surround their use. In J. VanTassel-Baska (Ed.), *Alternative assessment with gifted and talented students* (pp. 1–15). Waco, TX: Prufrock Press.

VanTassel-Baska, J. (2008). Using performance-based assessment to document authentic learning. In J. VanTassel-Baska (Ed.), *Alternative assessment with gifted and talented students* (pp. 285–308). Waco, TX: Prufrock Press.

VanTassel-Baska, J. (2008). Epilogue: What do we know about identifying and assessing the learning of gifted students? In J. VanTassel-Baska (Ed.), *Alternative assessment with gifted and talented students* (pp. 309–319). Waco, TX: Prufrock Press.

VanTassel-Baska, J., & MacFarlane, B. (2008). Science, secondary. In J. A. Plucker & C. M. Callahan (Eds.), *Critical issues and practices in gifted education: What the research says* (pp. 579–594). Waco, TX: Prufrock Press.

VanTassel-Baska, J., & MacFarlane, B. (2008). Writing. In J. A. Plucker & C. M. Callahan (Eds.), *Critical issues and practices in gifted education: What the research says* (pp. 749–760). Waco, TX: Prufrock Press.

VanTassel-Baska, J., & Wood, S. (2007). Curriculum development in gifted education: A challenge to provide optimal learning experiences. In F. Karnes & K. Stephens (Eds.), *Achieving excellence: Educating the gifted and talented* (pp. 209–229). Upper Saddle River, NJ: Pearson.

Bracken, B., VanTassel-Baska, J., Brown, E., & Feng, A. (2007). Project Athena: A tale of two studies. In J. VanTassel-Baska & T. Stambaugh (Eds.), *Overlooked gems: A national perspective on low-income promising learners* (pp. 63–67). Washington, DC: National Association for Gifted Children.

VanTassel-Baska, J. (2007). Introduction. In J. VanTassel-Baska & T. Stambaugh (Eds.), *Overlooked gems: A national perspective on low-income promising learners* (pp. 1–5). Washington, DC: National Association for Gifted Children.

VanTassel-Baska, J. (2007). Introduction and overview of the issues. In J. VanTassel-Baska (Ed.), *Serving gifted learners beyond the traditional classroom: A guide to alternative programs and services* (pp. 1–12). Waco, TX: Prufrock Press.

VanTassel-Baska, J. (2007). Alternative programs and services: A creative response to the unmet needs of gifted students. In J. VanTassel-Baska (Ed.), *Serving gifted learners beyond the traditional classroom: A guide to alternative programs and services* (pp. 241–256). Waco, TX: Prufrock Press.

VanTassel-Baska, J. (2006). Developing higher level thinking in gifted education. In J. Kauffman & J. Baer (Eds.), *The relationship between creativity, knowledge, and reason* (pp. 297–315). New York: Cambridge University Press.

VanTassel-Baska, J. (2006). State policies in gifted education. In J. Purcell & R. Eckert's (Eds.), *Designing services and programs for high-ability learners* (pp. 249–261). Washington, DC: National Association for Gifted Children.

VanTassel-Baska, J. (2006). Secondary affective curriculum and instruction for gifted learners. In F. A. Dixon & S. M. Moon (Eds.), *The handbook of secondary gifted education* (pp. 481–503), Waco. TX: Prufrock Press.

VanTassel-Baska, J. (2005). Domain-specific giftedness. In J. Davidson & R. Sternberg (Eds.), *Conceptions of giftedness* (2nd ed., pp. 358–376). New York: Cambridge University Press.

VanTassel-Baska, J., & Brown, E. (2004). An analysis of gifted education curricular models. In F. A. Karnes & S. M. Bean (Eds.), *Methods and materials for teaching the gifted* (2nd ed., pp. 75–101). Waco, TX: Prufrock Press.

VanTassel-Baska, J. (2004). Diversity curriculum. In D. Boothe & J. Stanley's (Eds.), *Giftedness and cultural diversity* (pp. 167–178). New York: Cambridge University Press.

VanTassel-Baska, J., & Worley, B. B., II. (2004). Giftedness and talent. In M. Friend's (Ed.), *Introduction to special education* (pp. 570–608). Needham Heights, MA: Allyn & Bacon.

VanTassel-Baska, J. (2004). Introduction to the William and Mary eclectic model of gifted program evaluation. In J. VanTassel-Baska & A. X. Feng (Eds.), *Designing and utilizing evaluation for gifted program improvement* (pp. 1–22). Waco, TX: Prufrock Press.

VanTassel-Baska, J. (2004). The processes in gifted program evaluation. In J. VanTassel-Baska & A. X. Feng (Eds.), *Designing and utilizing evaluation for gifted program improvement* (pp. 23–40). Waco, TX: Prufrock Press.

VanTassel-Baska, J. (2004). Assessing classroom practice: The use of a structured observation form. In J. VanTassel-Baska & A. X. Feng (Eds.), *Designing and utilizing evaluation for gifted program improvement* (pp. 87–108). Waco, TX: Prufrock Press.

VanTassel-Baska, J., & Feng, A. (2004). Collecting student impact data in gifted programs: Problems and processes. In J. VanTassel-Baska & A. X. Feng (Eds.), *Designing and utilizing evaluation for gifted program improvement* (pp. 133–154). Waco, TX: Prufrock Press.

VanTassel-Baska, J. (2004). Metafindings on the utilization of evaluations. In J. VanTassel-Baska & A. X. Feng (Eds.), *Designing and utilizing evaluation for gifted program improvement* (pp. 155–174). Waco, TX: Prufrock Press.

VanTassel-Baska, J. (2004). Metaevaluation findings: A call for gifted program quality. In J. VanTassel-Baska & A. X. Feng (Eds.), *Designing and utilizing evaluation for gifted program improvement* (pp. 227–245). Waco, TX: Prufrock Press.

VanTassel-Baska, J. (2003). Content-based curriculum for high-ability learners: An introduction. In J. VanTassel-Baska & C. A. Little (Eds.), *Content-based curriculum for high-ability learners* (pp. 1–23). Waco, TX: Prufrock Press.

VanTassel-Baska, J. (2003). Curriculum for the profoundly gifted. In K. Kay, D. Robson, & J. F. Brenneman (Eds.), *High IQ kids* (pp. 150–160). Minneapolis, MN: Free Spirit.

VanTassel-Baska, J. (2003). Curriculum policy development for gifted programs: Converting issues in the field to coherent practice. In J. H. Borland (Ed.), *Rethinking gifted education* (pp. 173–185). New York: Teachers College Press.

VanTassel-Baska, J. (2003). Implementing innovative curricular and instructional practices in classrooms and schools. In J. VanTassel-Baska & C. A. Little (Eds.), *Content-based curriculum for high-ability learners* (pp. 355–375). Waco, TX: Prufrock Press.

VanTassel-Baska, J., & Sher, B. (2003). Accelerating learning experiences in core content areas. In J. VanTassel-Baska & C. A. Little (Eds.), *Content-based curriculum for high-ability learners* (pp. 27–45). Waco, TX: Prufrock Press.

Zuo, L., & VanTassel-Baska, J. (2003). Assessing student learning. In J. VanTassel-Baska & C. A. Little (Eds.), *Content-based curriculum for high-ability learners* (pp. 305–325). Waco, TX: Prufrock Press.

VanTassel-Baska, J. (2002). What matters in curriculum for gifted learners: Reflections on theory, research, and practice. In G. A. Davis & N. Colangelo (Eds.), *Handbook on gifted education* (3rd ed., pp. 174–183). Boston: Allyn & Bacon.

VanTassel-Baska, J. (2000). Theory and research on curriculum development for the gifted. In K. Heller, F. J. Mönks, R. Sternberg, & R. Subotnik (Eds.), *International handbook of giftedness and talent* (2nd ed., pp. 345–365). London: Pergamon Press.

VanTassel-Baska, J., & Brown, E. F. (2000). An analysis of gifted education curriculum models. In F. A. Karnes & S. M. Bean (Eds.), *Methods and materials for teaching the gifted* (pp. 93–131). Waco, TX: Prufrock Press.

VanTassel-Baska, J. (1999). Infusing higher order thinking skills into science and language arts curriculum for high-ability learners. In B. Presseisen (Ed.), *Teaching for intelligence: A collection of articles* (pp. 319–332). Arlington Heights, IL: Skylight.

VanTassel-Baska, J. (1999). Making schools gifted. In K. Hegeman & S. Cline (Eds.), *Critical issues in gifted education* (pp. 265–274). Delray Beach, FL: Foundation for Concepts in Education.

VanTassel-Baska, J. (1999). The Brontë sisters. In M. Runco & S. Pritzer (Eds.), *Encyclopedia of creativity* (Vol 1., pp. 229–233). San Diego, CA: Academic Press.

VanTassel-Baska, J. (1998). A study of problem-based learning in teaching educational administration courses. In R. Muth & M. Martin (Eds.), *Toward the year 2000: Leadership for quality schools. 1998 NCPEA yearbook* (pp. 279–288). Denver: University of Colorado.

VanTassel-Baska, J. (1997). Gifted education and middle school education: Issues and answers. In C. Tomlinson (Ed.), *In search of common ground: What constitutes appropriate curriculum and instruction for middle schoolers?* (pp. 90–102). Washington, DC: National Association for Gifted Children.

VanTassel-Baska, J. (1996). What matters in curriculum for gifted learners: Reflections on theory, research, and practice. In G. A. Davis & N. Colangelo (Eds.), *Handbook on Gifted Education* (2nd ed., pp. 126–135). Boston: Allyn & Bacon.

VanTassel-Baska, J. (1996). Talent development in women writers: A study of Charlotte Brontë and Virginia Woolf. In K. D. Arnold, K. D. Noble, & R. F. Subotnik (Eds.), *Remarkable women: Perspectives on female talent development* (pp. 295–316). New York: Hampton Press.

VanTassel-Baska, J. (1996). The contribution of the talent search concept to gifted education. In C. Benbow & D. Lipinski (Eds.), *From psychometrics to giftedness: Essays in honor of Julian Stanley* (pp. 214–220). Baltimore: Johns Hopkins Press.

VanTassel-Baska, J. (1996). The process of talent development. In J. VanTassel-Baska, D. T. Johnson, and L. N. Boyce (Eds.), *Developing verbal talent: Ideas and strategies for teachers of elementary and middle school students* (pp. 3–22). Boston: Allyn & Bacon.

VanTassel-Baska, J. (1996). Creating a new language arts curriculum for high-ability learners. In J. VanTassel-Baska, D. T. Johnson, & L .N. Boyce (Eds.), *Developing verbal talent: Ideas and strategies for teachers of elementary and middle school students* (pp. 193–217). Boston: Allyn & Bacon.

VanTassel-Baska, J. (1994). A synthesis of perspectives: Another view. In J. Hanson & S. Hoover (Eds.), *Talent development: Theory and practice* (pp. 299–308). Dubuque, IA: Kendall/Hunt.

VanTassel-Baska, J. (1993). Research on special populations of gifted learners. In M. Wang (Section Ed.), *International encyclopedia of education* (pp. 77–101). London: Pergamon Press.

VanTassel-Baska, J. (1993). Developing self-esteem in gifted individuals. In G. McEachron-Hirsch (Ed.), *Integrating an image of self: A study of self-esteem in family and school environments* (pp. 311–344). Lancaster, PA: Technomic.

VanTassel-Baska, J. (1993). Theory and research on curriculum development for the gifted. In K. A. Heller, F. J. Mönks, & A. H. Passow (Eds.), *International handbook for research on giftedness and talent* (pp. 365–386). London: Pergamon Press.

VanTassel-Baska, J. (1992). The role of advocacy in local program development for the gifted. In J. Maker (Ed.), *Critical issues in gifted education* (Vol. 3, pp. 63–70). Rockville, MD: Aspen Systems.

VanTassel-Baska, J., & Baska, L. (1992). The role of school personnel in counseling gifted students. In L. Silverman (Ed.), *Counseling the gifted* (pp. 181–200). Denver, CO: Love.

VanTassel-Baska, J. (1992). Academic counseling for the gifted. In L. Silverman (Ed.), *Counseling the gifted* (pp. 201–214). Denver, CO: Love.

VanTassel-Baska, J. (1991). The identification of candidates for acceleration. In T. Southern & E. Jones (Eds.), *Educational acceleration* (pp. 148–161). New York: Teachers' College Press.

VanTassel-Baska, J. (1991). Special populations of gifted learners. In M. Wang & M. Reynolds (Eds.), *Review of educational research* (pp. 77–101). London: Pergamon Press.

VanTassel-Baska, J. (1991). The role of teachers in counseling the gifted. In R. Milgram (Ed.), *The development of the gifted* (pp. 37–52). Rockville, MD: ProEd.

VanTassel-Baska, J. (1990). Trends and issues in counseling the gifted. In J. VanTassel-Baska (Ed.), *A practical guide to counseling the gifted in a school setting* (pp. 6–14). Reston, VA: Council for Exceptional Children.

VanTassel-Baska, J. (1990). Collaboration of teachers and counselors in serving the affective needs of the gifted. In J. VanTassel-Baska (Ed.), *A practical guide to counseling the gifted in a school setting* (pp. 40–56). Reston, VA: Council for Exceptional Children.

Bailey, J., Boyce, L. N., & VanTassel-Baska, J. (1990). Writing, reading, and counseling connection: A framework for serving the gifted. In J. VanTassel-Baska (Ed.), *A practical guide to counseling the gifted in a school setting* (pp. 172–189). Reston, VA: Council for Exceptional Children.

VanTassel-Baska, J. (1989). Factors that characterize the development path of eminent individuals. In J. VanTassel-Baska & P. Olszewski-Kubilius (Eds.), *Patterns of influence: The home, the self, and the school* (pp. 146–162). New York: Teachers College Press.

VanTassel-Baska, J. (1989). Profiles of precocity: A three-year study of talented adolescents. In J. VanTassel-Baska & P. Olszewski-Kubilius (Eds.), *Patterns of influence: The home, the self, and the school* (pp. 29–39). New York: Teachers College Press.

VanTassel-Baska, J. (1989). The role of the family in the success of the disadvantaged gifted. In J. VanTassel-Baska & P. Olszewski-Kubilius (Eds.), *Patterns of influence: The home, the self, and the school* (pp. 60–80). New York: Teachers College Press.

VanTassel-Baska, J. (1986). The case for acceleration. In J. Maker (Ed.), *Critical issues in gifted education* (pp. 148–161). Rockville, MD: Aspen Systems.

VanTassel-Baska, J. (1985). Key administrative concepts in gifted program development. In J. Feldhusen (Ed.), *Toward excellence in gifted education* (pp. 85–104). Denver, CO: Love.

VanTassel-Baska, J. (1985). Appropriate curriculum for the gifted. In J. Feldhusen (Ed.), *Toward excellence in gifted education* (pp. 45–68). Denver, CO: Love.

VanTassel-Baska, J. (1983). State-wide replication in Illinois of the Johns Hopkins Study of Mathematically Precocious Youth. In C. P. Benbow & J. C. Stanley (Eds.), *Academic precocity: Aspects of its development* (pp. 179–191). Baltimore: Johns Hopkins University Press.

VanTassel-Baska, J. (1980). Evaluation of gifted programs. In J. Jordan & J. Grossi (Eds.), *An administrator's handbook on designing programs for the gifted and talented* (pp. 110–128). Reston, VA: Council for Exceptional Children.

VanTassel-Baska, J. (1980). Criteria for the selection of materials. In J. Jordan & J. Grossi (Eds.), *An administrator's handbook on designing programs for the gifted and talented* (pp. 102–109). Reston, VA: Council for Exceptional Children.

VanTassel-Baska, J. (1980). Needs assessment. In J. Jordan & J. Grossi (Eds.), *An administrator's handbook on designing programs for the gifted and talented* (pp. 23–37). Reston, VA: Council for Exceptional Children.

Selected Curriculum Units, Guides, and Reports

Authored or coauthored 45 curriculum materials, guides, and reports since 1976.

VanTassel-Baska, J., Chandler, K., & Robbins, J. (2009). *Curriculum modules for working with gifted learners.* Hong Kong: Hong Kong Ministry of Education.

VanTassel-Baska, J. (2008). *Budding botanists.* Williamsburg, VA: Center for Gifted Education.

VanTassel-Baska, J. (2008). *A guide to teaching language arts to gifted learners* (2nd ed.). Dubuque, IA: Kendall Hunt.

VanTassel-Baska, J. & Stambaugh, T. (Eds.). (2008). *What works: 20 years of curriculum development and research.* Waco, TX: Prufrock Press.

VanTassel-Baska, J., Stambaugh, T., French, H., & Drain, D. (2005). *Jacob's Ladder Reading Comprehension Program for 3rd, 4th, and 5th graders.* Williamsburg, VA: Center for Gifted Education.

VanTassel-Baska, J., Quek, C., Lee, F., & Chee, A. (2004). *Curriculum review of the Raffles Schools Integrated Units.* Williamsburg, VA: Center for Gifted Education.

VanTassel-Baska, J. (Ed.). (2003). *A guide to implementation of Project Athena.* Williamsburg, VA: Center for Gifted Education.

VanTassel-Baska, J. (Ed.). (2003). *Canadian unit on transformations, based on ICM and W&M models.* Calgary, Alberta, Canada: University of Calgary, Center for Gifted Education.

VanTassel-Baska, J. (2003). *A Utah curriculum framework for teaching gifted students in language arts.* Salt Lake City: Utah Association for the Gifted.

VanTassel-Baska, J., & Feng, A. (2003). *Advanced learning program curriculum study: Curriculum alignment* (Vols. 1 and 2). Greenwich, CT: Greenwich Public Schools.

VanTassel-Baska, J., & Gross, M. U. M. (Eds.). (2003). *Australian curriculum units on time, using the ICM model.* Sydney, Australia: University of New South Wales, GERRIC.

VanTassel-Baska, J. (2002). *Walk two moons.* Williamsburg, VA: Center for Gifted Education.

VanTassel-Baska, J., Pehkonen, L., & Buisman, J. (Eds.). (2002). *An Oregon guide to aligning gifted curriculum to Oregon standards.* Salem, OR: Department of Public Instruction.

VanTassel-Baska, J. (1997). *A proposed scope and sequence guide for gifted programs in South Carolina.* Columbus: South Carolina Department of Education.

Cawley, F. C., Johnson, D. T., VanTassel-Baska, J., & Boyce, L. N. (1994). *Journeys and destinations: The challenge of change.* Williamsburg, VA: College of William and Mary, Center for Gifted Education.

Coleman, S., Johnson, D. T., VanTassel-Baska, J., Boyce, L. N., & Hall, K. H. (1994). *Changing ideas and perspectives through persuasion.* Williamsburg, VA: College of William and Mary, Center for Gifted Education.

Crossett, B., Johnson, D. T., VanTassel-Baska, J., Boyce, L. N., & Hall, K. H. (1994). *Threads of change in 19th century American literature.* Williamsburg, VA: College of William and Mary, Center for Gifted Education.

Johnson, D. T., VanTassel-Baska, J., Boyce, L. N., & Hall, K. H. (1994). *Autobiographies: Personal odysseys for change.* Williamsburg, VA: College of William and Mary, Center for Gifted Education.

Moody, C., Johnson, D., VanTassel-Baska, J., Boyce, L. N., & Hall, K. H. (1994). *Literature of the 1940s: A decade of change*. Williamsburg, VA: College of William and Mary, Center for Gifted Education.

Prial, K. C., Johnson, D. T., VanTassel-Baska, J., Boyce, L. N., & Hall, K. H. (1994). *Literary reflections on personal and social change*. Williamsburg, VA: College of William and Mary, Center for Gifted Education.

VanTassel-Baska, J. (1993). *A guide to academic programs for talent search 5th and 6th graders*. Evanston, IL: Northwestern University, Center for Talent Development.

VanTassel-Baska, J. (1992). *A scope and sequence of curriculum and record of progress for the spectrum program*. Grand Rapids, MI: Grand Rapids Public Schools.

VanTassel-Baska, J. (1991). *A scope and sequence guide for curriculum for the gifted*. Fredericksburg, VA: Fredericksburg City School Division.

Bailey, J. M., & VanTassel-Baska, J. (1990). *A resource guide on teaching science to the gifted*. Richmond: State Council of Higher Education in Virginia.

Boyce, L. N., Bailey, J. M., & VanTassel-Baska, J. (1990). *Libraries link learning resource guide*. Richmond: Virginia State Library and Archives.

VanTassel-Baska, J. (Ed.). (1990). *Curriculum scope and sequence project*. Gary, IN: Gary Community School District.

VanTassel-Baska, J. (1990). *Secondary English curriculum guide for the gifted*. Atlanta: Georgia State Department of Education.

VanTassel-Baska, J., & Orehovec, J. (1989). *A resource guide on teaching mathematics to the gifted*. Richmond: State Council of Higher Education in Virginia.

Brown, C., & VanTassel-Baska, J. (1988). *Curriculum guide for academically gifted*. Bristol, VA: Bristol Public Schools.

VanTassel-Baska, J. (1987). *A scope and sequence guide in language arts programs for the gifted*. Williamsburg, VA: College of William and Mary, Center for Gifted Education.

VanTassel-Baska, J. (Ed.). (1986). *A curriculum guide to applications of science and technology for able learners*. Chicago: The Joyce Foundation.

VanTassel-Baska, J. (Ed.). (1986). *A curriculum guide to philosophy and methods of science for able learners*. Chicago: The Joyce Foundation.

VanTassel-Baska, J. (Ed.). (1986). *A curriculum guide to applications of mathematics and technology*. Chicago, IL: The Joyce Foundation.

VanTassel-Baska, J., & Feldhusen, J. (Eds.). (1981). *Concept curriculum for the gifted*. Washington, DC: United States Department of Education, Office of Gifted and Talented.

VanTassel-Baska, J. (1976). *Phoenix project curriculum guide*. Toledo, OH: Toledo Public Schools.

VanTassel-Baska, J. (1976). *The world of the gifted: K–6 curriculum guide*. Toledo, OH: Toledo Public Schools.

EVALUATION REPORTS

Authored or coauthored 50 evaluation reports since 1981. These reports included state evaluations in Ohio, Florida, and Idaho, and local school district evaluations in multiple states including Pennsylvania, Ohio, Michigan, Virginia, South Carolina, and Maryland. University program evaluations also were conducted, including international sites.

Book Reviews

Published 21 book reviews since 1971. These reviews have appeared in gifted education journals and other publications.

Nonrefereed Publications

Authored or coauthored 58 nonrefereed publications. These publications include special columns written while president of NAGC, special guides, and newsletter articles.

Research Reports From Grant or Contract Work

Authored or coauthored 41 research reports that summarize the research work done on relevant projects for federal and state grants. Wrote and served as principal investigator on 65 grants and contracts, totaling more than $15 million.

Publication Leadership

Editor, *Gifted and Talented International*, 1997–2005
Series Editor, Critical Issues in Equity and Excellence in Gifted Education, 2005–2009
Book Review Editor, *Gifted Child Quarterly*, 1997–2007
Editorial Board, *Gifted Child Quarterly*, 1984–1992, 1995–present
Coeditor (with A. H. Passow), special issue of *Gifted Child Quarterly* on curriculum, 1986, *30*(4)
Contributing Editor, *Roeper Review*. 1989–1993; reappointed 1993–1997; 2000–2003; 2002–2005; 2006–2008
Editorial Advisory Board, *Encyclopedia of Giftedness and Creativity* (Barbara Kerr, Ed.), 2007–2009
Editorial Advisory Board, *Journal for Advanced Academics*, 2008–2010
Editorial Advisor, *Asia Pacific Journal on Giftedness*, 2008–2010
Editorial Board, *Gifted Child Today*, 2006–2009
National Advisory Board, *Gifted Education Communicator*, California Association for the Gifted, 2000–2009
Coeditor, *Current Issues in Gifted Education*, a journal publication of the Center for Gifted Education, 2000
Editorial Advisory Board, Research Briefs, *Journal of Secondary Gifted Education*, 1997
Editorial Board, *Journal of Advanced Development*, 1989–present
Editorial Advisory Board, Critical Issues in Gifted Education series, ProEd Publications
Manuscript Review Editor, *Journal for the Education of the Gifted*, 1981–present
Column Editor, *Understanding the Gifted* newsletter (4 columns per year), 1989–1991
Executive Editor, *Systems* newsletter, Center for Gifted Education, 1992–2006

Publisher, *Talent Development Quarterly*, Center for Talent Development, Northwestern University, 1983–1987

Coeditor, *Connections*, newsletter of the Center for Gifted Education, 1990–1992

Member of Publications Committee, Council for Exceptional Children, 1981–1984

Manuscript reviewer for texts on gifted education: Allyn & Bacon, Houghton-Mifflin, Peacock Publishing Company, 1985–2000

ABOUT THE
EDITORS

Bronwyn MacFarlane is an assistant professor of gifted education in the Department of Educational Leadership at the University of Arkansas at Little Rock (UALR). She teaches graduate-level courses in gifted education and works with the UALR Center for Gifted Education. Prior to joining the UALR graduate school faculty, Dr. MacFarlane worked at the Center for Gifted Education at The College of William and Mary in Virginia as the research assistant to Dr. Joyce VanTassel-Baska for 3 years while earning her doctorate in educational policy, planning, and leadership with dual specializations in both gifted education program administration and K–12 school administration. She received the 2008 National Association for Gifted Children Outstanding Doctoral Student Award; the 2008 College of William and Mary School of Education Dean's Award for Excellence; the 2007 College of William and Mary Excellence in Gifted Education Doctoral Award; and the 2007 International P. E. O. Scholar Award. *Leading Change in Gifted Education* is Dr. MacFarlane's first edited volume.

Tamra Stambaugh is the director of programs for talented youth at Vanderbilt University. She is the coauthor (with Dr. Joyce VanTassel-Baska) of *Comprehensive Curriculum for Gifted Learners* and *Overlooked Gems: A National Perspective on Low-Income Promising Students*. In addition, Stambaugh has authored or coauthored journal articles; curriculum units including the *Jacob's Ladder Reading Comprehension Program*; and book chapters on topics including differentiation, leadership, curriculum and intervention studies, policy, effective programming, promising students of poverty, and gifted program evaluation. Her current research interests include the impact of accelerated curriculum on student achievement and talent development, especially for students of poverty, including those in rural areas. Stambaugh is the recipient of the National Association for Gifted Children Outstanding Doctoral Student Award, the College of William and Mary Center for Gifted Education Doctoral Student Award, and the College of William and Mary Margaret The Lady Thatcher Medallion for scholarship, service, and character. She was the previous director of grants and special projects, coordinating two Javits grants, at The College of William and Mary, Center for Gifted Education.

ABOUT THE AUTHORS

Linda D. Avery received her Ph.D. in educational policy, planning, and leadership from The College of William and Mary in 1999. She served as manager of the Center for Gifted Education until 2002, during which time she was integrally involved in Project STAR and Project Phoenix. Her earlier work was in state government programs, first in Michigan and then in Illinois. She has conducted several state and local gifted program evaluations and has published book chapters, journal articles, and research and evaluation reports.

Ariel Baska teaches Latin and drama in Fairfax County Public Schools, while pursuing her master's degree in gifted education at George Mason University. She received her bachelor's degree in classics from The College of William and Mary, where she received a scholarship to adapt and direct ancient plays. She has written two *Navigator* independent study activities for the Center for Gifted Education, and has cowritten a book chapter and an article with her mother, Joyce VanTassel-Baska, for publication.

Bruce Bracken currently is a professor in The College of William and Mary School of Education. During his career, Dr. Bracken has published more than 150 articles, reviews, book chapters, tests, books, curricula, training CDs, and videos. He cofounded the *Journal of Psychoeducational Assessment* and edited the journal for more than 20 years. He currently sits on the editorial boards of eight national and international educational and psychological journals. He is a Fellow of the APA in the Division of School Psychology (Div 16) and the Division of Child and Adolescent Psychology (Div 53). Dr. Bracken is a Diplomate and Fellow in the American Board of Assessment Psychology and a Fellow of the American Educational Research Association.

Linda E. Brody directs the Julian C. Stanley Study of Exceptional Talent (SET) at the Johns Hopkins Center for Talented Youth (CTY), which provides counseling services to students with exceptional academic abilities and studies their progress over time. She also supervises the counseling efforts of the Jack Kent Cooke Young Scholars program for CTY, the development of Cogito.org for top math and science students, and the publication of the award-winning *Imagine* magazine. Her research focuses on evaluating strategies to serve gifted students and on special populations including the highly gifted, gifted females, and twice-exceptional students. She earned her doctorate at Johns Hopkins.

Elissa F. Brown is the director of the Middle/High School Council for the North Carolina Department of Public Instruction where she facilitates statewide reform initiatives that impact middle and high schools. She came to the state agency in 2007 as the state consultant for gifted education. Prior to her appointment with the department, she was the director for the Center for Gifted Education at The College of William and Mary where she received her Ph.D. in educational policy planning and leadership with an emphasis in gifted education. She also is a former principal, teacher, and coordinator of gifted programs.

Brandy L. E. Buckingham is a doctoral student in learning sciences at Northwestern University. She holds a B.S. in cognitive science and theater from MIT as well as a M.A.Ed. in curriculum and instruction for gifted education from The College of William and Mary. Her broad research interests include the design of informal learning environments; the cognitive differences in learning from different media, artifacts, and environments; and the nature of intelligence and its impact on the design of learning environments.

Laurence J. Coleman is professor and holds the Judith Daso Herb Chair in Gifted Education at the University of Toledo in Ohio. He is the principal investigator of Accelerating Achievement in Math and Science in Urban Schools, a Javits-sponsored program. His scholarly interests include capturing the ordinary experience of gifted children and teachers in context and studying passions that fuel advanced development. Dr. Coleman coauthored *Being Gifted in School* with Tracy L. Cross, authored *Nurturing Talent in High Schools: Life in the Fast Lane*, served as editor of the *Journal for the Education of the Gifted*, and received the Distinguished Scholar Award from NAGC.

Lucas Cook is an intern with the American Psychological Association's Center for Gifted Education Policy. In addition to his contributions to the VanTassel-Baska festschrift chapter, he has played an important role in preparing the Center's professional development modules for teachers and in enhancing its Web site. He also is a full-time student at American University majoring in psychology and education.

Jennifer Riedl Cross received her Ph.D. in educational psychology from Ball State University, with a specialization in cognitive and social processes. She served 17 years as an assistant or managing editor for several different research journals in gifted education, including *Gifted Child Quarterly*, *Roeper Review*, and *Journal for the Education of the Gifted*. She has presented at numerous gifted education conferences at the local, regional, and international level and has conducted research concerning attitudes towards gifted students and their education.

Tracy L. Cross, George and Frances Ball Distinguished Professor of Psychology and Gifted Studies, is the associate dean for graduate studies, research, and assessment for Teachers College at Ball State University. For 9 years he served as the executive director of the Indiana Academy for Science, Mathematics, and Humanities, a public residential school for academically gifted adolescents. Dr. Cross has published more than 100 articles and book chapters, and a coauthored textbook, *Being Gifted in School: An Introduction to Development, Guidance, and Teaching*. He is the editor of the *Journal for the Education of the Gifted* and editor emeritus of the *Roeper Review*, *Gifted Child Quarterly*, and *Journal of Secondary Gifted Education*.

Andrew S. Davis is an associate professor of psychology at Ball State University and a licensed psychologist and school psychologist who specializes in pediatric neuropsychology. Dr. Davis is the editor of the upcoming *Handbook of Pediatric Neuropsychology* and has published or presented more than 100 research studies, book chapters, test reviews, and encyclopedia entries in the areas of clinical neuropsychology and school psychology. He is the clinical director of neurobehavioral health and his pediatric clinical practice primarily focuses on neurodevelopmental and genetic disorders and psychiatric disorders with a neurological component.

Joy L. Davis is a graduate of The College of William and Mary's master's and doctoral programs in gifted education. She has worked as a local and state administrator, adjunct instructor, and consultant specializing in the education of African American gifted learners. She currently is director of the Center for the Advancement of Academic Excellence at Virginia Union University and is serving her first term as chair of the NAGC's Diversity and Equity Committee.

Ashley Edmiston is a program officer for the American Psychological Association's Center for Psychology in Schools and Education (CPSE) and also acts as project director for the Catalyst program with the Center for Gifted Education Policy. She provides support and assists with projects involving psychology in schools and education and the Task Force on Classroom Violence Against Teachers. She holds a B.S. in psychology with a concentration on neuroscience from the University of Westminster.

Annie Xuemei Feng is a behavioral scientist, a SAIC Frederick contractor, supporting the Division of Cancer Control and Population Sciences at the National Cancer Institute (NCI). She is a member of the NCI evaluation team of cross-disciplinary initiatives, engaging in the study of team sciences. Previously, Dr. Feng was the director of research and evaluation at the Center for Gifted Education at The College of William and Mary. She also is a coprincipal investigator of the International Studies of Academic Olympiads. She received her B.A. in English language and literature from Jilin University in China and her doctorate in education from St. John's University in New York.

Melanie Frank served as an intern with the American Psychological Association's Center for Gifted Education Policy (CGEP) during 2008. She devoted much of her effort to the festschrift chapter as well as to helping CGEP write up an evaluation for the Center's Catalyst Project. Catalyst is one of CGEP's signature programs, providing adolescents with demonstrated high levels of motivation and accomplishment in the sciences access to eminent mentors in chemistry. She is currently a freshman psychology and education major at the University of Vermont.

Heather M. French is the director of education for The Riley Behavioral and Educational Center in Huntsville, AL, which provides comprehensive services for children with autism, pervasive developmental delay, and Asperger's syndrome. Dr. French holds a B.A. in English from Birmingham-Southern College, a M.S. in English education from Florida State University, and a Ph.D. in educational policy, planning, and leadership with an emphasis in gifted education from The College of William and Mary.

John P. Gaa is a professor of educational psychology and codirector of the Urban Talent Research Institute at the University of Houston. He has conducted research in a variety of areas including applied motivational interventions, goal-setting, locus of control, gender identity and sex role development, and ego and moral development. Most recently his research has focused on the affective and social-emotional development of gifted students, most specifically those students gifted in the arts.

Françoys Gagné obtained his Ph.D. in educational psychology (1966) at l'Université de Montréal. After devoting a decade to the study of student evaluations of teaching, he spent the rest of his career in the Department of Psychology, at l'Université du Québec à Montréal (UQAM). He has published extensively on theoretical matters, peer identification, and motivational issues and is known for his Differentiated Model of Giftedness and Talent (DMGT), which has been endorsed by educational authorities in many countries. Dr. Gagné has won major awards in the field of gifted education, among them NAGC's Distinguished Scholar Award (1996). Since retiring in 2001, Dr. Gagné has maintained international publishing and keynoting activities.

James Gallagher has spent more than 40 years in research and teaching on the subject of exceptional children. He has been a professor at the University of Illinois, the first director of the Bureau of Education for the Handicapped in the U.S. Office of Education, the director of the Frank Porter Graham Child Development Center at University of North Carolina–Chapel Hill for 17 years, and a Kenan Professor of Education for 32 years at the university. He has authored or edited more than 10 textbooks and more than 200 articles.

Shelagh A. Gallagher is a nationally recognized consultant in gifted education, who spent 10 years at the University of North Carolina at Charlotte as an associate professor in education where she directed two Javits grants. Prior to that, she worked at The College of William and Mary for a year and managed the Javits grant that produced the William and Mary problem-based learning (PBL) science units. She also has worked as research director for the Illinois Mathematics and Science Academy (IMSA). Dr. Gallagher has served two terms on the NAGC Board of Directors, has won two NAGC Curriculum Division awards, and the NAGC Article of the Year award. She and her father, James Gallagher, coauthored *Teaching the Gifted Child.* She is a doctoral graduate of the University of Arizona.

Leslie W. Grant is a visiting assistant professor in the curriculum and instruction and educational leadership areas at The College of William and Mary in Williamsburg, VA. She is the coauthor of *Teacher-Made Assessments: How to Connect Curriculum, Instruction, and Student Learning.* She has worked with school districts in the areas of teacher evaluation, student achievement goal setting, and student assessment. Her research interests include classroom-based assessments and teacher quality. Dr. Grant was a teacher and instructional leader before serving as a developer of state customized assessments for a major test publishing company. She received her doctoral degree from The College of William and Mary.

Miraca U. M. Gross is director of the Gifted Education Research, Resource, and Information Centre (GERRIC), at the University of New South Wales, Australia. Dr. Gross has won several international research awards including the Hollingworth Award for Excellence in Research in Gifted Education in 1987, and, in 1988 and 1990, the Mensa International Education and Research Foundation Awards for Excellence. In 2005, the National Association for Gifted Children honored her with its Distinguished Scholar Award—the first time this was awarded to a scholar outside North America. In 2008, she was appointed a Member of the Order of Australia in the Queen's Birthday Honours List for services to gifted education.

Suzanna E. Henshon graduated from The College of William and Mary in 2005 with a Ph.D. in gifted education and teaches creative writing and composition full time at Florida Gulf Coast University. She is the author of 150 publications, including three *Navigator* study guides; children's novels entitled *Mildew on the Wall* (2004) and *Spiders on the Ceiling* (2006); and numerous publications on the writing process, including *King Arthur's Academy: Descriptive and Narrative Writing Exercises* (2007), *Haunted House: Descriptive and Narrative Writing Exercises* (2007), and *Notes from a Writer* (2008).

Claire E. Hughes is an assistant professor in the School of Education at Bellarmine University. She graduated from The College of William and Mary with dual emphases in gifted education and special education in 2000 after being a graduate assistant at the Center for Gifted Education. She is a former elementary and middle school teacher, has presented at numerous national and state conferences, and has authored several articles and book chapters.

Susan E. Jackson is a doctoral student in educational psychology and individual differences and is associated with the Urban Talent Research Institute at the University of Houston. Her master's thesis focused on the effectiveness of the gifted program created by The Kids on the Block, Inc., and she anticipates her doctoral dissertation will entail research on the Renzulli Learning program. She has worked for many years with parent and community support groups in gifted education.

Susan K. Johnsen is a professor in the Department of Educational Psychology at Baylor University. She has written more than 150 articles, monographs, technical reports, and books related to gifted education. She is editor of *Gifted Child Today* and serves on the boards of *Gifted Child Quarterly*, *Journal for the Education of the Gifted*, and *Roeper Review*. She is the author of *Identifying Gifted Students: A Practical Guide* and coauthor of three tests used in identifying gifted students. She is president of The Association for the Gifted, Council for Exceptional Children and past president of the Texas Association for Gifted and Talented.

Patricia O'Connell Johnson is the Team Leader for both the Mathematics and Science Partnership program and the Javits Gifted and Talented Education program at the U.S. Department of Education. In 19 years with the Department, she also has managed the Eisenhower Math and Science National programs and the Fund for the Improvement of Education. Prior to joining the Department, she was associate director of Project 2061 at the American Association for the Advancement of Science (AAAS), director of academic programs with the Center for Talented Youth at Johns Hopkins University, and an education specialist with the Maine Department of Education. She received her undergraduate degree in anthropology from Beloit College, a master's of arts in teaching in museum education from George Washington University, and a master's in education degree in education policy from Harvard University.

Kyung Hee Kim is an assistant professor at the College of William and Mary. Her research interests include understanding the nature of creativity and characteristics of creatively gifted students; assessing creativity; and nurturing creativity, particularly concerning environmental and cultural interactions with creativity. She received the Hollingworth Award from the National Association for Gifted Children (NAGC) in 2008, the Ronald W. Collins Distinguished Faculty Research Award, the Outstanding Faculty Award in 2008, and the Faculty Scholarship Recognition Award in 2007 from Eastern Michigan University. She also received research awards from NAGC in 2005, from the American Creativity Association in 2005, and from the International Council of Psychologists in 2004.

Margie K. Kitano serves as associate dean of the College of Education and professor of special education at San Diego State University. She codeveloped and works with the San Diego Unified School District collaborative certificate in gifted education. The program combines current theory and research with best practices to support services to gifted students, with special attention to underrepresented populations. Her current research and publications focus on improving services to culturally and linguistically diverse gifted learners.

David W. Leslie is Chancellor Professor of Education Emeritus at The College of William and Mary. He was named an Alumni Fellow of the Pennsylvania State University in 2000, received the Research Achievement Award from the Association for the Study of Higher Education in 2002, and has served as a TIAA-CREF Institute Fellow (2004–2008). He taught and studied education policy at The College of William and Mary in Virginia.

Catherine A. Little is an assistant professor in educational psychology at the University of Connecticut. She teaches courses in gifted and talented education and in the undergraduate honors program. She previously served as visiting assistant professor in gifted education at The College of William and Mary, and as curriculum coordinator at the Center for Gifted Education there. Her research interests include professional development and curriculum differentiation. She coedited *Content-Based Curriculum for High-Ability Learners* with Joyce VanTassel-Baska.

David F. Lohman is a professor of educational psychology at the University of Iowa. He is a fellow of the American Psychological Association, the American Psychological Society, and the American Educational Research Association. He is the recipient of numerous awards, including a Fulbright Fellowship and the Iowa Regents Award for Faculty Excellence at the University of Iowa, *Gifted Child Quarterly* Research Paper of the year (2006 and 2008), and the NAGC Distinguished Scholar Award. He currently directs the Institute for Research and Policy on Acceleration at the Belin-Blank International Center for Gifted Education and Talent Development. Since 1998, he has coauthored the Cognitive Abilities Test with Elizabeth Hagen.

D. Betsy McCoach is an associate professor in the Educational Psychology Department in the Neag School of Education at the University of Connecticut, where she teaches graduate courses in measurement, educational statistics, and research design. Dr. McCoach's areas of substantive research interest include closing the achievement gap, the underachievement of academically able students, and motivation. Her methodological research interests include hierarchical linear modeling, instrument design and analysis, confirmatory factor analysis, structural equation modeling, latent growth modeling, and quantitative research methodology.

Susan McGowan is a National Board Certified Teacher with 15 years of classroom experience. She obtained her bachelor's degree from George Mason University and her master's degree in education from Marymount University in Arlington. Her interest in gifted education stems from her work with high-ability students at the middle school level and led her to work with Dr. VanTassel-Baska at The College of William and Mary, where she received her Ed.D. in educational policy planning and leadership with an emphasis in gifted education. She is an assistant professor of education at Longwood University.

Virginia L. McLaughlin is dean of the School of Education at The College of William and Mary. Dr. McLaughlin's teaching and research efforts have focused on program development and evaluation and collaborative service delivery for students with disabilities and those at risk. She has directed numerous grants supporting teacher and leadership development and leads several school-university partnerships to improve public education.

F. Richard "Rick" Olenchak is professor, psychologist, and codirector of the Urban Talent Research Institute at the University of Houston. Prior to his research career, he was a teacher, principal, and consulting psychologist. Having served in a number of ancillary professional roles, including service as president of the National Association for Gifted Children, he is interested in examining cognitive and affective interactions and exploring how educators and parents can enhance optimal development of young people.

Paula Olszewski-Kubilius is the director of the Center for Talent Development at Northwestern University and a professor in the School of Education and Social Policy. She has conducted research and published more than 80 articles or book chapters on issues of talent development, particularly the effects of accelerated educational programs and the needs of special populations of gifted children. She has served as the editor of *Gifted Child Quarterly* and as a coeditor of *The Journal of Secondary Gifted Education.* She also has served on the editorial advisory boards of the *Journal for the Education of the Gifted* and *Gifted Child International,* and was a consulting editor for *Roeper Review.* She currently is a member of the editorial board of *Gifted Child Today* and *Gifted Child Quarterly.*

William Orton has taught gifted learners in grades 2–8 over a 30-year period. Additionally, he has taught multiple gifted endorsement courses for two universities, directed the Saturday/Summer Enrichment Program through the Center for Gifted Education at William and Mary, and directed the Virginia Summer Residential Governor's School in Science, Math, and Technology. He also has served as coordinator of gifted education in Hampton City Schools. Dr. Orton holds a B.S. in engineering, an M.A. in education, and a Ph.D. in education administration-gifted from The College of William and Mary.

Jane Piirto is Trustees' Distinguished Professor at Ashland University in Ashland, OH. An award-winning novelist and poet, she is a specialist in creativity, the education of the gifted and talented, and qualitative research. Among her books are *Talented Children and Adults* (three editions), *Understanding Those Who Create* (two editions), *Understanding Creativity*, and *"My Teeming Brain": Understanding Creative Writers*. Her latest book of poetry is *Saunas*.

Sally M. Reis is a Board of Trustees Distinguished Professor and Teaching Fellow in educational psychology at the University of Connecticut, where she also serves as principal investigator of The National Research Center on the Gifted and Talented. She was a classroom teacher in public education as well as an administrator before coming to the University of Connecticut. She has authored and coauthored more than 140 articles, 12 books, 50 book chapters, and numerous monographs and technical reports, and worked on a research team that has generated more than $35 million in grants in the last 15 years.

Joseph S. Renzulli is the Neag Professor of Gifted Education and Talent Development at the University of Connecticut, where he also serves as the director of The National Research Center on the Gifted and Talented. He has served on numerous editorial boards in the fields of gifted education, educational psychology and research, and law and education. His major research interests are in identification and programming models for both gifted education and general school improvement.

Rochelle Rickoff is program officer at the American Psychological Association's Center for Psychology in Schools and Education (CPSE). She provides research and programmatic support to the CPSE director in developing and executing CPSE projects, including the National Science Foundation grant-funded study of the impact of specialized public high schools of science, mathematics, and technology. She has a BFA in theater studies from Boston University and a M.Ed. in international education policy from the Harvard Graduate School of Education.

Janice I. Robbins is the interim director of the Center for Gifted Education and adjunct professor in the School of Education at The College of William and Mary. She was formerly chief of curriculum and instruction for the Department of Defense Education Activity, directing curriculum, instruction, and assessment at stateside and overseas schools. Dr. Robbins is a former elementary and middle school principal and coordinator of the gifted program for Fairfax County Public Schools in Virginia. Janice earned her Ph.D. in educational research and evaluation from Virginia Tech and her master's in curriculum and instruction from George Mason University.

Ann Robinson is a professor of education and founding director of the Center for Gifted Education at the University of Arkansas at Little Rock. She is a former editor of *Gifted Child Quarterly* and serves as the Vice President of the National Association for Gifted Children. She coauthored *Recommended Practices in Gifted Education: A Critical Analysis,* identified as one of the 50 most influential works in gifted education by the Research & Evaluation Division of NAGC; and *Best Practices in Gifted Education: An Evidence-Based Guide.* She has been recognized as the Purdue University Alumna of Distinction and received awards for public service and faculty excellence in research from the University of Arkansas at Little Rock. In 2006, she received the NAGC Distinguished Service Award.

Nancy M. Robinson is Professor Emerita of Psychiatry and Behavioral Sciences at the University of Washington and former director of what is now known as the Halbert and Nancy Robinson Center for Young Scholars. Known previously for a 30-year career in mental retardation, her research interests since 1981 have focused on effects of marked academic acceleration to college, adjustment issues of gifted children, intellectual assessment, and verbal and mathematical precocity in very young children. She received the 1998 NAGC Distinguished Scholar Award and the 2007 NAGC Ann Isaacs Founders Memorial Award.

Karen B. Rogers is a professor of gifted studies in the Department of Special Education & Gifted Education in the College of Applied Professional Studies at the University of St. Thomas in Minneapolis. She is author of *Re-Forming Gifted Education: Matching the Program to the Child*, as well as several other books, chapters, articles, and program evaluations. She has written 36 differentiated units of instruction for gifted learners, including the Omnibus units. She is a past member of the NAGC Board of Directors, a past president and board member of The Association for the Gifted division of the Council for Exceptional Children, and current chair of the AERA special interest group, Research on Intellectual Giftedness.

Ken Seeley is president of the National Center for School Engagement in Denver, CO. As a professor of education at the University of Denver for 10 years, he created the teacher education program for gifted and advised doctoral research. He was principal of the Laboratory School at the University of Northern Colorado. As a community volunteer, Dr. Seeley has helped develop charter schools in Colorado, and served as the founding president of the KIPP Sunshine Peak Charter school in West Denver. He also serves as board president of Colorado Heritage Camps and Qualistar Early Learning Center in Denver.

Del Siegle is an associate professor of educational psychology in the Neag School of Education at the University of Connecticut where he was honored as a teaching fellow. Prior to earning his Ph.D., he worked as a gifted and talented coordinator in Montana. He is president of the National Association for Gifted Children and serves on the board of directors of The Association for the Gifted (CEC-TAG). He is coeditor of the *Journal of Advanced Academics* and authors a technology column for *Gifted Child Today*. Dr. Siegle's research interests include Web-based instruction, motivation of gifted students, and teacher bias in the identification of students for gifted programs.

Linda Kreger Silverman is a licensed clinical and counseling psychologist who has contributed more than 300 publications to the field, including the books, *Counseling the Gifted & Talented* and *Upside-Down Brilliance: The Visual-Spatial Learner*. She founded and directs the Institute for the Study of Advanced Development (ISAD), and its subsidiary, the Gifted Development Center (http://www.gifteddevelopment.com), which has assessed more than 5,500 children in the last 29 years. She is cochair of the NAGC Task Force on Assessment.

Frances R. Spielhagen is an associate professor of education at Mount Saint Mary College, Newburgh, NY. From 2003–2006, she was an AERA/IES Post-Doctoral Research Fellow at the Center for Gifted Education at The College of William and Mary in Williamsburg, VA. Her book, *Debating Single-Sex Education: Separate and Equal*, was published in December 2007. Her new book, *Unsolved Equations: The Algebra Solution to Mathematics Reform,* is based on her postdoctoral research. Dr. Spielhagen is a career educator with more than 30 years experience as a high school Latin teacher and coordinator of programs for gifted students.

Robert J. Sternberg is dean of the School of Arts and Sciences, professor of psychology, and adjunct professor of education at Tufts University. He also is Honorary Professor of Psychology at the University of Heidelberg. Prior to his appointment at Tufts, Sternberg was IBM Professor of Psychology and Education and professor of management at Yale University. Sternberg's Ph.D. is from Stanford University and he has 11 honorary doctorates. He is past president of the American Psychological Association.

James H. Stronge is the Heritage Professor in the educational policy, planning, and leadership area at The College of William and Mary, Williamsburg, VA. His research interests include policy and practice related to teacher quality and teacher and administrator evaluation. His work on teacher quality focuses on how to identify effective teachers and how to enhance teacher effectiveness. Stronge has authored, coauthored, or edited 19 books and more than 90 articles, chapters, and technical reports.

Rena F. Subotnik is director of the Center for Psychology in Schools and Education (CPSE) and the Center for Gifted Education Policy (CGEP). CPSE's mission is to promote applications of psychological science to teaching and learning in precollegiate education. CGEP's mission is to generate and advocate for high-quality research, policy, and practice concerning gifted children and adults in the arts, science, sport, and the professions.

Carol L. Tieso is an associate professor at The College of William and Mary where she teaches courses in gifted education. Before joining the faculty at The College of William and Mary, she served as program coordinator for Programs in Gifted Education at The University of Alabama. Her research interests include examining the effects of differentiated curriculum and instruction and addressing specific affective and personality characteristics of gifted and talented students.

Kimberly M. Tyler is an assistant professor of education at Texas Wesleyan University. Before moving to higher education, she spent 14 years teaching in public schools. Dr. Tyler earned her undergraduate degree in elementary education from Louisiana State University and a master's degree in special education with an emphasis in gifted education from the University of Southern Mississippi. She did her doctoral work at The College of William and Mary where she earned a Ph.D. in educational policy, planning, and leadership with an emphasis in gifted education.

Susannah M. Wood received her B.A. in psychology and English from the University of Richmond. She completed her M.Ed. in school counseling and her Ph.D. in counselor education with a cognate in gifted education at The College of William and Mary. She won the Margaret, The Lady Thatcher Medallion for academic excellence. She currently is an assistant professor at the University of Iowa where she teaches both doctoral students and students who are pursuing their master's in school counseling with an emphasis in gifted education. She is a faculty partner with the Belin-Blank Center for Gifted Education and Talent Development.

Frank C. Worrell is a professor at the University of California, Berkeley, where he also is director of the School Psychology program and faculty director of the Academic Talent Development Program. He serves as director for research and development for the California College Preparatory Academy, a charter school partnership involving UC Berkeley and Aspire Public Schools. His research interests include academic talent development, at-risk youth, scale development and validation, and teacher effectiveness.